W9-CKM-503

Creativity 36
Annual Awards

CREATIVITY 36
Annual Awards

Edited by

THE CREATIVITY AWARDS
Board of Editors

COLLINS | DESIGN
An Imprint of HarperCollins*Publishers*

CREATIVITY 36

HarperCollins books may be purchased for educational, business, or sales promotional use. For information, please write: Special Markets Department, HarperCollins Publishers, 10 East 53rd Street, New York, NY 10022.

First Edition

First published in 2007 by:
Collins Design
An Imprint of HarperCollins*Publishers*
10 East 53rd Street
New York, NY 10022
Tel: (212) 207-7000
Fax: (212) 207-7654
collinsdesign@harpercollins.com
www.harpercollins.com

Distributed throughout the world by:
HarperCollins*Publishers*
10 East 53rd Street
New York, NY 10022
Fax: (212) 207-7654

Special thanks to Tim Moran, for seamlessly organizing the 2006 competition and judging procedures.

Cover and page design by Joe Weber

Additional photography provided by Melissa McIntosh, www.1214.biz

Production and book design by Designs on You! • Anthony and Suzanna Stephens

Library of Congress Control Number: 2007925502

ISBN: 978-0-06-125572-4
ISBN-10: 0-06-125572-6

Produced by Crescent Hill Books, Louisville, KY.
Printed in China by Everbest Printing Company through Crescent Hill Books, Louisville, Kentucky.

First Printing, 2007

TABLE OF CONTENTS

MEDAL DESIGNATIONS

Ⓟ **Platinum**—This symbol designates a Platinum Award winning design. Our most prestigious award is reserved for the Best in Category. Only one design is awarded per category.

Ⓖ **Gold**—This symbol designates a Gold Award winning design. The top 10% of designs in each category are selected for the Gold Award.

Ⓢ **Silver**—This symbol designates a Silver Award winning design. The top 25% of designs in each category are selected for the Silver Award.

Creative Firm: **A3 DESIGN — CHARLOTTE, NC**
Creative Team: **ALAN ALTMAN, AMANDA ALTMAN**
Client: **MATTAMY HOMES**

Creative Firm: **ORIGINAL IMPRESSIONS — MIAMI, FL**
Creative Team: **LISA CUERVO**
Client: **SUNSET HEIGHTS**

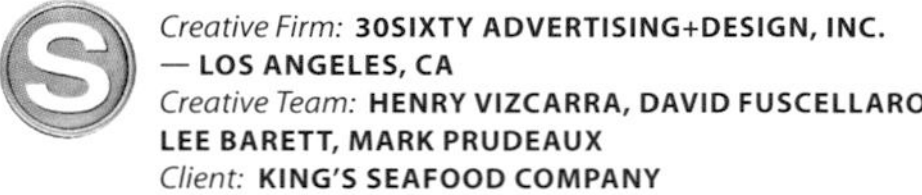

Creative Firm: **30SIXTY ADVERTISING+DESIGN, INC. — LOS ANGELES, CA**
Creative Team: **HENRY VIZCARRA, DAVID FUSCELLARO, LEE BARETT, MARK PRUDEAUX**
Client: **KING'S SEAFOOD COMPANY**

Creative Firm: **HORNALL ANDERSON DESIGN WORKS — SEATTLE, WA**
Creative Team: **DAVID BATES, YURI SHVETS, JACOB CARTER**
Client: **WET PAINT**

Creative Firm: **MT&L PUBLIC RELATIONS LTD. — HALIFAX, NS, CANADA**
Creative Team: **PAUL WILLIAMS**
Client: **AIRFIRE WIRELESS CONNECTIVITY**

Creative Firm: **STEPHEN LONGO DESIGN ASSOCIATES — WEST ORANGE, NJ**
Creative Team: **STEPHEN LONGO**
Client: **THE HEARING GROUP**

Creative Firm: **SNAP CREATIVE — ST. CHARLES, MO**
Creative Team: **ANGELA NEAL, HILARY CLEMENTS**
Client: **MIDWEST INDUSTRIAL**

Creative Firm: **VERY MEMORABLE DESIGN — NEW YORK, NY**
Creative Team: **MICHAEL PINTO**
Client: **WEINER ASSOCIATES**

Creative Firm: **KAREN SKUNTA & COMPANY — CLEVELAND, OH**
Creative Team: **KAREN SKUNTA, JAMIE FINKELHOR**
Client: **THE CLEVELAND PLAY HOUSE**

Creative Firm: **VINCE RINI DESIGN — HUNTINGTON BEACH, CA**
Creative Team: **VINCE RINI**
Client: **NEWPORT ORTHOPEDIC INSTITUTE**

Creative Firm: **GROUP T DESIGN — WASHINGTON, DC**
Creative Team: **TOM KLINEDINST**
Client: **BLUE GIN**

Creative Firm: **MAD STUDIOS — HONG KONG**
Creative Team: **BRIAN YEE HUAN LAU, LILIAN LAI YEE CHAN**
Client: **VISIONQUEST INTERNATIONAL**

iCONCLUDE

Creative Firm: **CONNIE HWANG DESIGN — GAINESVILLE, FL**
Creative Team: **CONNIE HWANG**
Client: **ICONCLUDE**

Creative Firm: **NEURON SYNDICATE INC. —SANTA MONICA, CA**
Creative Team: **SEAN ALATORRE, RYAN CRAMER, JASON BURNAM**
Client: **20TH CENTURY FOX MOBILE DIVISION**

Creative Firm: **PLUMBLINE STUDIOS, INC — NAPA, CA**
Creative Team: **DOM MORECI**
Client: **MASHERY**

Creative Firm: **SILVER CREATIVE GROUP — SOUTH NORWALK, CT**
Creative Team: **BONNIE HARRIMAN, DONNA BONATO**
Client: **SOUNDTANKER CHARTERING**

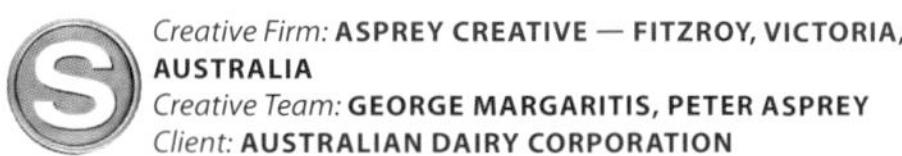

Creative Firm: **ASPREY CREATIVE — FITZROY, VICTORIA, AUSTRALIA**
Creative Team: **GEORGE MARGARITIS, PETER ASPREY**
Client: **AUSTRALIAN DAIRY CORPORATION**

Creative Firm: **MCGUFFIE DESIGN — NORTH VANCOUVER, BC, CANADA**
Creative Team: **STEVE MCGUFFIE**
Client: **VANCOUVER BOARD OF PARKS AND RECREATION**

Creative Firm: **BREEDWORKS — ONEONTA, NY**
Creative Team: **SUSAN MUTHER**
Client: **SUN KING ALPACAS**

Creative Firm: **LEVERAGE MARKETING GROUP — NEWTOWN, CT**
Creative Team: **DON WHELAN, DAVID GOODWICK, TOM MARKS, BECKY KOROL, RICH BRZOZOWSKI**
Client: **SEALED AIR CORPORATION**

Creative Firm: **MAD DOG GRAPHX — ANCHORAGE, AK**
Creative Team: **KRIS RYAN-CLARKE**
Client: **SIMPLIFY**

Creative Firm: **RODGERS TOWNSEND — ST. LOUIS, MO**
Creative Team: **KRIS WRIGHT**
Client: **RODGERS TOWNSEND GOLF TOURNAMENT**

Creative Firm: **KOMP|REHENSIVE DESIGN — KING OF PRUSSIA, PA**
Creative Team: **JEANNE KOMP**
Client: **GOLD LION ASSOCIATES**

Creative Firm: **DANIEL GREEN EYE-D DESIGN — GREEN BAY, WI**
Creative Team: **DANIEL GREEN**
Client: **GREEN BAY EAST HIGH SOCCER BOOSTER CLUB**

Creative Firm: **KOR GROUP — BOSTON, MA**
Creative Team: **KAREN DENDY SMITH, KJERSTIN WESTGAARD OH**
Client: **BOSTON PROPERTIES**

Creative Firm: **JANIS BROWN & ASSOCIATES — CARLSBAD, CA**
Creative Team: **TRACY SABIN, JANIS BROWN**
Client: **GARRETT RANCH**

Creative Firm: **SMITH + BARTELS — BERKELEY, CA**
Creative Team: **DON BARTELS, NANCY SMITH**
Client: **AGILENT TECHNOLOGIES, INC.**

Creative Firm: **MARK OLIVER, INC.—SOLVANG, CA**
Creative Team: **MARK OLIVER, TOM HENNESSY**
Client: **SANTA RITA HILLS WINEGROWERS ALLIANCE**

Creative Firm: **STELLAR DEBRIS — HADANO-SHI, KANAGAWA-KEN, JAPAN**
Creative Team: **CHRISTOPHER JONES**
Client: **STELLAR DEBRIS**

Creative Firm: **DESIGNSKI L.L.C. — TOLEDO, OH**
Creative Team: **DENNY KREGER**
Client: **NICK PINOTTI**

Creative Firm: **FITTING GROUP — PITTSBURGH, PA**
Creative Team: **ANDREW ELLIS, TRAVIS NORRIS, ANDREA FITTING**
Client: **PRODUCT STRATEGY NETWORK**

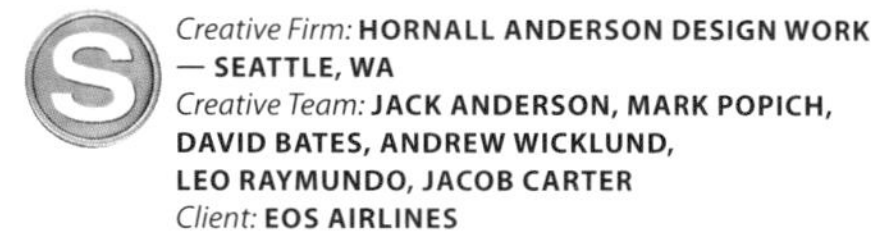

Creative Firm: **HORNALL ANDERSON DESIGN WORKS — SEATTLE, WA**
Creative Team: **JACK ANDERSON, MARK POPICH, DAVID BATES, ANDREW WICKLUND, LEO RAYMUNDO, JACOB CARTER**
Client: **EOS AIRLINES**

i-Squared
making information make sense

Creative Firm: **INFORMATION EXPERTS — RESTON, VA**
Creative Team: **ELICIA ROBERTS, JERRY SMITH**
Client: **COMMDEV**

Creative Firm: **HITCHCOCK FLEMING & ASSOCIATES INC. — AKRON, OH**
Creative Team: **NICK BETRO, TODD MOSER**
Client: **VERITAS**

Creative Firm: **FITTING GROUP — PITTSBURGH, PA**
Creative Team: **TRAVIS NORRIS, ANDREW ELLIS, ANDREA FITTING**
Client: **I-SQUARED**

Creative Firm: **FITTING GROUP — PITTSBURGH, PA**
Creative Team: **ANDREW ELLIS, TRAVIS NORRIS**
Client: **BLACK KNIGHT SECURITY**

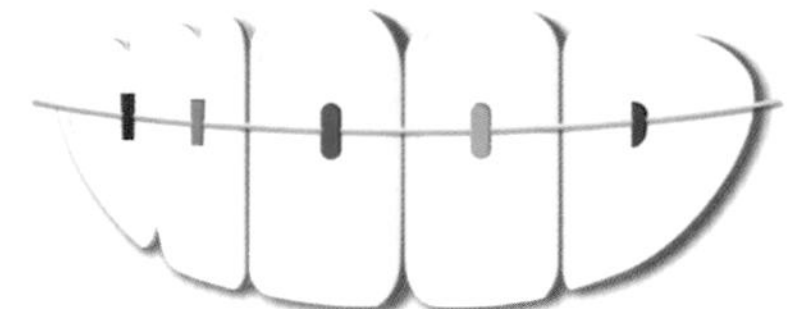

Creative Firm: **ATOMIC DESIGN — CROWLEY, TX**
Creative Team: **LEWIS GLASER**
Client: **STEVEN C. WOOD**

Creative Firm: **ENGINE, LLC — SAN FRANCISCO, CA**
Creative Team: **LOTUS CHILD, GEOFF SKIGEN**
Client: **MEDJOOL**

Creative Firm: **SPRINGBOARD CREATIVE — MISSION, KS**
Creative Team: **KEVIN FULLERTON**
Client: **SPRINGBOARD CREATIVE**

Creative Firm: **LORENC+YOO DESIGN — ROSWELL, GA**
Creative Team: **JAN LORENC, DAVID PARK, JISUN AN**
Client: **GENERAL GROWTH PROPERTIES**

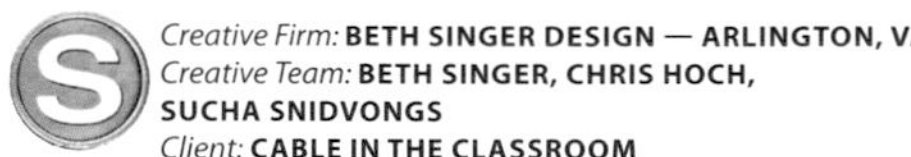
Creative Firm: **BETH SINGER DESIGN — ARLINGTON, VA**
Creative Team: **BETH SINGER, CHRIS HOCH, SUCHA SNIDVONGS**
Client: **CABLE IN THE CLASSROOM**

Creative Firm: **DESIGN OBJECTIVES PTE LTD — SINGAPORE**
Creative Team: **RONNIE S C TAN**
Client: **JW MARRIOTT HOTEL, BEIJING**

Creative Firm: **VENTRESS DESIGN GROUP — FRANKLIN, TN**
Creative Team: **TOM VENTRESS**
Client: **SUSAN GRAY SCHOOL**

Creative Firm: **KELLY BREWSTER — CHARLOTTE, NC**
Creative Team: **KELLY BREWSTER**
Client: **BURTIN POLYMER LABORATORIES**

Creative Firm: **BRAND ENGINE — SAUSALITO, CA**
Creative Team: **ANDREW OTTO, MEGHAN ZODROW, KONRAD TSE, ISKRA JOHNSON**
Client: **PLUM ORGANICS**

Creative Firm: **TD2, S.C. — MEXICO CITY, D.F., MEXICO**
Creative Team: **JOSE LUIS (PAT) PATIÑO, R. RODRIGO CORDOVA, RAFAEL TREVINO**
Client: **COA**

Creative Firm: **ZENN GRAPHIC DESIGN — LOS ANGELES, CA**
Creative Team: **ZENGO YOSHIDA, MARK WOOD**
Client: **MARK WOOD DESIGN OFFICE**

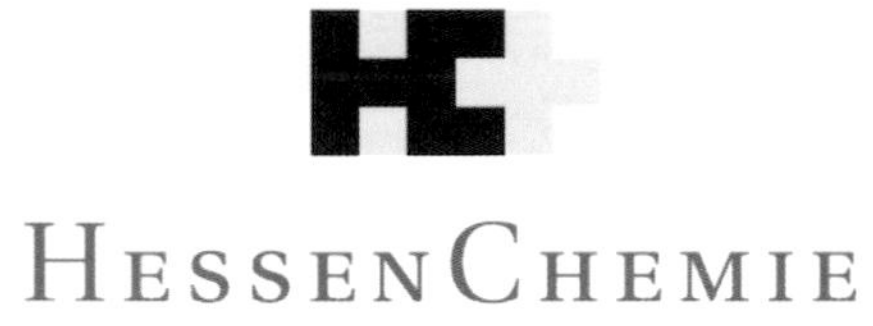

Creative Firm: **Q — WIESBADEN, GERMANY**
Creative Team: **THILO VON DEBSCHITZ, LAURENZ NIELBOCK, MARCEL KUMMERER, CHRISTOPH DAHINTEN**
Client: **HESSENCHEMIE**

Creative Firm: **KOLANO DESIGN — PITTSBURGH, PA**
Creative Team: **BILL KOLANO, TIM CARRERA**
Client: **NICHOLE GOLDSMITH, WORLD SHOE TRAVELERS ASSOCIATION**

Creative Firm: **BAER DESIGN GROUP — EVANSTON, IL**
Creative Team: **DAVE SEIDLER, TODD BAER**
Client: **SOMMERS ORGANIC**

Creative Firm: **TOM FOWLER, INC. — NORWALK, CT**
Creative Team: **ELIZABETH P. BALL**
Client: **SERVICEMACS LLC**

Creative Firm: **WHET DESIGN, INC. — NEW YORK, NY**
Creative Team: **CHERYL OPPENHEIM, CRISTINA LAGORIO**
Client: **EMPLOYEES ONLY**

Creative Firm: **VISUALLY SPEAKING — BALTIMORE, MD**
Creative Team: **CRAIG KIRBY**
Client: **RED ABBEY CAPITAL MANAGEMENT**

Creative Firm: **ELEVATOR — SPLIT, CROATIA (HRVATSKA)**
Creative Team: **TONY ADAMIC, LANA VITAS, GORANA MARSIC**
Client: **BIOLAB**

Creative Firm: **REDUCED FAT — SARATOGA SPRINGS, NY**
Creative Team: **JOHN BOLSTER**
Client: **DEBRA DOCYK**

Creative Firm: **MIKE SALISBURY EFFECTIVE CREATIVE STRATEGIES — VENICE, CA**
Creative Team: **MIKE SALISBURY, MATT BRIGHT**
Client: **DISNEY'S CALIFORNIA ADVENTURE**

Creative Firm: **OCTAVO DESIGNS — FREDERICK, MD**
Creative Team: **SUE HOUGH, MARK BURRIER**
Client: **STRATEGIC PARTNERSHIPS INTERNATIONAL**

Creative Firm: **FUTUREBRAND — NEW YORK, NY**
Creative Team: **DIEGO KOLSKY, MIKE WILLIAMS, CHERYL HILLS, STEPHANIE CARROLL, WILLIAM SHINTANI, RAYMOND CHAN**
Client: **ARCAPITA**

Creative Firm: **DEVER DESIGNS — LAUREL, MD**
Creative Team: **JEFFREY DEVER**
Client: **TAKOMA ACADEMY JAMAICA TOUR**

Creative Firm: **DESIGN OBJECTIVES PTE LTD — SINGAPORE**
Creative Team: **RONNIE S C TAN**
Client: **BEAUFORT SENTOSA DEVELOPMENT PTE LTD**

Creative Firm: **OJO DESIGN LIMITED — KOWLOON BAY, HONG KONG**
Creative Team: **ONG JOEL NG, ONG CHAN CHUNG CHUN, ONG JESSIKA OLIVE**
Client: **CARITAS YOUTH & COMMUNITY SERVICE**

Creative Firm: **MAD DOG GRAPHX — ANCHORAGE, AK**
Creative Team: **MICHAEL ARDAIZ**
Client: **GREAT CIRCLE FLIGHT SERVICES**

Creative Firm: **MORNINGSTAR DESIGN, INC. — FREDERICK, MD**
Creative Team: **MISTI MORNINGSTAR**
Client: **FUSION NIGHTCLUB**

Creative Firm: **ZERO GRAVITY DESIGN GROUP — SMITHTOWN, NY**
Creative Team: **ZERO GRAVITY DESIGN GROUP**
Client: **DIRECT ACCESS PARTNERS**

Creative Firm: **BETH SINGER DESIGN — ARLINGTON, VA**
Creative Team: **BETH SINGER, SUCHA SNIDVONGS**
Client: **TCI**

Creative Firm: **AF&A BRANDTELLIGENCE — PITTSBURGH, PA**
Creative Team: **ROBERT ADAM, BLAIR GOOD, RALPH RUSSINI**
Client: **PIETRAGALLO, BOSICK & GORDON, LLP**

Creative Firm: **CONNIE HWANG DESIGN — GAINESVILLE, FL**
Creative Team: **CONNIE HWANG**
Client: **JITTERBIT**

Creative Firm: **SILVER COMMUNICATIONS INC — NEW YORK, NY**
Creative Team: **GREGG SIBERT, CHRISTINA WEISSMAN**
Client: **EAST MIDTOWN ASSOCIATION**

Creative Firm: **SABINGRAFIK, INC. — CARLSBAD, CA**
Creative Team: **TRACY SABIN**
Client: **SABINGRAFIK, INC.**

Creative Firm: **SPEEDY MOTORCYCLE STUDIO, LTD. — PHILADELPHIA, PA**
Creative Team: **E. JUNE ROBERTS-LUNN**
Client: **SPEEDY MOTORCYCLE STUDIO, LTD.**

Creative Firm: **DESIGN NUT — KENSINGTON, MD**
Creative Team: **WENDY BOGART, BRENT ALMOND**
Client: **COUNCIL FOR ADVANCEMENT AND SUPPORT OF EDUCATION**

Creative Firm: **MARK DEITCH & ASSOCIATES, INC. — BURBANK, CA**
Creative Team: **DVORJAC RIEMERSMA**
Client: **AEG**

Creative Firm: **BRAND ENGINE — SAUSALITO, CA**
Creative Team: **ERIC READ, AILEEN KENDLE-SMITH, CORALIE RUSSO**
Client: **SUGAR BOWL BAKERY**

Creative Firm: **CONRY DESIGN — TOPANGA, CA**
Creative Team: **RHONDA CONRY**
Client: **THE JOB COACH**

Creative Firm: **GROUP T DESIGN — WASHINGTON, DC**
Creative Team: **TOM KLINEDINST**
Client: **MANA WAERE**

Creative Firm: **MEGAN BOYER — ENCINITAS, CA**
Creative Team: **MEGAN BOYER, HEATHER HOOGENDAM**
Client: **SOUTHERN CALIFORNIA VACATION RENTALS**

Creative Firm: **BERRY DESIGN INC — ALPHARETTA, GA**
Creative Team: **BOB BERRY, CHIP WALLER**
Client: **CRABAPPLE TAVERN**

Creative Firm: **FAINE-OLLER PRODUCTIONS — SEATTLE, WA**
Creative Team: **CATHERINE OLLER, BRUCE HALE, NANCY STENTZ**
Client: **COLESON FOODS, INC.**

Creative Firm: **MAD STUDIOS — HONG KONG**
Creative Team: **BRIAN YEE HUAN LAU, LILIAN LAI YEE CHAN**
Client: **BABYFIRST**

Creative Firm: **CROXSON DESIGN — HOUSTON, TX**
Creative Team: **STEPHEN CROXSON, RICHARD BYRD**
Client: **HOUSTON AREA WOMEN'S CENTER**

Creative Firm: **VINCE RINI DESIGN — HUNTINGTON BEACH, CA**
Creative Team: **VINCE RINI**
Client: **BLUE COW**

Creative Firm: **AIJALON — LINCOLN, NE**
Creative Team: **LANCE FORD**
Client: **DYNAMIC HOLDINGS**

Creative Firm: **KIKU OBATA & COMPANY — ST. LOUIS, MO**
Creative Team: **ELEANOR SAFE**
Client: **SMARTCARE**

Creative Firm: **GRAFIK MARKETING COMMUNICATIONS — ALEXANDRIA, VA**
Creative Team: **KRISTIN MOORE, MELISSA WILETS, HAL SWETNAM, HEATH DWIGGINS**
Client: **WASHINGTON COURT HOTEL**

Creative Firm: **ORIGINAL IMPRESSIONS — MIAMI, FL**
Creative Team: **LISA CUERVO**
Client: **THE ALEDAN GROUP**

Creative Firm: **GRAPHICAT LTD. — WANCHAI, HONG KONG**
Creative Team: **COLIN TILLYER**
Client: **JC HOLDINGS LTD.**

Creative Firm: **GREENFIELD/BELSER LTD. — WASHINGTON, DC**
Creative Team: **BURKEY BELSER, CAROLYN SEWELL**
Client: **CHOATE HALL & STEWART LLP**

Creative Firm: **A3 DESIGN — CHARLOTTE, NC**
Creative Team: **ALAN ALTMAN, AMANDA ALTMAN**
Client: **GOODY'S PAINT INC.**

Creative Firm: **ACME COMMUNICATIONS, INC. — NEW YORK, NY**
Creative Team: **KIKI BOUCHER**
Client: **BEACH HOUSE SUPPLY CO.**

Creative Firm: **DESIGNSKI L.L.C. — TOLEDO, OH**
Creative Team: **DENNY KREGER**
Client: **COMMERCIAL INTERIORS**

sweetgrass
NATURAL FIBERS

Creative Firm: **KINESIS — ASHLAND, OR**
Creative Team: **SHAWN BUSSE, MICHELLE CHENEY**
Client: **SWEETGRASS NATURAL FIBERS**

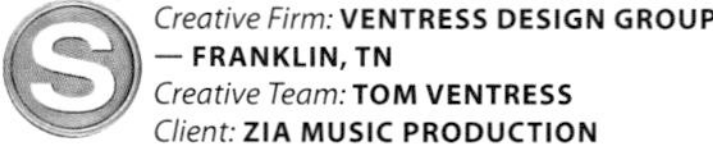

Creative Firm: **VENTRESS DESIGN GROUP — FRANKLIN, TN**
Creative Team: **TOM VENTRESS**
Client: **ZIA MUSIC PRODUCTION**

Creative Firm: **ACOSTA DESIGN INC — NEW YORK, NY**
Creative Team: **MAURICIO ACOSTA**
Client: **ACOSTA DESIGN INC**

Creative Firm: **FIVESTONE — BUFORD, GA**
Creative Team: **JASON LOCY, PATRICIO JUAREZ**
Client: **RETHINK GROUP**

Creative Firm: **TOM FOWLER, INC. — NORWALK, CT**
Creative Team: **THOMAS G. FOWLER, ELIZABETH P. BALL, STEPHANIE JOHNSON**
Client: **THE CONNECTICUT GRAND OPERA & ORCHESTRA**

Creative Firm: **A3 DESIGN — CHARLOTTE, NC**
Creative Team: **ALAN ALTMAN, AMANDA ALTMAN, SCOTT ELLIOTT**
Client: **MATTAMY HOMES**

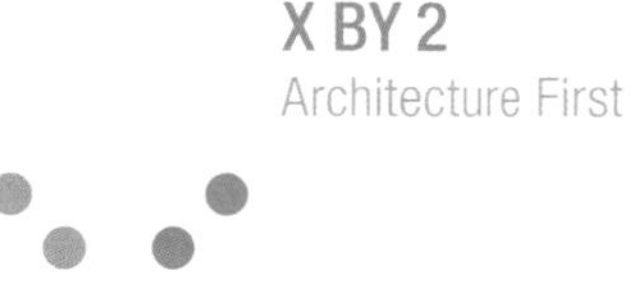

Creative Firm: **BBK STUDIO — GRAND RAPIDS, MI**
Creative Team: **SHARON OLENICZAK, KEVIN BUDELMANN, BRIAN HAUCH, TIM CALKINS**
Client: **XBY2**

Creative Firm: **INFORMATION EXPERTS — RESTON, VA**
Creative Team: **ELICIA ROBERTS, JERRY SMITH**
Client: **CRISIS PARTNERS INTERNATIONAL**

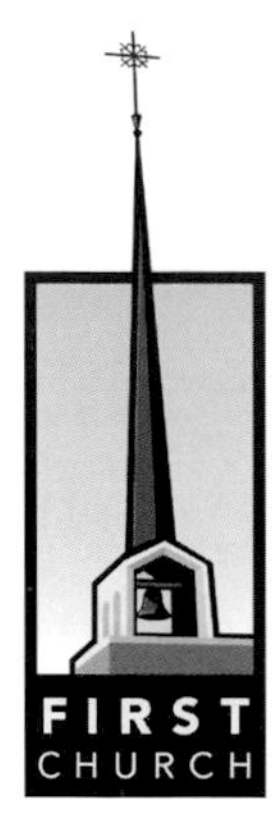

Creative Firm: **VANPELT CREATIVE — GARLAND, TX**
Creative Team: **CHIP VANPELT**
Client: **FIRST UNITED METHODIST CHURCH OF GARLAND**

Creative Firm: **GRAFIK MARKETING COMMUNICATIONS — ALEXANDRIA, VA**
Creative Team: **KRISTIN MOORE, MELISSA WILETS, HAL SWETNAM, HEATH DWIGGINS**
Client: **WASHINGTON COURT HOTEL**

Creative Firm: **TANGRAM STRATEGIC DESIGN — NOVARA, ITALY**
Creative Team: **ENRICO SEMPI, ANDREA SEMPI**
Client: **CARLO FILIPPO FOLLIS**

Creative Firm: **DEVER DESIGNS — LAUREL, MD**
Creative Team: **JEFFREY DEVER**
Client: **NATIONAL ASSOCIATION OF COUNTIES**

Creative Firm: **DESIGN GROUP WEST — CARLSBAD, CA**
Creative Team: **TRACY SABIN, JIM NAEGELI**
Client: **UNIVERSITY OF SAN DIEGO**

Creative Firm: **TOM FOWLER, INC. — NORWALK, CT**
Creative Team: **MARY ELLEN BUTKUS, ELIZABETH P. BALL**
Client: **ACME UNITED CORPORATION**

Creative Firm: **MAD STUDIOS — HONG KONG**
Creative Team: **BRIAN YEE HUAN LAU, LILIAN LAI YEE CHAN**
Client: **ECCHINESE**

Creative Firm: **ACART COMMUNICATIONS — OTTAWA, ON, CANADA**
Creative Team: **KERRY CAVLOVIC, VERNON LAI, TOM MEGGINSON, JOHN STARESINIC, CRAIG CEBRYK**
Client: **WORLD JUNIOR CHAMPIONSHIP**

Creative Firm: **TD2, S.C. — MEXICO CITY, D.F., MEXICO**
Creative Team: **GABRIELA ZAMORA, R. RODRIGO CORDOVA, RAFAEL TREVINO**
Client: **CIE**

Creative Firm: **BRIGHT RAIN CREATIVE — ST. LOUIS, MO**
Creative Team: **KEVIN HOUGH, MATT MARINO**
Client: **BRIGHT RAIN CREATIVE**

Creative Firm: **MAD DOG GRAPHX — ANCHORAGE, AK**
Creative Team: **MICHAEL ARDAIZ**
Client: **HARBOR DINNER CLUB**

Creative Firm: **BRAND ENGINE — SAUSALITO, CA**
Creative Team: **ERIC READ, ROBERT BURNS, YUSUKE ASAKA**
Client: **BRAND ENGINE**

Creative Firm: **HBO OFF-AIR CREATIVE SERVICES — NEW YORK, NY**
Creative Team: **VENUS DENNISON, ANA RACELIS, CARLOS TEJEDA**
Client: **HBO PRODUCT DEVELOPMENT**

Creative Firm: **KOR GROUP —BOSTON, MA**
Creative Team: **JIM GIBSON**
Client: **KERWIN**

Creative Firm: **TYPE G DESIGN — CARLSBAD, CA**
Creative Team: **TRACY SABIN, MIKE NELSON**
Client: **PASTA PASTA RESTAURANT**

Creative Firm: **BRIGHT RAIN CREATIVE — ST. LOUIS, MO**
Creative Team: **MATT MARINO, KEVIN HOUGH**
Client: **SMOKIN' DICK'S BBQ**

Creative Firm: **HORNALL ANDERSON DESIGN WORKS — SEATTLE, WA**
Creative Team: **JACK ANDERSON, LARRY ANDERSON, JAY HILBURN, BRUCE STIGLER, ELMER DELA CRUZ, DAYMON BRUCK, HAYDEN SCHOEN**
Client: **WIDMER BROTHERS BREWERY**

*

Creative Firm: **CBX — NEW YORK, NY**
Client: **NEIGHBOURS**

Creative Firm: **BRAND ENGINE — SAUSALITO, CA**
Creative Team: **ERIC READ, MEGHAN ZODROW, ROBERT BURNS, AILEEN KENDLE-SMITH**
Client: **PACKAGE DESIGN MAGAZINE: DESIGN CHALLENGE 2005**

Creative Firm: **A3 DESIGN — CHARLOTTE, NC**
Creative Team: **ALAN ALTMAN, AMANDA ALTMAN**
Client: **HOT SAKE CREATIVE**

Creative Firm: **TD2, S.C. — MEXICO CITY, D.F., MEXICO**
Creative Team: **R. RODRIGO CORDOVA, MAURICIO MUÑOZ**
Client: **CHIN-AI BAR**

Creative Firm: **DON SCHAAF & FRIENDS, INC. — WASHINGTON, DC**
Creative Team: **DON SCHAAF**
Client: **HONESTY ONLINE**

Creative Firm: **DEVER DESIGNS — LAUREL, MD**
Creative Team: **JEFFREY DEVER**
Client: **NATIONAL ASSOCIATION OF COUNTIES**

Creative Firm: **VENTRESS DESIGN GROUP — FRANKLIN, TN**
Creative Team: **TOM VENTRESS**
Client: **COMMUNITY INITIATIVE**

Creative Firm: **AF&A BRANDTELLIGENCE — PITTSBURGH, PA**
Creative Team: **ROBERT ADAM, RALPH RUSSINI, BLAIR GOOD**
Client: **ONE OCEAN**

Creative Firm: **FITTING GROUP — PITTSBURGH, PA**
Creative Team: **TRAVIS NORRIS, ANDREW ELLIS, ANDREA FITTING**
Client: **THE FRENCH TART**

Creative Firm: **PATRICIA LOPEZ-HURTADO — SAN MATEO, CA**
Client: **COLLEGE OF SAN MATEO**

Creative Firm: **TOM FOWLER, INC. — NORWALK, CT**
Creative Team: **BRIEN O'REILLY, THOMAS G. FOWLER**
Client: **WESTCHESTER SPORTS AND WELLNESS**

Creative Firm: **ELLEN BRUSS DESIGN — DENVER, CO**
Creative Team: **ELLEN BRUSS**
Client: **UNIVERSITY OF DAYTON**

Creative Firm: **ELEVATOR — SPLIT, CROATIA (HRVATSKA)**
Creative Team: **TONY ADAMIC, LANA VITAS**
Client: **ASFALTNA CESTA**

Creative Firm: **KARACTERS DESIGN GROUP/DDB CANADA — VANCOUVER, BC, CANADA**
Creative Team: **JAMES BATEMAN, MARSHA LARKIN, HELEN WYNNE, PHIL COLLINS, MARK FINN, RUSS HORII**
Client: **NORTHLANDS**

Creative Firm: **BRIGHT RAIN CREATIVE — ST. LOUIS, MO**
Creative Team: **MATT MARINO**
Client: **PLAY 54, LLC**

Creative Firm: **PHOENIX CREATIVE GROUP, LLC — POTOMAC FALLS, VA**
Creative Team: **SEAN MULLINS, NICK LUTKINS, CHRISTIAN MUSSELMAN**
Client: **URBAN LAND INSTITUTE**

Creative Firm: **HOTSAUCE — NEW YORK, NY**
Creative Team: **WYNDY SLOAN**
Client: **VIRGIN COMICS**

Oogle&beyond

Creative Firm: **DESIGN SYSTEMAT, INC. — MAKATI, MANILA, PHILIPPINES**
Creative Team: **STEFANO PAOLO BUNAG, GERONIMO SANTOS**
Client: **OOGLE AND BEYOND**

Creative Firm: **SINGULARITY DESIGN, INC. — PHILADELPHIA, PA**
Creative Team: **OWEN LINTON, JOSHUA COHEN**
Client: **PENN IMAGE COMPUTING & SCIENCE LAB**

Creative Firm: **SERAN DESIGN — KEEZLETOWN, VA**
Creative Team: **SANG YOON**
Client: **COLLEGE OF VISUAL & PERFORMING ARTS, JAMES MADISON UNIVERSITY**

Creative Firm: **A3 DESIGN — CHARLOTTE, NC**
Creative Team: **ALAN ALTMAN, AMANDA ALTMAN**
Client: **MATTAMY HOMES**

Creative Firm: **G2 — NEW YORK, NY**
Creative Team: **LOU ANTONUCCI, ANDRE KALLAUR**
Client: **AEROBED**

Creative Firm: **LISKA + ASSOCIATES — CHICAGO, IL**
Creative Team: **TANYA QUICK, FERNANDO MUNOZ**
Client: **AROMAFLORIA**

Creative Firm: **BBK STUDIO — GRAND RAPIDS, MI**
Creative Team: **KEVIN BUDELMANN, BRIAN HAUCH, TIM CALKINS**
Client: **1TO3.ORG**

Creative Firm: **ORIGINAL IMPRESSIONS — MIAMI, FL**
Creative Team: **FRANK IRIAS**
Client: **VILLAS AT JASMINE PARK**

Creative Firm: **HELENA SEO DESIGN — SUNNYVALE, CA**
Client: **VIVENDI DEVELOPMENT**

Creative Firm: **BETH SINGER DESIGN — ARLINGTON, VA**
Creative Team: **BETH SINGER, SUCHA SNIDVONGS**
Client: **PARTNERSHIP FOR JEWISH LIFE AND LEARNING (PJLL)**

Creative Firm: **RULE29 — GENEVA, IL**
Creative Team: **JUSTIN AHERNS, KERRI LIU**
Client: **AGROPURE**

Creative Firm: **GREEN CAT DZINE — ISSAQUAH, WA**
Creative Team: **ELISABETH RUMPELSBERGER**
Client: **HJORTEN GROUP**

Creative Firm: **A3 DESIGN — CHARLOTTE, NC**
Creative Team: **ALAN ALTMAN, AMANDA ALTMAN**
Client: **CROWN COMMUNICATIONS**

Creative Firm: **ORIGINAL IMPRESSIONS — MIAMI, FL**
Creative Team: **FRANK IRIAS**
Client: **YACHTSMAN'S COVE**

cincinnati art museum

Creative Firm: **LIBBY PERSZYK KATHMAN — CINCINNATI, OH**
Creative Team: **PETER BOROWSKI, ANNELLE STOTZ**
Client: **CINCINNATI ART MUSEUM**

Creative Firm: **LISKA + ASSOCIATES — CHICAGO, IL**
Creative Team: **STEVE LISKA**
Client: **JOHN MICHAEL KOHLER ARTS CENTER**

Creative Firm: **CRABTREE & COMPANY — FALLS CHURCH, VA**
Creative Team: **SUSAN ANGRISANI, JOE VELASQUEZ**
Client: **EVENTOLOGY, LLC**

UNION CHARTER

Creative Firm: **ORIGINAL IMPRESSIONS — MIAMI, FL**
Creative Team: **FRANK IRIAS**
Client: **UNION CHARTER**

Creative Firm: **DESIGN OBJECTIVES PTE LTD — SINGAPORE**
Creative Team: **RONNIE S C TAN**
Client: **SHERATON TAIPEI HOTEL**

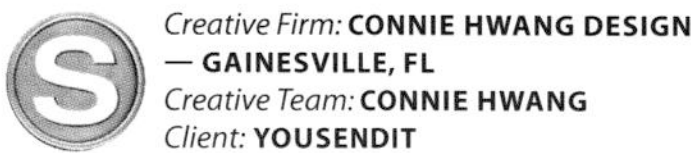
Creative Firm: **CONNIE HWANG DESIGN — GAINESVILLE, FL**
Creative Team: **CONNIE HWANG**
Client: **YOUSENDIT**

Creative Firm: **MCMILLIAN DESIGN — BROOKLYN, NY**
Creative Team: **WILLIAM MCMILLIAN**
Client: **JASON RICHELSON**

Creative Firm: **HORNALL ANDERSON DESIGN WORKS — SEATTLE, WA**
Creative Team: **JACK ANDERSON, LARRY ANDERSON, HOLLY CRAVEN, JAY HILBURN, CHRIS FREED**
Client: **COLD STANDARD**

Creative Firm: **DESIGN OBJECTIVES PTE LTD — SINGAPORE**
Creative Team: **RONNIE S C TAN**
Client: **BEAUFORT SENTOSA DEVELOPMENT PTE LTD**

Creative Firm: **FUTUREBRAND — NEW YORK, NY**
Creative Team: **DIEGO KOLSKY, MIKE WILLIAMS, CHERYL HILLS, BRENDAN O'NEILL, SAMAR SAMUEL, RITA PINTO**
Client: **DUBAI AEROSPACE ENTERPRISE**

Creative Firm: **PLUMBLINE STUDIOS, INC — NAPA, CA**
Creative Team: **DOM MORECI**
Client: **ON THE HOOK RECORDINGS**

Creative Firm: **HORNALL ANDERSON DESIGN WORKS — SEATTLE, WA**
Creative Team: **JACK ANDERSON, JAMES TEE, ANDREW WICKLUND, ELMER DELA CRUZ, HOLLY CRAVEN, JAY HILBURN**
Client: **WEYERHAEUSER CORP.**

Creative Firm: **GREENFIELD/BELSER LTD. — WASHINGTON, DC**
Creative Team: **BURKEY BELSER, JONATHAN BRUNS, ALYSON FIELDMAN**
Client: **CAMELLIA HOME HEALTH & HOSPICE**

Creative Firm: **VSA PARTNERS, INC. — CHICAGO, IL**
Creative Team: **CURT SCHREIBER, STEVE RYAN, ASHLEY LIPPARD, SILAS MUNRO, WENDY BELT,**
Client: **IBM CORPORATION**

Creative Firm: **KELLY BREWSTER, — CHARLOTTE, NC**
Creative Team: **KELLY BREWSTER**
Client: **BELLA TUNNO LLC**

Creative Firm: **SUBSTANCE — CHICAGO, IL**
Creative Team: **MATTHEW BRETT**
Client: **LAKEWOOD REHABILITATION CENTER**

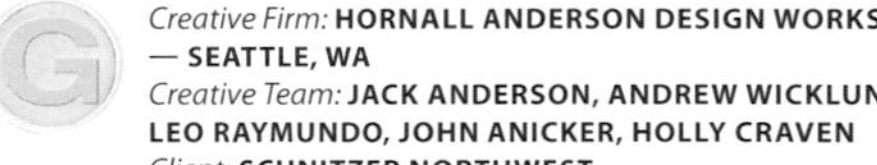

Creative Firm: **HORNALL ANDERSON DESIGN WORKS — SEATTLE, WA**
Creative Team: **JACK ANDERSON, ANDREW WICKLUND, LEO RAYMUNDO, JOHN ANICKER, HOLLY CRAVEN**
Client: **SCHNITZER NORTHWEST**

Creative Firm: **WHET DESIGN, INC. — NEW YORK, NY**
Creative Team: **CHERYL OPPENHEIM**
Client: **LORELEI ENTERPRISES & EVENTS**

Creative Firm: **ADVANTAGE LTD — HAMILTON, BERMUDA**
Creative Team: **SUSAN TANG-PETERSEN**
Client: **THE PROPERTY GROUP LTD.**

Creative Firm: **CROXSON DESIGN — HOUSTON, TX**
Creative Team: **STEPHEN CROXSON, RICHARD BYRD**
Client: **M.D. ANDERSON CANCER CENTER**

Creative Firm: **DESIGN OBJECTIVES PTE LTD — SINGAPORE**
Creative Team: **RONNIE S C TAN**
Client: **PEARL ENERGY LIMITED**

Creative Firm: **RED CANOE — DEER LODGE, TN**
Creative Team: **DEB KOCH, CAROLINE KAVANAGH**
Client: **LITTLE MARKET STREET PACKAGE CO.**

Creative Firm: **DESIGN OBJECTIVES PTE LTD — SINGAPORE**
Creative Team: **RONNIE S C TAN**
Client: **SHERATON TAIPEI HOTEL**

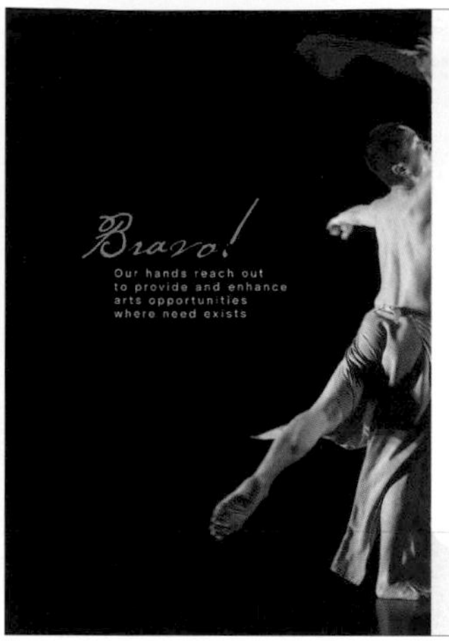

Creative Firm: **HERBERGER COLLEGE OF FINE ARTS — TEMPE, AZ**
Creative Team: **AMY NG, LAURA TOUSSAINT, TRACEY BENSON, STACEY SHAW**
Client: **HERBERGER COLLEGE OF FINE ARTS**

Creative Firm: **EMERSON, WAJDOWICZ STUDIOS — NEW YORK, NY**
Creative Team: **JUREK WAJDOWICZ , LISA LAROCHELLE, MANNY MENDEZ, STEVEN MANNING, PETER BIRO, SCOTT ANGER AND OTHERS**
Client: **INTERNATIONAL RESCUE COMMITTEE**

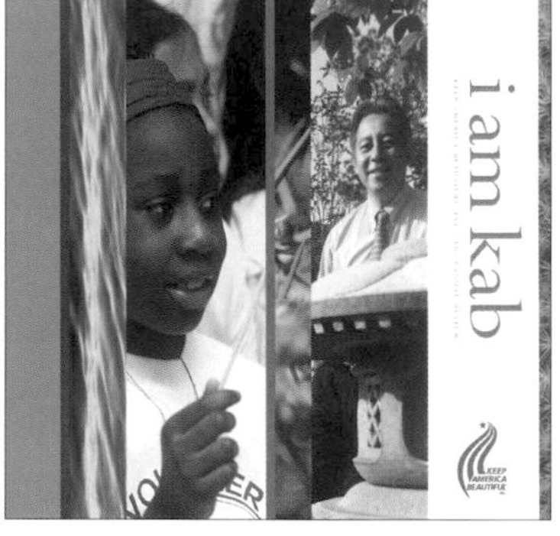

Creative Firm: **TAYLOR DESIGN — STAMFORD, CT**
Creative Team: **MARLE BARRETT, LARRY KAUFMAN, ROB WALLACE, DAN TAYLOR**
Client: **KEEP AMERICA BEAUTIFUL**

Creative Firm: **ADDISON — NEW YORK, NY**
Creative Team: **DAVID KOHLER, MIHO NISHIMANIWA**
Client: **GATX**

Creative Firm: **HULL CREATIVE GROUP — BROOKLINE, MA**
Creative Team: **CARYL H. HULL, AMY BRADDOCK, RUSS SHLEIPMAN**
Client: **DYAX**

Creative Firm: **KOLBRENER INC. — PITTSBURGH, PA**
Creative Team: **MICHAEL KOLBRENER, DECK SLONE, KIM LINK, KIRK LITTELL**
Client: **ARCH COAL INC.**

Creative Firm: **DEVON ENERGY - IN HOUSE — OKLAHOMA CITY, OK**
Creative Team: **TIM LANGENBERG, ZACK HAGAR, SHEA SNYDER, CHIP MINTY, SCOTT RAFFE**
Client: **DEVON ENERGY CORPORATION**

Creative Firm: **Q-PLUS DESIGN PTE LTD. — SINGAPORE**
Creative Team: **DILLON J., MARK SIDWELL**
Client: **PACIFIC INTERNET LIMITED**

Creative Firm: **RWI — NEW YORK, NY**
Creative Team: **MICHAEL DEVOURSNEY, ROBERT WEBSTER**
Client: **VNU**

Creative Firm: **DESIGN OBJECTIVES PTE LTD — SINGAPORE**
Creative Team: **RONNIE S C TAN**
Client: **SP CHEMICALS LTD**

Creative Firm: **CREDENCE PARTNERSHIP PTE LTD — SINGAPORE**
Creative Team: **FRANCIS SKG, RESHMA, STEPHEN**
Client: **MULTIVISION INTELLIGENT SURVEILLANCE LIMITED**

Creative Firm: **GRAPHICAT LTD. — WANCHAI, HONG KONG**
Creative Team: **COLIN TILLYER**
Client: **NOBLE GROUP LTD.**

Creative Firm: **Q-PLUS DESIGN PTE LTD. — SINGAPORE**
Creative Team: **DILLON J., LI SAR SNG**
Client: **LOW KENG HUAT LTD.**

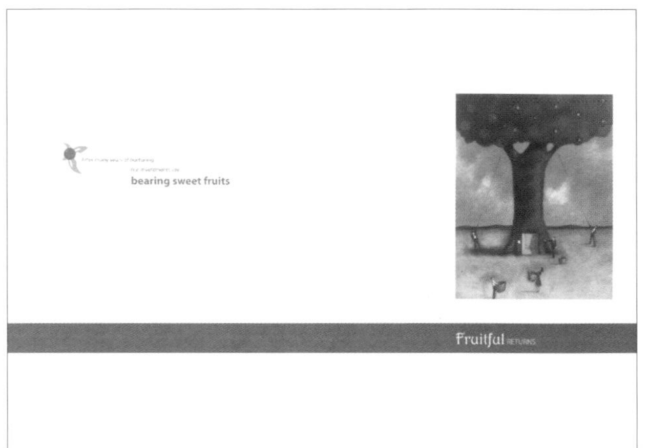

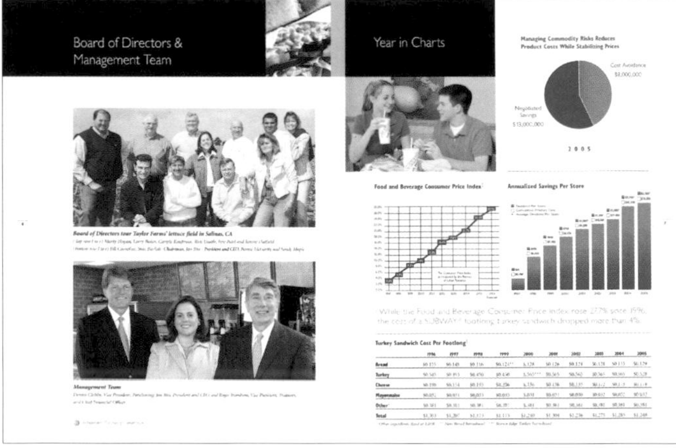

Creative Team: **ORIGINAL IMPRESSIONS — MIAMI, FL**
Art directors: **LISA CUERVO**
Client: **IPC**

Creative Firm: **GODBE COMMUNICATIONS — HALF MOON BAY, CA**
Client: **LUCILE PACKARD CHILDREN'S HOSPITAL**

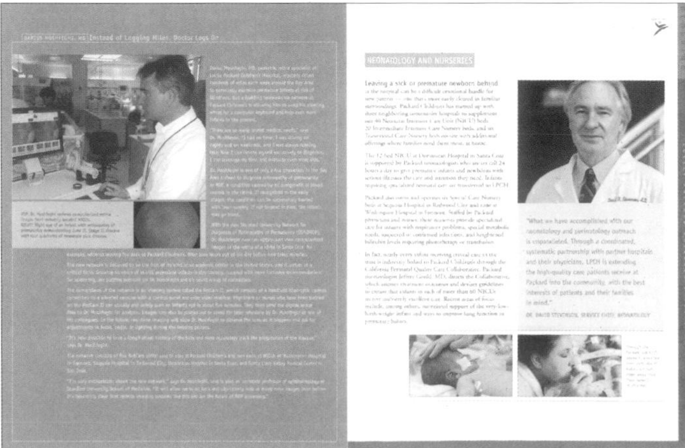

Creative Team: **SIGNI — MEXICO CITY, D.F., MEXICO**
Art directors: **RENE GALINDO, PABLO GARCIA**
Client: **ALSEA**

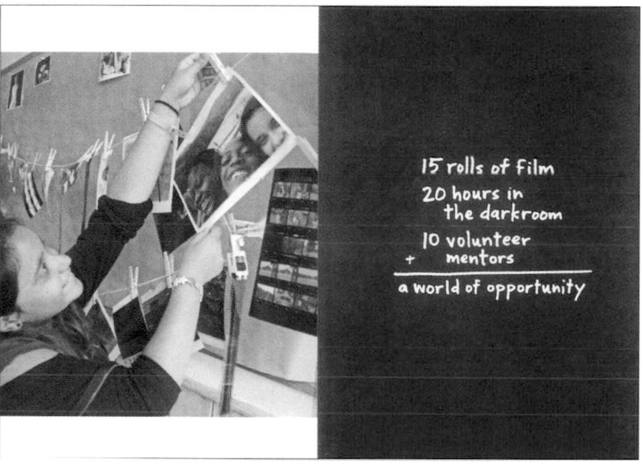

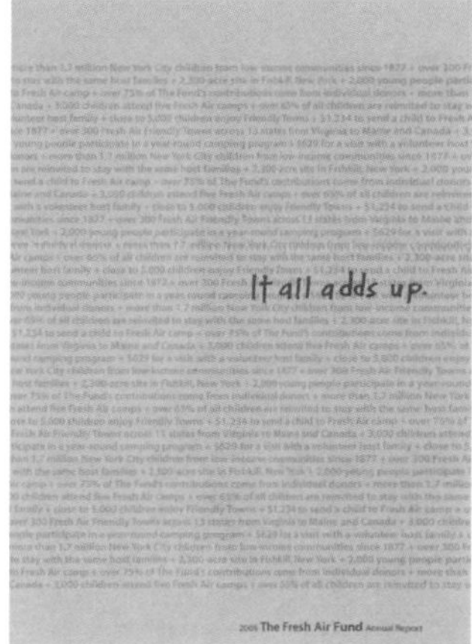

Creative Firm: **SUKA DESIGN — NEW YORK, NY**
Creative Team: **MARIA BELFIORE**
Client: **THE FRESH AIR FUND**

Creative Firm: **Q-PLUS DESIGN PTE LTD. — SINGAPORE**
Creative Team: **DILLON J., MARK SIDWELL**
Client: **SINGAPORE AIRPORT TERMINAL SERVICE LTD.**

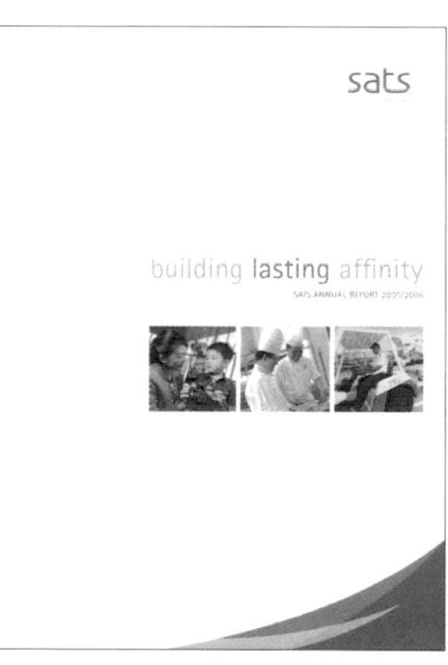

Creative Firm: **VSA PARTNERS, INC. — CHICAGO, IL**
Creative Team: **CURT SCHREIBER, STEVE RYAN, JEN ORTH, MICHAEL FREIMUTH, AZURE DAVIS, RICHARD RENNO**
Client: **IBM CORPORATION**

Creative Team: **BCN COMMUNICATIONS — CHICAGO, IL**
Art directors: **CARA CARPENTER, JAMES PITROSKI, MICHAEL NEU, JAMES SCHNEPF, TED STOIK**
Client: **HNI CORPORATION**

Creative Firm: **MEDIACONCEPTS CORPORATION — ASSONET, MA**
Creative Team: **MEDIACONCEPTS CORPORATION, GREG DOBOS**
Client: **OCEAN SPRAY**

Creative Firm: **PARAGRAPHS DESIGN — CHICAGO, IL**
Creative Team: **JIM CHILCUTT, ROBIN ZVONEK**
Client: **HOSPIRA**

Creative Firm: **SIGNI — MEXICO CITY, D.F., MEXICO**
Creative Team: **DANIEL CASTELAO, ODETTE EDWARDS**
Client: **WAL-MART MEXICO**

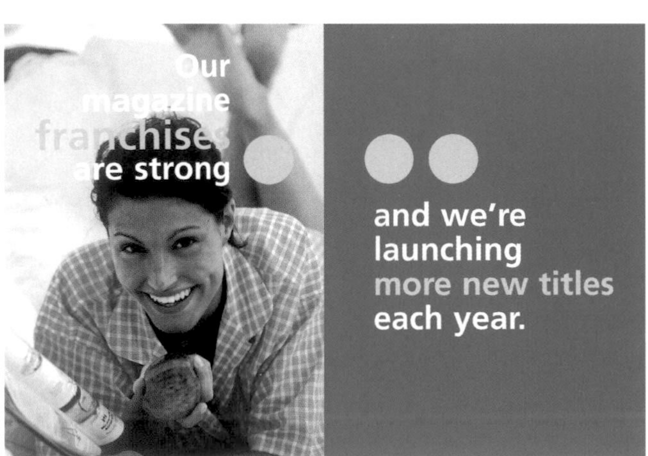

Creative Firm: **TAYLOR & IVES INCORPORATED — NEW YORK, NY**
Creative Team: **ALISA ZAMIR, PAMELA BROOKS**
Client: **THE READER'S DIGEST ASSOCIATION, INC.**

Creative Firm: **ADDISON — NEW YORK, NY**
Creative Team: **DAVID KOHLER, JASON MILLER**
Client: **SL GREEN REALTY CORP.**

Creative Firm: **PARAGRAPHS DESIGN — CHICAGO, IL**
Creative Team: **DORA RODRIGUEZ, RACHEL RAPTKE, ROBIN ZVONEK**
Client: **COCA-COLA FEMSA**

Creative Firm: **DEVER DESIGNS — LAUREL, MD**
Creative Team: **JEFFREY DEVER, KIM POLLOCK**
Client: **SOCIETY FOR NEUROSCIENCE**

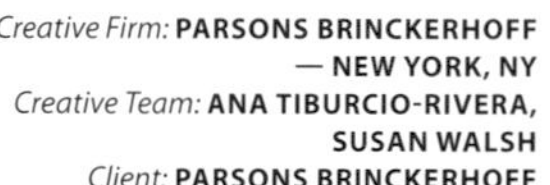

Creative Firm: **PARSONS BRINCKERHOFF — NEW YORK, NY**
Creative Team: **ANA TIBURCIO-RIVERA, SUSAN WALSH**
Client: **PARSONS BRINCKERHOFF**

Creative Firm: **MEDIACONCEPTS CORPORATION — ASSONET, MA**
Creative Team: **MEDIACONCEPTS CORPORATION, GREG DOBOS**
Client. **SEPRACOR**

Creative Firm: **ALL MEDIA PROJECTS LIMITED — PORT OF SPAIN, TRINIDAD AND TOBAGO**
Creative Team: **SHELLEY HOSEIN, ANTHONY MOORE, DEBBIE GARRAWAY, JULIEN GREENIDGE, CARIBBEAN PAPER AND PRINTED PRODUCTS (1993) LTD ,**
Client: **CLICO**

Creative Firm: **MAD DOG GRAPHX — ANCHORAGE, AK**
Creative Team: **KRIS RYAN CLARKE**
Client: **ALASKA COMMUNITY FOUNDATION**

Creative Firm: **COATES AND COATES — NAPERVILLE, IL**
Creative Team: **CAROLIN COATES, RON COATES, JAMES SCHNEPF, STEVEN MCDONALD, ANDY GOODWIN**
Client: **SARA LEE CORPORATION**

Creative Firm: **ADDISON — NEW YORK, NY**
Creative Team: **RICHARD COLBOURNE, JASON MILLER**
Client: **AVERY DENNISON**

Creative Firm: **MEDIACONCEPTS CORPORATION — ASSONET, MA**
Creative Team: **MEDIACONCEPTS CORPORATION, GREG DOBOS**
Client: **CRITICAL THERAPEUTICS, INC.**

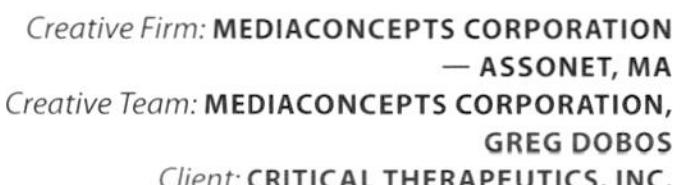

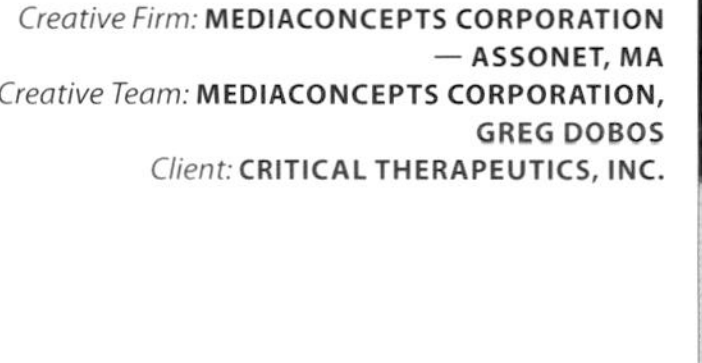

Creative Firm: **DESIGN OBJECTIVES PTE LTD — SINGAPORE**
Creative Team: **RONNIE S C TAN**
Client: **BEAUTY CHINA HOLDINGS LIMITED**

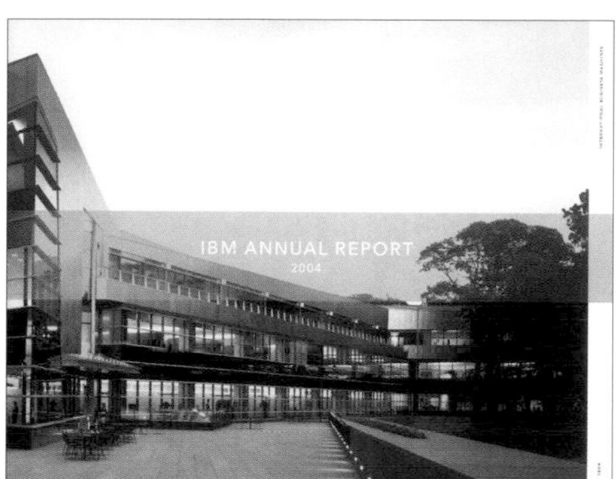

Creative Firm: **VSA PARTNERS, INC. — CHICAGO, IL**
Creative Team: **CURT SCHREIBER, STEVE RYAN, ASHLEY LIPPARD, WENDY BELT, SILAS MUNRO, RICHARD RENNO**
Client: **IBM CORPORATION**

Creative Firm: **Q-PLUS DESIGN PTE LTD. — SINGAPORE**
Creative Team: **DILLON J., MARK SIDWELL**
Client: **DMX TECHNOLOGIES GROUP LIMITED**

Creative Firm: **SUKA DESIGN — NEW YORK, NY**
Creative Team: **LOLA BERNABE**
Client: **THE FUND FOR PUBLIC SCHOOL**

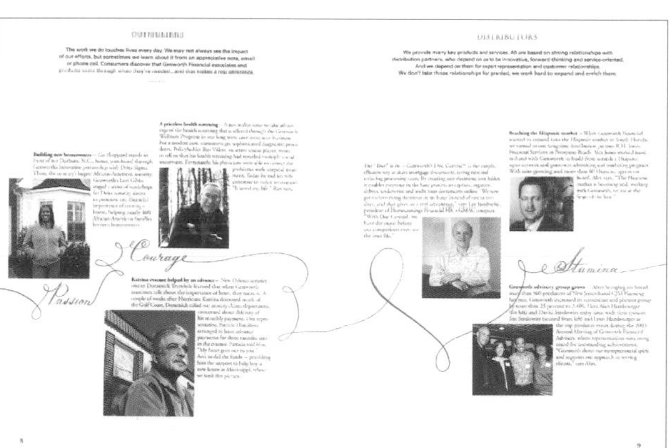

Creative Firm: **ADDISON — NEW YORK, NY**
Creative Team: **DAVID KOHLER, CHRISTINA ANTONOPOULOS**
Client: **GENWORTH FINANCIAL**

Creative Firm: **SIGNI — MEXICO CITY, D.F., MEXICO**
Creative Team: **RENE GALINDO**
Client: **CEMEX**

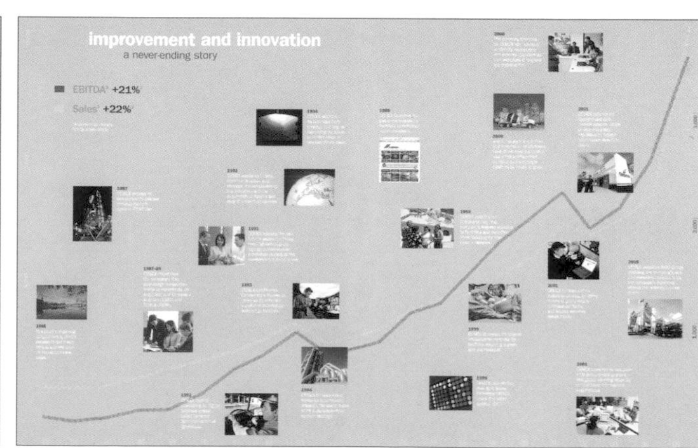

Creative Firm: **EMERSON, WAJDOWICZ STUDIOS — NEW YORK, NY**
Creative Team: **LISA LAROCHELLE, JUREK WAJDOWICZ, YOKO YOSHIDA, TRICKLE UP PROGRAM**
Client: **TRICKLE UP PROGRAM**

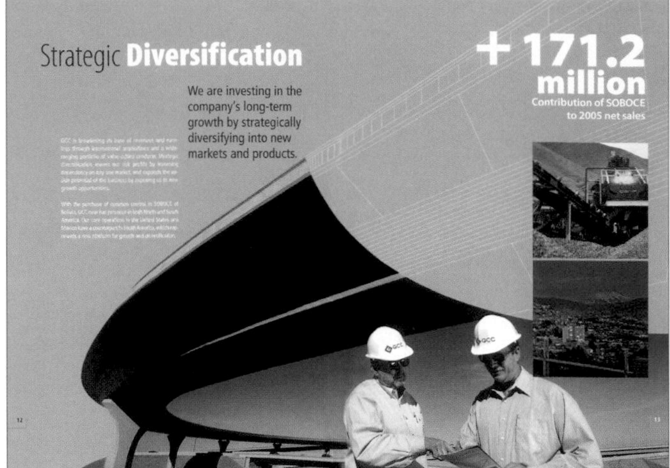

Creative Firm: **SIGNI — MEXICO CITY, D.F., MEXICO**
Creative Team: **DANIEL CASTELAO, PABLO GARCIA**
Client: **GRUPO CEMENTOS DE CHIHUAHUA**

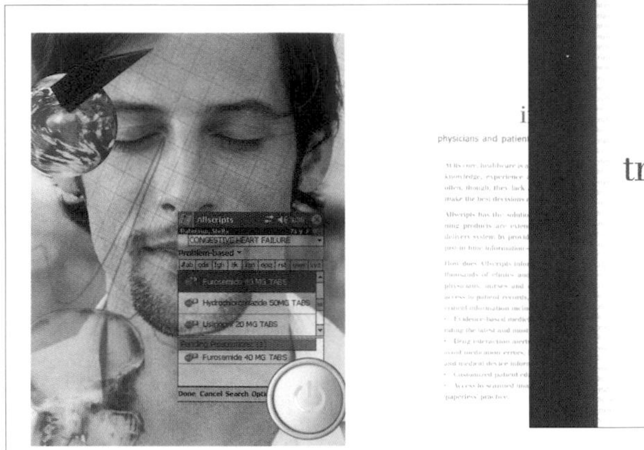

Creative Firm: **PARAGRAPHS DESIGN — CHICAGO, IL**
Creative Team: **DORA RODRIGUEZ, RACHEL RADKE, ROBIN ZVONEX**
Client: **ALLSCRIPTS**

Creative Firm: **KAN & LAU DESIGN CONSULTANTS — KOWLOON TONG, HONG KONG**
Creative Team: **FREEMAN LAU SIU HONG, KO SI HONG, JAN HAU**
Client: **ROADSHOW HOLDINGS LTD.**

Creative Firm: **SIGNI — MEXICO CITY, D.F., MEXICO**
Creative Team: **DANIEL CASTELAO, FELIPE SALAS**
Client: **AMERICA MOVIL**

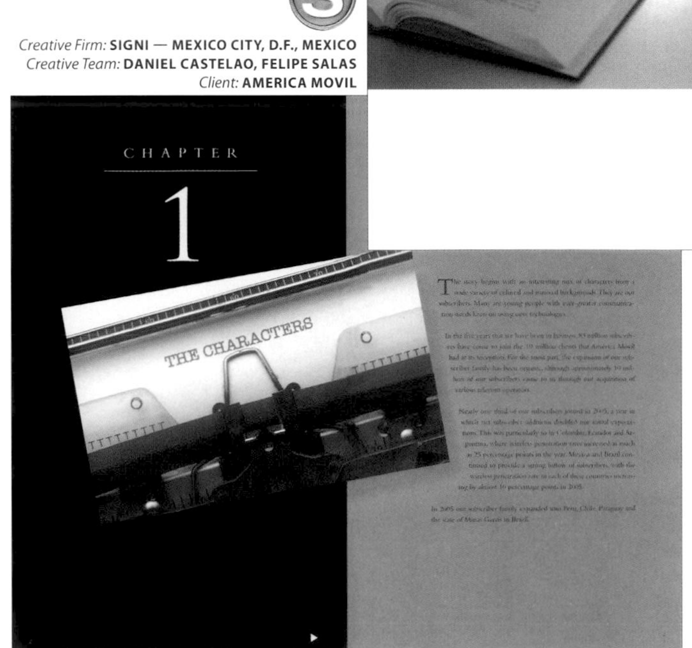

Creative Firm: **PARAGRAPHS DESIGN — CHICAGO, IL**
Creative Team: **MEOW VATANATUMRAK, RACHEL RADTKE, CARY MARTIN**
Client: **SUNTRUST BANKS, INC.**

Creative Firm: **EMERSON, WAJDOWICZ STUDIOS— NEW YORK, NY**
Creative Team: **L. LAROCHELLE, J. WAJDOWICZ, Y. YOSHIDA, M. MENDEZ , P. PETTERSSON, R. HAVIV, B. STEVENS, P. BONET, S. BOELSCH AND OTHERS**
Client: **MÉDECINS SANS FRONTIÈRES / DOCTORS WITHOUT BORDERS**

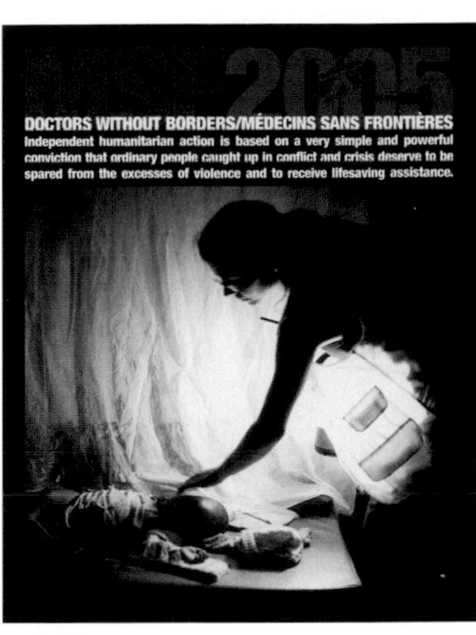

Creative Firm: **TAYLOR & IVES INCORPORATED — NEW YORK, NY**
Creative Team: **ALISA ZAMIR, TREVOR PACCIONE**
Client: **THE HERSHEY COMPANY**

Creative Firm: **SIGNI — MEXICO CITY, D.F., MEXICO**
Creative Team: **RENE GALINDO, ODETTE EDWARDS**
Client: **TELEVISA**

Creative Firm: **SUKA DESIGN — NEW YORK, NY**
Creative Team: **BRIAN WONG**
Client: **GAY, LESBIAN, AND STRAIGHT EDUCATION NETWORK**

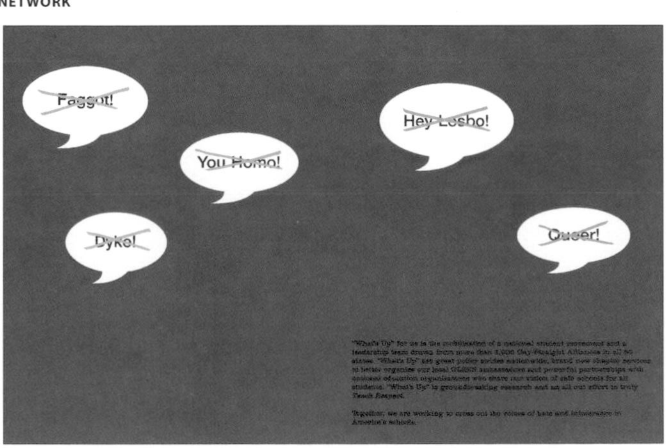

Creative Firm: **BCN COMMUNICATIONS — CHICAGO, IL**
Creative Team: **MICHAEL O'BRIEN, HARRI BOLLER, MICHAEL NEU, ROTH & RAMBERG PHOTOGRAPHY , TED STOIK**
Client: **CN**

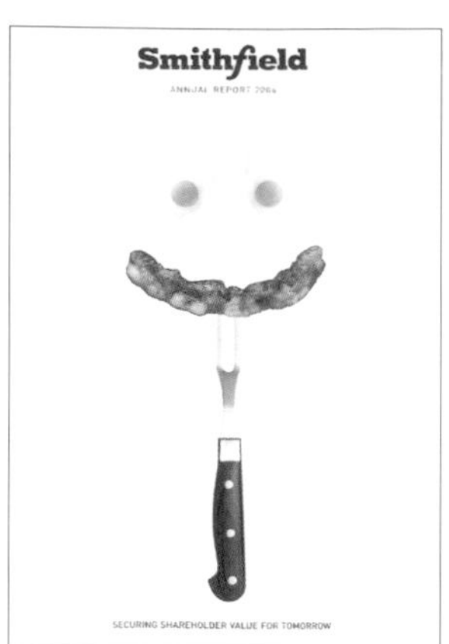

Creative Firm: **TAYLOR & IVES INCORPORATED — NEW YORK, NY**
Creative Team: **ALISA ZAMIR, DANIEL CASPESCHA**
Client: **SMITHFIELD FOODS, INC.**

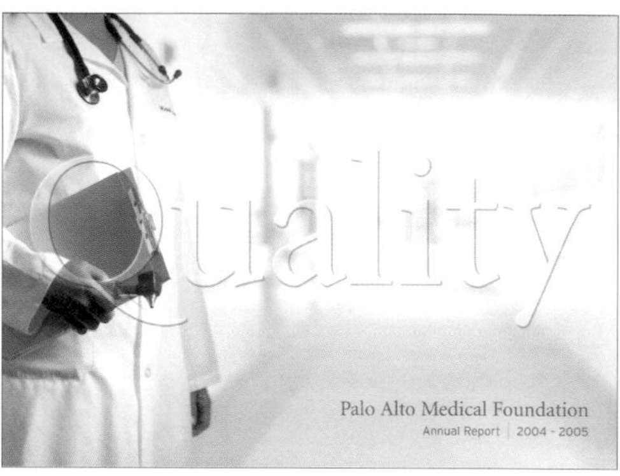

Creative Firm: **VOICEBOX CREATIVE — SAN FRANCISCO, CA**
Creative Team: **JACQUES ROSSOUW, MARK TUSCHMAN, SUSAN SHARPE**
Client: **PALO ALTO MEDICAL FOUNDATION**

Creative Firm: **PHOENIX CREATIVE GROUP, LLC — POTOMAC FALLS, VA**
Creative Team: **NICOLE KASSOLIS, SEAN MULLINS, C&R PRINTING, JUPITER IMAGES, AGE FOTOSTOCK, MASTERFILE, PICTUREQUEST**
Client: **ICI MUTUAL**

Creative Firm: **SILVER COMMUNICATIONS INC — NEW YORK, NY**
Creative Team: **GREGG SIBERT, CHRISTINA WEISSMAN**
Client: **EAST MIDTOWN ASSOCIATION**

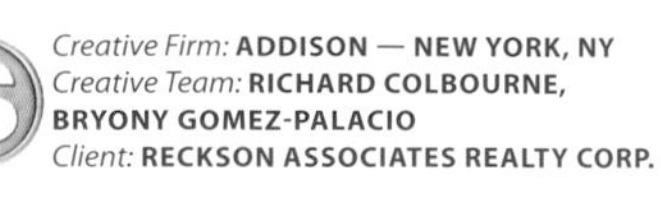

Creative Firm: **ADDISON — NEW YORK, NY**
Creative Team: **RICHARD COLBOURNE, BRYONY GOMEZ-PALACIO**
Client: **RECKSON ASSOCIATES REALTY CORP.**

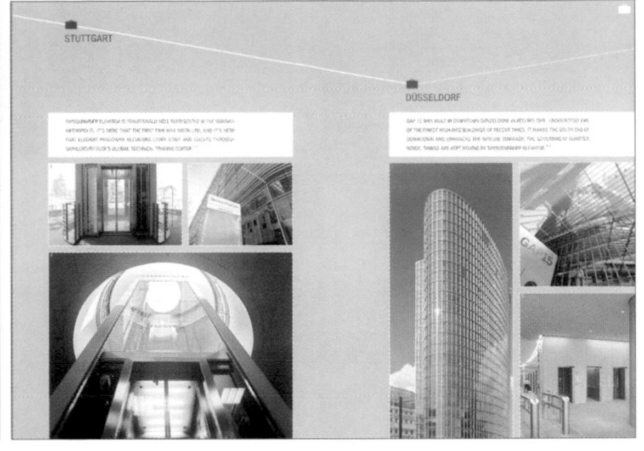

Creative Firm: **RTS RIEGER TEAM WERBEAGENTUR GMBH — DÜSSELDORF, GERMANY**
Creative Team: **MICHAELA MÜLLER, VEREUA TRURNIT, ULRICH GIELISCH, FRANCISCO NAVARRO Y GOMES**
Client: **THYSSENKRUPP ELEVATOR AG**

Creative Team: **KATE FERRY, RAYMOND HEBERT**
Client: **COMMUNITY FOUNDATION OF ACADIANA**

Creative Firm: **ORIGINAL IMPRESSIONS — MIAMI, FL**
Creative Team: **LISA CUERVO**
Client: **BURGER KING/MCLAMORE FOUNDATION**

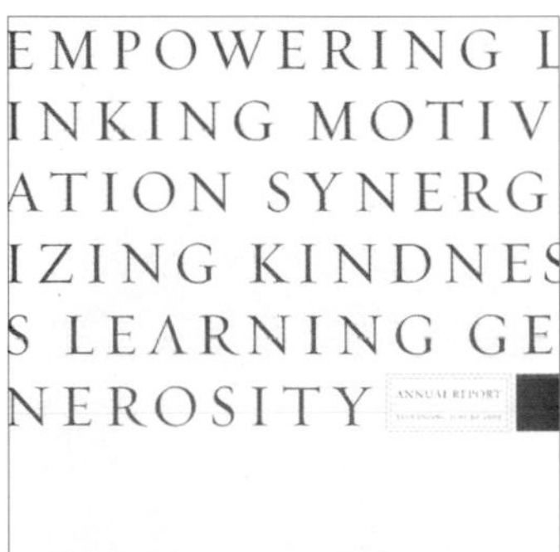

Creative Firm: **THE DESIGN STUDIO AT KEAN UNIVERSITY— UNION, NJ**
Creative Team: **ANIA MURRAY, ERIN SMITH**
Client: **KEAN UNIVERSITY FOUNDATION**

Creative Firm: **ADDISON — NEW YORK, NY**
Creative Team: **DAVID KOHLER, RICK SLUSHER**
Client: **ENGELHARD**

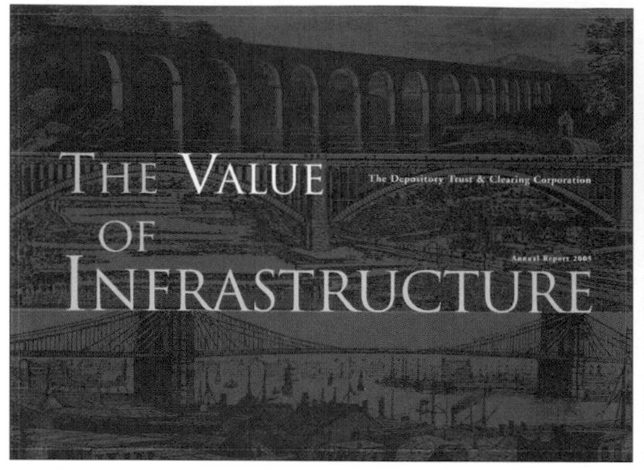

Creative Firm: **TAYLOR & IVES INCORPORATED — NEW YORK, NY**
Creative Team: **ALISA ZAMIR, PAMELA BROOKS**
Client: **THE DEPOSITORY TRUST & CLEARING CORPORATION**

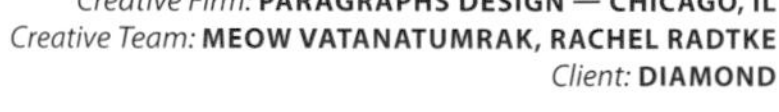

Creative Firm: **PARAGRAPHS DESIGN — CHICAGO, IL**
Creative Team: **MEOW VATANATUMRAK, RACHEL RADTKE**
Client: **DIAMOND**

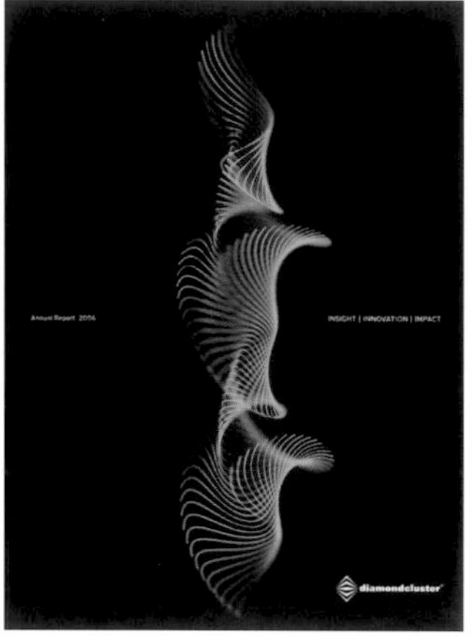

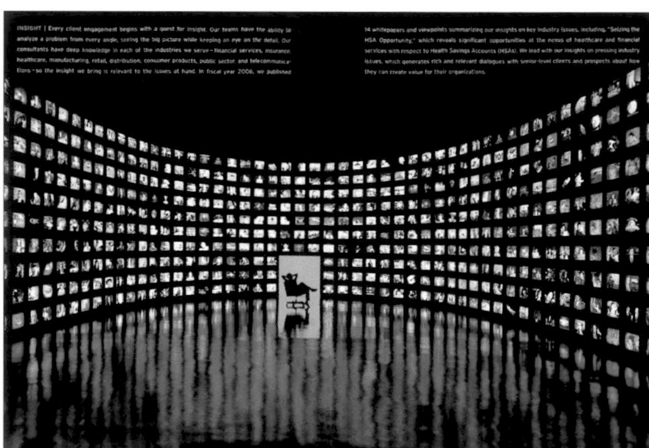

Creative Firm: **EMERSON, WAJDOWICZ STUDIOS — NEW YORK, NY**
Creative Team: **JUREK WAJDOWICZ, LISA LAROCHELLE, MANNY MENDEZ, JONAS BENDIKSEN**
Client: **THE ROCKEFELLER FOUNDATION**

Creative Firm: **ADDISON — NEW YORK, NY**
Creative Team: **DAVID KOHLER, BRYONY GOMEZ-PALACIO**
Client: **AES CORPORATION**

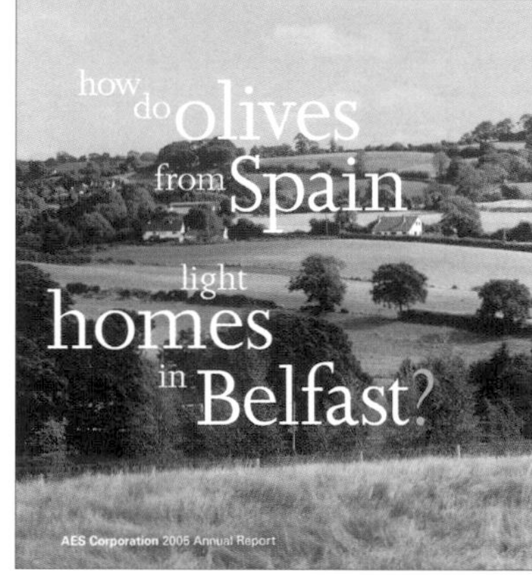

Creative Firm: **KAN & LAU DESIGN CONSULTANTS — KOWLOON TONG, HONG KONG**
Creative Team: **KAN TAI-KEUNG, CARMEN KWOK, JUSTIN YU**
Client: **HYSAN DEVELOPMENT CO. LTD.**

Creative Firm: **KOLBRENER INC. — PITTSBURGH, PA**
Creative Team: **MICHAEL KOLBRENER, YVONNE ROEBUCK**
Client: **PRESSLEY RIDGE**

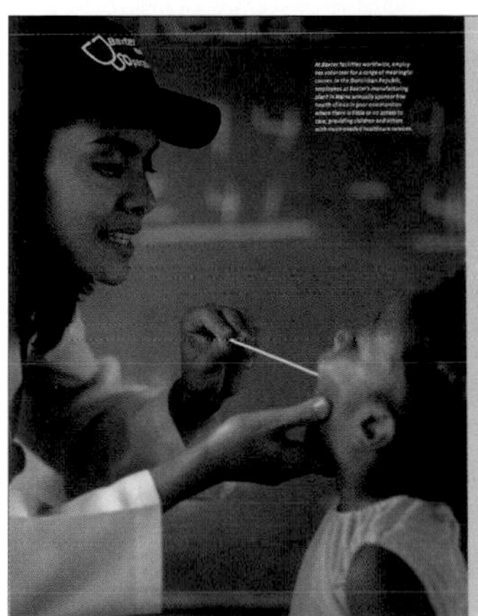

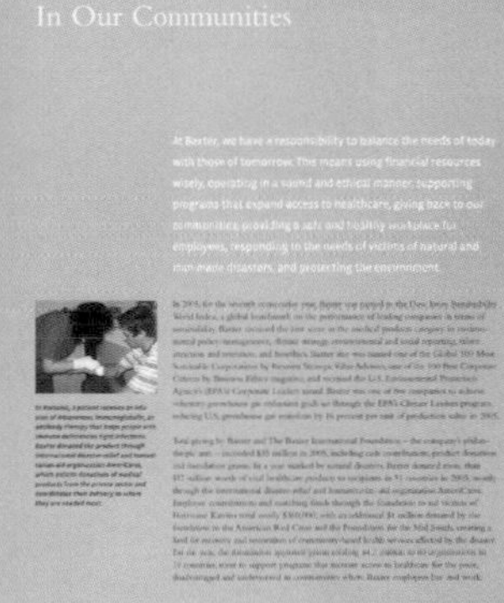

Creative Firm: **PARAGRAPHS DESIGN — CHICAGO, IL**
Creative Team: **MEOW VATANATUMRAK, ROBIN ZVONEK**
Client: **BAXTER INTERNATIONAL INC.**

Creative Firm: **TAYLOR & IVES INCORPORATED — NEW YORK, NY**
Creative Team: **ALISA ZAMIR, DANIEL CASPESCHA**
Client: **BLACKROCK**

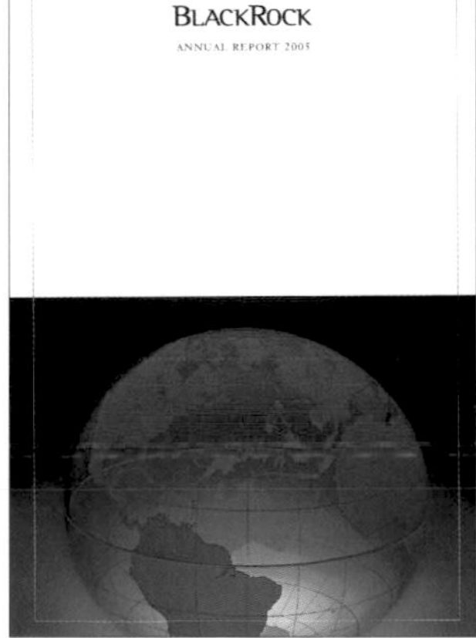

Creative Firm: **HENRYGILL ADVERTISING — DENVER, CO**
Creative Team: **BRYANT FERNANDEZ**
Client: **BLACK HILLS CORPORATION**

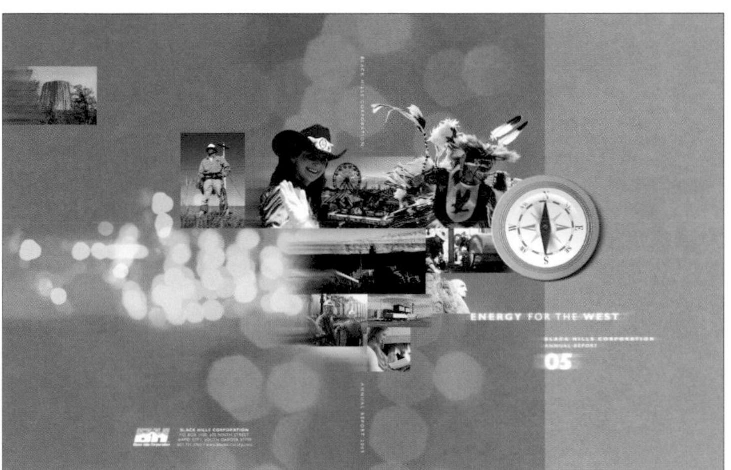

Creative Firm: **GRAPHICAT LTD. — WANCHAI, HONG KONG**
Creative Team: **COLIN TILLYER**
Client: **ASIA SATELLITE TELECOMMUNICATIONS HOLDINGS LTD.**

Creative Firm: **ADDISON — NEW YORK, NY**
Creative Team: **RICHARD COLBOURNE, CHRISTINA ANTONOPOULOS**
Client: **ISTAR FINANCIAL**

Creative Firm: **COATES AND COATES — NAPERVILLE, IL**
Creative Team: **CAROLIN COATES, RON COATES**
Client: **PROLOGIS**

Creative Firm: **ADDISON — NEW YORK, NY**
Creative Team: **DAVID KOHLER, RICK SLUSHER**
Client: **THE MCGRAW-HILL COMPANIES, INC.**

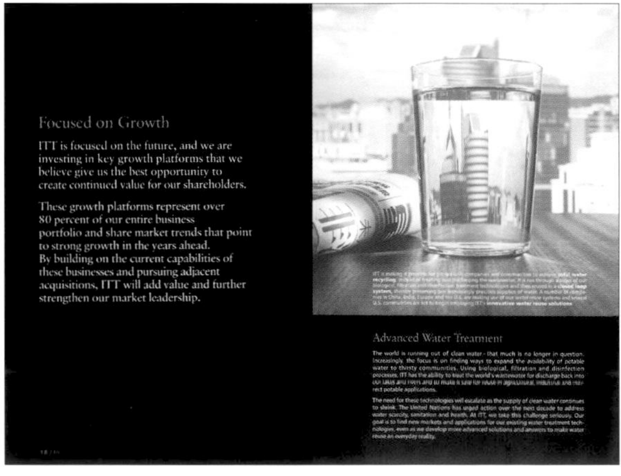

Creative Firm: **ADDISON — NEW YORK, NY**
Creative Team: **RICHARD COLBOURNE, JASON MILLER**
Client: **ITT**

Creative Firm: **HERMAN MILLER, INC. — ZEELAND, MI**
Creative Team: **STEVE FRYKHOLM, ANDREW DULL, CLARK MALCOLM, MARLENE CAPOTOSTO**
Client: **HERMAN MILLER, INC.**

Creative Firm: **PARAGRAPHS DESIGN — CHICAGO, IL**
Creative Team: **JIM CHILCUTT, ROBIN ZVONEK**
Client: **EXELON CORPORATION**

Creative Firm: **COATES AND COATES — NAPERVILLE, IL**
Creative Team: **CAROLIN COATES, RON COATES, TED STOIK**
Client: **MOLSON COORS BREWING COMPANY**

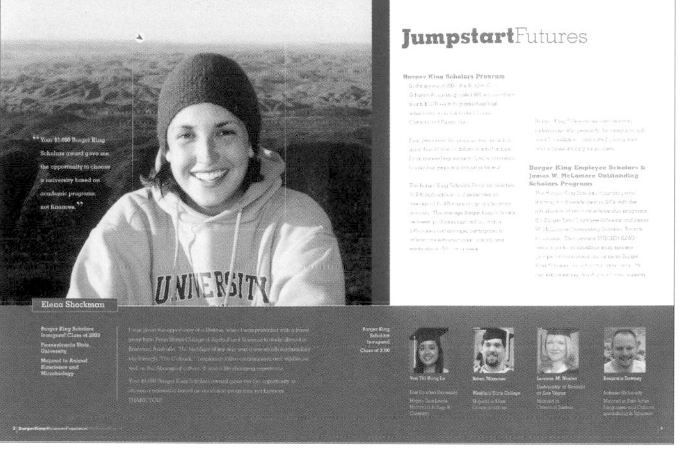

Creative Firm: **ORIGINAL IMPRESSIONS — MIAMI, FL**
Creative Team: **LISA CUERVO**
Client: **BURGER KING/MCLAMORE FOUNDATION**

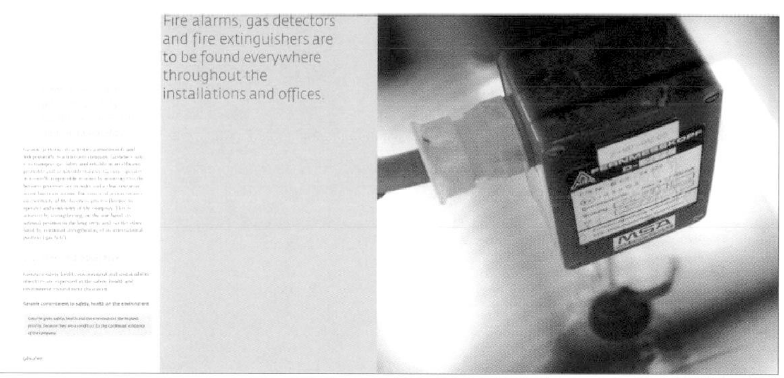

Creative Firm: **ERWIN ZINGER GRAPHIC DESIGN — GRONINGEN, NETHERLANDS**
Creative Team: **ERWIN ZINGER, DESIRÉE DIJKSTRA, TEACKELE SOEPBOER**
Client: **N.V. NEDERLANDSE GASUNIE**

Creative Firm: **SIGNI — MEXICO CITY, D.F., MEXICO**
Creative Team: **RENE GALINDO, FELIPE SALAS**
Client: **CASAS GEO**

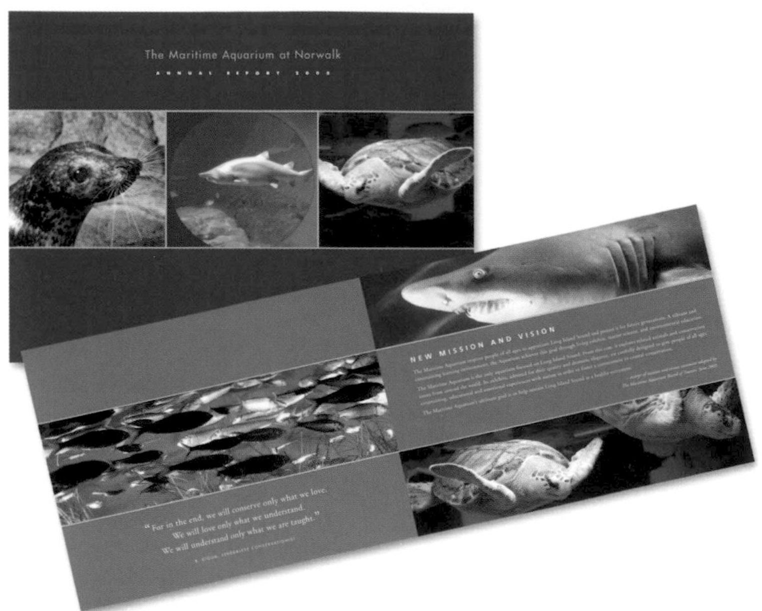

Creative Firm: **TOM FOWLER, INC. — NORWALK, CT**
Creative Team: **ELIZABETH P. BALL, BRIEN O'REILLY, THOMAS G. FOWLER**
Client: **THE MARITIME AQUARIUM AT NORWALK**

Creative Firm: **COASTLINES CREATIVE GROUP — VANCOUVER, BC, CANADA**
Creative Team: **BYRON DOWLER, MICHAEL SINANAN, ERIK PROSSER, KAREN SPEIRS**
Client: **CHROMOS MOLECULAR SYSTEMS**

Creative Firm: **KOR GROUP — BOSTON, MA**
Creative Team: **ANNE CALL, JIM GIBSON, LEN RUBENSTEIN, BETSY CULLEN**
Client: **BETH ISRAEL DEACONESS MEDICAL CENTER**

Creative Firm: **BCN COMMUNICATIONS — CHICAGO, IL**
Creative Team: **JAMES PITROSKI, MICHAEL O'BRIEN, MICHAEL NEU, JAMES SCHNEPF**
Client: **GENERAL MOTORS CORPORATION**

Creative Firm: **PHOENIX CREATIVE GROUP, LLC — POTOMAC FALLS, VA**
Creative Team: **SEAN MULLINS, NICOLE KASSOLIS, THERESA WALLACE, S&S GRAPHICS**
Client: **AMERICAN WOODWORK CORPORATION**

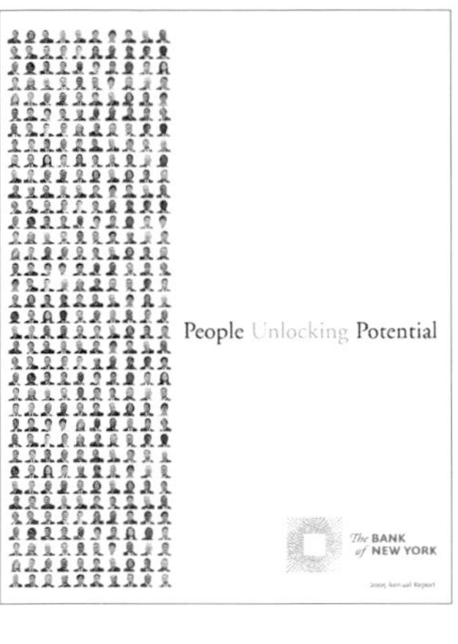

Creative Firm: **TAYLOR & IVES INCORPORATED — NEW YORK, NY**
Creative Team: **ALISA ZAMIR, DANIEL CASPESCHA**
Client: **THE BANK OF NEW YORK, INC.**

Creative Firm: **STAN GELLMAN GRAPHIC DESIGN INC.— ST. LOUIS, MO**
Creative Team: **MEGAN MILLER, BARRY TILSON, GREG KIGER, COLLEEN CLEMENTS**
Client: **LABARGE INC.**

Creative Firm: **SPLASH PRODUCTIONS PTE LTD — SINGAPORE**
Creative Team: **TERRY LEE, STANLEY TAP, NORMAN LAI**
Client: **STRATECH SYSTEMS LIMITED**

Creative Firm: **NAMARO GRAPHIC DESIGNS, INC. — RHINEBECK, NY**
Creative Team: **NADINE ROBBINS, WENDY MACOMBER**
Client: **NATIONAL EQUITY FUND INC.**

I'M MORE THAN A PATIENT.

Creative Firm: **SUKA DESIGN — NEW YORK, NY**
Creative Team: **BRIAN WONG, LOLA BERNABE**
Client: **VISITING NURSE SERVICE OF NEW YORK**

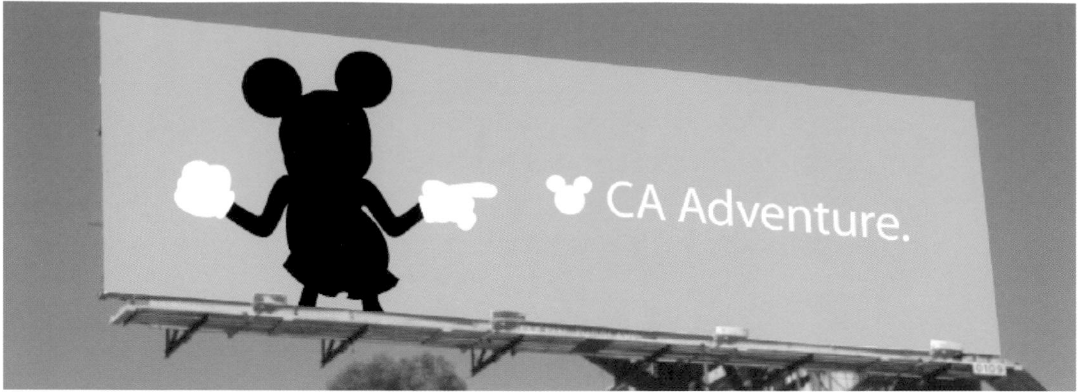

Creative Firm: **MIKE SALISBURY EFFECTIVE CREATIVE STRATEGIES — VENICE, CA**
Creative Team: **MIKE SALISBURY, MATT BRIGHT, GUSTAVO MORAIS**
Client: **DISNEY'S CALIFORNIA ADVENTURE**

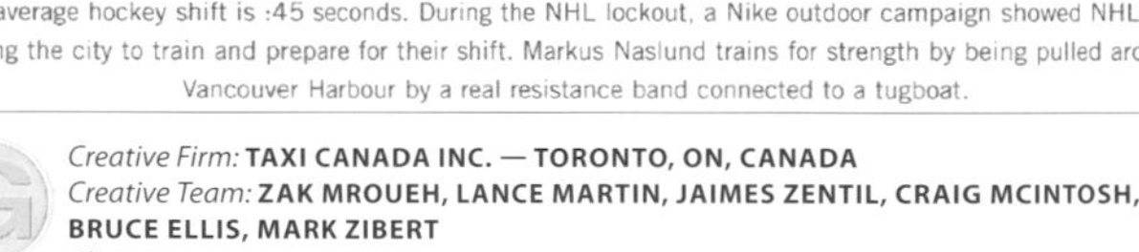
The average hockey shift is :45 seconds. During the NHL lockout, a Nike outdoor campaign showed NHL stars using the city to train and prepare for their shift. Markus Naslund trains for strength by being pulled around Vancouver Harbour by a real resistance band connected to a tugboat.

Creative Firm: **TAXI CANADA INC. — TORONTO, ON, CANADA**
Creative Team: **ZAK MROUEH, LANCE MARTIN, JAIMES ZENTIL, CRAIG MCINTOSH, BRUCE ELLIS, MARK ZIBERT**
Client: **NIKE CANADA**

Creative Firm: **HEYE&PARTNER GMBH — UNTERHACHING, BAVARIA, GERMANY**
Creative Team: **JAN WOELFEL, LUKAS BECKER, MARKUS LANGE, MICHAEL STEMPROCK**
Client: **MCDONALD'S GERMANY**

Creative Firm: **HOFFMAN/LEWIS — SAN FRANCISCO, CA**
Creative Team: **SHARON KRINSKY, JAMES CABRAL, RONDA DUNN, JASON HEADLEY**
Client: **HENRY'S**

Creative Firm: **HOFFMAN/LEWIS — SAN FRANCISCO, CA**
Creative Team: **SHARON KRINSKY, JAMES CABRAL**
Client: **TOYOTA**

S

Creative Firm: **RUSTY GEORGE DESIGN — TACOMA, WA**
Creative Team: **RYAN MELINE, RUSTY GEORGE DESIGN**
Client: **NORTHWEST TREK**

Creative Firm: **HOFFMAN/LEWIS — SAN FRANCISCO, CA**
Creative Team: **SHARON KRINSKY, JAMES CABRAL, RONDA DUNN, JASON HEADLEY**
Client: **HENRY'S**

Creative Firm: **CREATIVE ALLIANCE — LOUISVILLE, KY**
Creative Team: **JOE ADAMS, ERIC HAHN, CHRISTINA KNOPF**
Client: **NANZ & KRAFT FLORISTS**

Creative Firm: **YOUNG & RUBICAM GMBH & CO. KG — FRANKFURT AM MAIN, HESSEN, GERMANY**
Creative Team: **CHRISTIAN DAUL, ULRIKE JOST, ROBIN EBENER**
Client: **COLGATE PALMOLIVE**

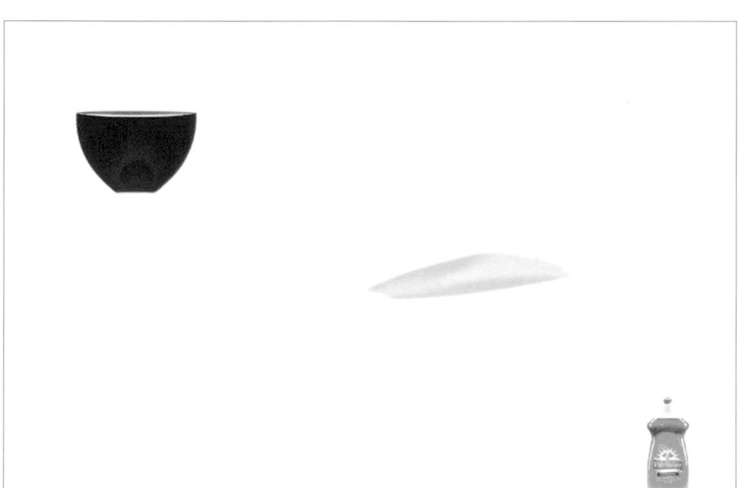

Creative Firm: **HEYE&PARTNER GMBH — UNTERHACHING, BAVARIA, GERMANY**
Creative Team: **THOMAS ALEXY, MATTHIAS REMMLING**
Client: **STEPPENWOLF GMBH MOUNTAINBIKES**

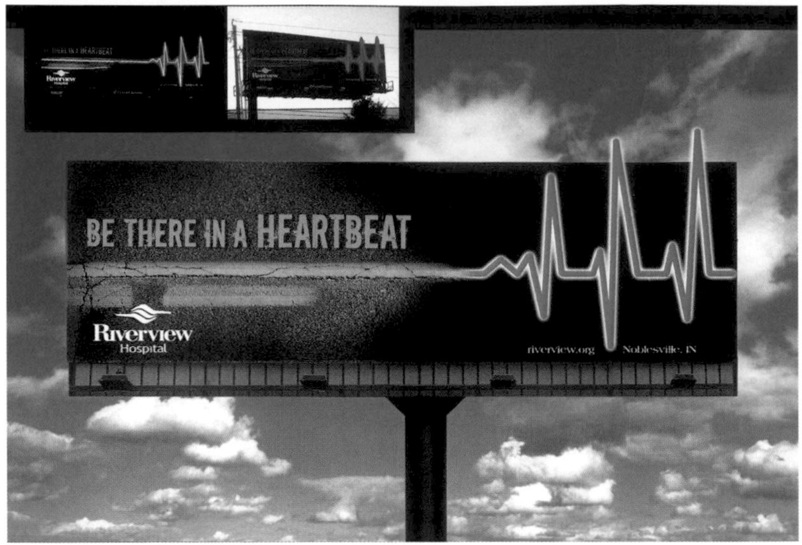

Creative Firm: **KELLER CRESCENT — EVANSVILLE, IN**
Creative Team: **RANDALL ROHN, LEE BRYANT**
Client: **RIVERVIEW HOSPITAL**

The average hockey shift is :45 seconds. During the NHL lockout, a Nike outdoor campaign showed NHL stars using the city to train and prepare for their shift. A crane erected alongside a major motorway shows a larger than life Jarome Iginla training for strength by doing leg lifts.

Creative Firm: **TAXI CANADA INC. — TORONTO, ON, CANADA**
Creative Team: **ZAK MROUEH, LANCE MARTIN, JAIMES ZENTIL, CRAIG MCINTOSH, BRUCE ELLIS, MARK ZIBERT**
Client: **NIKE CANADA**

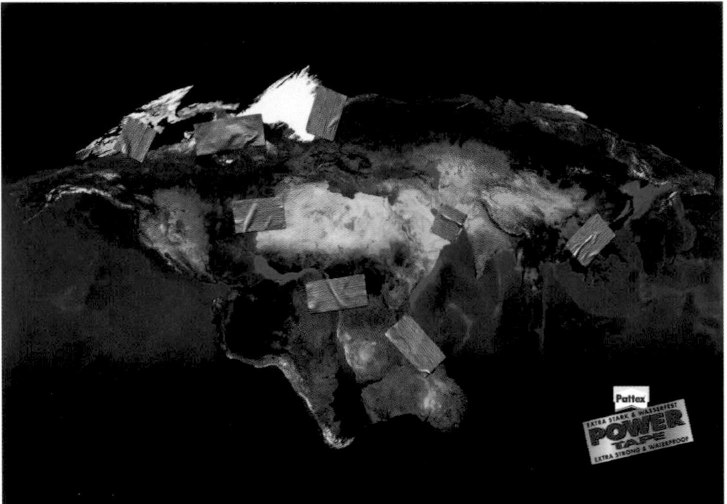

Creative Firm: **HEYE&PARTNER GMBH — UNTERHACHING, BAVARIA, GERMANY**
Creative Team: **HANNES CIATTI, GUNNAR IMMISCH, JAN OKUSLUK, OLIVER DIEHR**
Client: **HENKEL/PATTEX POWERTAPE**

Creative Firm: **YELLOW SHOES CREATIVE WEST, DISNEYLAND RESORT — ANAHEIM, CA**
Creative Team: **SCOTT STARKEY, MARTY MULLER, JACQUELYN MOE, WES CLARK JIM ST. AMANT**
Client: **DISNEYLAND RESORT**

Creative Firm: **DISNEYLAND RESORT — ANAHEIM, CA**
Creative Team: **SCOTT STARKEY, MARTY MULLER, JACQUELYN MOE, WES CLARK**
Client: **DISNEYLAND RESORT**

Creative Firm: **PETERSON MILLA HOOKS — MINNEAPOLIS, MN**
Creative Team: **DAVE PETERSON, SUE KAASE, ELLEN FREGO, CATHERINE IRMITER, KENNETH WILLARDT**
Client: **TARGET**

Creative Firm: **DISNEYLAND RESORT — ANAHEIM, CA**
Creative Team: **SCOTT STARKEY, WES CLARK, JANE ROHAN, MARTY MULLER, JACQUELYN MOE**
Client: **DISNEYLAND RESORT**

Creative Firm: **TAXI CANADA — MONTRÉAL, QC, CANADA**
Creative Team: **STÉPHANE CHARIER, PATRICK CHAUBET, BRIAN GILL, ELYSE NOËL DE TILLY, GUILLAUME BLANCHET, BARRY HARRIS**
Client: **REITMANS/CASSIS**

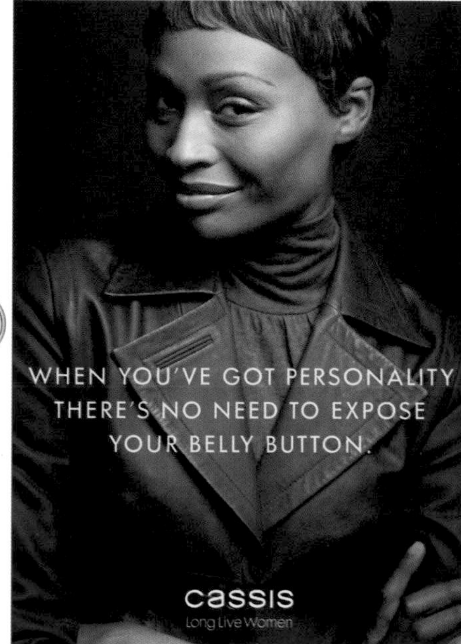

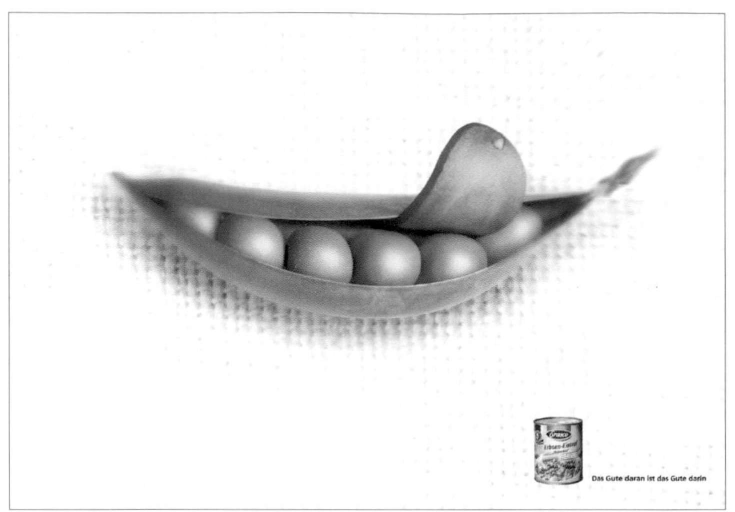

Creative Firm: **YOUNG & RUBICAM GMBH & CO. KG — FRANKFURT AM MAIN, HESSEN, GERMANY**
Creative Team: **CHRISTIAN DAUL, BRUNO PETZ, THOMAS BALZER, MARC WUCHNER**
Client: **CAMPBELL'S GERMANY GMBH**

Creative Firm: **TV LAND — NEW YORK, NY**
Creative Team: **KIM ROSENBLUM, DOMINIQUE VITALI, KEVIN HARTMAN, CHELSEA MOST, MONIQUE SANKEY, TONY D'ORIO**
Client: **TV LAND**

Creative Firm: **YELLOW SHOES CREATIVE WEST, DISNEYLAND RESORT — ANAHEIM, CA**
Creative Team: **SCOTT STARKEY, MARTY MULLER, JACQUELYN MOE, WES CLARK, JIM ST. AMANT, JANE ROHAN**
Client: **DISNEYLAND RESORT**

Creative Firm: **RUSTY GEORGE DESIGN — TACOMA, WA**
Creative Team: **RYAN MELINE**
Client: **WASHINGTON STATE HISTORY MUSEUM**

Creative Firm: **THE FOUNDATION FOR A BETTER LIFE — DENVER, CO**
Creative Team: **BERNIE HOGYA, RON WACHINO, RUSSELL DIXON**
Client: **THE FOUNDATION FOR A BETTER LIFE**

Creative Firm: **DISNEYLAND RESORT — ANAHEIM, CA**
Creative Team: **SCOTT STARKEY, WES CLARK, JACQUELYN MOE, MARTY MULLER, JIM ST. AMANT**
Client: **DISNEYLAND RESORT**

Creative Firm: **LEO BURNETT/YELLOW SHOES CREATIVE WEST, DISNEYLAND RESORT — ANAHEIM, CA**
Creative Team: **SCOTT STARKEY, MARTY MULLER, JACQUELYN MOE, WES CLARK, JIM ST. AMANT**
Client: **DISNEYLAND RESORT**

Creative Firm: **YELLOW SHOES CREATIVE WEST, DISNEYLAND RESORT — ANAHEIM, CA**
Creative Team: **DATHAN SHORE, WES CLARK, MARTY MULLER, JACQUELYN MOE, JIM ST. AMANT**
Client: **DISNEYLAND**

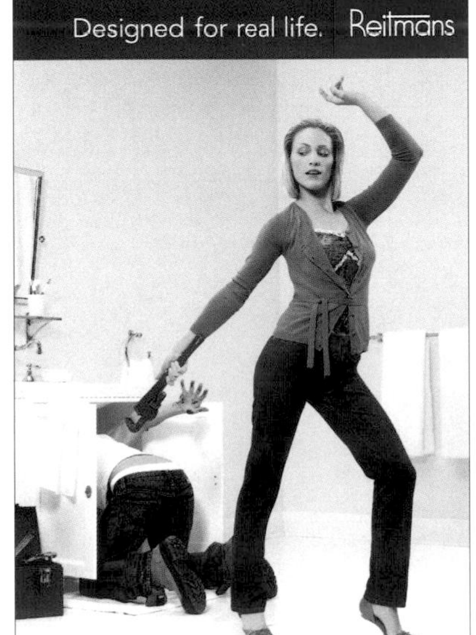

Creative Firm: **TAXI CANADA — MONTRÉAL, QC, CANADA**
Creative Team: **STÉPHANE CHARIER, PATRICK CHAUBET, BRIAN GILL**
Client: **REITMANS**

Creative Firm: **IM-AJ COMMUNICATIONS & DESIGN, INC. — WEST KINGSTON, RI**
Creative Team: **JAMI OUELLETTE, LESLIE EMERT**
Client: **RHODE ISLAND HOUSING**

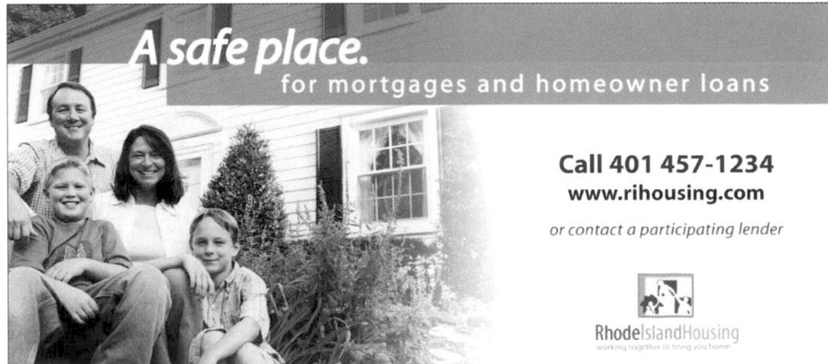

Creative Firm: **PRIMARY DESIGN, INC. — HAVERHILL, MA**
Creative Team: **LIZ FEDORZYN, VITA MIRONOVA, SHARYN ROGERS, JULES EPSTEIN, ALLISON DAVIS**
Client: **ABBOTT HOMES**

Creative Firm: **VH1 — NEW YORK, NY**
Client: **VH1**

Creative Firm: **RUDER FINN DESIGN — NEW YORK, NY**
Creative Team: **LISA GABBAY, SAL CATANIA, KAVEN LAM, JOHN GRUEN**
Client: **TRANSPLACE**

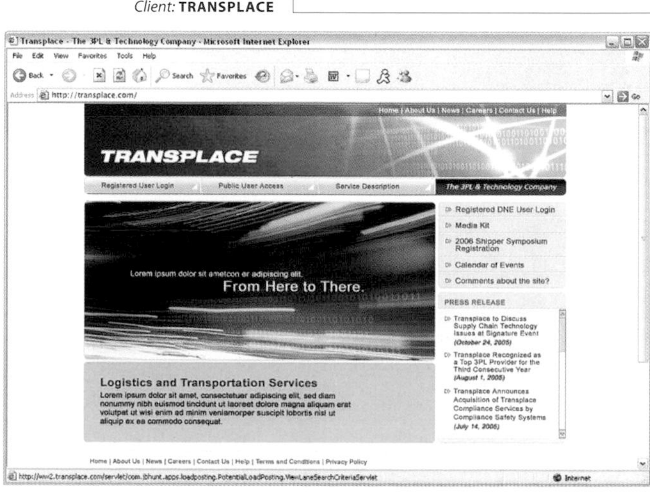

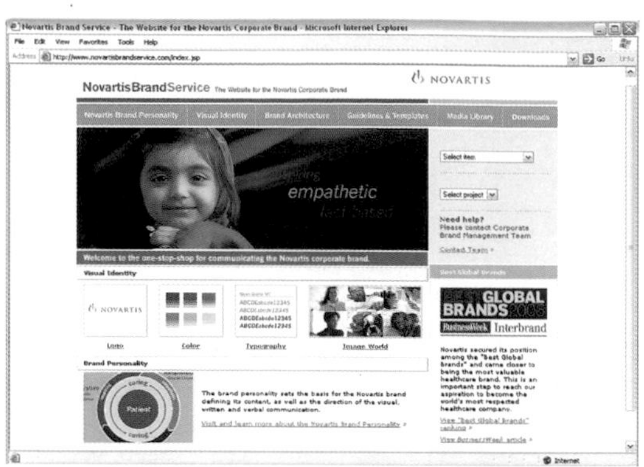

Caring and curing
At Novartis, we are committed to answering the unmet needs of patients around the world.

Breakthrough medicines are our highest priority — they open up healthcare's frontier and answer unmet needs. But no two patients are exactly alike. That's why at Novartis we go beyond breakthrough medicines to offer disease prevention, generic alternatives and access to medicines.

Creative Firm: **RUDER FINN DESIGN — NEW YORK, NY**
Creative Team: **MICHAEL SCHUBERT, LISA GABBAY, SAL CATANIA, DIANA YEO, KEI CHAN, JEEYOON RHEE**
Client: **NOVARTIS**

Creative Firm: **PRIMARY DESIGN, INC. — HAVERHILL, MA**
Creative Team: **DAVID VADALA, JULES EPSTEIN**
Client: **ARBORS INDEPENDENT LIVING**

Creative Firm: **PRIMARY DESIGN, INC. — HAVERHILL, MA**
Creative Team: **ALLISON DAVIS, JULES EPSTEIN, KRISTEN LOSSMAN, SHARYN ROGERS, VITA MIRONOVA**
Client: **GILLIS HOMES**

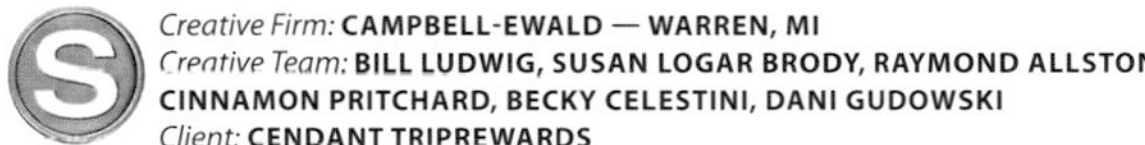
Creative Firm: **CAMPBELL-EWALD — WARREN, MI**
Creative Team: **BILL LUDWIG, SUSAN LOGAR BRODY, RAYMOND ALLSTON, CINNAMON PRITCHARD, BECKY CELESTINI, DANI GUDOWSKI**
Client: **CENDANT TRIPREWARDS**

Creative Firm: **ENGINE, LLC — SAN FRANCISCO, CA**
Creative Team: **LOTUS CHILD, GEOFF SKIGEN**
Client: **MEDJOOL**

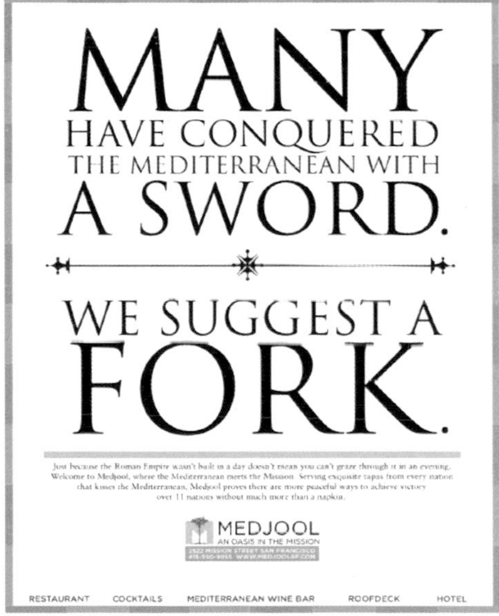

Creative Firm: **STRATEGY ONE — WOODBUY, MN**
Creative Team: **JASON THOMPSON, BRIAN DANAHER, TODD BAXTER, JOHN PHOTOS, SUSAN JENKS**
Client: **HIWIN**

Creative Firm: **BMR (BROOKS MARKETING RESOURCES) — SAULT STE. MARIE, ON, CANADA**
Creative Team: **MARK FALKINS**
Client: **OLG**

Creative Firm: **ALEXANDER MARKETING SERVICES INC. — BUFFALO GROVE, IL**
Creative Team: **TRISH RADAJ, LYNN WIER**
Client: **INITIAL TROPICAL PLANTS**

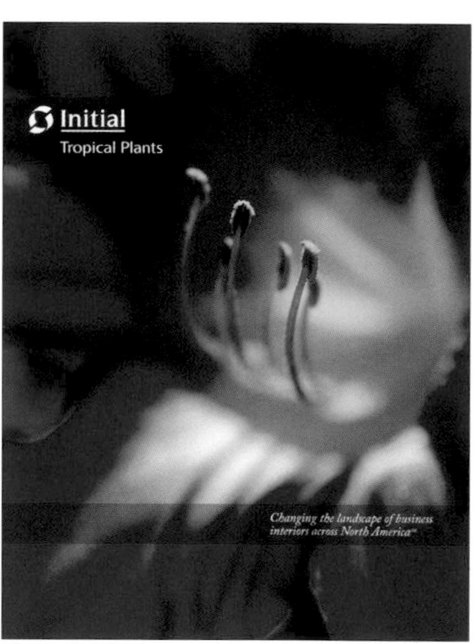

Creative Firm: **INCA TANVIR ADVERTISING — SHARJAH, UNITED ARAB EMIRATES**
Creative Team: **ERNEST DESAI, MAX D'LIMA**
Client: **JASHANMAL NATIONAL COMPANY LLC**

HERON CREST

Creative Firm: **PRIMARY DESIGN, INC. — HAVERHILL, MA**
Creative Team: **ALLISON DAVIS, JULES EPSTEIN, DAVID VADALA**
Client: **GLOBAL PROPERTY DEVELOPMENT**

HERON CREST

HERON CREST

631 East Street, Mansfield, MA 02048 · TEL: 888-261-6685 · www.HeronCrest55.com

Creative Firm: **RUDER FINN DESIGN — NEW YORK, NY**
Creative Team: **LISA GABBAY, SAL CATANIA, DIANA YEO, KEI CHAN, EMILY KORSMO, DAVID NICOLAOU**
Client: **INTERNATIONAL CENTER OF PHOTOGRAPHY**

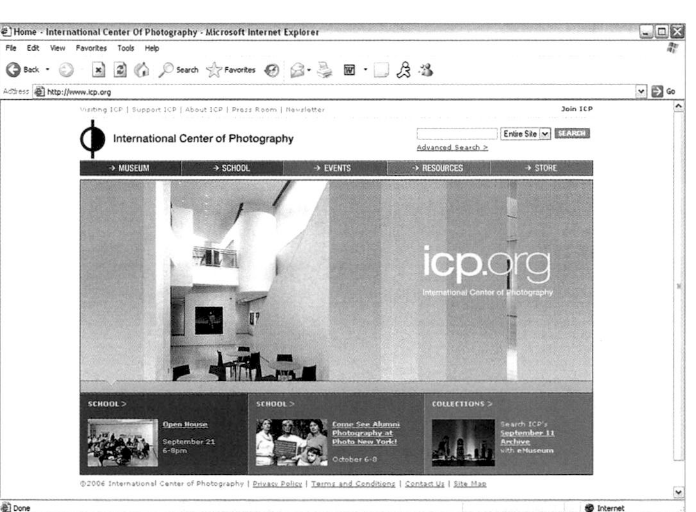

Creative Firm: **RUDER FINN DESIGN — NEW YORK, NY**
Creative Team: **LISA GABBAY, SAL CATANIA, JEEYOON RHEE, KEI CHAN**
Client: **CHIRON - A NOVARTIS COMPANY**

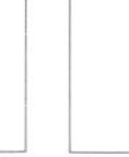

Creative Firm: **DESIGN NUT — KENSINGTON, MD**
Creative Team: **BRENT ALMOND, STEVE SMITH**
Client: **ART DIRECTORS CLUB OF METROPOLITAN WASHINGTON**

Creative Firm: **BUITENKANT ADVERTISING & DESIGN — FLUSHING, NY**
Creative Team: **VAVA BUITENKANT, DEBBIE MCCARTHY, DAN PALLOTTA, JOYCE ANDERSON , RALPH L. CWERMAN, DEENA PLOTKA**
Client: **CONNIE'S BAKERY & GENERAL STORE**

Creative Firm: **VH1 — NEW YORK, NY**
Client: **VH1**

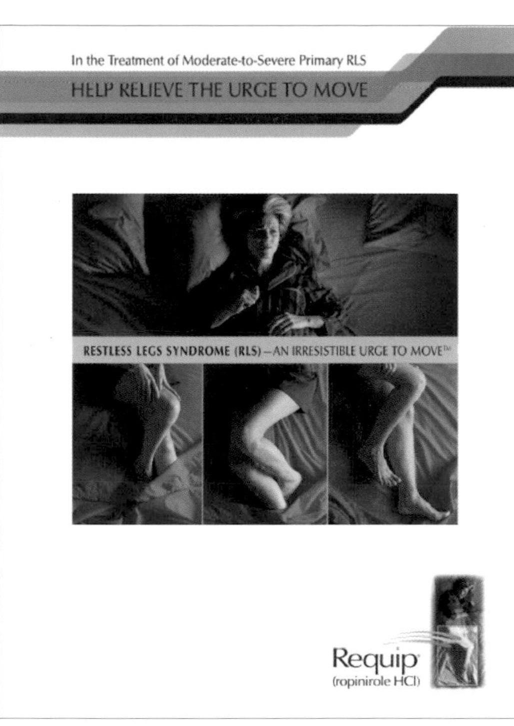

Creative Firm: **BRC MARKETING,INC — DAYTON, OH**
Creative Team: **DOM CIMEI, MARK MARTEL, TERRY NEUBERG, AMBER MOORE, BLAIR BOONE, JIM STONE**
Client: **TERADATA**

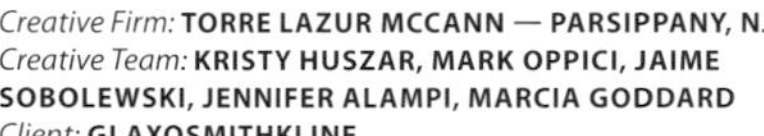

Creative Firm: **TORRE LAZUR MCCANN — PARSIPPANY, NJ**
Creative Team: **KRISTY HUSZAR, MARK OPPICI, JAIME SOBOLEWSKI, JENNIFER ALAMPI, MARCIA GODDARD**
Client: **GLAXOSMITHKLINE**

Creative Firm: **KARAKTER LTD — LONDON, UNITED KINGDOM**
Creative Team: **CLIVE ROHALD, MEI WING CHAN, KAM DEVSI, SHAHAR SILBERSHATZ, PIERRE VINSOT**
Client: **CSA CZECH AIRLINES**

Creative Firm: **TORRE LAZUR MCCANN — PARSIPPANY, NJ**
Creative Team: **ANNEMARIE ANESES, MEGAN DILLEY, DEBRA FEATH, TATIANA LYONS, STACEY DUSKIN, JENNIFER / MARCIA ALAMPI / GODDARD**
Client: **EISAI / PRICARA**

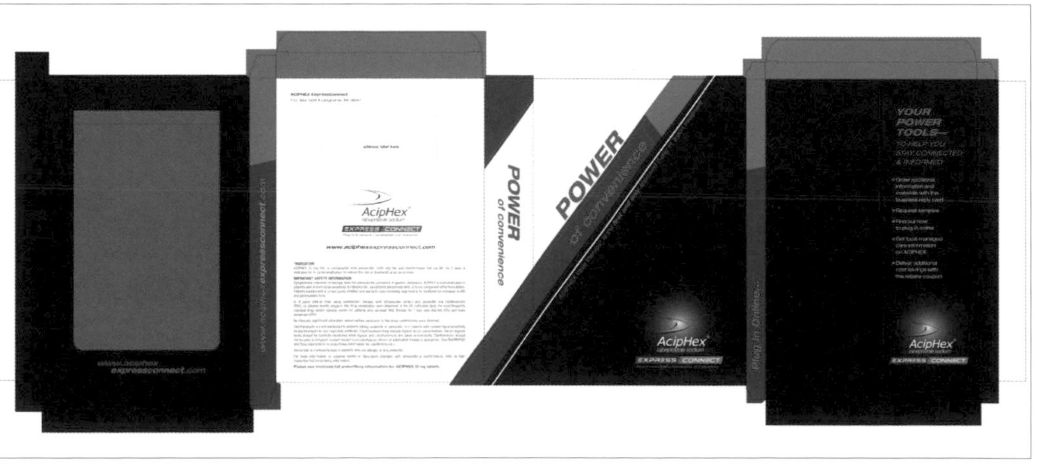

Creative Firm: **ATOMZ I! PTE LTD — SINGAPORE**
Creative Team: **PATRICK LEE, ALBERT LEE, KESTREL LEE**
Client: **ECONOMIC DEVELOPMENT BOARD**

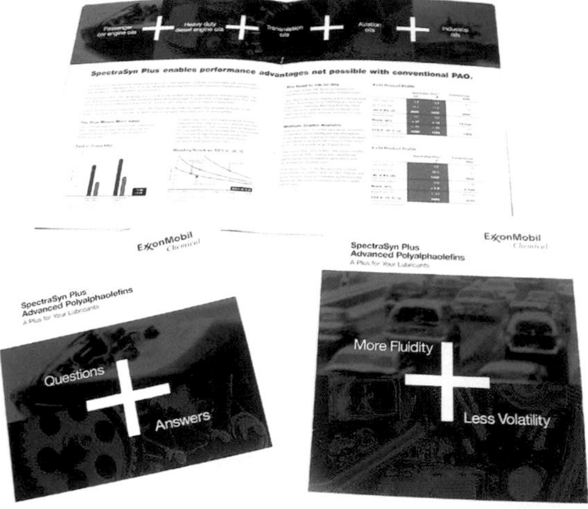

Creative Firm: **CROXSON DESIGN — HOUSTON, TX**
Creative Team: **STEPHEN CROXSON, MICHAEL RATCLIFF, RICHARD BYRD**
Client: **EXXONMOBIL CHEMICAL COMPANY**

Creative Firm: **HOTSAUCE — NEW YORK, NY**
Creative Team: **WYNDY SLOAN, ALICIA DOTTER**
Client: **LENOX HILL VETERINARIANS**

Creative Firm: **TORRE LAZUR MCCANN — PARSIPPANY, NJ**
Creative Team: **KRISTY HUSZAR, MARK OPPICI, JENNIFER ALAMPI, MARCIA GODDARD**
Client: **GLAXOSMITHKLINE**

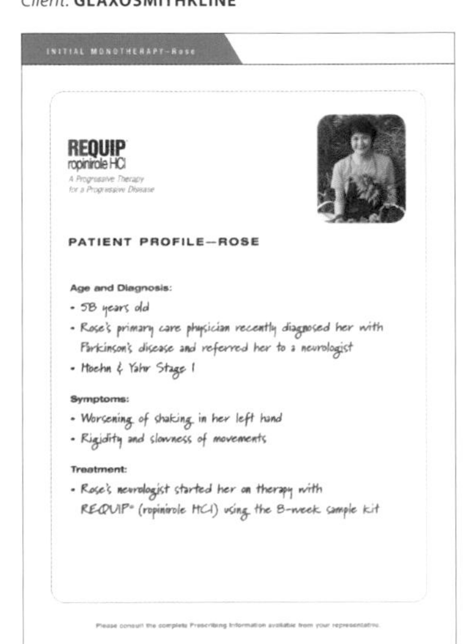

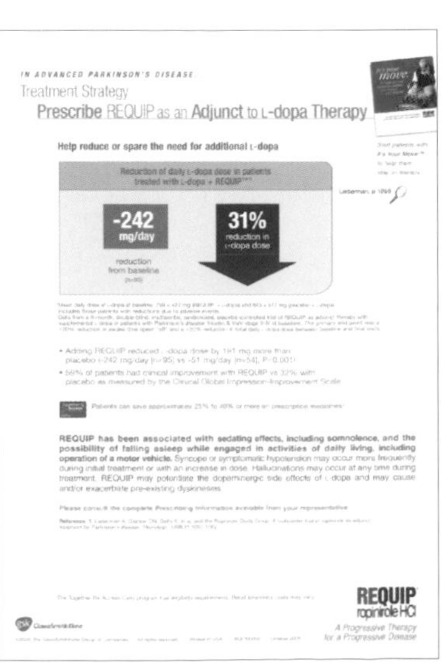

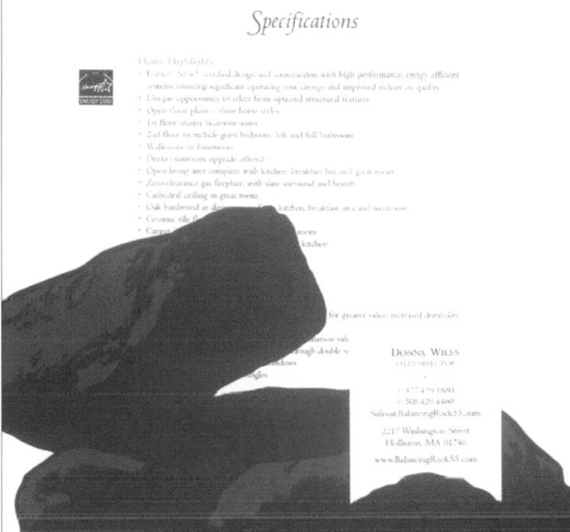

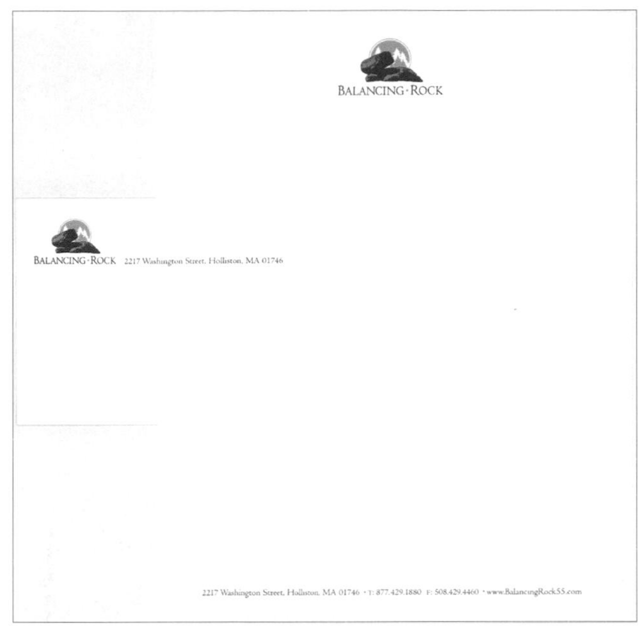

Creative Firm: **PRIMARY DESIGN, INC. — HAVERHILL, MA**
Creative Team: **DAVID VADALA, JULES EPSTEIN, LIZ FEDORZYN, SHARYN ROGERS, VITA MIRONOVA**
Client: **OXBOW DEVELOPMENT**

Creative Firm: **ALEXANDER MARKETING SERVICES INC. — BUFFALO GROVE, IL**
Creative Team: **DOUG WAYNER, LAURIE BRAMMER, DIANE PRAIS**
Client: **JUNO LIGHTING GROUP**

Creative Firm: **JPL PRODUCTIONS — HARRISBURG, PA**
Creative Team: **JIM MITCHELL, DAVE ROBERTSON, MATT DALY, CHELSIE MARKEL**
Client: **HARRISBURG UNIVERSITY OF SCIENCE AND TECHNOLOGY**

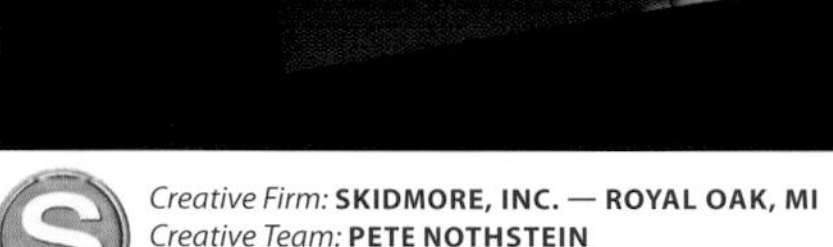

Creative Firm: **SKIDMORE, INC. — ROYAL OAK, MI**
Creative Team: **PETE NOTHSTEIN**
Client: **HARLEY ELLIS DEVEREAUX**

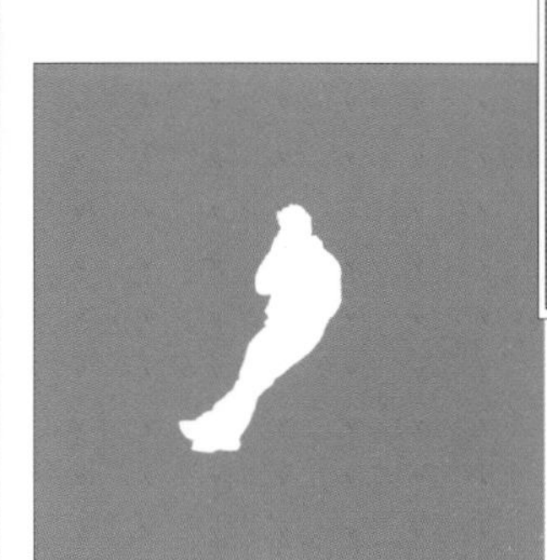

Creative Firm: **STELLAR DEBRIS — HADANO-SHI, KANAGAWA-KEN, JAPAN**
Creative Team: **CHRISTOPHER JONES**
Client: **STELLAR DEBRIS**

Creative Firm: **BUCK & PULLEYN — PITTSFORD, NY**
Creative Team: **BRENDA BRODSKY, DAN MULCAHY, PJ GALGAY, WAYNE CALABRESE**
Client: **EASTMAN KODAK COMPANY**

Creative Firm: **MENDES PUBLICIDADE — BELÉM, PARÁ, BRAZIL**
Creative Team: **OSWALDO MENDES, MARIA ALICE PENNA, LUIZ BRAGA, OCTAVIO CARDOSO, JOÃO RAMID**
Client: **BENEDITO MUTRAN**

Creative Firm: **HULL CREATIVE GROUP — BROOKLINE, MA**
Creative Team: **CARYL H. HULL, AMY BRADDOCK, SHELBY HYPES**
Client: **ICOSYSTEM**

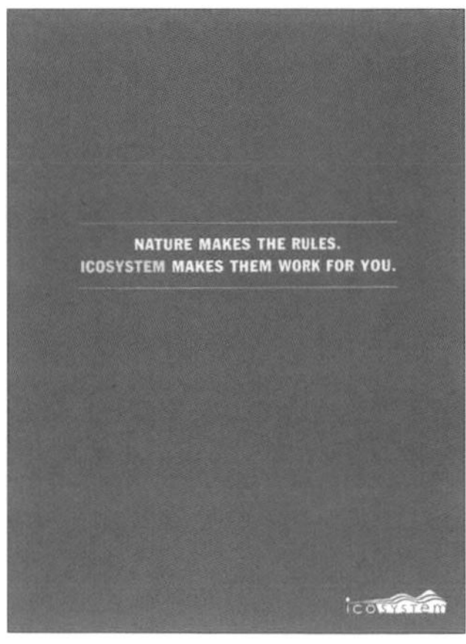

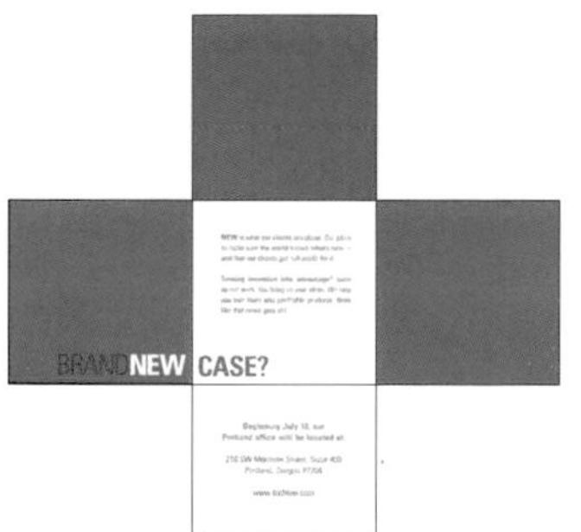

Creative Firm: **GREENFIELD/BELSER LTD. — WASHINGTON, DC**
Creative Team: **BURKEY BELSER, CAROLYN SEWELL, GEORGE KELL, JAIME CHIRINOS**
Client: **MARGER JOHNSON & MCCOLLOM PC**

Creative Firm: **HORNALL ANDERSON DESIGN WORKS — SEATTLE, WA**
Creative Team: **J. ANDERSON, J. TEE, A. WICKLUND, E. DELA CRUZ, H. CRAVEN, J. HILBURN, H. SCHOEN, B. BOWLING, Y. SHVETS, M. CONNORS**
Client: **WEYERHAEUSER CORP.**

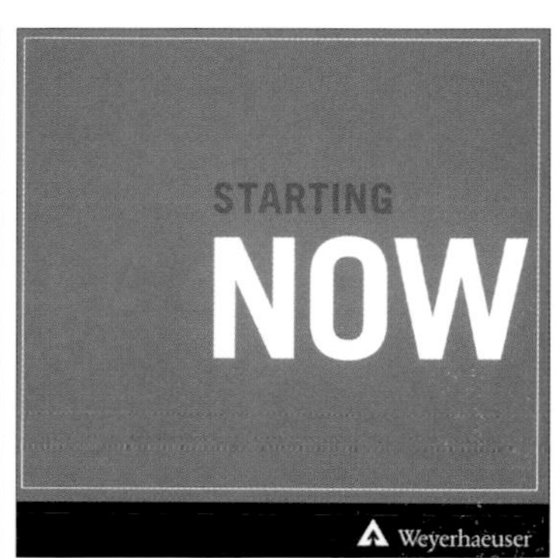

Creative Firm: **KELLER CRESCENT — EVANSVILLE, IN**
Creative Team: **GERRY ULRICH, MARY REILLY, LYNNE MLADY, RANDY ROHN**
Client: **HEAVEN HILL**

Creative Firm: **CROXSON DESIGN — HOUSTON, TX**
Creative Team: **STEPHEN CROXSON, MICHAEL RATCLIFF**
Client: **EXXONMOBIL CHEMICAL COMPANY**

Creative Firm: **MYTTON WILLIAMS — BATH, BANES, UNITED KINGDOM**
Creative Team: **BOB MYTTON, TRACEY BOWES, TOM CHESHIRE, SIMON JONES**
Client: **INK COPYWRITERS**

Words are a little like icebergs. Beneath the elegant bits on the surface is an unseen force holding everything together. In writing, this is the thought behind the words; the strategy that makes your communication stand out. So before we put pen to paper, we pause for a while.

More than you'd expect:

Copy strategy: developing and implementing a language that reflects your brand. Training: helping organisations improve writing skills and express their brand in communications. Translation: adapting copy for most international languages using only the best mother-tongue writers. Editing and proofing: providing a complete editorial service, from magazine content plans to fully proofing every item for printing.

think

Creative Firm: **Q — WIESBADEN, GERMANY**
Creative Team: **MATTHIAS FREY, LAURENZ NIELBOCK, CHRISTOPH DAHINTEN, UTE DERSCH, FRANK C. LAMBERRY**
Client: **HESSENCHEMIE**

Creative Firm: **BRIGHT RAIN CREATIVE — ST. LOUIS, MO**
Creative Team: **KEVIN HOUGH, MATT MARINO**
Client: **ST. LOUIS YPO**

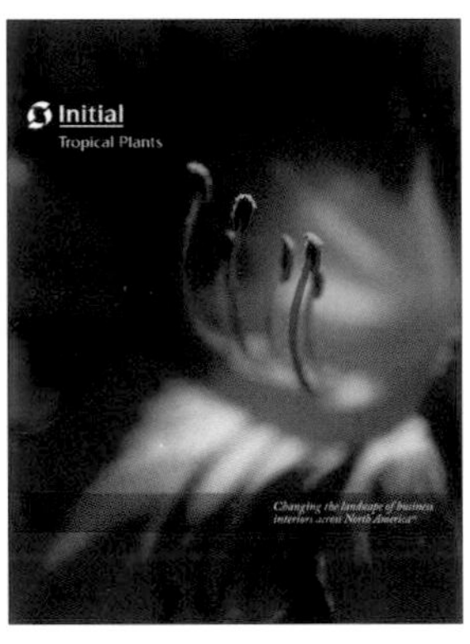

Creative Firm: **ALEXANDER MARKETING SERVICES INC. — BUFFALO GROVE, IL**
Creative Team: **TRISH RADAJ, LYNN WIER**
Client: **INITIAL TROPICAL PLANTS**

Creative Firm: **HERMAN MILLER, INC. — ZEELAND, MI**
Creative Team: **ANDREW DULL, JUSTIN MACOHOCHIE, MARLENE CAPOTOSTO**
Client: **HERMAN MILLER, INC.**

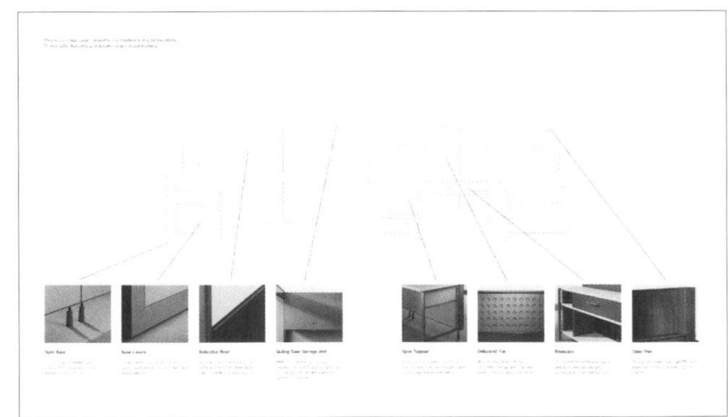

Creative Firm: **KELLER CRESCENT — EVANSVILLE, IN**
Creative Team: **RANDALL ROHN, LYNNE MLADY, MARY REILLY, GERRY ULRICH, RANDY ROHN, PAT FAGAN**
Client: **HEAVEN HILL**

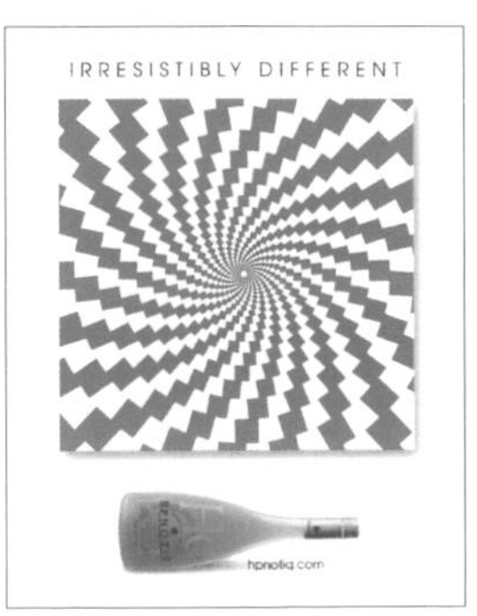

Creative Firm: **CSC'S P2 COMMUNICATIONS SERVICES — FALLS CHURCH, VA**
Creative Team: **AARON KOBILIS, TERRY WILSON, JOHN FARQUHAR, MAURICE COTTINGHAM**
Client: **CSC TMG**

Creative Firm: **RTS RIEGER TEAM WERBEAGENTUR GMBH — DÜSSELDORF, GERMANY**
Creative Team: **MICHAELA MÜLLER, DANIELA SCHÄFER, ULRICH GIELISCH, FRANCISCO NAVARRO Y GOMES**
Client: **THYSSENKRUPP ELEVATOR AG**

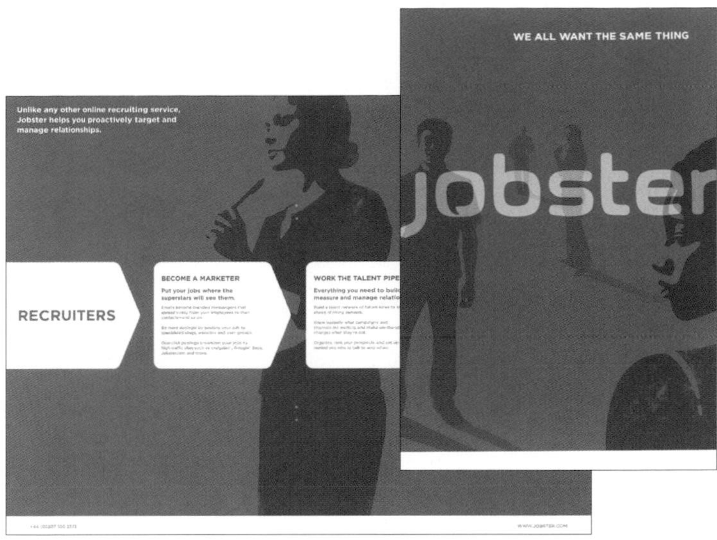

Creative Firm: **HORNALL ANDERSON DESIGN WORKS — SEATTLE, WA**
Creative Team: **JACK ANDERSON, MICHAEL CONNORS, LEO RAYMUNDO, ENSI MOFASSER**
Client: **JOBSTER**

Creative Firm: **CROXSON DESIGN HOUSTON, TX**
Creative Team: **STEPHEN CROXSON, RICHARD BYRD, MICHAEL RATCLIFF**
Client: **THE BURKE GROUP**

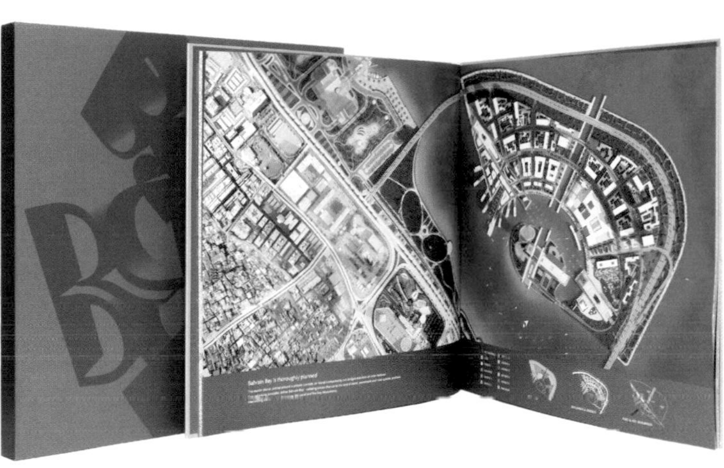

Creative Firm: **FUTUREBRAND BRAND EXPERIENCE — NEW YORK, NY**
Creative Team: **DIEGO KOLSKY, CHERYL HILLS, ANTONIO BAGLIONE, STEPHANIE CARROLL, WILLIAM SHINTANI, RAYMOND CHAN**
Client: **ARCAPITA**

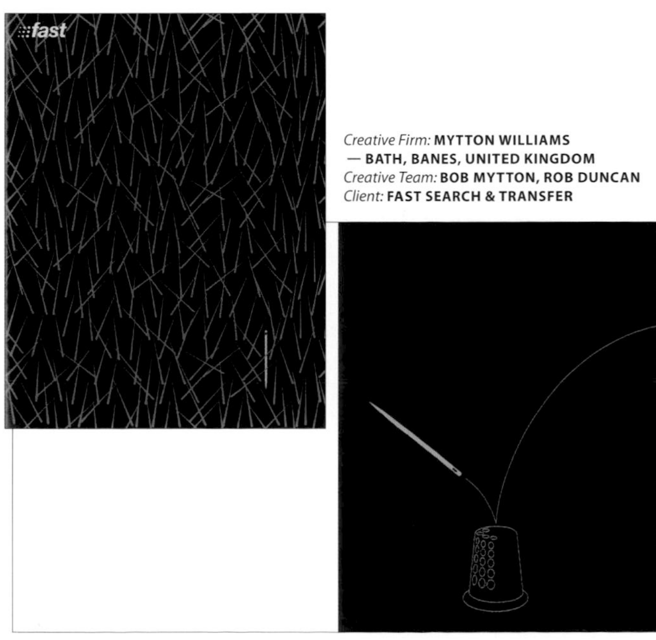

Creative Firm: **MYTTON WILLIAMS — BATH, BANES, UNITED KINGDOM**
Creative Team: **BOB MYTTON, ROB DUNCAN**
Client: **FAST SEARCH & TRANSFER**

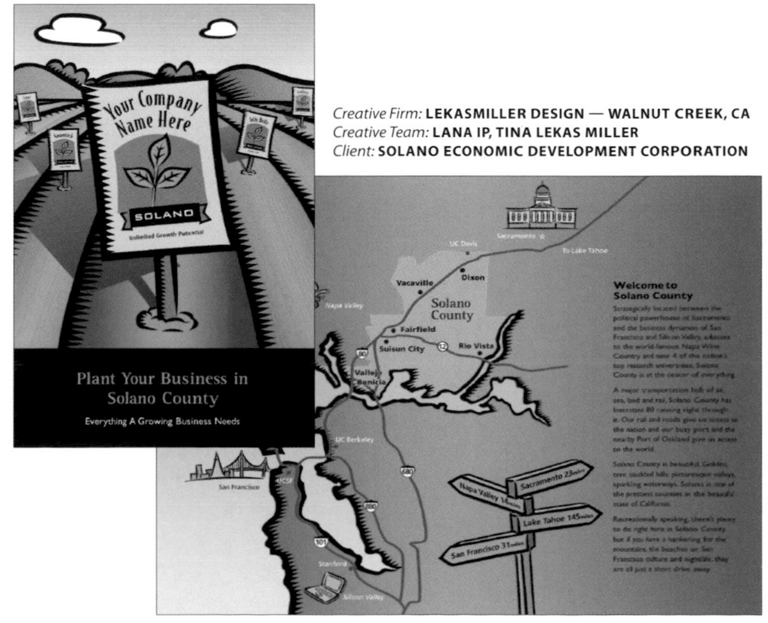

Creative Firm: **LEKASMILLER DESIGN — WALNUT CREEK, CA**
Creative Team: **LANA IP, TINA LEKAS MILLER**
Client: **SOLANO ECONOMIC DEVELOPMENT CORPORATION**

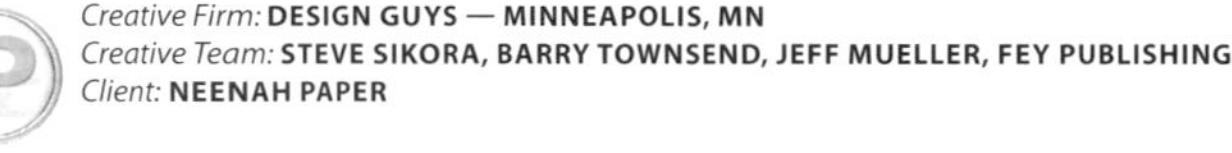

Creative Firm: **DESIGN GUYS — MINNEAPOLIS, MN**
Creative Team: **STEVE SIKORA, BARRY TOWNSEND, JEFF MUELLER, FEY PUBLISHING**
Client: **NEENAH PAPER**

Creative Firm: **CROXSON DESIGN — HOUSTON, TX**
Creative Team: **STEPHEN CROXSON, RICHARD BYRD, JOHN SMALLWOOD**
Client: **M.D. ANDERSON CANCER CENTER**

Creative Firm: **QUALCOMM — SAN DIEGO, CA**
Creative Team: **FRANK BERNAS, CHRIS LEE**

Creative Firm: **RTS RIEGER TEAM WERBEAGENTUR GMBH — LEINFELDEN-ECHTERDINGEN, GERMANY**
Creative Team: **INA RALL, DAVID ZEIFERT**
Client: **MAHR GMBH**

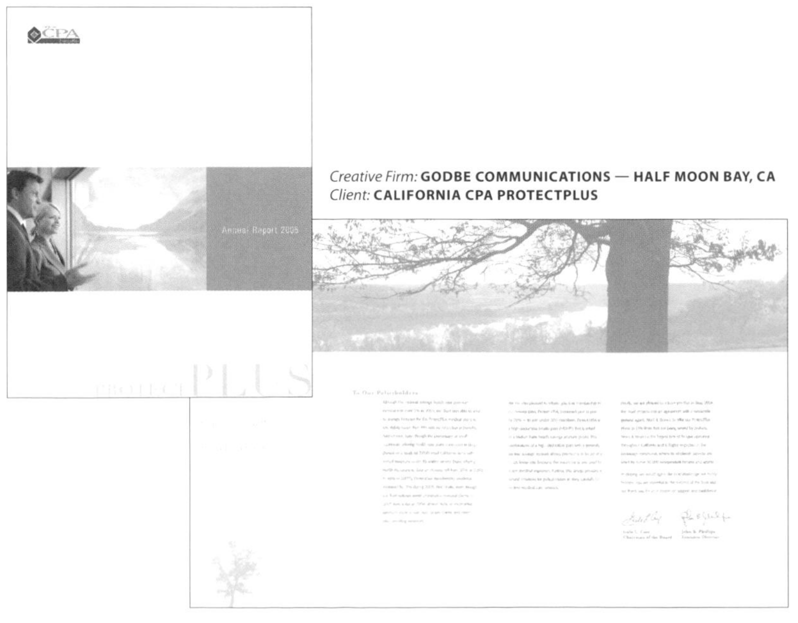

Creative Firm: **GODBE COMMUNICATIONS — HALF MOON BAY, CA**
Client: **CALIFORNIA CPA PROTECTPLUS**

Creative Firm: **PARAGRAPHS DESIGN — CHICAGO, IL**
Creative Team: **JIM CHILCUTT**
Client: **KAUFMANHALL**

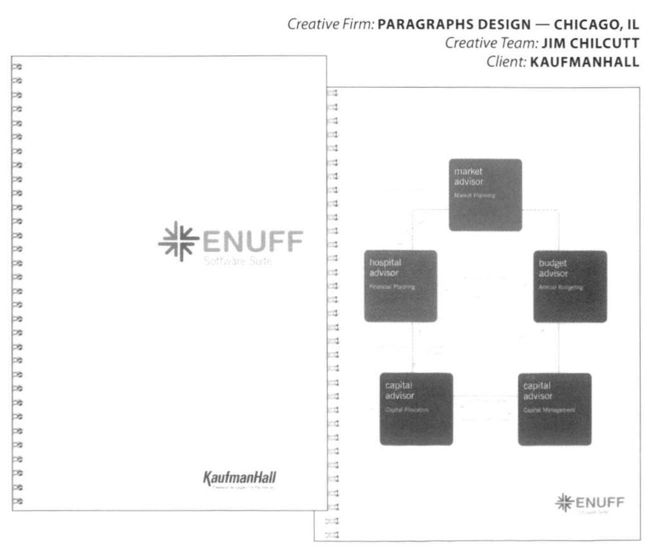

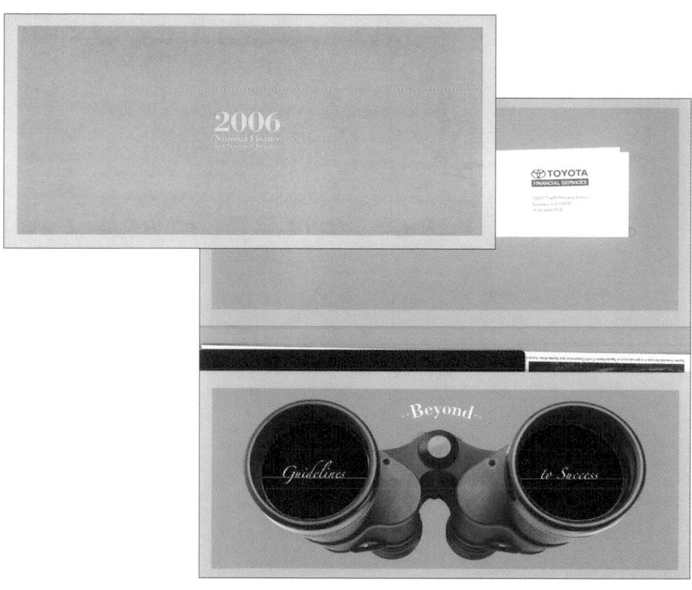

Creative Firm: **TOYOTA FINANCIAL SERVICES MEDIA DESIGN — TORRANCE, CA**
Creative Team: **DANIEL KO**
Client: **TOYOTA FINANCIAL SERVICES**

Creative Firm: **RTS RIEGER TEAM WERBEAGENTUR GMBH — DÜSSELDORF, GERMANY**
Creative Team: **MICHAELA MÜLLER, KERSTIN OYDA, HEINZ ZANDER**
Client: **WEIDMÜLLER INTERFACE GMBH & CO.**

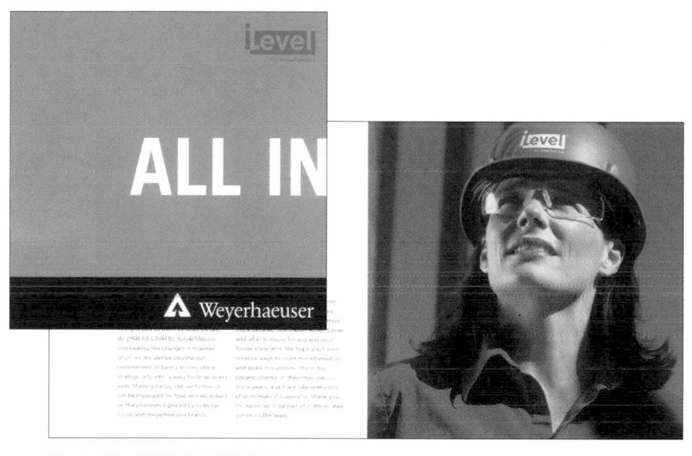

Creative Firm: **HORNALL ANDERSON DESIGN WORKS — SEATTLE, WA**
Creative Team: **J. ANDERSON, J. TEE, A. WICKLUND, E. DELA CRUZ, H. CRAVEN, J. HILBURN, H. SCHOEN, B. BOWLING, Y. SHVETS, M. CONNORS**
Client: **WEYERHAEUSER CORP.**

Creative Firm: **LISKA + ASSOCIATES — CHICAGO, IL**
Creative Team: **STEVE LISKA, VANESSA OLTMANNS, ANN MARIE GRAY**
Client: **CRANE & CO. PAPER**

Creative Firm: **GREENFIELD/BELSER LTD. — WASHINGTON, DC**
Creative Team: **BURKEY BELSER, SIOBHAN DAVIS, JOE WALSH**
Client: **ERS GROUP**

Creative Firm: **DON SCHAAF & FRIENDS, INC. — WASHINGTON, DC**
Creative Team: **DON SCHAAF**
Client: **FLOWSERVE**

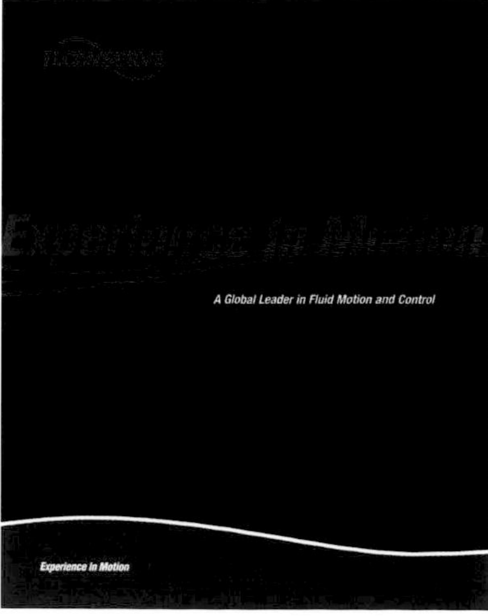

Creative Firm: **HITCHCOCK FLEMING & ASSOCIATES INC. — AKRON, OH**
Creative Team: **NICK BETRO, KIM BRUNS, TODD MOSER**
Client: **VERITAS**

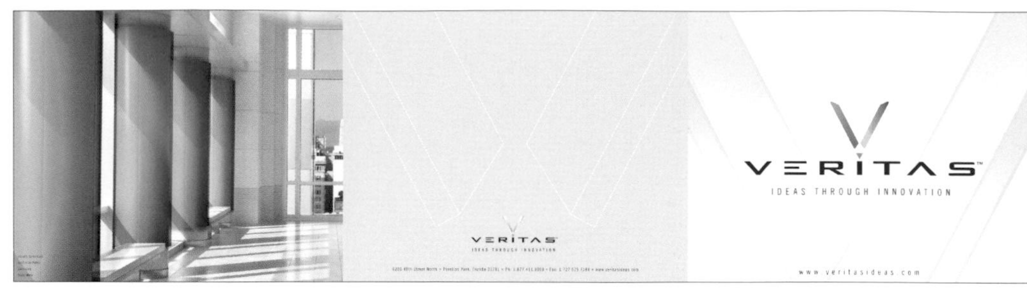

Creative Firm: **EFFECTIVENESS THROUGH COMMUNICATION — EL CAJON, CA**
Creative Team: **MARIE HORN**
Client: **ELEMENTARY INSTITUTE OF SCIENCE**

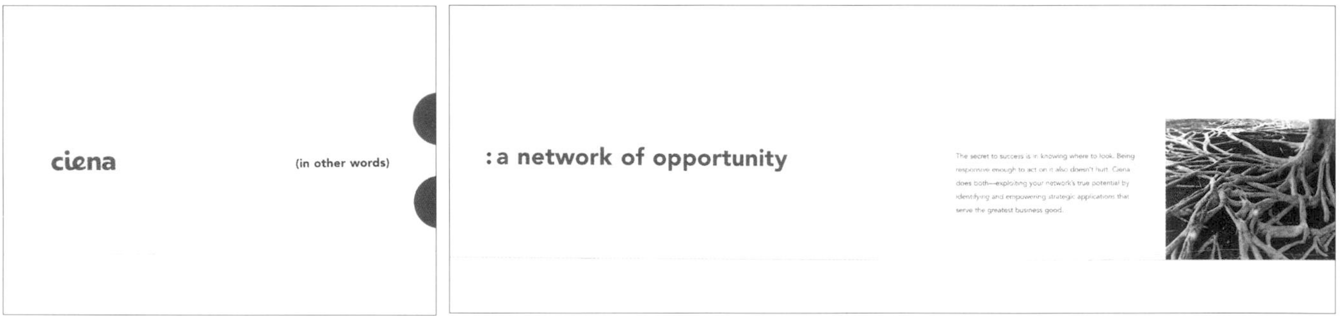

Creative Firm: **HORNALL ANDERSON DESIGN WORKS — SEATTLE, WA**
Creative Team: **JACK ANDERSON, ANDY DAVIDHAZY, HOLLY CRAVEN, SONJA MAX, YURI SHVETS, ANDREW WICKLUND, KRIS DELANEY**
Client: **CIENA**

Creative Firm: **TAYLOR DESIGN — STAMFORD, CT**
Creative Team: **SUZANNE REUSCH, DAN TAYLOR, CRAIG FRAZIER**
Client: **MASTERCARD**

Creative Firm: **QUALCOMM — SAN DIEGO, CA**
Creative Team: **LUISA LOPEZ, CHRIS LEE**

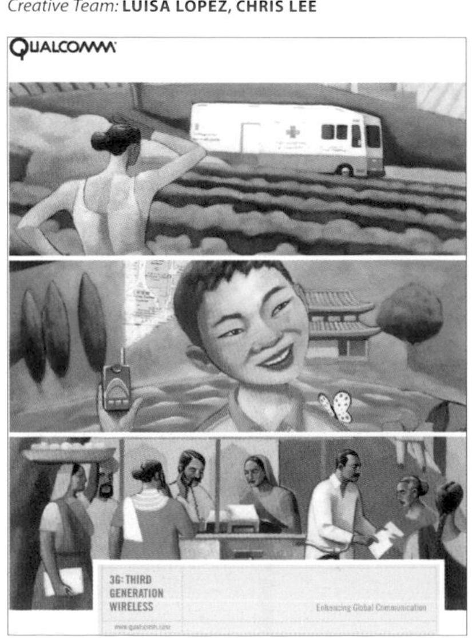

Creative Firm: **GODBE COMMUNICATIONS — HALF MOON BAY, CA**
Client: **PACIFIC CAPITAL INVESTMENTS**

Creative Firm: **DOUBLE TAKE CREATIVE — LAWRENCEVILLE, GA**
Creative Team: **VINCENT MARASCHIELLO, AMY POWERS**
Client: **DESIGN TYPE PRINTING SERVICES**

Creative Firm: **HORNALL ANDERSON DESIGN WORKS — SEATTLE, WA**
Creative Team: **J. ANDERSON, M. CONNORS, L. A. JOHNSON, L. RAYMUNDO, Y. SHVETS, E. LEE, K. SAITO, B. STIGLER, D. BATES**
Client: **JOBSTER**

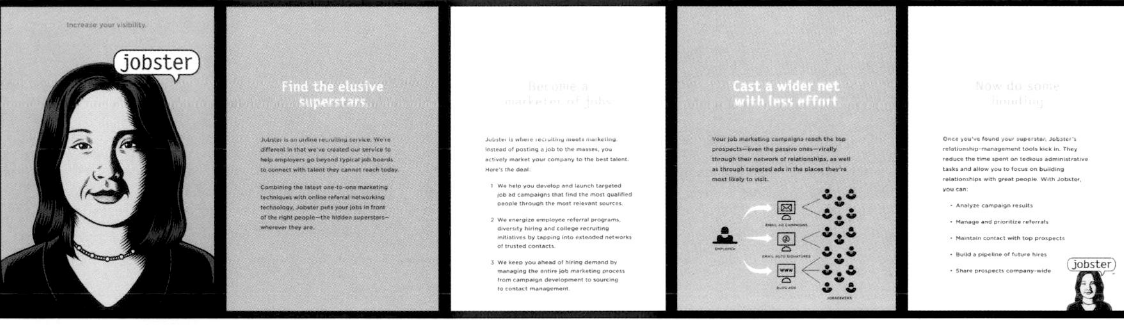

Creative Firm: **PLUMBLINE STUDIOS, INC — NAPA, CA**
Creative Team: **DOM MORECI, MARK JORDAN, CRAIG SHEROD**
Client: **WYSE**

Creative Firm: **PHOENIX CREATIVE GROUP, LLC — POTOMAC FALLS, VA**
Creative Team: **NICOLE KASSOLIS, SEAN MULLINS, GARFUNKLE & ASSOCIATES, STOCK BYTE**
Client: **MAINSTREET BANK, HERNDON, VA**

Creative Firm: **FITTING GROUP — PITTSBURGH, PA**
Creative Team: **TRAVIS NORRIS**
Client: **SCHOOL OF COMPUTER SCIENCE AT CARNEGIE MELLON UNIVERSITY**

Creative Firm: **TD2, S.C. — MEXICO CITY, D.F., MEXICO**
Creative Team: **RAFAEL TREVIÑO, R. RODRIGO CORDOVA, DAMARIS TAMBORRELL**
Client: **GFA ARCHITECTS**

Creative Firm: **Q — WIESBADEN, GERMANY**
Creative Team: **KATIA WITTROWSKI, THILO VON DEBSCHITZ, UTE DERSCH**
Client: **ICR, WESTPORT/CT**

Creative Firm: **PLUMBLINE STUDIOS, INC — NAPA, CA**
Creative Team: **DOM MORECI, TERRY LORANT**
Client: **COBLENTZ, PATCH, DUFFY & BASS, LLP**

Creative Firm: **HORNALL ANDERSON DESIGN WORKS — SEATTLE, WA**
Creative Team: **J. ANDERSON, J. TEE, A. WICKLUND, E. DELA CRUZ, H. CRAVEN, J. HILBURN, H. SCHOEN, B. BOWLING, Y. SHVETS, M. CONNORS**
Client: **WEYERHAEUSER CORP.**

Creative Firm: **TOYOTA FINANCIAL SERVICES MEDIA DESIGN — TORRANCE, CA**
Creative Team: **DANIEL KO**
Client: **TOYOTA FINANCIAL SERVICES**

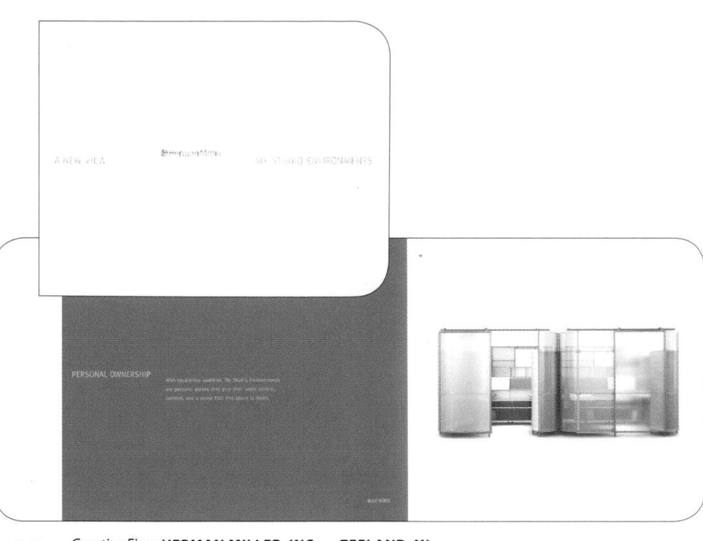

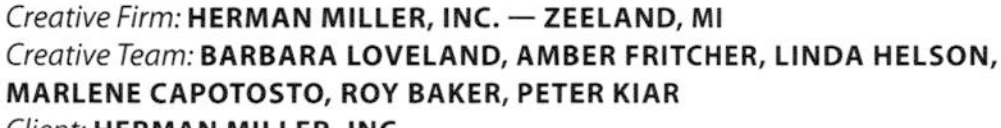

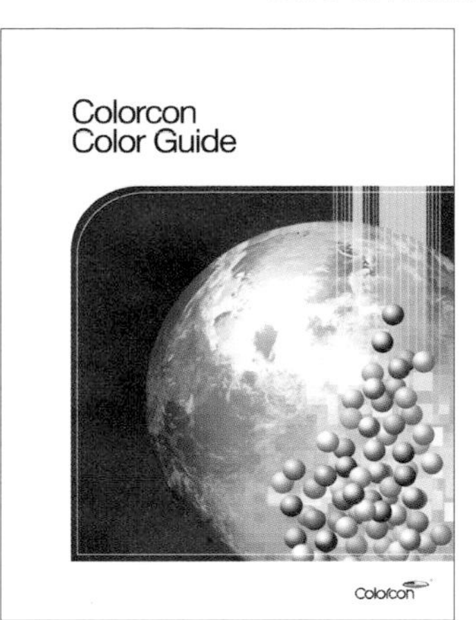

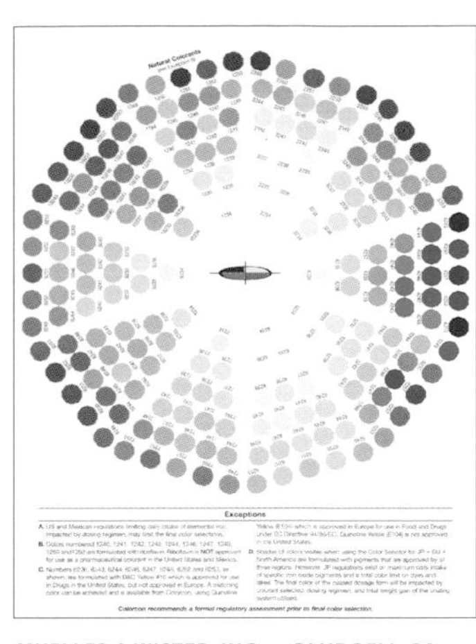

Creative Firm: **MUELLER & WISTER, INC. — BLUE BELL, PA**
Creative Team: **WOLFGANG MUELLER, CLARK MILLS, ANNE TELLEFSEN**
Client: **COLORCON**

Creative Firm: **HERMAN MILLER, INC. — ZEELAND, MI**
Creative Team: **BARBARA LOVELAND, AMBER FRITCHER, LINDA HELSON, MARLENE CAPOTOSTO, ROY BAKER, PETER KIAR**
Client: **HERMAN MILLER, INC.**

Creative Firm: **DESIGN GUYS — MINNEAPOLIS, MN**
Creative Team: **STEVE SIKORA, BARRY TOWNSEND, JAY THEIGE, KAREN LOKENSGARD, POMCO GRAPHIC ARTS**
Client: **NEENAH PAPER**

Creative Firm: **HORNALL ANDERSON DESIGN WORKS — SEATTLE, WA**
Creative Team: **JOHN ANICKER, JACK ANDERSON, ANDREW WICKLUND, LEO RAYMUNDO, CHRIS FREED, KATHLEEN GIBSON**
Client: **SCHNITZER NORTHWEST**

Creative Firm: **GREENFIELD/BELSER LTD. — WASHINGTON, DC**
Creative Team: **BURKEY BELSER, GEORGE KELL, JOHN MITRIONE, MOSAIC**
Client: **WOMBLE CARLYLE SANDRIDGE & RICE, PLLC**

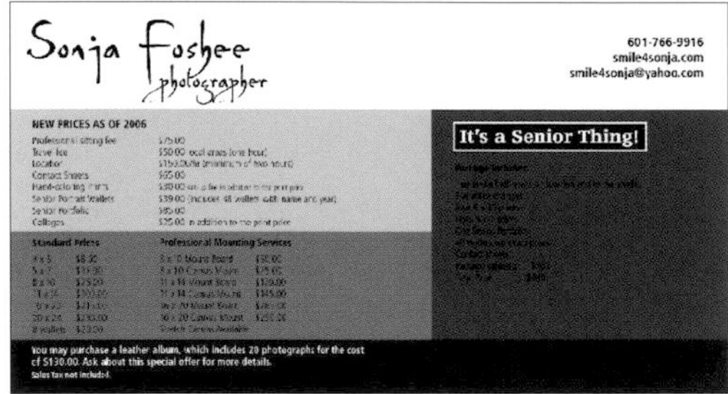

Creative Firm: **LITTLE BIRD COMMUNICATIONS — MOBILE, AL**
Creative Team: **DIANE GIBBS, SONJA FOSHEE**
Client: **SONJA FOSHEE PHOTOGRAPHER**

Creative Firm: **CREATIVE MINDWORKS — MIAMI LAKES, FL**
Creative Team: **ANGELICA MARTINEZ, RAISA SIRES, LIZETTE FERNANDEZ**
Client: **PRESTIGE BUILDERS PARTNERS**

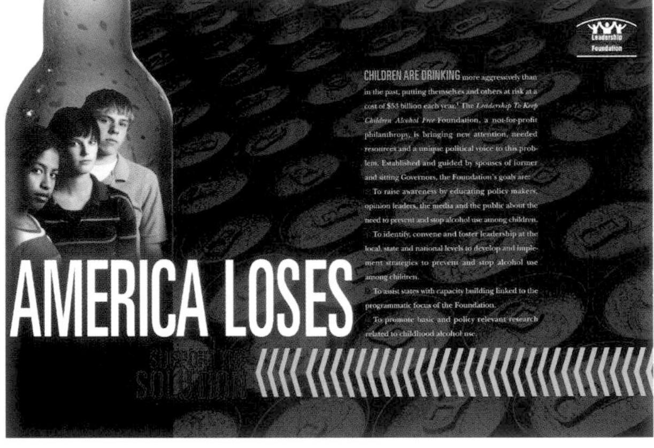

Creative Firm: **DEVER DESIGNS — LAUREL, MD**
Creative Team: **JEFFREY DEVER, KIM POLLOCK**
Client: **LEADERSHIP TO KEEP CHILDREN ALCOHOL FREE**

Creative Firm: **HULL CREATIVE GROUP — BROOKLINE, MA**
Creative Team: **CARYL H. HULL, CAROLYN COLONNA, STUART DANFORTH**
Client: **DANFORTH ASSOCIATES**

Creative Firm: **SHERIFF DESIGN — ELKINS PARK, PA**
Creative Team: **PAUL SHERIFF, DR. AMY SCHLEVEL, JUDY FOX, HEIDI WIRTH**
Client: **TUFTS UNIVERSITY**

Creative Firm: **KAA DESIGN GROUP, INC. - GRAPHICS STUDIO — LOS ANGELES, CA**
Creative Team: **MELANIE ROBINSON**
Client: **FIRSTSTEPS FOR KIDS, INC.**

Creative Firm: **MCGUFFIE DESIGN — NORTH VANCOUVER, BC, CANADA**
Creative Team: **STEVE MCGUFFIE**
Client: **CANACCORD CAPITAL**

Creative Firm: **SILVER CREATIVE GROUP — SOUTH NORWALK, CT**
Creative Team: **PAUL ZULLO, SUZANNE PETROW**
Client: **ROCKROSE DEVELOPMENT CORP.**

Creative Firm: **HOWARD HANNA SMYTHE CRAMER — CLEVELAND , OH**
Creative Team: **AIMEE CAMPBELL**
Client: **RYSAR PROPERTIES**

Creative Firm: **THE DESIGNQUARTERS — SINGAPORE**
Creative Team: **DEBORAH ANG**
Client: **R.I.K. INDUSTRIES PTE. LTD.**

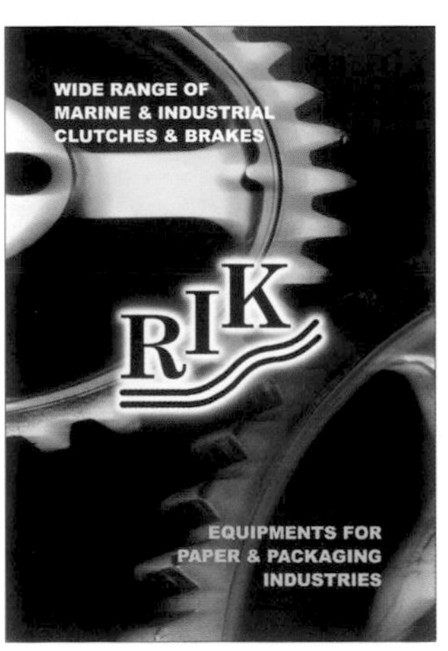

Creative Firm: **BRIAN J. GANTON & ASSOCIATES — CEDAR GROVE, NJ**
Creative Team: **MARK GANTON, BRIAN J. GANTON JR., PAT PALMIERI, BRIAN J. GANTON SR., CHRISTOPHER GANTON, JOHN HOVELL**
Client: **BELGARD**

Creative Firm: **BURROWS — BRENTWOOD, ESSEX, UNITED KINGDOM**
Creative Team: **DEREK PRICE, ROYDON HEARNE, MARK ELLIS, ZOE FOWLER, NIGEL HALL**
Client: **FORD MOTOR COMPANY (EUROPE)**

Creative Firm: **HERBERGER COLLEGE OF FINE ARTS — TEMPE, AZ**
Creative Team: **AMY NG, MARTHA KNIGHT, STACEY SHAW, TIM TRUMBLE**
Client: **HERBERGER COLLEGE FOR KIDS/AT LARGE**

Creative Firm: **ALL MEDIA PROJECTS LIMITED — PORT OF SPAIN, TRINIDAD AND TOBAGO**
Creative Team: **CATHLEEN JONES, MARISA CAMEJO, JULIEN GREENIDGE, JOSIANE KHAN**
Client: **BP TRINIDAD AND TOBAGO (BPTT)**

Creative Firm: **RODGERS TOWNSEND — ST. LOUIS, MO**
Creative Team: **ERIK MATHRE, LIZ FORSYTHE, BILL ECKLOFF, CHERYL SPARKS**
Client: **THE BLACK REP**

Creative Firm: **HORNALL ANDERSON DESIGN WORKS — SEATTLE**
Creative Team: **JACK ANDERSON, JULIE LOCK, LAURA JAKOBSEN BECKON WYLD**
Client: **EOS AIRLINES**

Creative Firm: **DEVER DESIGNS — LAUREL, MD**
Creative Team: **JEFFREY DEVER, KRISTIN DEUEL DUFFY, FATIMA AMEEN**
Client: **NAT'L INSTITUTES OF HEALTH/ NAT'L INSTITUTE OF AGING**

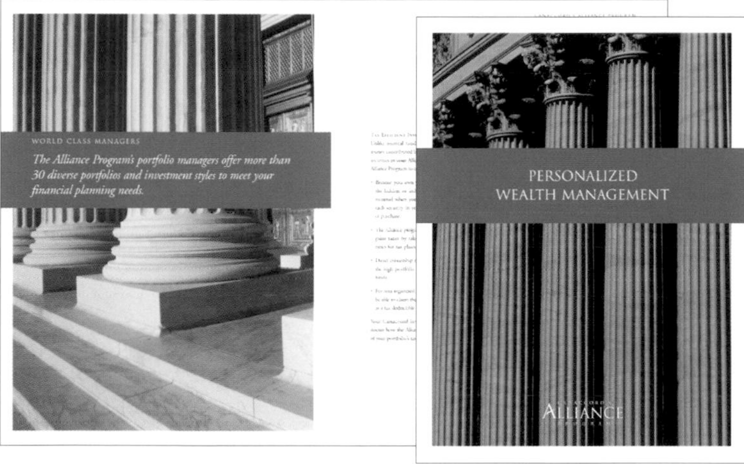

Creative Firm: **MCGUFFIE DESIGN NORTH VANCOUVER, BC, CANADA**
Creative Team: **STEVE MCGUFFIE**
Client: **CANACCORD CAPITAL**

Creative Firm: **HELENA SEO DESIGN — SUNNYVALE, CA**
Creative Team: **HELENA SEO, BILL O'SUCH**
Client: **INEKE, LLC**

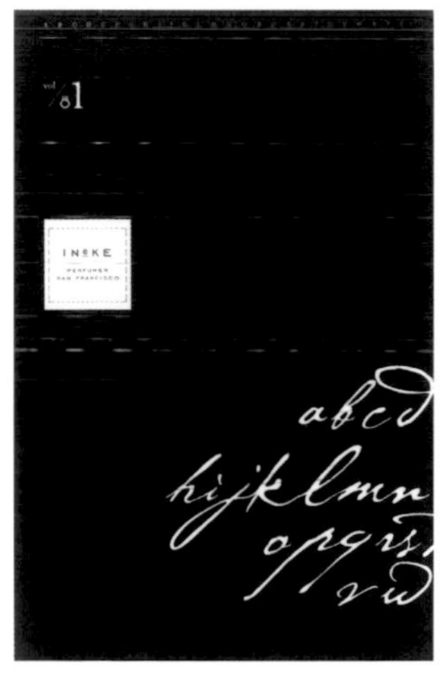

Creative Firm: **SPLASH PRODUCTIONS PTE LTD — SINGAPORE**
Creative Team: **TERRY LEE, LOW JAT LENG, BRICE LI, STANLEY TAP**
Client: **MINDEF SCHOLARSHIP CENTRE**

Creative Firm: **WESTGROUP CREATIVE — NEW YORK, NY**
Creative Team: **CHIP TOLANEY, MARVIN BERK, PETER SAKAS, MAX SHUPPERT**
Client: **IPSILON MUSIC SERVICES**

Creative Firm: **SCOTT ADAMS DESIGN ASSOCIATES — COLUMBUS, OH**
Creative Team: **SCOTT ADAMS, MANDY MILLER, COLIN MCGUIRE, TOM GRIFFIN, NATHAN KRAFT**
Client: **NATIONWIDE REALTY INVESTORS**

Creative Firm: **ORIGINAL IMPRESSIONS — MIAMI, FL**
Creative Team: **FRANK IRIAS**
Client: **OCEAN REEF CLUB**

Creative Firm: **TTA ADVERTISING — PHOENIX, AZ**
Creative Team: **RUSTY PILE, SWAPNA SALGAR**
Client: **DIAMOND SHOWCASE**

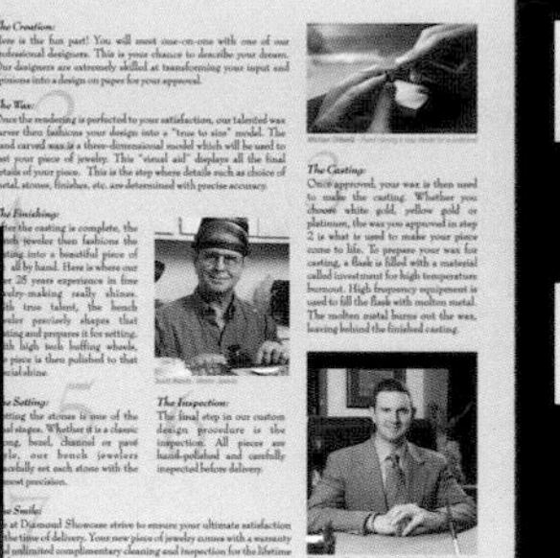

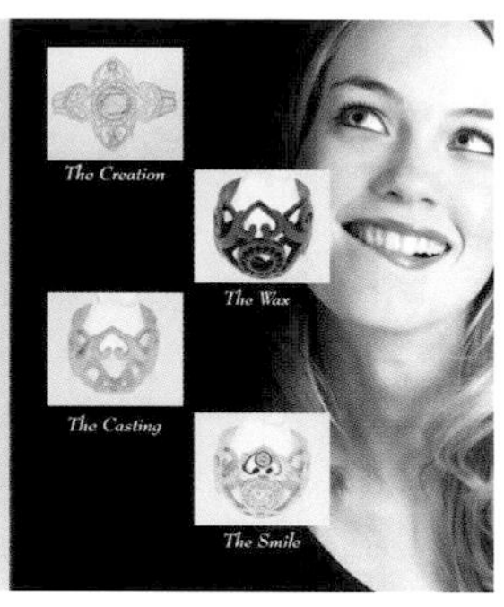

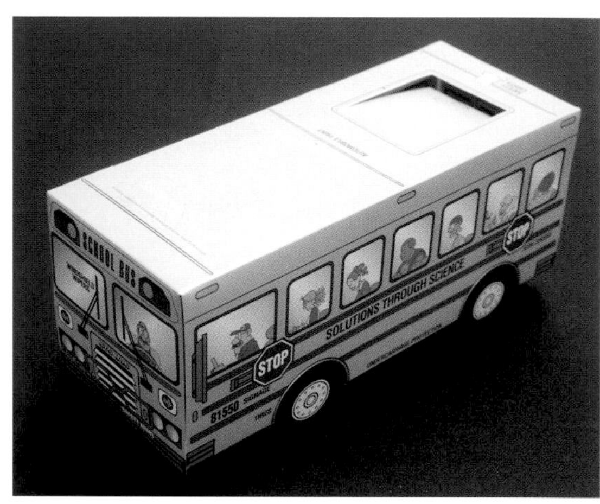

Creative Firm: **HARRIS, DEVILLE & ASSOCIATES, INC. — BATON ROUGE, LA**
Creative Team: **ELIZABETH PERRY, STAN TAYLOR, BEVERLY SMILEY**
Client: **SOLUTIONS THROUGH SCIENCE**

Creative Firm: **VANPELT CREATIVE — GARLAND, TX**
Creative Team: **CHIP VANPELT, TODD BRASHEAR, J.W. BURKEY**
Client: **AM APPLIANCE GROUP**

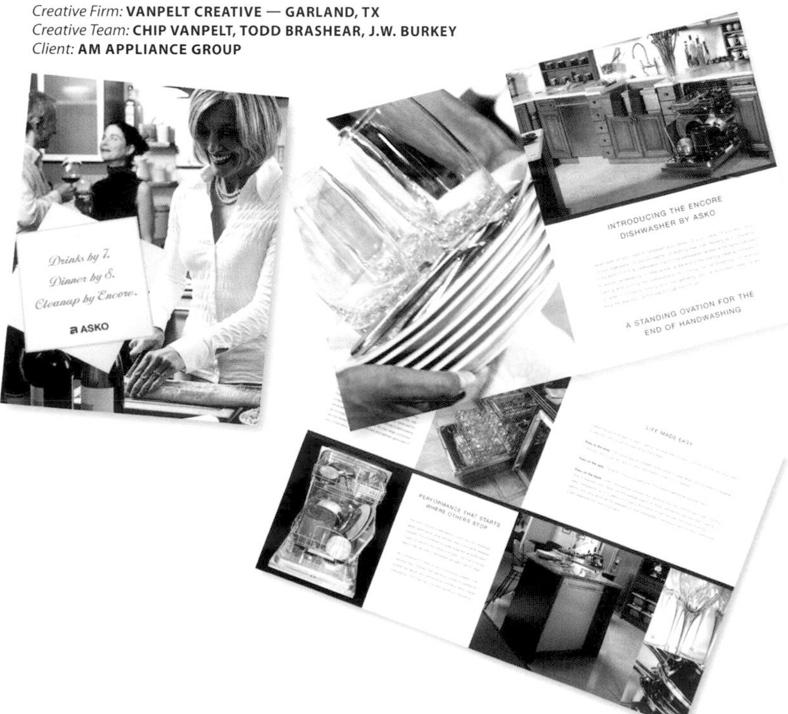

Creative Firm: **WESTGROUP CREATIVE — NEW YORK, NY**
Creative Team: **CHIP TOLANEY, MARVIN BERK**
Client: **AMERICAN GLOBE THEATRE**

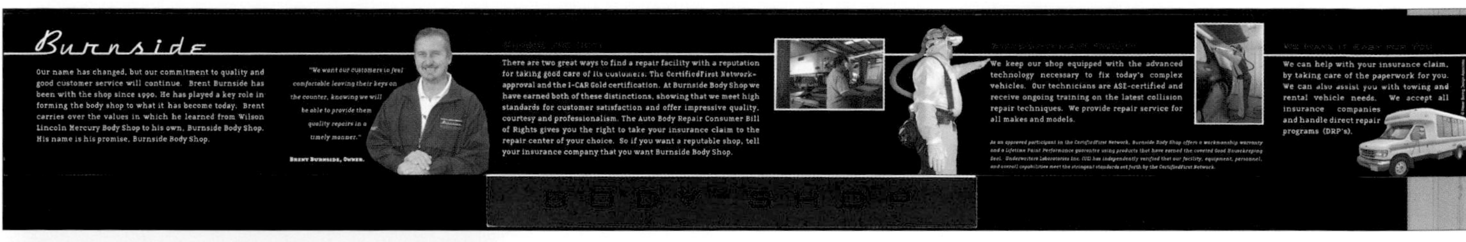

Burnside

Burnside Body Shop is an independent, family-owned and operated facility. Our shop opened in the 1960's as Wilson Lincoln Mercury Body Shop and has remained a prominent collision repair facility in the area. We have built our reputation on meeting the highest quality standards with friendly service. From the insurance company to the customer, everyone is treated fairly, with honesty and integrity.

BODY SHOP

Creative Firm: **NEVER BORING DESIGN ASSOCIATES — MODESTO, CA**
Creative Team: **KATRINA FURTON**
Client: **BURNSIDE BODY SHOP**

Creative Firm: **LEKASMILLER DESIGN — WALNUT CREEK, CA**
Creative Team: **LANA IP**
Client: **THE RESTAURANT AT WENTE VINEYARDS**

Creative Firm: **A3 DESIGN — CHARLOTTE, NC**
Creative Team: **ALAN ALTMAN, AMANDA ALTMAN**
Client: **CARMAL COUNTRY CLUB**

Creative Firm: **GRAFIK MARKETING COMMUNICATIONS — ALEXANDRIA, VA**
Creative Team: **MICHELLE MAR COLLINS, JOHNNY VITOROVICH, HAL SWETNAM, IVAN HOOKER, CINDY COLE, DEAN ALEXANDER**
Client: **EYA**

Creative Firm: **KOR GROUP — BOSTON, MA**
Creative Team: **MB JAROSIK, JAMES GRADY**
Client: **THE CONGRESS GROUP**

Creative Firm: **HUGHES HUNTER, INC. — THOUSAND OAKS, CA**
Creative Team: **JIM HUGHES, BRUCE POLKES, KIRSTEN MCGUIRE**
Client: **AVEX AVIATION**

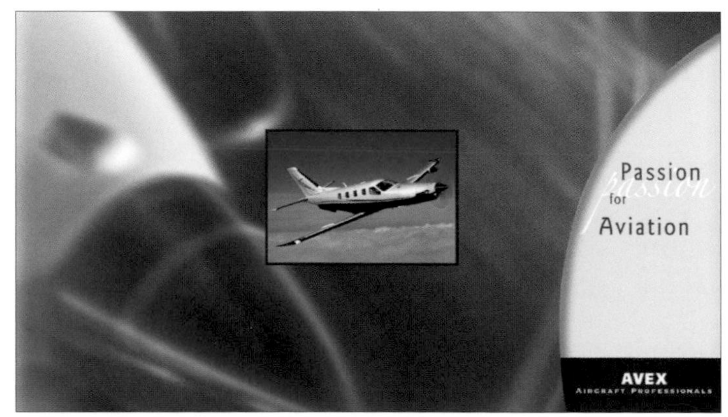

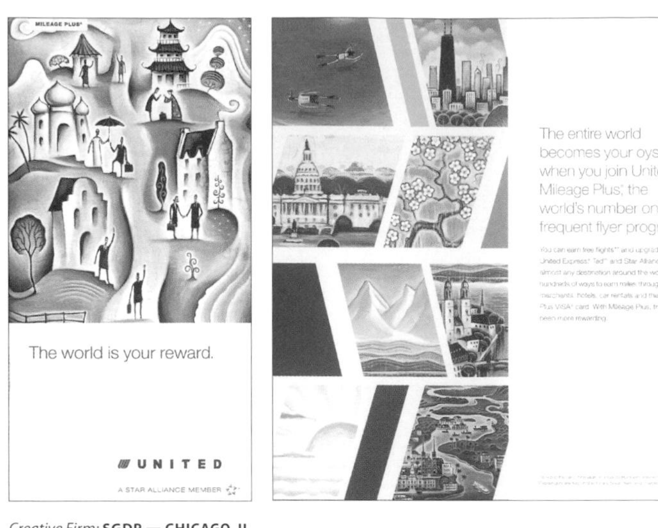

Creative Firm: **SGDP — CHICAGO, IL**
Creative Team: **KIM TERZIS, ALBENA IVANOVA, KEVIN KLEBER**
Client: **UNITED AIRLINES**

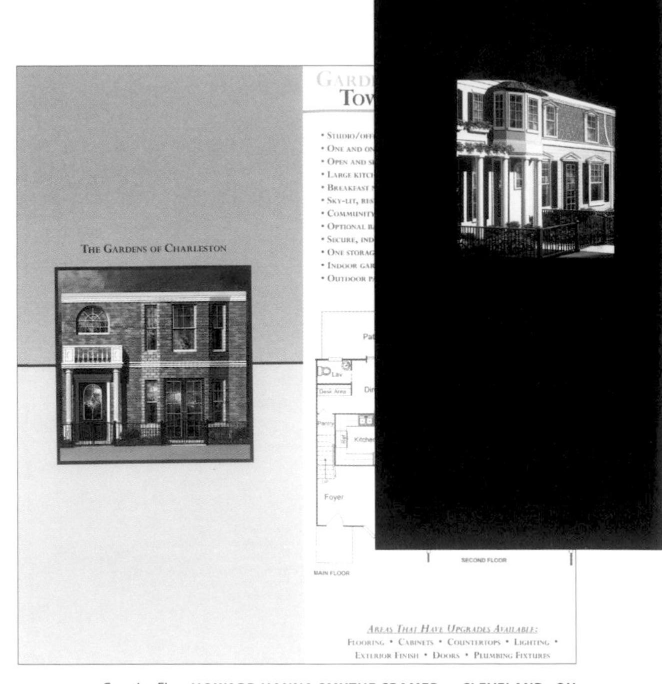

Creative Firm: **HOWARD HANNA SMYTHE CRAMER — CLEVELAND , OH**
Creative Team: **AIMEE CAMPBELL**
Client: **GARDENS OF CHARLESTON**

Creative Firm: **RUDER FINN DESIGN — NEW YORK, NY**
Creative Team: **LISA GABBAY, SAL CATANIA, AARON WILSON**
Client: **NEW YORK THEATRE WORKSHOP**

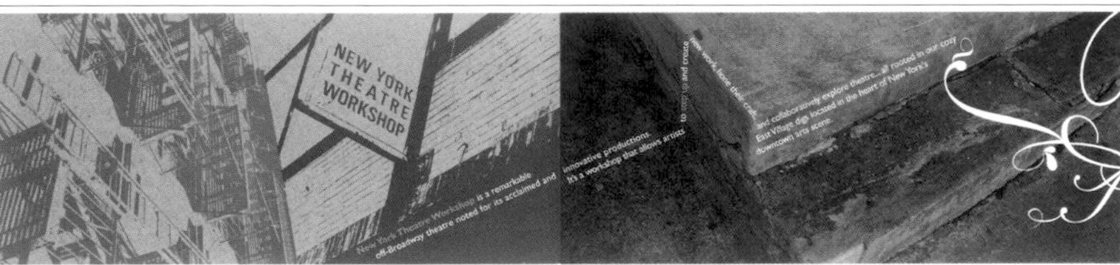

Creative Firm: **SUBPLOT DESIGN INC. — VANCOUVER, BC, CANADA**
Creative Team: **MATTHEW CLARK, ROY WHITE, STEPH GIBSON**
Client: **RYDERS EYEWEAR**

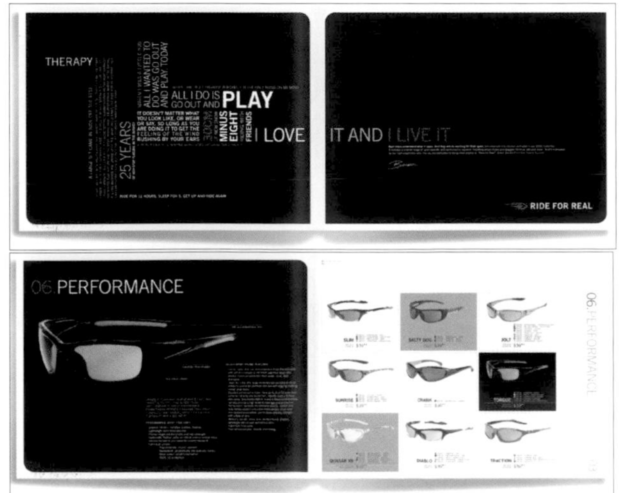

Creative Firm: **HORNALL ANDERSON DESIGN WORKS — SEATTLE, WA**
Creative Team: **MARK POPICH, PETER ANDERSON, YURI SHVETS, MICHAEL BRUGMAN**
Client: **ONREQUEST**

Creative Firm: **GAMMON RAGONESI ASSOCIATES — NEW YORK, NY**
Creative Team: **MARY RAGONESI, YARITSA ARENAS**
Client: **NESTLE**

East Midtown

Where New York Gets Its Style

The Guide

Whether you're traveling for business or pleasure, East Midtown is the ideal place to stay. It's convenient to everything New York has to offer, and great shopping and dining are just around the corner. East Midtown offers a range of accommodations, from world-renowned establishments to distinctive boutique hotels.

www.eastmidtown.org

Creative Firm: **SILVER COMMUNICATIONS INC — NEW YORK, NY**
Creative Team: **GREGG SIBERT, CHRISTINA WEISSMAN**
Client: **EAST MIDTOWN ASSOCIATION**

Creative Firm: **SUKA DESIGN — NEW YORK, NY**
Creative Team: **BRIAN WONG**
Client: **THE BRONX HIGH SCHOOL OF SCIENCE**

Creative Firm: **RUDER FINN DESIGN — NEW YORK, NY**
Creative Team: **LISA GABBAY, SAL CATANIA, DIANA YEO**
Client: **NOVARTIS**

Creative Firm: **TRIPLE 888 STUDIOS — PARRAMATTA, NSW, AUSTRALIA**
Creative Team: **TRIPLE 888 CREATIVE TEAM**
Client: **SIRTEX MEDICAL**

Creative Firm: **KELLER CRESCENT — EVANSVILLE, IN**
Creative Team: **RANDALL ROHN, LYNNE MLADY, GERRY ULRICH**
Client: **HEAVEN HILL**

Creative Firm: **HORNALL ANDERSON DESIGN WORKS — SEATTLE, WA**
Creative Team: **JACK ANDERSON, YURI SHVETS, KATHA DALTON, SARA SIMON**
Client: **AISH SEATTLE**

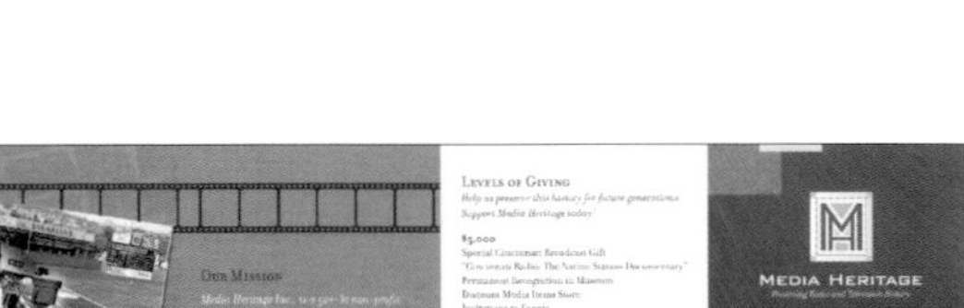

Creative Firm: **BELYEA — SEATTLE, WA**
Creative Team: **RON HANSEN, ANNE BRYANT, SHERI-LOU STANNARD**
Client: **HOLY NAMES ACADENY**

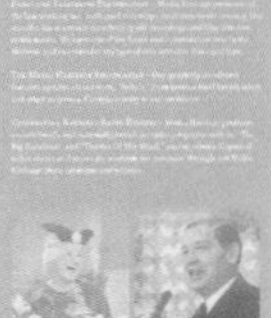

Creative Firm: **FIVE VISUAL COMMUNICATION & DESIGN — WEST CHESTER, OH**
Creative Team: **RONDI TSCHOPP**
Client: **MEDIA HERITAGE INC.**

Creative Firm: **BBK STUDIO — GRAND RAPIDS, MI**
Creative Team: **YANG KIM, MICHELE CHARTIER, KRISTIN TENANT, DEAN VAN DIS, SVH GROUP**
Client: **IZZYDESIGN**

Creative Firm: **SGDP — CHICAGO, IL**
Creative Team: **KIM TERZIS, ALBENA IVANOVA, STEVE BATTERSON**
Client: **UNITED AIRLINES**

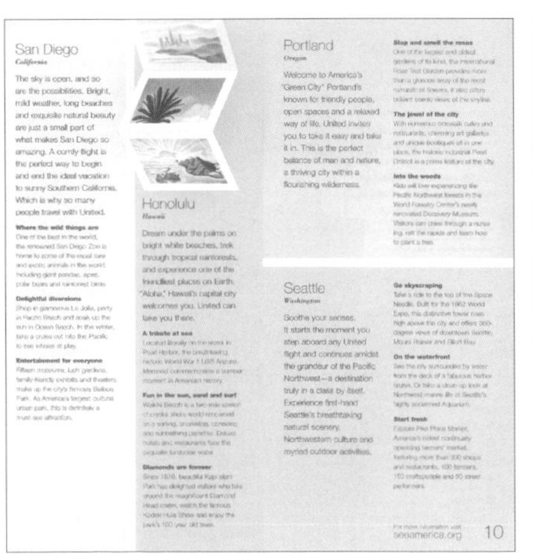

Creative Firm: **GRAFIK MARKETING COMMUNICATIONS — ALEXANDRIA, VA**
Creative Team: **MICHELLE MAR COLLINS, LYNN MURPHY, JOHNNY VITOROVICH, HAL SWETNAM, REGINA ESPOSITO, IVAN HOOKER**
Client: **EYA**

Creative Firm: **QUALCOMM — SAN DIEGO, CA**
Creative Team: **FRANK BERNAS, CHRIS LEE**
Client: **RANCHO SANTA FE GOLF CLUB**

Creative Firm: **THE COLLEGE OF SAINT ROSE — ALBANY, NY**
Creative Team: **MARK HAMILTON, CHRIS PARODY, MEREDITH ROSE**
Client: **THE COLLEGE OF SAINT ROSE**

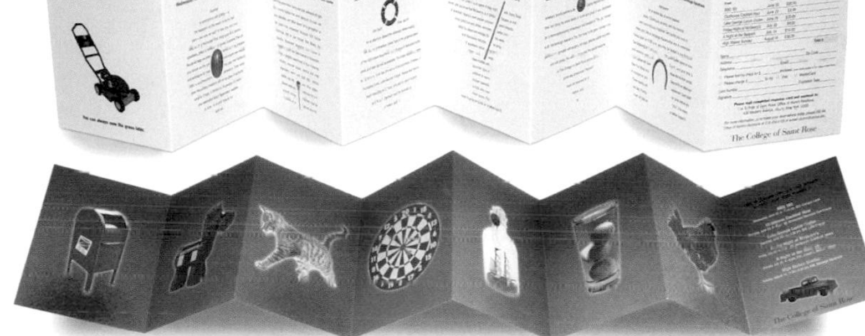

Creative Firm: **HARRIS, DEVILLE & ASSOCIATES, INC. — BATON ROUGE, LA**
Creative Team: **ELIZABETH PERRY, STAN TAYLOR, BEVERLY SMILEY**
Client: **SOLUTIONS THROUGH SCIENCE**

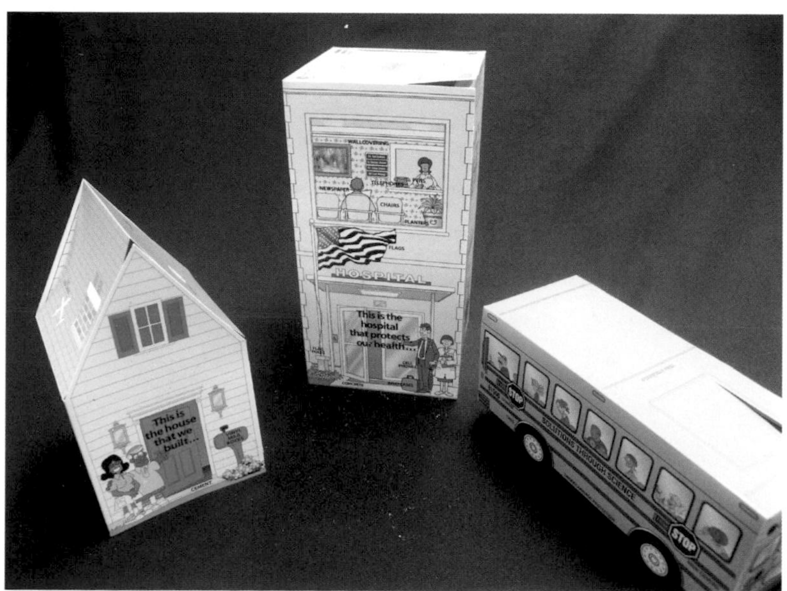

Creative Firm: **THE COLLEGE OF SAINT ROSE — ALBANY, NY**
Creative Team: **MARK HAMILTON, CHRIS PARODY, JOHN HUNTER**
Client: **THE COLLEGE OF SAINT ROSE**

Creative Firm: **SPLASH PRODUCTIONS PTE LTD — SINGAPORE**
Creative Team: **TERRY LEE, NORMAN LAI**
Client: **SURBANA INTERNATIONAL CONSULTANTS PTE. LTD.**

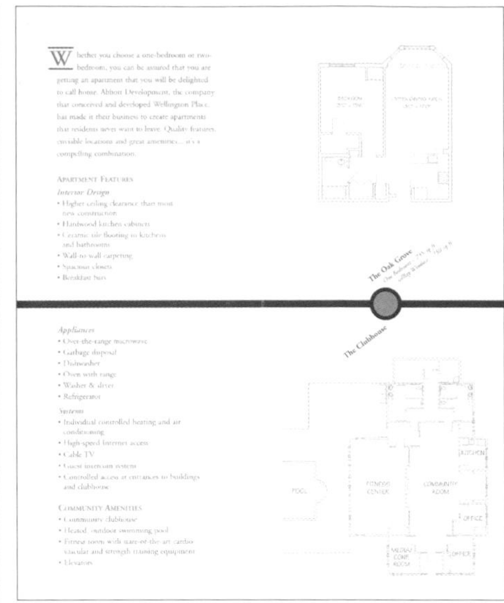

Creative Firm: **PRIMARY DESIGN, INC. — HAVERHILL, MA**
Creative Team: **JULES EPSTEIN, DAVID VADALA, SHARYN ROGERS, ALLISON DAVIS**
Client: **ABBOTT DEVELOPMENT**

Creative Firm: **VANPELT CREATIVE — GARLAND, TX**
Creative Team: **CHIP VANPELT, TODD BRASHEAR, J.W. BURKEY**
Client: **AM APPLIANCE GROUP**

Creative Firm: **SUKA DESIGN — NEW YORK, NY**
Creative Team: **LAURA PLOSZAJ**
Client: **APOLLO THEATRE FOUNDATION**

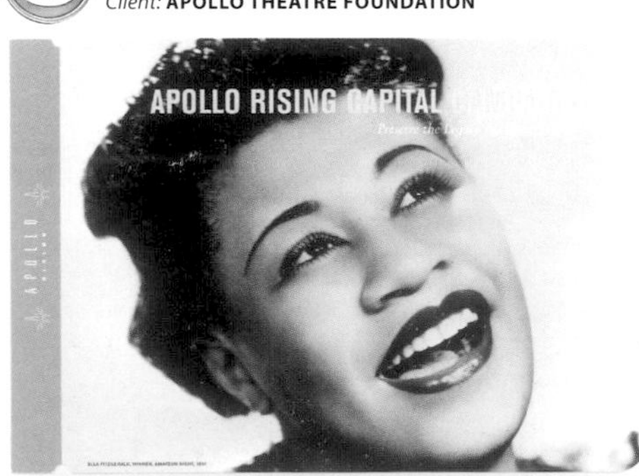

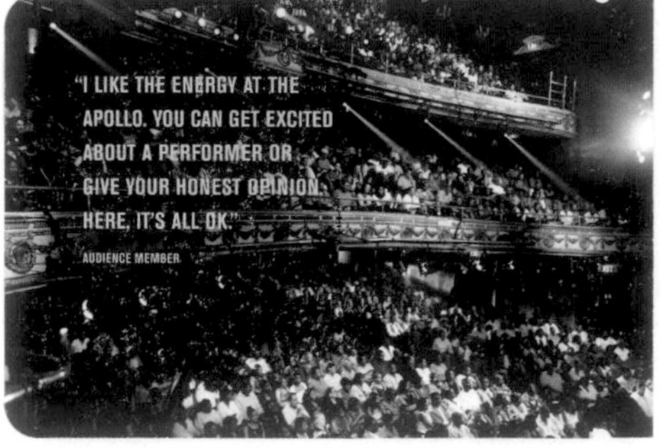

Creative Firm: **SPLASH PRODUCTIONS PTE LTD — SINGAPORE**
Creative Team: **TERRY LEE, LOW JAT LENG, STANLEY TAP, BRICE LI**
Client: **MINDEF SCHOLARSHIP CENTRE**

Creative Firm: **WESTGROUP CREATIVE — NEW YORK, NY**
Creative Team: **CHIP TOLANEY, MARVIN BERK**
Client: **NEW DANCE GROUP**

Creative Firm: **YELLOW SHOES CREATIVE WEST, DISNEYLAND RESORT — ANAHEIM, CA**
Creative Team: **STEVEN GERRY, WES CLARK, JACQUELYN MOE, ANIKO BOTA, CLAIRE BILBY**
Client: **ORANGE COUNTY VISITORS & CONVENTION BUREAU**

Creative Firm: **KOR GROUP — BOSTON, MA**
Creative Team: **JIM GIBSON, TONY RINALIDO**
Client: **BEAVER COUNTRY DAY SCHOOL**

Creative Firm: **BELYEA — SEATTLE, WA**
Creative Team: **RON HANSEN, ANNE BRYANT, SHERI-LOU STANNARD**
Client: **HOLY NAMES ACADEMY**

Creative Firm: **VENTRESS DESIGN GROUP — FRANKLIN, TN**
Creative Team: **TOM VENTRESS, ERIC VENTRESS, BILL COVERT, DAN LOFTIN, SANDY CAMPBELL**
Client: **VANDERBILT UNIVERSITY LAW SCHOOL**

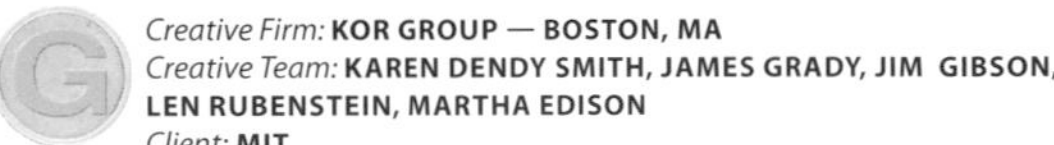

Creative Firm: **KOR GROUP — BOSTON, MA**
Creative Team: **KAREN DENDY SMITH, JAMES GRADY, JIM GIBSON, LEN RUBENSTEIN, MARTHA EDISON**
Client: **MIT**

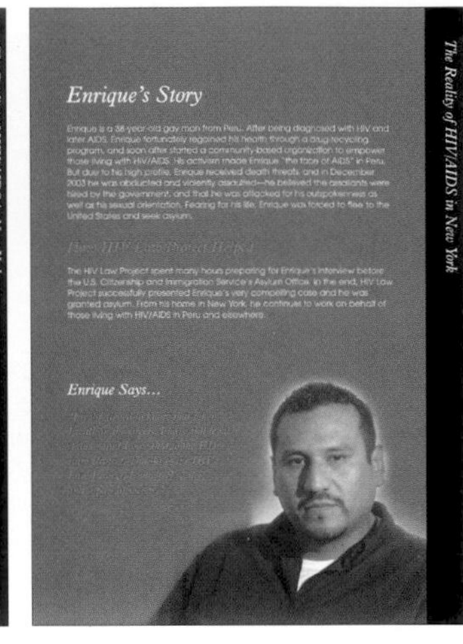

Creative Firm: **TAPROOT FOUNDATION — BROOKLYN, NY**
Creative Team: **CHIP TOLANEY, LINDSAY MERGENS, PETER DOLCHIN, BERNARD LEIBOV, ANNE OLDEROG, ANDREW GRYN**
Client: **THE HIV LAW PROJECT**

Creative Firm: **GRAFIK MARKETING COMMUNICATIONS — ALEXANDRIA, VA**
Creative Team: **GREGG GLAVIANO, LYNN MURPHY, HEATH DWIGGINS**
Client: **FM STRATEGIC COMMUNICATIONS**

Creative Firm: **SUKA DESIGN — NEW YORK, NY**
Creative Team: **LOLA BERNABE**
Client: **THE EAST HARLEM SCHOOL**

Creative Firm: **ORIGINAL IMPRESSIONS — MIAMI, FL**
Creative Team: **FRANK IRIAS**
Client: **OCEAN REEF CLUB**

Creative Firm: **ORIGINAL IMPRESSIONS — MIAMI, FL**
Creative Team: **FRANK IRIAS**
Client: **VILLAS AT JASMINE PARK**

Creative Firm: **A3 DESIGN — CHARLOTTE, NC**
Creative Team: **ALAN ALTMAN, AMANDA ALTMAN**
Client: **MATTAMY HOMES**

Creative Firm: **KOR GROUP — BOSTON, MA**
Creative Team: **ANNE CALLAHAN, JIM GIBSON, LEN RUBENSTEIN**
Client: **RAMAPO COLLEGE**

Creative Firm: **FUTURA DDB — LJUBLANA, SLOVENIA**
Creative Team: **ZARE KERIN, MARKO VICIC, MATEJA PODMENIK**

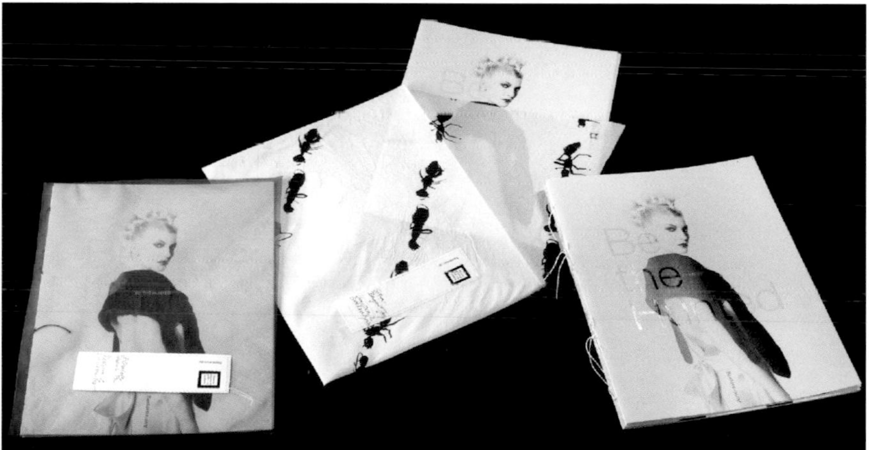

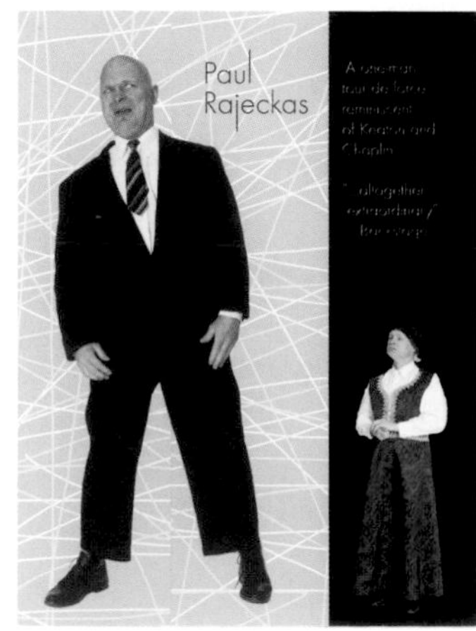

Creative Firm: **WESTGROUP CREATIVE — NEW YORK, NY**
Creative Team: **CHIP TOLANEY, MARVIN BERK, NOEL HAYASHI, CAROL ROSEGG**
Client: **PAUL RAJECKAS**

Creative Firm: **STUDIO FIVE — NEW YORK, NY**
Creative Team: **TATIANA AROCHA, MELISSA GORMAN**
Client: **EXPANSION TEAM**

1001 PARK AVENUE
NEW YORK, NY 10028
(917) 648-8397
PHIL.SHIPPER@GMAIL.COM

Creative Firm: **ACME COMMUNICATIONS, INC. — NEW YORK, NY**
Creative Team: **KIKI BOUCHER, ANDREA ROSS BOYLE**
Client: **PHILIP SHIPPER**

Creative Firm: **RUDER FINN DESIGN — NEW YORK, NY**
Creative Team: **LISA GABBAY, SAL CATANIA, DIANA YEO, KAVEN LAM, RUBEN MERCADO, JEFF GILLAM**
Client: **RUDER FINN DESIGN**

Creative Firm: **PERCEPT CREATIVE GROUP — CRONULLA, NSW, AUSTRALIA**
Creative Team: **LEWIS JENKINS**
Client: **CARMENS NIGHT CLUB / MIRANDA HOTEL**

Jake Smack
Director of eMarketing
jsmack@bluesqstudios.com
21410 N 19th Avenue, Ste 143
Phoenix, Arizona 85027
T 623.466.6600
D 623.466.6610
F 623.466.6601
www.bluesqstudios.com

Creative Firm: **RULE29 — GENEVA, IL**
Creative Team: **JUSTIN AHERNS, O'NEIL PRINTING**
Client: **BLUE SQUARE STUDIOS**

Creative Firm: **HERE! NETWORKS — NEW YORK, NY**
Creative Team: **ERIC FELDMAN, CRAIG OELRICH**
Client: **HERE! NETWORKS.**

Creative Firm: **MODERN MARKETING CONCEPTS — LOUISVILLE, KY**
Creative Team: **MARK A. GROVES**
Client: **MODERN MARKETING CONCEPTS**

MARK DEITCH
president
mark deitch & associates, inc.
4444 riverside drive, suite 202
burbank, ca 91505-4048
p. 818.558.1010
f. 818.558.1515
markd@markdeitch.com
www.WebSiteDesigns.com

Creative Firm: **MARK DEITCH & ASSOCIATES, INC. — BURBANK, CA**
Creative Team: **LISA CLARK**
Client: **MARK DEITCH & ASSOCIATES, INC.**

Creative Firm: **MT&L PUBLIC RELATIONS LTD. — HALIFAX, NS, CANADA**
Creative Team: **DANNY GODFREY, PAUL WILLIAMS**
Client: **AIRFIRE WIRELESS CONNECTIVITY**

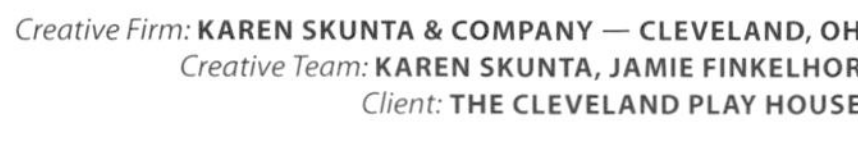

Creative Firm: **KAREN SKUNTA & COMPANY — CLEVELAND, OH**
Creative Team: **KAREN SKUNTA, JAMIE FINKELHOR**
Client: **THE CLEVELAND PLAY HOUSE**

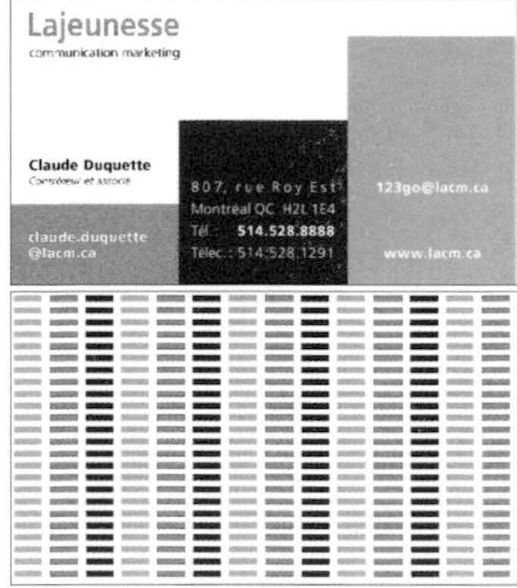

Creative Firm: **LAJEUNESSE COMMUNICATION MARKETING — MONTREAL, QC, CANADA**
Creative Team: **YVES DUQUETTE, NATHALIE DAIGLE**

Creative Firm: **BRIGHT RAIN CREATIVE — ST. LOUIS, MO**
Creative Team: **MATT MARINO, KEVIN HOUGH**
Client: **REDLINE PRODUCTION & POST**

Creative Firm: **MTV OFF AIR CREATIVE — NEW YORK, NY**
Creative Team: **JEFFREY KEYTON, JIM DEBARROS, KAREN WEISS, STACY DRUMMOND**
Client: **MTV NETWORKS**

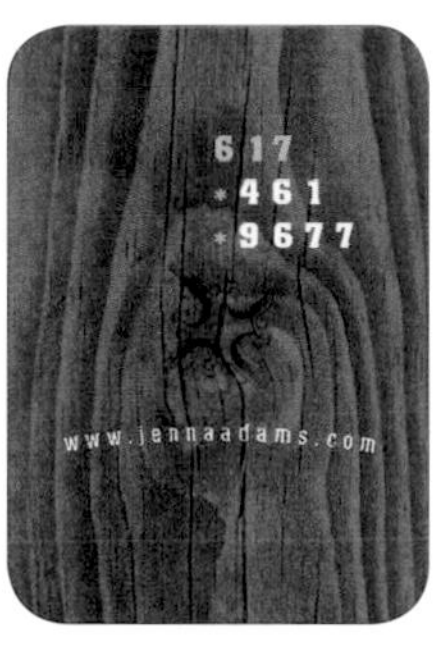

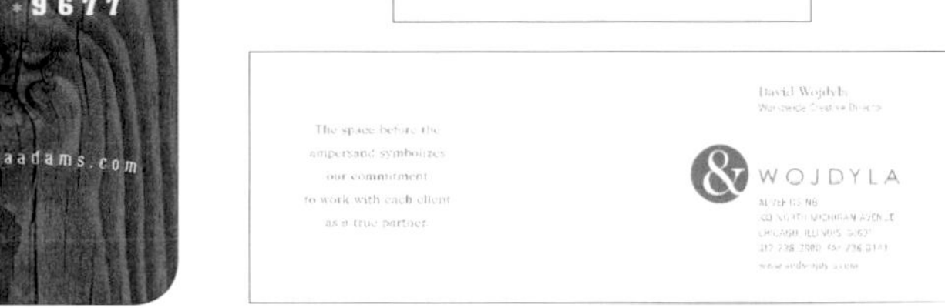

Creative Firm: **INTERROBANG DESIGN COLLABORATIVE, INC. — RICHMOND, VT**
Creative Team: **MARK D. SYLVESTER**
Client: **JENNA ADAMS / STYLIST**

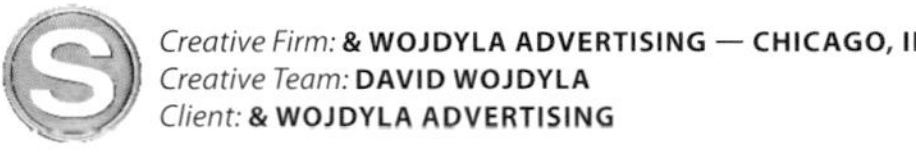

Creative Firm: **& WOJDYLA ADVERTISING — CHICAGO, IL**
Creative Team: **DAVID WOJDYLA**
Client: **& WOJDYLA ADVERTISING**

Creative Firm: **KARACTERS DESIGN GROUP/DDB CANADA — VANCOUVER, BC, CANADA**
Creative Team: **MARIA KENNEDY, MARSHA LARKIN, HELEN WYNNE, MARK FINN, RUSS HORII**
Client: **KARACTERS DESIGN GROUP**

Pushkar Thakur. Creative Director. +91.9811510755 pushkarthakur@thegrafiosi.com. http://www.thegrafiosi.com

Creative Firm: **THE GRAFIOSI — NEW DELHI, INDIA**
Creative Team: **PUSHKAR THAKUR**
Client: **THE GRAFIOSI**

Creative Firm: **MC CREATIONS DESIGN STUDIO, INC. — JERICHO, NY**
Creative Team: **MICHAEL CALI, CYNTHIA MORILLO**

Creative Firm: **VOICEBOX CREATIVE — SAN FRANCISCO, CA**
Creative Team: **JACQUES ROSSOUW, VOICEBOX TEAM, GREG CLARKE, JAN DENTON**
Client: **VINTAGE POINT**

Creative Firm: **STELLAR DEBRIS — HADANO-SHI, KANAGAWA-KEN, JAPAN**
Creative Team: **CHRISTOPHER JONES**
Client: **STELLAR DEBRIS**

Creative Firm: **CJ DESIGN — SANTA CRUZ, CA**
Creative Team: **CHRIS MARK, CHRIS MARK, DAN JENKINS, NIKKI BROOKS, ART DURAND**
Client: **AIKANE**

Creative Firm: **NINA DAVID KOMMUNIKATIONSDESIGN — DUESSELDORF, NRW, GERMANY**
Creative Team: **NINA DAVID, NINA DAVID**
Client: **FONT-O-RAMA**

Creative Firm: **RTS RIEGER TEAM WERBEAGENTUR GMBH — LEINFELDEN-ECHTERDINGEN, GERMANY**
Creative Team: **ANNETTE PIENTKA, CHRISTINE GRAF**
Client: **H. STOLL GMBH & CO. KG**

Creative Firm: **PHOENIX CREATIVE GROUP, LLC — POTOMAC FALLS, VA**
Creative Team: **NICOLE KASSOLIS, SEAN MULLINS, HICKORY PRINTING, ALDERMAN STUDIOS**
Client: **TIMBERLAKE / AMERICAN WOODWORK**

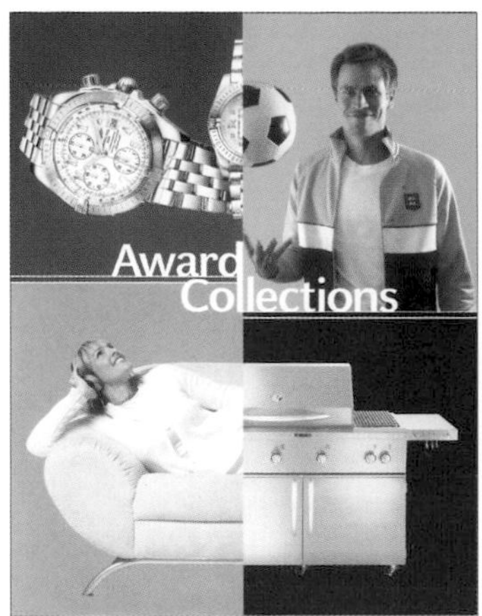

Creative Firm: **STAN GELLMAN GRAPHIC DESIGN INC. — ST. LOUIS, MO**
Creative Team: **JILL FRANTTI, DIANA DOERR, BARRY TILSON**
Client: **HINDA INCENTIVES**

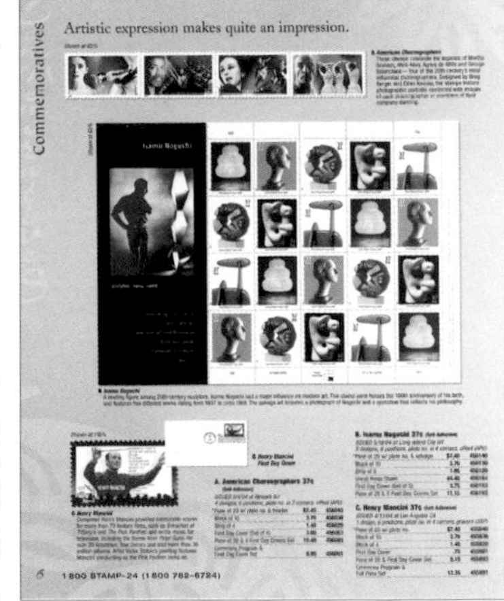

Creative Firm: **UNITED STATES POSTAL SERVICE — ARLINGTON, VA**

Creative Firm: **BOOMM! MARKETING & COMMUNICATIONS — WESTCHESTER, IL**
Client: **MCCAIN FOODS USA**

Creative Firm: **LTD CREATIVE — FREDERICK, MD**
Creative Team: **LOUANNE WELGOSS, TIMOTHY FINNEN, BRIDGIT KEARNS**
Client: **HANLEY WOOD, LLC**

Creative Firm: **LTD CREATIVE — FREDERICK, MD**
Creative Team: **LOUANNE WELGOSS, TIMOTHY FINNEN, KIMBERLY DOW, SARA TOBIN**
Client: **HANLEY WOOD, LLC**

Creative Firm: **UIUC SCHOOL OF ART AND DESIGN — CHAMPAIGN, IL**
Creative Team: **JENNIFER GUNJI, ANNETTE ROTZ-GLEASON, KRISTINE DECHAVEZ, TIRZAH ROSE**
Client: **SCHOOL OF ART AND DESIGN**

Creative Firm: **UNITED STATES POSTAL SERVICE — ARLINGTON, VA**

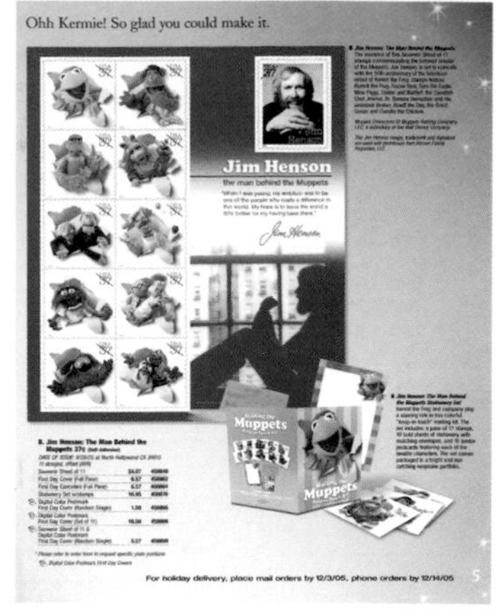

Creative Firm: **UNITED STATES POSTAL SERVICE — ARLINGTON, VA**

Creative Firm: **UNITED STATES POSTAL SERVICE — ARLINGTON, VA**

Creative Firm: **UNITED STATES POSTAL SERVICE — ARLINGTON, VA**

Creative Firm: **CJ DESIGN — SANTA CRUZ, CA**
Creative Team: **CHRIS MARK, ART DURAND**
Client: **AIKANE**

Creative Firm: **CROSLEY RADIO — LOUISVILLE, KY**
Creative Team: **MARK A. GROVES**
Client: **CROSLEY RADIO**

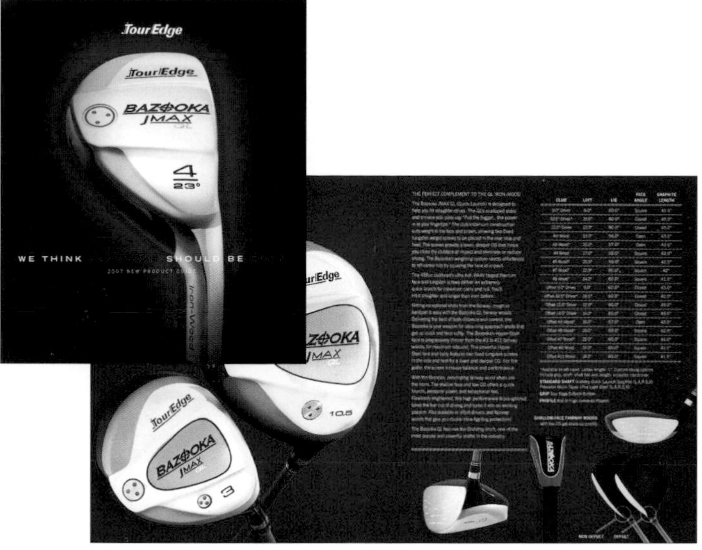

Creative Firm: **RULE29 — GENEVA, IL**
Creative Team: **JUSTIN AHERNS, JOSH JENSEN**
Client: **TOUR EDGE**

Creative Firm: **THE DESIGN STUDIO AT KEAN UNIVERSITY — UNION, NJ**
Creative Team: **STEVEN BROWER, TRICIA DECKER, STEPHANIE HELLER**
Client: **CAS GALLERY, KEAN UNIVERSITY**

Creative Firm: **BRIAN J. GANTON & ASSOCIATES — CEDAR GROVE, NJ**
Creative Team: **CHRISTOPHER GANTON, BRIAN GANTON JR., MARK GANTON**
Client: **BELGARD**

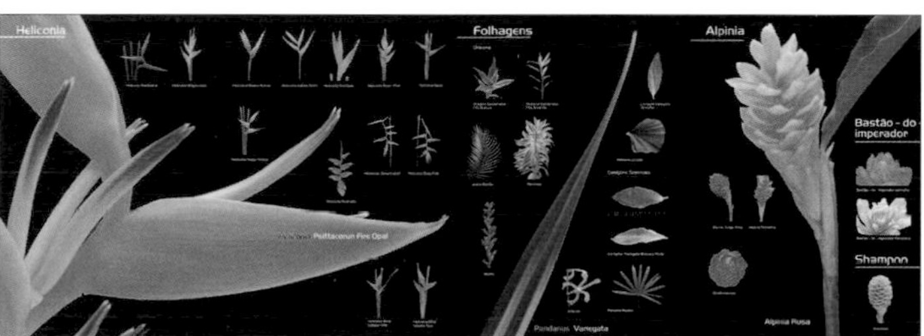

Creative Firm: **MENDES PUBLICIDADE — BELÉM, PARÁ, BRAZIL**
Creative Team: **OSWALDO MENDES, DALMIRO FREITAS, MARCEL CHAVES**
Client: **SEBRAE/PA**

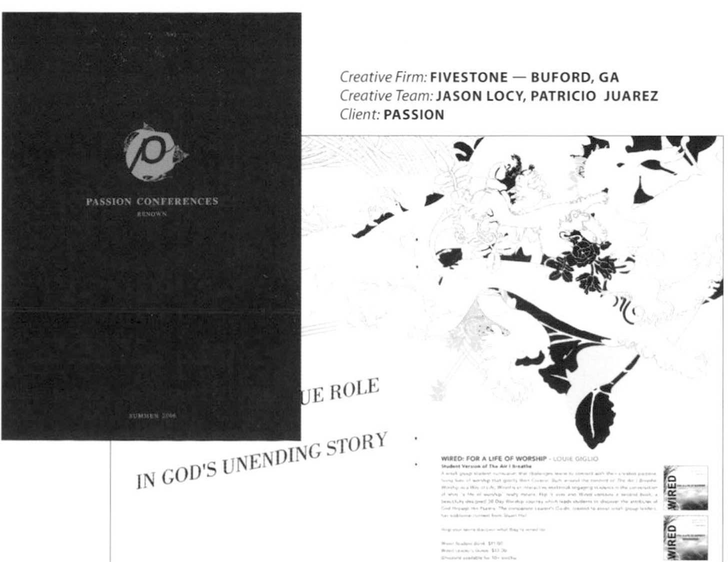

Creative Firm: **FIVESTONE — BUFORD, GA**
Creative Team: **JASON LOCY, PATRICIO JUAREZ**
Client: **PASSION**

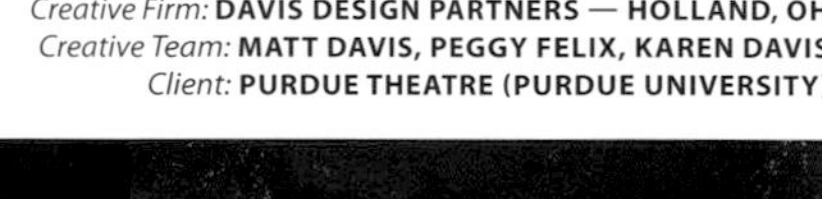

Creative Firm: **DAVIS DESIGN PARTNERS — HOLLAND, OH**
Creative Team: **MATT DAVIS, PEGGY FELIX, KAREN DAVIS**
Client: **PURDUE THEATRE (PURDUE UNIVERSITY)**

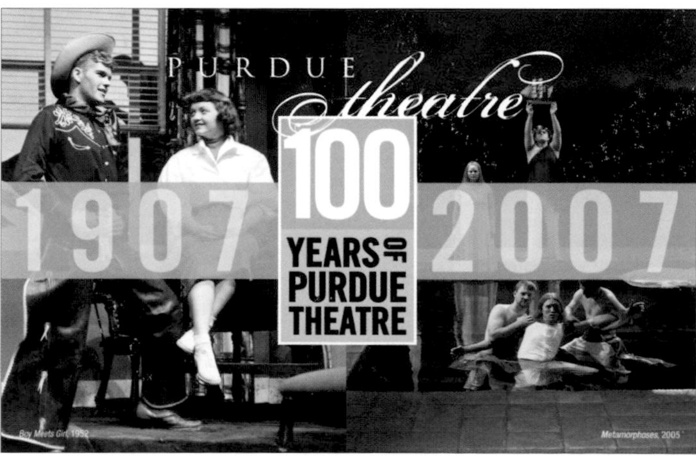

Creative Firm: **JONI RAE AND ASSOCIATES — ENCINO, CA**
Creative Team: **JONI RAE RUSSELL, BEVERLY TRENGOVE**
Client: **THERMAFUSE**

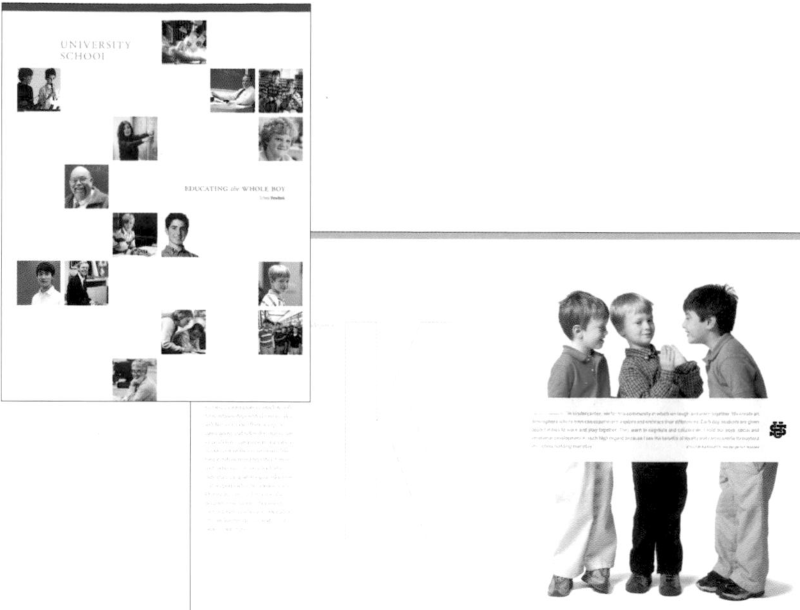

Creative Firm: **DAVIS DESIGN PARTNERS — HOLLAND, OH**
Creative Team: **MATT DAVIS, KAREN MEYERS, GABRIEL AMADEAUS COONEY, KAREN DAVIS, FIONA REILLY**
Client: **UNIVERSITY SCHOOL**

Creative Firm: **DESIGN GUYS — MINNEAPOLIS, MN**
Creative Team: **STEVE SIKORA, KELLY MUNSON, GEORGE HEINRICH, JEFF MUELLER, POMCO GRAPHIC ARTS**
Client: **LAZOR OFFICE**

Creative Firm: **RUDER FINN DESIGN — NEW YORK, NY**
Creative Team: **LISA GABBAY, SAL CATANIA, EMILY KORSMO**
Client: **RUDER FINN PRESS**

Creative Firm: **Q — WIESBADEN, GERMANY**
Creative Team: **MATTHIAS FREY, MICHAEL LINK**
Client: **ANJA GOCKEL - LONDON**

Creative Firm: **SGDP — CHICAGO, IL**
Creative Team: **KIM TERZIS, ALBENA IVANOVA, KEVIN KLEBER**
Client: **UNITED AIRLINES**

Creative Firm: **HUGHES HUNTER, INC. — THOUSAND OAKS, CA**
Creative Team: **JIM HUGHES, BRUCE POLKES, RENEE AIRINGTON, LIZ FIELDS, JODY LEVITAN, CAROL GRAVELLE**
Client: **FLEETWOOD RV**

Creative Firm: **ELLEN BRUSS DESIGN — DENVER, CO**
Creative Team: **ELLEN BRUSS, CHARLES CARPENTER, STEVE RURA**
Client: **HYDE PARK JEWLERS**

Creative Firm: **ORANGESEED DESIGN — MINNEAPOLIS, MN**
Creative Team: **DAMIEN WOLF, DALE MUSTFUL, ROB REBISCHKE**
Client: **MONTANA LEGEND**

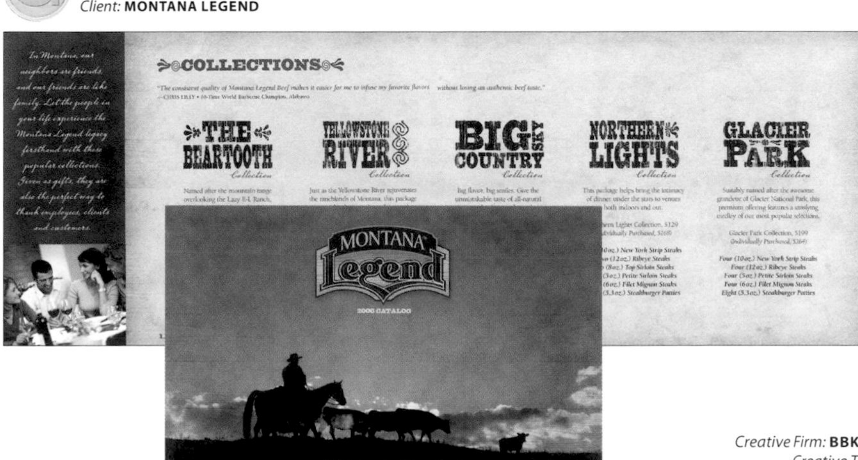

Creative Firm: **BBK STUDIO — GRAND RAPIDS, MI**
Creative Team: **YANG KIM, BRIAN HAUCH, JASON MURRAY, JEREMY FRECHETTE, DAVID KNORR**
Client: **STEELCASE**

Creative Firm: **COMEDY CENTRAL — NEW YORK, NY**
Creative Team: **ROLYN BARTHELMAN**

Creative Firm: **GRIZZELL & CO. — ST. LOUIS, MO**
Creative Team: **JOHN H. GRIZZELL**
Client: **FRIENDS OF KATHERINE DUNHAM**

Creative Firm: **CMT — NEW YORK, NY**
Creative Team: **JAMES HITCHCOCK, AMIE NGUYEN, NORA GAFFNEY**
Client: **CMT**

Creative Firm: **HULL CREATIVE GROUP — BROOKLINE, MA**
Creative Team: **CARYL H. HULL, SUSAN ZANEY**
Client: **DANFORTH MUSEUM OF ART**

Creative Firm: **TORRE LAZUR MCCANN — PARSIPPANY, NJ**
Creative Team: **DAVID PROUDFOOT, KATHRYN LIEBERTHAL, JULIET ALVAREZ, JENNIFER ALAMPI, MARCIA GODDARD**
Client: **BMS / SANOFI**

Creative Firm: **TLC DESIGN — CHURCHVILLE, VA**
Creative Team: **TRUDY L. COLE**
Client: **TLC DESIGN**

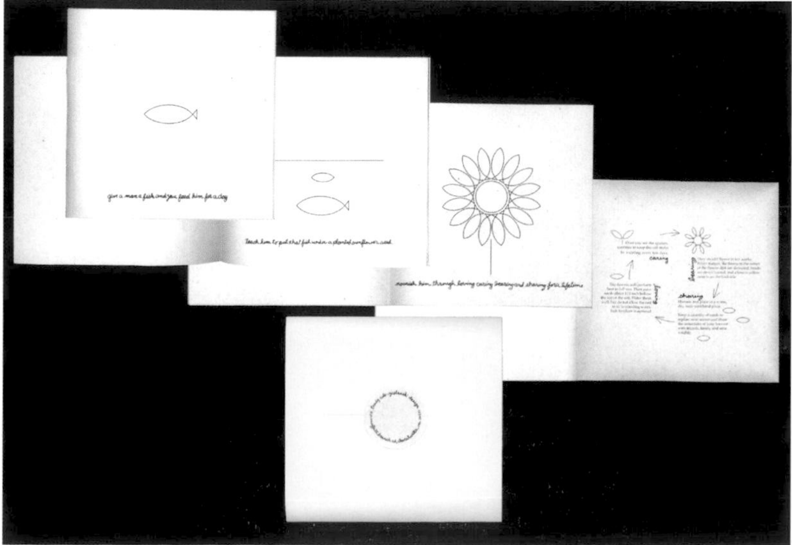

Creative Firm: **PATRICK HENRY CREATIVE PROMOTIONS, INC. — STAFFORD, TX**
Creative Team: **CATHY DONALDSON**
Client: **PATRICK HENRY CREATIVE PROMOTIONS, INC.**

Creative Firm: **FIVE VISUAL COMMUNICATION & DESIGN — WEST CHESTER, OH**
Creative Team: **RONDI TSCHOPP**
Client: **FAIRFIELD COMMUNITY ARTS CENTER**

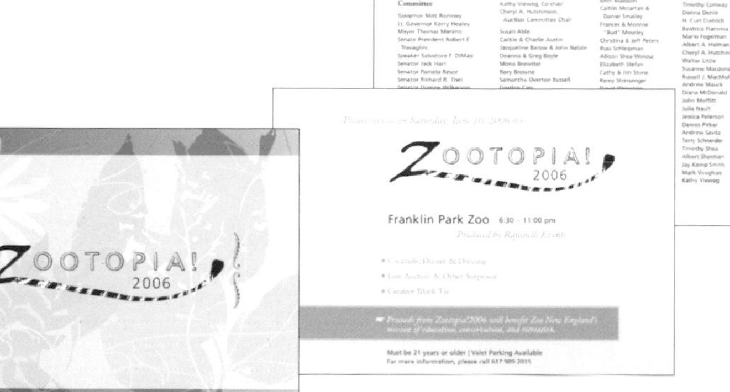

Creative Firm: **KOR GROUP — BOSTON, MA**
Creative Team: **KAREN DENDY SMITH, BRIGITTE TING**
Client: **ZOO NEW ENGLAND**

Creative Firm: **DISCO DOG DESIGN — SAUSALITO, CA**
Creative Team: **BETHANIE MURGUIA**

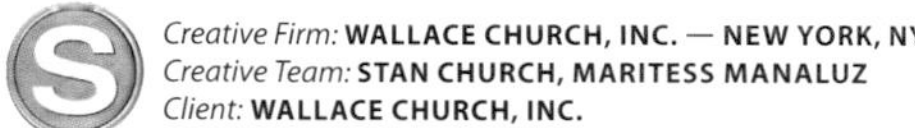

Creative Firm: **WALLACE CHURCH, INC. — NEW YORK, NY**
Creative Team: **STAN CHURCH, MARITESS MANALUZ**
Client: **WALLACE CHURCH, INC.**

Creative Firm: **BRC MARKETING,INC — DAYTON, OH**
Creative Team: **DOM CIMEI, JASON KANTER, MARY FRANCES RODRIGUEZ, AMBER MOORE**
Client: **BRC**

Creative Firm: **WALLACE CHURCH, INC. — NEW YORK, NY**
Creative Team: **STAN CHURCH, JHOMY IRRAZABA, RICH RICKABY, SHERRI SEBASTIAN**
Client: **WALLACE CHURCH, INC.**

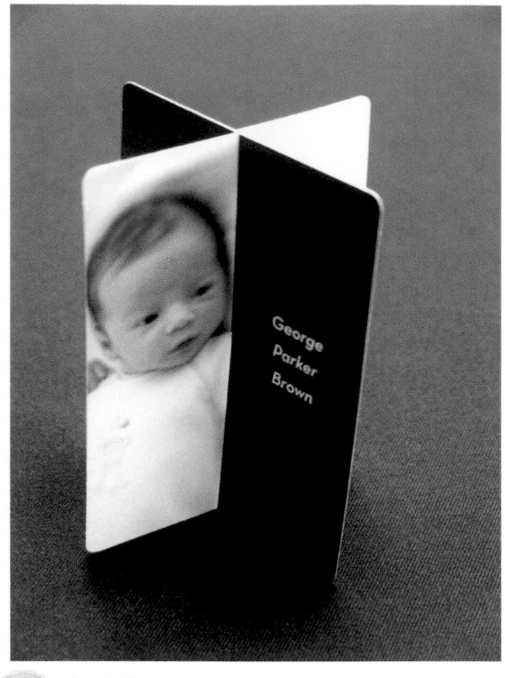

Creative Firm: **ELLEN BRUSS DESIGN — DENVER, CO**
Creative Team: **ELLEN BRUSS, CHARLES CARPENTER**
Client: **MARK AND RACHEL BROWN**

Creative Firm: **NICKTOONS — NEW YORK, NY**
Creative Team: **TERRY MCCORMICK, SUE KIM**
Client: **NICKTOONS NETWORK**

Creative Firm: **ORIGINAL IMPRESSIONS — MIAMI, FL**
Creative Team: **FRANK IRIAS**
Client: **ST. THOMAS UNIVERSITY**

Creative Firm: **PARSONS BRINCKERHOFF — NEW YORK, NY**
Creative Team: **ANA TIBURCIO-RIVERA**
Client: **PARSONS BRINCKERHOFF**

Creative Firm: **GRAFIK MARKETING COMMUNICATIONS — ALEXANDRIA, VA**
Creative Team: **MICHELLE MAR COLLINS, MICHAEL MATEOS, LYNN UMEMOTO**
Client: **MCKEE NELSON, LLP**

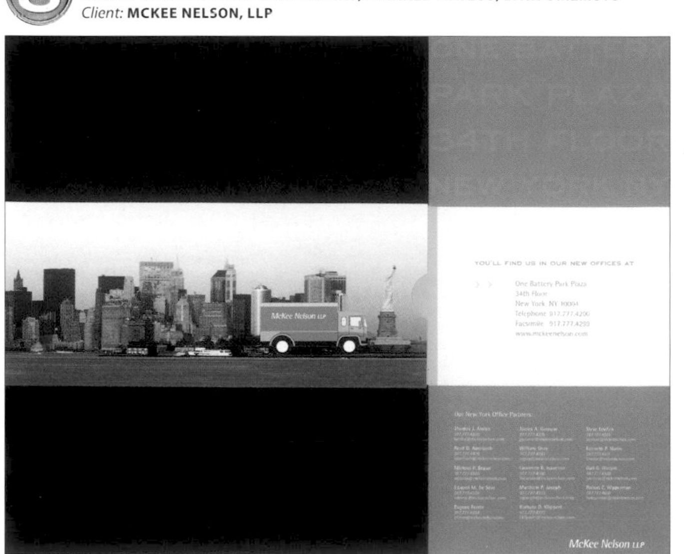

Creative Firm: **GRAFIK MARKETING COMMUNICATIONS — ALEXANDRIA, VA**
Creative Team: **GREGG GLAVIANO, MILA ARRISUENO, LYNN MURPHY, REGINA ESPOSITO**
Client: **SMITHSONIAN LATINO CENTER**

Creative Firm: **PHP COMMUNICATIONS — BIRMINGHAM, AL**
Creative Team: **BRYAN CHACE, LYNN SMITH**
Client: **PHP COMMUNICATIONS**

Creative Firm: **HERBERGER COLLEGE OF FINE ARTS — TEMPE, AZ**
Creative Team: **AMY NG, MARTHA KNIGHT, STACEY SHAW, TIM TRUMBLE**
Client: **HERBERGER COLLEGE OF FINE ARTS**

Creative Firm: **THE HUMANE SOCIETY OF THE UNITED STATES — WASHINGTON, DC**
Creative Team: **PAULA JAWORSKI, ANNE LEUCK FELDHAUS**
Client: **THE HUMANE SOCIETY OF THE UNITED STATES**

Creative Firm: **HBO OFF-AIR CREATIVE SERVICES — NEW YORK, NY**
Creative Team: **VENUS DENNISON, IVY CALAHORRANO, JOSE MENDEZ, IMELDA MOCARSKI**
Client: **HBO MEDIA RELATIONS**

Creative Firm: **CSC'S P2 COMMUNICATIONS SERVICES — FALLS CHURCH, VA**
Creative Team: **NANCY NAUGHTON, TERRY WILSON, AARON KOBILIS, LYNN JEUNETTE, ADAM DONOVAN**
Client: **CSC CORPORATE**

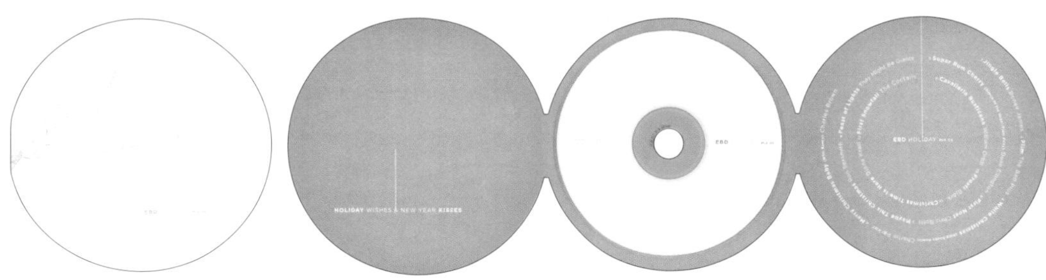

Creative Firm: **ELLEN BRUSS DESIGN — DENVER, CO**
Creative Team: **ELLEN BRUSS, CHARLES CARPENTER**
Client: **ELLEN BRUSS DESIGN**

Creative Firm: **CRABTREE & COMPANY — FALLS CHURCH, VA**
Creative Team: **SUSAN ANGRISANI, TAMERA FINN**
Client: **DISCOVERY CREEK**

Creative Firm: **CREATIVE ALLIANCE — LOUISVILLE, KY**
Creative Team: **JOE ADAMS, ERIC HA**
Client: **CREATIVE ALLIANCE**

Creative Firm: **BELYEA — SEATTLE, WA**
Creative Team: **RON HANSEN, NAOMI COX, SHERI-LOU STANNARD**
Client: **COLORGRAPHICS**

Creative Firm: **GEE + CHUNG DESIGN — SAN FRANCISCO, CA**
Creative Team: **EARL GEE, EARL GEE, FANI CHUNG, EARL GEE, KEVIN NG**
Client: **DCM**

Creative Firm: **A3 DESIGN — CHARLOTTE, NC**
Creative Team: **ALAN ALTMAN, AMANDA ALTMAN, MARIE LORIMER**
Client: **MATTAMY HOMES**

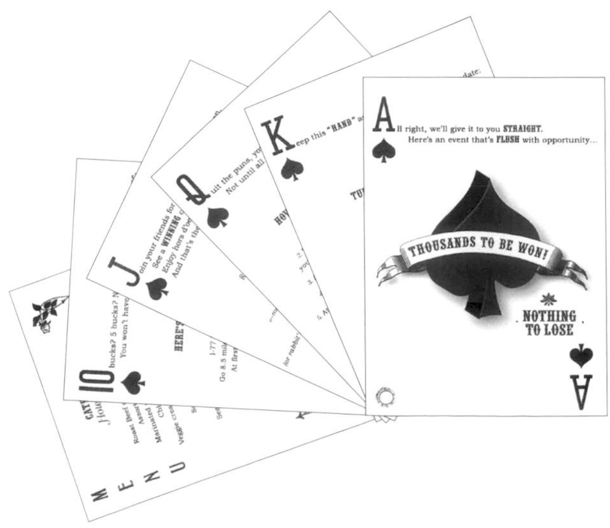

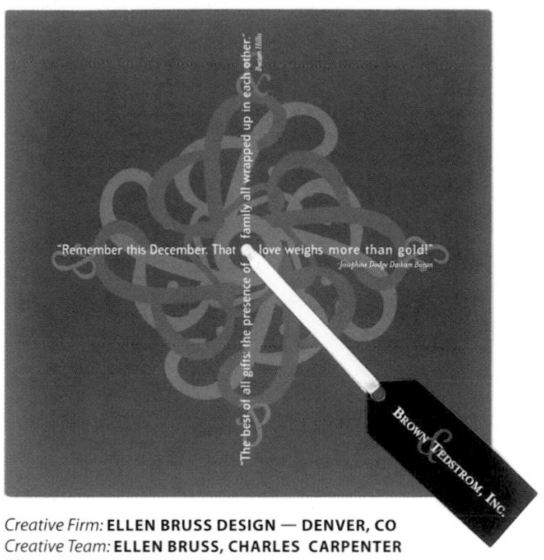

Creative Firm: **ELLEN BRUSS DESIGN — DENVER, CO**
Creative Team: **ELLEN BRUSS, CHARLES CARPENTER**
Client: **BROWN AND TEDSTROM**

Creative Firm: **PHOENIX CREATIVE GROUP, LLC — POTOMAC FALLS, VA**
Creative Team: **SEAN MULLINS**
Client: **BATES-WHITE**

Creative Firm: **THE HUMANE SOCIETY OF THE UNITED STATES — WASHINGTON, DC**
Creative Team: **PAULA JAWORSKI, PATTI GAY**
Client: **THE HUMANE SOCIETY OF THE UNITED STATES**

Creative Firm: **IGNITED MINDS, LLC — MARINA DEL REY, CA**
Creative Team: **OOGIE LEE, PERRY SIEWERT, DAMIAN FRATICELLI, CARDS OF WOOD**
Client: **IGNITED MINDS, LLC**

Creative Firm: **LYNN CYR DESIGN — ST-JEAN-DE-LA-LANDE, QC, CANADA**
Creative Team: **LYNN CYR**
Client: **LYNN CYR DESIGN**

Creative Firm: **SPIKE TV — NEW YORK, NY**
Creative Team: **ANDRE RAZO, BOB SALAZAR, MILINDA ZUMPANO**
Client: **SPIKE**

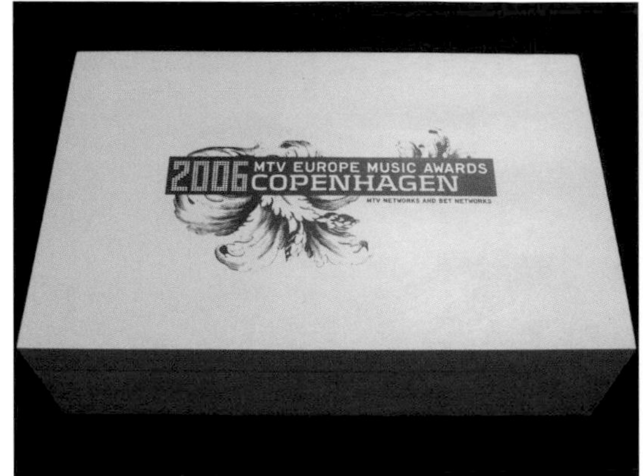

Creative Firm: **MTV NETWORKS CREATIVE SERVICES — NEW YORK, NY**

The International Center for Research on Women
cordially invites you to attend our
30th Anniversary Gala

Celebrating the Power of Partnerships

on International Women's Day
Wednesday, March 8, 2006 at 6:30 pm
The John F. Kennedy Center for the Performing Arts
Washington, DC
Black tie optional

Presenting Sponsor
MAC VIVA GLAM

Creative Firm: **GREENFIELD/BELSER LTD. — WASHINGTON, DC**
Creative Team: **MARK LEDGERWOOD, SHIKHA SAVDAS, CAROLYN SEWELL, GENE SHAFFER**
Client: **INTERNATIONAL CENTER FOR RESEARCH ON WOMEN**

Creative Firm: **PEGGY LAURITSEN DESIGN GROUP — MINNEAPOLIS, MN**
Creative Team: **BRIAN DANAHER**

Creative Firm: **GEE + CHUNG DESIGN — SAN FRANCISCO, CA**
Creative Team: **EARL GEE, EARL GEE, FANI CHUNG, EARL GEE**
Client: **DCM**

Creative Firm: **DESIGN GUYS — MINNEAPOLIS, MN**
Creative Team: **STEVE SIKORA, BARRY TOWNSEND, JAY THEIGE, JAY THEIGE, KAREN LOKENSGARD, SHAPCO PRINTING**
Client: **MINNESOTA PUBLIC RADIO**

Creative Firm: **19NOVANTA COMMUNICATION PARTNERS — ROME, ITALY**
Creative Team: **CONSUELO UGHI, ANDREA PROVVIDENZA, LUCA BALDI, VALERIA CIARDULLI, ROCCO VIGGIANO, MARIO BIZZARRI**

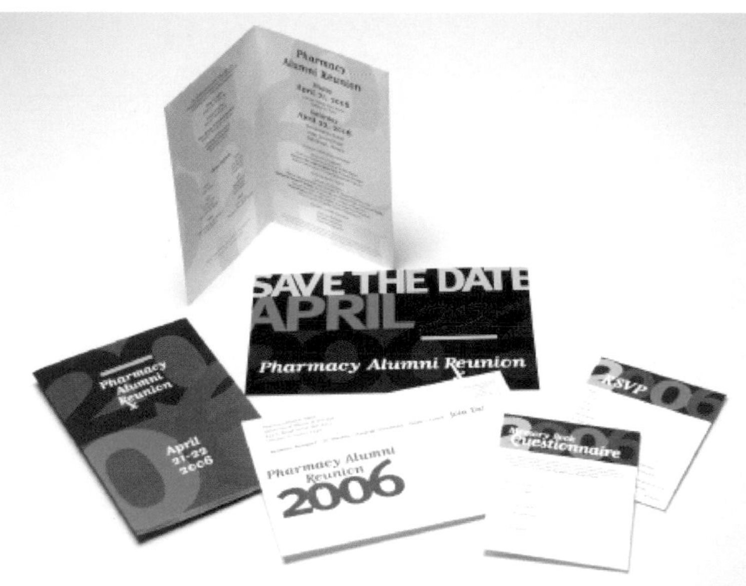

Creative Firm: **DAWN DESIGN — CHICAGO, IL**
Creative Team: **DAWN PECCATIELLO**
Client: **UIC- COLLEGE OF PHARMACY**

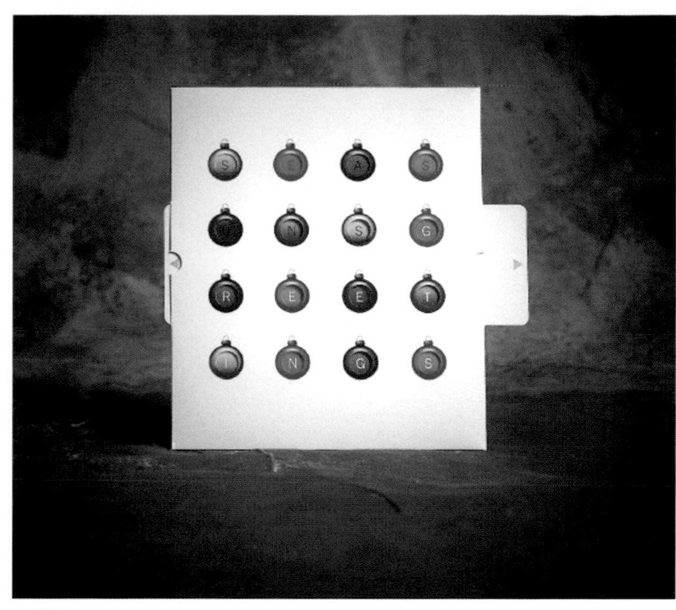

Creative Firm: **BRC MARKETING INC — DAYTON, OH**
Creative Team: **DOM CIMEI, MARK MARTEL, AMBER MOORE**

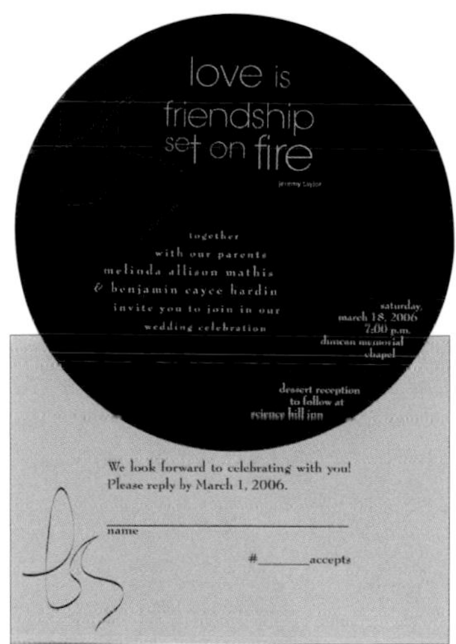

Creative Firm: **AD HARVEST — SIMPSONVILLE, KY**
Creative Team: **MARK GROVES**
Client: **MELINDA & BEN HARDIN**

Creative Firm: **BELYEA — SEATTLE, WA**
Creative Team: **RON HANSEN**
Client: **MCKINSTRY**

Creative Firm: **TOM FOWLER, INC. — NORWALK, CT**
Creative Team: **ELIZABETH P. BALL**
Client: **NORWALK EMERGENCY SHELTER**

Creative Firm: **ELLEN BRUSS DESIGN — DENVER, CO**
Creative Team: **ELLEN BRUSS, STEVE RURA**
Client: **THE LAB AT BELMAR**

Creative Firm: **LAJEUNESSE COMMUNICATION MARKETING — MONTREAL, QC, CANADA**
Creative Team: **YVES DUQUETTE, NATHALIE DAIGLE**

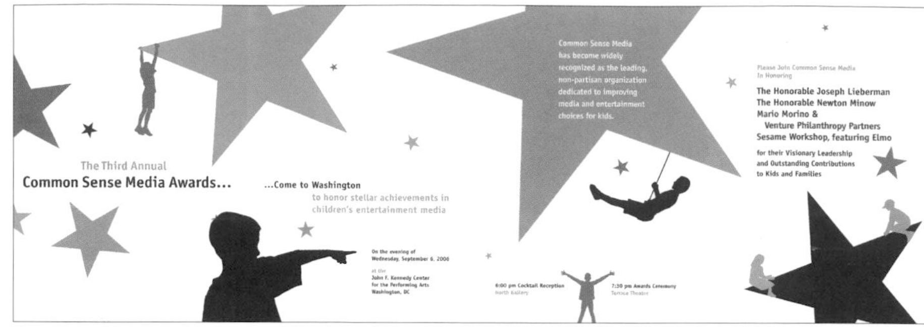

Creative Firm: **CRABTREE & COMPANY — FALLS CHURCH, VA**
Creative Team: **SUSAN ANGRISANI, ROD VERA**
Client: **COMMON SENSE MEDIA**

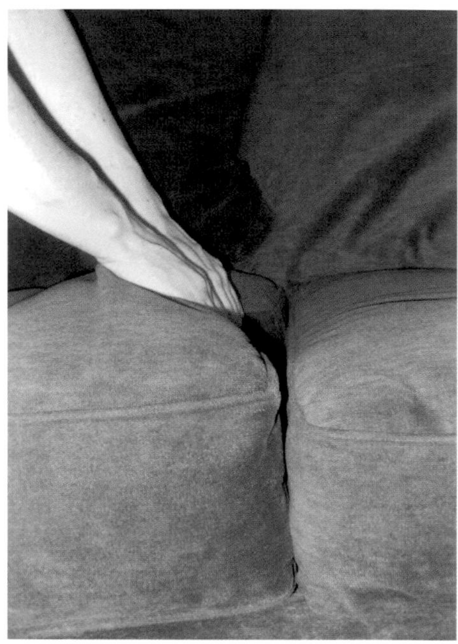

Creative Firm: **PRIMARY DESIGN, INC. — HAVERHILL, MA**
Creative Team: **LIZ FEDORZYN, JULES EPSTEIN, SHARYN ROGERS**
Client: **PRIMARY DESIGN, INC.**

Creative Firm: **AD HARVEST — SIMPSONVILLE, KY**
Creative Team: **MARK GROVES**
Client: **SHELBY COUNTY REUNION**

Creative Firm: **MTV NETWORKS CREATIVE SERVICES — NEW YORK, NY**

Creative Firm: **ELEVATOR — SPLIT, CROATIA (HRVATSKA)**
Creative Team: **TONY ADAMIC, GORANA MARSIC**
Client: **PORTUS ADRIA**

Creative Firm: **THE HUMANE SOCIETY OF THE UNITED STATES — WASHINGTON, DC**
Creative Team: **PAULA JAWORSKI**
Client: **THE HUMANE SOCIETY OF THE UNITED STATES**

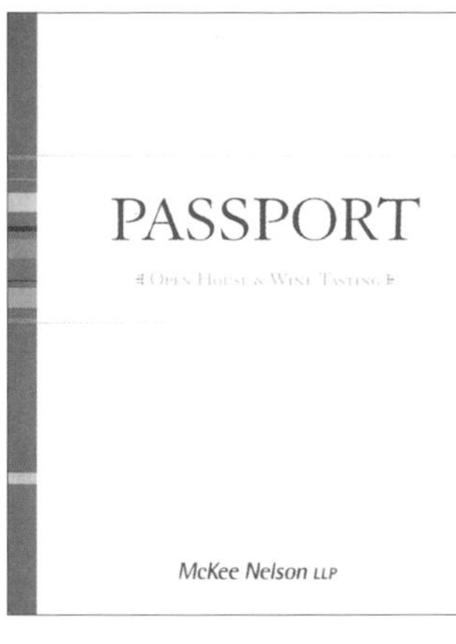

Creative Firm: **GRAFIK MARKETING COMMUNICATIONS — ALEXANDRIA, VA**
Creative Team: **MICHELLE MAR COLLINS, MILA ARRISUENO, LYNN UMEMOTO, HEATH DWIGGINS, REGINA ESPOSITO**
Client: **MCKEE NELSON, LLP**

Creative Firm: **JACK NADEL INTERNATIONAL — LOS ANGELES, CA**
Creative Team: **SCOTT BROWN, SAM MINSTER**
Client: **JACK NADEL INTERNATIONAL**

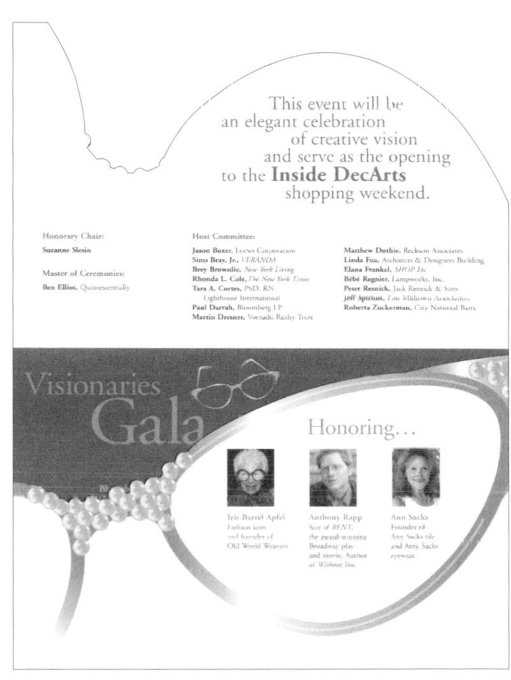

Creative Firm: **SILVER COMMUNICATIONS INC — NEW YORK, NY**
Creative Team: **GREGG SIBERT, CHRISTINA WEISSMAN**
Client: **EAST MIDTOWN ASSOCIATION**

Creative Firm: **CRABTREE & COMPANY — FALLS CHURCH, VA**
Client: **CRABTREE & COMPANY**

Creative Firm: **ELLEN BRUSS DESIGN — DENVER, CO**
Creative Team: **ELLEN BRUSS, STEVE RURA**
Client: **THE LAB AT BELMAR**

Creative Firm: **SUBSTANCE151 — BALTIMORE, MD**
Creative Team: **IDA CHEINMAN, RICK SALZMAN**
Client: **ADVERTISING ASSOCIATION OF BALTIMORE**

Creative Firm: **VINCE RINI DESIGN — HUNTINGTON BEACH, CA**
Creative Team: **VINCE RINI**
Client: **NEWPORT ORTHOPEDIC INSTITUTE**

Creative Firm: **THE COLLEGE OF SAINT ROSE — ALBANY, NY**
Creative Team: **MARK HAMILTON, CHRIS PARODY, LUIGI BENINCASA, KRISTINE HERRICK**
Client: **THE COLLEGE OF SAINT ROSE**

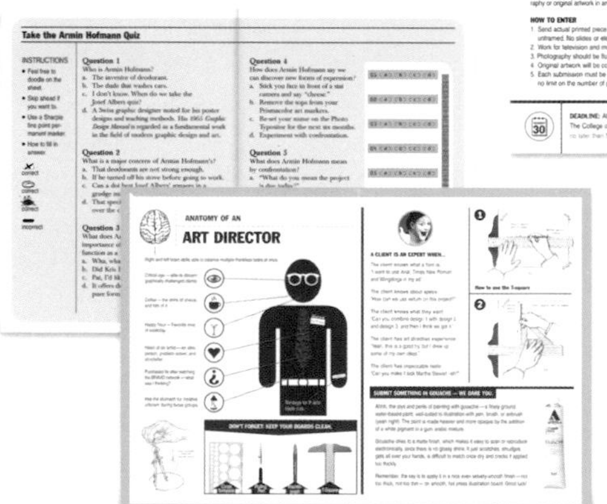

Creative Firm: **LOGO — NEW YORK, NY**
Creative Team: **NANCY BENNETT, TOM BAYER, VALENTINA AKERMAN, WAGNER WAGNER, VINNY LOPEZ**
Client: **LOGO MARKETING**

BACK

Creative Firm: **ALOFT GROUP, INC. — NEWBURYPORT, MA**
Creative Team: **DON CRANE, KIM CILLEY**
Client: **DICTAPHONE HEALTHCARE**

Creative Firm: **BRC MARKETING,INC — DAYTON, OH**
Creative Team: **MARY FRANCES RODRIGUEZ, DOM CIMEI, JASON KANTNER, JEFFREY DUSKO, VIRVE TREMBLAY, AMBER MOORE**
Client: **NCR**

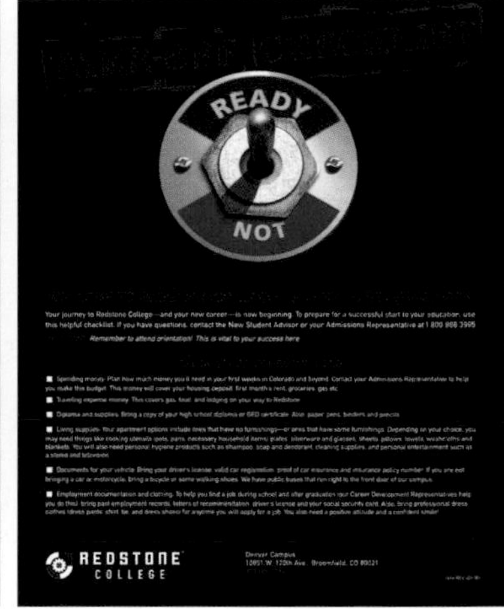

Creative Firm: **HENRYGILL ADVERTISING — DENVER, CO**
Creative Team: **BRYANT FERNANDEZ**
Client: **REDSTONE COLLEGE**

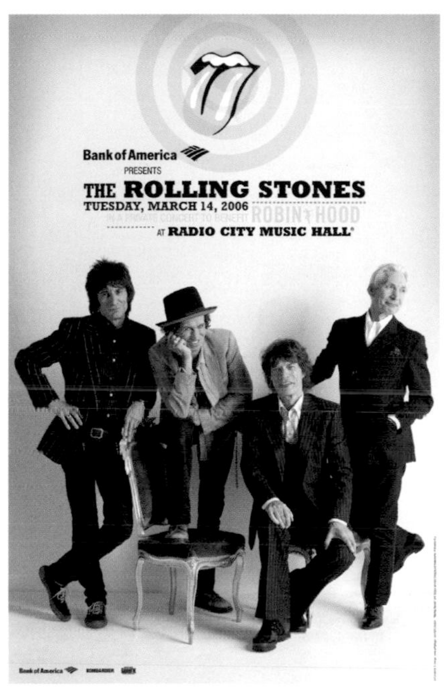

Creative Firm: **JEFF GILLIGAN — NEW YORK, NY**
Creative Team: **JEFF GILLIGAN, GSG DESIGN**
Client: **ROBIN HOOD FOUNDATION/GSG DESIGN**

Creative Firm: **YOUNG & RUBICAM GMBH & CO. KG — FRANKFURT AM MAIN, HESSEN, GERMANY**
Creative Team: **CHRISTIAN DAUL, UWE MARQUARDT, MONIKA SPIRKL**
Client: **FRAUENNOTRUF FRANKFURT (WOMEN'S EMERGENCY CALL)**

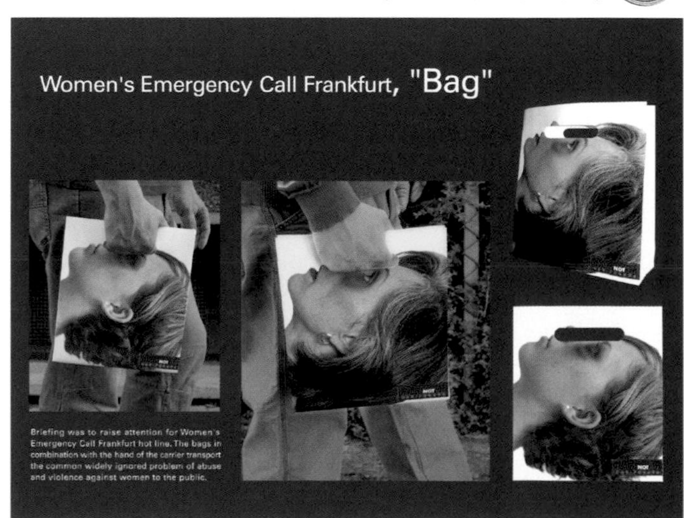

Creative Firm: **YELLOW SHOES CREATIVE WEST, DISNEYLAND RESORT — ANAHEIM, CA**
Creative Team: **DATHAN SHORE, WES CLARK, MARTY MULLER, JACQUELYN MOE, KEVIN YONEDA**
Client: **DISNEYLAND RESORT**

Creative Firm: **MNA CREATIVE — DANBURY, CT**
Creative Team: **MNA CREATIVE - THE ENTIRE AGENCY**
Client: **TSINGTAO**

Creative Firm: **PALIO COMMUNICATIONS — SARATOGA SPRINGS, NY**
Creative Team: **TOM ROTHERMEL, LEAH DWORNIK, ANALIA DEL GIORGIO, NICK PARSLOW, ALEN MERCIER, MIREK JANCHOR**
Client: **SARATOGA SHAKESPEARE COMPANY**

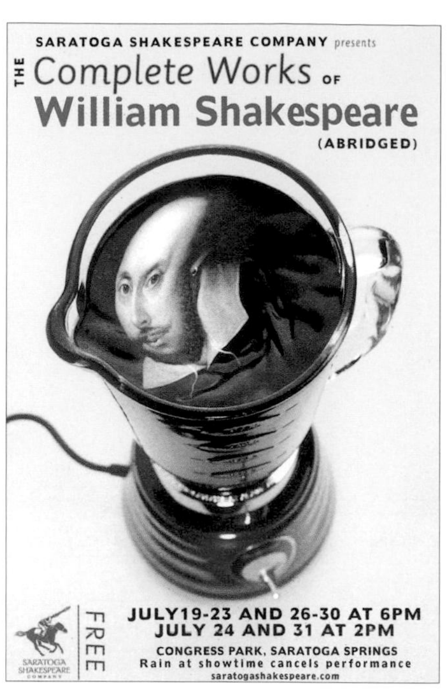

To announce its arrival, Electric Bikes were locked up to the top of hydro poles around the city.

Creative Firm: **TAXI CANADA INC. — TORONTO, ON, CANADA**
Creative Team: **ZAK MROUEH, LANCE MARTIN, SAM CERULLO, JOSEPH BONNICI, KIRA THOMSON, CHERYL MCKENZIE**
Client: **CANADIAN TIRE**

Creative Firm: **MT&L PUBLIC RELATIONS LTD. — HALIFAX, NS, CANADA**
Creative Team: **PAUL WILLIAMS, KELLY CLARK, ANNMARIE GREENE**
Client: **SAINT MARY'S UNIVERSITY**

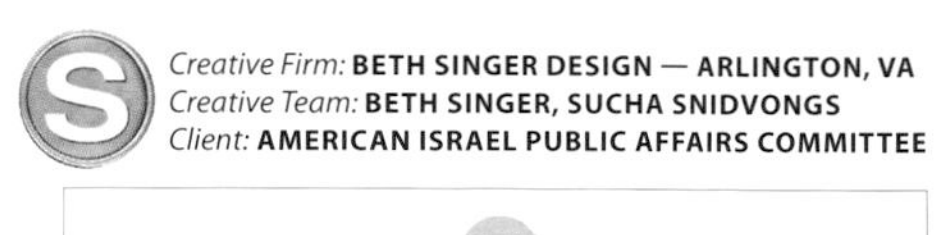

Creative Firm: **BETH SINGER DESIGN — ARLINGTON, VA**
Creative Team: **BETH SINGER, SUCHA SNIDVONGS**
Client: **AMERICAN ISRAEL PUBLIC AFFAIRS COMMITTEE**

Creative Firm: **KOCH CREATIVE GROUP — WICHITA, KS**
Creative Team: **KAY DAVIS, DUSTIN COMMER**
Client: **YOUTH ENTREPRENEURS OF KANSAS**

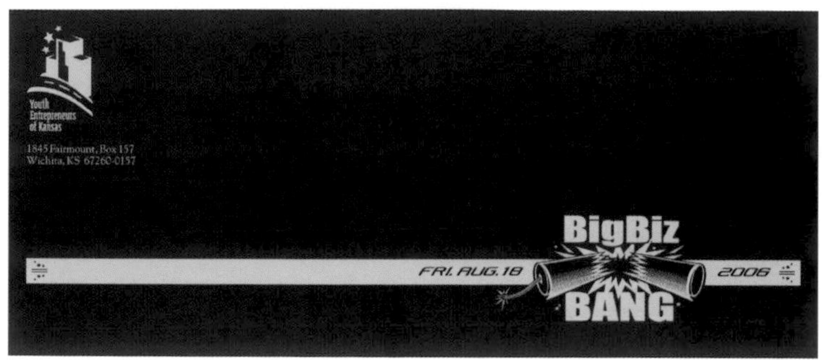

Creative Firm: **RULE29 — GENEVA, IL**
Creative Team: **JUSTIN AHERNS, JOSH JENSEN, KERRI LIU, DAN HASSENPLUG, BRIAN MACDONALD, TERRY MARKS**
Client: **O'NEIL PRINTING**

Creative Firm: **REVOLUZION ADVERTISING & DESIGN — NEUHAUSEN OB ECK, GERMANY**
Creative Team: **BERND LUZ, CHRISTOS SCHWEEN**
Client: **ALLEZ-Y SÉJOURS LINGUISTIQUES**

Creative Firm: **TROUTMAN/DEWERTH DESIGN — AKRON, OH**
Creative Team: **JANICE TROUTMAN, BRITTYN DEWERTH, KEVIN OLDS, DUNCAN PRESS**
Client: **EMILY DAVIS GALLERY/THE UNIVERSITY OF AKRON**

Creative Firm: **FITTING GROUP — PITTSBURGH, PA**
Creative Team: **ANDREW ELLIS, TRAVIS NORRIS**
Client: **BLACK KNIGHT SECURITY**

Creative Firm: **MAD DOG GRAPHX — ANCHORAGE, AK**
Creative Team: **KRIS RYAN-CLARKE**
Client: **NANA MANAGEMENT SERVICES**

Creative Firm: **COMCAST SPOTLIGHT — MALVERN, PA**
Creative Team: **CARA NGO, ANN LETIZI**
Client: **COMCAST SPOTLIGHT**

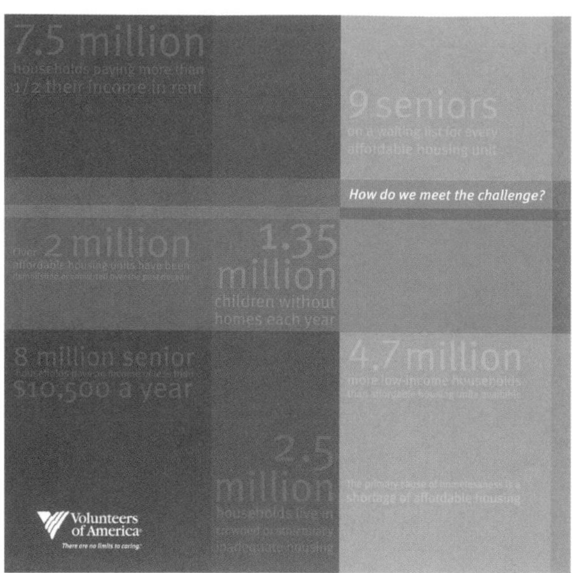

Creative Firm: **GRAFIK MARKETING COMMUNICATIONS — ALEXANDRIA, VA**
Creative Team: **KRISTIN MOORE, MILA ARRISUENO, MELBA BLACK, IVAN HOOKER**
Client: **VOLUNTEERS OF AMERICA**

Creative Firm: **OCTAVO DESIGNS — FREDERICK, MD**
Creative Team: **SUE HOUGH, MARK BURRIER**
Client: **FREDERICK COUNTY OFFICE OF ECONOMIC DEVELOPMENT**

Creative Firm: **ACOSTA DESIGN INC — NEW YORK, NY**
Creative Team: **MAURICIO ACOSTA**
Client: **NCG**

Creative Firm: **KOLANO DESIGN — PITTSBURGH, PA**
Creative Team: **BILL KOLANO, TIMOTHY CARRERA**
Client: **DONNA HOLDORF — NATIONAL ROAD HERTIAGE CORRIDOR**

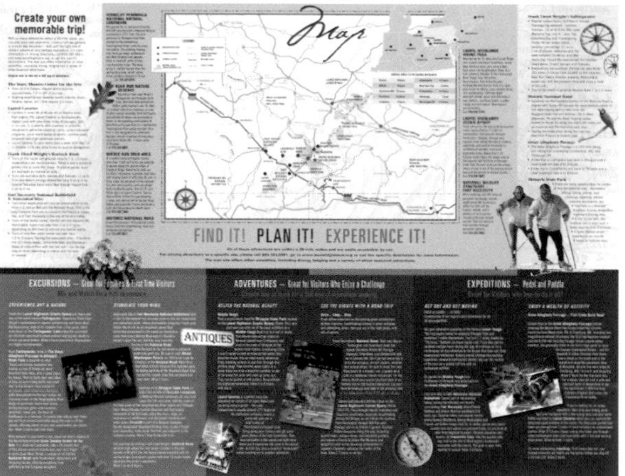

Creative Firm: **DESIGN OBJECTIVES PTE LTD — SINGAPORE**
Creative Team: **RONNIE S C TAN**
Client: **MERITUS SUITES STATE TOWER. BANGKOK**

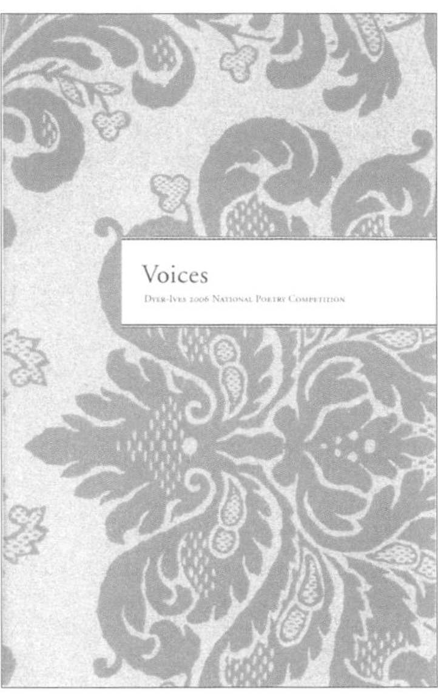

Creative Firm: **BBK STUDIO — GRAND RAPIDS, MI**
Creative Team: **MICHELE CHARTIER, TIM CALKINS**
Client: **DYER-IVES FOUNDATION**

Creative Firm: **THINKHOUSE CREATIVE — ATLANTA, GA**
Client: **PUGET SOUND ENERGY**

Creative Firm: **DESIGN GUYS — MINNEAPOLIS, MN**
Creative Team: **STEVE SIKORA, KELLY MUNSON, JEFF MUELLER, GEORGE HEINRICH**
Client: **NEENAH PAPER**

Creative Firm: **G2 — NEW YORK, NY**
Creative Team: **BEN GOLD, RAY MARRERO, DANIELA MASIELLO, JIHEE KIM, MEGAN TRINIDAD**
Client: **RUSHMORE**

Creative Firm: **DAVIS DESIGN PARTNERS — HOLLAND, OH**
Creative Team: **MATT DAVIS, KAREN DAVIS, GABRIEL AMADEAUS COONEY, JOSEPH W. DARWAL, UNIVERSITY SCHOOL ARCHIVES**
Client: **UNIVERSITY SCHOOL**

Creative Firm: **YELLOW SHOES CREATIVE WEST, DISNEYLAND RESORT — ANAHEIM, CA**
Creative Team: **DATHAN SHORE, WES CLARK, MARTY MULLER, JACQUELYN MOE, JIM ST. AMANT, SHAG**
Client: **DISNEYLAND RESORT**

Creative Firm: **VELOCITY DESIGN WORKS — WINNIPEG, MB, CANADA**
Creative Team: **LASHA ORZECHOWSKI**
Client: **EDWARD CARRIERE**

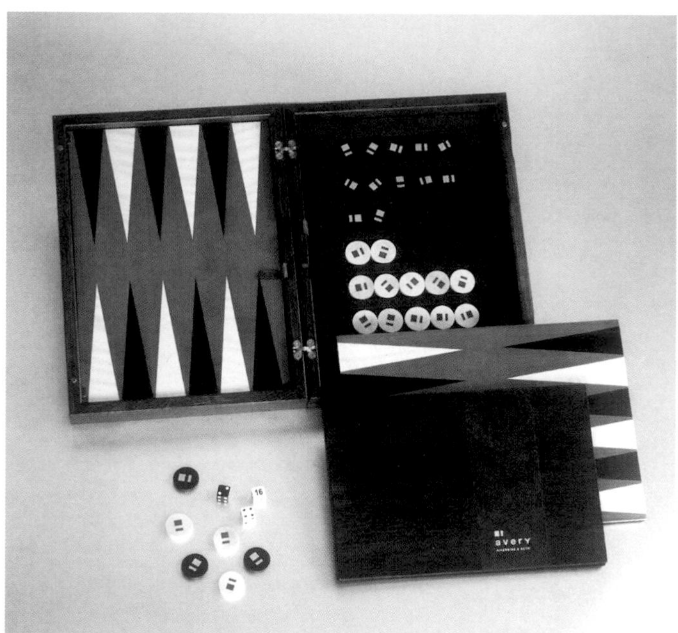

Creative Firm: **G2 — NEW YORK, NY**
Creative Team: **BEN GOLD, RAY MARRERO, DANIELA MASIELLO**
Client: **AVERY**

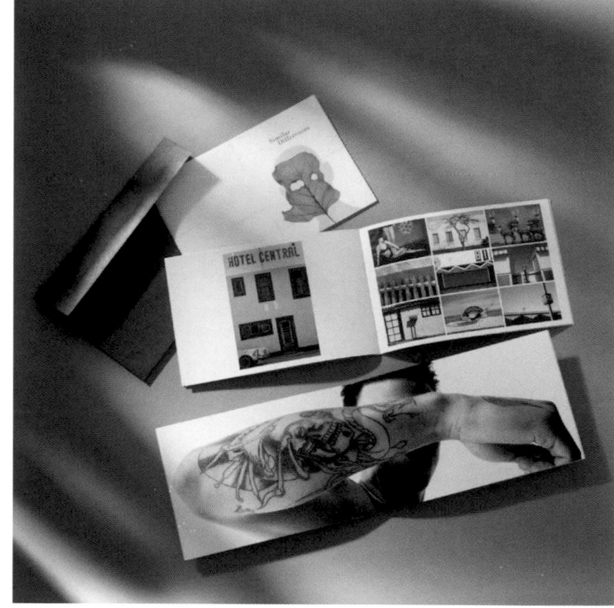

Creative Firm: **INTERROBANG DESIGN COLLABORATIVE, INC. — RICHMOND, VT**
Creative Team: **MARK D. SYLVESTER, BOB PACKERT, SHARON WHITE**
Client: **WHITE / PACKERT PHOTOGRAPHY**

Creative Firm: **NBC UNIVERSAL GLOBAL NETWORKS ITALIA SRL — ROME, ITALY**

QUANDO INDAGHI SUL CINEMA,
OGNI SCENA È QUELLA DEL CRIMINE.

Creative Firm: **CRABTREE & COMPANY — FALLS CHURCH, VA**
Creative Team: **SUSAN ANGRISANI, TAMERA FINN**
Client: **NATIONAL ASSOCIATION OF REALTORS®**

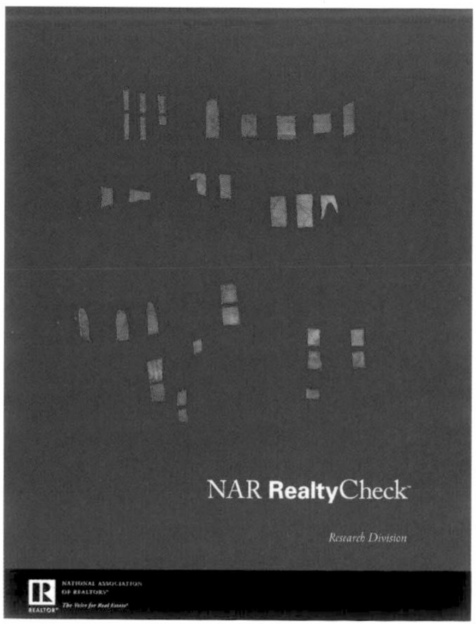

Creative Firm: **AD HARVEST — SIMPSONVILLE, KY**
Creative Team: **MARK GROVES**
Client: **SHELBY COUNTY COMMUNITY THEATRE**

Creative Firm: **YELLOW SHOES CREATIVE WEST, DISNEYLAND RESORT — ANAHEIM, CA**
Creative Team: **STEVEN GERRY, WES CLARK, MARTY MULLER, JACQUELYN MOE, ANIKO BOTA**
Client: **DISNEYLAND RESORT**

Creative Firm: **CAMPBELL-EWALD — WARREN, MI**
Creative Team: **BILL LUDWIG, SUSAN LOGAR BRODY, RAYMOND ALLSTON, ILYA HARDEY, DAVID BARLOW, CHAD WOOLUMS**
Client: **THE UNITED STATES NAVY**

Creative Firm: **GRAFIK MARKETING COMMUNICATIONS — ALEXANDRIA, VA**
Creative Team: **GREGG GLAVIANO, MILA ARRISUENO, REGINA ESPOSITO, IVAN HOOKER**
Client: **UNITED WAY**

Creative Firm: **WHITNEY EDWARDS LLC — EASTON, MD**
Creative Team: **CHARLENE EDWARDS, CHARLENE EDWARDS, PAT VOJTECH**
Client: **WILDLIFE INTERNATIONAL, LTD.**

Creative Firm: **DESIGN HOCH DREI — STUTTGART, BADEN-WÜRTTEMBERG, GERMANY**
Creative Team: **SUSANNE WACKER, TOBIAS KOLLMANN, IOANNIS KARANASIOS**
Client: **DAIMLER CHRYSLER AG**

Creative Firm: **YELLOW SHOES CREATIVE WEST, DISNEYLAND RESORT — ANAHEIM, CA** *Creative Team:* **DATHAN SHORE, WES CLARK, JACQUELYN MOE, JIM ST. AMANT, MICHAEL FIRMAN**
Client: **DISNEYLAND RESORT**

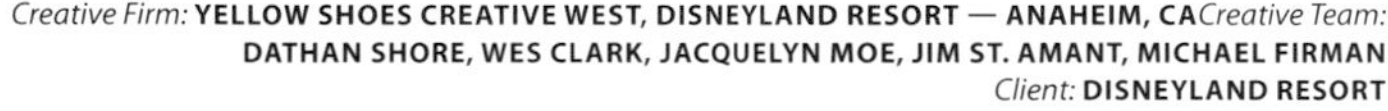

Creative Firm: **HELENA SEO DESIGN & SCHULTE DESIGN — SUNNYVALE, CA**
Client: **MPM CAPITAL**

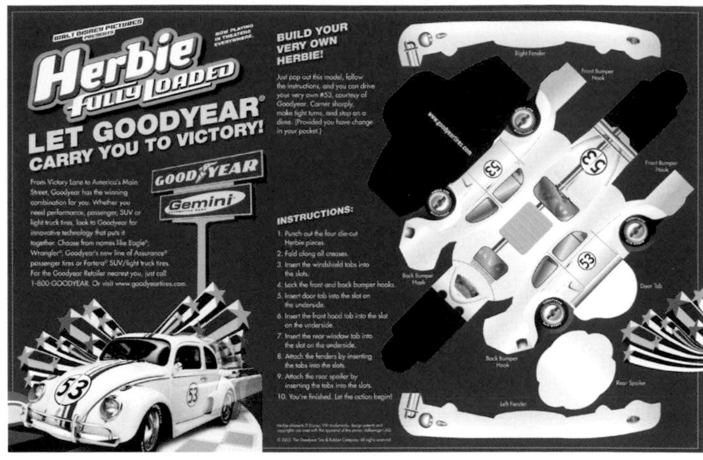

Creative Firm: **HITCHCOCK FLEMING & ASSOCIATES INC. — AKRON, OH**
Creative Team: **NICK BETRO, CHUCK REPEDE, LENNY SPENGLER, MATT MCCALLUM**
Client: **GOODYEAR TIRE & RUBBER COMPANY**

Creative Firm: **RODGERS TOWNSEND — ST. LOUIS, MO**
Creative Team: **ERIK MATHRE, MARK ARNOLD, TODD MITCHELL, CHERYL SPARKS**
Client: **HUMANE SOCIETY OF MISSOURI**

Creative Firm: **SUKA DESIGN — NEW YORK, NY**
Creative Team: **MARIA BELFIORE**
Client: **THE POLLOCK-KRASNER REPORT**

Creative Firm: **ORIGINAL IMPRESSIONS — MIAMI, FL**
Creative Team: **LISA CUERVO**
Client: **YACHTSMAN'S COVE**

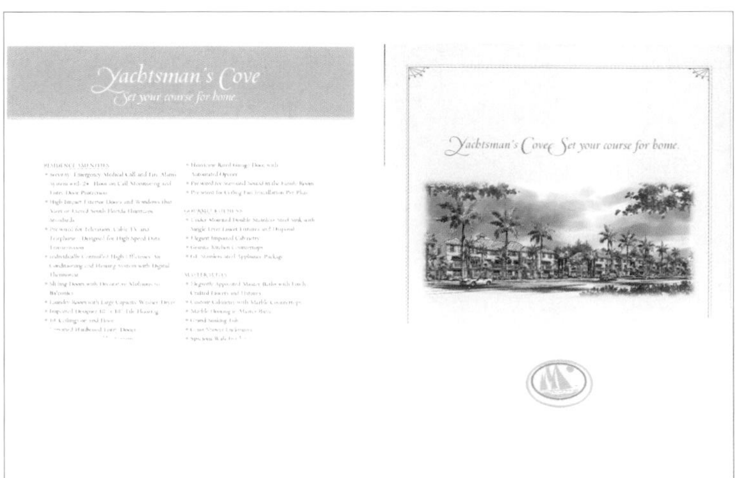

Creative Firm: **ALCONE MARKETING — IRVINE, CA**
Creative Team: **CARLOS MUSQUEZ, JULIE KIMURA, SHIVONNE MILLER, LUIS CAMANO**
Client: **EBAY**

Creative Firm: **GRAFIK MARKETING COMMUNICATIONS — ALEXANDRIA, VA**
Creative Team: **MICHAEL MATEOS, HAL SWETNAM, IVAN HOOKER, MAX HIRSHFELD**
Client: **WASHINGTON METROPOLITAN SCHOLARS**

Creative Firm: **ORIGINAL IMPRESSIONS — MIAMI, FL**
Creative Team: **FRANK IRIAS**
Client: **ROYAL CARIBBEAN INTERNATIONAL**

Creative Firm: **CSC'S P2 COMMUNICATIONS SERVICES — FALLS CHURCH, VA**
Creative Team: **NANCY NAUGHTON, JENNIFER VOLTAGGIO, AARON KOBILIS, TERRY WILSON, JOHN LANCASTER, LALITHA SUNDARAM**
Client: **CSC GLOBAL LEARNING DEVELOPMENT MANAGEMENT (GLDM)**

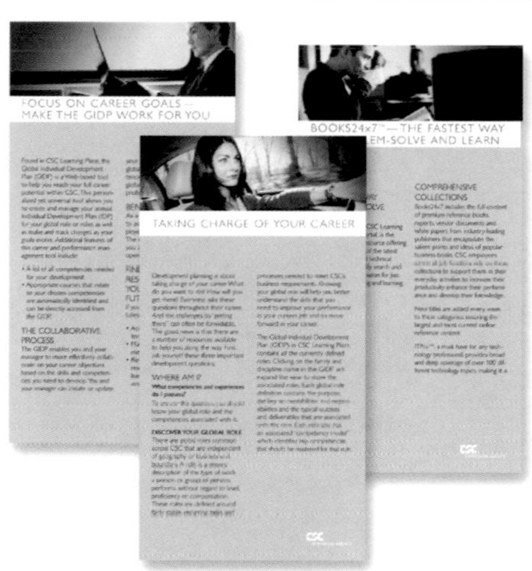

Creative Firm: **BETH SINGER DESIGN — ARLINGTON, VA**
Creative Team: **BETH SINGER, HOWARD SMITH, DON WHELAN, ELLEN KARDELL, LISA CORDES, TRACI SLATER-RIGAUD**
Client: **PRESIDENT'S COMMITTEE ON THE ARTS AND HUMANITIES**

Creative Firm: **MCGRAW-HILL CORPORATE CREATIVE SERVICES — NEW YORK, NY**
Creative Team: **MARIANNE JOHNSTON, PAUL BIEDERMANN**
Client: **MCGRAW-HILL CORPORATE ROYALTY OPERATIONS**

Creative Firm: **ORANGESEED DESIGN — MINNEAPOLIS, MN**
Creative Team: **DAMIEN WOLF, JOHN WIELAND, REBECCA AVIÑA**
Client: **TWIN CITIES MARATHON**

Creative Firm: **Q — WIESBADEN, GERMANY**
Creative Team: **THILO VON DEBSCHITZ, MATTHIAS FREY, UTE DERSCH**
Client: **ARJOWIGGINS**

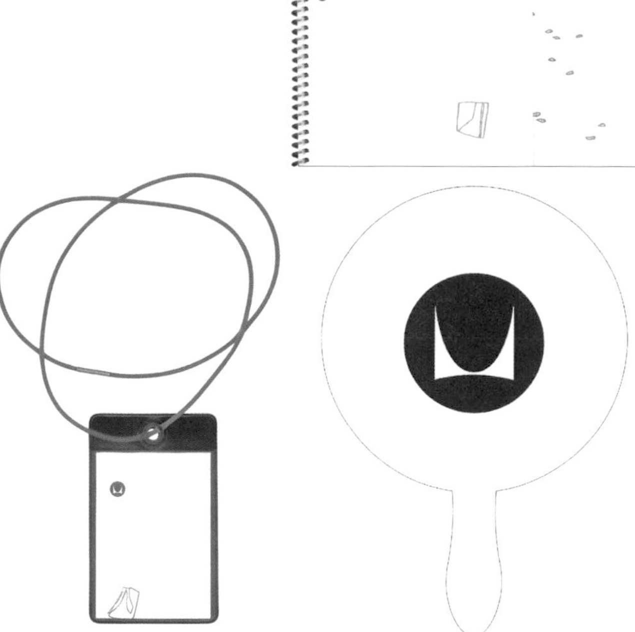

Creative Firm: **BBK STUDIO — GRAND RAPIDS, MI**
Creative Team: **SHARON OLENICZAK, BRIAN HAUCH, TIM CALKINS, YANG KIM**
Client: **HERMAN MILLER**

Creative Firm: **HOFFMAN/LEWIS — SAN FRANCISCO, CA**
Creative Team: **SHARON KRINSKY, JAMES CABRAL, RONDA DUNN, JASON HEADLEY**
Client: **HENRY'S**

Creative Firm: **A3 DESIGN — CHARLOTTE, NC**
Creative Team: **ALAN ALTMAN, AMANDA ALTMAN**
Client: **LIMERICK STUDIOS**

Creative Firm: **MCGRAW-HILL CORPORATE CREATIVE SERVICES — NEW YORK, NY**
Creative Team: **MARIANNE JOHNSTON, PAUL BIEDERMANN**
Client: **MCGRAW-HILL CORPORATE HUMAN RESOURCES**

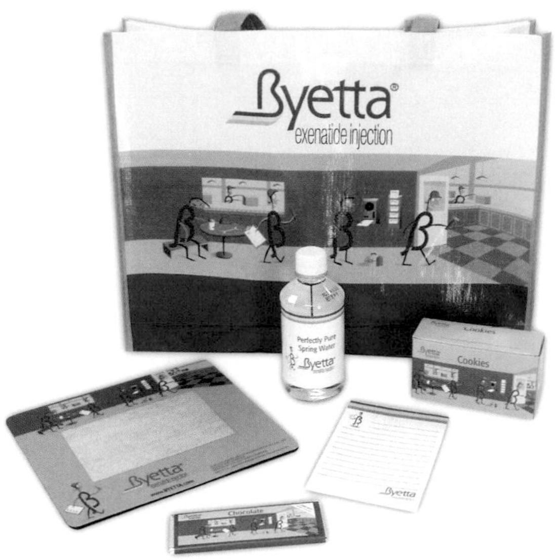

Creative Firm: **JACK NADEL INTERNATIONAL — LOS ANGELES, CA**
Creative Team: **SHELLEY SLUBOWSKI, AMYLIN PHARMECEUTICALS ART DIRECTION**
Client: **AMYLIN PHARMACEUTICALS / ELI LILLY**

Creative Firm: **ISLAND OASIS — WALPOLE, MA**
Creative Team: **JENNY KEECH**
Client: **ISLAND OASIS**

PRODUCT / SELL SHEETS

Creative Firm: **TOM FOWLER, INC. — NORWALK, CT**
Creative Team: **MARY ELLEN BUTKUS, BRIEN O'REILLY, THOMAS G. FOWLER**
Client: **HONEYWELL CONSUMER PRODUCTS**

CORPORATE ID MANUALS, *SINGLE*

Creative Firm: **SUBPLOT DESIGN INC. — VANCOUVER, BC, CANADA**
Creative Team: **ROY WHITE, MATTHEW CLARK, STEPH GIBSON**
Client: **VANCOUVER AQUARIUM**

Creative Firm: **YELLOW SHOES CREATIVE WEST, DISNEYLAND RESORT — ANAHEIM, CA**
Creative Team: **STEVEN GERRY, WES CLARK, MARTY MULLER, JACQUELYN MOE, ANIKO BOTA, CLAIRE BILBY**
Client: **DISNEYLAND RESORT**

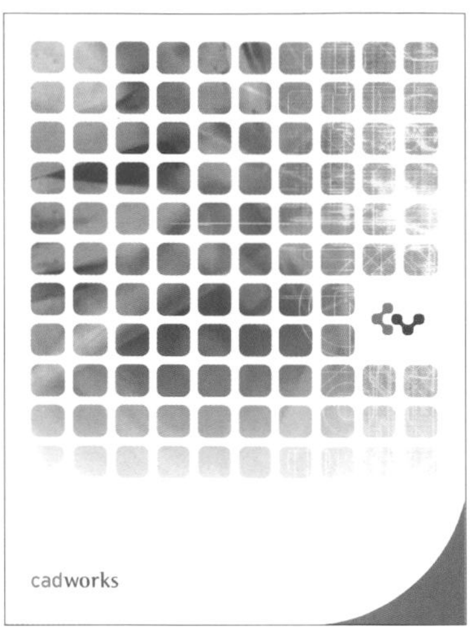

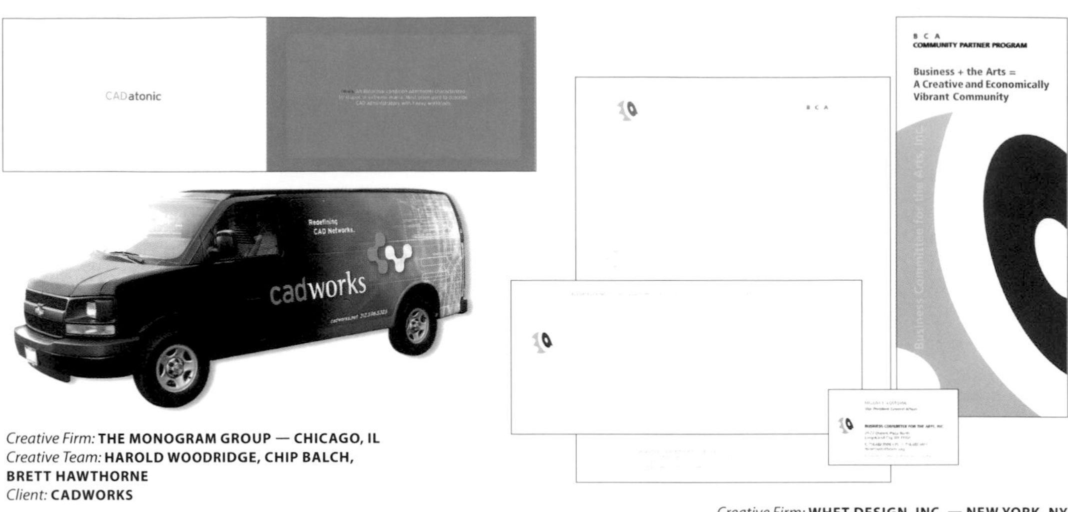

Creative Firm: **THE MONOGRAM GROUP — CHICAGO, IL**
Creative Team: **HAROLD WOODRIDGE, CHIP BALCH, BRETT HAWTHORNE**
Client: **CADWORKS**

Creative Firm: **WHET DESIGN, INC. — NEW YORK, NY**
Creative Team: **CHERYL OPPENHEIM, JOHN WATERS, YOHEI TAKESHITA**
Client: **BUSINESS COMMITTEE FOR THE ARTS, INC.**

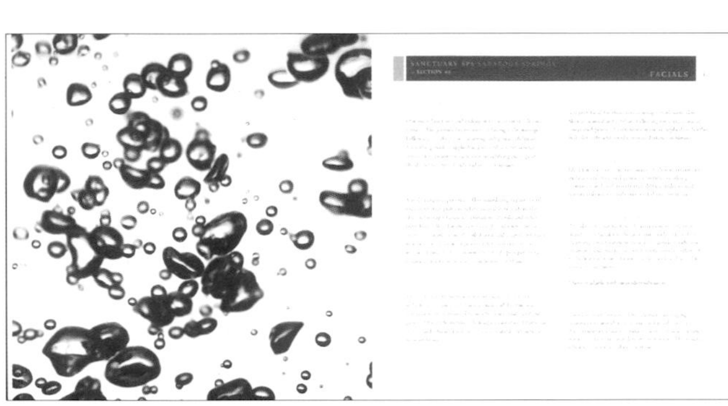

Creative Firm: **REDUCED FAT — SARATOGA SPRINGS, NY**
Creative Team: **JOHN BOLSTER, JOHN MISSALE**
Client: **DEBRA DOCYK**

Creative Firm: **30SIXTY ADVERTISING+DESIGN, INC. — LOS ANGELES, CA**
Creative Team: **HENRY VIZCARRA, DAVID FUSCELLARO, LEE BARETT, SUZANA LAKATOS, YUJIN ONO, BRUCE VENTANILLA**
Client: **DISNEY CONSUMER PRODUCTS**

Creative Firm: **KARACTERS DESIGN GROUP/DDB CANADA — VANCOUVER, BC, CANADA**
Creative Team: **MARIA KENNEDY, JAMES BATEMAN, MONICA MARTINEZ, TIM HOFFPAUIR, ANNE FARRER, HELEN WYNNE**
Client: **VANCOUVER 2010 OLYMPIC COMMITTEE**

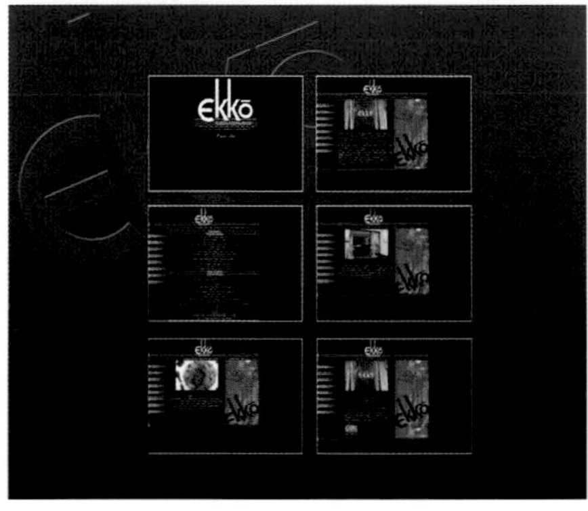

Creative Firm: **STEPHEN LONGO DESIGN ASSOCIATES — WEST ORANGE, NJ**
Creative Team: **STEPHEN LONGO**
Client: **EKKO RESTAURANT**

Creative Firm: **TM&N DESIGN AND BRAND CONSULTANTS LTD. — HONG KONG**
Creative Team: **LEILA NACHTIGALL, JILLIAN LEE, LIEM CHEUNG**
Client: **ZENIKA HOLDINGS LIMITED**

RETROSPECTIVA DEL PREMIO QUORUM

Creative Firm: **SIGNI — MEXICO CITY, D.F., MEXICO**
Creative Team: **RENE GALINDO**
Client: **QUORUM**

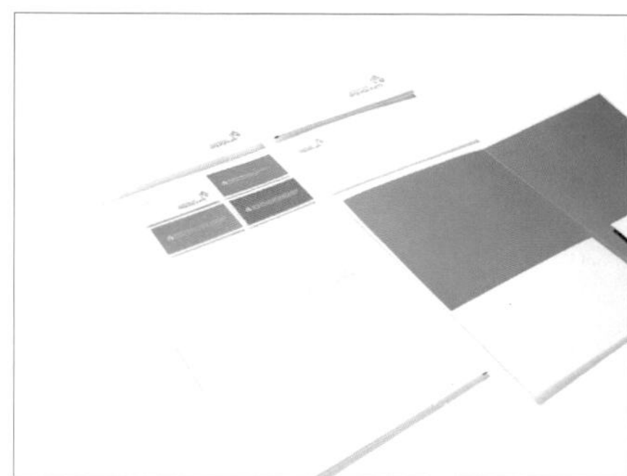

Creative Firm: **SUBPLOT DESIGN INC. — VANCOUVER, BC, CANADA**
Creative Team: **ROY WHITE, MATTHEW CLARK, STEPH GIBSON**
Client: **VANCOUVER AQUARIUM**

Creative Firm: **RUDER FINN DESIGN — NEW YORK, NY**
Creative Team: **MICHAEL SCHUBERT, LISA GABBAY, SAL CATANIA, DIANA YEO, EMILY KORSMO, LAURA VINCHESI**
Client: **NOVARTIS**

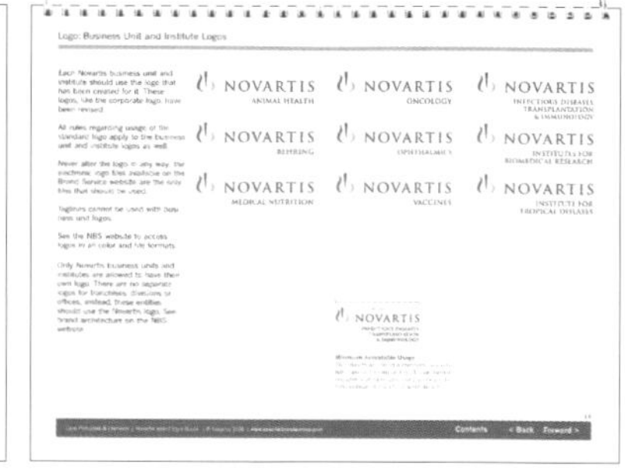

Creative Firm: **DON SCHAAF & FRIENDS, INC. — WASHINGTON, DC**
Creative Team: **DON SCHAAF, BRUCE MACINDOE**
Client: **OFFIT KURMAN**

Creative Firm: **KARACTERS DESIGN GROUP/DDB CANADA — VANCOUVER, BC, CANADA**
Creative Team: **JAMES BATEMAN, KARA BOHL, ANNE FARRER, HELEN WYNNE, SCOTT RUSSELL, MARK FINN**
Client: **MOUNTAIN EQUIPMENT CO-OP**

Creative Firm: **SIGNI — MEXICO CITY, D.F., MEXICO**
Creative Team: **RENE GALINDO**
Client: **CICOM**

Creative Firm: **NAMARO GRAPHIC DESIGNS, INC. — RHINEBECK, NY**
Creative Team: **NADINE ROBBINS, MOLLY AHEARN, WENDY MACOMBER**
Client: **CANON USA**

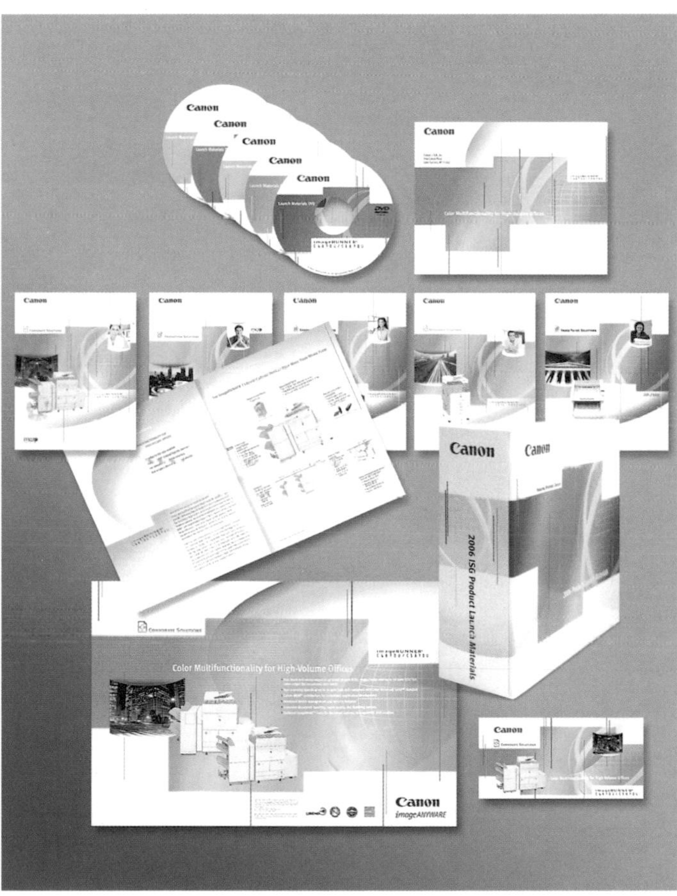

Creative Firm: **NAMARO GRAPHIC DESIGNS, INC. — RHINEBECK, NY**
Creative Team: **NADINE ROBBINS, MOLLY AHEARN**
Client: **NATIONAL EQUITY FUND INC.**

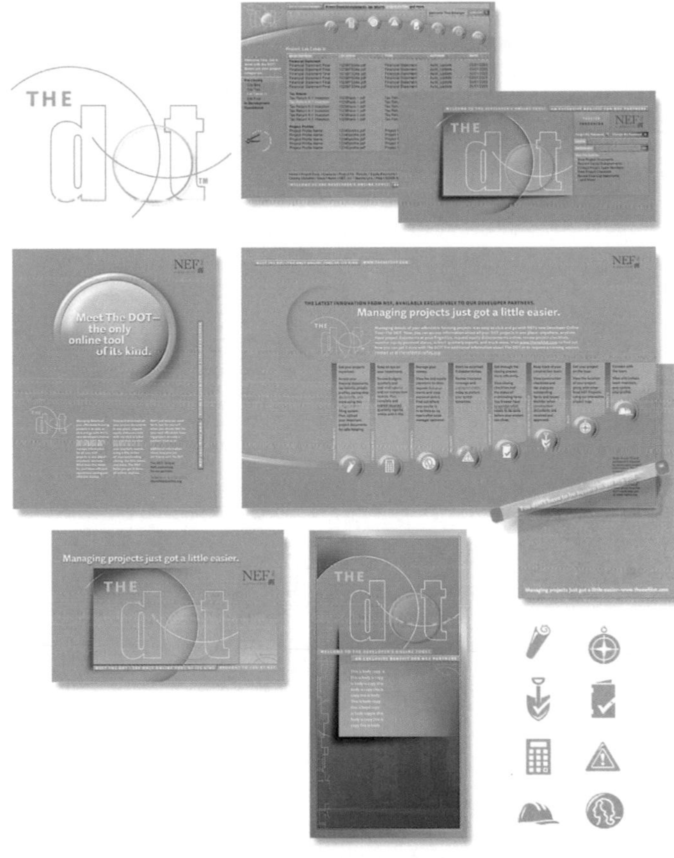

Creative Firm: **KARACTERS DESIGN GROUP/DDB CANADA — VANCOUVER, BC, CANADA**
Creative Team: **JAMES BATEMAN, MARSHA LARKIN, NIKI MATSUMOTO, HELEN WYNNE, MARK FINN, PHIL COLLINS, RUSS HORII**
Client: **NORTHLANDS**

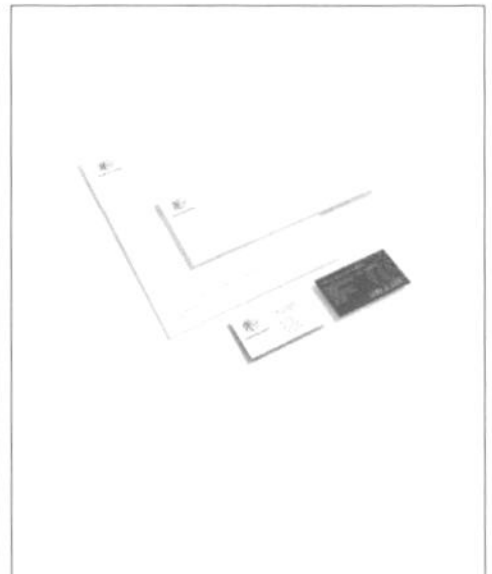

Creative Firm: **SUNSPOTS CREATIVE — FRANKLIN LAKES, NJ**
Creative Team: **RICK BONELLI, DEENA HARTLEY, DAVE VIOREANU**
Client: **SUNSPOTS CREATIVE**

Creative Firm: **LEVINE & ASSOCIATES — WASHINGTON, DC**
Creative Team: **GREG SITZMANN, JENNIE JARIEL, MEGAN RIORDAN, MONICA SNELLINGS, LENA MARKLEY**
Client: **LEVINE & ASSOCIATES**

Creative Firm: **KARACTERS DESIGN GROUP/DDB CANADA — VANCOUVER, BC, CANADA**
Creative Team: **MARIA KENNEDY, ALAN RUSSELL, KARA BOHL, JAMES LEE, HELEN WYNNE, LISA GOOD, MARK FINN**
Client: **DDB CANADA**

Creative Firm: **TD2, S.C. — MEXICO CITY, D.F., MEXICO**
Creative Team: **VANESSA GARCIA**
Client: **TD2**

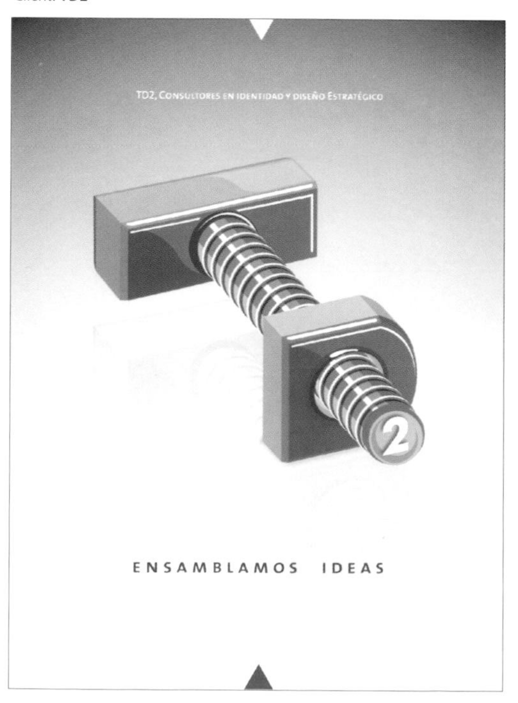

Creative Firm: **DESIGN 446 — MANASQUAN, NJ**
Creative Team: **BRIAN STERN**
Client: **DESIGN 446**

Creative Firm: **ALEXANDER ISLEY — REDDING, CT**
Creative Team: **ALEXANDER ISLEY, GEORGE KOKKINIDIS, CHERITH VICTORINO**
Client: **ALEXANDER ISLEY INC.**

Creative Firm: **BRIGHT RAIN CREATIVE — ST. LOUIS, MO**
Creative Team: **KEVIN HOUGH, DAVID HOUGH**
Client: **BRIGHT RAIN CREATIVE**

Creative Firm: **ROTTMAN CREATIVE GROUP — LA PLATA, MD**
Creative Team: **GARY ROTTMAN**
Client: **ROTTMAN CREATIVE GROUP, INC.**

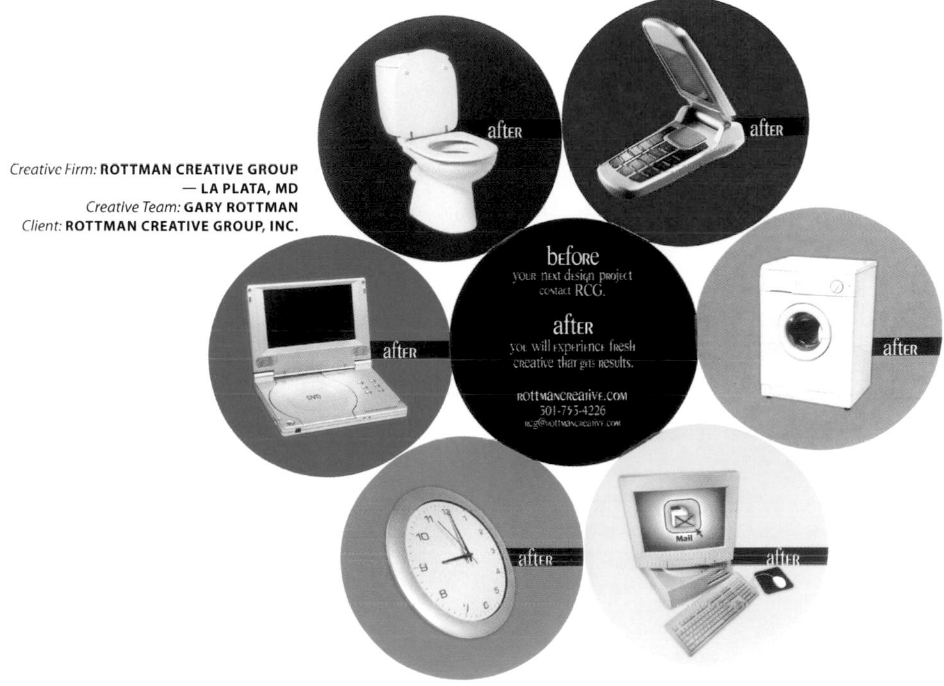

Creative Firm: **THE DAVE AND ALEX SHOW — REDDING, CT**
Creative Team: **AMY UNIKEWICZ, DAVE GOLDENBERG**
Client: **THE DAVE AND ALEX SHOW**

Creative Firm: **PHP COMMUNICATIONS — BIRMINGHAM, AL**
Creative Team: **LYNN SMITH**
Client: **PHP COMMUNICATIONS**

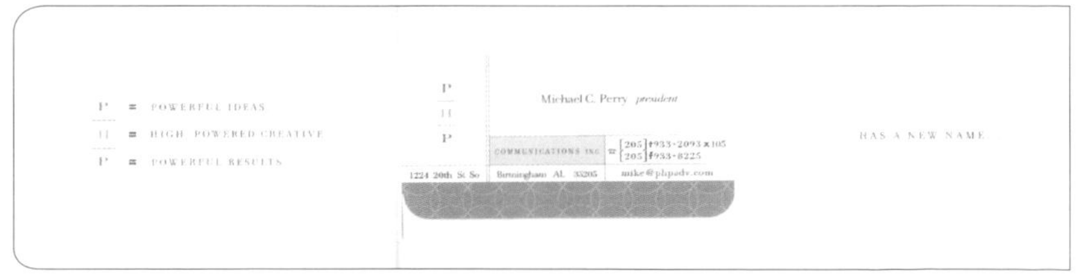

Creative Firm: **TD2, S.C. — MEXICO CITY, D.F., MEXICO**
Creative Team: **R. RODRIGO CORDOVA**
Client: **TD2**

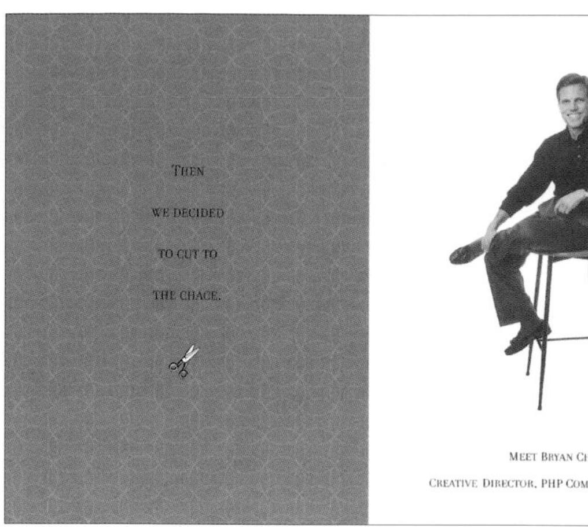

Creative Firm: **PHP COMMUNICATIONS — BIRMINGHAM, AL**
Creative Team: **BRYAN CHACE, LYNN SMITH**
Client: **PHP COMMUNICATIONS**

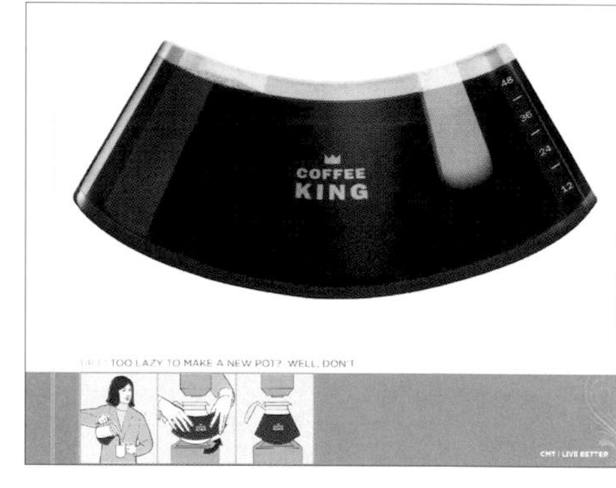

Creative Firm: **CMT — NEW YORK, NY**
Creative Team: **JAMES HITCHCOCK, AMIE NGUYEN, NORA GAFFNEY**
Client: **CMT**

Creative Firm: **OCTAVO DESIGNS — FREDERICK, MD**
Creative Team: **SUE HOUGH, MARK BURRIER**
Client: **OCTAVO DESIGNS**

Creative Firm: **LISKA + ASSOCIATES — CHICAGO, IL**
Creative Team: **STEVE LISKA, SABINE KRAUSS, ANN MARIE GRAY**
Client: **BRININSTOOL + LYNCH**

Creative Firm: **BCN COMMUNICATIONS — CHICAGO, IL**
Creative Team: **JAMES PITROSKI, MICHAEL NEU**
Client: **BCN COMMUNICATIONS**

Creative Firm: **TAYLOR DESIGN — STAMFORD, CT**
Creative Team: **SUZANNE REUSCH, HANNAH FICHANDLER, MARLE BARRETTI, KEN HOCKER, STEVE HABERSANG, MIKE KRAUZ, MICHELLE DOVE**
Client: **TAYLOR DESIGN**

Creative Firm: **DOUBLE TAKE CREATIVE — LAWRENCEVILLE, GA**
Creative Team: **AMY POWERS, VINCENT MARASCHIELLO**
Client: **DOUBLE TAKE CREATIVE**

Creative Firm: **BCN COMMUNICATIONS — CHICAGO, IL**
Creative Team: **MICHAEL O'BRIEN, MICHAEL NEU**
Client: **BCN COMMUNICATIONS**

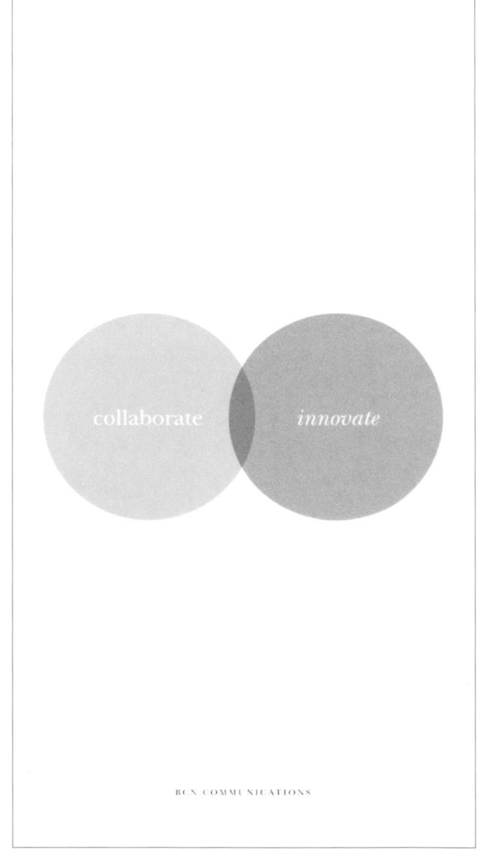

Creative Firm: **PHP COMMUNICATIONS — BIRMINGHAM, AL**
Creative Team: **BRYAN CHACE, LYNN SMITH**
Client: **PHP COMMUNICATIONS**

Creative Firm: **MARKET STREET MARKETING — REDDING, CA**
Creative Team: **KATHLEEN DOWNS**
Client: **MARKET STREET MARKETING**

Creative Firm: **BCN COMMUNICATIONS — CHICAGO, IL**
Creative Team: **JAMES PITROSKI, MICHAEL NEU**
Client: **BCN COMMUNICATIONS**

Creative Firm: **PERCEPT CREATIVE GROUP — CRONULLA, NSW, AUSTRALIA**
Creative Team: **LEWIS JENKINS**
Client: **PERCEPT CREATIVE GROUP**

Creative Firm: **JACK NADEL INTERNATIONAL — LOS ANGELES, CA**
Creative Team: **SCOTT BROWN, ROBERT BUCKINGHAM, STEVE WIDDECOMBE**
Client: **JACK NADEL INTERNATIONAL**

Creative Firm: **MYTTON WILLIAMS — BATH, BANES, UNITED KINGDOM**
Creative Team: **BOB MYTTON, GARY MARTYNIAK**

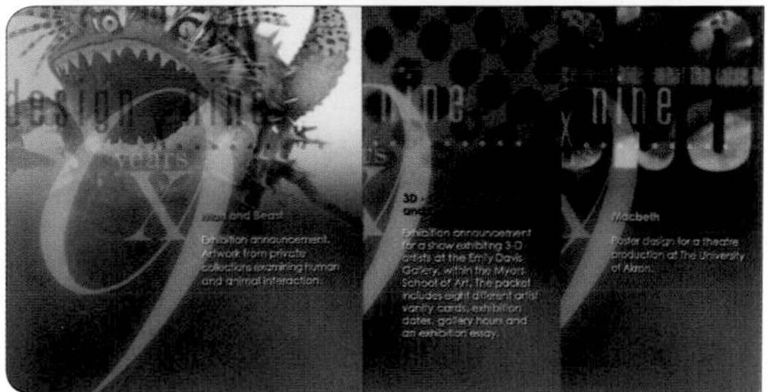

Creative Firm: **UNIVERSITY OF AKRON/DESIGN X NINE — AKRON, OH**
Creative Team: **JANICE TROUTMAN, JOHN MORRISON, DESIGN X NINE TEAM**
Client: **DESIGN X NINE**

Creative Firm: **WALLACE CHURCH, INC. — NEW YORK, NY**
Creative Team: **STAN CHURCH, JHOMY IRRAZABA, RICH RICKABY, SHERRI SEBASTIAN**
Client: **WALLACE CHURCH, INC.**

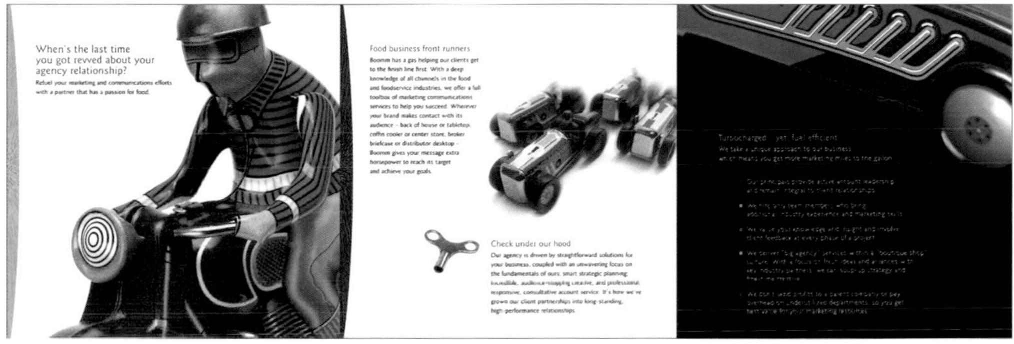

Creative Firm: **BOOMM! MARKETING & COMMUNICATIONS — WESTCHESTER, IL**
Client: **BOOMM! MARKETING & COMMUNICATIONS**

Creative Firm: **GRIFFO — BELÉM, PARÁ, BRAZIL**
Creative Team: **EDGAR CARDOSO, SERGIO BASTOS, ANTÔNIO NATSUO**
Client: **GRIFFO**

Creative Firm: **KAA DESIGN GROUP, INC. - GRAPHICS STUDIO — LOS ANGELES, CA**
Creative Team: **MELANIE ROBINSON, LOUIS-PHILIPPE CARRETTA, WELDON BREWSTER PHOTOGRAPHY, PHILIP CLAYTON THOMPSON PHOTOGRAPHY, BRANDIE HANDELMANN**
Client: **KAA DESIGN GROUP, INC.**

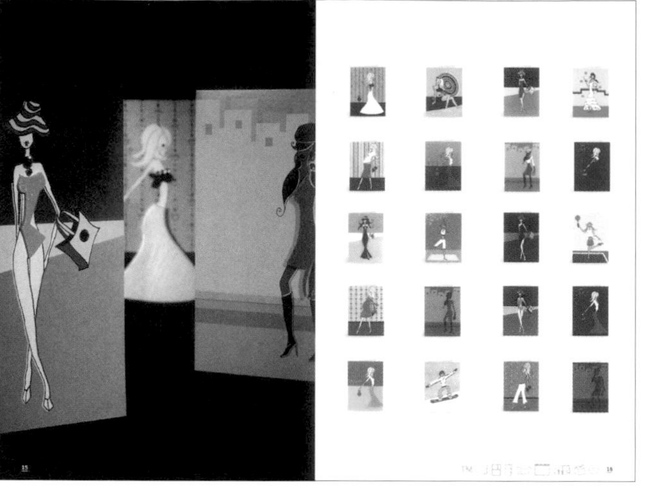

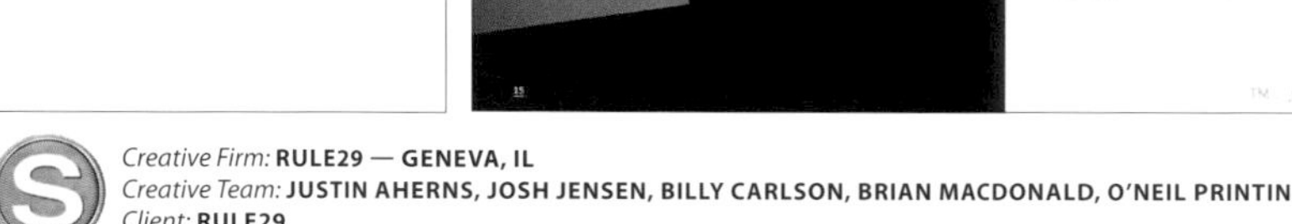

Creative Firm: **RULE29 — GENEVA, IL**
Creative Team: **JUSTIN AHERNS, JOSH JENSEN, BILLY CARLSON, BRIAN MACDONALD, O'NEIL PRINTING**
Client: **RULE29**

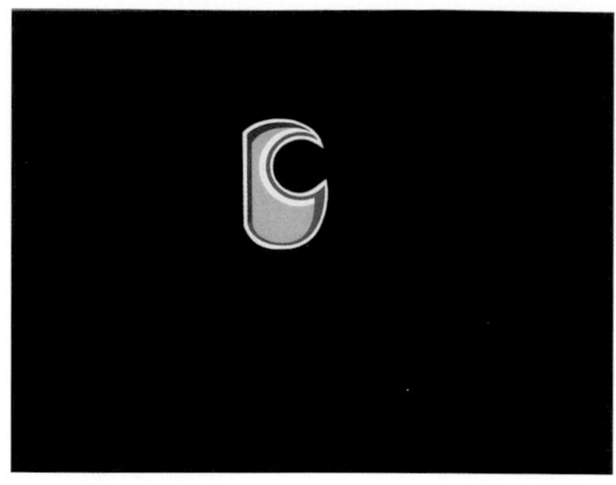

Creative Firm: **ROTTMAN CREATIVE GROUP — LA PLATA, MD**
Creative Team: **GARY ROTTMAN**
Client: **ROTTMAN CREATIVE GROUP, INC.**

Creative Firm: **JACK NADEL INTERNATIONAL — LOS ANGELES, CA**
Creative Team: **SCOTT BROWN, SAM MINSTER**
Client: **JACK NADEL INTERNATIONAL**

Creative Firm: **UNIVERSITY OF AKRON/DESIGN X NINE — AKRON, OH**
Creative Team: **JANICE TROUTMAN, JOHN MORRISON, NATHAN MUELLER**
Client: **SHERRY SIMMS**

Creative Firm: **PHP COMMUNICATIONS — BIRMINGHAM, AL**
Creative Team: **BRYAN CHACE, LYNN SMITH**
Client: **PHP COMMUNICATIONS**

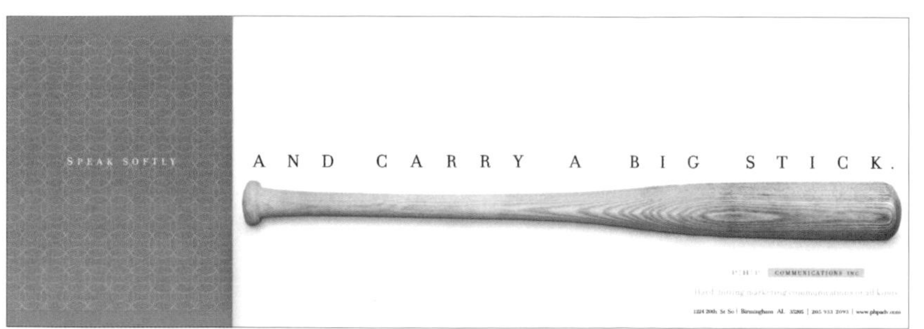

Creative Firm: **30SIXTY ADVERTISING+DESIGN, INC. — LOS ANGELES, CA**
Creative Team: **HENRY VIZCARRA, DAVID FUSCELLARO, MARISA GHIGLIERI, OLEG ZATLER, SCOTT HENSEL**
Client: **30SIXTY ADVERTISING+DESIGN, INC.**

Creative Firm: **BETH SINGER DESIGN — ARLINGTON, VA**
Creative Team: **BETH SINGER, CHRIS HOCH**
Client: **BETH SINGER DESIGN**

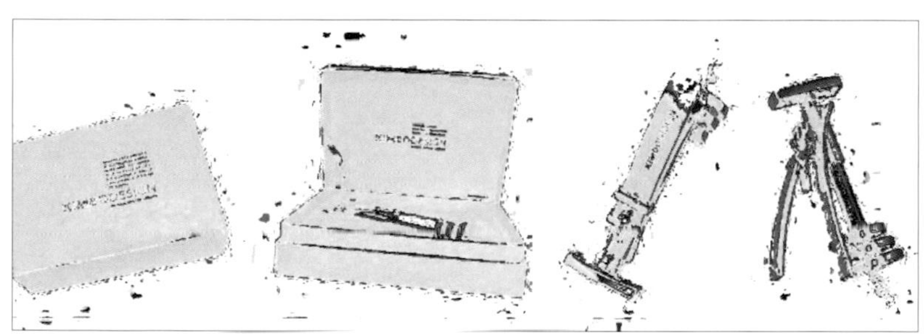

Creative Firm: **KIMBO DESIGN — VANCOUVER, BC, CANADA**
Creative Team: **KIM PICKETT, BUDIANTO NASRUN**
Client: **KIMBO DESIGN**

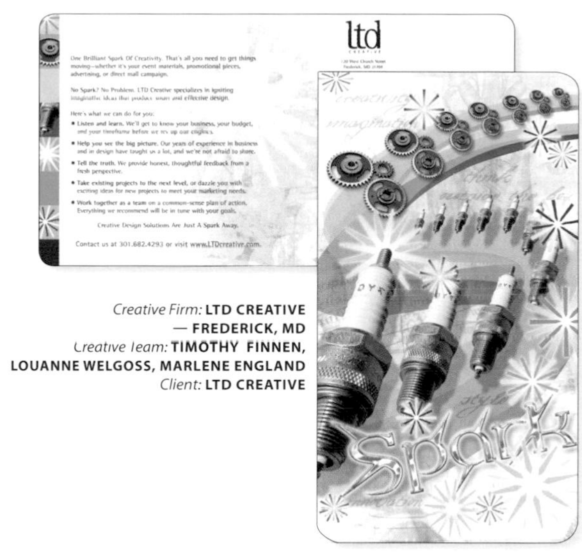

Creative Firm: **LTD CREATIVE — FREDERICK, MD**
Creative Team: **TIMOTHY FINNEN, LOUANNE WELGOSS, MARLENE ENGLAND**
Client: **LTD CREATIVE**

Creative Firm: **LTD CREATIVE — FREDERICK, MD**
Creative Team: **TIMOTHY FINNEN, LOUANNE WELGOSS, KIMBERLY DOW, EVAN WIEGAND, MARLENE ENGLAND**
Client: **LTD CREATIVE**

Creative Firm: **30SIXTY ADVERTISING+DESIGN, INC. — LOS ANGELES, CA**
Creative Team: **HENRY VIZCARRA, DAVID FUSCELLARO, MARISA GHIGLIERI**
Client: **30SIXTY ADVERTISING+DESIGN, INC.**

Creative Firm: **ORANGESEED DESIGN — MINNEAPOLIS, MN**
Creative Team: **DAMIEN WOLF, REBECCA AVIÑA, ROGER LUNDQUIST**
Client: **ORANGESEED DESIGN**

Creative Firm: **GROUP 55 MARKETING — DETROIT, MI**
Creative Team: **JEANNETTE GUTIERREZ, HEATHER SOWINSKI, JENNIFER REWITZ, DAVE WARNER**
Client: **GROUP FIFTY-FIVE MARKETING**

Creative Firm: **ROTTMAN CREATIVE GROUP — LA PLATA, MD**
Creative Team: **GARY ROTTMAN, MARY ROTTMAN, TANIA BAUMLER, NIKKI PLASCHKO, ROBERT WHETZEL**
Client: **ROTTMAN CREATIVE GROUP, INC.**

Creative Firm: **TOM FOWLER, INC. — NORWALK, CT**
Creative Team: **MARY ELLEN BUTKUS, ELIZABETH P. BALL, THOMAS G. FOWLER, STEPHANIE JOHNSON**
Client: **TOM FOWLER, INC.**

Creative Firm: **GROUP 55 MARKETING — DETROIT, MI**
Creative Team: **JEANNETTE GUTIERREZ**
Client: **GROUP FIFTY-FIVE MARKETING**

Creative Firm: **TOM FOWLER, INC. — NORWALK, CT**
Creative Team: **ELIZABETH P. BALL**
Client: **TOM FOWLER, INC.**

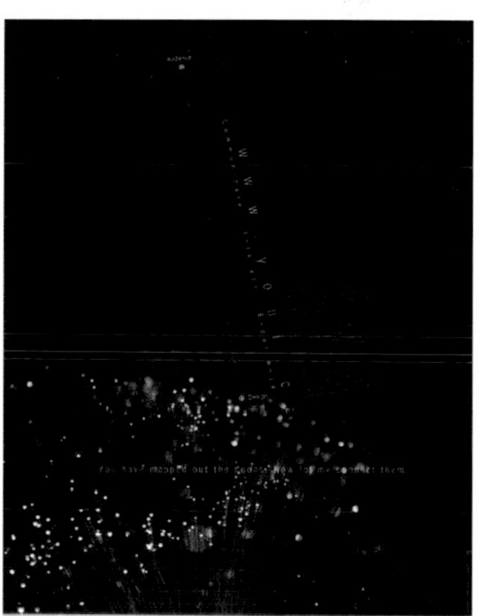

Creative Firm: **YOUI — SURREY, BC, CANADA**
Creative Team: **SIONG CHAN**

Creative Firm: **G2 — NEW YORK, NY**
Creative Team: **JASON BORZOUYEH, STEVE BROCKWAY, KURT HAIMAN**
Client: **G2**

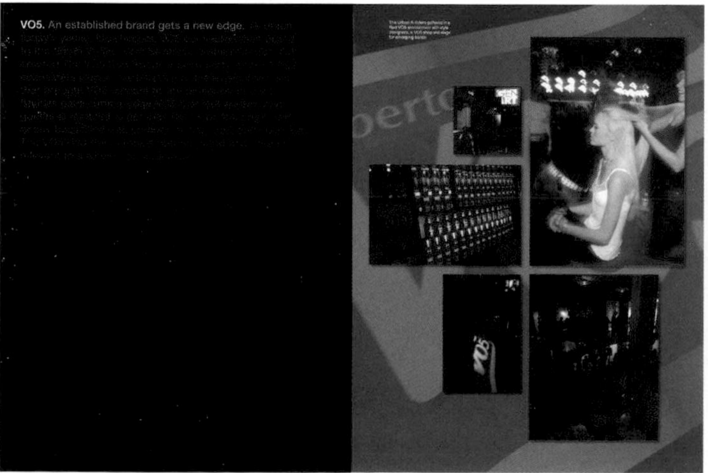

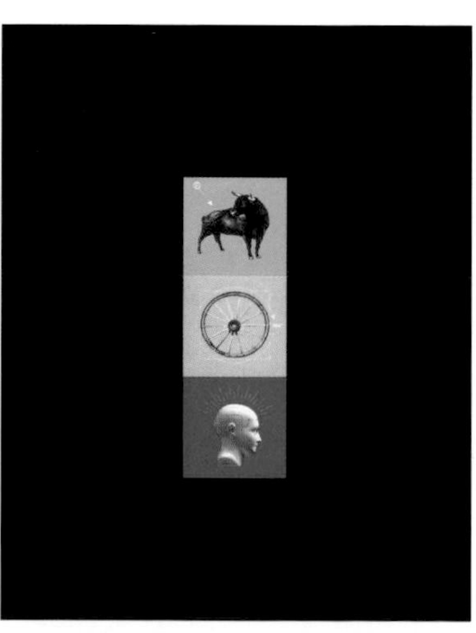

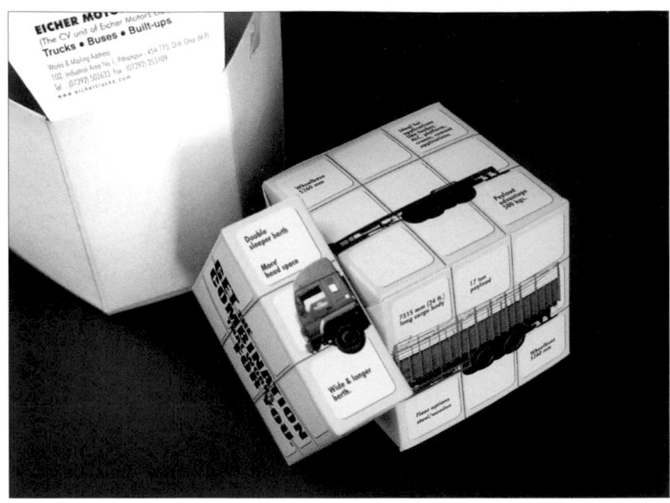

Creative Firm: **PURPLE FOCUS PVT. LTD. — INDORE, MADHYA PRADESH, INDIA**
Creative Team: **SAMEER DIXIT, ANURAG YADAV, PRAVEEN KARPE**
Client: **EICHER MOTORS LTD.**

Creative Firm: **DESIGN GUYS — MINNEAPOLIS, MN**
Creative Team: **STEVE SIKORA, JAY THEIGE**
Client: **TARGET**

Creative Firm: **ALEXANDER MARKETING SERVICES INC. — BUFFALO GROVE, IL**
Creative Team: **LAURIE BRAMMER, LYNN WIER**
Client: **ITW PASLODE**

Creative Firm: **RODGERS TOWNSEND — ST. LOUIS, MO**
Creative Team: **ERIK MATHRE, LIZ FORSYTHE, BILL ECKLOF**
Client: **THE BLACK REP**

Creative Firm: **CAMPBELL-EWALD — WARREN, MI**
Creative Team: **SUSAN LOGAR BRODY, JOEL BENAY, MICHELLE KRYSZAK, BOB HUFFMAN, BRANDI GEUY, TOM FORDE**
Client: **GM**

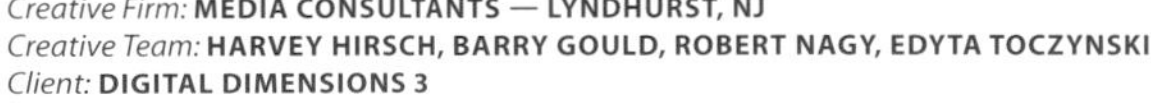

Creative Firm: **MEDIA CONSULTANTS — LYNDHURST, NJ**
Creative Team: **HARVEY HIRSCH, BARRY GOULD, ROBERT NAGY, EDYTA TOCZYNSKI**
Client: **DIGITAL DIMENSIONS 3**

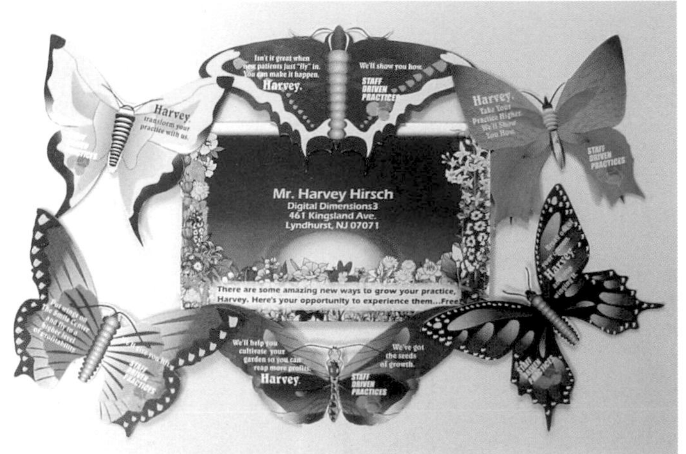

Creative Firm: **HITCHCOCK FLEMING & ASSOCIATES INC. — AKRON, OH**
Creative Team: **NICK BETRO, TONY CARTER, TONY FANIZZI, MATT WEISS, KEVIN KINSLEY**
Client: **LP BUILDING PRODUCTS**

Creative Firm: **MORNINGSTAR DESIGN, INC. — FREDERICK, MD**
Creative Team: **MISTI MORNINGSTAR, MELISSA NEAL, EMILY POTTHAST, RACHEL RABAT**

Creative Firm: **SUNSPOTS CREATIVE — FRANKLIN LAKES, NJ**
Creative Team: **RICK BONELLI, DAVE VIOREANU, DEENA HARTLEY**
Client: **MEDIA SCIENCES**

Creative Firm: **MEDIA CONSULTANTS INC. — LYNDHURST, NJ**
Creative Team: **HARVEY HIRSCH, BARRY GOULD, ROBERT NAGY, EDYTA TOCZYNSKI**
Client: **DIGITAL DIMENSIONS 3**

Creative Firm: **FIRST MARKETING — POMPANO BEACH, FL**
Creative Team: **KEITH JOHNSON, SUSIE REKECHENSKY, MELISSA KIESEY**
Client: **NEXTEL PARTNERS**

Creative Firm: **RODGERS TOWNSEND — ST. LOUIS, MO**
Creative Team: **ERIK MATHRE, MICHELLE VESTH**
Client: **SBC COMMUNICATIONS, INC**

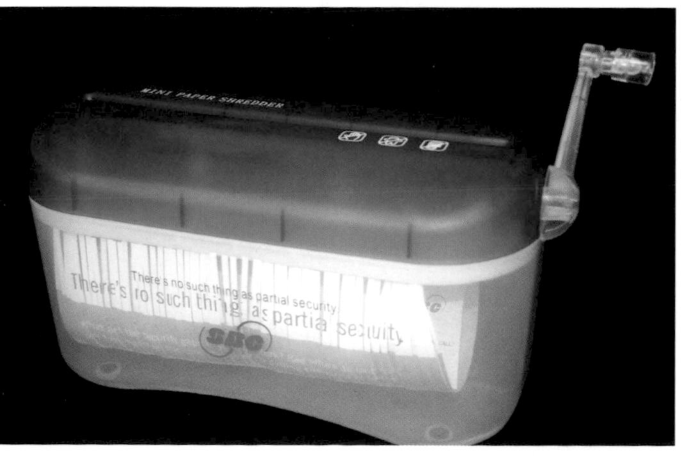

Creative Firm: **JACK NADEL INTERNATIONAL — LOS ANGELES, CA**
Creative Team: **SCOTT BROWN, ROBERT BUCKINGHAM, STEVE WIDDECOMBE**
Client: **JACK NADEL INTERNATIONAL**

Creative Firm: **AOL | 360 CREATIVE — NEW YORK, NY**
Creative Team: **ANTHONY FARIA, ERIC LANE, TOM POLLEY, ERIKA ALONSO**
Client: **AOL MEDIA NETWORKS**

Creative Firm: **DESIGN GUYS — MINNEAPOLIS, MN**
Creative Team: **STEVE SIKORA, BARRY TOWNSEND, JAY THEIGE, FEY PUBLISHING**
Client: **NEENAH PAPER**

Creative Firm: **PEGGY LAURITSEN DESIGN GROUP — MINNEAPOLIS, MN**
Creative Team: **BRIAN DANAHER**
Client: **DATALINK**

Creative Firm: **RODGERS TOWNSEND — ST. LOUIS, MO**
Creative Team: **MICHELLE VESTH, ERIK MATHRE**
Client: **SBC COMMUNICATIONS, INC**

Creative Firm: **OLSON/KOTOWSKI, INC. — TORRANCE, CA**
Creative Team: **JANICE OLSON, KEVIN KOTOWSKI, STEVE MURPHY, JEFF GUIDO**
Client: **INTUIT**

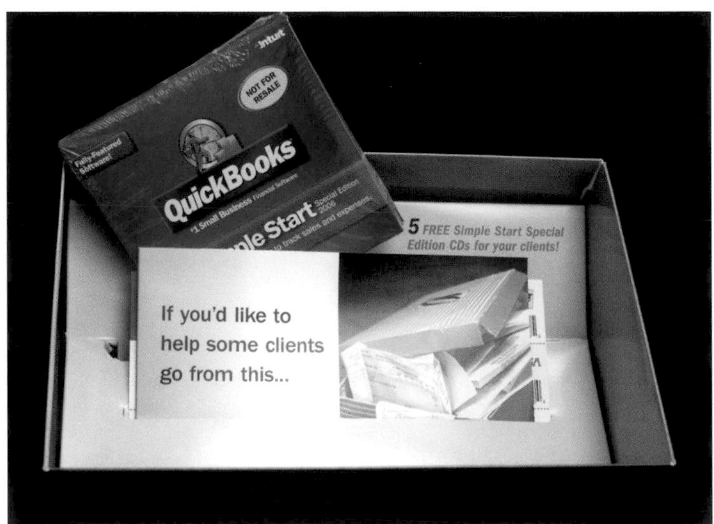

Creative Firm: **CAMPBELL-EWALD — WARREN, MI**
Creative Team: **BILL LUDWIG, ANNE MOORE, JOE PAS, SUSAN BERRY, JENNIFER BEAUDOIN, JOHN WOODWARD**
Client: **NATIONAL CITY CORPORATION**

Creative Firm: **EPOS, INC. — SANTA MONICA, CA**
Creative Team: **BRANDON FALL, GABRIELLE RAUMBERGER**
Client: **LOS ANGELES PUBLIC LIBRARY**

Creative Firm: **KOR GROUP — BOSTON, MA**
Creative Team: **ANNE CALLAHAN, KAREN DENDY SMITH, MB JAROSIK, JIM GIBSON, JAMES GRADY, RACHEL JOHNSON**
Client: **KOR GROUP**

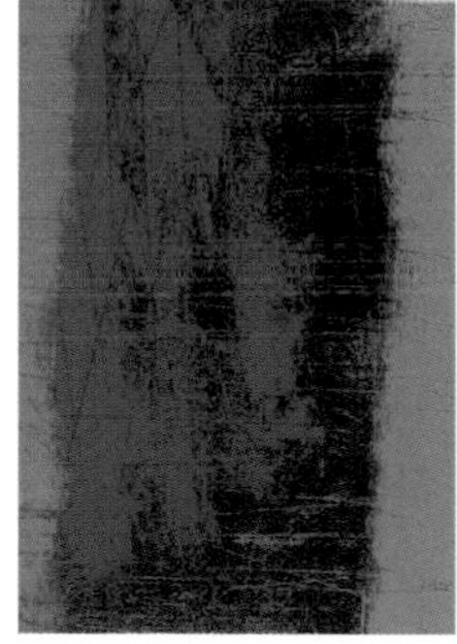

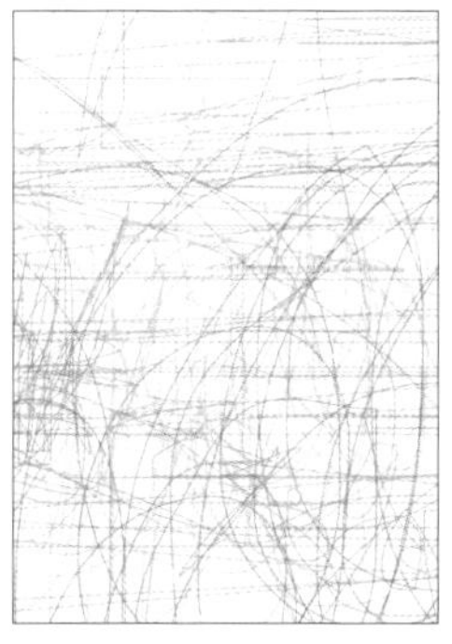

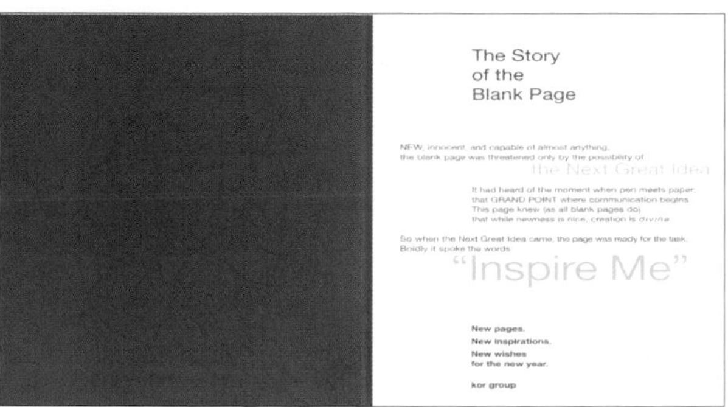

Creative Firm: **HOWARD HANNA SMYTHE CRAMER — CLEVELAND , OH**
Creative Team: **AIMEE CAMPBELL**
Client: **K&D GROUP**

Creative Firm: **YELLOW SHOES CREATIVE WEST, DISNEYLAND RESORT — ANAHEIM, CA**
Creative Team: **JANE ROHAN, WES CLARK, JACQUELYN MOE, JIM ST. AMANT**
Client: **DISNEYLAND RESORT**

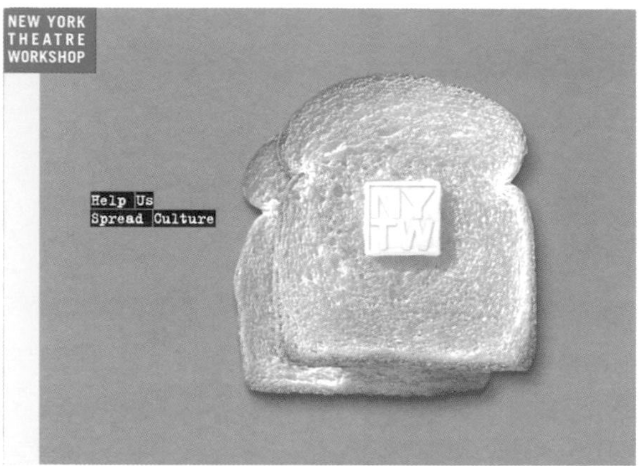

Creative Firm: **RUDER FINN DESIGN — NEW YORK, NY**
Creative Team: **LISA GABBAY, SAL CATANIA, AARON WILSON**
Client: **NEW YORK THEATRE WORKSHOP**

Creative Firm: **PUBLICIS DIALOG — SAN FRANCISCO, CA**
Creative Team: **LYLE LIM, MICHAEL AYHAN, KRISTY WARNER, BRIAN TYLER, CATHY KUZIA, CHRISTOPHER NELSON**
Client: **HP**

Creative Firm: **FITTING GROUP — PITTSBURGH, PA**
Creative Team: **TRAVIS NORRIS, AMY CHIAVERINI**
Client: **WOMEN & GIRLS FOUNDATION**

Creative Firm: **MEDIA CONSULTANTS — LYNDHURST, NJ**
Creative Team: **HARVEY HIRSCH, BARRY GOULD, ROBERT NAGY, EDYTA TOCZYNSKI**
Client: **DIGITAL DIMENSIONS 3**

Creative Firm: **THE BUDDY PROJECT/SQUAREHAND — ASTORIA, NY**
Creative Team: **DAVID SACKS, MÓNICA TORREJÓN KELLY**
Client: **DAVID SACKS PHOTOGRAPHY**

Creative Firm: **POSTCARD MANIA — CLEARWATER, FL**
Creative Team: **JOE NIEWIERSICI, JUDAA DOBIN**
Client: **POSTCARD MANIA**

Creative Firm: **PUBLICIS DIALOG — SAN FRANCISCO, CA**
Creative Team: **JONATHAN BUTTS, ALEX GROSSMAN, CHRISTOPHER ST. JOHN, BLAIR CERNY, BRIAN TYLER, MARTIN KOJNOK**
Client: **SPRINT**

Creative Firm: **YELLOW SHOES CREATIVE WEST, DISNEYLAND RESORT — ANAHEIM, CA**
Creative Team: **DATHAN SHORE, WES CLARK, MARTY MULLER, JACQUELYN MOE, KEVIN YONEDA**
Client: **DISNEYLAND RESORT**

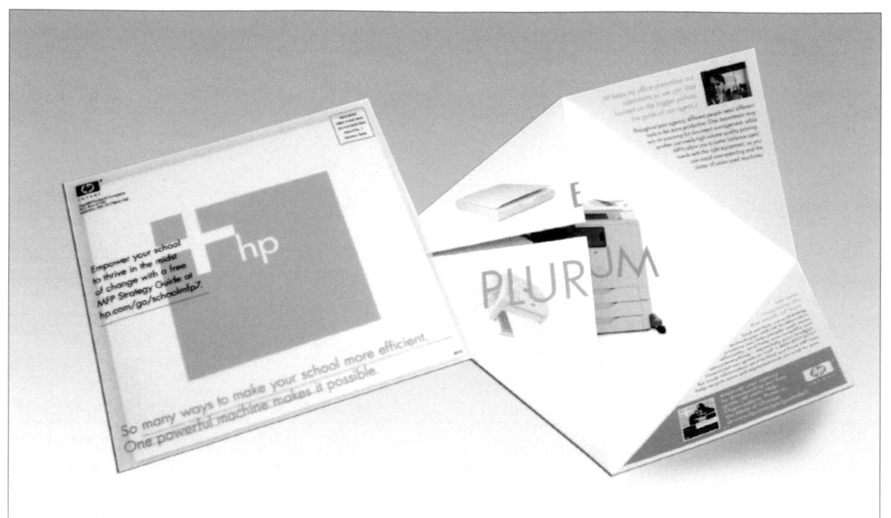

Creative Firm: **PUBLICIS DIALOG — SAN FRANCISCO, CA**
Creative Team: **LYLE LIM, KRISTY WARNER, JASON LAKIS, CATHY KUZIA, CHRISTOPHER NELSON**
Client: **HP**

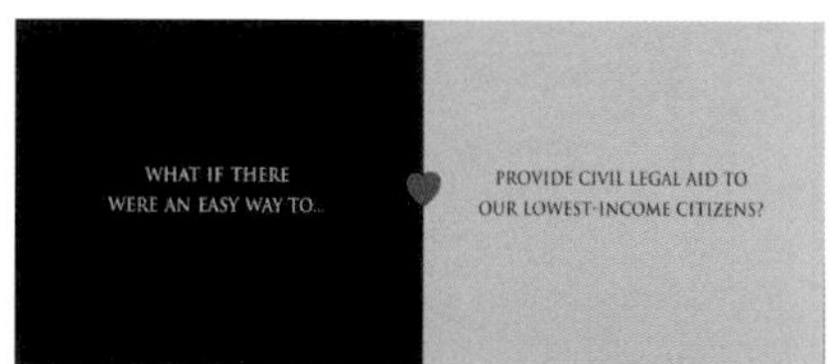

Creative Firm: **PHP COMMUNICATIONS — BIRMINGHAM, AL**
Creative Team: **BRYAN CHACE, LYNN SMITH**
Client: **LEGAL SERVICES ALABAMA**

Creative Firm: **POSTCARD MANIA — CLEARWATER, FL**
Creative Team: **JOE NIEWIERSICI**
Client: **POSTCARD MANIA**

Creative Firm: **RUSTY GEORGE DESIGN — TACOMA, WA**
Creative Team: **LANCE KAGEY, RUSTY GEORGE DESIGN**
Client: **SEATTLE DIRECT MARKETING ASSOCIATION**

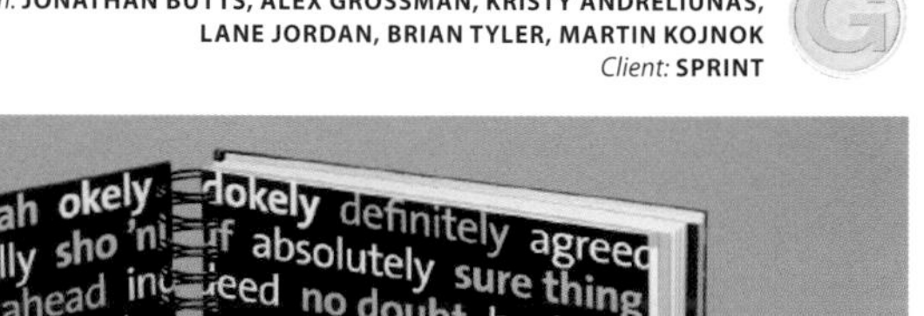
Creative Firm: **PUBLICIS DIALOG — SAN FRANCISCO, CA**
Creative Team: **JONATHAN BUTTS, ALEX GROSSMAN, KRISTY ANDRELIUNAS, LANE JORDAN, BRIAN TYLER, MARTIN KOJNOK**
Client: **SPRINT**

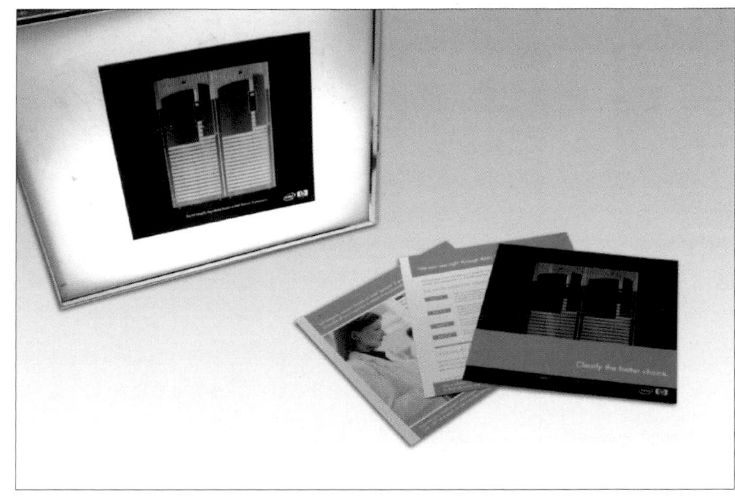

Creative Firm: **PUBLICIS DIALOG — SAN FRANCISCO, CA**
Creative Team: **JONATHAN BUTTS, KATIE HOPKINS, SHAWN POE, SIOW WEI KAY, MARTIN KOJNOK**
Client: **SPRINT**

Creative Firm: **PUBLICIS DIALOG — SAN FRANCISCO, CA**
Creative Team: **LYLE LIM, THERESA LEE, LEANNE MILWAY, ANTHONY BORDERS, CHRISTOPHER NELSON**
Client: **HP**

Creative Firm: **GREENFIELD/BELSER LTD. — WASHINGTON, DC**
Creative Team: **CAROLYN SEWELL, JOE WALSH, GENE SHAFFER**
Client: **GOODWIN PROCTER LLP**

Creative Firm: **A3 DESIGN — CHARLOTTE, NC**
Creative Team: **ALAN ALTMAN, AMANDA ALTMAN, SUSAN WALKER**
Client: **THE LIGHT FACTORY**

Creative Firm: **PUBLICIS DIALOG — SAN FRANCISCO, CA**
Creative Team: **JONATHAN BUTTS, ALEX GROSSMAN, JASON LAKIS, JASON BLACK, MARTIN KOJNOK, CHRISTOPHER NELSON**
Client: **SPRINT**

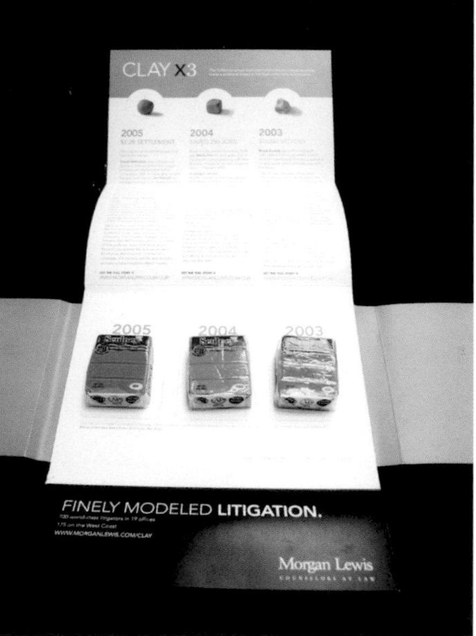

Creative Firm: **GREENFIELD/BELSER LTD. — WASHINGTON, DC**
Creative Team: **BURKEY BELSER, JOE WALSH, SIOBHAN DAVIS, GEORGE KELL, CHRIS ATKIN, CAVANAUGH PRESS**
Client: **MORGAN, LEWIS & BOCKIUS LLP**

Creative Firm: **DEZAINWERKZ — SINGAPORE**
Creative Team: **XAVIER SANJIMAN, FLUX FOTOGRAPHY, JEANETTE LAU, CHUA CHYE TECK**
Client: **TOSHIBA SINGAPORE**

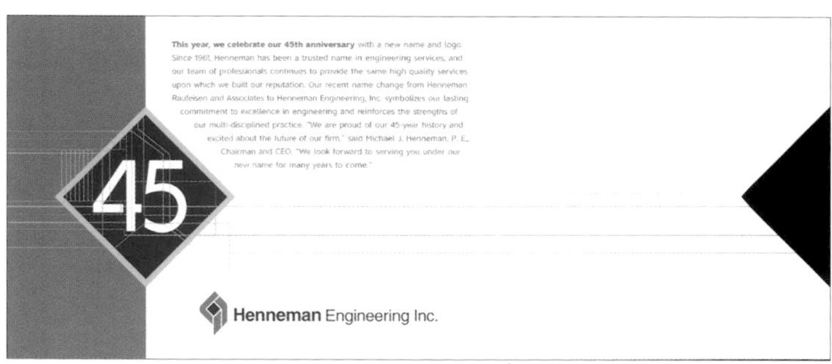

Creative Firm: **STAN GELLMAN GRAPHIC DESIGN INC. — ST. LOUIS, MO**
Creative Team: **JILL FRANTTI, BARRY TILSON, KAREN ROGERS**
Client: **HENNEMAN ENGINEERING INC.**

Creative Firm: **PUBLICIS DIALOG — SAN FRANCISCO, CA**
Creative Team: **JONATHAN BUTTS, ALEX GROSSMAN, LEANNE MILWAY, TEIJA KUOSKU, SUSAN SYMMONS, ERIC CHOI**
Client: **BERMUDA TOURISM**

Creative Firm: **PURPLE FOCUS PVT. LTD. — INDORE, MADHYA PRADESH, INDIA**
Creative Team: **AARISH NANDEDKAR, ANURAG YADAV, VINOD BHARGAV**
Client: **NAIDUNIYA**

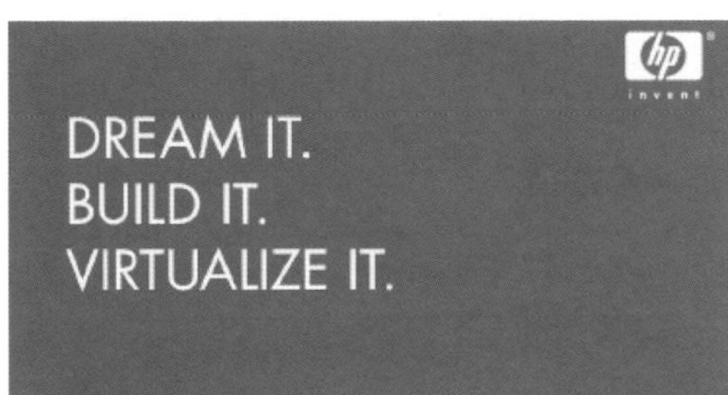

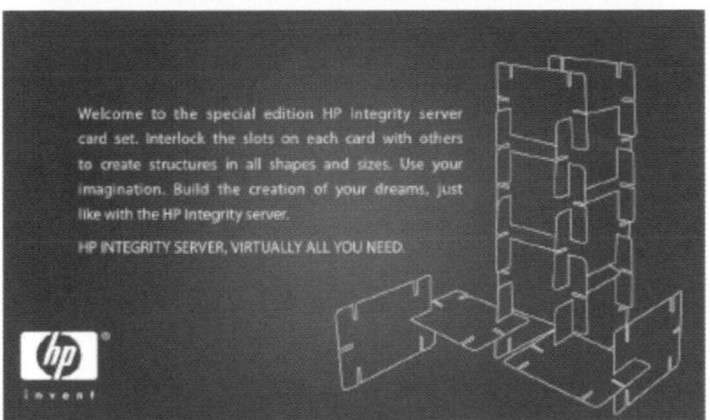

Creative Firm: **PUBLICIS DIALOG — SAN FRANCISCO, CA**
Creative Team: **LYLE LIM, LANE JORDAN, JASON BLACK, CATHY KUZIA**
Client: **HP**

Creative Firm: **PUBLICIS DIALOG — SAN FRANCISCO, CA**
Creative Team: **KATIE HOPKINS, ANTHONY BORDERS, IAN GOLDER**
Client: **SPRINT**

Creative Firm: **GREENFIELD/BELSER LTD. — WASHINGTON, DC**
Creative Team: **DONNA GREENFIELD, AARON HANSEN**
Client: **BURKE SCHOOL**

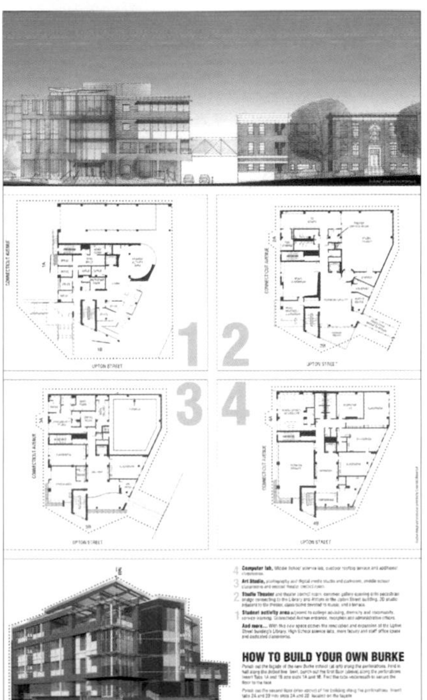

Creative Firm: **PUBLICIS DIALOG — SAN FRANCISCO, CA**
Creative Team: **JONATHAN BUTTS, CHRISTOPHER ST. JOHN, THERESA LEE, IAN GOLDER, MARTIN KOJNOK**
Client: **SPRINT**

Creative Firm: **TAPAGE COMMUNICATION — BLAINVILLE, QC, CANADA**
Creative Team: **CHRISTINE EMOND, ISABELLE GAGNÉ**
Client: **GROUPE DOMCO**

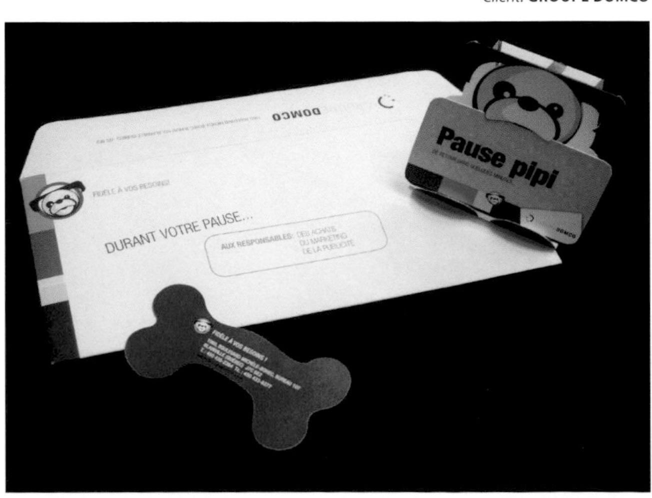

Creative Firm: **JACK NADEL INTERNATIONAL — LOS ANGELES, CA**
Creative Team: **SCOTT BROWN, ROBERT BUCKINGHAM, STEVE WIDDECOMBE**
Client: **JACK NADEL INTERNATIONAL**

Creative Firm: **YELLOW SHOES CREATIVE WEST, DISNEYLAND RESORT — ANAHEIM, CA**
Creative Team: **JANE ROHAN, WES CLARK, JACQUELYN MOE, JIM ST. AMANT**
Client: **DISNEYLAND RESORT**

Creative Firm: **MEDIA CONSULTANTS — LYNDHURST, NJ**
Creative Team: **HARVEY HIRSCH, BARRY GOULD, ROBERT NAGY, EDYTA TOCZYNSKI**
Client: **DIGITAL DIMENSIONS 3**

Creative Firm: **REDUCED FAT — SARATOGA SPRINGS, NY**
Creative Team: **JOHN BOLSTER**
Client: **DEBRA DOCYK**

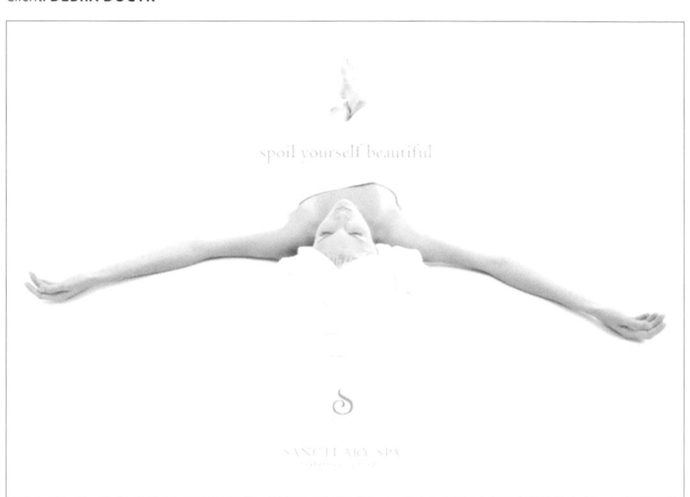

Creative Firm: **PUBLICIS DIALOG — SAN FRANCISCO, CA**
Creative Team: **ALEX GROSSMAN, BLAIR CERNY, JASON BLACK, MARTIN KOJNOK, TOM HOWARD, MADELYN HAPPEL**
Client: **SPRINT**

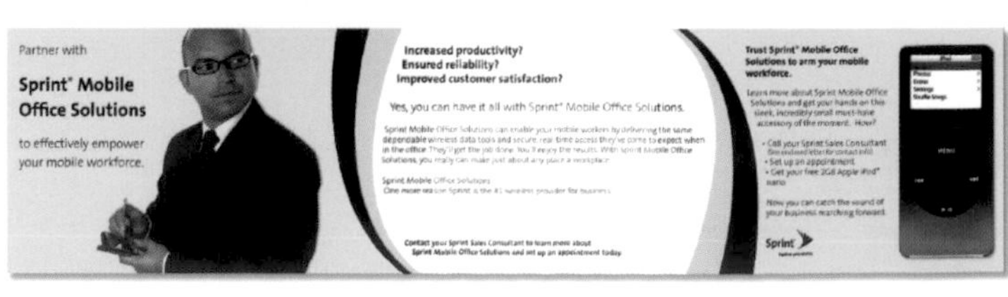

Creative Firm: **PUBLICIS DIALOG — SAN FRANCISCO, CA**
Creative Team: **CHRISTOPHER ST. JOHN, TEIJA KUOSKU**
Client: **GREATER SAN FRANCISCO AD CLUB**

Creative Firm: **PUBLICIS DIALOG — SAN FRANCISCO, CA**
Creative Team: **CHRISTOPHER ST. JOHN, KARLYN NEEL, JILL WHYSEL**
Client: **GREATER SAN FRANCISCO AD CLUB**

Creative Firm: **MAD DOG GRAPHX — ANCHORAGE, AK**
Creative Team: **MICHAEL ARDAIZ**
Client: **ALASKA STOCK**

Creative Firm: **STRATEGY ONE — WOODBUY, MN**
Creative Team: **JASON THOMPSON, BRIAN DANAHER**
Client: **GRAND THEATER CORPORATION**

Creative Firm: **PUBLICIS DIALOG — SAN FRANCISCO, CA**
Creative Team: **KATIE HOPKINS, THERESA LEE, JASON BLACK, TOM HOWARD, NICOLE HOGARTY**
Client: **SPRINT**

Creative Firm: **PUBLICIS DIALOG — SAN FRANCISCO, CA**
Creative Team: **CHRISTOPHER ST. JOHN, KARLYN NEEL, JILL WHYSEL**
Client: **GREATER SAN FRANCISCO AD CLUB**

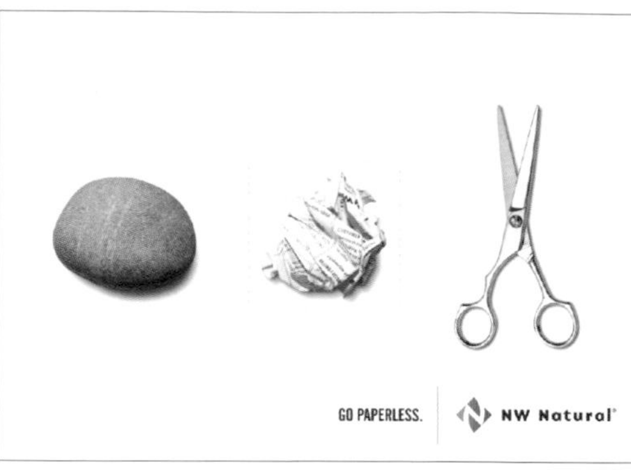

Creative Firm: **MAGNETO BRAND ADVERTISING — PORTLAND, OR**
Creative Team: **R. CRAIG OPFER, JAY FAWCETT, MIKE TERRY**
Client: **NW NATURAL**

Creative Firm: **PAT SLOAN DESIGN — FORT WORTH, TX**
Creative Team: **PAT SLOAN**
Client: **UNIVERSITY ART GALLERY-TCU**

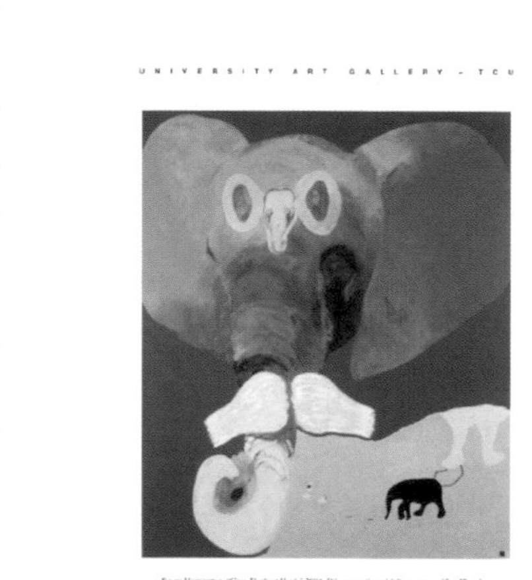

Creative Firm: **BRIGHT ORANGE ADVERTISING — RICHMOND, VA**
Creative Team: **BRUCE GOLDMAN, DANIEL GOLDMAN**
Client: **JEWISH FEDERATION OF GREATER HARTFORD**

Creative Firm: **PUBLICIS DIALOG — SAN FRANCISCO, CA**
Creative Team: **JONATHAN BUTTS, ALEX GROSSMAN, LANE JORDAN, JASON BLACK, ANDY ROSS, CATHY KUZIA**
Client: **SPRINT**

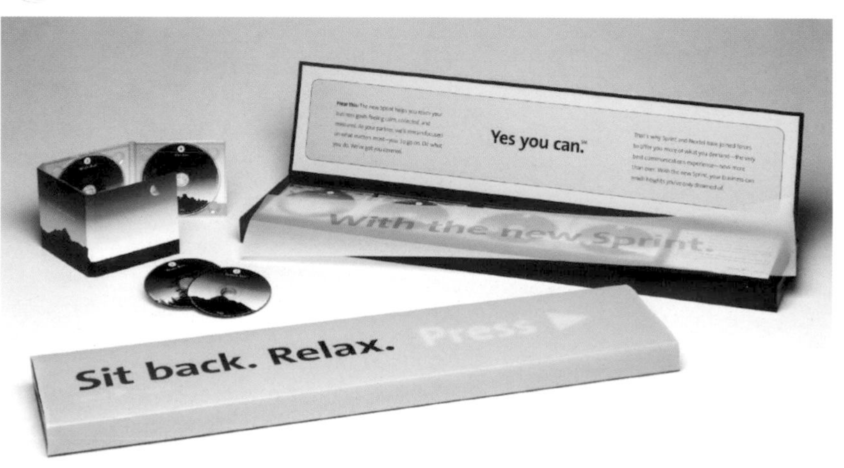

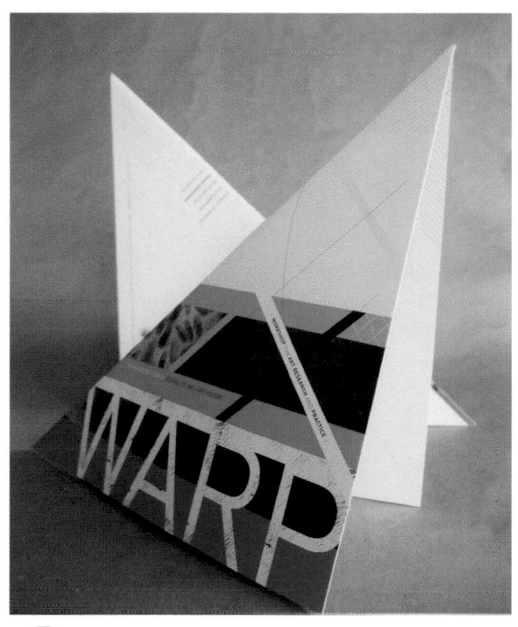

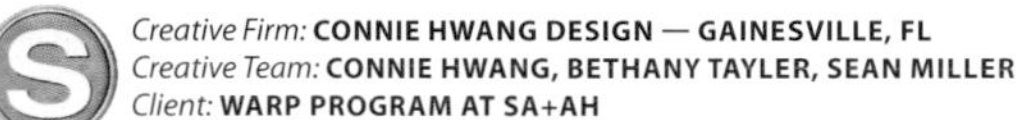

Creative Firm: **CONNIE HWANG DESIGN — GAINESVILLE, FL**
Creative Team: **CONNIE HWANG, BETHANY TAYLER, SEAN MILLER**
Client: **WARP PROGRAM AT SA+AH**

WE TOLD 10 PEOPLE
THAT *Buntin Reid*
IS HAVING ANOTHER
PAPER SHOW AT
THE HARD ROCK CAFÉ
AND THIS IS WHAT
THEY HAD TO SAY:

Creative Firm: **KOLEGRAM — GATNINEAU, QC, CANADA**
Creative Team: **GONTRAN BLAIS, YANNICE BEAUVALET**
Client: **BUNTIN REID**

Creative Firm: **DEZAINWERKZ — SINGAPORE**
Creative Team: **XAVIER SANJIMAN, SIMON LOW, JEANETTE LAU**
Client: **FLUX FOTOGRAPHY**

Creative Firm: **PUBLICIS DIALOG — SAN FRANCISCO, CA**
Creative Team: **JONATHAN BUTTS, ALEX GROSSMAN, LEANNE MILWAY, LANE JORDAN, MARTIN KOJNOK**
Client: **SPRINT**

Creative Firm: **ACME COMMUNICATIONS, INC. — NEW YORK, NY**
Creative Team: **KIKI BOUCHER, ANDREA ROSS BOYLE**
Client: **DIRTWORKS, PC**

DIRTWORKS, PC
LANDSCAPE ARCHITECTURE
200 PARK AVENUE SOUTH
NEW YORK, NEW YORK 10003

NEW Projects

NEW Photos

NEW Information

Company News

Dirtworks invites you to look at their updated web site.

www.dirtworks.us
TEL 212-529-2263 FAX 212-505-0904
EMAIL INFO@DIRTWORKS.US

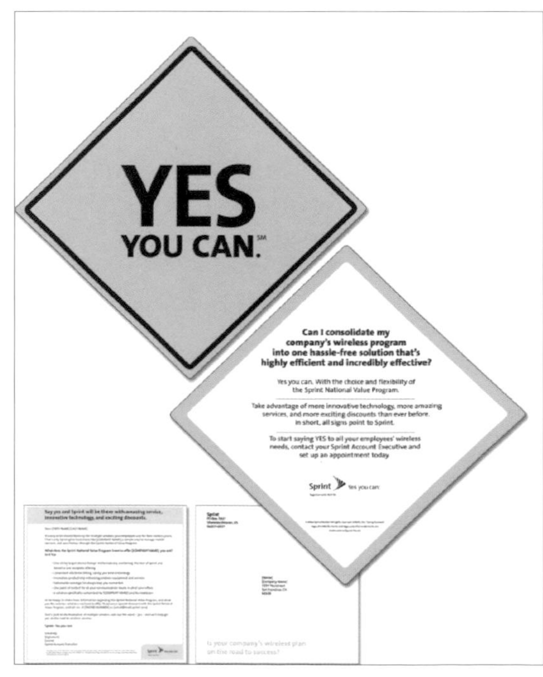

Creative Firm: **WESTGROUP CREATIVE — NEW YORK, NY**
Creative Team: **CHIP TOLANEY, MARVIN BERK**
Client: **NEW DANCE GROUP**

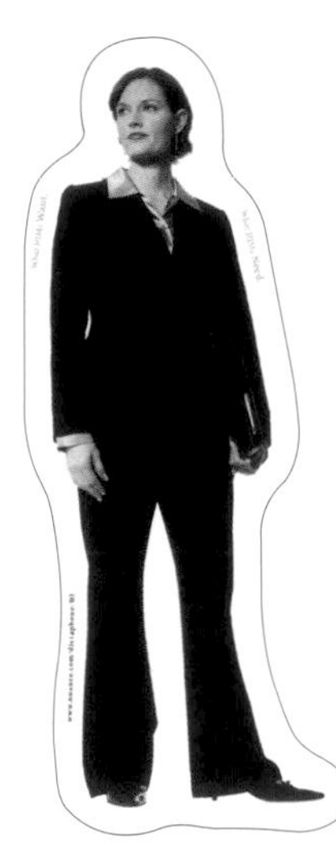

Creative Firm: **ALOFT GROUP, INC. — NEWBURYPORT, MA**
Creative Team: **DON CRANE, KIM CILLEY, MICHAEL INDRESANO**
Client: **DICTAPHONE HEALTHCARE**

Creative Firm: **BRC MARKETING — DAYTON, OH**
Creative Team: **DOM CIMEI, JASON KANTER, MICHAEL BOYD, AMBER MOORE**
Client: **CINTAS**

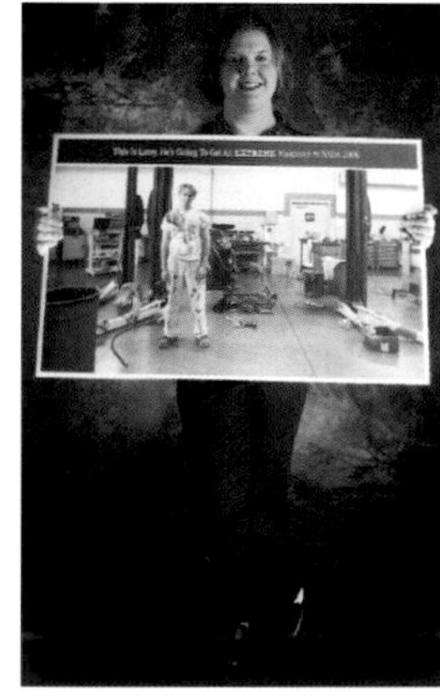

Creative Firm: **SNAP CREATIVE — ST. CHARLES, MO**
Creative Team: **ANGELA NEAL, HILARY CLEMENTS**
Client: **JACQUIN STUDIOS**

Creative Firm: **PUBLICIS DIALOG — SAN FRANCISCO, CA**
Creative Team: **JONATHAN BUTTS, ALEX GROSSMAN, LANE JORDAN, JASON BLACK, CATHY KUZIA, MARTIN KOJNOK**
Client: **SPRINT**

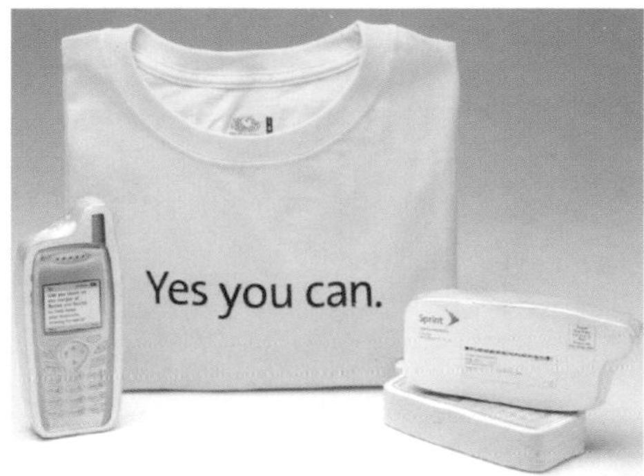

Creative Firm: **RUDER FINN DESIGN — NEW YORK, NY**
Creative Team: **LISA GABBAY, SAL CATANIA, KEI CHAN**
Client: **HUNTER MOUNTAIN**

Creative Firm: **MAD DOG GRAPHX — ANCHORAGE, AK**
Creative Team: **MICHAEL ARDAIZ**
Client: **ALASKA STOCK**

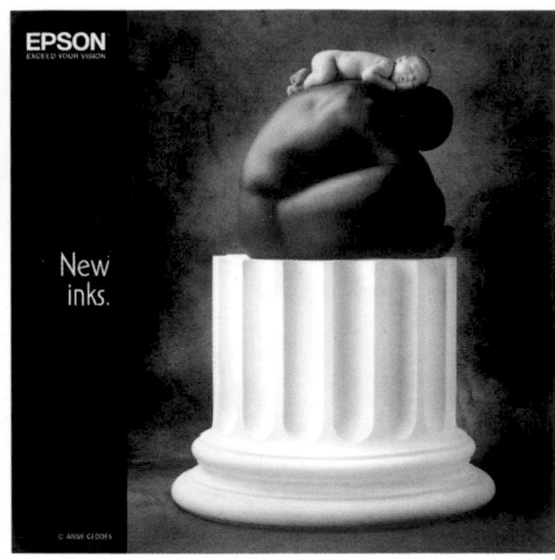

Creative Firm: **OLSON/KOTOWSKI, INC. — TORRANCE, CA**
Creative Team: **JANICE OLSON, KEVIN KOTOWSKI, MOIRA DYER, JEFF GUIDO, DONNA JOHNSON, THAD WAWRO**
Client: **EPSON**

Creative Firm: **ORANGESEED DESIGN — MINNEAPOLIS, MN**
Creative Team: **DAMIEN WOLF, REBECCA AVIÑA, STAFFORD PHOTOGRAPHY**
Client: **STAFFORD PHOTOGRAPHY**

Creative Firm: **G2 — NEW YORK, NY**
Creative Team: **VICTOR MAZZEO, ELEANOR ZACH, PHIL KONTRIS, MEGAN TRINIDAD**
Client: **CACHE**

Creative Firm: **CRABTREE & COMPANY — FALLS CHURCH, VA**
Creative Team: **SUSAN ANGRISANI, TAMERA FINN**
Client: **INTERNATIONAL SPY MUSEUM**

Creative Firm: **PUBLICIS DIALOG — SAN FRANCISCO, CA**
Creative Team: **JONATHAN BUTTS, CHRISTOPHER ST. JOHN, TEIJA KUOSKU, MARTIN KOJNOK**
Client: **GREATER SAN FRANCISCO AD CLUB**

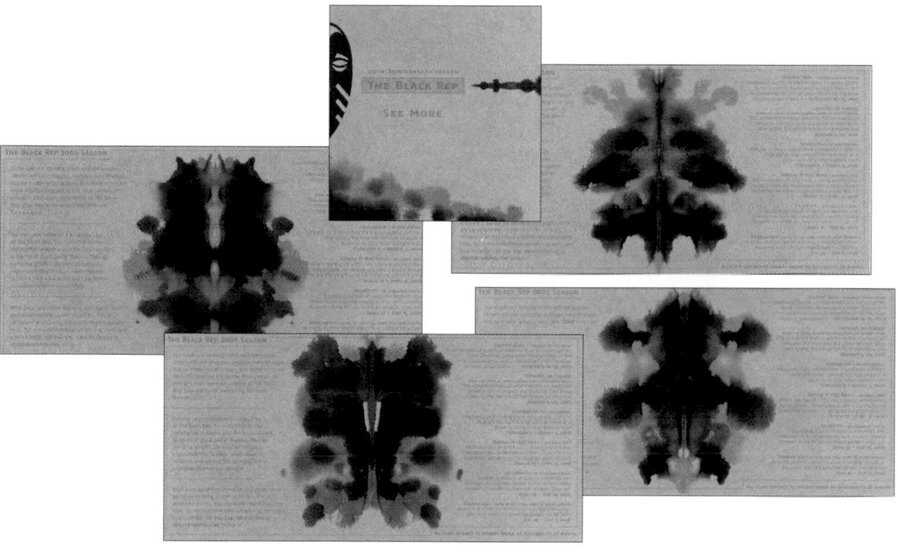

Creative Firm: **RODGERS TOWNSEND — ST. LOUIS, MO**
Creative Team: **ERIK MATHRE, RON COPELAND, RYAN MCMICHAEL**
Client: **THE BLACK REP**

Creative Firm: **PEGGY LAURITSEN DESIGN GROUP — MINNEAPOLIS, MN**
Creative Team: **BRIAN DANAHER, HIGH POINT CREATIVE**
Client: **AMERICAN MEDICAL SYSTEMS**

Creative Firm: **TORRE LAZUR MCCANN — PARSIPPANY, NJ**
Creative Team: **DANIELLE TERMINI, JILL LESIAK, ALBERT MAURIELLO, LINDA CICCARELLI, JENNIFER ALAMPI, MARCIA GODDARD**
Client: **EISAI / PFIZER**

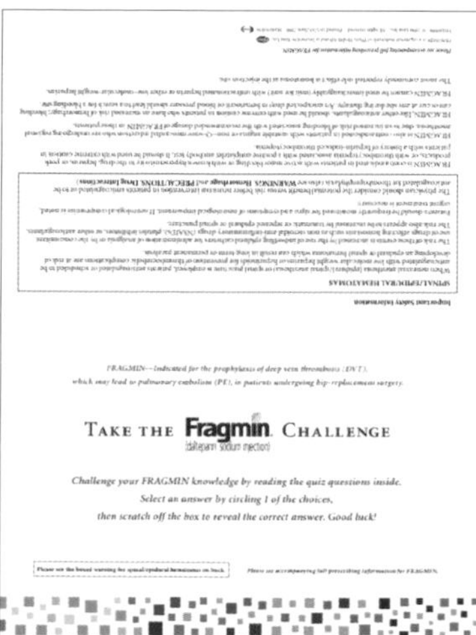

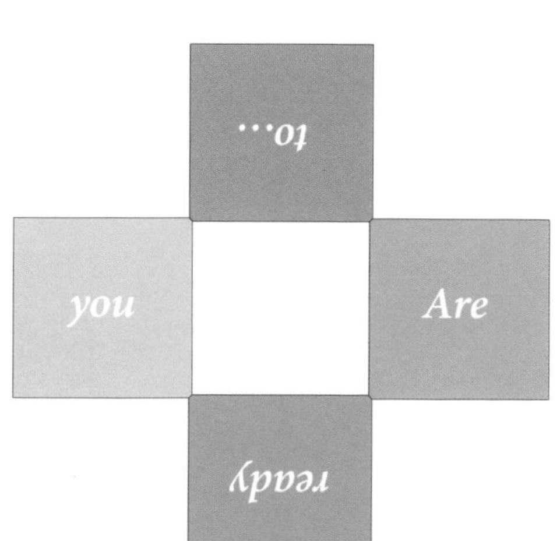

Creative Firm: **STEPHEN LONGO DESIGN ASSOCIATES — WEST ORANGE, NJ**
Creative Team: **STEPHEN LONGO**
Client: **EKKO RESTAURANT**

Creative Firm: **ALTERNATIVES — NEW YORK, NY**
Creative Team: **JULIE KOCH-BEINKE, MARK KOCH**
Client: **CADBURY SCHWEPPES**

Creative Firm: **ADSYSTEMS INTERNATIONAL — MAKATI, MANILA, PHILIPPINES**
Creative Team: **MA. PILAR BUNAG, STEFANO PAOLO BUNAG**
Client: **BAKER FRESH FOODS PHILIPPINES, INC. (DELIFRANCE)**

Creative Firm: **JGA — SOUTHFIELD, MI**
Creative Team: **KEN NISCH, KATHI MCWILLIAMS**
Client: **GODIVA CHOCOLATIER**

Creative Firm: **BETH SINGER DESIGN — ARLINGTON, VA**
Creative Team: **BETH SINGER, HOWARD SMITH, LOLAN O'ROURKE**
Client: **NATIONAL ASSOCIATION OF REALTORS**

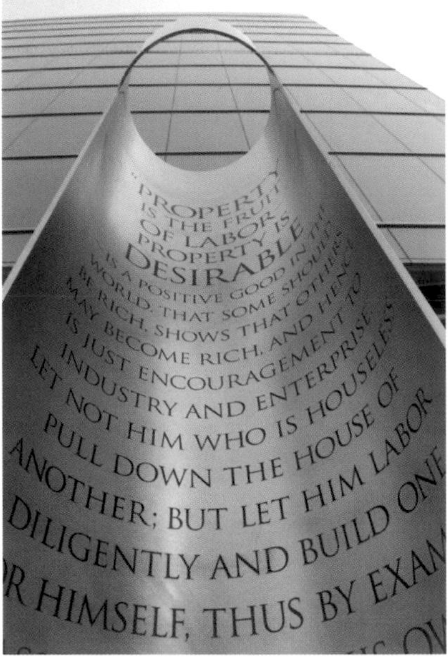

Creative Firm: **EPOS, INC. — SANTA MONICA, CA**
Creative Team: **BRANDON FALL, GABRIELLE RAUMBERGER**
Client: **LOS ANGELES PUBLIC LIBRARY**

Creative Firm: **JGA — SOUTHFIELD, MI**
Creative Team: **KEN NISCH, GORDON EASON**
Client: **HERSHEY FOODS CORPORATION**

Creative Firm: **JGA — SOUTHFIELD, MI**
Creative Team: **DAVID NELSON, GORDON EASON**
Client: **PULTE HOMES, INC.**

Creative Firm: **BUITENKANT ADVERTISING & DESIGN — FLUSHING, NY**
Creative Team: **VAVA BUITENKANT, DEBBIE MCCARTHY, RALPH L. CWERMAN, DEENA PLOTKA**
Client: **CONNIE'S BAKERY & GENERAL STORE**

Creative Firm: **HORNALL ANDERSON DESIGN WORKS — SEATTLE, WA**
Creative Team: **JACK ANDERSON, SKB ARCHITECTS**
Client: **HORNALL ANDERSON DESIGN WORKS**

Creative Firm: **LORENC+YOO DESIGN — ROSWELL, GA**
Creative Team: **JAN LORENC, CHUNG YOUL YOO, STEVE MCCALL, DAVID PARK, JISUN AN, KEN BOYD**
Client: **MAYO CLINIC**

Creative Firm: **KARACTERS DESIGN GROUP/DDB CANADA — VANCOUVER, BC, CANADA**
Creative Team: **JAMES BATEMAN, KARA BOHL, DAN O'LEARY, HELEN WYNNE, SCOTT RUSSELL, MARK FINN**
Client: **MOUNTAIN EQUIPMENT CO-OP**

Creative Firm: **FUTUREBRAND — NEW YORK, NY**
Creative Team: **TOM LI, MIKE WILLIAMS, BRENDAN O'NEILL, ANTHONY DECOSTA, JAE HWANG, TESS ABRAHAM**
Client: **NAKHEEL**

Creative Firm: **RALPH APPELBAUM ASSOCIATES — NEW YORK, NY**
Creative Team: **RALPH APPELBAUM, DENNIS COHEN, KAI CHIU, VIVI HSIN-YI HSU, MADELINE CHINNICI, IDA BACHTIAR**
Client: **S'PORE DISCOVERY CENTRE**

Creative Firm: **CBX — NEW YORK, NY**
Client: **NEIGHBOURS**

Creative Firm: **DESIGN OBJECTIVES PTE LTD — SINGAPORE**
Creative Team: **RONNIE S C TAN**
Client: **RAFFLES INTERNATIONAL**

Creative Firm: **KAREN SKUNTA & COMPANY — CLEVELAND, OH**
Creative Team: **KAREN SKUNTA, BECKY RALICH-SPAK, JAMIE FINKELHOR, JENNY PAN, TRG STUDIOS**
Client: **THE CLEVELAND PLAY HOUSE**

Creative Firm: **RALPH APPELBAUM ASSOCIATES — NEW YORK, NY**
Creative Team: **RALPH APPELBAUM, RICK SOBEL, MIA BUERSKENS, SYLVIA JURAN, KYLE CHEPULIS, AUDIO VIDEO AND CONTROLS**
Client: **EDISON PRESERVATION FOUNDATION**

Creative Firm: **DON SCHAAF & FRIENDS, INC. — WASHINGTON, DC**
Creative Team: **DON SCHAAF, BRUCE MACINDOE**
Client: **HEART RHYTHM SOCIETY**

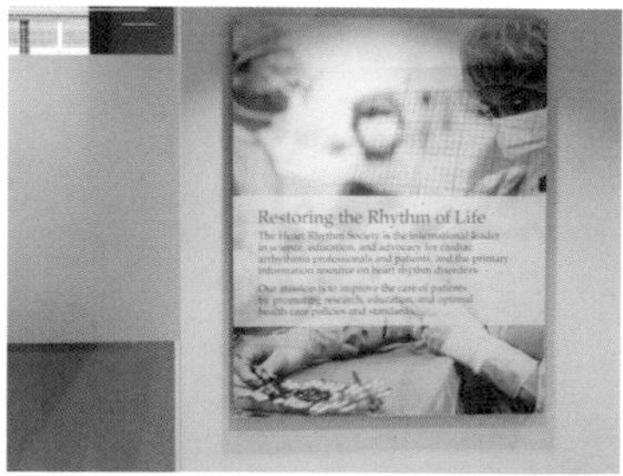

Creative Firm: **LORENC+YOO DESIGN — ROSWELL, GA**
Creative Team: **JAN LORENC, STEVE MCCALL, DAVID PARK**
Client: **PHILLIPS EDISON & COMPANY**

Creative Firm: **DESIGN OBJECTIVES PTE LTD — SINGAPORE**
Creative Team: **RONNIE S C TAN**
Client: **SHERATON TAIPEI HOTEL**

Creative Firm: **KIMAK DESIGN — ORANGEBURG, NY**
Creative Team: **JAMES KIMAK, CHILDRENS' ART COURTESY OF TRI-STATE AREA SCHOOLS**
Client: **NEW YORK PRESBYTERIAN HOSTPITAL**

Creative Firm: **FUTUREBRAND — NEW YORK, NY**
Creative Team: **ALEX SUGAI, TOM LI, CHERYL HILLS, ANTHONY DECOSTA, SAGAYARAJ PRASANNA, JAE HWANG**
Client: **DUBAI AEROSPACE ENTERPRISE**

Creative Firm: **LORENC+YOO DESIGN — ROSWELL, GA**
Creative Team: **JAN LORENC, STEVE MCCALL, KEN BOYD**
Client: **THE RELATED COMPANIES**

Creative Firm: **FUTUREBRAND — NEW YORK, NY**
Creative Team: **DIEGO KOLSKY, CHERYL HILLS, BRENDAN O'NEILL, ANTONIO BAGLIONE, SAGAYARAJ PRASANNA, JAE HWANG**
Client: **DUBAI AEROSPACE ENTERPRISE**

Creative Firm: **KIKU OBATA & COMPANY — ST. LOUIS, MO**
Creative Team: **LAURA MCCANNA, RICH NELSON, RUSSELL BUCHANAN, JR., DAVID LEAVEY, TODD MAYBERRY, CAROLE JEROME**
Client: **THE ST. LOUIS CARDINALS/BUSCH STADIUM**

Creative Firm: **30SIXTY ADVERTISING+DESIGN, INC. — LOS ANGELES, CA**
Creative Team: **HENRY VIZCARRA, DAVID FUSCELLARO, YUJIN ONO**
Client: **KING'S SEAFOOD COMPANY**

Creative Firm: **DOUBLE TAKE CREATIVE — LAWRENCEVILLE, GA**
Creative Team: **AMY POWERS, VINCENT MARASCHIELLO**
Client: **DOUBLE TAKE CREATIVE**

Creative Firm: **VINCE RINI DESIGN — HUNTINGTON BEACH, CA**
Creative Team: **VINCE RINI**
Client: **BLUE COW**

Creative Firm: **MAYHEM STUDIOS — LOS ANGELES, CA**
Creative Team: **CALVIN LEE**
Client: **EMTEK PRODUCTS, INC.**

Creative Firm: **RIORDON DESIGN — OAKVILLE, ON, CANADA**
Creative Team: **ALAN KRPAN, RIC RIORDON**
Client: **ADRIANA TONCIC INTERIORS**

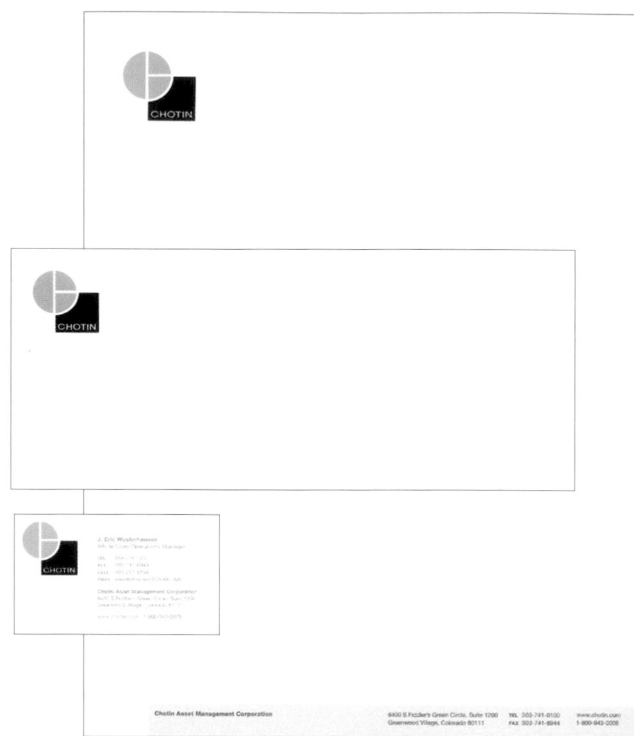

Creative Firm: **ELLEN BRUSS DESIGN — DENVER, CO**
Creative Team: **ELLEN BRUSS, RYAN NEE**
Client: **THE CHOTIN GROUP**

Creative Firm: **HORNALL ANDERSON DESIGN WORKS — SEATTLE, WA**
Creative Team: **DAYMON BRUCK, YURI SHVETS, HILLARY RADBILL**
Client: **BLRB ARCHITECTS**

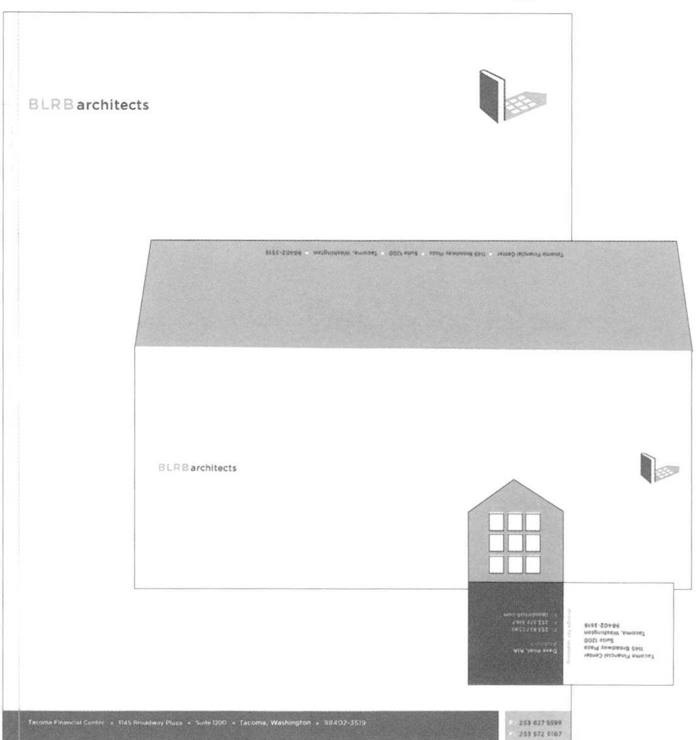

Creative Firm: **STELLAR DEBRIS — HADANO-SHI, KANAGAWA-KEN, JAPAN**
Creative Team: **CHRISTOPHER JONES**
Client: **STELLAR DEBRIS**

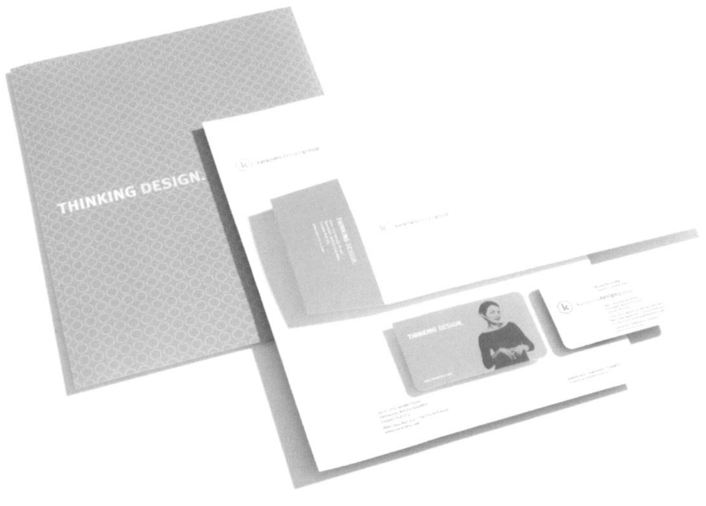

Creative Firm: **KARACTERS DESIGN GROUP/DDB CANADA — VANCOUVER, BC, CANADA**
Creative Team: **MARIA KENNEDY, MARSHA LARKIN, HELEN WYNNE, RUSS HORII, MARK FINN**
Client: **KARACTERS DESIGN GROUP**

Creative Firm: **ZERO GRAVITY DESIGN GROUP — SMITHTOWN, NY**
Creative Team: **ZERO GRAVITY DESIGN GROUP**
Client: **ATTWOOD EQUESTRIAN SURFACES**

Creative Firm: **RIORDON DESIGN — OAKVILLE, ON, CANADA**
Creative Team: **DAWN CHARNEY, SHIRLEY RIORDON**
Client: **CHELSTER HALL**

Creative Firm: **HITCHCOCK FLEMING & ASSOCIATES INC. — AKRON, OH**
Creative Team: **NICK BETRO, TODD MOSER, RENE MCCANN**
Client: **VERITAS**

Creative Firm: **ZERO GRAVITY DESIGN GROUP — SMITHTOWN, NY**
Creative Team: **ZERO GRAVITY DESIGN GROUP**
Client: **U.S. COFFEE**

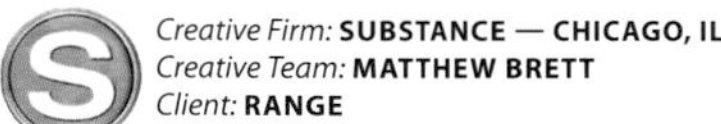

Creative Firm: **SUBSTANCE — CHICAGO, IL**
Creative Team: **MATTHEW BRETT**
Client: **RANGE**

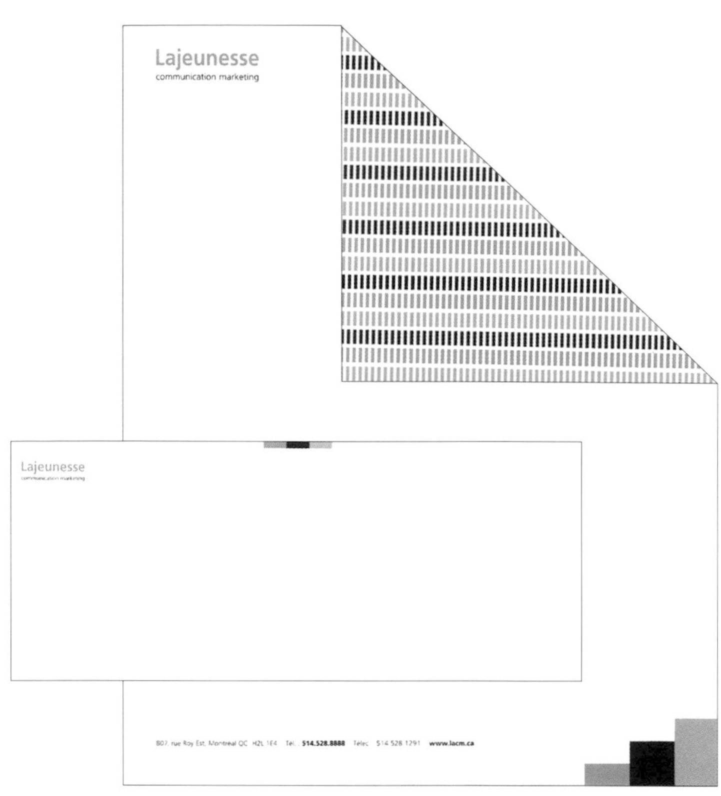

Creative Firm: **LAJEUNESSE COMMUNICATION MARKETING — MONTREAL, QC, CANADA**
Creative Team: **YVES DUQUETTE, NATHALIE DAIGLE**

Creative Firm: **SCOTT ADAMS DESIGN ASSOCIATES — COLUMBUS, OH**
Creative Team: **SCOTT ADAMS**
Client: **ASSET STRATEGIES GROUP**

Creative Firm: **STRATEGY ONE — WOODBUY, MN**
Creative Team: **JASON THOMPSON**
Client: **COLLEGE CHURCH**

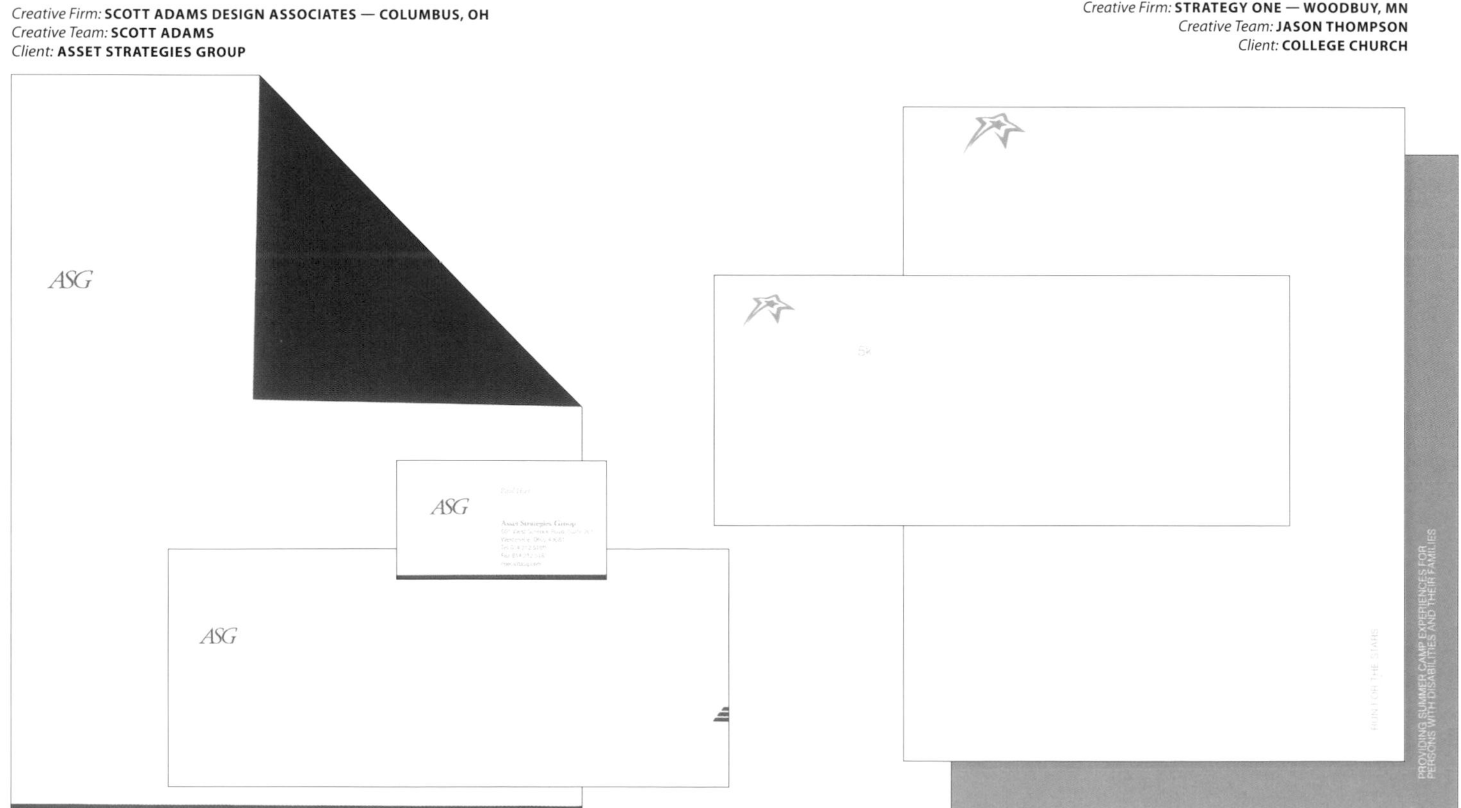

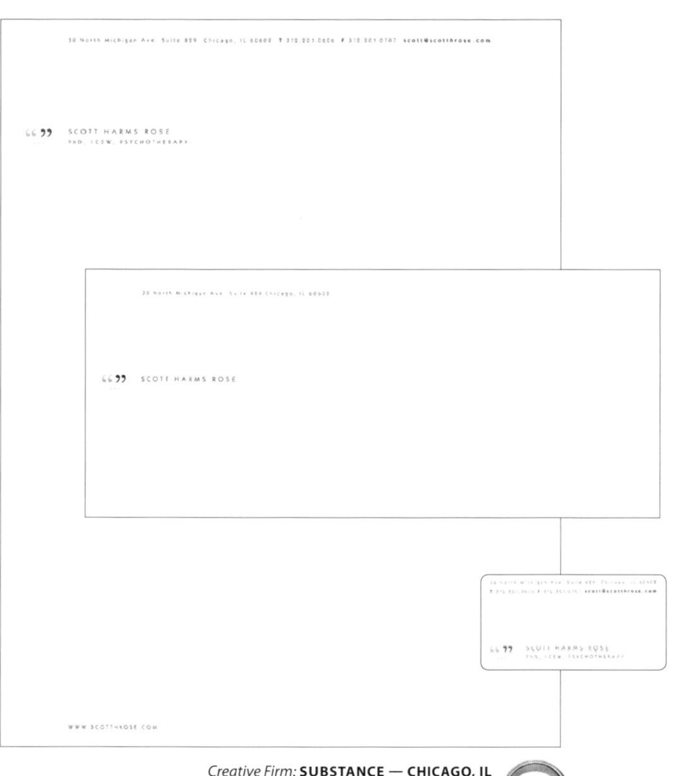

Creative Firm: **SUBSTANCE — CHICAGO, IL**
Creative Team: **MATTHEW BRETT**
Client: **SCOTT HARMS ROSE, PSYCHOTHERAPIST**

Creative Firm: **VOICEBOX CREATIVE — SAN FRANCISCO, CA**
Creative Team: **JACQUES ROSSOUW, KRISTIE WISE**
Client: **SBRAGIA FAMILY VINEYARDS**

Creative Firm: **HELENA SEO DESIGN — SUNNYVALE, CA**
Client: **ANGARA, INC.**

Creative Firm: **VOICEBOX CREATIVE — SAN FRANCISCO, CA**
Creative Team: **JACQUES ROSSOUW, VOICEBOX TEAM, GREG CLARKE, JAN DENTON**
Client: **VINTAGE POINT**

Creative Firm: **ZERO GRAVITY DESIGN GROUP — SMITHTOWN, NY**
Creative Team: **ZERO GRAVITY DESIGN GROUP**
Client: **DIRECT ACCESS PARTNERS**

Creative Firm: **HERE! NETWORKS — NEW YORK, NY**
Creative Team: **ERIC FELDMAN, CRAIG OELRICH**

Creative Firm: **MODERN MARKETING CONCEPTS — LOUISVILLE,KY**
Creative Team: **MARK GROVES**
Client: **MODERN MARKETING CONCEPTS**

Creative Firm: **SIMPATICO DESIGN STUDIO — ALEXANDRIA, VA**
Creative Team: **AMY SIMPSON**
Client: **SIMPATICO DESIGN STUDIO**

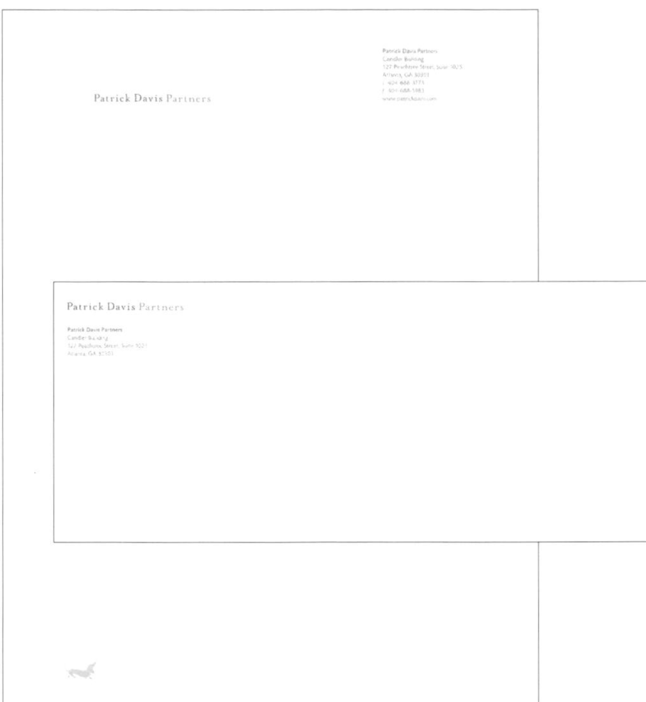

Creative Firm: **KIKU OBATA & COMPANY — ST. LOUIS, MO**
Creative Team: **JOE FLORESCA, ELEANOR SAFE**
Client: **PATRICK DAVIS PARTNERS**

Creative Firm: **ALTERNATIVES — NEW YORK, NY**
Creative Team: **LISA PAWSON**
Client: **AMY TUCKER**

Creative Firm: **SPRINGBOARD CREATIVE — MISSION, KS**
Creative Team: **KEVIN FULLERTON**
Client: **SPRINGBOARD CREATIVE**

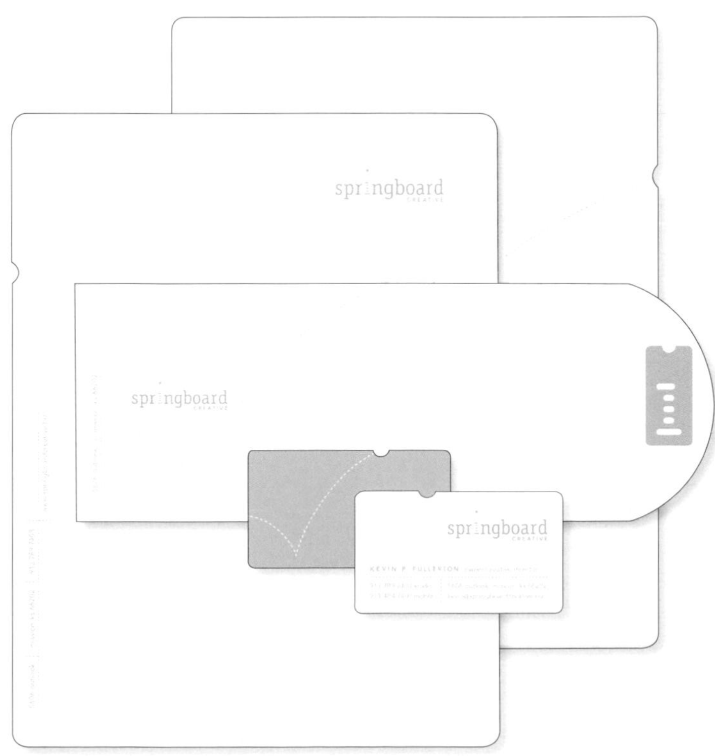

Creative Firm: **ELLEN BRUSS DESIGN — DENVER, CO**
Creative Team: **ELLEN BRUSS, JORGE LAMORA**
Client: **THE LAB AT BELMAR**

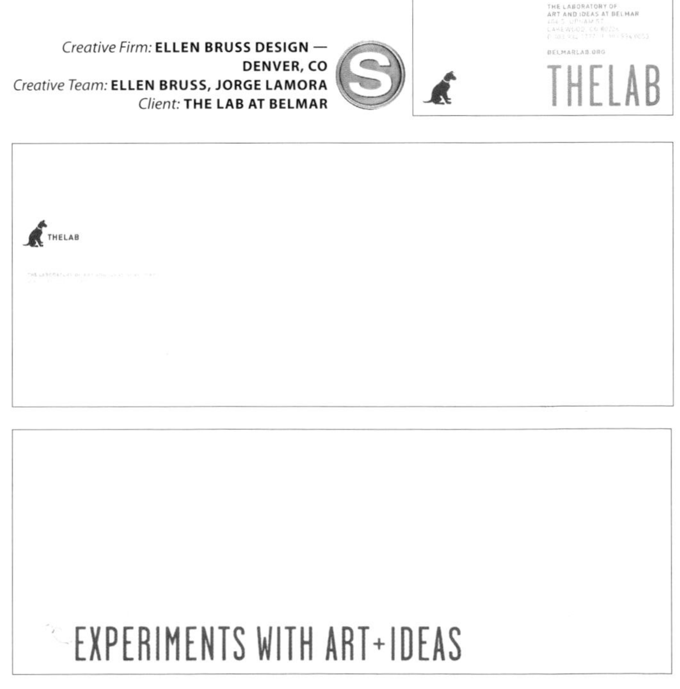

Creative Firm: **STUDIO FIVE — NEW YORK, NY**
Creative Team: **TATIANA AROCHA, MELISSA GORMAN**
Client: **EXPANSION TEAM**

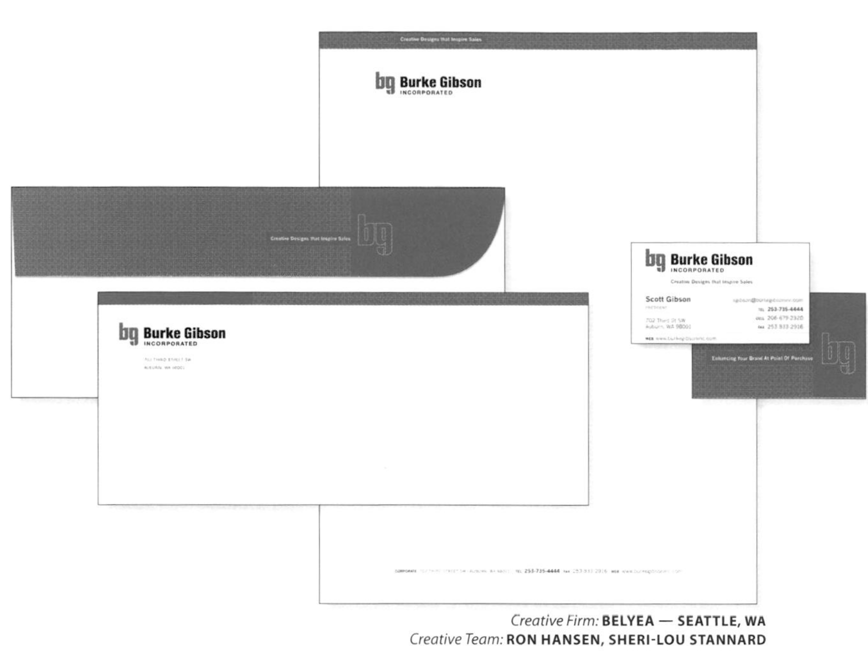

Creative Firm: **BELYEA — SEATTLE, WA**
Creative Team: **RON HANSEN, SHERI-LOU STANNARD**
Client: **BURKE GIBSON**

Creative Firm: **BELYEA — SEATTLE, WA**
Creative Team: **RON HANSEN, SHERI-LOU STANNARD**
Client: **LAIRD NORTON TYEE**

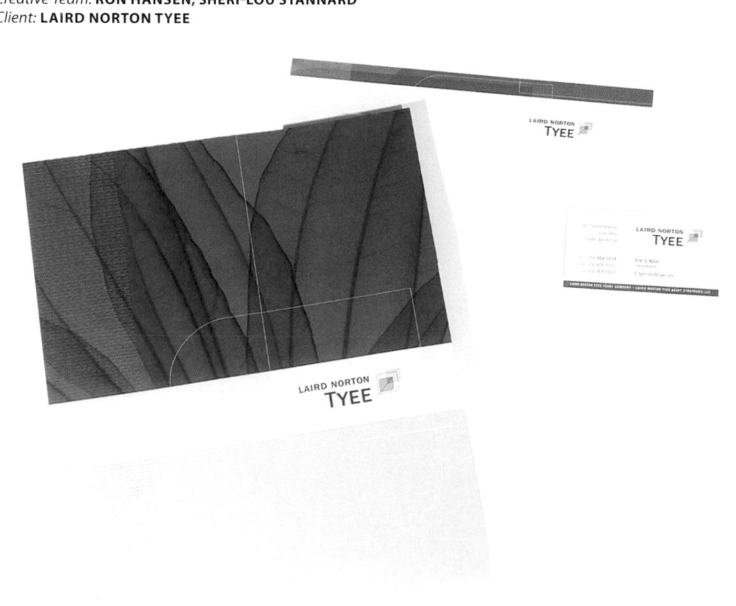

Creative Firm: **JONI RAE AND ASSOCIATES — ENCINO, CA**
Creative Team: **JONI RAE RUSSELL, BEVERLY TRENGOVE**
Client: **JONI RAE AND ASSOCIATES**

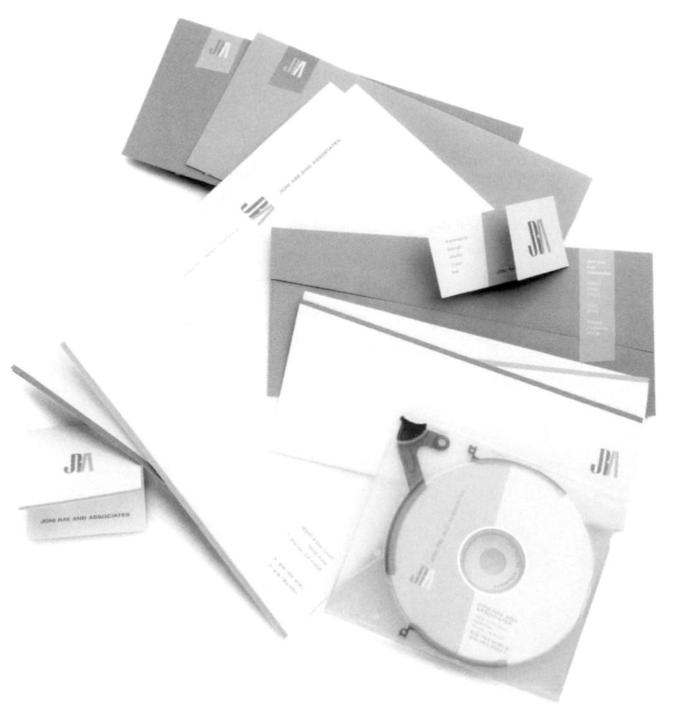

Creative Firm: **HOLOHAN DESIGN — PHILADELPHIA, PA**
Creative Team: **KELLY HOLOHAN, THE IMAGING GROUP , RIS PAPER COMPANY**
Client: **THE HURRICANE POSTER PROJECT**

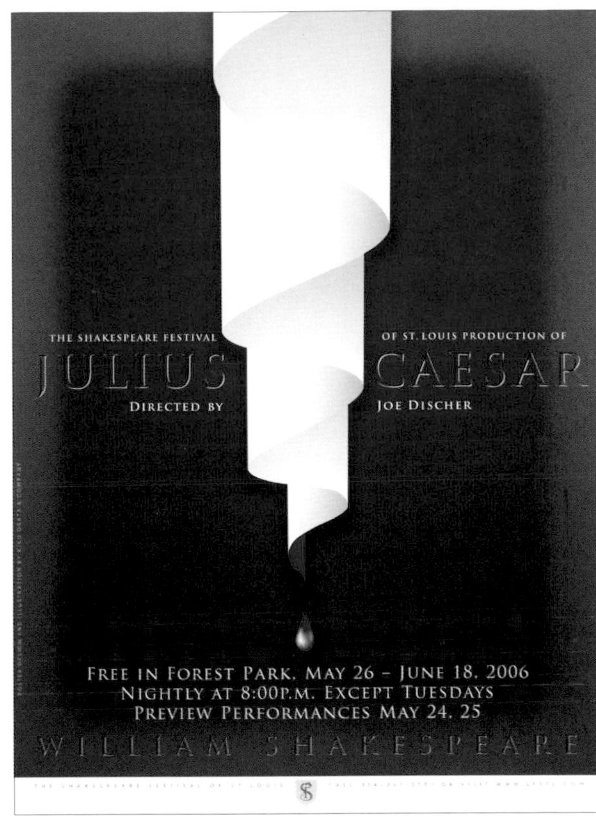

Creative Firm: **KIKU OBATA & COMPANY — ST. LOUIS, MO**
Creative Team: **RICH NELSON**
Client: **THE SHAKESPEARE FESTIVAL OF ST. LOUIS**

Creative Firm: **HERMAN MILLER, INC. — ZEELAND, MI**
Creative Team: **ANDREW DULL, MARLENE CAPOTOSTO**
Client: **HERMAN MILLER, INC.**

Creative Firm: **WESTGROUP CREATIVE — NEW YORK, NY**
Creative Team: **CHIP TOLANEY, MARVIN BERK**
Client: **NEW DANCE GROUP**

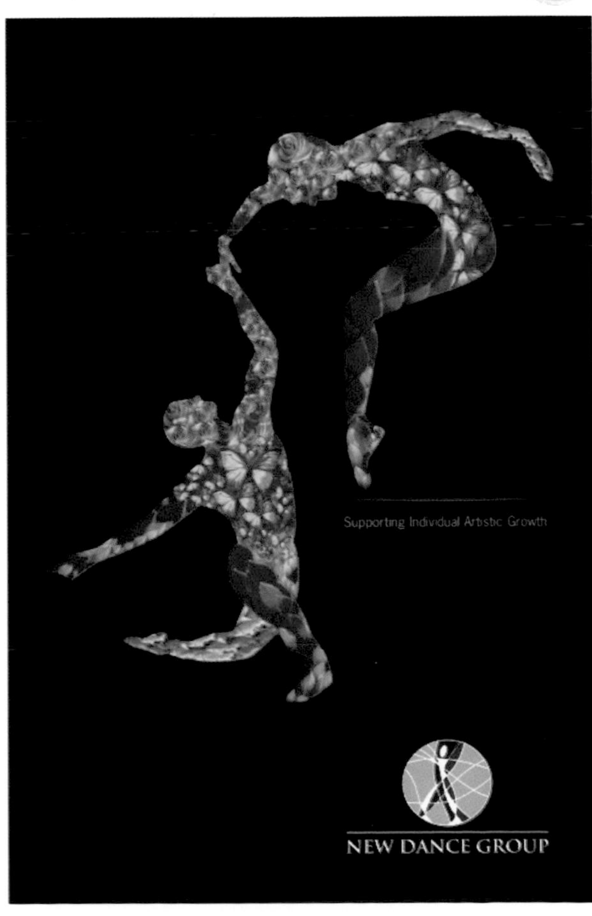

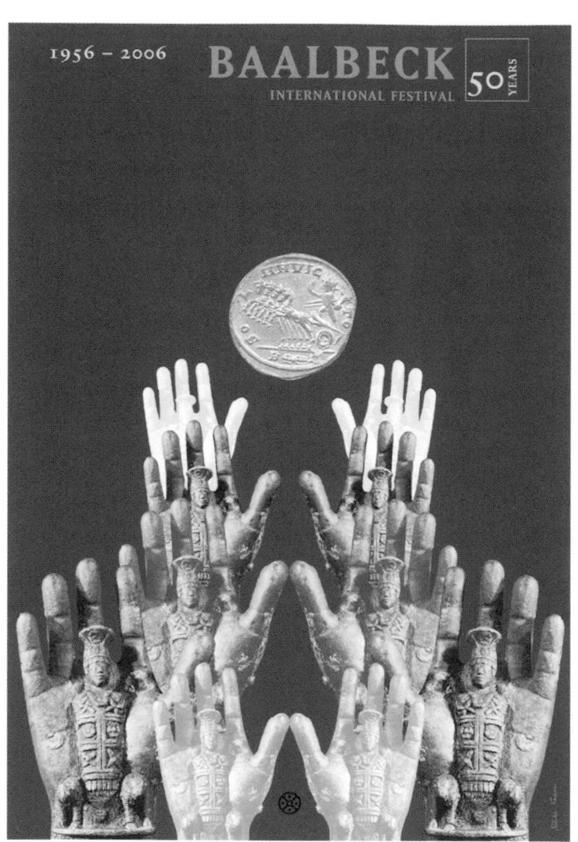

Creative Firm: **NASSAR DESIGN — BROOKLINE, MA**
Creative Team: **NELIDA NASSAR**
Client: **BAALBECK INTERNATIONAL FESTIVAL**

Creative Firm: **RODGERS TOWNSEND — ST. LOUIS, MO**
Creative Team: **TOM HUDDER, LUKE PART, JAKE EDINGER, JAMES SCHWARTZ, CHERYL SPARKS**
Client: **ARTS & EDUCATION COUNCIL OF GREATER ST. LOUIS**

Creative Firm: **AD HARVEST — SIMPSONVILLE, KY**
Creative Team: **MARK GROVES**
Client: **SHELBY COUNTY FAIR**

Creative Firm: **ZYGO COMMUNICATIONS — WYNCOTE, PA**
Creative Team: **SCOTT LASEROW**
Client: **THE HURRICANE POSTER PROJECT**

Creative Firm: **ZERO GRAVITY — SAN MARCOS, TX**
Creative Team: **IVANETE BLANCO**
Client: **JAMES HOUSEFIELD**

Creative Firm: **ATOMIC DESIGN — CROWLEY, TX**
Creative Team: **LEWIS GLASER**
Client: **ELLEN SHELTON/TCU BALLET & MODERN DANCE**

Creative Firm: **RODGERS TOWNSEND — ST. LOUIS, MO**
Creative Team: **TOM HUDDER, MARK ARNOLD, TODD MITCHELL, CHERYL SPARKS**
Client: **CIRCUS FLORA**

Creative Firm: **MCCANN ERICKSON, NEW YORK — NEW YORK, NY**
Creative Team: **BILL OBERLANDER, TOM SULLIVAN, LARRY PLATT, WENDY LEAHY, JOYCE KING THOMAS**
Client: **NIKON**

Creative Firm: **RODGERS TOWNSEND — ST. LOUIS, MO**
Creative Team: **ERIK MATHRE, LIZ FORSYTHE, BILL ECKLOFF, CHERYL SPARKS**
Client: **THE BLACK REP**

Creative Firm: **THE MILLER GROUP — LOS ANGELES, CA**
Creative Team: **RENEE MILLER, SHIN KAWASE, CHRIS ROBB, JOHN HAGE, ERNEST VON ROSEN**
Client: **CHIN CHIN**

Creative Firm: **ALCONE MARKETING — IRVINE, CA**
Creative Team: **CARLOS MUSQUEZ, JULIE KIMURA, SHIVONNE MILLER, LUIS CAMANO, ROBERT WAGT**
Client: **EBAY**

Creative Firm: **RODGERS TOWNSEND — ST. LOUIS, MO**
Creative Team: **TOM HUDDER, JENNY STORINO, JAKE EDINGER, CHERYL SPARKS**
Client: **THE DUBLINER**

Creative Firm: **ONE HUNDRED CHURCH STREET — LOGAN, UT**
Creative Team: **R.P. BISSLAND**
Client: **USU MUSIC DEPARTMENT**

Creative Firm: **LEE STEWART'S CREATIVE WORKS! — CHARLOTTE, NC**
Creative Team: **LEE STEWART, ADAM LINGLE**
Client: **ROWAN REGIONAL MEDICAL CENTER**

Creative Firm: **THE DESIGN CONSORTIUM — NEWARK, NJ**
Creative Team: **NED DREW**
Client: **WHYWEHIDE.COM**

Creative Firm: **MENDES PUBLICIDADE — BELÉM, PARÁ, BRAZIL**
Creative Team: **OSWALDO MENDES, MARIA ALICE PENNA, OCTAVIO CARDOSO**
Client: **DIRETORIA DA FESTA DE NAZARÉ**

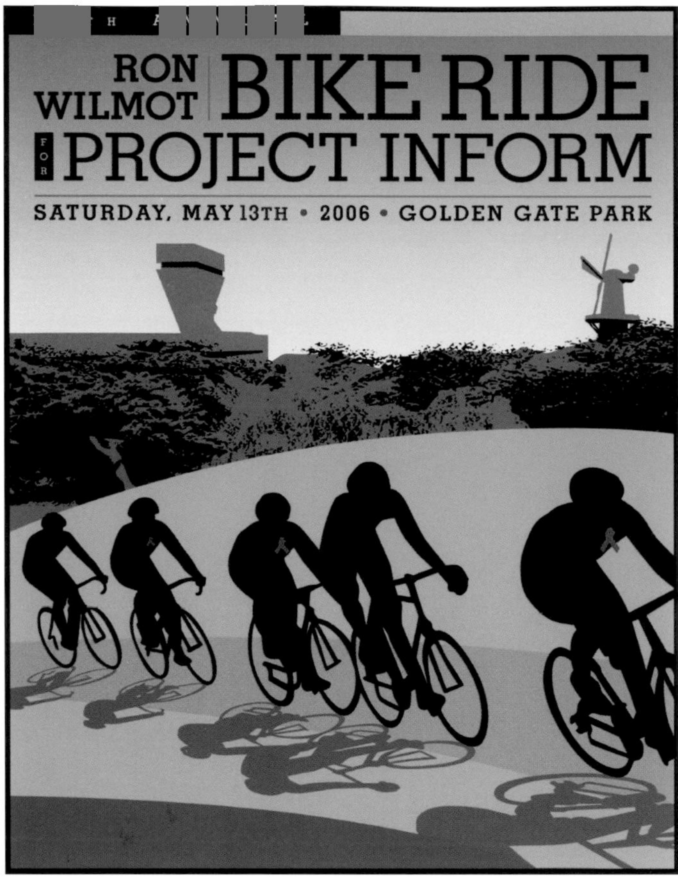

Creative Firm: **BIGWIG DESIGN — SAN FRANCISCO, CA**
Creative Team: **RICHARD LEEDS**
Client: **PROJECT INFORM**

Creative Firm: **HBO OFF-AIR CREATIVE SERVICES — NEW YORK, NY**
Creative Team: **VENUS DENNISON, MARY TCHORBAJIAN, CARLOS TEJEDA, LARRY BURNETT**
Client: **HBO DOCUMENTARY FILMS**

Creative Firm: **RODGERS TOWNSEND — ST. LOUIS, MO**
Creative Team: **TOM HUDDER, LUKE PARTRIDGE, MICHAEL MCCORMICK, BRIAN KUHLMAN, CHERYL SPARKS**
Client: **CARNIVALE D' ART**

Creative Firm: **CSC'S P2 COMMUNICATIONS SERVICES — FALLS CHURCH, VA**
Creative Team: **AARON KOBILIS, TERRY WILSON, TIM DEWAELE, LYNN JEUNETTE, ADAM DONOVAN**
Client: **CSC CORPORATE**

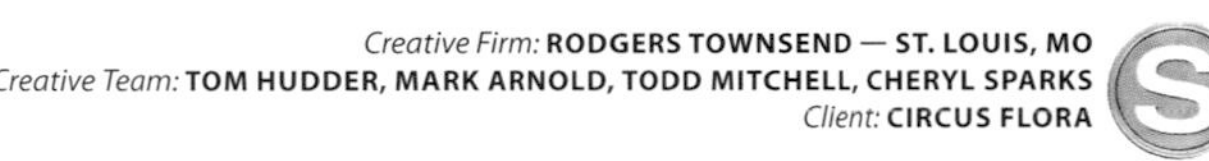

Creative Firm: **RODGERS TOWNSEND — ST. LOUIS, MO**
Creative Team: **TOM HUDDER, MARK ARNOLD, TODD MITCHELL, CHERYL SPARKS**
Client: **CIRCUS FLORA**

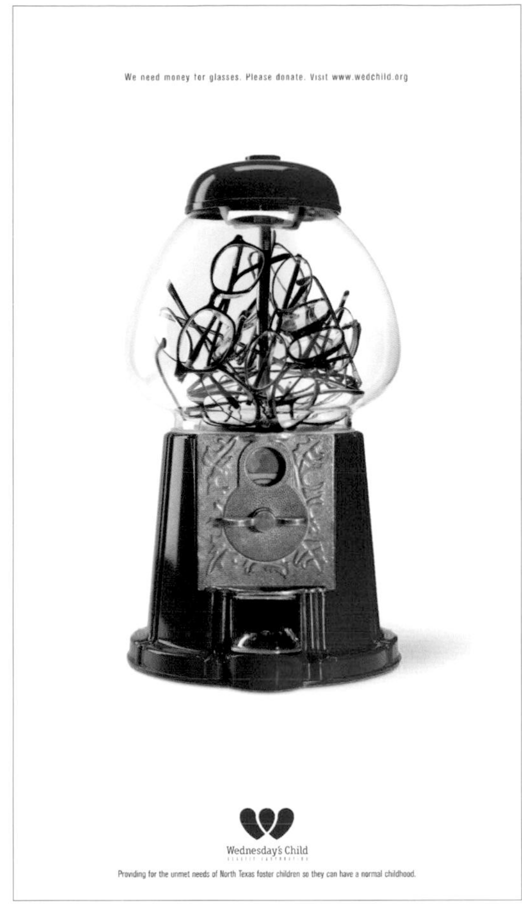

Creative Firm: **DIESTE HARMEL & PARTNERS — DALLAS, TX**
Creative Team: **ALDO QUEVEDO, JAIME ANDRADE, GABRIEL PUERTO, JOSE SUASTE, ALEX TOEDTLI**
Client: **WEDNESDAY'S CHILD BENEFIT CORP.**

Creative Firm: **GREENLIGHT DESIGNS — N. HOLLYWOOD, CA**
Creative Team: **TAMI MAHNKEN, DARRYL SHELLY, MELISSA IRWIN, SHAUN WOOD**
Client: **MILLENIUM FILMS**

Creative Firm: **RODGERS TOWNSEND — ST. LOUIS, MO**
Creative Team: **TOM HUDDER, LUKE PARTRIDGE, MICHAEL MCCORMICK, BRIAN KUHLMAN, CHERYL SPARKS**
Client: **CARNIVALE D' ART**

Creative Firm: **RODGERS TOWNSEND — ST. LOUIS, MO**
Creative Team: **TOM HUDDER, JENNY STORINO, JAKE EDINGER, CHERYL SPARKS**
Client: **THE DUBLINER**

Creative Firm: **BIGWIG DESIGN — SAN FRANCISCO, CA**
Creative Team: **RICHARD LEEDS**
Client: **ACTORS ENSEMBLE OF BERKELEY**

Creative Firm: **RODGERS TOWNSEND — ST. LOUIS, MO**
Creative Team: **ERIK MATHRE, LIZ FORSYTHE, BILL ECKLOFF, CHERYL SPARKS**
Client: **THE BLACK REP**

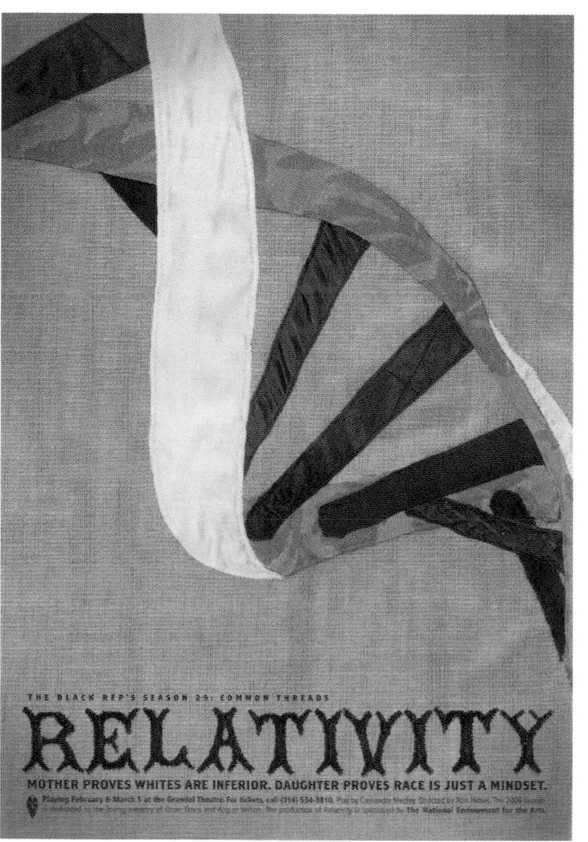

Creative Firm: **INTELLIGENT FISH STUDIO — WOODBUY, MN**
Creative Team: **BRIAN DANAHER, JOHN PHOTOS**
Client: **ACE HARDWARE CORP**

Creative Firm: **RODGERS TOWNSEND — ST. LOUIS, MO**
Creative Team: **ERIK MATHRE, LIZ FORSYTHE, BILL ECKLOFF, CHERYL SPARKS**
Client: **THE BLACK REP**

Creative Firm: **30SIXTY ADVERTISING+DESIGN, INC. — LOS ANGELES, CA**
Creative Team: **HENRY VIZCARRA, PÄR LARSSON, DAVID FUSCELLARO, BRUCE VENTANILLA, TUYET VONG**
Client: **BEYOND THE BELL**

Creative Firm: **THE MONOGRAM GROUP — CHICAGO, IL**
Creative Team: **HAROLD WOODRIDGE, BRETT HAWTHORNE, CHRISTA VELBEL**
Client: **VICTORY GARDENS THEATER**

Creative Firm: **HOTSAUCE — NEW YORK, NY**
Creative Team: **WYNDY SLOAN, ANASTASIA VASILAKIS**
Client: **NYC AFFILIATE OF THE SUSAN G. KOMEN FOUNDATION**

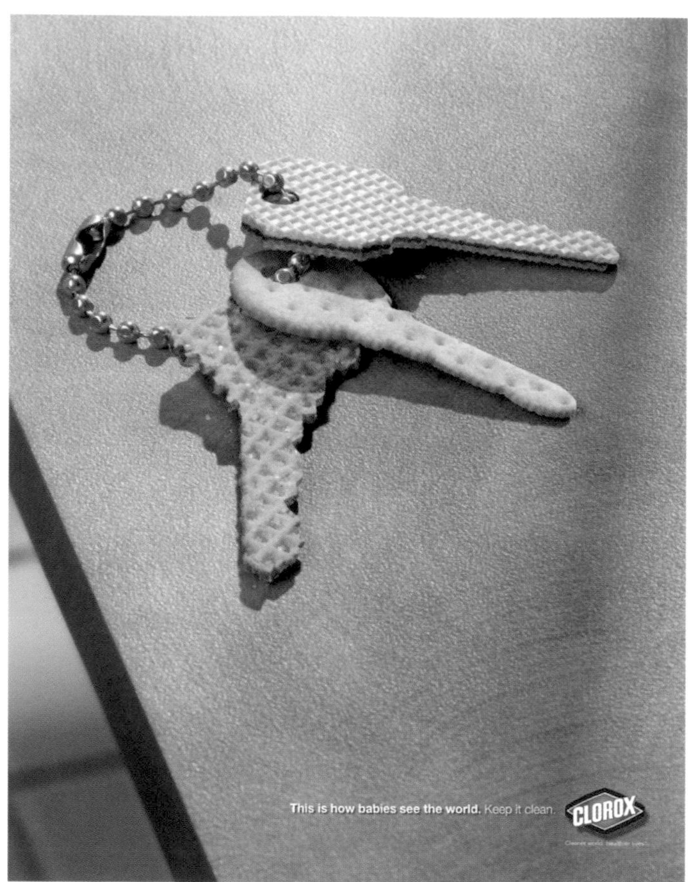

Creative Firm: **DIESTE HARMEL & PARTNERS — DALLAS, TX**
Creative Team: **ALDO QUEVEDO, CARLOS TOURNE, PATRICIA MARTINEZ, RAYMUNDO VALDEZ, DIEGO DUPRAT**
Client: **CLOROX**

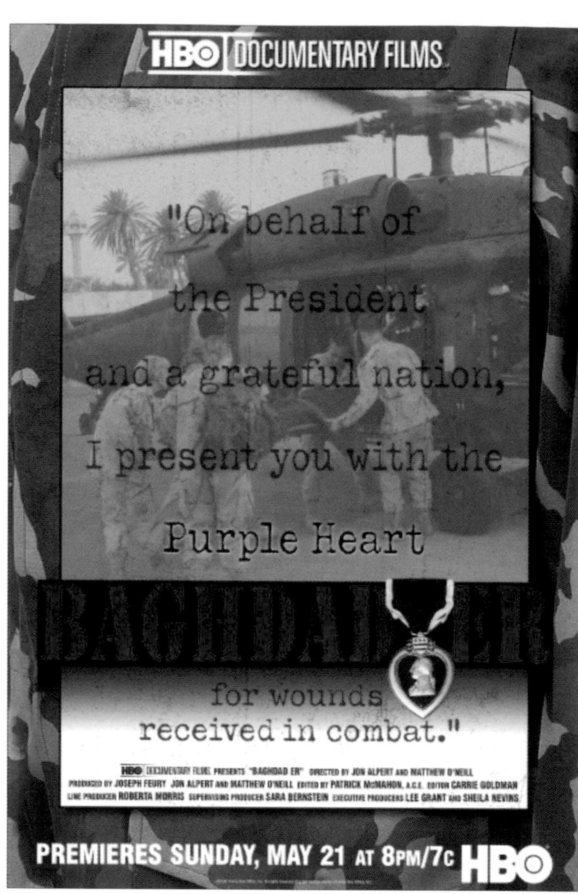

Creative Firm: **HBO OFF-AIR CREATIVE SERVICES — NEW YORK, NY**
Creative Team: **MARY TCHORBAJIAN, TONY VIOLA, VENUS DENNISON**
Client: **HBO DOCUMENTARY FILMS**

Creative Firm: **AD HARVEST — SIMPSONVILLE, KY**
Creative Team: **MARK GROVES**
Client: **SHELBYVILLE HORSE SHOW**

Creative Firm: **RODGERS TOWNSEND — ST. LOUIS, MO**
Creative Team: **ERIK MATHRE, LIZ FORSYTHE, BILL ECKLOFF, CHERYL SPARKS**
Client: **THE BLACK REP**

Creative Firm: **HOLOHAN DESIGN — PHILADELPHIA, PA**
Creative Team: **KELLY HOLOHAN**
Client: **TYLER SCHOOL OF ART**

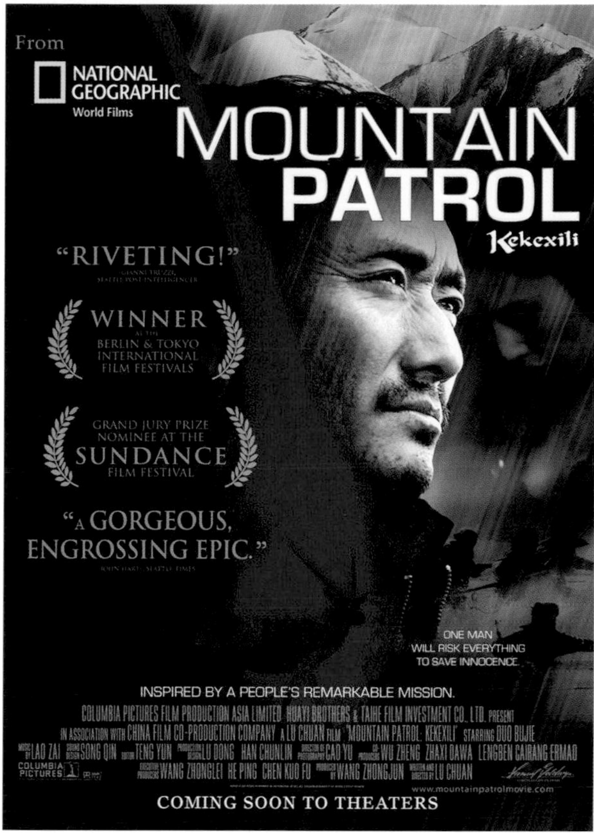

Creative Firm: **GREENLIGHT DESIGNS — N. HOLLYWOOD, CA**
Creative Team: **TAMI MAHNKEN, DARRYL SHELLY, MELISSA IRWIN, SHAUN WOOD**
Client: **COLUMBIA PICTURES**

Creative Firm: **RODGERS TOWNSEND — ST. LOUIS, MO**
Creative Team: **TOM HUDDER, MARK ARNOLD, TODD MITCHELL, CHERYL SPARKS**
Client: **CIRCUS FLORA**

Creative Firm: **HBO OFF-AIR CREATIVE SERVICES — NEW YORK, NY**
Creative Team: **JOSE MENDEZ, IVY CALAHORRANO, VENUS DENNISON**
Client: **HBO LATINO**

Creative Firm: **HBO OFF-AIR CREATIVE SERVICES — NEW YORK, NY**
Creative Team: **JOSE MENDEZ, IVY CALAHORRANO, VENUS DENNISON**
Client: **HBO SEGMENT MARKETING**

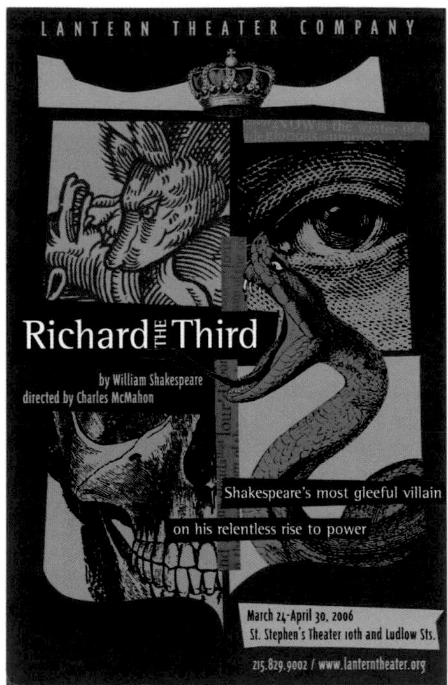

Creative Firm: **SHERIFF DESIGN — ELKINS PARK, PA**
Creative Team: **PAUL SHERIFF**
Client: **LANTERN THEATER COMPANY**

Creative Firm: **CHASE CREATIVE — ST. PETE BEACH, FL**
Creative Team: **GEORGE CHASE**
Client: **BAMBOOZLE**

Creative Firm: **RODGERS TOWNSEND — ST. LOUIS, MO**
Creative Team: **TOM HUDDER, LUKE PARTRIDGE, MICHAEL MCCORMICK, BRIAN KUHLMAN, CHERYL SPARKS**
Client: **CARNIVALE D' ART**

Creative Firm: **RODGERS TOWNSEND — ST. LOUIS, MO**
Creative Team: **TOM HUDDER, JENNY STORINO, JAKE EDINGER, CHERYL SPARKS**
Client: **THE DUBLINER**

Creative Firm: **YOUNG & RUBICAM GMBH & CO. KG — FRANKFURT AM MAIN, HESSEN, GERMANY**
Creative Team: **UWE MARQUARDT, XENIA KLEIN**
Client: **ASITA GMBH**

Creative Firm: **HBO OFF-AIR CREATIVE SERVICES — NEW YORK, NY**
Creative Team: **ANA RACELIS, JOSE MENDEZ, VENUS DENNISON, LARRY BURNETT**
Client: **HBO PPV SPORT**

Creative Firm: **DIESTE HARMEL & PARTNERS — DALLAS, TX**
Creative Team: **ALDO QUEVEDO, JAIME ANDRADE, GABRIEL PUERTO, JOSE SUASTE, ALEX TOEDTLI**
Client: **WEDNESDAY'S CHILD BENEFIT CORP.**

Creative Firm: **GRAFISK DESIGN — ASTORIA, NY**
Creative Team: **JOHN FISK**
Client: **LIP THEATRE COMPANY**

Creative Firm: **RODGERS TOWNSEND — ST. LOUIS, MO**
Creative Team: **TOM HUDDER, JENNY STORINO, JAKE EDINGER, CHERYL SPARKS**
Client: **THE DUBLINER**

Creative Firm: **QUALCOMM — SAN DIEGO, CA**
Creative Team: **TYLER MOLHOOK, CHRIS LEE**
Client: **SOUTHERN CAREGIVER RESOURCE CENTER**

Creative Firm: **RODGERS TOWNSEND — ST. LOUIS, MO**
Creative Team: **ERIK MATHRE, LIZ FORSYTHE, BILL ECKLOFF, CHERYL SPARKS**
Client: **THE BLACK REP**

Creative Firm: **ERIC CAI DESIGN CO. — BEIJING, CHINA**
Creative Team: **ERIC CAI SHI WEI, ESTHER TAN YAN**
Client: **ERIC CAI DESIGN CO.**

Creative Firm: **AGENCY X ADS — SAN FRANCISCO, CA**
Creative Team: **LOTUS CHILD, DENISE ST. LOUIS**
Client: **ALICE RADIO**

Creative Firm: **VENTRESS DESIGN GROUP — FRANKLIN, TN**
Creative Team: **TOM VENTRESS, ERIC VENTRESS**
Client: **FRIST CENTER FOR THE VISUAL ARTS**

Creative Firm: **ALCONE MARKETING — IRVINE, CA**
Creative Team: **LUIS CAMANO, SHIVONNE MILLER, JULIE KIMURA**
Client: **CALIFORNIA LOTTERY**

Creative Firm: **RAVENHOUSE DESIGN PRACTICE — TACOMA, WA**
Creative Team: **JAY HEMBER, LANCE KAGEY, TOM LLEWELLYN**
Client: **WINTERGRASS**

Creative Firm: **GRAFISK DESIGN — ASTORIA, NY**
Creative Team: **JOHN FISK**
Client: **LIP THEATRE COMPANY**

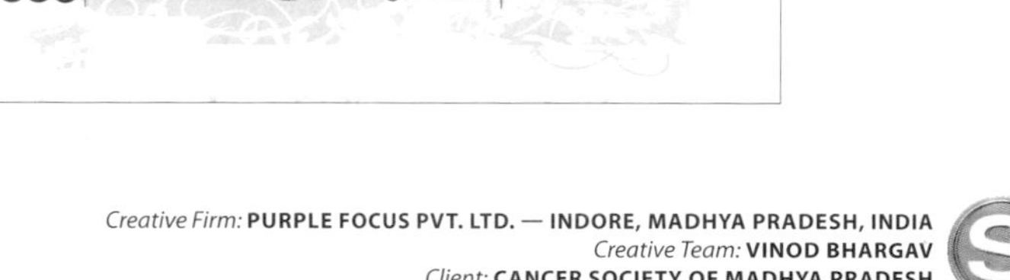
Creative Firm: **PURPLE FOCUS PVT. LTD. — INDORE, MADHYA PRADESH, INDIA**
Creative Team: **VINOD BHARGAV**
Client: **CANCER SOCIETY OF MADHYA PRADESH**

Creative Firm: **HOFFMAN/LEWIS — SAN FRANCISCO, CA**
Creative Team: **SHARON KRINSKY, JAMES CABRAL, MELISSA LACHANCE, JOE GATTI**
Client: **TOYOTA**

Creative Firm: **RODGERS TOWNSEND — ST. LOUIS, MO**
Creative Team: **TOM HUDDER, JENNY STORINO, JAKE EDINGER, CHERYL SPARKS**
Client: **THE DUBLINER**

Creative Firm: **VANPELT CREATIVE — GARLAND, TX**
Creative Team: **CHIP VANPELT, JOHN EVANS**
Client: **MUSEUM OF THE BIG BEND**

Creative Firm: **RODGERS TOWNSEND — ST. LOUIS, MO**
Creative Team: **TOM HUDDER, VALERIE TERILLA, KAY COCHRAN, STEFAN HESTER, CHERYL SPARKS**
Client: **HUMANE SOCIETY OF MISSOURI**

Creative Firm: **AD PLANET GROUP / ACE: DAYTONS ADVERTISING — SINGAPORE**
Creative Team: **ALFRED TEO, JOE TAN, AMOUS SEOW, LOUISE BOLO, ANTHONY SIOW, BEN LIM**
Client: **NATURE SOCIETY SINGAPORE**

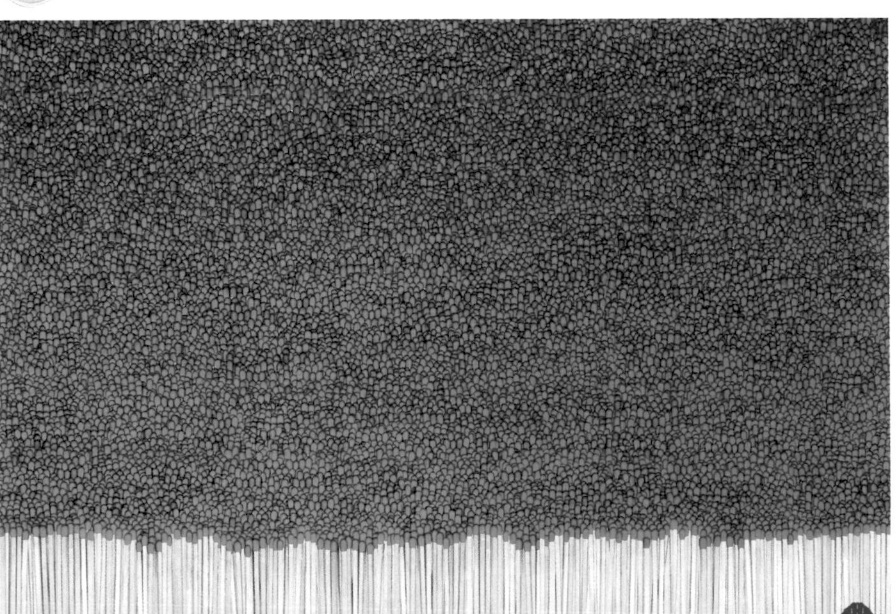

Creative Firm: **ALCONE MARKETING — IRVINE, CA**
Creative Team: **LUIS CAMANO, SHIVONNE MILLER**
Client: **CALIFORNIA LOTTERY**

Creative Firm: **AD PLANET GROUP / ACE: DAYTONS ADVERTISING — SINGAPORE**
Creative Team: **LEO TECK CHONG, ALFRED TEO, KIM TAN, JENNIFER OU, BEN LIM, JAMES TAN**
Client: **PEEP ONE EROTIC DRINK**

Creative Firm: **PATRICK HENRY CREATIVE PROMOTIONS, INC. — STAFFORD, TX**
Creative Team: **PHCP PRESTIGE ART TEAM, DAVE PAPAZIAN**
Client: **RED LION HOTELS CORPORATION**

Creative Firm: **HBO OFF-AIR CREATIVE SERVICES — NEW YORK, NY**
Creative Team: **SETH LUTSKY, ANA RACELIS, VENUS DENNISON**
Client: **HBO SEGMENT MARKETING**

Creative Firm: **PURPLE FOCUS PVT. LTD. — INDORE, MADHYA PRADESH, INDIA**
Creative Team: **SATYAJIT RAI, VINOD BHARGAV**
Client: **CHANNEL SITI**

Creative Firm: **RODGERS TOWNSEND — ST. LOUIS, MO**
Creative Team: **TOM HUDDER, VALERIE TIRELLA, KAY COCHRAN, STEFAN HESTER, CHERYL SPARKS**
Client: **HUMANE SOCIETY OF MISSOURI**

Creative Firm: **DIESTE HARMEL & PARTNERS — DALLAS, TX**
Creative Team: **ALDO QUEVEDO, CARLOS TOURNE, PATRICIA MARTINEZ, RAYMUNDO VALDEZ, DIEGO DUPRAT**
Client: **CLOROX**

Creative Firm: **RODGERS TOWNSEND — ST. LOUIS, MO**
Creative Team: **TOM HUDDER, VALERIE TIRELLA, KAY COCHRAN, STEFAN HESTER, CHERYL SPARKS**
Client: **HUMANE SOCIETY OF MISSOURI**

Creative Firm: **BRUKETA&ZINIC — ZAGREB, CROATIA (HRVATSKA)**
Creative Team: **IMELDA RAMOVIC, MIREL HADZIJUSUFOVIC**
Client: **QUEER ZAGREB**

Creative Firm: **RODGERS TOWNSEND — ST. LOUIS, MO**
Creative Team: **TOM HUDDER, LUKE PARTRIDGE, JAKE EDINGER, JAMES SCHWARTZ, CHERYL SPARKS**
Client: **ARTS & EDUCATION COUNCIL OF GREATER ST. LOUIS**

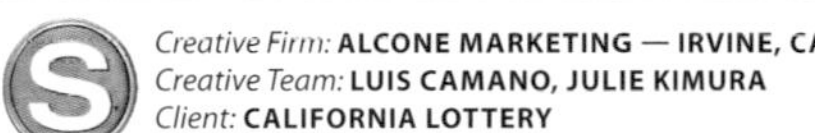

Creative Firm: **ALCONE MARKETING — IRVINE, CA**
Creative Team: **LUIS CAMANO, JULIE KIMURA**
Client: **CALIFORNIA LOTTERY**

Creative Firm: **RODGERS TOWNSEND — ST. LOUIS, MO**
Creative Team: **ERIK MATHRE, MARK ARNOLD, TODD MITCHELL, CHERYL SPARKS**
Client: **HUMANE SOCIETY OF MISSOURI**

Creative Firm: **MARIBETH KRADEL-WEITZEL DESIGN — POTTSTOWN, PA**
Creative Team: **MARIBETH KRADEL-WEITZEL**
Client: **THE HURRICANE POSTER PROJECT**

Creative Firm: **SOMMESE DESIGN — PORT MATILDA, PA**
Creative Team: **LANNY SOMMESE**
Client: **CENTRAL PENNSYLVANIA FESTIVAL OF THE ARTS**

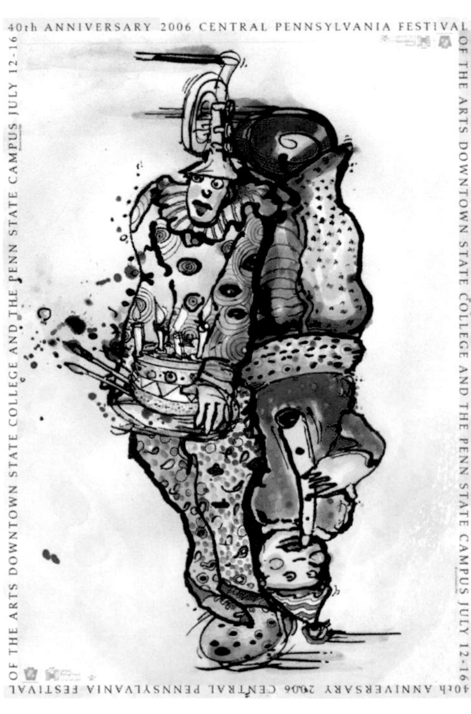

Creative Firm: **ACART COMMUNICATIONS — OTTAWA, ON, CANADA**
Creative Team: **VERNON LAI, TOM MEGGINSON, JOHN STARESINIC, DONNA STOTT**
Client: **CUTA**

Creative Firm: **RODGERS TOWNSEND — ST. LOUIS, MO**
Creative Team: **TOM HUDDER, JENNY STORINO, JAKE EDINGER, CHERYL SPARKS**
Client: **THE DUBLINER**

Creative Firm: **SERAN DESIGN — KEEZLETOWN, VA**
Creative Team: **SANG YOON**
Client: **SCHOOL OF MUSIC, JAMES MADISON UNIVERSITY**

Creative Firm: **DEVER DESIGNS — LAUREL, MD**
Creative Team: **JEFFREY DEVER**
Client: **DEVER DESIGNS**

Creative Firm: **ALL MEDIA PROJECTS LIMITED — PORT OF SPAIN, TRINIDAD AND TOBAGO**
Creative Team: **RICHARD RYAN, BRENT MATTHEW, DEBBIE GARRAWAY, JULIEN GREENIDGE**
Client: **CLICO**

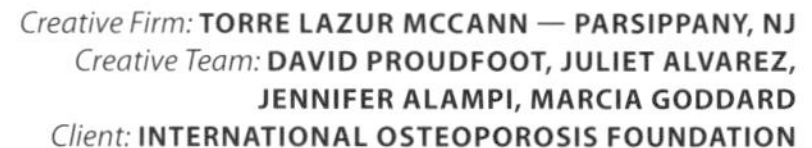

Creative Firm: **TORRE LAZUR MCCANN — PARSIPPANY, NJ**
Creative Team: **DAVID PROUDFOOT, JULIET ALVAREZ, JENNIFER ALAMPI, MARCIA GODDARD**
Client: **INTERNATIONAL OSTEOPOROSIS FOUNDATION**

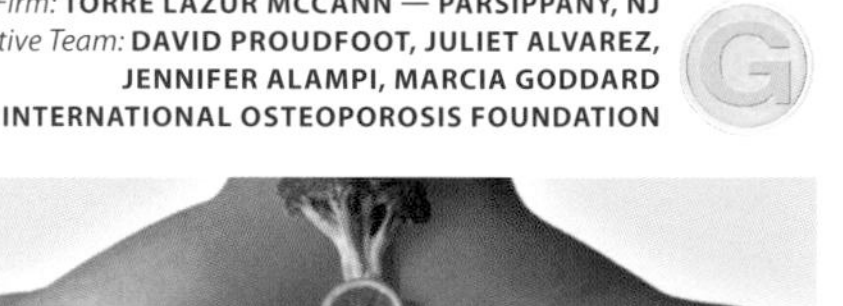

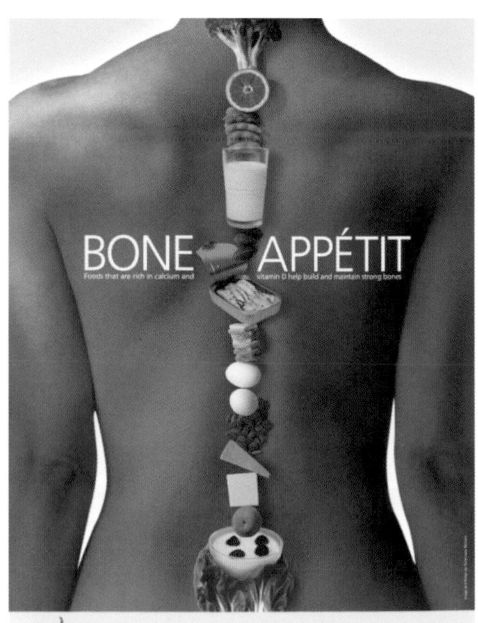

Creative Firm: **HBO — NEW YORK, NY**
Creative Team: **VENUS DENNISON, MARY TCHORBAJIAN, CARLOS TEJEDA**
Client: **HBO DOCUMENTARY FILMS**

Creative Firm: **MARIBETH KRADEL-WEITZEL DESIGN — POTTSTOWN, PA**
Creative Team: **MARIBETH KRADEL-WEITZEL**
Client: **PHILADELPHIA UNIVERSITY**

Creative Firm: **RODGERS TOWNSEND — ST. LOUIS, MO**
Creative Team: **TOM HUDDER, LUKE PARTRIDGE, JAKE EDINGER, JAMES SCHWARTZ, CHERYL SPARKS**
Client: **ARTS & EDUCATION COUNCIL OF GREATER ST. LOUIS**

NEVER UNDERESTIMATE THE POWER OF ART.

Creative Firm: **VANPELT CREATIVE — GARLAND, TX**
Creative Team: **CHIP VANPELT, J.W. BURKEY, MICHAEL EGAN**
Client: **CHAMBER MUSIC INTERNATIONAL**

Creative Firm: **ONE HUNDRED CHURCH STREET — LOGAN, UT**
Creative Team: **R.P. BISLAND**
Client: **CACHE VALLEY GARDENERS MARKET**

Creative Firm: **MARIBETH KRADEL-WEITZEL DESIGN — POTTSTOWN, PA**
Creative Team: **MARIBETH KRADEL-WEITZEL**
Client: **AIGA PHILADELPHIA**

Creative Firm: **YELLOW SHOES CREATIVE WEST, DISNEYLAND RESORT — ANAHEIM, CA**
Creative Team: **SCOTT STARKEY, JANE ROHAN, WES CLARK, MARTY MULLER, JACQUELYN MOE**
Client: **DISNEYLAND RESORT**

Creative Firm: **RUSTY GEORGE DESIGN — TACOMA, WA**
Creative Team: **RYAN MELINE**
Client: **POINT DEFIANCE ZOO & AQUARIUM**

Creative Firm: **BBK STUDIO — GRAND RAPIDS, MI**
Creative Team: **YANG KIM, JASON MURRAY, MICHELE CHARTIER, INTEGRA**
Client: **CMP**

Creative Firm: **RODGERS TOWNSEND — ST. LOUIS, MO**
Creative Team: **TOM HUDDER, LUKE PARTRIDGE, JAKE EDINGER, JAMES SCHWARTZ, CHERYL SPARKS**
Client: **ARTS & EDUCATION COUNCIL OF GREATER ST. LOUIS**

Creative Firm: **HITCHCOCK FLEMING & ASSOCIATES INC. — AKRON, OH**
Creative Team: **NICK BETRO, CHUCK REPEDE, LENNY SPENGLER, MATT MCCALLUM**
Client: **GOODYEAR TIRE & RUBBER COMPANY**

Creative Firm: **WESTERN MICHIGAN UNIVERSITY — KALAMAZOO, MI**
Creative Team: **PRAVIN SEVAK, ARVIND SEVAK, KALPESH PATEL**
Client: **PRAVIN C SEVAK**

Creative Firm: **RODGERS TOWNSEND — ST. LOUIS, MO**
Creative Team: **TOM HUDDER, MARK ARNOLD, TODD MITCHELL, CHERYL SPARKS**
Client: **CIRCUS FLORA**

Creative Firm: **YOUNG & RUBICAM GMBH & CO. KG — FRANKFURT AM MAIN, HESSEN, GERMANY**
Creative Team: **CHRISTIAN DAUL, UWE MARQUARDT, HELGE KNIESS, KARSTEN RUTZ, THOMAS BALZER**
Client: **DIALOGMUSEUM**

Creative Firm: **MCCANN ERICKSON, NEW YORK — NEW YORK, NY**
Creative Team: **CHRIS CEREDA, JOYCE KING THOMAS, SONIA ZOBEL, ROBERT FISCHER**
Client: **MASTERCARD AFFLUENT CAMPAIGN**

Creative Firm: **FRY HAMMOND BARR — ORLANDO, FL**
Creative Team: **TIM FISHER, SEAN BRUNSON, SANDRA LAWTON, JOHN DEEB, STEPHANIE RUELKE**
Client: **ORLANDO SCIENCE CENTER**

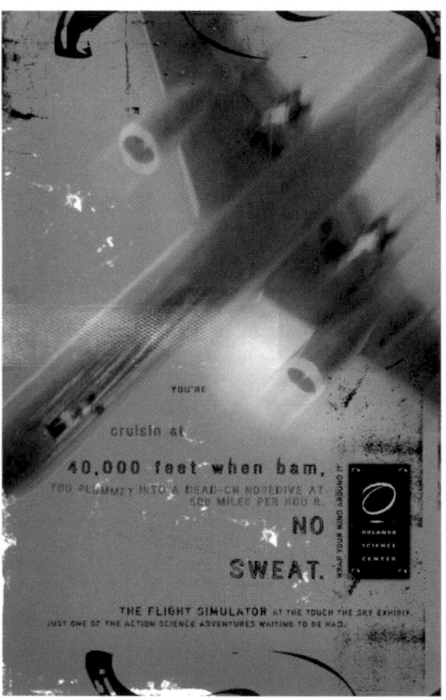

Creative Firm: **AD PLANET GROUP / ACE: DAYTONS ADVERTISING — SINGAPORE**
Creative Team: **LEO TECK CHONG, ALFRED TEO, CHEN YILONG, ANDREW LEONG KAR POH**
Client: **SINGAPORE TRAFFIC POLICE**

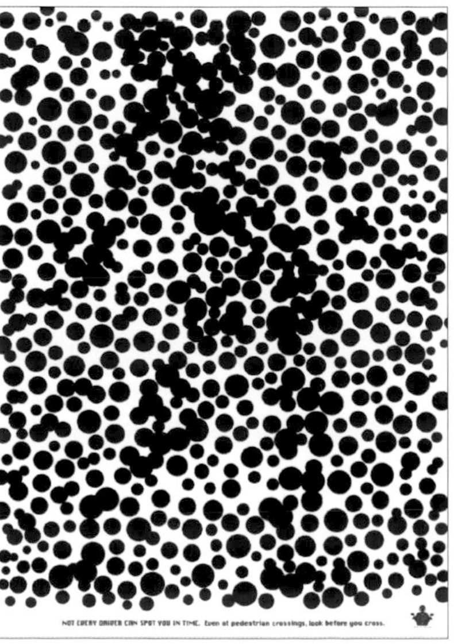

Creative Firm: **ALCONE MARKETING — IRVINE, CA**
Creative Team: **LUIS CAMANO, CARLOS MUSQUEZ, SHIVONNE MILLER, JULIE KIMURA**
Client: **CALIFORNIA LOTTERY**

Creative Firm: **TAXI CANADA INC. — TORONTO, ON, CANADA**
Creative Team: **ZAK MROUEH, ROSE SAUQUILLO, JOHNNIE INGRAM, ALEXIS GROPPER, JEREMY DIMMOCK, AMANDA GASPARD**
Client: **FLOW 93.5**

Creative Firm: **CSC'S P2 COMMUNICATIONS SERVICES — FALLS CHURCH, VA**
Creative Team: **MARK RICHARDS, TERRY WILSON, LALITHA SUNDARAM**
Client: **CSC'S P2 COMMUNICATIONS SERVICES - SELF-PROMOTION**

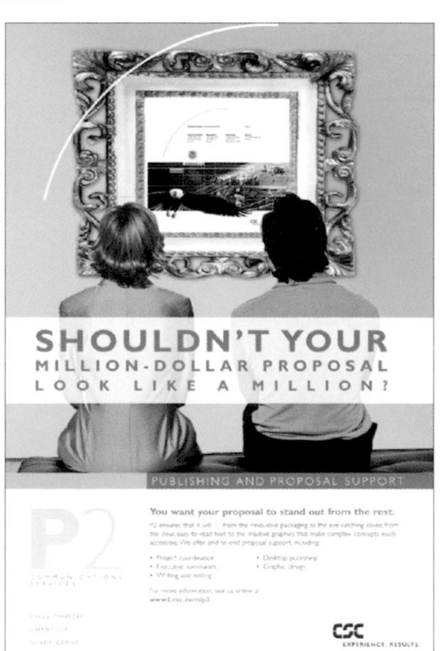

Creative Firm: **RODGERS TOWNSEND — ST. LOUIS, MO**
Creative Team: **ERIK MATHRE, LIZ FORSYTHE, BILL ECKLOFF, CHERYL SPARKS**
Client: **THE BLACK REP**

Creative Firm: **MIKE SALISBURY EFFECTIVE CREATIVE STRATEGIES — VENICE, CA**
Creative Team: **MIKE SALISBURY, JIM SHOEMAKER**
Client: **TRIUMPH USA**

Creative Firm: **ALL MEDIA PROJECTS LIMITED — PORT OF SPAIN, TRINIDAD AND TOBAGO**
Creative Team: **CLINT WILLIAMS, MARISA CAMEJO, RICHARD RYAN, JULIEN GREENIDGE, JOSIANE KHAN**
Client: **BP TRINIDAD AND TOBAGO (BPTT)**

Creative Firm: **RODGERS TOWNSEND — ST. LOUIS, MO**
Creative Team: **TOM HUDDER, LUKE PARTRIDGE, JAKE EDINGER, JAMES SCHWARTZ, CHERYL SPARKS**
Client: **ARTS & EDUCATION COUNCIL OF GREATER ST. LOUIS**

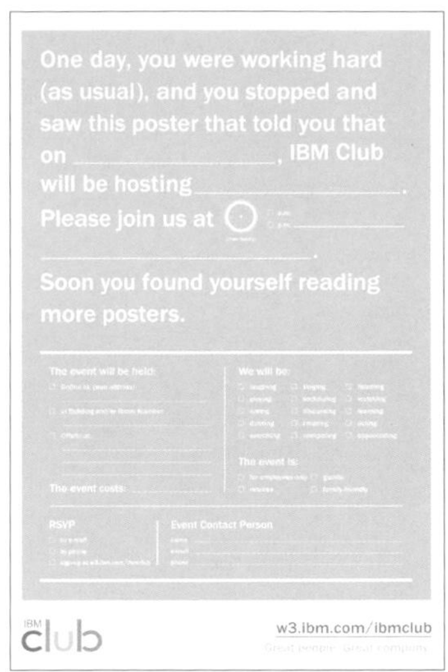

Creative Firm: **VSA PARTNERS, INC. — CHICAGO, IL**
Creative Team: **CURT SCHREIBER, STEVE RYAN, ASHLEY LIPPARD, WENDY BELT**
Client: **IBM CORPORATION**

Creative Firm: **CMT — NEW YORK, NY**
Creative Team: **JAMES HITCHCOCK, AMIE NGUYEN, LINDA ZACK**
Client: **CMT**

Creative Firm: **RODGERS TOWNSEND — ST. LOUIS, MO**
Creative Team: **TOM HUDDER, LUKE PARTRIDGE, MICHAEL MCCORMICK, BRIAN KUHLMAN, CHERYL SPARKS**
Client: **CARNIVALE D' ART**

Creative Firm: **ERIC CAI DESIGN CO. — BEIJING, CHINA**
Creative Team: **ERIC CAI SHI WEI, DUAN LIAN, ESTHER TAN YAN**
Client: **CITY CLUB MAGAZINE**

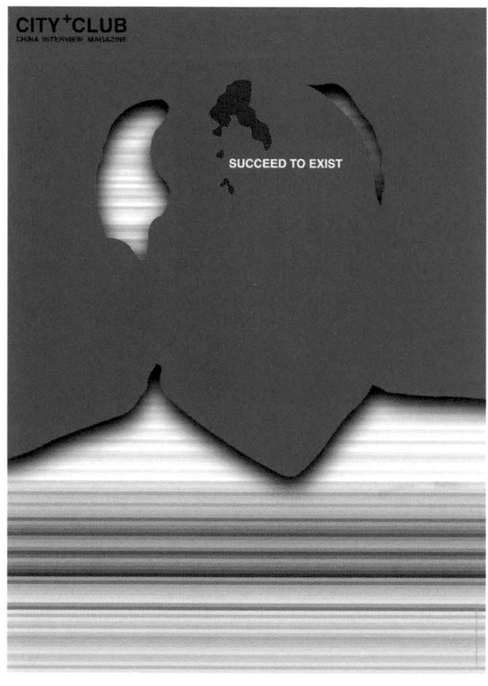

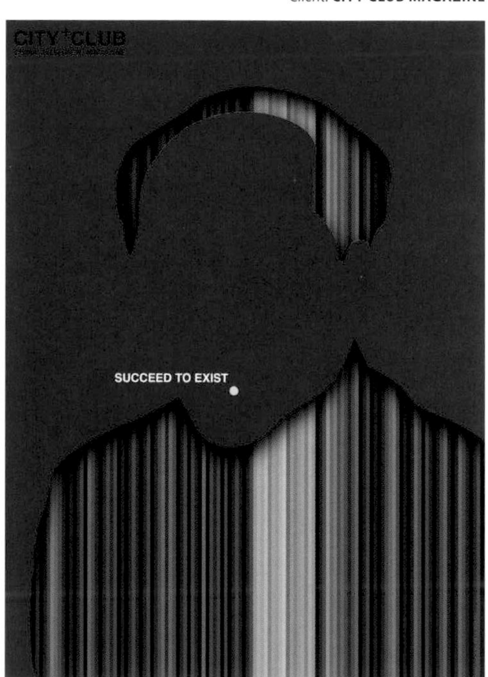

Creative Firm: **KOCH CREATIVE GROUP — WICHITA, KS**
Creative Team: **JASON GRAMKE, JASON FORTUNE, DUSTIN JOYCE, GAVIN PETERS**
Client: **FLINT HILLS RESOURCES**

Creative Firm: **THE MONOGRAM GROUP — CHICAGO, IL**
Creative Team: **HAROLD WOODRIDGE, BRETT HAWTHORNE, CHRISTA VELBEL**
Client: **VICTORY GARDENS THEATER**

Creative Firm: **LEBOW — TORONTO, ON, CANADA**
Creative Team: **RONNIE LEBOW**
Client: **INTERNATIONAL POKER TOURS**

Creative Firm: **RODGERS TOWNSEND — ST. LOUIS, MO**
Creative Team: **TOM HUDDER, VALERIE TIRELLA, KAY COCHRAN, STEFAN HESTER, CHERYL SPARKS**
Client: **HUMANE SOCIETY OF MISSOURI**

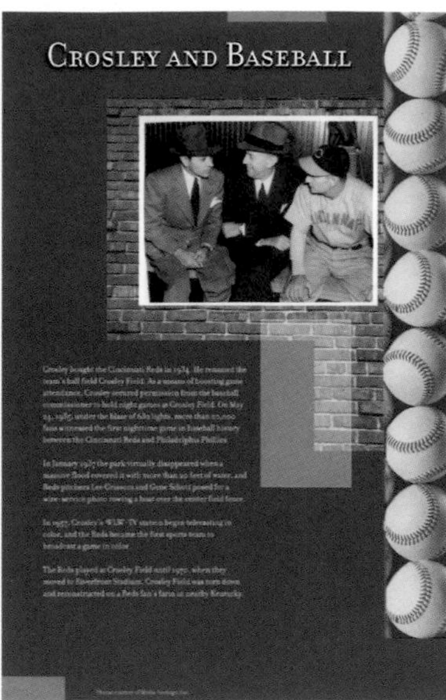

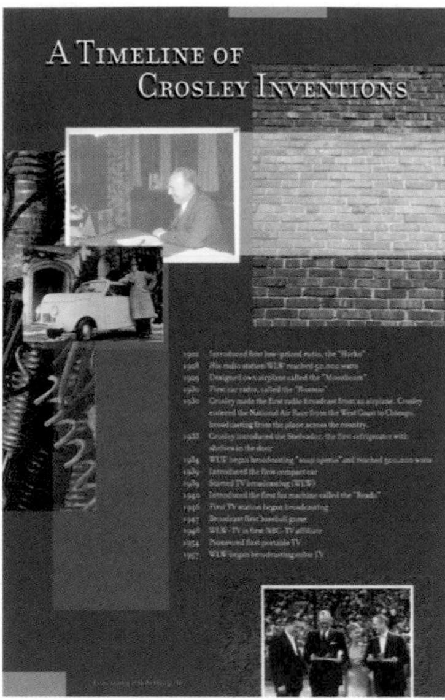

Creative Firm: **FIVE VISUAL COMMUNICATION & DESIGN — WEST CHESTER, OH**
Creative Team: **RONDI TSCHOPP**
Client: **MERCY HEALTH PARTNERS**

Creative Firm: **HULL CREATIVE GROUP — BROOKLINE, MA**
Creative Team: **CARYL H. HULL, HEIDI PRINCE, FOSTER PARENTS**
Client: **DARE FAMILY SERVICES**

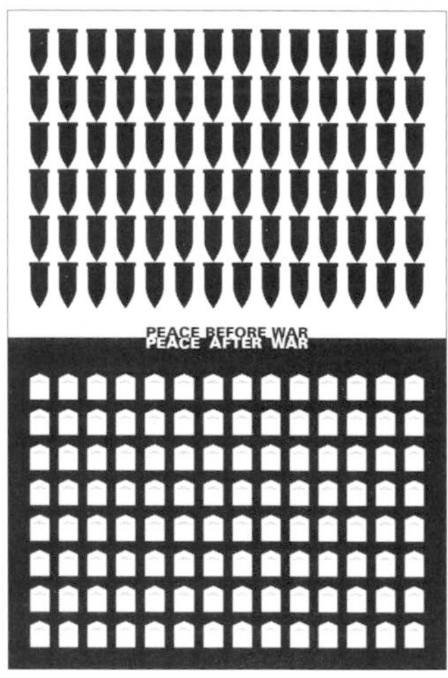

Creative Firm: **WESTERN MICHIGAN UNIVERSITY — KALAMAZOO, MI**
Creative Team: **PRAVIN SEVAK, ARVIND SEVAK, KALPESH PATEL**
Client: **PRAVIN C SEVAK**

Creative Firm: **SUBPLOT DESIGN INC. — VANCOUVER, BC, CANADA**
Creative Team: **MATTHEW CLARK, ROY WHITE, WALDY MARTENS**
Client: **RYDERS EYEWEAR**

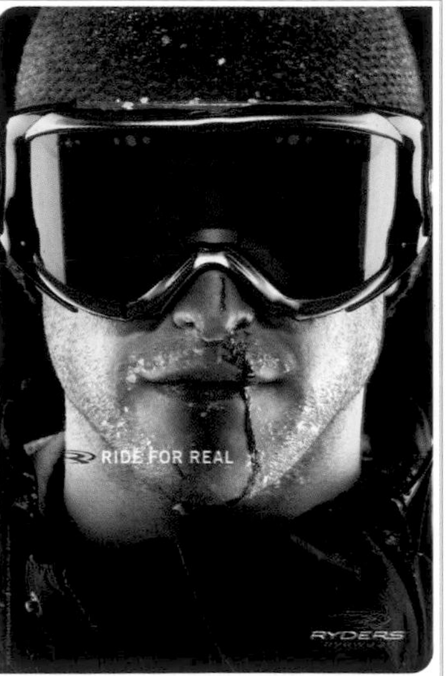

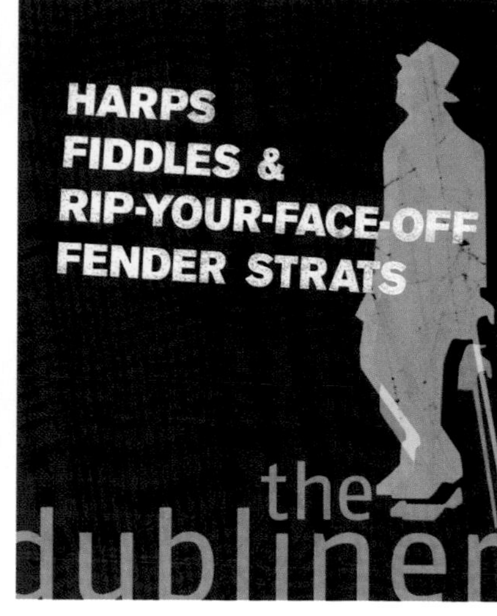

Creative Firm: **RODGERS TOWNSEND — ST. LOUIS, MO**
Creative Team: **TOM HUDDER, JENNY STORINO, JAKE EDINGER, CHERYL SPARKS**
Client: **THE DUBLINER**

Creative Firm: **ERIC CAI DESIGN CO. — BEIJING, CHINA**
Creative Team: **ERIC CAI SHI WEI, XU ZHI HONG**
Client: **NANJING MASSACRE MEMORIAL**

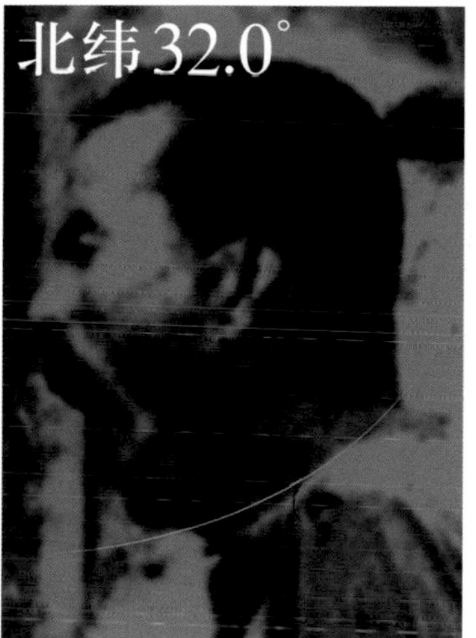

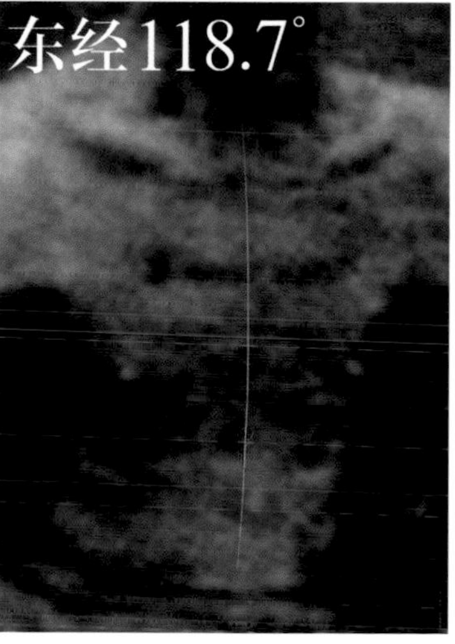

Creative Firm: **ADVANTAGE LTD — HAMILTON, BERMUDA**
Creative Team: **SAMI LILL, MEREDITH ANDREWS**
Client: **PARLIAMENTARY REGISTRY**

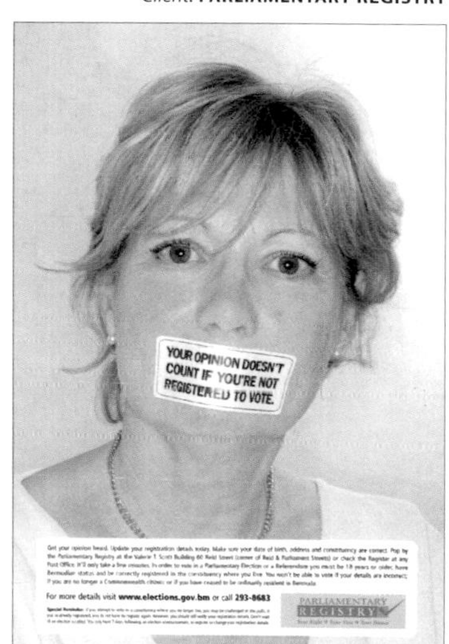

Creative Firm: **DAVIS DESIGN PARTNERS — HOLLAND, OH**
Creative Team: **MATT DAVIS, KAREN DAVIS, PEGGY FELIX**
Client: **PURDUE THEATRE (PURDUE UNIVERSITY)**

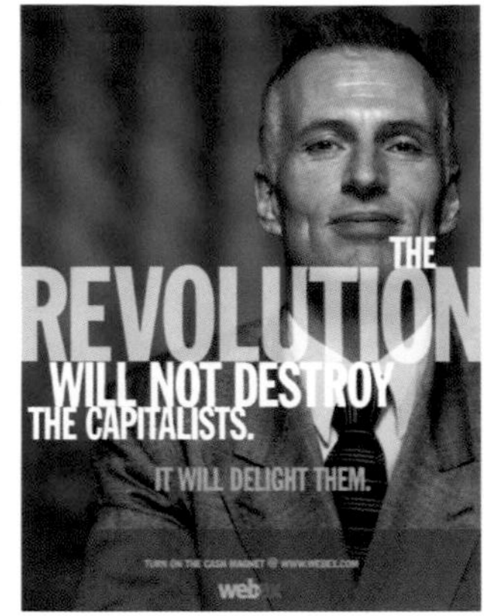

Creative Firm: **PUBLICIS DIALOG — SAN FRANCISCO, CA**
Creative Team: **JOE LIN, CHRISTOPHER ST. JOHN, THERESA LEE, SHAWN POE, CLAUDIA GOETZELMAN**
Client: **WEBEX COMMUNICATIONS, INC.**

Creative Firm: **DISNEYLAND RESORT — ANAHEIM, CA**
Creative Team: **DATHAN SHORE, WES CLARK, JACQUELYN MOE, JIM ST. AMANT, SCOTT STARKEY, JANE ROHAN**
Client: **DISNEYLAND RESORT**

Creative Firm: **HULL CREATIVE GROUP — BROOKLINE, MA**
Creative Team: **CARYL H. HULL, DIANE RIPSTEIN, FAY FOTO**
Client: **TEMPLE SANAI**

Creative Firm: **RODGERS TOWNSEND — ST. LOUIS, MO**
Creative Team: **TOM HUDDER, JENNY STORINO, JAKE EDINGER, CHERYL SPARKS**
Client: **THE DUBLINER**

Creative Firm: **RODGERS TOWNSEND — ST. LOUIS, MO**
Creative Team: **TOM HUDDER, MARK ARNOLD, TODD MITCHELL, CHERYL SPARKS**
Client: **CIRCUS FLORA**

Creative Firm: **ATOMZ I! PTE LTD — SINGAPORE**
Creative Team: **PATRICK LEE, ALBERT LEE, KESTREL LEE, LOUIS CHEW**
Client: **AGRI-FOOD & VETERINARY AUTHORITY OF SINGAPORE**

Creative Firm: **ALL MEDIA PROJECTS LIMITED — PORT OF SPAIN, TRINIDAD AND TOBAGO**
Creative Team: **CLINT WILLIAMS, CHRISTOPHER WILCOX, MARQUITA CELESTINE**
Client: **BP TRINIDAD AND TOBAGO (BPTT)**

Creative Firm: **AD PLANET GROUP / ACE: DAYTONS ADVERTISING — SINGAPORE**
Creative Team: **LEO TECK CHONG, ALFRED TEO, JOE TAN, SERENE GOH, BEN LIM, JAMES TAN**
Client: **SARA LEE SINGAPORE PTE LTD**

Creative Firm: **WALLACH GLASS STUDIO — SANTA ROSA, CA**
Creative Team: **CHRISTINA WALLACH, ARLENE RHODEN, TIM FELDMAN**
Client: **UC MERCED**

Creative Firm: **HUGHES HUNTER, INC. — THOUSAND OAKS, CA**
Creative Team: **JIM HUGHES, BRUCE POLKES, DENNIS RICCI, CAROL GRAVELLE**
Client: **LEXUS**

Creative Firm: **MAYHEM STUDIOS — LOS ANGELES, CA**
Creative Team: **CALVIN LEE**
Client: **FAMILY MEDICAL CENTER**

Creative Firm: **ASPREY CREATIVE — FITZROY, VICTORIA, AUSTRALIA**
Creative Team: **RITA PALMIERI TRSAN, PETER ASPREY**
Client: **TRE BICCHIERI**

Creative Firm: **RANDI WOLF DESIGN — GLASSBORO, NJ**
Creative Team: **RANDI WOLF, ASTRO SIGNS, JOHN & TRACIE SPERRATORE**
Client: **THE FOUNDERS INN BED & BREAKFAST**

Creative Firm: **MODREN MARKETING CONCEPTS — LOUISVILLE, KY**
Creative Team: **MARK GROVES**
Client: **MODREN MARKETING CONCEPTS**

Steak & Shrimp
COMBO MAMBO
New!
$5.99
Natural Caribbean Flavor.
Pollo Tropical

Creative Firm: **ORIGINAL IMPRESSIONS — MIAMI, FL**
Creative Team: **RAFAEL BAEZA**
Client: **POLLO TROPICAL**

CAUTION
SLIPPERY WHEN WET
INSIDEHER
Erotisches für Frauen

InsideHer is the first women-only-erotic-shop in town. It offers a special choice of lingerie, toys and erotic articles. The promotion signs were placed outside and inside of the shop to get the attention of female pedestrians and to invite them in.

Creative Firm: **YOUNG & RUBICAM GMBH & CO. KG — FRANKFURT AM MAIN, HESSEN, GERMANY**
Creative Team: **CHRISTIAN DAUL, MAJA MILOSEVIC, ANNA-KARINA KORN, THOMAS BALZER**
Client: **INSIDEHER - EROTIC ACCESSORIES FOR WOMEN**

Creative Firm: **GAMMON RAGONESI ASSOCIATES — NEW YORK, NY**
Creative Team: **MARY RAGONESI, JILLSHELLHORN**
Client: **NESTLE**

Creative Firm: **YOUNG & RUBICAM GMBH & CO. KG — FRANKFURT AM MAIN, HESSEN, GERMANY**
Creative Team: **CHRISTIAN DAUL, UWE MARQUARDT, MONIKA SPIRKL, BRUNO PETZ, HERIBERT BURKERT**
Client: **SHARKPROJECT E.V.**

Creative Firm: **ORIGINAL IMPRESSIONS — MIAMI, FL**
Creative Team: **RAFAEL BAEZA**
Client: **POLLO TROPICAL**

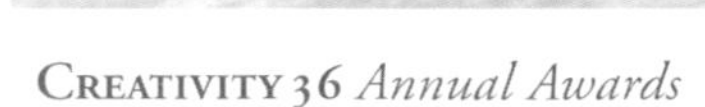

Creative Firm: **WALLACH GLASS STUDIO — SANTA ROSA, CA**
Creative Team: **CHRISTINA WALLACH, ARLENE RHODEN, ART VIGER, JENNIFER SEROTA, TIM FELDMAN, NELS ACKERLUND**
Client: **ROCKFORD MEMORIAL HOSPITAL**

Creative Firm: **PETERSON MILLA HOOKS — MINNEAPOLIS, MN**
Creative Team: **DAVE PETERSON, GAYLE MALCOLM, ELLEN FREGO**
Client: **TARGET**

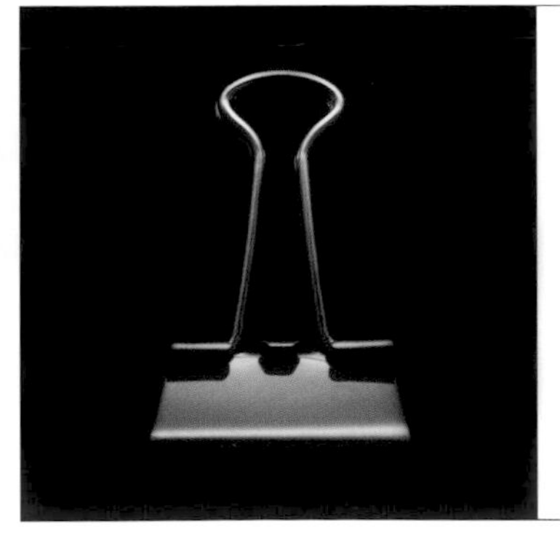

Creative Firm: **WALLACH GLASS STUDIO — SANTA ROSA, CA**
Creative Team: **CHRISTINA WALLACH, ARLENE RHODEN, TIM FELDMAN, NELS ACKERLUND**
Client: **ROCKFORD MEMORIAL HOSPITAL**

Creative Firm: **QUALCOMM — SAN DIEGO, CA**
Creative Team: **FRANK BERNAS, CHRIS LEE**

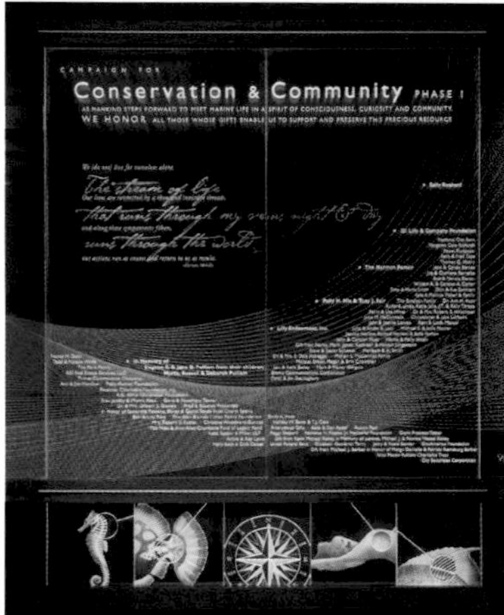

Creative Firm: **WALLACH GLASS STUDIO — SANTA ROSA, CA**
Creative Team: **CHRISTINA WALLACH, ARLENE RHODEN, TIM FELDMAN**
Client: **INDIANAPOLIS ZOO**

Creative Firm: **WINDCHASER PRODUCTS, INC — MARINA DEL REY, CA**
Creative Team: **NATHAN ADAMS, JOEY GARCIA**
Client: **WINDCHASER PRODUCTS, INC**

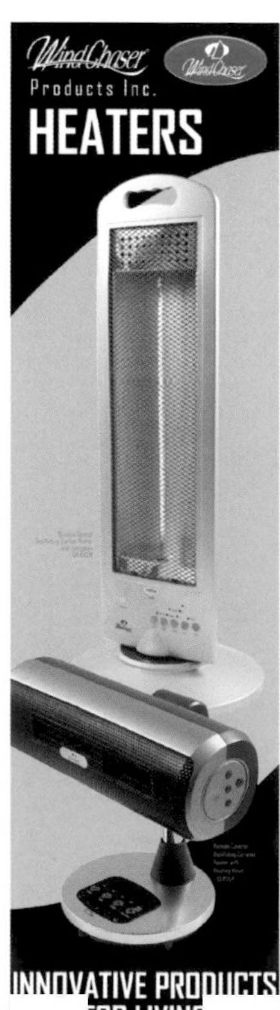

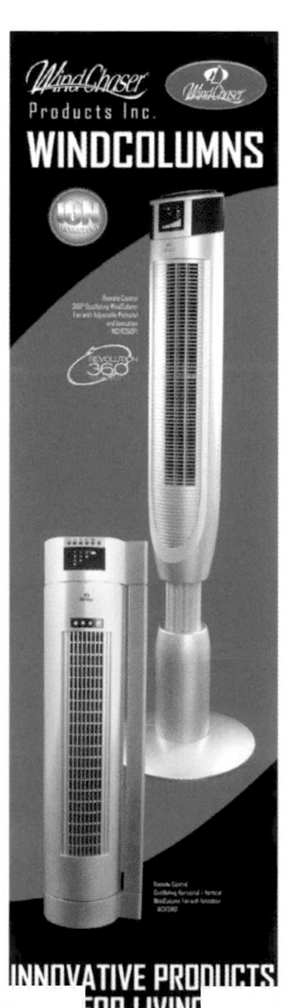

Creative Firm: **BETH SINGER DESIGN — ARLINGTON, VA**
Creative Team: **BETH SINGER, CHRIS HOCH, DEBORAH ECKBRETH, HOWARD SMITH**
Client: **AMERICAN ISRAEL PUBLIC AFFAIRS COMMITTEE**

Creative Firm: **HORNALL ANDERSON DESIGN WORKS — SEATTLE, WA**
Creative Team: **JACK ANDERSON, MARK POPICH, LARRY ANDERSON**
Client: **EOS AIRLINES**

Creative Firm: **REVOLUZION ADVERTISING & DESIGN — NEUHAUSEN OB ECK, GERMANY**
Creative Team: **BERND LUZ, THOMAS BRECHT**
Client: **TÜRK+HILLINGER HEATING ELEMENTS**

Creative Firm: **MTV NETWORKS CREATIVE SERVICES — NEW YORK, NY**
Client: **MTV NETWORKS AFFILIATE SALES**

Creative Firm: **PURE DESIGN CO. LLC—LEVERETT, MA**
Creative Team: **DAN MISHKIND, MARY KATE MARCHAND**
Client: **GOOD FOOD ORGANICS, INC.**

Creative Firm: **GEE + CHUNG DESIGN — SAN FRANCISCO, CA**
Creative Team: **EARL GEE, ANDY CAULFIELD, HOOD EXHIBITS**
Client: **QUALYS, INC.**

Creative Firm: **ORIGINAL IMPRESSIONS — MIAMI, FL**
Creative Team: **FRANK IRIAS**
Client: **ROYAL CARIBBEAN INTERNATIONAL**

Creative Firm: **JGA — SOUTHFIELD, MI**
Creative Team: **DAVID NELSON, TAMI JO URBAN, GORDON EASON**
Client: **PHOTO MARKETING ASSOCIATION**

Creative Firm: **PETERSON MILLA HOOKS — MINNEAPOLIS, MN**
Creative Team: **DAVE PETERSON, AARON POLLOCK, CATHERINE IRMITER, ELLEN FREGO, MICHAEL SHARP**
Client: **TARGET**

Creative Firm: **THE MONOGRAM GROUP — CHICAGO, IL**
Creative Team: **HAROLD WOODRIDGE, CHIP BALCH, SAVERIO TRUGLIA**
Client: **CHICAGO SYMPHONY ORCHESTRA**

Creative Firm: **RODGERS TOWNSEND — ST. LOUIS, MO**
Creative Team: **TOM HUDDER, TOM TOWNSEND, CHERYL SPARKS**
Client: **ST. LOUIS RAMS**

Creative Firm: **HOFFMAN/LEWIS — SAN FRANCISCO, CA**
Creative Team: **SHARON KRINSKY, JAMES CABRAL, RONDA DUNN, JASON HEADLEY**
Client: **HENRY'S**

Creative Firm: **RODGERS TOWNSEND — ST. LOUIS, MO**
Creative Team: **TOM HUDDER, TOM TOWNSEND, CHERYL SPARKS**
Client: **ST. LOUIS RAMS**

Creative Firm: **RODGERS TOWNSEND — ST. LOUIS, MO**
Creative Team: **TOM HUDDER, TOM TOWNSEND, CHERYL SPARKS**
Client: **ST. LOUIS RAMS**

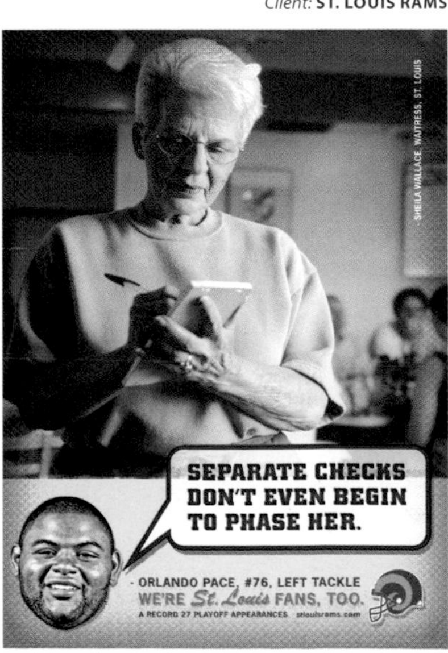

Creative Firm: **PETERSON MILLA HOOKS — MINNEAPOLIS, MN**
Creative Team: **DAVE PETERSON, SUE KAASE, GAYLE MALCOLM, ELLEN FREGO, KENNETH WILLARDT**
Client: **TARGET**

Creative Firm: **VOICEBOX CREATIVE — SAN FRANCISCO, CA**
Creative Team: **JACQUES ROSSOUW, PATRICK MCFARLIN**
Client: **FOSTER'S WINE ESTATES**

Creative Firm: **HERE! NETWORKS — NEW YORK, NY**
Creative Team: **ERIC FELDMAN, MEGAN ELLIS**

Creative Firm: **RODGERS TOWNSEND — ST. LOUIS, MO**
Creative Team: **TOM HUDDER, TOM TOWNSEND, CHERYL SPARKS**
Client: **ST. LOUIS RAMS**

Creative Firm: **RODGERS TOWNSEND — ST. LOUIS, MO**
Creative Team: **TOM HUDDER, TOM TOWNSEND, CHERYL SPARKS**
Client: **ST. LOUIS RAMS**

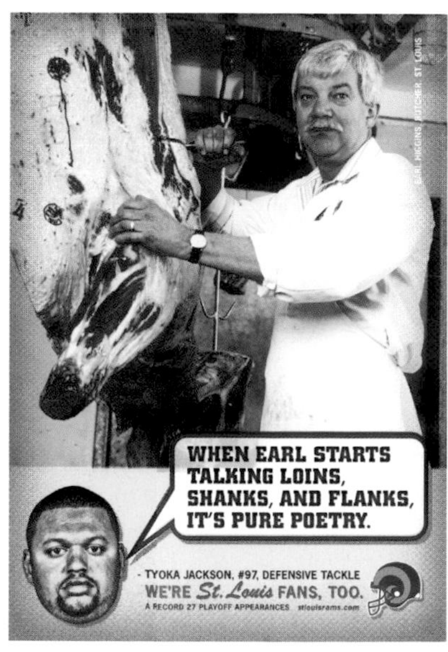

Creative Firm: **RODGERS TOWNSEND — ST. LOUIS, MO**
Creative Team: **TOM HUDDER, TOM TOWNSEND, CHERYL SPARKS**
Client: **ST. LOUIS RAMS**

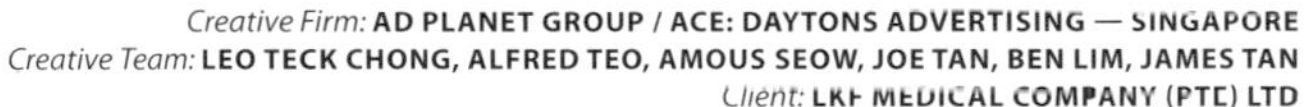

Creative Firm: **AD PLANET GROUP / ACE: DAYTONS ADVERTISING — SINGAPORE**
Creative Team: **LEO TECK CHONG, ALFRED TEO, AMOUS SEOW, JOE TAN, BEN LIM, JAMES TAN**
Client: **LKF MEDICAL COMPANY (PTE) LTD**

Creative Firm: **LEO BURNETT/YELLOW SHOES CREATIVE WEST, DISNEYLAND RESORT — ANAHEIM, CA**
Creative Team: **DATHAN SHORE, MARTY MULLER, WES CLARK, JACQUELYN MOE, JIM ST. AMANT, ROSANNA AGUILAR**
Client: **DISNEYLAND RESORT**

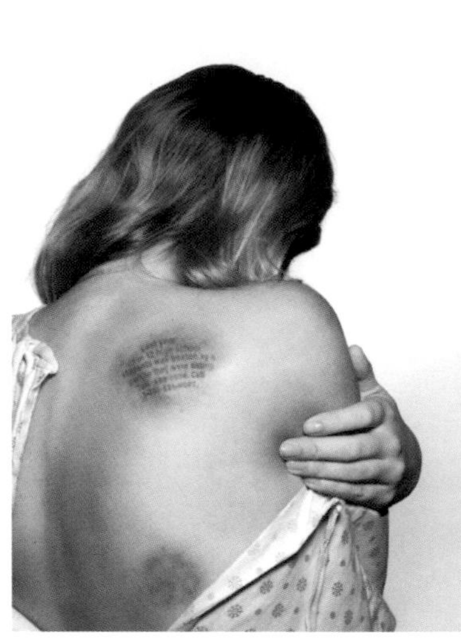

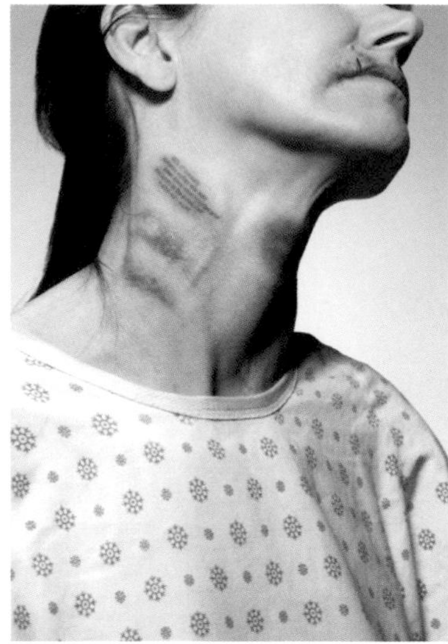

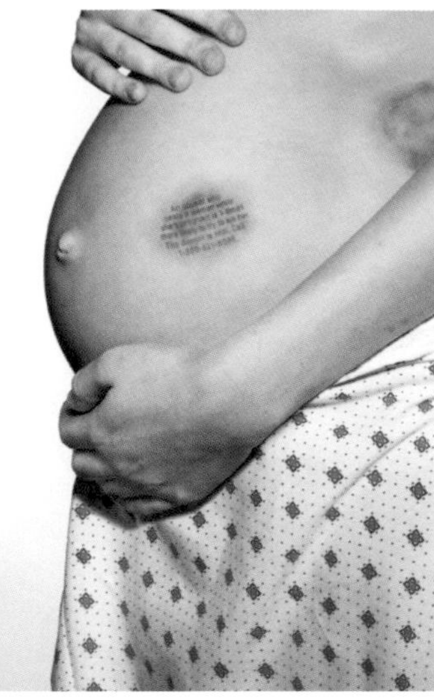

Creative Firm: **MCCANN ERICKSON, NEW YORK — NEW YORK, NY**
Creative Team: **LESLIE SIMS, AUDREY HUFFENREUTER, JOYCE KING THOMAS, ANDREA KAYE, LEON STEELE, APRIL GALLO**
Client: **CITY OF NEW YORK, MAYOR BLOOMBERG'S OFFICE**

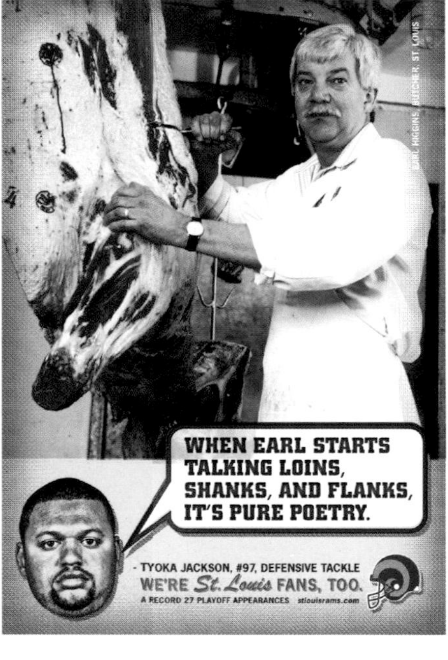

Creative Firm: **RODGERS TOWNSEND — ST. LOUIS, MO**
Creative Team: **TOM HUDDER, TOM TOWNSEND, CHERYL SPARKS**
Client: **ST. LOUIS RAMS**

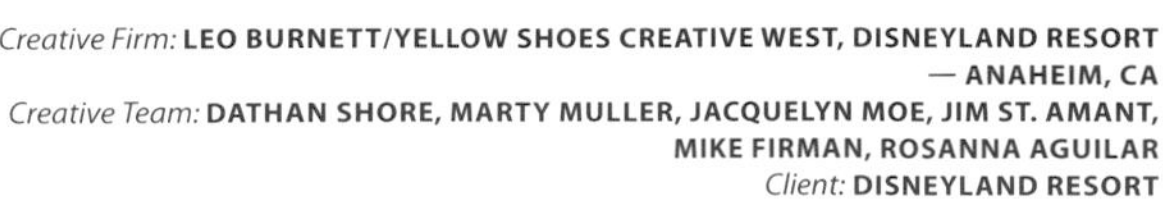

Creative Firm: **LEO BURNETT/YELLOW SHOES CREATIVE WEST, DISNEYLAND RESORT — ANAHEIM, CA**
Creative Team: **DATHAN SHORE, MARTY MULLER, JACQUELYN MOE, JIM ST. AMANT, MIKE FIRMAN, ROSANNA AGUILAR**
Client: **DISNEYLAND RESORT**

Creative Firm: **VH1 — NEW YORK, NY**
Client: **VH1**

Creative Firm: **THE MONOGRAM GROUP — CHICAGO, IL**
Creative Team: **HAROLD WOODRIDGE, CHIP BALCH, SAVERIO TRUGLIA**
Client: **CHICAGO SYMPHONY ORCHESTRA**

Creative Firm: **YELLOW SHOES CREATIVE WEST, DISNEYLAND RESORT — ANAHEIM, CA**
Creative Team: **DATHAN SHORE, MARTY MULLER, JACQUELYN MOE, WES CLARK**
Client: **DISNEYLAND RESORT**

Creative Firm: **LEO BURNETT/YELLOW SHOES CREATIVE WEST, DISNEYLAND RESORT — ANAHEIM, CA**
Creative Team: **DATHAN SHORE, MARTY MULLER, JACQUELYN MOE, WES CLARK**
Client: **DISNEYLAND RESORT**

Creative Firm: **FRY HAMMOND BARR — ORLANDO, FL**
Creative Team: **TIM FISHER, RAY KILINSKI, TOM KANE, STEPHANIE RUELKE, ARTISTIC IMAGE**
Client: **KENNEDY SPACE CENTER**

Creative Firm: **NICK AT NITE — NEW YORK, NY**
Creative Team: **KENNA KAY, NATIONAL TELEVISION, CATHERINE MULCAHY**
Client: **NICK AT NITE**

Creative Firm: **MIKE SALISBURY EFFECTIVE CREATIVE STRATEGIES — VENICE, CA**
Creative Team: **MIKE SALISBURY, GUSTAVO MORAIS**
Client: **TRIUMPH USA**

Creative Firm: **YELLOW SHOES CREATIVE WEST, DISNEYLAND RESORT — ANAHEIM, CA**
Creative Team: **SCOTT STARKEY, JACQUELYN MOE, CLAIRE BILBY**
Client: **DISNEYLAND RESORT**

Creative Firm: **GAMMON RAGONESI ASSOCIATES — NEW YORK, NY**
Creative Team: **MARY RAGONESI, KELLY MUDGE, YARITSA ARENAS**
Client: **NESTLE**

Creative Firm: **HORNALL ANDERSON DESIGN WORKS — SEATTLE, WA**
Creative Team: **J. ANDERSON, M. POPICH, D. BATES, L. ANDERSON, A. WICKLUND, L. RAYMUNDO, J. CARTER, Y. SHVETS**
Client: **EOS AIRLINES**

Creative Firm: **TTA ADVERTISING — PHOENIX, AZ**
Creative Team: **RUSTY PILE, ROB TINSMAN**
Client: **MONUMENT HOSPITALITY**

Creative Firm: **AD HARVEST — SIMPSONVILLE, KY**
Creative Team: **MARK GROVES**
Client: **B. P. CONCEPTS AND AFLAC**

Creative Firm: **YELLOW SHOES CREATIVE WEST, DISNEYLAND RESORT — ANAHEIM, CA**
Creative Team: **MIKE PUCHALSKI, MARTY MULLER, JACQUELYN MOE, WES CLARK, ANIKO BOTA, CLAIRE BILBY**
Client: **DISNEYLAND RESORT**

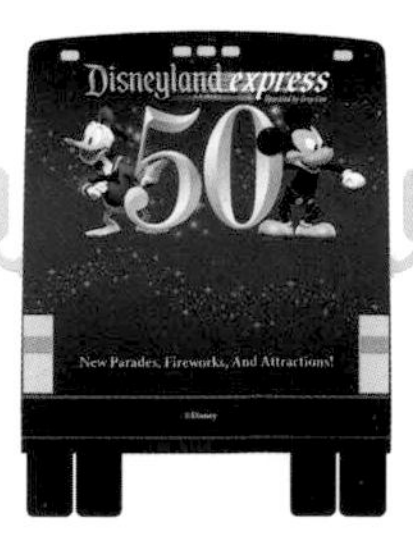

Creative Firm: **MIRACLE GRAPHICS CO. WLL — MANAMA, BAHRAIN**
Creative Team: **KHALID JUMAN, JAY BHAGAWATI, PAUL WARRENER, GEIR ERDAL**
Client: **SHEIKH EBRAHIM CENTRE FOR CULTURE & RESEARCH**

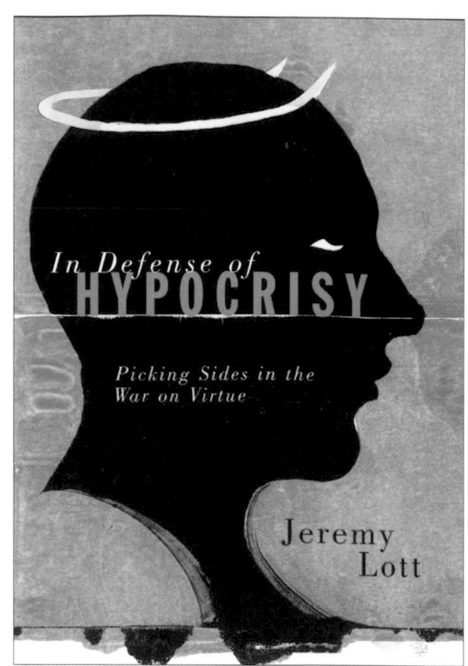

Creative Firm: **RED CANOE — DEER LODGE, TN**
Creative Team: **DEB KOCH, KAREN PHILLIPS, CAROLINE KAVANAGH, DANIEL BEJAR, JEREMY LOTT**
Client: **THOMAS NELSON PUBLISHERS**

Creative Firm: **SCHOOL OF VISUAL ARTS — NEW YORK, NY**
Creative Team: **PAULA SCHER, RICHARD WILDE, LENNY NAAR, JULIA HOFFMAN**
Client: **SCHOOL OF VISUAL ARTS**

Creative Firm: **VSA PARTNERS, INC. — CHICAGO, IL**
Creative Team: **CURT SCHREIBER, ASHLEY LIPPARD, AMY GLAIBERMAN, RICHARD RENNO, DREW BROOKS, ROBYN PAPROCKI**
Client: **ATRIA BOOKS**

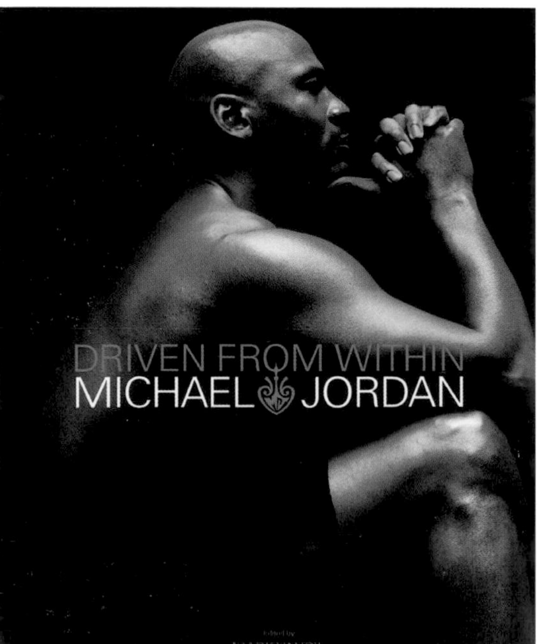

Creative Firm: **RED CANOE — DEER LODGE, TN**
Creative Team: **DEB KOCH, BELINDA BASS, CAROLINE KAVANAGH, ABM, RON LAMBERT, TOM PARKER**
Client: **THOMAS NELSON PUBLISHERS**

Creative Firm: **TD2, S.C. — MEXICO CITY, D.F., MEXICO**
Creative Team: **R. RODRIGO CORDOVA**
Client: **MICHELLE MORALES - WRITER**

Creative Firm: **RED CANOE — DEER LODGE, TN**
Creative Team: **DEB KOCH, BELINDA BASS, CAROLINE KAVANAGH, DR. TONY ZEISS, TYLER BOLEY**
Client: **THOMAS NELSON PUBLISHERS**

Creative Firm: **DESIGN GUYS — MINNEAPOLIS, MN**
Creative Team: **STEVE SIKORA, BARRY TOWNSEND, DARRELL EAGER, POMCO GRAPHIC ARTS**
Client: **NEENAH PAPER**

Creative Firm: **RED CANOE — DEER LODGE, TN**
Creative Team: **DEB KOCH, KAREN PHILLIPS, CAROLINE KAVANAGH, IAN LAWRENCE, KATHERINE ALBRECHT, LIZ MCINTYRE**
Client: **THOMAS NELSON PUBLISHERS**

Creative Firm: **MIRACLE GRAPHICS CO. WLL — MANAMA, BAHRAIN**
Creative Team: **KHALID JUMAN, JAY BHAGAWATI, GEIR ERDEL**

Creative Firm: **ROBINLANDA.COM — NEW YORK, NY**
Creative Team: **ROBIN LANDA, DENISE ANDERSON, CHRISTOPHER NAVETTA, MENZA LAURA F.**
Client: **THOMSON**

Creative Firm: **UNIVERSITY OF SOUTH ALABAMA — MOBILE, AL**
Creative Team: **MATTHEW JOHNSON**
Client: **SWF PUBLISHING HAUS**

Creative Firm: **RED CANOE — DEER LODGE, TN**
Creative Team: **DEB KOCH, KAREN PHILLIPS, CAROLINE KAVANAGH, HENRI SILBERMAN, STAR PARKER,**
Client: **THOMAS NELSON PUBLISHERS**

Creative Firm: **HULL CREATIVE GROUP — BROOKLINE, MA**
Creative Team: **CARYL H. HULL, JILL WINITZER**
Client: **JUSTIN, CHARLES & CO.**

Creative Firm: **COASTLINES CREATIVE GROUP — VANCOUVER, BC, CANADA**
Creative Team: **BYRON DOWLER, PATRICK MCKENNA, GERRY NISKIN**
Client: **EDGE INTERNATIONAL**

Creative Firm: **HULL CREATIVE GROUP — BROOKLINE, MA**
Creative Team: **CARYL H. HULL, CAROLYN COLONNA**
Client: **JUSTIN, CHARLES & CO.**

Creative Firm: **ROBINLANDA.COM — NEW YORK, NY**
Creative Team: **ROBIN LANDA, DENISE ANDERSON, GISH JAMES**
Client: **THOMSON LEARNING**

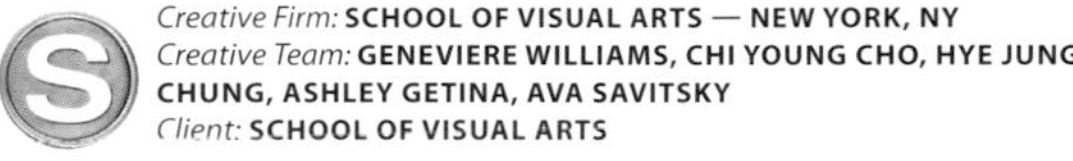

Creative Firm: **SCHOOL OF VISUAL ARTS — NEW YORK, NY**
Creative Team: **GENEVIERE WILLIAMS, CHI YOUNG CHO, HYE JUNG CHUNG, ASHLEY GETINA, AVA SAVITSKY**
Client: **SCHOOL OF VISUAL ARTS**

Creative Firm: **VERY MEMORABLE DESIGN — NEW YORK, NY**
Creative Team: **MICHAEL PINTO**
Client: **JOHN WILEY & SONS, INC.**

Creative Firm: **RED CANOE — DEER LODGE, TN**
Creative Team: **DEB KOCH, MARK ROSS, CAROLINE KAVANAGH, LAURA JENSEN WALKER,**
Client: **THOMAS NELSON PUBLISHERS**

I DID NOT WANT TO GO TO THE NIKE MEETING.
I DIDN'T KNOW NIKE.
I DIDN'T THINK I LIKED NIKE.

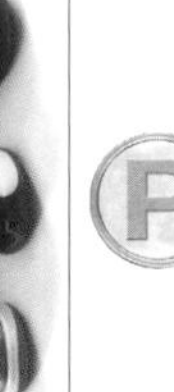

Creative Firm: **VSA PARTNERS, INC. — CHICAGO, IL**
Creative Team: **CURT SCHREIBER, ASHLEY LIPPARD, AMY GLAIBERMAN, RICHARD RENNO, DREW BROOKS, ROBYN PAPROCKI**
Client: **ATRIA BOOKS**

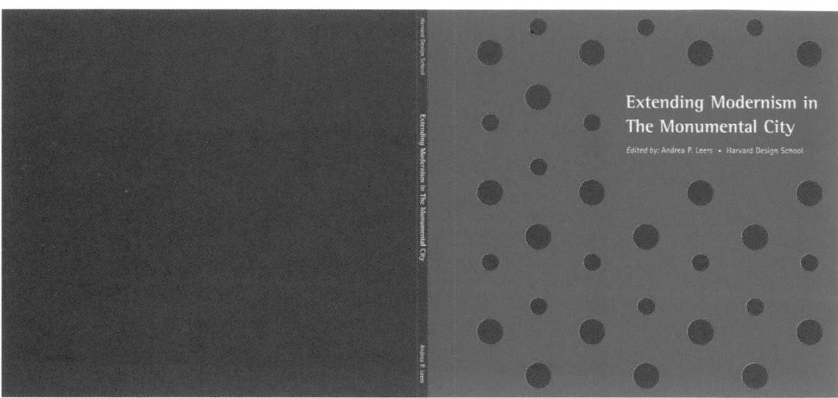

Creative Firm: **NASSAR DESIGN — BROOKLINE, MA**
Creative Team: **NELIDA NASSAR**
Client: **HARVARD DESIGN SCHOOL**

< A 1953 Herman Miller ad designed by the Eames Office to introduce the plastic side chair, the upholstered armchair and the Eames Storage Unit

Early vinyl and fabric upholstered drafting armchair (622NA-99)

> Dining or desk side chairs with "Eiffel Tower" wire bases (DSR)

52

Creative Firm: **DESIGN GUYS — MINNEAPOLIS, MN**
Creative Team: **STEVE SIKORA, BARRY TOWNSEND, EAMES OFFICE , HERMAN MILLER , DANIEL OSTROFF, EAMES DEMETRIOS**
Client: **NEENAH PAPER**

Creative Firm: **MIRACLE GRAPHICS CO. WLL — MANAMA, BAHRAIN**
Creative Team: **KHALID JUMAN, JAY BHAGAWATI, GEIR ERDEL**

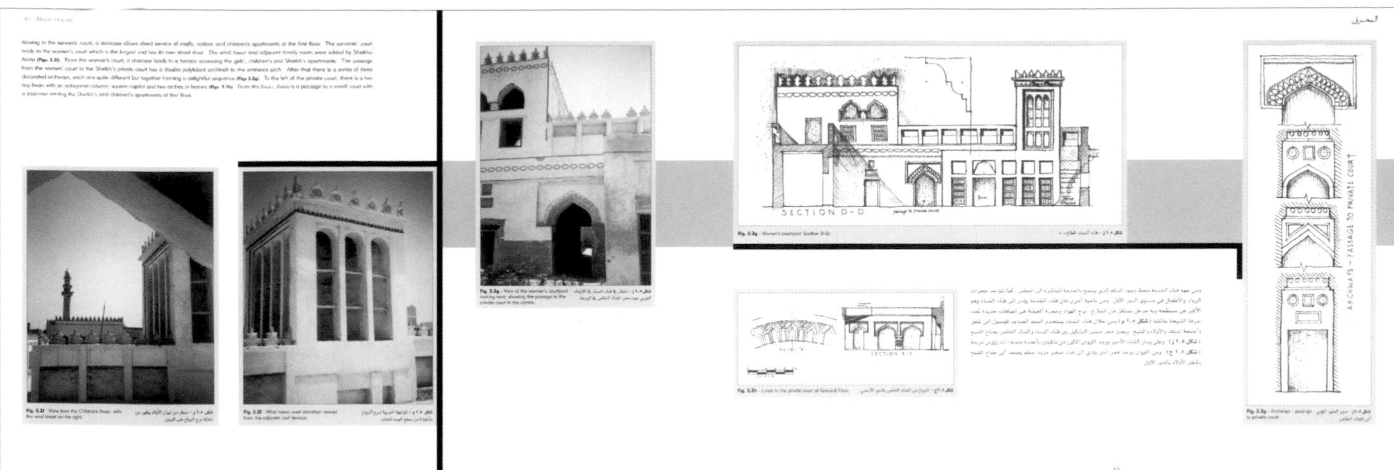

Creative Firm: **MIRACLE GRAPHICS CO. WLL — MANAMA, BAHRAIN**
Creative Team: **KHALID JUMAN, JAY BHAGAWATI, PAUL WARRENER, GEIR ERDAL**
Client: **SHEIKH EBRAHIM CENTRE FOR CULTURE & RESEARCH**

Creative Firm: **GLOW PUBLISHING — DHAKA, BANGLADESH**
Creative Team: **LAURA BONAPACE, REENA ABRAHAM, GMB AKASH**
Client: **GMB AKASH**

Creative Firm: **VH1 — NEW YORK, NY**
Client: **VH1**

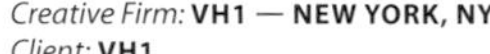

Creative Firm: **MASTRO PHOTOGRAPHY+DESIGN — MOBILE, AL**
Creative Team: **MICHAEL MASTRO, ARCHBISHOP OSCAR H. LIPSCOMB, ANDY ZAK, JOHN STROPE**
Client: **ARCHDIOCESE OF MOBILE**

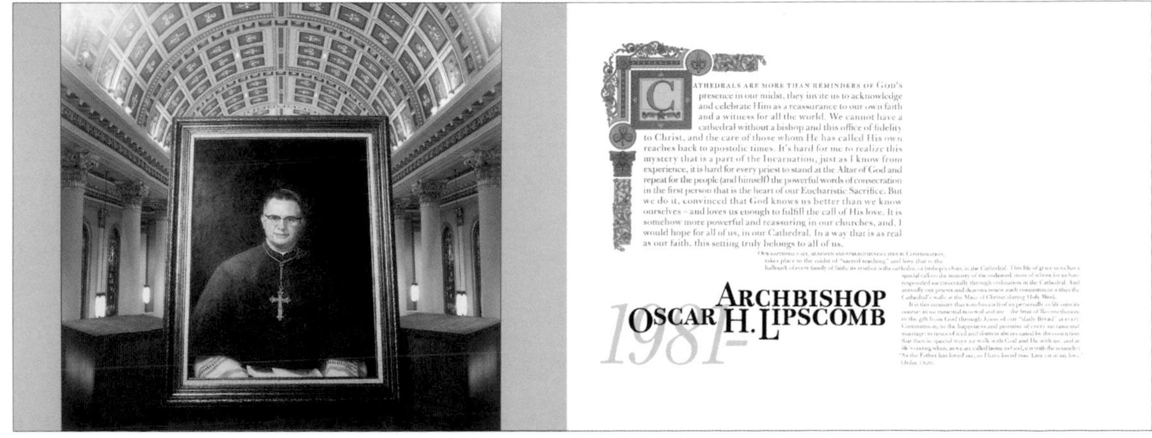

Creative Firm: **UIUC SCHOOL OF ART AND DESIGN — CHAMPAIGN, IL**
Creative Team: **JENNIFER GUNJI, NAN GOGGIN, DEANA MCDONAGH**
Client: **PROFESSOR DEANA MCDONAGH**

Creative Firm: **SCOTT ADAMS DESIGN ASSOCIATES — COLUMBUS, OH**
Creative Team: **SCOTT ADAMS, JARRON TERRY, NATHAN KRAFT**
Client: **NATIONWIDE REALTY INVESTORS**

Creative Firm: **COMPANY STANDARD — BROOKLYN, NY**
Creative Team: **MELISSA GORMAN**
Client: **ARCADIA UNIVERSITY ART GALLERY**

Creative Firm: **DESIGNLORE — PHILADELPHIA, PA**
Creative Team: **LAURIE CHURCHMAN**
Client: **ARCADIA UNIVERSITY**

Creative Firm: **KOLEGRAM — GATNINEAU, QC, CANADA**
Creative Team: **GAETAN ALBERT, TONY FOUHSE, DWAYNE BROWN**
Client: **KOLEGRAM**

Creative Firm: **COMEDY CENTRAL — NEW YORK, NY**
Creative Team: **DZP , BRIAN DIECKS**

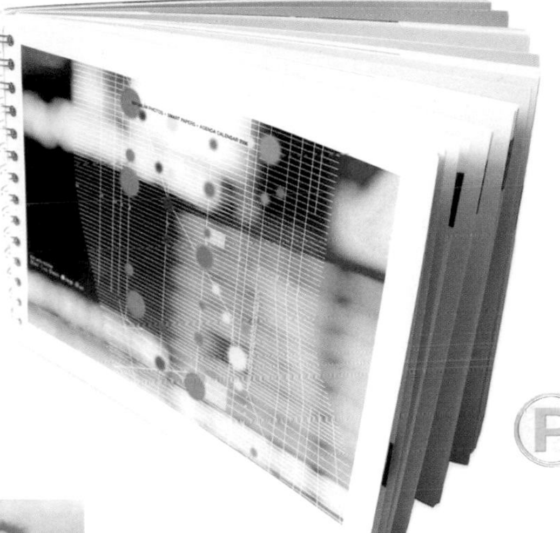

Creative Firm: **YELLOW SHOES CREATIVE WEST, DISNEYLAND RESORT — ANAHEIM, CA**
Creative Team: **DATHAN SHORE, WES CLARK, JACQUELYN MOE, KEVIN YONEDA**
Client: **DISNEYLAND RESORT**

Creative Firm: **EMERSON, WAJDOWICZ STUDIOS — NEW YORK, NY**
Creative Team: **LISA LAROCHELLE, YOKO YOSHIDA, MANNY MENDEZ, JUREK WAJDOWICZ, 17 MAGNUM PHOTOGRAPHERS**
Client: **MAGNUM PHOTOS AND SMART PAPERS**

Creative Firm: **THE HUMANE SOCIETY OF THE UNITED STATES — WASHINGTON, DC**
Creative Team: **PAULA JAWORSKI, ELIZABETH MCNULTY**
Client: **THE HUMANE SOCIETY OF THE UNITED STATES**

Creative Firm: **MTV OFF AIR CREATIVE — NEW YORK, NY**
Creative Team: **JEFFREY KEYTON, JIM DEBARROS, KAREN WEISS, CHIE ARAKI**
Client: **MTV NETWORKS**

Creative Firm: **FUTURA DDB — LJUBLANA, SLOVENIA**
Creative Team: **ZARE KERIN, MATJAZ ZORC**
Client: **BELINKA**

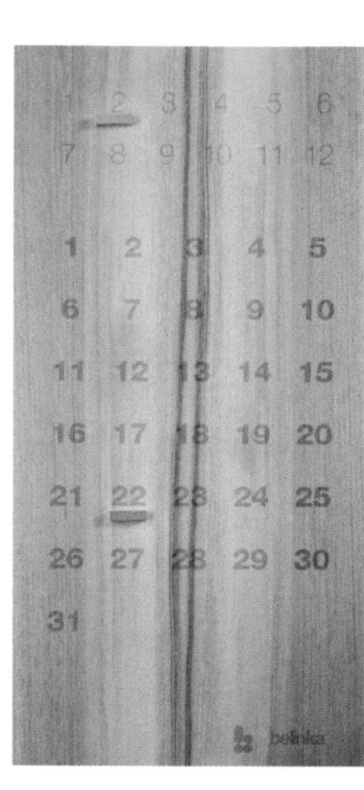

Creative Firm: **AMERICAN RED CROSS BLOOD SERVICES, WEST DIVISION — POMONA, CA**
Creative Team: **MARC JACKSON, SAUNDRA DAVISON, DONNA ANAYA, STEPHEN WHITBURN**

Creative Firm: **ALL MEDIA PROJECTS LIMITED — PORT OF SPAIN, TRINIDAD AND TOBAGO**
Creative Team: **CLINT WILLIAMS, CATHLEEN JONES, MARISA CAMEJO, ANTHONY MOORE, JULIEN GREENIDGE, JOSIANE KHANI**
Client: **BP TRINIDAD AND TOBAGO (BPTT)**

Creative Firm: **SELLING POWER MAGAZINE — FREDERICKSBURG, VA**
Creative Team: **COLLEEN QUINNELL, PATRICK SWIRC / CORBIS OUTLINE**
Client: **SELLING POWER**

Creative Firm: **DEVER DESIGNS — LAUREL, MD**
Creative Team: **JEFFREY DEVER, JIM DANDY/IMAGES.COM**
Client: **PSYCHOTHERAPY NETWORKER MAGAZINE**

Creative Firm: **EMPHASIS MEDIA LIMITED — HONG KONG**
Creative Team: **TERESITA KHAW**
Client: **THAI AIRWAYS INTERNATIONAL**

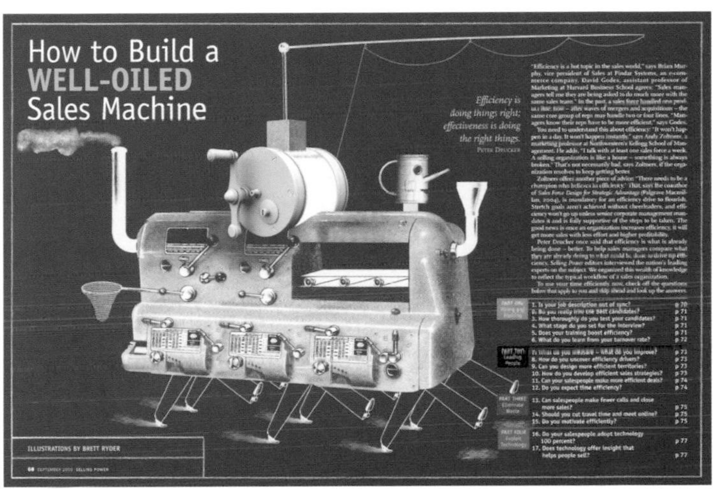

Creative Firm: **SELLING POWER MAGAZINE — FREDERICKSBURG, VA**
Creative Team: **COLLEEN QUINNELL, BRETT RYDER**
Client: **SELLING POWER**

Creative Firm: **DEVER DESIGNS — LAUREL, MD**
Creative Team: **JEFREY DEVER, KRISTIN DEUÈL DUFFY, WILLIAM RIESER**
Client: **AIPCS MAGAZINE**

Creative Firm: **SELLING POWER MAGAZINE — FREDERICKSBURG, VA**
Creative Team: **MICHAEL AUBRECHT, BROOKS KRAFT / CORBIS**
Client: **SELLING POWER**

Creative Firm: **DEVER DESIGNS — LAUREL, MD**
Creative Team: **JEFFREY DEVER, AARON JASINSKI**
Client: **PSYCHOTHERAPY NETWORKER MAGAZINE**

Creative Firm: **EMPHASIS MEDIA LIMITED — HONG KONG**
Creative Team: **PERCY CHUNG, HOWARD LEUNG, JENNIFER SPENCER-KENTRUP**
Client: **CATHAY PACIFIC AIRWAYS**

Creative Firm: **BUSINESS TRAVEL NEWS — MALVERNE, NY**
Creative Team: **TERESA M. CARBONI, DIGITAL VISION**
Client: **BUSINESS TRAVEL NEWS**

Creative Firm: **CCM IN-HOUSE — WEST ORANGE, NJ**
Creative Team: **STEPHEN LONGO, JENNIFER BASSORA, JOHN FARISCHON, CHRISTOPHER WARZOCHA, PATRICK BOBER, TREBOR RICADELA**
Client: **COUNTY COLLEGE OF MORRIS**

Creative Firm: **SELLING POWER MAGAZINE — FREDERICKSBURG, V4**
Creative Team: **COLLEEN QUINNELL**
Client: **SELLING POWER**

Creative Firm: **EMPHASIS MEDIA LIMITED — HONG KONG**
Creative Team: **LOCKY LAI**
Client: **CHINA AIRLINES**

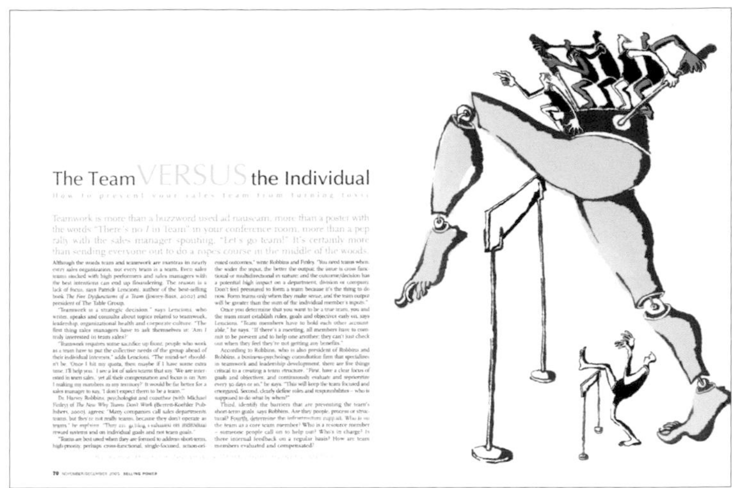

Creative Firm: **SELLING POWER MAGAZINE — FREDERICKSBURG, VA**
Creative Team: **MICHAEL AUBRECHT, BELLE MELLOR**
Client: **SELLING POWER**

Creative Firm: **BUSINESS TRAVEL NEWS — MALVERNE, NY**
Creative Team: **TERESA M. CARBONI, PAUL STODDARD**
Client: **BUSINESS TRAVEL NEWS**

Creative Firm: **EMPHASIS MEDIA LIMITED — HONG KONG**
Creative Team: **TERESITA KHAW, JENNIFER SPENCER-KENTRUP**
Client: **THAI AIRWAYS INTERNATIONAL**

Creative Firm: **SELLING POWER MAGAZINE — FREDERICKSBURG, VA**
Creative Team: **TARVER HARRIS, JON KRAUSE**
Client: **SELLING POWER**

Creative Firm: **DEVER DESIGNS — LAUREL, MD**
Creative Team: **JEFFREY DEVER, ROBERT PIZZO**
Client: **APICS MAGAZINE**

Creative Firm: **DEVER DESIGNS — LAUREL, MD**
Creative Team: **JEFFREY DEVER, CHARLIE POWELL**
Client: **LIBERTY MAGAZINE**

Creative Firm: **SELLING POWER MAGAZINE — FREDERICKSBURG, VA**
Creative Team: **MICHAEL AUBRECHT, ROBERT PIZZO**
Client: **SELLING POWER**

Creative Firm: **SELLING POWER MAGAZINE — FREDERICKSBURG, VA**
Creative Team: **TARVER HARRIS**
Client: **SELLING POWER**

Creative Firm: **BUSINESS TRAVEL NEWS — MALVERNE, NY**
Creative Team: **TERESA M. CARBONI, PHOTODISC**
Client: **BUSINESS TRAVEL NEWS**

Creative Firm: **BUSINESS TRAVEL NEWS — MALVERNE, NY**
Creative Team: **TERESA M. CARBONI, DARREN HOPES**
Client: **BUSINESS TRAVEL NEWS**

Creative Firm: **SELLING POWER MAGAZINE — FREDERICKSBURG, VA**
Creative Team: **TARVER HARRIS, SERGE BLOCH**
Client: **SELLING POWER**

Creative Firm: **EYEBALLNYC — NEW YORK, NY**
Creative Team: **L. SHUR, J. BEVAN, R. SIMONIAN, F. SAENZ RECIO, J. BRENNICK, T. JURKIEWICZ, M. EASTWOOD, E. EHRICH, G. HEFFRON, S. MEISE**
Client: **VOGUE ITALIA**

Creative Firm: **MPHASIS ON FRONTIER — DENVER, CO**
Creative Team: **DANA BARAK**
Client: **WILD BLUE YONDER MAGAZINE**

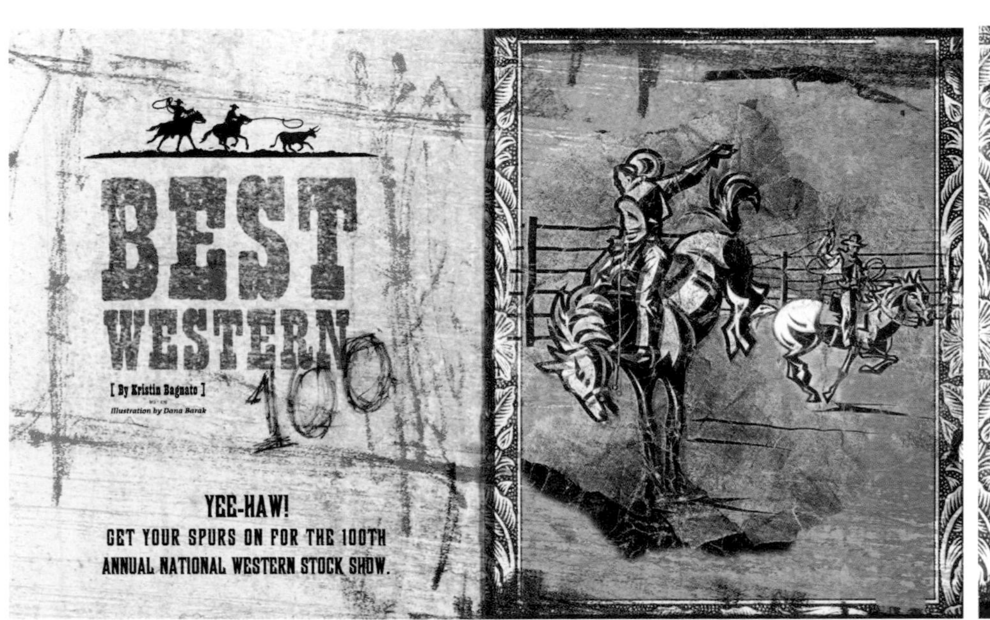

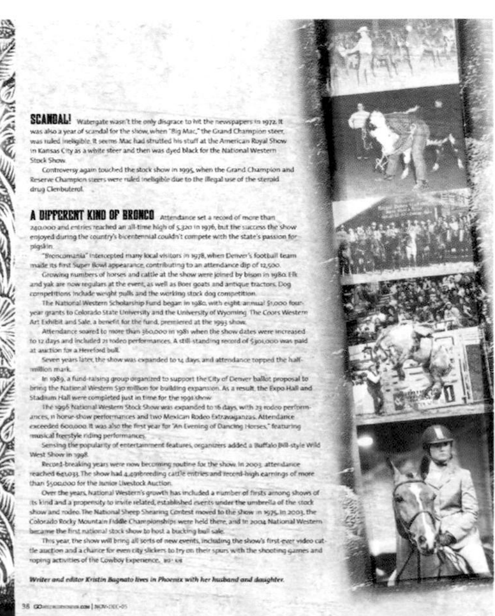

SCANDAL! Watergate wasn't the only disgrace to hit the newspapers in 1972. It was also a year of scandal for the show, when "Big Mac," the Grand Champion steer, was ruled ineligible. It seems Mac had strutted his stuff at the American Royal Show in Kansas City as a white steer and then was dyed black for the National Western Stock Show.

Controversy again touched the stock show in 1995, when the Grand Champion and Reserve Champion steers were ruled ineligible due to the illegal use of the steroid drug Clenbuterol.

A DIFFERENT KIND OF BRONCO Attendance set a record of more than 240,000 and entries reached an all-time high of 5,320 in 1976, but the success the show enjoyed during the country's bicentennial couldn't compete with the state's passion for pigskin.

"Broncomania" intercepted many local visitors in 1978, when Denver's football team made its first Super Bowl appearance, contributing to an attendance dip of 12,500.

Growing numbers of horses and cattle at the show were joined by bison in 1980. Elk and yak are now regulars at the event, as well as Boer goats and antique tractors. Dog competitions include weight pulls and the working stock dog competition.

The National Western Scholarship Fund began in 1980, with eight annual $1,000 four-year grants to Colorado State University and the University of Wyoming. The Coors Western Art Exhibit and Sale, a benefit for the fund, premiered at the 1993 show.

Attendance soared to more than 360,000 in 1981 when the show dates were increased to 12 days and included 21 rodeo performances. A still-standing record of $301,000 was paid at auction for a Hereford bull.

Seven years later, the show was expanded to 14 days and attendance topped the half-million mark.

In 1989, a fund-raising group organized to support the City of Denver ballot proposal to bring the National Western $30 million for building expansion. As a result, the Expo Hall and Stadium Hall were completed just in time for the 1991 show.

The 1996 National Western Stock Show was expanded to 16 days, with 23 rodeo performances, 11 horse-show performances and two Mexican Rodeo Extravaganzas. Attendance exceeded 600,000. It was also the first year for "An Evening of Dancing Horses," featuring musical freestyle riding performances.

Sensing the popularity of entertainment features, organizers added a Buffalo Bill-style Wild West Show in 1998.

Record-breaking years were now becoming routine for the show. In 2003, attendance reached 641,033. The show had 4,491 breeding cattle entries and record-high earnings of more than $500,000 for the Junior Livestock Auction.

Over the years, National Western's growth has included a number of firsts among shows of its kind and a propensity to invite related, established events under the umbrella of the stock show and rodeo. The National Sheep Shearing Contest moved to the show in 1975. In 2003, the Colorado Rocky Mountain Fiddle Championships were held there, and in 2004 National Western became the first national stock show to host a bucking bull sale.

This year, the show will bring all sorts of new events, including the show's first-ever video cattle auction and a chance for even city slickers to try on their spurs with the shooting games and roping activities of the Cowboy Experience.

Writer and editor Kristin Bagnato lives in Phoenix with her husband and daughter.

38 | NOV-DEC-05

Creative Firm: **MPHASIS ON FRONTIER — DENVER, CO**
Creative Team: **BRYANT FERNANDEZ, JOE HANCOCK**
Client: **WILD BLUE YONDER MAGAZINE**

Creative Firm: **STELLAR DEBRIS — HADANO-SHI, KANAGAWA-KEN, JAPAN**
Creative Team: **CHRISTOPHER JONES**
Client: **RENO-TAHOE AMERICAN MARKETING ASSOCIATION**

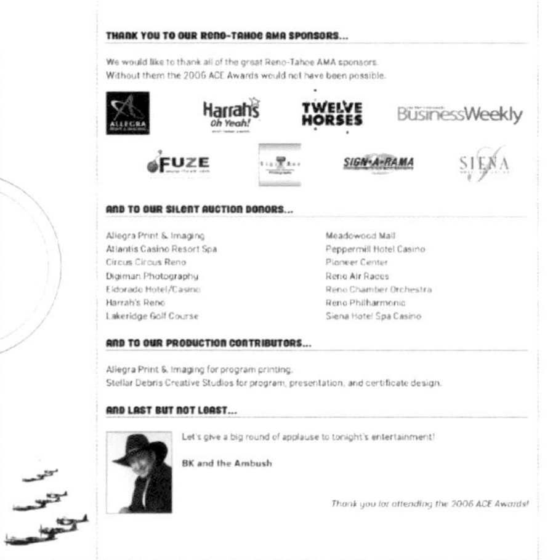

Creative Firm: **MPHASIS ON FRONTIER — DENVER, CO**
Creative Team: **BRYANT FERNANDEZ, HOWARD SOKOL**
Client: **WILD BLUE YONDER MAGAZINE**

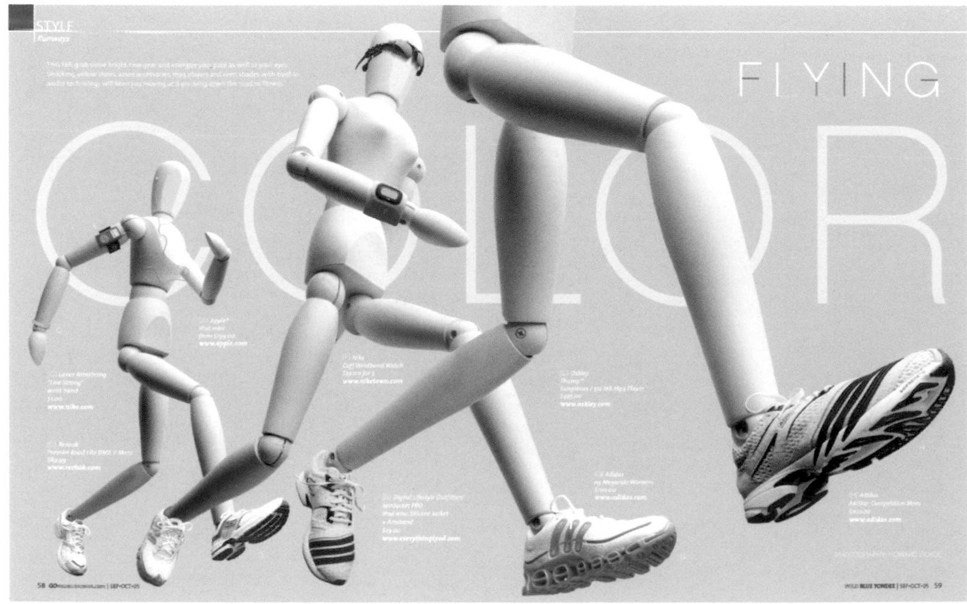

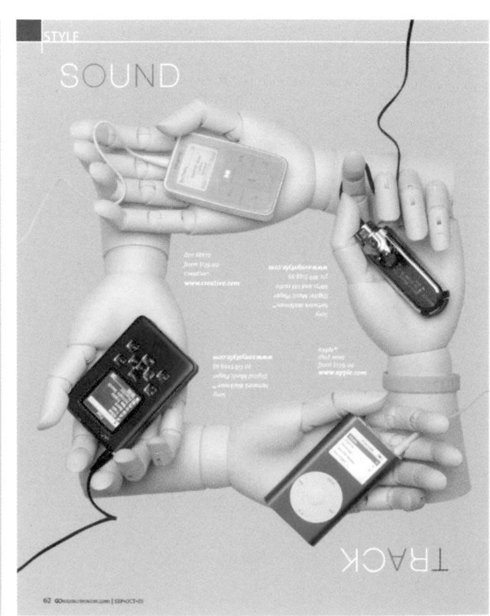

Creative Firm: **TAXI CANADA INC. — TORONTO, ON, CANADA**
Creative Team: **ZAK MROUEH, MARK SCOTT, IRFAN KHAN, DEREK SHAPTON, MARK PROLE, BRUCE ELLIS**
Client: **IHAVEANIDEA**

Pomegranate Perfected.

Consumers are clamoring for drinks that feature the flavor of pomegranate. Now there's PAMA, the world's first true pomegranate liqueur that captures the deep crimson color and complex sweet yet tart taste of all-natural California pomegranates. It's the perfect way to satisfy your customers.

PAMA
POMEGRANATE LIQUEUR
pamaliqueur.com

Creative Firm: **KELLER CRESCENT — EVANSVILLE, IN**
Creative Team: **GERRY ULRICH, LYNNE MLADY, RANDY ROHN**

Creative Firm: **FITTING GROUP — PITTSBURGH, PA**
Creative Team: **TRAVIS NORRIS, BECKY THURNER**
Client: **FITTING GROUP**

Creative Firm: **GREENLIGHT DESIGNS — N. HOLLYWOOD, CA**
Creative Team: **TAMI MAHNKEN, DARRYL SHELLY, MELISSA IRWIN, SHAUN WOOD**
Client: **LIONSGATE FILMS**

Creative Firm: **RODGERS TOWNSEND — ST. LOUIS, MO**
Creative Team: **TOM HUDDER, LUKE PARTRIDGE, MICHAEL MCCORMICK, JEFF MINTON, CHERYL SPARKS**
Client: **AT&T**

Creative Firm: **RODGERS TOWNSEND — ST. LOUIS, MO**
Creative Team: **TOM HUDDER, LUKE PARTRIDGE, MICHAEL MCCORMICK, JEFF MINTON, CHERYL SPARKS**
Client: **AT&T**

Creative Firm: **RODGERS TOWNSEND — ST. LOUIS, MO**
Creative Team: **TOM HUDDER, LUKE PARTRIDGE, MICHAEL MCCORMICK, JEFF MINTON, CHERYL SPARKS**
Client: **AT&T**

Creative Firm: **RODGERS TOWNSEND — ST. LOUIS, MO**
Creative Team: **TOM HUDDER, LUKE PARTRIDGE, MICHAEL MCCORMICK, JEFF MINTON, CHERYL SPARKS**
Client: **AT&T**

Creative Firm: **RODGERS TOWNSEND — ST. LOUIS, MO**
Creative Team: **TOM HUDDER, LUKE PARTRIDGE, MICHAEL MCCORMICK, JEFF MINTON, CHERYL SPARKS**
Client: **AT&T**

Creative Firm: **RODGERS TOWNSEND — ST. LOUIS, MO**
Creative Team: **TOM HUDDER, LUKE PARTRIDGE, MICHAEL MCCORMICK, JEFF MINTON, CHERYL SPARKS**
Client: **AT&T**

Creative Firm: **RODGERS TOWNSEND — ST. LOUIS, MO**
Creative Team: **TOM HUDDER, LUKE PARTRIDGE, MICHAEL MCCORMICK, JEFF MINTON, CHERYL SPARKS**
Client: **AT&T**

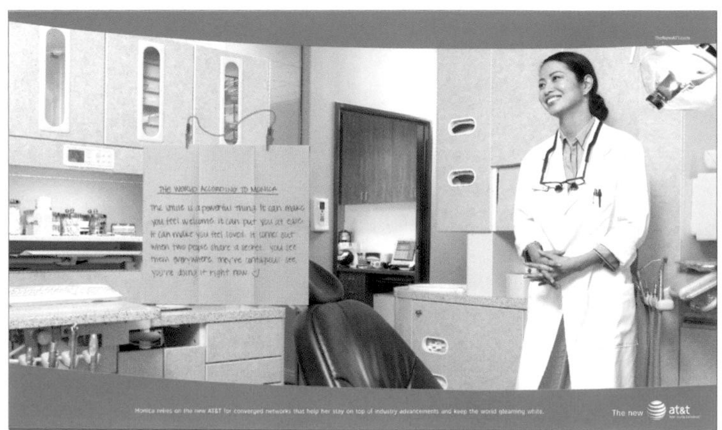

Creative Firm: **RODGERS TOWNSEND — ST. LOUIS, MO**
Creative Team: **TOM HUDDER, MIKE DILLON, FRANK SCHOTT, CHERYL SPARKS**
Client: **AT&T**

Creative Firm: **RODGERS TOWNSEND — ST. LOUIS, MO**
Creative Team: **TOM HUDDER, FRANK SCHOTT, CHRIS HANLEY, CHERYL SPARKS**
Client: **AT&T**

Creative Firm: **RODGERS TOWNSEND — ST. LOUIS, MO**
Creative Team: **TOM HUDDER, MARK ARNOLD, TODD MITCHELL, FRANK SCHOTT, CHERYL SPARKS**
Client: **AT&T**

Creative Firm: **RODGERS TOWNSEND — ST. LOUIS, MO**
Creative Team: **TOM HUDDER, LUKE PARTRIDGE, MICHAEL MCCORMICK, FRANK SCHOTT, CHERYL SPARKS,**
Client: **AT&T**

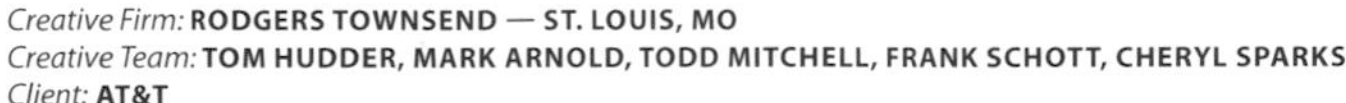

Creative Firm: **RODGERS TOWNSEND — ST. LOUIS, MO**
Creative Team: **TOM HUDDER, MARK ARNOLD, TODD MITCHELL, FRANK SCHOTT, CHERYL SPARKS**
Client: **AT&T**

Creative Firm: **RODGERS TOWNSEND — ST. LOUIS, MO**
Creative Team: **TOM HUDDER, MARK ARNOLD, TODD MITCHELL, FRANK SCHOTT, CHERYL SPARKS**
Client: **AT&T**

Creative Firm: **RODGERS TOWNSEND — ST. LOUIS, MO**
Creative Team: **TOM HUDDER, MIKE DILLON, FRANK SCHOTT, CHERYL SPARKS**
Client: **AT&T**

Creative Firm: **RODGERS TOWNSEND — ST. LOUIS, MO**
Creative Team: **TOM HUDDER, MIKE DILLON, FRANK SCHOTT, CHERYL SPARKS**
Client: **AT&T**

Creative Firm: **RODGERS TOWNSEND — ST. LOUIS, MO**
Creative Team: **TOM HUDDER, LUKE PARTRIDGE, MICHAEL MC CORMICK, FRANK SCHOTT, CHERYL SPARKS**
Client: **AT&T**

Creative Firm: **BUCK & PULLEYN — PITTSFORD, NY**
Creative Team: **DAN MULCAHY, DONA BAGLEY, PJ GALGAY, BRENDA BRODSKY, SUE STOJANOVICH**
Client: **KODAK ENTERTAINMENT IMAGING**

Creative Firm: **RODGERS TOWNSEND — ST. LOUIS, MO**
Creative Team: **TOM HUDDER, MARK ARNOLD, TODD MITCHELL, FRANK SCHOTT, CHERYL SPARKS**
Client: **AT&T**

Creative Firm: **RODGERS TOWNSEND — ST. LOUIS, MO**
Creative Team: **TOM HUDDER, MARK ARNOLD, TODD MITCHELL, FRANK SCHOTT, CHERYL SPARKS**
Client: **AT&T**

Creative Firm: **RODGERS TOWNSEND — ST. LOUIS, MO**
Creative Team: **TOM HUDDER, MARK ARNOLD, TODD MITCHELL, FRANK SCHOTT, CHERYL SPARKS**
Client: **AT&T**

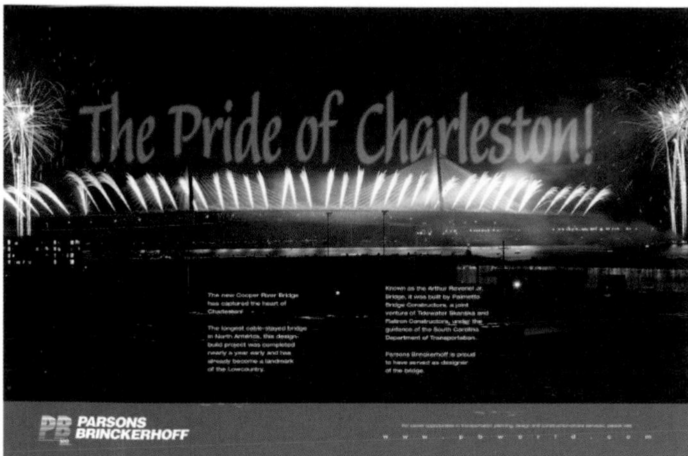

Creative Firm: **PARSONS BRINCKERHOFF — NEW YORK, NY**
Creative Team: **ANA TIBURCIO-RIVERA, TOM MALCOLM, TONY WINN**
Client: **PARSONS BRINCKERHOFF**

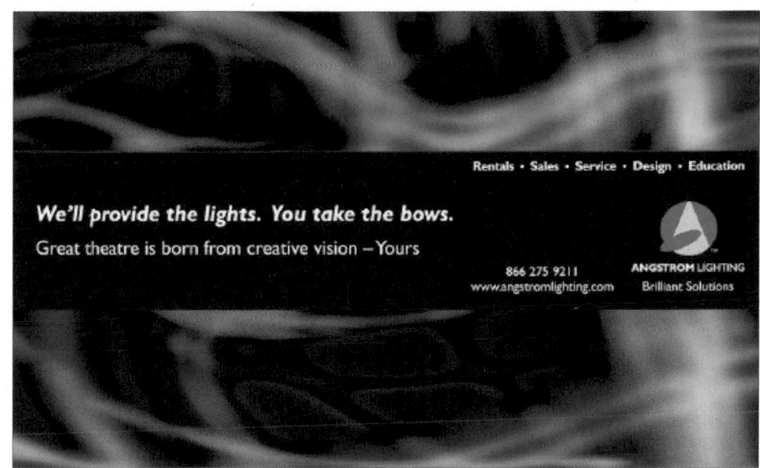

Creative Firm: **SHIMOKOCHI-REEVES — LOS ANGELES, CA**
Creative Team: **MAMORU SHIMOKOCHI, ANNE REEVES, MARTY LIPKIN**
Client: **ANGSTROM LIGHTING**

Creative Firm: **NEURON SYNDICATE INC. — SANTA MONICA, CA**
Creative Team: **SEAN ALATORRE, RYAN CRAMER**
Client: **WARNER BROS.**

Creative Firm: **MT&L PUBLIC RELATIONS LTD. — HALIFAX, NS, CANADA**
Creative Team: **PAUL WILLIAMS, GETTY IMAGES STOCK**
Client: **HALIFAX PORT AUTHORITY**

Creative Firm: **HITCHCOCK FLEMING & ASSOCIATES INC. — AKRON, OH**
Creative Team: **NICK BETRO, TODD MOSER, GREG PFIFFNER, MARK COLLINS**
Client: **LP BUILDING PRODUCTS**

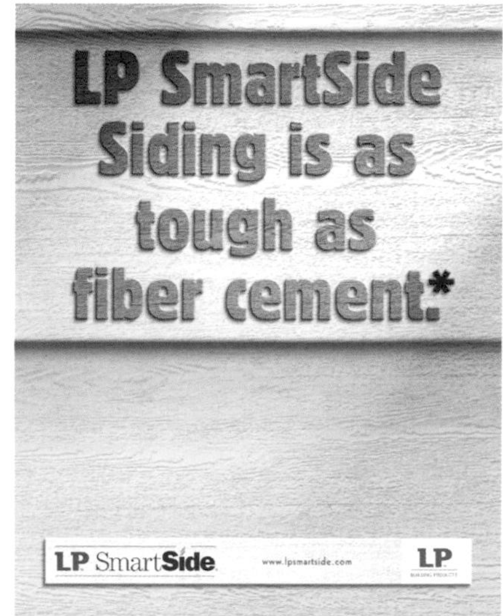

Creative Firm: **SPIKE TV — NEW YORK, NY**
Creative Team: **BOB SALAZAR, NIELS SCHUURMANS, GREG DALY**
Client: **SPIKE**

Creative Firm: **BOOMM! MARKETING & COMMUNICATIONS — WESTCHESTER, IL**
Client: **ALCAN PACKAGING**

Creative Firm: **RODGERS TOWNSEND — ST. LOUIS, MO**
Creative Team: **TOM HUDDER, TOM TOWNSEND, CHERYL SPARKS**
Client: **SBC COMMUNICATIONS, INC**

Creative Firm: **RODGERS TOWNSEND — ST. LOUIS, MO**
Creative Team: **TOM HUDDER, LUKE PARTRIDGE, MICHAEL MCCORMICK, CHERYL SPARKS**
Client: **SBC COMMUNICATIONS, INC**

Creative Firm: **BRIGHT ORANGE ADVERTISING — RICHMOND, VA**
Creative Team: **BRUCE GOLDMAN, DANIEL GOLDMAN**
Client: **OAKLEA PRESS**

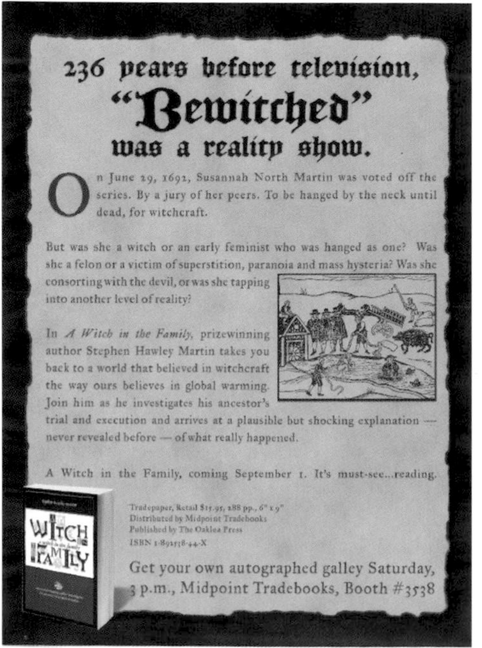

Creative Firm: **SILVER COMMUNICATIONS INC — NEW YORK, NY**
Creative Team: **GREGG SIBERT, CHRISTINA WEISSMAN, JEFF EWEN**
Client: **BNY BROKERAGE**

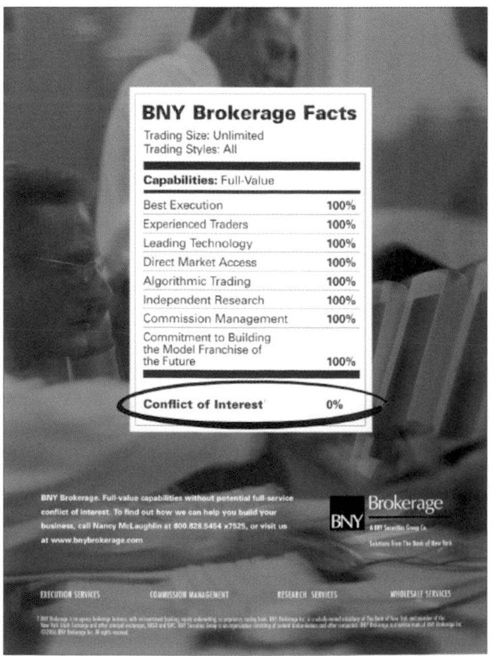

Creative Firm: **RODGERS TOWNSEND — ST. LOUIS, MO**
Creative Team: **TOM HUDDER, TON TOWNSEND**
Client: **SBC COMMUNICATIONS, INC**

Creative Firm: **TAXI CANADA INC.—TORONTO, ON, CANADA**
Creative Team: **ZAK MROUEH, JOHNNIE INGRAM, RON SMRCZEK, ALEXIS GROPPER, TRACY HAAPAMAKI, TOM FEILER**
Client: **IHAVEANIDEA**

Creative Firm: **BSY ASSOCIATES INC. — HOLMDEL, NJ**
Creative Team: **LARRY RAVINETT, GORDON FORSYTH IV, JOHN BRADY**
Client: **NATIONAL RETAIL SYSTEMS INC.**

Creative Firm: **RODGERS TOWNSEND — ST. LOUIS, MO**
Creative Team: **TOM HUDDER, LUKE PARTRIDGE, MICHAEL MCCORMICK, JEFF MINTON, CHERYL SPARKS**
Client: **AT&T**

Creative Firm: **VANPELT CREATIVE — GARLAND, TX**
Creative Team: **CHIP VANPELT, BRYAN MATTHEWS, LEWIS LEE**
Client: **VARI LITE**

Creative Firm: **SILVER COMMUNICATIONS INC — NEW YORK, NY**
Creative Team: **GREGG SIBERT, CHRISTINA WEISSMAN, JEFF EWEN**
Client: **BNY BROKERAGE**

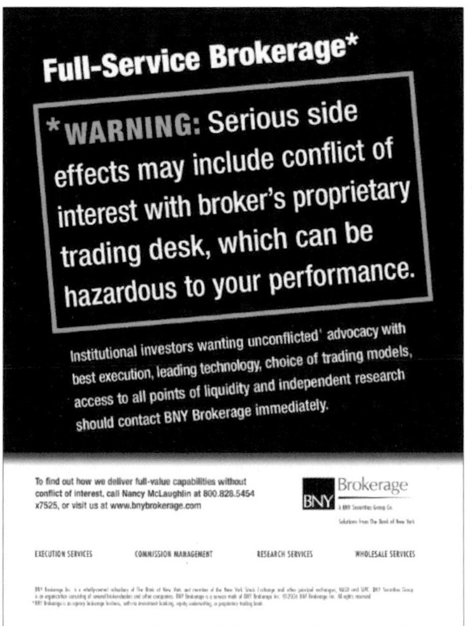

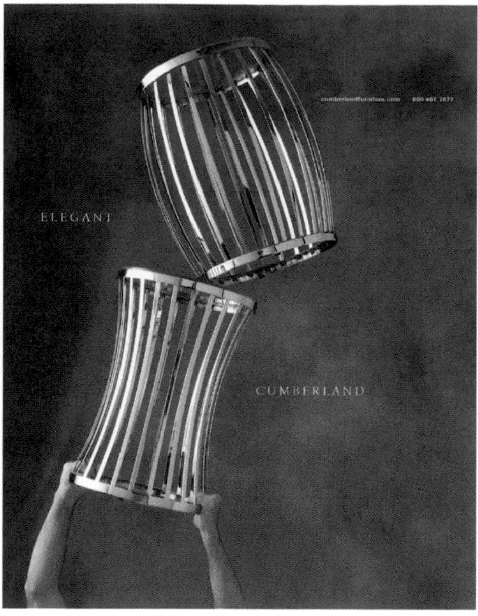

Creative Firm: **BBK STUDIO — GRAND RAPIDS, MI**
Creative Team: **KEVIN BUDELMANN, BRIAN HAUCH, CHUCK SHOTWELL**
Client: **CUMBERLAND FURNITURE**

Creative Firm: **GREENFIELD/BELSER LTD. — WASHINGTON, DC**
Creative Team: **BURKEY BELSER, GEORGE KELL, CHRIS ATKIN, JAIME CHIRINOS**
Client: **CHOATE HALL & STEWART LLP**

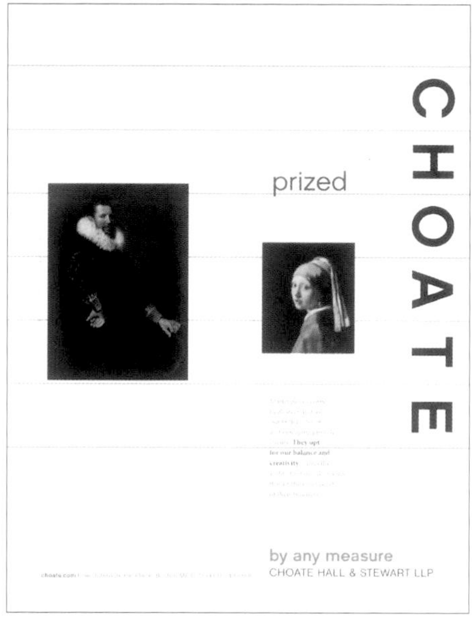

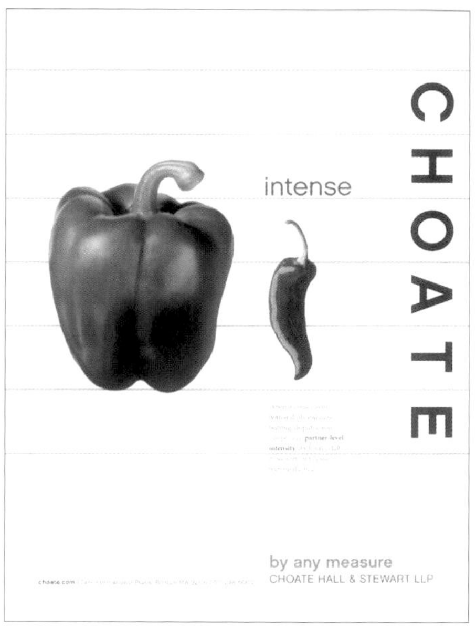

Creative Firm: **YOUNG & RUBICAM GMBH & CO. KG — FRANKFURT AM MAIN, HESSEN, GERMANY**
Creative Team: **UWE MARQUARDT, CHRISTIAN DAUL, INGMAR KRANNICH, KAJO STRAUCH**
Client: **NEUDORFF**

Creative Firm: **RODGERS TOWNSEND — ST. LOUIS, MO**
Creative Team: **TOM HUDDER, LUKE PARTRIDGE, MICHAEL MCCORMICK, CHRIS HANLEY, CHERYL SPARKS**
Client: **AT&T**

Creative Firm: **GREENFIELD/BELSER LTD. — WASHINGTON, DC**
Creative Team: **BURKEY BELSER, JOE WALSH, CRAIG FRAZIER, GEORGE KELL, CHRIS ATKIN**
Client: **NAVIGANT CONSULTING**

Creative Firm: **STELLAR DEBRIS — HADANO-SHI, KANAGAWA-KEN, JAPAN**
Creative Team: **CHRISTOPHER JONES**
Client: **BYTWARE, INC.**

Creative Firm: **CMT — NEW YORK, NY**
Creative Team: **JAMES HITCHCOCK, MICHAEL ENGLEMAN, AMIE NGUYEN, LINDA ZACK**
Client: **CMT**

Creative Firm: **RODGERS TOWNSEND — ST. LOUIS, MO**
Creative Team: **TOM HUDDER, TOM TOWNSEND**
Client: **SBC COMMUNICATIONS, INC**

Creative Firm: **GREENFIELD/BELSER LTD. — WASHINGTON, DC**
Creative Team: **BURKEY BELSER, MATT MASON, MARK THOMAS, GEORGE KELL, GENE SHAFFER, JAIME CHIRINOS**
Client: **FORD & HARRISON, LLP**

Creative Firm: **SILVER COMMUNICATIONS INC — NEW YORK, NY**
Creative Team: **GREGG SIBERT, CHRISTINA WEISSMAN, JEFF EWEN**
Client: **ADP CLEARING & OUTSOURCING SERVICES**

Creative Firm: **RODGERS TOWNSEND — ST. LOUIS, MO**
Creative Team: **TOM HUDDER, LUKE PARTRIDGE, MARK ARNOLD, FRANK SCHOTT**
Client: **AT&T**

Creative Firm: **RTS RIEGER TEAM WERBEAGENTUR GMBH — LEINFELDEN-ECHTERDINGEN, GERMANY**
Creative Team: **UTE WITZMANN, CHRISTIAN GRIMM**
Client: **CHRISTIAN WINKLER GMBH & CO. KG**

Creative Firm: **LEVERAGE MARKETING GROUP — NEWTOWN, CT**
Creative Team: **DAVID GOODWICK , RICH BRZOZOWSKI, TOM MARKS**
Client: **GE SECURITY**

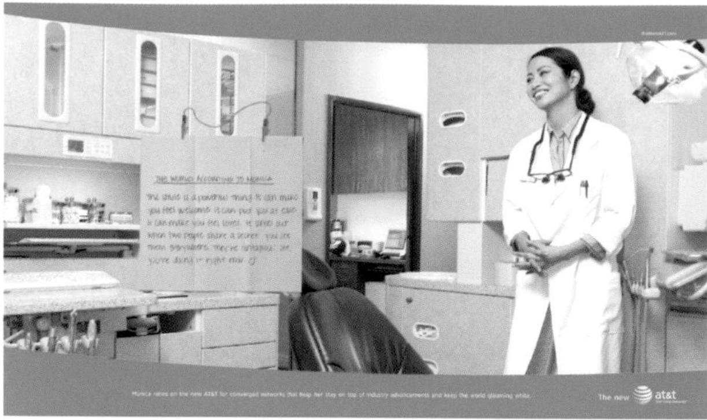

Creative Firm: **RODGERS TOWNSEND — ST. LOUIS, MO**
Creative Team: **TOM HUDDER, LUKE PARTRIDGE, MICHAEL MCCORMICK, CHRIS HANLEY, CHERYL SPARKS**
Client: **AT&T**

Creative Firm: **THE MONOGRAM GROUP — CHICAGO, IL**
Creative Team: **HAROLD WOODRIDGE, CHIP BALCH, CHRISTA VELBEL**
Client: **MFC CAPITAL**

Creative Firm: **RODGERS TOWNSEND — ST. LOUIS, MO**
Creative Team: **TOM HUDDER, LUKE PARTRIDGE, MARK ARNOLD, FRANK SCHOTT, CHERYL SPARKS**
Client: **AT&T**

Creative Firm: **SILVER COMMUNICATIONS INC — NEW YORK, NY**
Creative Team: **GREGG SIBERT, CHRISTINA WEISSMAN, JEFF EWEN**
Client: **BNY GLOBAL TRANSITION MANAGEMENT**

Creative Firm: **RTS RIEGER TEAM WERBEAGENTUR GMBH — LEINFELDEN-ECHTERDINGEN, GERMANY**
Creative Team: **ANNETTE PIENTKA, FRIEDERIKE APEL, SIEGRIED SCHAAL**
Client: **NEOMAN BUS GMBH**

Creative Firm: **GREENFIELD/BELSER LTD. — WASHINGTON, DC**
Creative Team: **BURKEY BELSER, SIOBHAN DAVIS, ALYSON FIELDMAN, BRANDEE CAHIR**
Client: **WEINTRAUB GENSHLEA CHEDIAK**

Creative Firm: **JWT DUESSELDORF — DUESSELDORF, NRW, GERMANY**
Creative Team: **EDDY GREENWOOD, JOHN ABEL, MARTIJN OORT, NORBERT ANDRUP, ELKE BOLL, ALEXANDRA LAUFF**
Client: **MAZDA MOTOR EUROPE**

Creative Firm: **PETERSON MILLA HOOKS — MINNEAPOLIS, MN**
Creative Team: **DAVE PETERSON, ERIKA WALDEN, CATHERINE IRMITER, ELLEN FREGO, KEN BARLAGE**
Client: **TARGET**

Creative Firm: **PURPLE FOCUS PVT. LTD. — INDORE, MADHYA PRADESH, INDIA**
Creative Team: **SATYAJIT RAI, JITENDRA RAMPURIA, VINOD BHARGAV, PURPLE PRODUCTIONS**
Client: **PINNACLE INDUSTRIES**

Creative Firm: **ENGINE, LLC — SAN FRANCISCO, CA**
Creative Team: **LOTUS CHILD, GEOFF SKIGEN**
Client: **MEDJOOL**

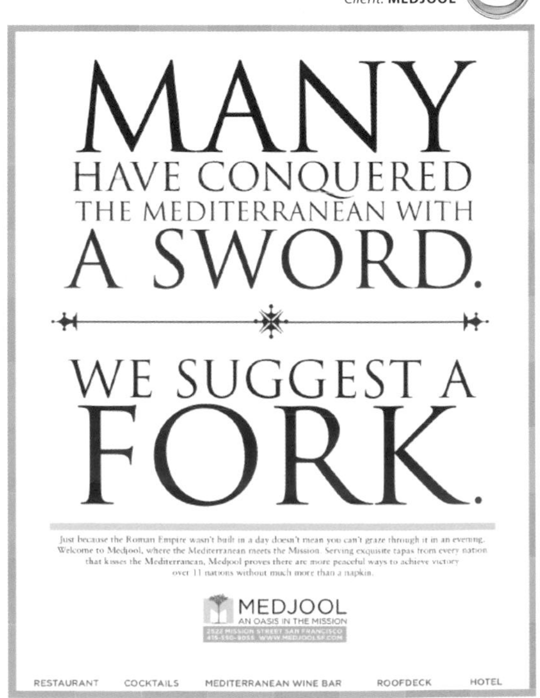

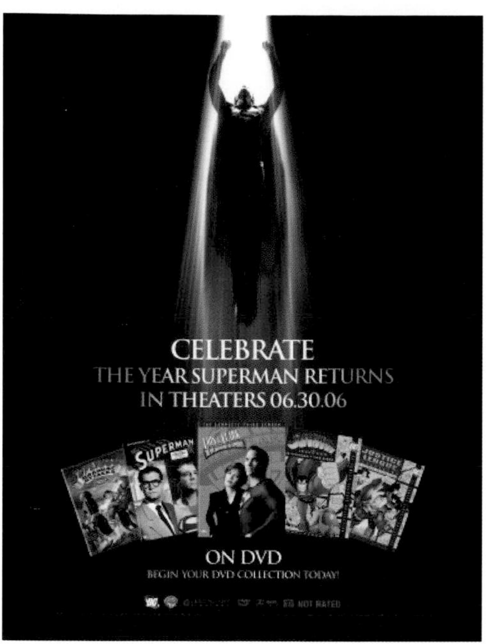

Creative Firm: **NEURON SYNDICATE INC. — SANTA MONICA, CA**
Creative Team: **RYAN CRAMER, SEAN ALATORRE**
Client: **WARNER BROS.**

Creative Firm: **JWT DUESSELDORF — DUESSELDORF, NRW, GERMANY**
Creative Team: **EDDY GREENWOOD, JOHN ABEL, BO HYLEN, BLAKE DUERDEN, ELKE BOLL, ALEXANDRA LAUFF**
Client: **MAZDA MOTOR EUROPE**

Creative Firm: **COMEDY CENTRAL — NEW YORK, NY**
Creative Team: **SHILO, ROLYN BARTHELMAN**

Creative Firm: **SPIKE TV — NEW YORK, NY**
Creative Team: **ANDRE RAZO, BOB SALAZAR, NIELS SCHUURMANS**
Client: **SPIKE**

Creative Firm: **COMEDY CENTRAL — NEW YORK, NY**
Creative Team: **CHARLES HAMILTON, STEPHEN KAMSLER, ROLYN BARTHELMAN**

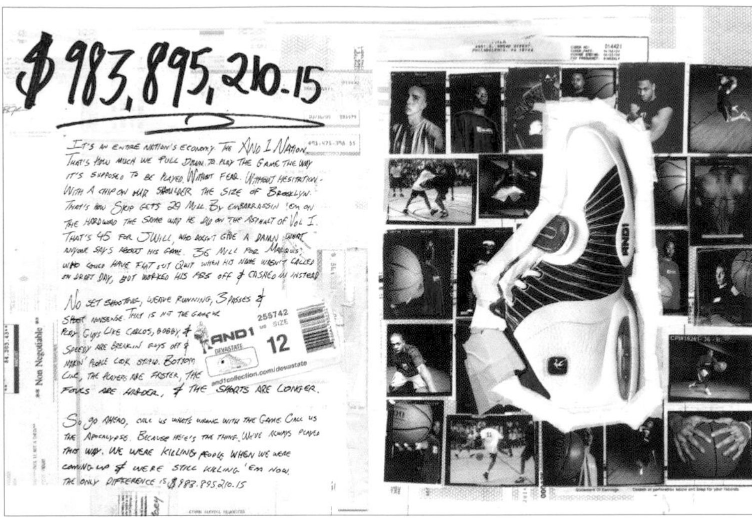

Creative Firm: **160 OVER 90 — PHILADELPHIA, PA**
Creative Team: **DARRYL CILLI, JIM WALLS, DAN SHEPELAVY, GIACOMO CIMINELLO, STEPHEN PENNING, BRENDAN QUINN**
Client: **AND1 BASKETBALL**

C'mon Jews...
show them who *really* runs Hollywood.
L RON HUBBARD'S SCIENTOLOGY Celebrity Center
Comedy Central congratulates SOUTH PARK on your Primetime Emmy nomination, OUTSTANDING ANIMATED PROGRAM (For Programming Less Than One Hour) "Trapped in the Closet"
comedycentral.com

Creative Firm: **COMEDY CENTRAL — NEW YORK, NY**
Creative Team: **STEPHEN KAMSLER, JOHN LEFTERATOS, ROLYN BARTHELMAN**

Creative Firm: **TAXI CANADA — MONTRÉAL, QC, CANADA**
Creative Team: **STÉPHANE CHARIER, ELYSE NOËL DE TILLY, BRIAN GILL, ROBERTO BAIBICH, PATRICK CHAUBET, LEDA & ST-JACQUES**
Client: **DERMETK PHARMACEUTIQUE (ROBERT LAVOIE-PRESIDENT)**

Creative Firm: **TIME MARKETING - CREATIVE SERVICES — NEW YORK, NY**
Creative Team: **LIZA GREENE, ANDREA COSTA, CINDY MURPHY**
Client: **KELLOGG'S**

Creative Firm: **PETERSON MILLA HOOKS — MINNEAPOLIS, MN**
Creative Team: **DAVE PETERSON, SUE KAASE, ELLEN FREGO, CARRIE REAY, GAYLE MALCOLM**
Client: **TARGET**

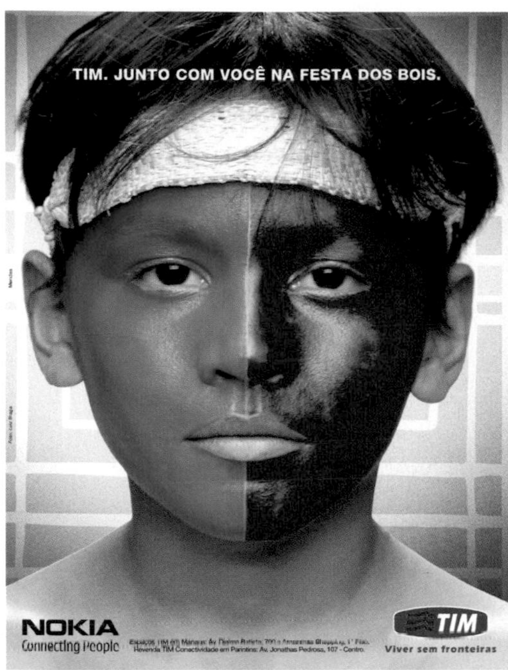

Creative Firm: **MENDES PUBLICIDADE — BELÉM, PARÁ, BRAZIL**
Creative Team: **OSWALDO MENDES, MARCELO AMORIM**
Client: **TIM NORTE**

Creative Firm: **COMEDY CENTRAL — NEW YORK, NY**
Creative Team: **ROLYN BARTHELMAN, STEPHEN KAMSLER**

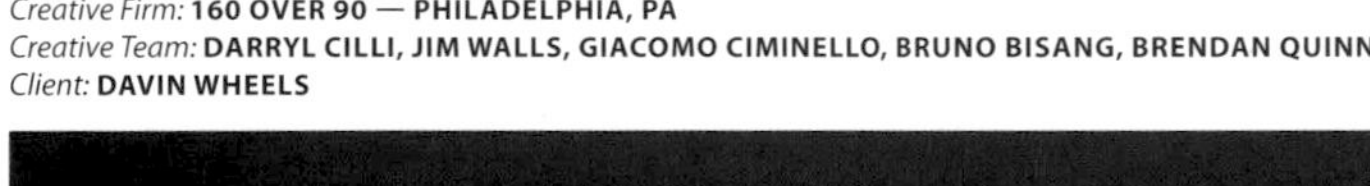

Creative Firm: **BURROWS — BRENTWOOD, ESSEX, UNITED KINGDOM**
Creative Team: **ROYDON HEARNE, DARRYL SMITH, AARON HULSIZER, LUCY WELDON**
Client: **VOLVO CARS**

Creative Firm: **160 OVER 90 — PHILADELPHIA, PA**
Creative Team: **DARRYL CILLI, JIM WALLS, GIACOMO CIMINELLO, BRUNO BISANG, BRENDAN QUINN**
Client: **DAVIN WHEELS**

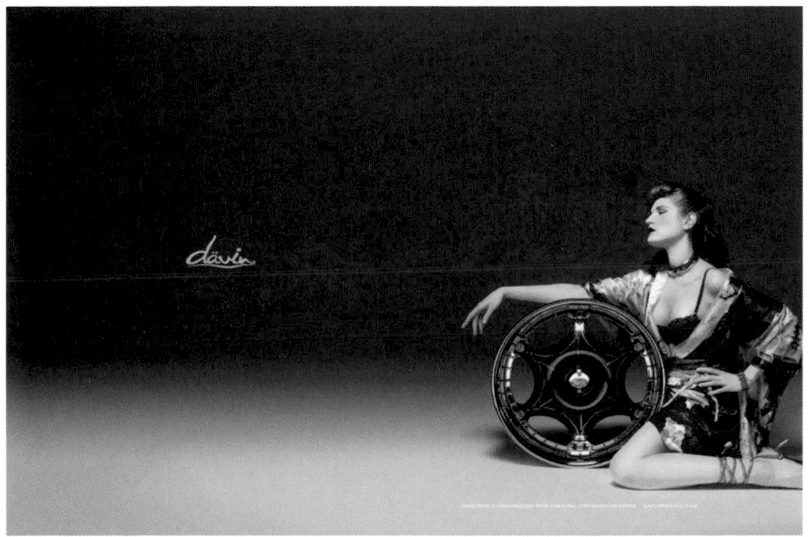

Creative Firm: **HERE! NETWORKS — NEW YORK, NY**
Creative Team: **ERIC FELDMAN, MEGAN ELLIS**

Creative Firm: **CREATIVE ALLIANCE — LOUISVILLE, KY**
Creative Team: **SCOTT BOSWELL, MARK ROSENTHAL**
Client: **CHS HOSPITALS**

Creative Firm: **HBO OFF-AIR CREATIVE SERVICES — NEW YORK, NY**
Creative Team: **VENUS DENNISON, ANA RACELIS, CARLOS TEJEDA, JOSE MENDEZ**
Client: **HBO LATINO**

Creative Firm: **NEURON SYNDICATE INC. — SANTA MONICA, CA**
Creative Team: **SEAN ALATORRE, RYAN CRAMER, JASON BURNAM, PHIL MCKENNA**
Client: **WARNER BROS.**

Creative Firm: **RODGERS TOWNSEND — ST. LOUIS, MO**
Creative Team: **TOM HUDDER, RYAN SMITH, TODD MITCHELL, CHERYL SPARKS**
Client: **ST. LOUIS CHILDREN'S HOSPITAL**

Creative Firm: **COMEDY CENTRAL — NEW YORK, NY**
Creative Team: **BUCK, LAURIE HINZMAN WHITE**

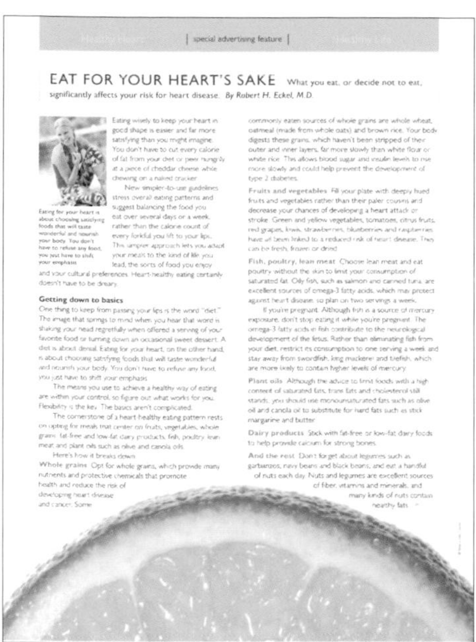

| special advertising feature |

EAT FOR YOUR HEART'S SAKE What you eat, or decide not to eat, significantly affects your risk for heart disease. By Robert H. Eckel, M.D.

Creative Firm: **TIME MARKETING - CREATIVE SERVICES — NEW YORK, NY**
Creative Team: **LIZA GREENE, RAY RUALO, CINDY MURPHY, TIM CALLAHAN**
Client: **TIME MAGAZINE**

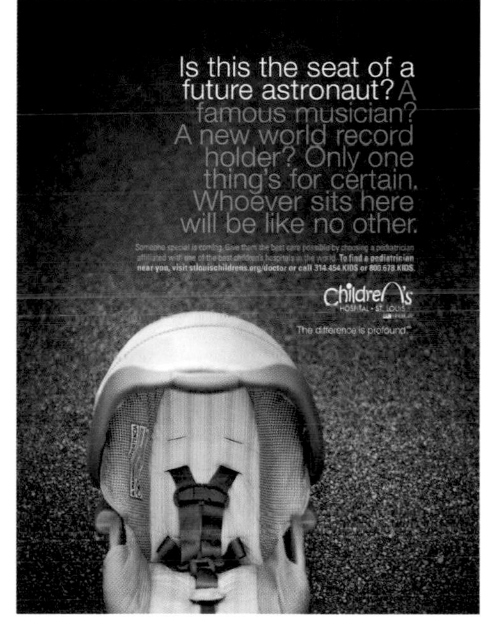

Creative Firm: **SILVER CREATIVE GROUP — SOUTH NORWALK, CT**
Creative Team: **PAUL ZULLO, TRACY WAXENBERG, SUZANNE PETROW**
Client: **THOMPSON BRANDS**

Creative Firm: **RODGERS TOWNSEND — ST. LOUIS, MO**
Creative Team: **TOM HUDDER, RYAN SMITH, TODD MITCHELL, CHERYL SPARKS**
Client: **ST. LOUIS CHILDREN'S HOSPITAL**

Creative Firm: **COMEDY CENTRAL — NEW YORK, NY**
Creative Team: **ROLYN BARTHELMAN, STEPHEN KAMSLER**

Creative Firm: **PLANET ADS AND DESIGN P/L — SINGAPORE**
Creative Team: **MICHELLE LAURIDSEN, HAL SUZUKI, KITANO TOMOYA**
Client: **DISCOVERY NETWORKS ASIA**

Creative Firm: **BURROWS — BRENTWOOD, ESSEX, UNITED KINGDOM**
Creative Team: **ROYDON HEARNE, ANDREW NICHOLSON, AARON HULSIZER, LUCY WELDON**
Client: **VOLVO CARS UK**

Creative Firm: **KELLER CRESCENT — EVANSVILLE, IN**
Creative Team: **RANDALL ROHN, GERRY ULRICH, RANDY ROHN**
Client: **HEAVEN HILL**

Creative Firm: **LEKASMILLER DESIGN — WALNUT CREEK, CA**
Creative Team: **LANA IP, TINA LEKAS MILLER**
Client: **MAIN STREET PROPERTIES**

Creative Firm: **HERE! NETWORKS — NEW YORK, NY**
Creative Team: **ERIC FELDMAN, MEGAN ELLIS**

Creative Firm: **CREATIVE ALLIANCE — LOUISVILLE, KY**
Creative Team: **SCOTT BOSWELL, MARK ROSENTHAL**
Client: **CHS HOSPITALS**

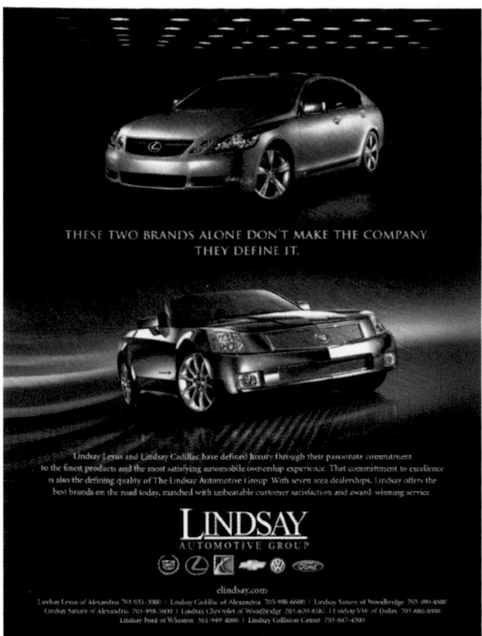

Creative Firm: **SIMPATICO DESIGN STUDIO — ALEXANDRIA, VA**
Creative Team: **AMY SIMPSON**
Client: **LINDSAY LEXUS AND LINDSAY CADILLAC**

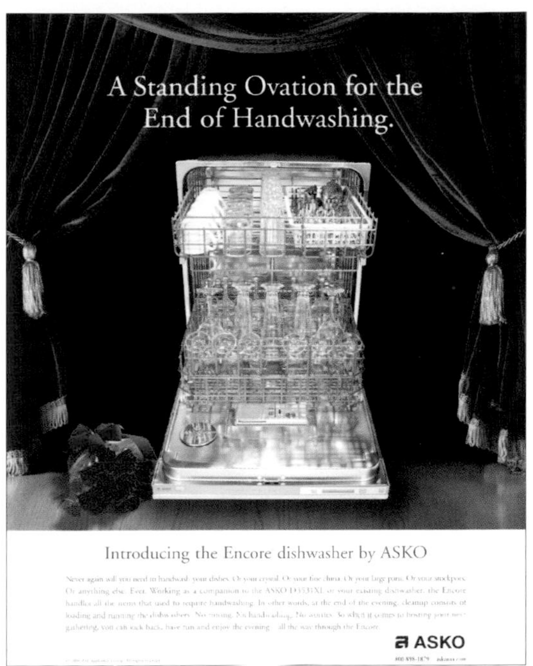

Creative Firm: **VANPELT CREATIVE — GARLAND, TX**
Creative Team: **CHIP VANPELT, TODD BRASHEAR, J.W. BURKEY**
Client: **AM APPLIANCE GROUP**

Creative Firm: **ENGINE, LLC — SAN FRANCISCO, CA**
Creative Team: **LOTUS CHILD, GEOFF SKIGEN**
Client: **MEDJOOL**

Creative Firm: **BURROWS — BRENTWOOD, ESSEX, UNITED KINGDOM**
Creative Team: **ROYDON HEARNE, MARK ELLIS, AARON HULSIZER, LUCY WELDON**
Client: **VOLVO CARS UK**

Creative Firm: **COMEDY CENTRAL — NEW YORK, NY**
Creative Team: **MICHELLE WILLEMS, LAURIE HINZMAN WHITE**

Creative Firm: **CREATIVE ALLIANCE — LOUISVILLE, KY**
Creative Team: **JOE ADAMS, SCOTT BOSWELL**
Client: **NANZ & KRAFT FLORISTS**

Creative Firm: **ENGINE, LLC — SAN FRANCISCO, CA**
Creative Team: **LOTUS CHILD, GEOFF SKIGEN**
Client: **MEDJOOL**

Creative Firm: **BURROWS — BRENTWOOD, ESSEX, UNITED KINGDOM**
Creative Team: **ROYDON HEARNE, ANDREW NICHOLSON, AARON HULSIZER, LUCY WELDON**
Client: **VOLVO CARS UK**

Creative Firm: **FUTURA DDB — LJUBLANA, SLOVENIA**
Creative Team: **ZORAN GABRIJAN, MARKO VICIC, ZARE KERIN, MARUSA KOZELJ**
Client: **DONAT**

Creative Firm: **PETERSON MILLA HOOKS — MINNEAPOLIS, MN**
Creative Team: **DAVE PETERSON, ERIKA WALDEN, CATHERINE IRMITER, ELLEN FREGO, KEN BARLAGE**
Client: **TARGET**

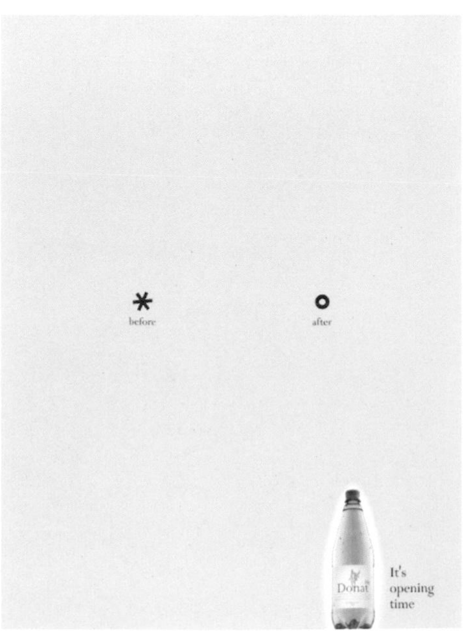

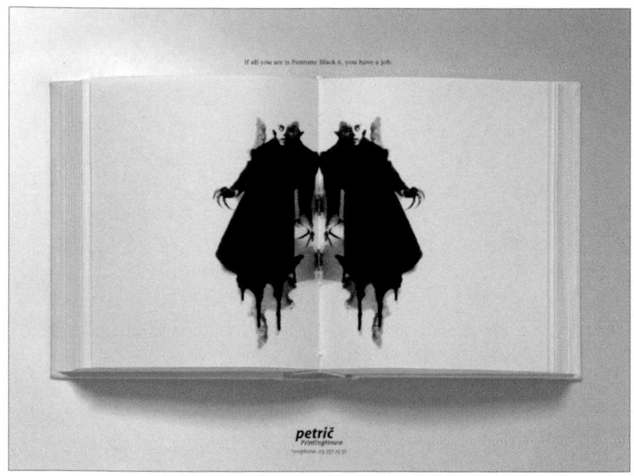

Creative Firm: **FUTURA DDB — LJUBLANA, SLOVENIA**
Creative Team: **ZARE KERIN, ZORAN GABRIAJAN, MIHA GROBLER**
Client: **PRINTING HOUSE PETRIC**

Creative Firm: **PETERSON MILLA HOOKS — MINNEAPOLIS, MN**
Creative Team: **DAVE PETERSON, SUE KAASE, ELLEN FREGO, CARRIE REAY, GAYLE MALCOLM**
Client: **TARGET**

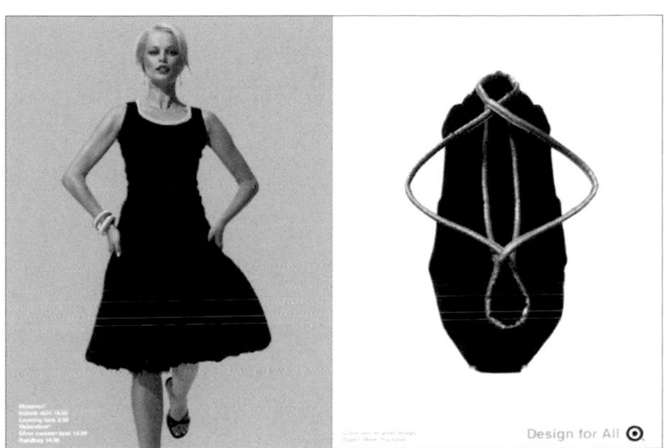

Creative Firm: **PETESON MILLA HOOKS —MINNEAPOLIS, MN**
Creative Team: **DAVE PETERSON, JENNY SHEARS, CARRIE REAY, ILAN RUBIN**
Client: **TARGET**

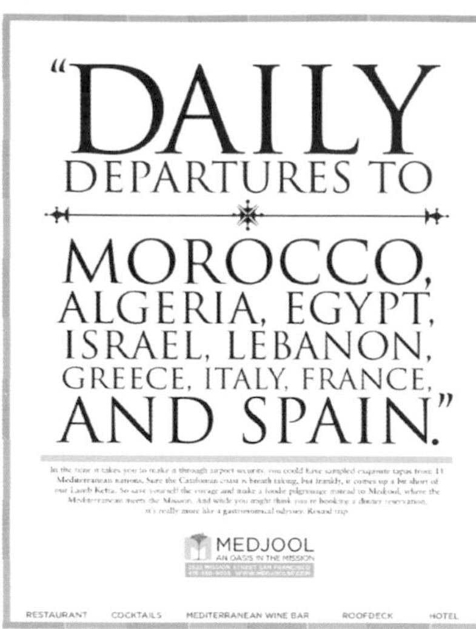

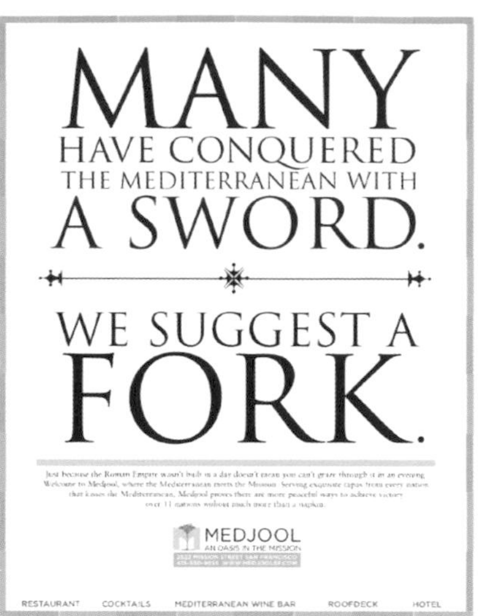

Creative Firm: **ENGINE, LLC— SAN FRANCISCO, CA**
Creative Team: **LOTUS CHILD, GEOFF SKIGEN**
Client: **MEDJOOL**

Creative Firm: **160 OVER 90 — PHILADELPHIA, PA**
Creative Team: **DARRYL CILLI, JIM WALLS, GIACOMO CIMINELLO, BRUNO BISANG, BRENDAN QUINN**
Client: **DAVIN WHEELS**

Creative Firm: **30SIXTY ADVERTISING+DESIGN, INC. — LOS ANGELES, CA**
Creative Team: **HENRY VIZCARRA, PÄR LARSSON, KASEY CHATILA, BRUCE VENTANILLA**
Client: **MGM HOME ENTERTAINMENT**

Creative Firm: **LAUNCH CREATIVE MARKETING**
Creative Team: **BRUCE BUTCHER, CHRISTINE MONAHAN**
Client: **UNITED STATIONERS**

Creative Firm: **ADVANTAGE LTD — HAMILTON, BERMUDA**
Creative Team: **SHEILA SEMOS, SAMI LILL**
Client: **BELCO LTD.**

Creative Firm: **PETERSON MILLA HOOKS — MINNEAPOLIS, MN**
Creative Team: **DAVE PETERSON, SUE KAASE, GAYLE OBODZINSKI, ELLEN FREGO, KENNETH WILLARDT, CATHERINE IRMITER**
Client: **TARGET**

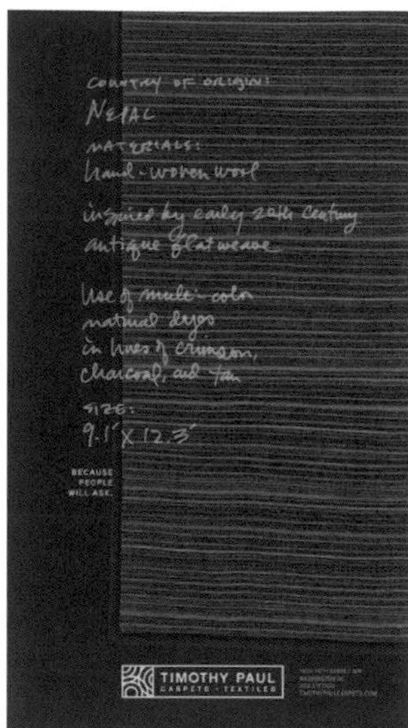

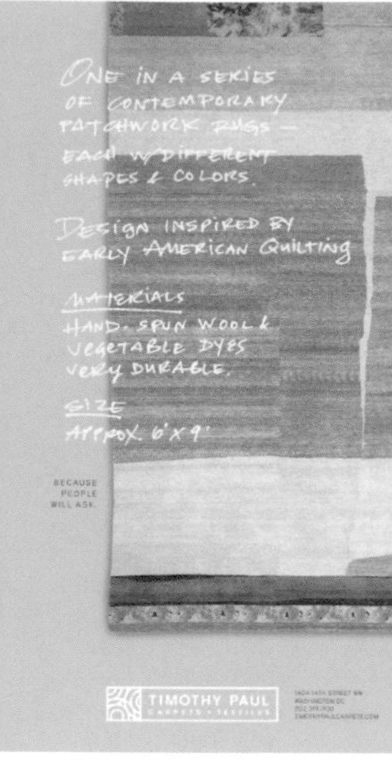

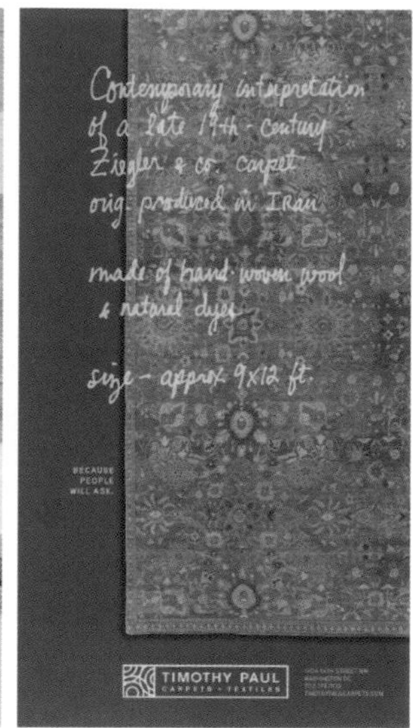

Creative Firm: **DESIGN NUT — KENSINGTON, MD**
Creative Team: **BRENT ALMOND, TIMOTHY WORRELL, THOMAS DEMARCO**
Client: **TIMOTHY PAUL CARPETS + TEXTILES**

Creative Firm: **NAMARO GRAPHIC DESIGNS, INC. — RHINEBECK, NY**
Creative Team: **NADINE ROBBINS, WENDY MACOMBER**
Client: **ORTHOPEDIC ASSOCIATES OF DUTCHESS COUNTY**

Creative Firm: **D'ADDA, LORENZINI, VIGORELLI, BBDO — ROME, ITALY**
Creative Team: **GIANPIERO VIGORELLI, ALESSANDRO FRUSCELLA, LETIZIA ZIACO, RITA DELLA PORTA, LUCA BERNASCONI**
Client: **NBC UNIVERSAL GLOBAL NETWORKS ITALIA SRL**

Creative Firm: **PETERSON MILLA HOOKS — MINNEAPOLIS, MN**
Creative Team: **DAVE PETERSON, SUE KAASE, ELLEN FREGO, CARRIE REAY, GAYLE MALCOLM**
Client: **TARGET**

Creative Firm: **CREATIVE ALLIANCE — LOUISVILLE, KY**
Creative Team: **SCOTT BOSWELL, MARK ROSENTHAL, ALBERT LEGGETT**
Client: **CABBAGE PATCH SETTLEMENT HOUSE**

Creative Firm: **INTERNO OTTO SRL — ROME, ITALY**
Creative Team: **MICHELE BELSANTI, ROBERTO MENELAO, VALERIO DE BERARDINIS**
Client: **NBC UNIVERSAL GLOBAL NETWORKS ITALIA SRL**

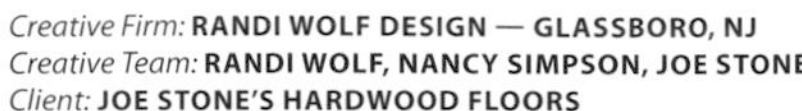

Creative Firm: **RANDI WOLF DESIGN — GLASSBORO, NJ**
Creative Team: **RANDI WOLF, NANCY SIMPSON, JOE STONE**
Client: **JOE STONE'S HARDWOOD FLOORS**

Creative Firm: **D'ADDA, LORENZINI, VIGORELLI, BBDO — ROME, ITALY**
Creative Team: **GIANPIERO VIGORELLI, NICOLA LAMPUGNANI, LETIZIA ZIACO, RITA DELLA PORTA, LUCA BERNASCONI**
Client: **NBC UNIVERSAL GLOBAL NETWORKS ITALIA SRL**

Creative Firm: **160 OVER 90 — PHILADELPHIA, PA**
Creative Team: **DARRYL CILLI, JIM WALLS, DAN SHEPELAVY, GIACOMO CIMINELLO, STEVE PENNING, BRENDAN QUINN**
Client: **AND1 BASKETBALL**

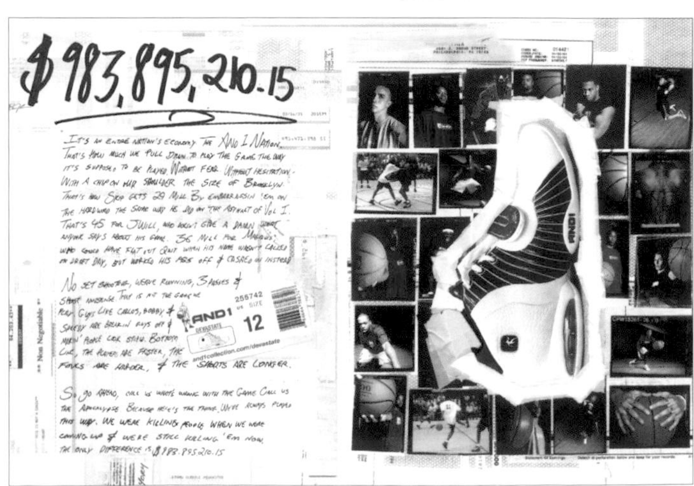

Creative Firm: **REDIFFUSION DYR — NEW DELHI, INDIA**
Creative Team: **ANIRUDH VERMA, PRADYUMNA CHAUHAN, PRAMOD PURANIK, SUDHIR GAUTAM**
Client: **PVR CINEMAS**

Creative Firm: **FUTURA DDB — LJUBLANA, SLOVENIA**
Creative Team: **ZORAN GABRIJAN, ZARE KERIN, MIHA GROBLER, JANEZ PUKSIC**
Client: **PIVK**

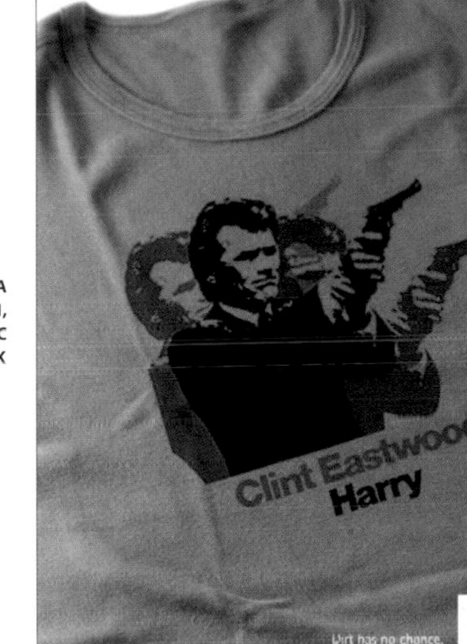

Creative Firm: **MADARA DESIGN — LANCASTER, PA**
Creative Team: **JOHN MADARA, JOHN ZESWITZ, BILL SIMONE**
Client: **JOHN A. WEIERBACH II, DMD**

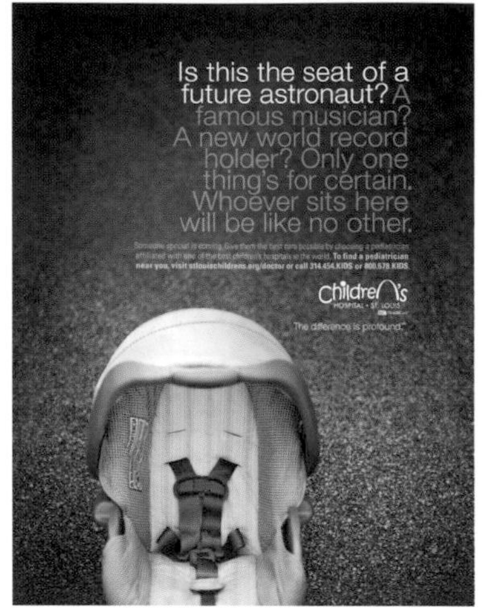

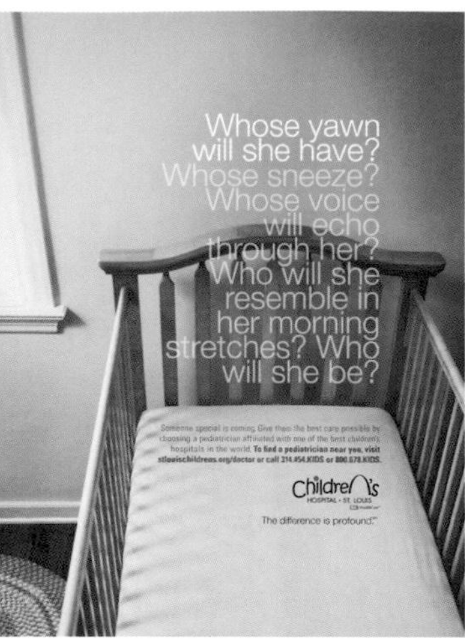

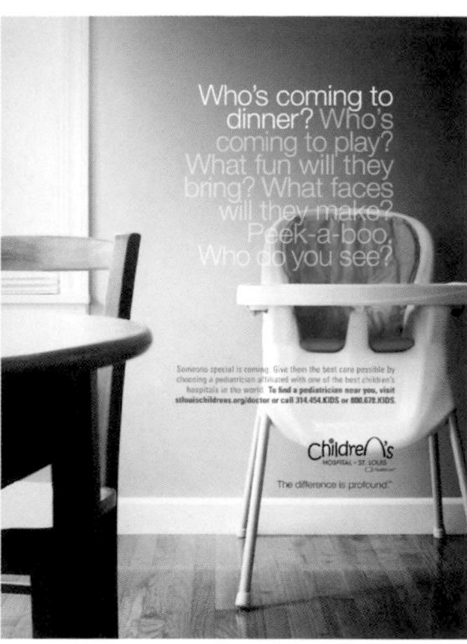

Creative Firm: **RODGERS TOWNSEND — ST. LOUIS, MO**
Creative Team: **TOM HUDDER, RYAN SMITH, TODD MITCHELL, CHERYL SPARKS**
Client: **ST. LOUIS CHILDREN'S HOSPITAL**

Creative Firm: **PHP COMMUNICATIONS — BIRMINGHAM, AL**
Creative Team: **BRYAN CHACE, LYNN SMITH**
Client: **THE CROSSINGS AT DEERFOOT**

Creative Firm: **LEKASMILLER DESIGN — WALNUT CREEK, CA**
Creative Team: **LANA IP, TINA LEKAS MILLER**
Client: **CASTELLANA HOMES**

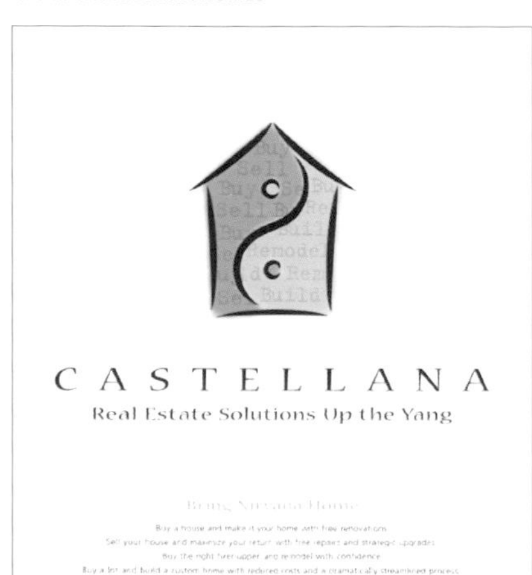

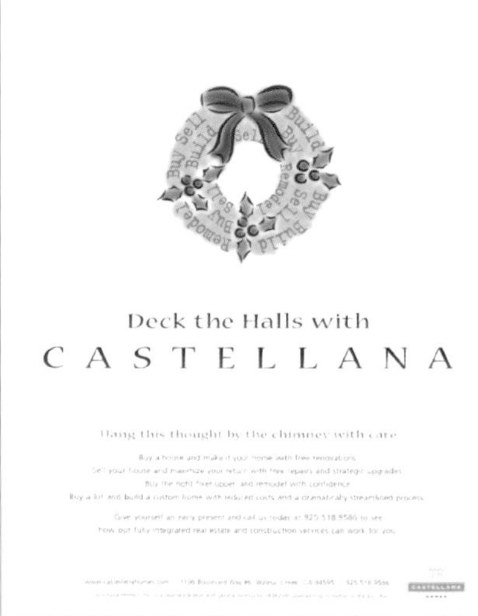

Creative Firm: **RTS RIEGER TEAM WERBEAGENTUR GMBH — LEINFELDEN-ECHTERDINGEN, GERMANY**
Creative Team: **UTE WITZMANN, ANTIE KRAY, WALFGANG KRÖPER, MARKUS KOCH**
Client: **METABOWERKE GMBH**

Creative Firm: **AMERICAN RED CROSS BLOOD SERVICES, WEST DIVISION — POMONA, CA**
Creative Team: **MARC JACKSON, SAUNDRA KEENAN DAVISON, DONNA ANAYA**

Creative Firm: **THE HUMANE SOCIETY OF THE UNITED STATES — WASHINGTON, DC**
Creative Team: **PAULA JAWORSKI**
Client: **THE HUMANE SOCIETY OF THE UNITED STATES**

Creative Firm: **THE HUMANE SOCIETY OF THE UNITED STATES — WASHINGTON, DC**
Creative Team: **PAULA JAWORSKI**
Client: **THE HUMANE SOCIETY OF THE UNITED STATES**

Creative Firm: **ACART COMMUNICATIONS — OTTAWA, ON, CANADA**
Creative Team: **RYAN ABBOTT, KERRY CAVLOVIC, VERNON LAI, JOHN STARESINIC**
Client: **ACART COMMUNICATIONS**

Creative Firm: **& WOJDYLA ADVERTISING — CHICAGO, IL**
Creative Team: **MICHAEL JOHN, FRANKIE TRULL, DAVID WOJDYLA, BARBARA LIVINGSTON**
Client: **FOUNDATION FOR BIOMEDICAL RESEARCH**

Creative Firm: **MTV OFF AIR CREATIVE — NEW YORK, NY**
Creative Team: **JEFFREY KEYTON, JIM DEBARROS, LANCE RUSOFF, THOMAS BERGER, SARAH JAMES, NICK SONDERUP**
Client: **MTV NETWORKS**

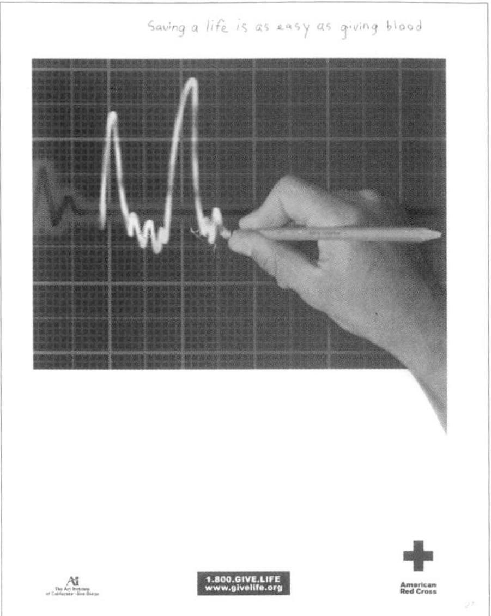

Creative Firm: **ART INSTITUE OF CALIFORNIA, SAN DIEGO — SAN DIEGO, CA**
Creative Team: **LOGAN BAILEY**
Client: **AMERICAN RED CROSS BLOOD SERVICES**

Creative Firm: **THE HUMANE SOCIETY OF THE UNITED STATES — WASHINGTON, DC**
Creative Team: **PAULA JAWORSKI**
Client: **THE HUMANE SOCIETY OF THE UNITED STATES**

Creative Firm: **THE HUMANE SOCIETY OF THE UNITED STATES — WASHINGTON, DC**
Creative Team: **PAULA JAWORSKI**
Client: **THE HUMANE SOCIETY OF THE UNITED STATES**

Creative Firm: **MPHASIS ON FRONTIER — DENVER, CO**
Creative Team: **BRYANT FERNANDEZ, BRUCE FERNANDEZ FUTAGO IMAGES**
Client: **WILD BLUE YONDER MAGAZINE**

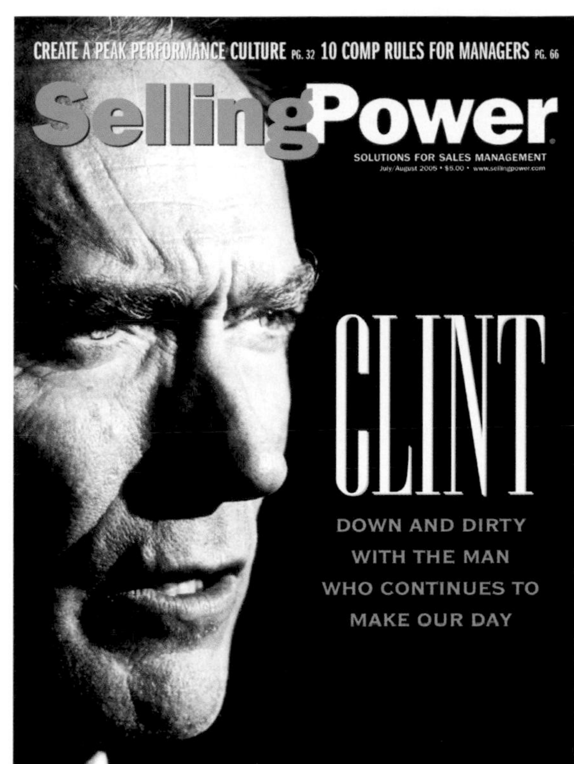

Creative Firm: **SELLING POWER MAGAZINE — FREDERICKSBURG, VA**
Creative Team: **COLLEEN QUINNELL, BRYN COLTON / CORBIS**
Client: **SELLING POWER**

Creative Firm: **ALOFT GROUP, INC. — NEWBURYPORT, MA**
Creative Team: **DON CRANE, ROBBIE MACDONALD**
Client: **DICTAPHONE HEALTHCARE**

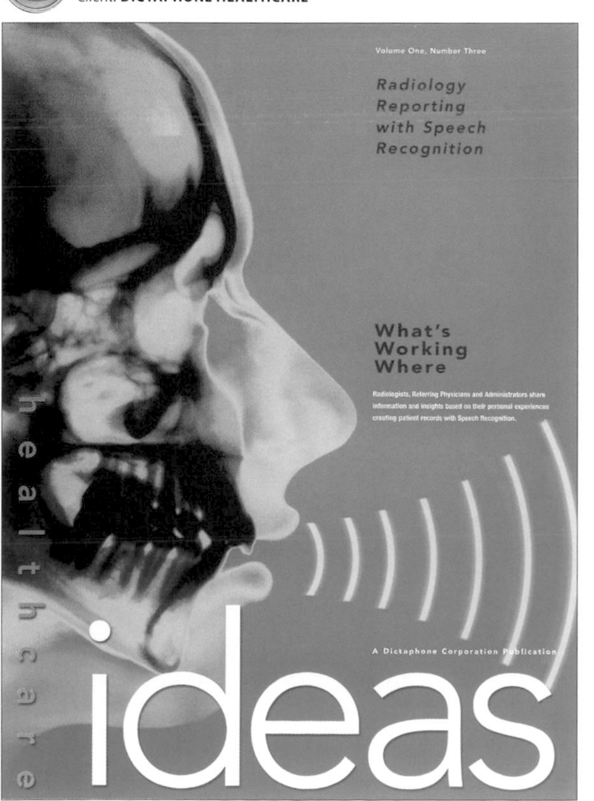

Creative Firm: **EYEBALLNYC — NEW YORK, NY**
Client: **VOGUE ITALIA**

Creative Firm: **EMPHASIS MEDIA LIMITED — HONG KONG**
Creative Team: **PERCY CHUNG, HOWARD LEUNG, JENNIFER SPENCER-KENTRUP**
Client: **CATHAY PACIFIC AIRWAYS**

Creative Firm: **MPHASIS ON FRONTIER — DENVER, CO**
Creative Team: **JEFF SWAIM**
Client: **WILD BLUE YONDER MAGAZINE**

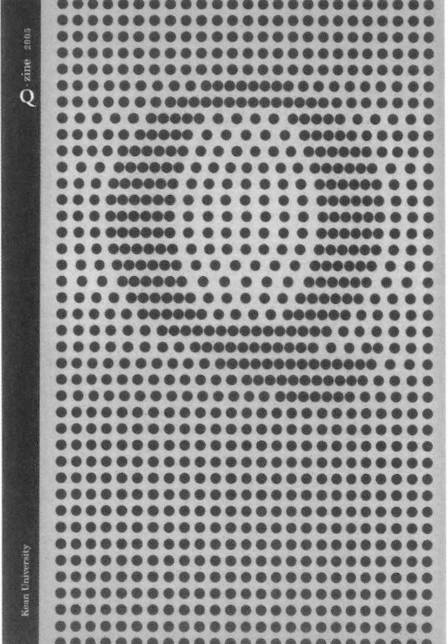

Creative Firm: **THE DESIGN STUDIO AT KEAN UNIVERSITY — UNION, NJ**
Creative Team: **STEVEN BROWER, BRIAN RUTTACAÚOLE**
Client: **OFFICE OF RESEARCH & SPONSORED PROGRAMS**

Creative Firm: **STAN GELLMAN GRAPHIC DESIGN INC. — ST. LOUIS, MO**
Creative Team: **MEG ZELENOVICH, BRITNI EGGERS, MEGAN MILLER, BRYAN WAKELAND, JILL FRANTTI, BARRY TILSON**
Client: **ST. LOUIS COMMERCE MAGAZINE**

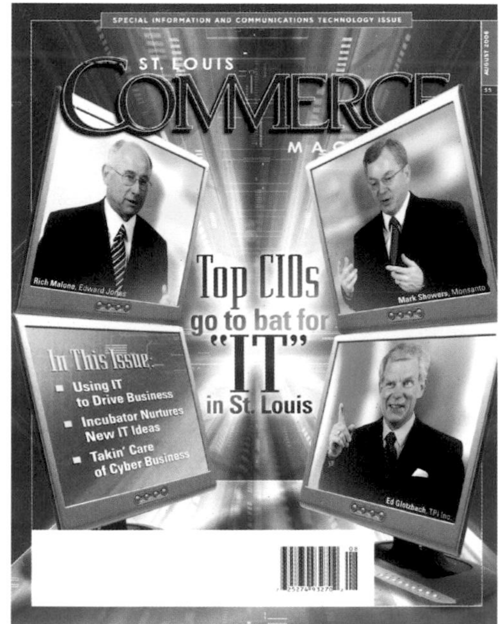

Creative Firm: **EMPHASIS MEDIA LIMITED — HONG KONG**
Creative Team: **PERCY CHUNG, RAYMOND HO, JENNIFER SPENCER-KENTRUP**
Client: **CATHAY PACIFIC AIRWAYS**

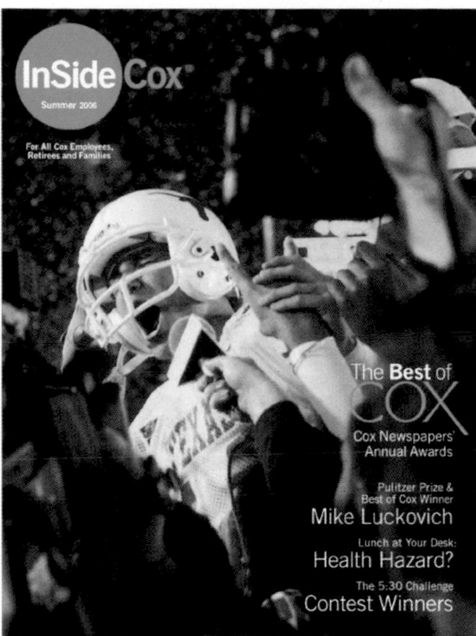

Creative Firm: **THINKHOUSE CREATIVE — ATLANTA, GA**
Client: **COX ENTERPRISES, INC.**

Creative Firm: **RUDER FINN DESIGN — NEW YORK, NY**
Creative Team: **MICHAEL SCHUBERT, LISA GABBAY, SAL CATANIA, DIANA YEO, KAVEN LAM**
Client: **RUDER FINN INC.**

Creative Firm: **EMPHASIS MEDIA LIMITED — HONG KONG**
Creative Team: **JULIE MAN, JENNIFER SPENCER-KENTRUP**
Client: **PERNOD RICARD ASIA**

Creative Firm: **PEO — TORONTO, ON, CANADA**
Creative Team: **ASH KOUSA R.G.D., JENNIFER COOMBES, CONNIE MUCKLESTONE**
Client: **ENGINEERING DIMENSIONS MAGAZINE**

Creative Firm: **STAN GELLMAN GRAPHIC DESIGN INC. — ST. LOUIS, MO**
Creative Team: **MEG ZELENOVICH, BRITNI EGGERS, MEGAN MILLER, BRYAN WAKELAND, JILL FRANTTI, BARRY TILSON**
Client: **ST. LOUIS COMMERCE MAGAZINE**

Creative Firm: **DEVER DESIGNS — LAUREL, MD**
Creative Team: **JEFFREY DEVER, PAUL ANDERSON**
Client: **PSYCHOTHERAPY NETWORKER MAGAZINE**

Creative Firm: **STAN GELLMAN GRAPHIC DESIGN INC. — ST. LOUIS, MO**
Creative Team: **MEG ZELENOVICH, BRITNI EGGERS, MEGAN MILLER, BRYAN WAKELAND, JILL FRANTTI, BARRY TILSON**
Client: **ST. LOUIS COMMERCE MAGAZINE**

Creative Firm: **EMPHASIS MEDIA LIMITED — HONG KONG**
Creative Team: **ALISON LAM, CONNIE CHU**
Client: **DRAGONAIR**

Creative Firm: **EMPHASIS MEDIA LIMITED — HONG KONG**
Creative Team: **ALISON LAM, CONNIE CHU**
Client: **DRAGONAIR**

Creative Firm: **THINKHOUSE CREATIVE — ATLANTA, GA**
Client: **COX ENTERPRISES, INC.**

RE-THINKING

ENVIRONMENTS

FOR

HEALTHCARE

Photography by Nathan Perkel

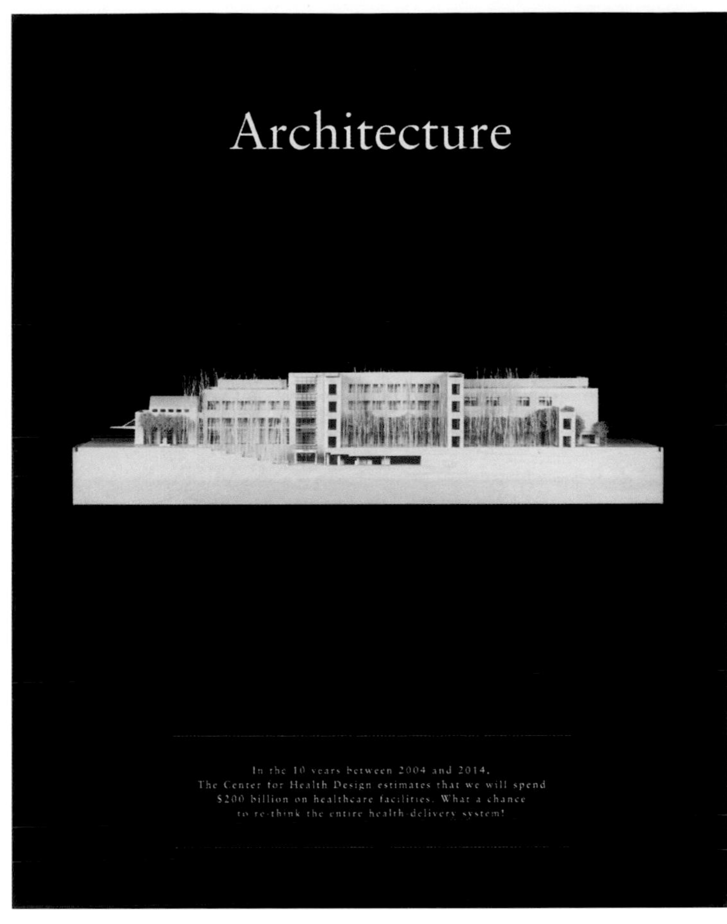

Architecture

In the 10 years between 2004 and 2014,
The Center for Health Design estimates that we will spend
$200 billion on healthcare facilities. What a chance
to re-think the entire health delivery system!

Creative Firm: **CAHAN & ASSOCIATES — ZEELAND, MI**
Creative Team: **T. RICHARDS, E. ADAMS, C. RHINELANDER, S. FRYKHOLM, C. MALCOLM, G. STROBEL, M. CAPOTOSTO**
Client: **HERMAN MILLER, INC.**

Creative Firm: **TAYLOR DESIGN — STAMFORD, CT**
Creative Team: **DAN TAYLOR, HANNAH FICHANDLER, ANDREW LICHTENSTEIN, DON HAMERMAN, AARON MERSHON**
Client: **SARAH LAWRENCE COLLEGE**

ALUMNAE/I PLAY THE GAME OF

GIFT

AND EVERYONE WINS!

SARAH LAWRENCE

I BEQUEATH

MARIELA CISNEROS-MESTRE

"I want to improve education in Venezuela to change the generations that follow. Exchanging information from different countries or communities may be the most enriching way to achieve progress for the whole international educational community."

In the SLC Child Development Institute, Mariela Cisneros-Mestre '86 found a way to enhance her interest in improving Venezuelan education. Eager to share the College's educational resources, she sponsored five Venezuelan elementary school educators to participate in the CDI's Empowering Teachers Summer Institute for two years. Her generosity meant that the Venezuelans brought new perspectives to the Bronxville program, returning home to share the SLC model with their community.

MEG QUINN COULTER

"If the College empowered you and made you a fully realized person, how can you **not** want to nurture that in the coming generations?"

Meg Quinn Coulter '60 is an explorer—and her enthusiasm is multifaceted. She's taught high school English and creative writing, been a school psychologist, traveled throughout the world, and collected treasures and artifacts, some of which she sells annually at a boutique in her home to benefit the SLC Scholarship Fund. She is now establishing, via a planned gift, the **Meg Quinn Coulter Chair in Interdisciplinary Studies**. Meg could find no better way to honor a College where students and faculty are encouraged to evolve, to explore and to cross unexpected bridges.

ALLEN E. SHAY

"Meaningful employment on campus fueled my education and propelled me into the future, and I can only hope that this fund will help other students to supplement their academic study in the same way."

As a student, Allen Shay worked for a faculty member, a job that exposed him to the practical application of his education and stimulated his interest in his future career. Sixteen years later, as a direct result of his own experience, he created the **Allen Shay Fund for Student Employment** to encourage and enable students to develop responsibility, confidence and skills through meaningful employment on campus. The fund gives particular preference to students in situations where they will be learning while teaching others: helping faculty create Web sites, or tutoring their peers, for example. Allen happily renewed the fund in April, 2005.

"We thought about giving a tree or a bench, but then we decided that this was something that we could keep giving to for years to come." —Talia Shalev '05, Senior Gift Committee

The Class of 2004 wanted to give back to Sarah Lawrence but weren't sure how—until they found a non-traditional solution. Raising money for a scholarship fund. It was the largest single graduating class gift ever, with what was then the highest participation rate (41% of students and parents). Not to be outdone, the Class of 2005 created a fund to help future SLC students through financial aid and scholarships. Their turnout? A new participation high of 47 percent.

SENIOR CLASS '04 & '05

PALMER GROSS DUCOMMUN

"A love of Sarah Lawrence has crossed generations in my family. I adored my three years there, and my mother-in-law, Palmer, adored her four. It's just a superb education." —Lynn Ducommun '75

As a tribute to his wife Palmer—a former trustee of the College—and her love for painting while an SLC student, Charles Ducommun established the **Palmer Gross Ducommun Fund** in 1987, celebrating Palmer's life by supporting the arts program. Palmer's children, Electra and Robert, have seen to it that the fund remained strong through the help of the family's foundation. Palmer's daughter-in-law, Lynn, has also been a strong family supporter. In 2004, in honor of the College's 75th anniversary and the new Heimbold Visual Arts Center, the Ducommun family made a new pledge to the fund from their family foundation.

SUSAN STRAUSBERG

"I'd been giving consistently to the College for years, but it was only when I returned to campus after 30 years, and saw the Heimbold Center, that my commitment to the College became stronger than ever."

Always a consistent giver to the **Fund for Sarah Lawrence**, it was only recently that Susan Strausberg '62 really reconnected to the College. Susan returned to campus last year to see what all of the 75th anniversary buzz was about, touring the Heimbold Visual Arts Center and returning later to attend the annual Women's History Conference; later, she met with President Michele Myers. This Sarah Lawrence interaction renewed her sense of commitment, and she decided that it was time to increase her FSL gifts to provide more support for the cost of a labor-intensive, highly individualized education.

Meshon 05

Creative Firm: **UIUC SCHOOL OF ART AND DESIGN — CHAMPAIGN, IL**
Creative Team: **JENNIFER GUNJI, JODEE STANLEY, JOSEPH SQUIER, NAN GOGGIN**
Client: **UIUC DEPARTMENT OF ENGLISH**

Creative Firm: **BENSON & HEPKER DESIGN — IOWA CITY, IA**
Creative Team: **ROBYN HEPKER, DEE ANN REXROAT, CEDAR GRAPHICS**
Client: **CORNELL COLLEGE**

Creative Firm: **RUDER FINN DESIGN — NEW YORK, NY**
Creative Team: **MICHAEL SCHUBERT, LISA GABBAY, SAL CATANIA, DIANA YEO, KAVEN LAM,**
Client: **RUDER FINN INC**

Creative Firm: **THE COLLEGE OF SAINT ROSE — ALBANY, NY**
Creative Team: **LISA HALEY THOMSON, MARK HAMILTON, RENEE ISGRO KELLY, CHRIS PARODY, LUIGI BENINCASA**
Client: **THE COLLEGE OF SAINT ROSE**

Creative Firm: **RTS RIEGER TEAM WERBEAGENTUR GMBH — DÜSSELDORF, GERMANY**
Creative Team: **MICHAELA MÜLLER, ULRICH GIELISCH**
Client: **BALL PACKAGING EUROPE HOLDING GMBH & CO. KG**

Creative Firm: **FIVESTONE — BUFORD, GA**
Creative Team: **JASON LOCY, PATRICIO JUAREZ**
Client: **INJOY**

Creative Firm: **ERWIN ZINGER GRAPHIC DESIGN — GRONINGEN, GRONINGEN, NETHERLANDS**
Creative Team: **ERWIN ZINGER, MARIO MORTIER**
Client: **AVENTURA ENTERTAINMENT**

Creative Firm: **ALOFT GROUP, INC. — NEWBURYPORT, MA**
Creative Team: **DON CRANE, ROBBIE MACDONALD**
Client: **DICTAPHONE HEALTHCARE**

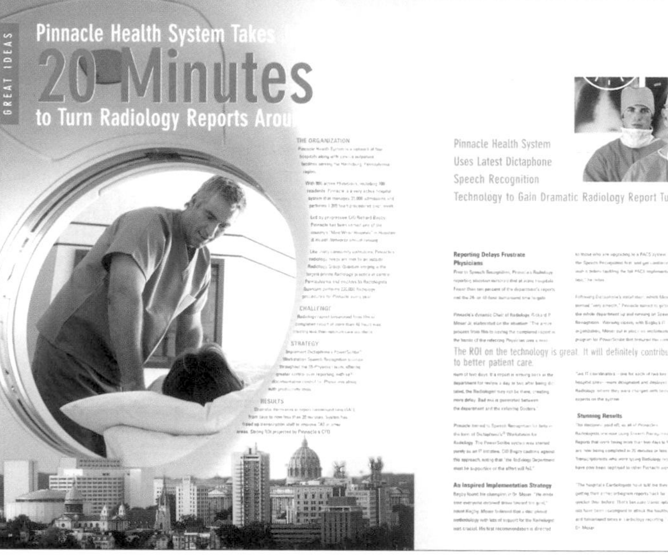

Creative Firm: **CCM — WEST ORANGE, NJ**
Creative Team: **STEPHEN LONGO, JENNIFER BASSORA, JOHN FARISCHON, CHRISTOPHER WARZOCHA**
Client: **COUNTY COLLEGE OF MORRIS**

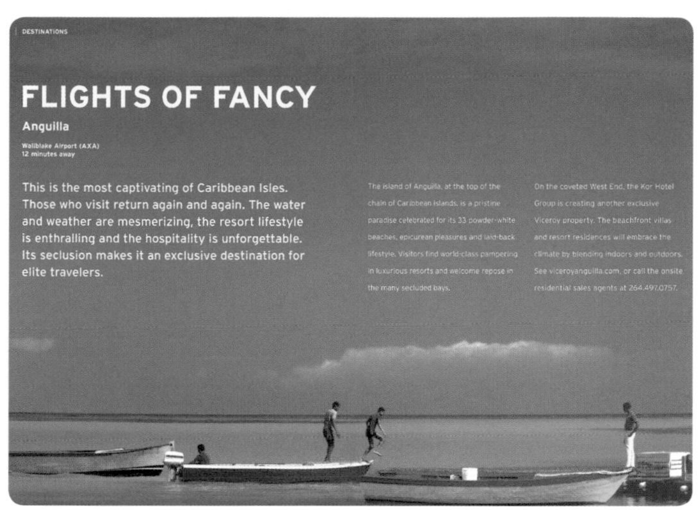
DESTINATIONS

FLIGHTS OF FANCY

Anguilla

Wallblake Airport (AXA)
12 minutes away

This is the most captivating of Caribbean Isles. Those who visit return again and again. The water and weather are mesmerizing, the resort lifestyle is enthralling and the hospitality is unforgettable. Its seclusion makes it an exclusive destination for elite travelers.

The island of Anguilla, at the top of the chain of Caribbean islands, is a pristine paradise celebrated for its 33 powder-white beaches, epicurean pleasures and laid-back lifestyle. Visitors find world-class pampering in luxurious resorts and welcome repose in the many secluded bays.

On the coveted West End, the Kor Hotel Group is creating another exclusive Viceroy property. The beachfront villas and resort residences will embrace the climate by blending indoors and outdoors. See viceroyanguilla.com, or call the onsite residential sales agents at 264.497.0757.

Creative Firm: **HORNALL ANDERSON DESIGN WORKS — SEATTLE, WA**
Creative Team: **JACK ANDERSON, KATHY SAITO, HENRY YIU, ALAN COPELAND**
Client: **CITATIONSHARES**

Creative Firm: **REDPOINT DESIGN DIRECTION — MIDLAND, MI**
Creative Team: **CLARK MOST**
Client: **CENTRAL MICHIGAN UNIVERSITY**

Creative Firm: **HORNALL ANDERSON DESIGN WORKS — SEATTLE, WA**
Creative Team: **JACK ANDERSON, KATHY SAITO, HENRY YIU, ALAN COPELAND**
Client: **CITATIONSHARES**

DESTINATIONS

UP, UP, AND FAIRWAY

Faster than you can say "pooling your resources," savvy golfers have discovered that with careful planning foursomes can fly by private jet to their favorite resorts—for not much more than it costs to go first-class. John Steinbreder hops aboard.

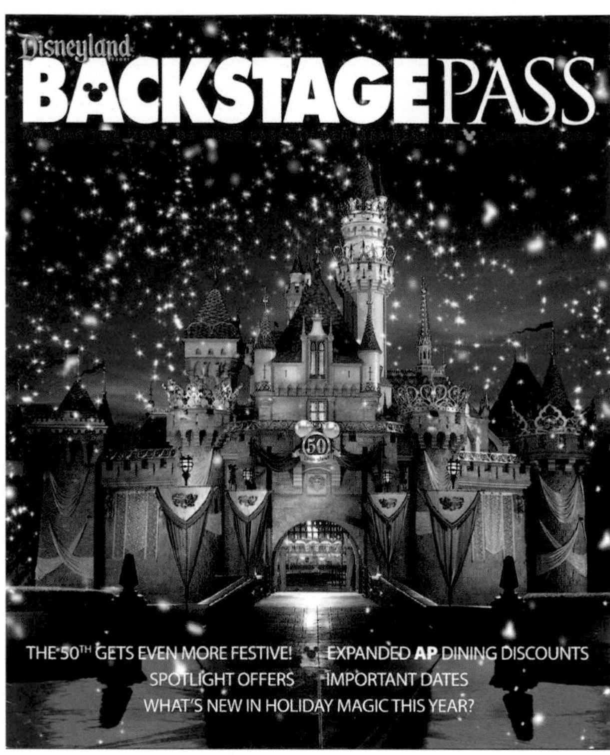

Creative Firm: **YELLOW SHOES CREATIVE WEST, DISNEYLAND RESORT — ANAHEIM, CA**
Creative Team: **DATHAN SHORE, WES CLARK, MARTY MULLER, JACQUELYN MOE, KEVIN YONEDA**
Client: **DISNEYLAND RESORT**

Creative Firm: **PHOENIX CREATIVE GROUP, LLC — POTOMAC FALLS, VA**
Creative Team: **NICOLE KASSOLIS, SEAN MULLINS, KATHLEEN RUSH, MATTHEW BORKOWSKI, JUPITER IMAGES**
Client: **HOMESTEAD FUNDS**

Creative Firm: **FIRST MARKETING — POMPANO BEACH, FL**
Creative Team: **DAN GARLENSKI, JESS FARBER, MAURICIO ABELA, KEITH JOHNSON, ADRIANA NAYLOR, MICHAEL CADIEUX**
Client: **REGENT SEVEN SEAS CRUISES**

Creative Firm: **SPLASH PRODUCTIONS PTE LTD — SINGAPORE**
Creative Team: **STANLEY TAP**
Client: **CLUB RAINBOW SINGAPORE**

Creative Firm: **VH1 — NEW YORK, NY**
Client: **VH1**

Creative Firm: **AMERICAN RED CROSS BLOOD SERVICES, WEST DIVISION — POMONA, CA**
Creative Team: **M. JACKSON, D. ANAYA, S. WHITBURN, R. HERON, MD, G. GARRATTY, PHD FRC PATH, B. MEDINA, S. DAVISON**
Client: **PUBLIC AFFAIRS & COMMUNICATIONS DEPT.**

Creative Firm: **PUBLICIS DIALOG — SAN FRANCISCO, CA**
Creative Team: **CHRISTOPHER ST. JOHN, THERESA LEE, JASON BLACK, BRIAN TYLER**
Client: **GREATER SAN FRANCISCO AD CLUB**

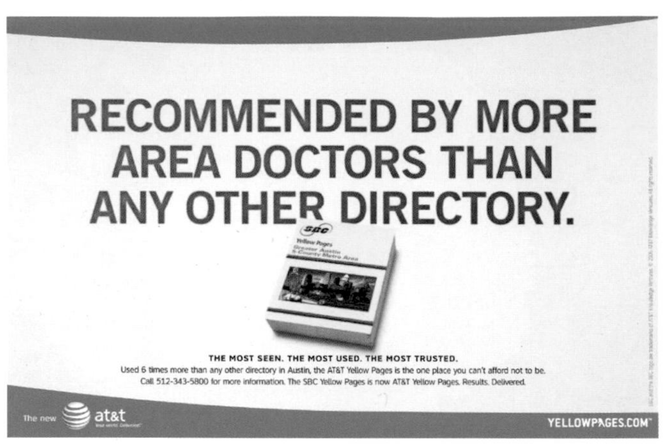

Creative Firm: **RODGERS TOWNSEND — ST. LOUIS, MO**
Creative Team: **TOM HUDDER, MARK ARNOLD, TODD MITCHELL, CHERYL SPARKS**
Client: **AT&T YELLOW PAGES**

Creative Firm: **RODGERS TOWNSEND — ST. LOUIS, MO**
Creative Team: **TOM HUDDER, MARK ARNOLD, TODD MITCHELL, CHERYL SPARKS**
Client: **AT&T YELLOW PAGES**

Creative Firm: **RODGERS TOWNSEND — ST. LOUIS, MO**
Creative Team: **TOM HUDDER, MARK ARNOLD, TODD MITCHELL, CHERYL SPARKS**
Client: **AT&T YELLOW PAGES**

Creative Firm: **RODGERS TOWNSEND — ST. LOUIS, MO**
Creative Team: **TOM HUDDER, MARK ARNOLD, TODD MITCHELL, CHERYL SPARKS**
Client: **AT&T YELLOW PAGES**

Creative Firm: **RODGERS TOWNSEND — ST. LOUIS, MO**
Creative Team: **TOM HUDDER, MARK ARNOLD, TODD MITCHELL, CHERYL SPARKS**
Client: **AT&T YELLOW PAGES**

Creative Firm: **MT&L PUBLIC RELATIONS LTD. — HALIFAX, NS, CANADA**
Creative Team: **DANNY GODFREY, PAUL WILLIAMS, JOHN SHERLOCK, SARAH MOSES**
Client: **MCINNES COOPER**

NEWSPAPER AD, *BUSINESS TO BUSINESS,* CAMPAIGN

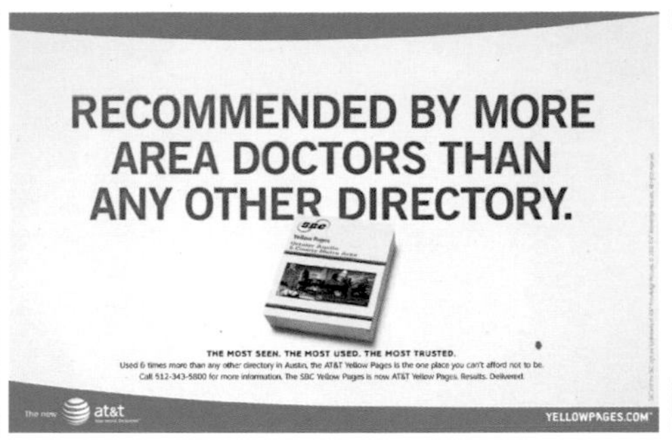

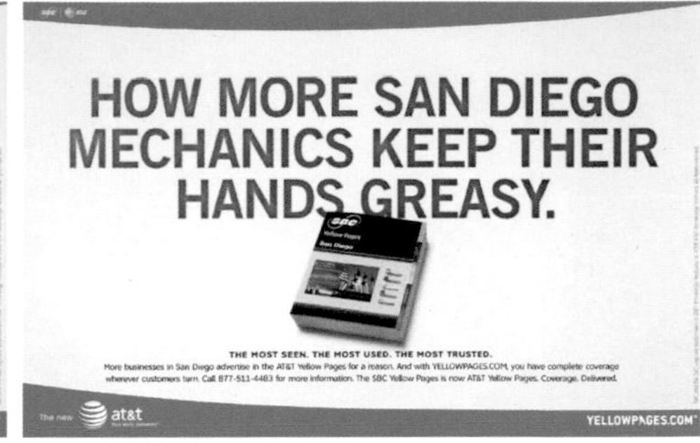

Creative Firm: **RODGERS TOWNSEND — ST. LOUIS, MO**
Creative Team: **TOM HUDDER, MARK ARNOLD, TODD MITCHELL, CHERYL SPARKS**
Client: **AT&T YELLOW PAGES**

Creative Firm: **RODGERS TOWNSEND — ST. LOUIS, MO**
Creative Team: **TOM HUDDER, MARK ARNOLD, TODD MITCHELL, CHERYL SPARKS**
Client: **AT&T YELLOW PAGES**

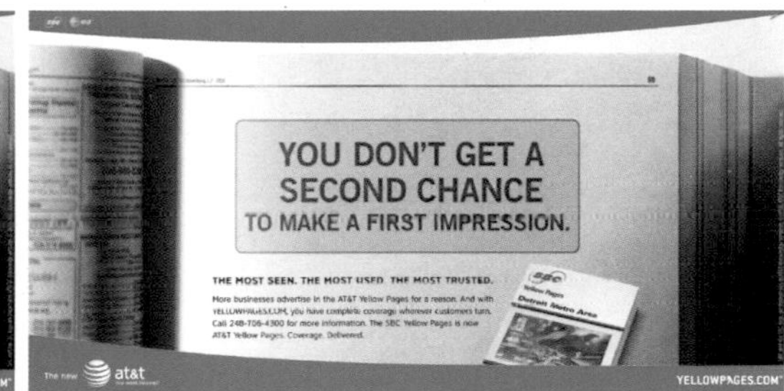

NEWSPAPER AD, *PUBLIC SERVICE,* CAMPAIGN

Creative Firm: **ALL MEDIA PROJECTS LIMITED — PORT OF SPAIN, TRINIDAD AND TOBAGO**
Creative Team: **ANTHONY MOORE, JOSIANE KHAN, GLENN FORTE, BERTRAND DE PEAZA**
Client: **BP TRINIDAD AND TOBAGO (BPTT)**

Creative Firm: **ALL MEDIA PROJECTS LIMITED — PORT OF SPAIN, TRINIDAD AND TOBAGO**
Creative Team: **ANTHONY MOORE, GLENN FORTE, CATHLEEN JONES, REVELINO GUEVARA, CARL HARDING,**
Client: **SFA COMMUNICATIONS**

HO HO HO HOMELESS

Christmas isn't Merry for everyone. More than 300 Bermudians will be sleeping rough this winter, including women and children. So as you carve your big juicy turkey, please spare them a thought. Better still, show that you care by giving a donation to The Bermuda Salvation Army. **Call Carmelita on 292 0601** or send a cheque to P.O. Box HM 2259, Hamilton HM JX, made out to 'The Bermuda Salvation Army'. Thank you for your support.

Creative Firm: **ADVANTAGE LTD — HAMILTON, BERMUDA**
Creative Team: **SAMI LILL**
Client: **SALVATION ARMY**

Creative Firm: **PLANET ADS AND DESIGN P/L — SINGAPORE**
Creative Team: **HAL SUZUKI, MICHELLE LAURIDSEN, HANS IBRAHIM**
Client: **CARREFOUR SINGAPORE PTE LTD**

Creative Firm: **MENDES PUBLICIDADE — BELÉM, PARÁ, BRAZIL**
Creative Team: **OSWALDO MENDES, MARCELO AMORIM**
Client: **INSTITUTO CRIANÇA VIDA**

Creative Firm: **ACART COMMUNICATIONS — OTTAWA, ON, CANADA**
Creative Team: **TOM MEGGINSON, JOHN STARESINIC, JAVIER FRUTOS, VERNON LAI, CHANTAL VALLERAND, DONNA STOTT**
Client: **VIA RAIL CANADA**

Creative Firm: **PURPLE FOCUS PVT. LTD. — INDORE, MADHYA PRADESH, INDIA**
Creative Team: **MANSI JUNEJA, VIPIN RATHORE, MILIND BHAVSAR, SATYAJIT RAI, VINOD BHARGAV**
Client: **EICHER MOTORS LTD.**

Creative Firm: **DC3/UNICOM — BELÉM, PARÁ, BRAZIL**
Creative Team: **ALEXANDRE HELMUT, STEVEN DOLZANE, GLAUCO LIMA, HAROLDO VALENTE**
Client: **JOVEM PAN FM**

Creative Firm: **TV LAND — NEW YORK, NY**
Creative Team: **KIM ROSENBLUM, DOMINQUE VITALI, KEVIN HARTMAN, CHELSEA MOST, MONIQUE SANKEY, TONY D'ORIO**
Client: **TV LAND**

Creative Firm: **YOUNG & RUBICAM GMBH & CO. KG — FRANKFURT AM MAIN, HESSEN, GERMANY**
Creative Team: **CHRISTIAN DAUL, BRUNO PETZ**
Client: **HARLEY DAVIDSON FACTORY**

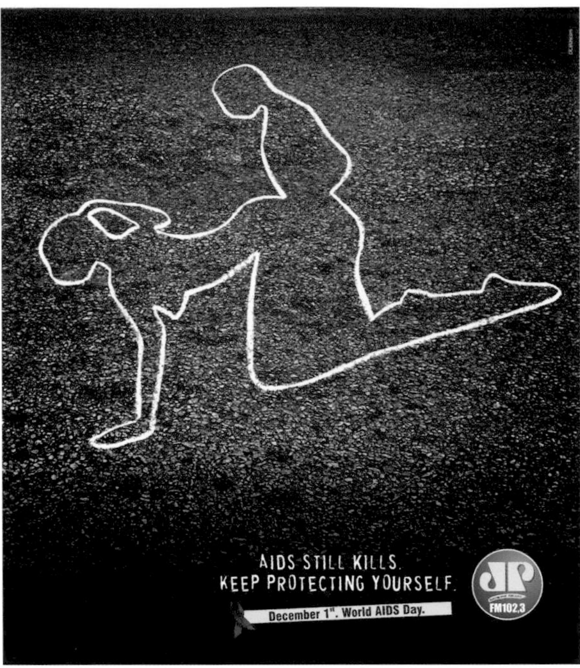

Creative Firm: **DC3/UNICOM — BELÉM, PARÁ, BRAZIL**
Creative Team: **ALEXANDRE HELMUT, RENATA SEGTOWICK, GLAUCO LIMA, HAROLDO VALENTE**
Client: **JOVEM PAN FM**

Creative Firm: **KELLER CRESCENT — EVANSVILLE, IN**
Creative Team: **RANDALL ROHN, LEE BRYANT, RANDY ROHN**
Client: **RIVERVIEW HOSPITAL**

Creative Firm: **RODGERS TOWNSEND — ST. LOUIS, MO**
Creative Team: **TOM HUDDER, MARK ARNOLD, TODD MITCHELL, CHERYL SPARKS**
Client: **AT&T YELLOW PAGES**

Creative Firm: **DC3/UNICOM — BELÉM, PARÁ, BRAZIL**
Creative Team: **ALEXANDRE HELMUT, FERNANDO FAÇANHA, DANIEL JACOB, GLAUCO LIMA, HAROLDO VALENTE**
Client: **JOVEM PAN FM**

Creative Firm: **DC3/UNICOM — BELÉM, PARÁ, BRAZIL**
Creative Team: **ALEXANDRE HELMUT, FERNANDO FAÇANHA, DANIEL JACOB, GLAUCO LIMA, HAROLDO VALENTE,**
Client: **ORM CABO**

Creative Firm: **THE UNGAR GROUP — CHICAGO, IL**
Creative Team: **TOM UNGAR, JIM FURRH**
Client: **CHICAGO SINFONIETTA**

Creative Firm: **NEURON SYNDICATE INC. — SANTA MONICA, CA**
Creative Team: **SEAN ALATORRE, RYAN CRAMER, TIM CALIA**
Client: **20TH CENTURY FOX**

Creative Firm: **BUCK & PULLEYN — PITTSFORD, NY**
Creative Team: **DAN MULCAHY, ANNE ESSE, CHRIS CAPONE, STEVE SAFRAN**
Client: **UNITY HEALTH SYSTEM**

Creative Firm: **DC3/UNICOM — BELÉM, PARÁ, BRAZIL**
Creative Team: **DANIEL JACOB, RENATA SEGTOWICK, ALEXANDRE HELMUT, GLAUCO LIMA, HAROLDO VALENTE**
Client: **JOVEM PAN FM**

Creative Firm: **PLANET ADS AND DESIGN P/L — SINGAPORE**
Creative Team: **HAL SUZUKI, SUZANNE LAURIDSEN, KITANO TOMOYA**
Client: **DISCOVERY NETWORKS ASIA**

Creative Firm: **ALL MEDIA PROJECTS LIMITED — PORT OF SPAIN, TRINIDAD AND TOBAGO**
Creative Team: **ANTHONY MOORE, CHRISTOPHER WILCOX, CARL HARDING**
Client: **TRINIDAD AND TOBAGO ELECTRICITY COMMISSION (T&TEC)**

Creative Firm: **GRIFFO — BELÉM, PARÁ, BRAZIL**
Creative Team: **EDGAR CARDOSO, SERGIO BASTOS, ANTÔNIO NATSUO**
Client: **ORM**

Creative Firm: **DC3/UNICOM — BELÉM, PARÁ, BRAZIL**
Creative Team: **DANIEL JACOB, RENATA SEGTOWICK, ALEXANDRE HELMUT, GLAUCO LIMA, HAROLDO VALENTE,**
Client: **JOVEM PAN FM**

Creative Firm: **PURPLE FOCUS PVT. LTD. — INDORE, MADHYA PRADESH, INDIA**
Creative Team: **SATYAJIT RAI, JITENDRA RAMPURIA, VINOD BHARGAV, PURPLE PRODUCTIONS**
Client: **PINNACLE INDUSTRIES**

Creative Firm: **GRIFFO — BELÉM, PARÁ, BRAZIL**
Creative Team: **EDGAR CARDOSO, SERGIO BASTOS, ANTÔNIO NATSUO**
Client: **ORM**

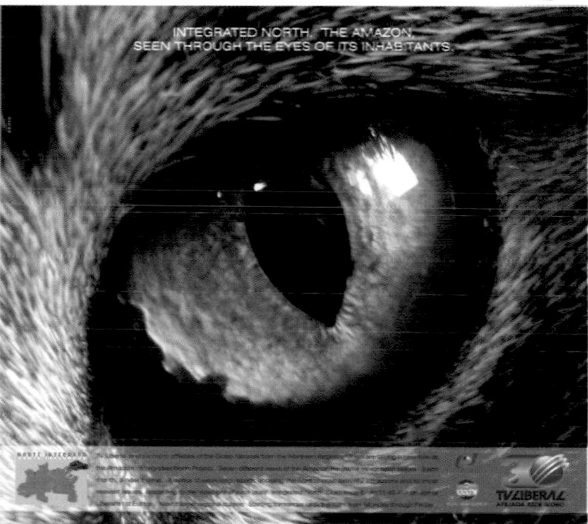

Creative Firm: **YELLOW SHOES CREATIVE WEST, DISNEYLAND RESORT — ANAHEIM, CA**
Creative Team: **SCOTT STARKEY, WES CLARK, JACQUELYN MOE, JIM ST. AMANT**
Client: **DISNEYLAND RESORT**

Creative Firm: **PURPLE FOCUS PVT. LTD. — INDORE, MADHYA PRADESH, INDIA**
Creative Team: **AARISH NANDEDKAR, PRAVEEN KARPE, VINOD BHARGAV**
Client: **DAINIK BHASKAR**

Creative Firm: **LEO BURNETT/YELLOW SHOES CREATIVE WEST, DISNEYLAND RESORT — ANAHEIM, CA**
Creative Team: **JANE ROHAN, WES CLARK, MARTY MULLER, JACQUELYN MOE, JIM ST. AMANT**
Client: **DISNEYLAND RESORT**

Creative Firm: **YELLOW SHOES CREATIVE WEST, DISNEYLAND RESORT — ANAHEIM, CA**
Creative Team: **SCOTT STARKEY, WES CLARK, MARTY MULLER, JIM ST. AMANT, JACQUELYN MOE**
Client: **DISNEYLAND RESORT**

Creative Firm: **GODBE COMMUNICATIONS — HALF MOON BAY, CA**
Client: **LUCILE PACKARD CHILDREN'S HOSPITAL**

Creative Firm: **PRIMARY DESIGN, INC. — HAVERHILL, MA**
Creative Team: **KRISTEN LOSSMAN, SHARYN ROGERS, JULES EPSTEIN**
Client: **AVALON AT CHESTNUT HILL, AVALON BAY COMMUNITIES**

Creative Firm: **ALL MEDIA PROJECTS LIMITED — PORT OF SPAIN, TRINIDAD AND TOBAGO**
Creative Team: **CLINT WILLIAMS, MARISA CAMEJO, SHELLEY HOSEIN, ANTHONY MOORE, DAMIAN BENGOCHEA, DEBBIE GARRAWAY**
Client: **CLICO**

Creative Firm: **YELLOW SHOES CREATIVE WEST, DISNEYLAND RESORT — ANAHEIM, CA**
Creative Team: **SCOTT STARKEY, MARTY MULLER, JACQUELYN MOE, WES CLARK, JIM ST. AMANT**
Client: **DISNEYLAND RESORT**

Creative Firm: **YELLOW SHOES CREATIVE WEST, DISNEYLAND RESORT — ANAHEIM, CA**
Creative Team: **SCOTT STARKEY, WES CLARK, MARTY MULLER, JACQUELYN MOE, JIM ST. AMANT**
Client: **DISNEYLAND RESORT**

Creative Firm: **YELLOW SHOES CREATIVE WEST, DISNEYLAND RESORT — ANAHEIM, CA**
Creative Team: **SCOTT STARKEY, WES CLARK, JANE ROHAN, MARTY MULLER, JACQUELYN MOE, JIM ST. AMANT**
Client: **DISNEYLAND RESORT**

Creative Firm: **GRIFFO — BELÉM, PARÁ, BRAZIL**
Creative Team: **EDGAR CARDOSO, SERGIO BASTOS, ANTÔNIO NATSUO**
Client: **ORM**

Creative Firm: **THE UNGAR GROUP — CHICAGO, IL**
Creative Team: **TOM UNGAR, JIM FURRH**
Client: **ROGERS AUTO GROUP**

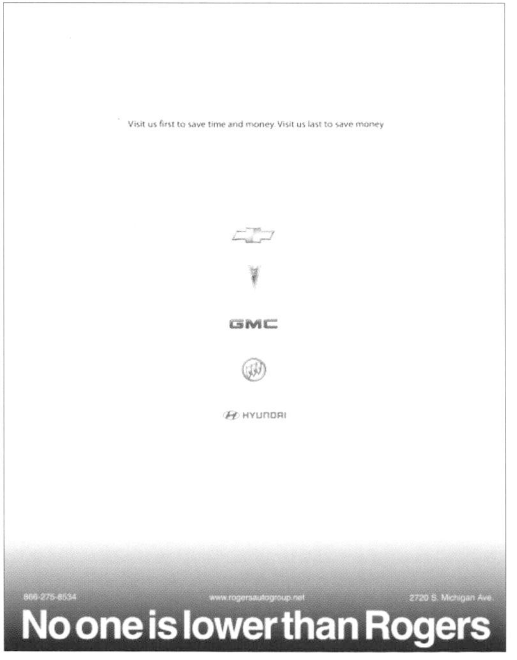

Creative Firm: **LEO BURNETT/YELLOW SHOES CREATIVE WEST, DISNEYLAND RESORT — ANAHEIM, CA**
Creative Team: **SCOTT STARKEY, MARTY MULLER, WES CLARK, JACQUELYN MOE, JIM ST. AMANT, MIKE PUCHALSKI**
Client: **DISNEYLAND RESORT**

Creative Firm: **TAXI CANADA INC. — TORONTO, ON, CANADA**
Creative Team: **ZAK MROUEH, TROY MCGUINESS, JORDAN DOUCETTE, LYNNETTE FERNANDES, BARRY TEPLICKY, DARYN SUTHERLAND**
Client: **MINI CANADA**

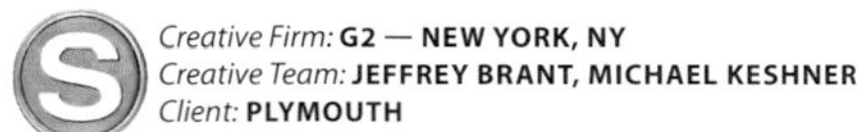

Creative Firm: **G2 — NEW YORK, NY**
Creative Team: **JEFFREY BRANT, MICHAEL KESHNER**
Client: **PLYMOUTH**

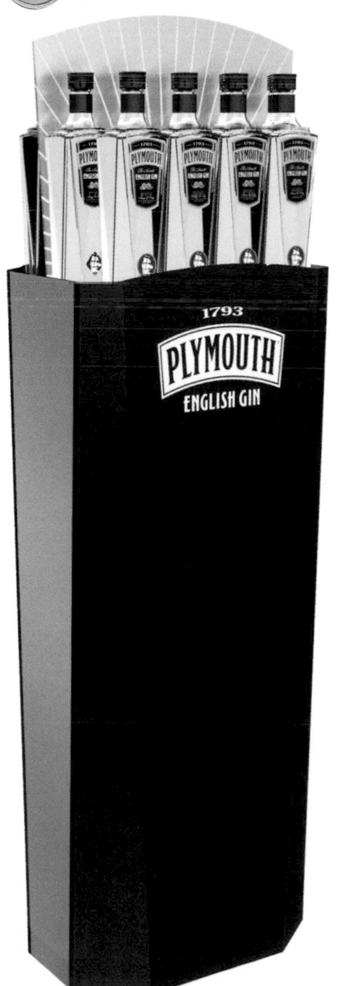

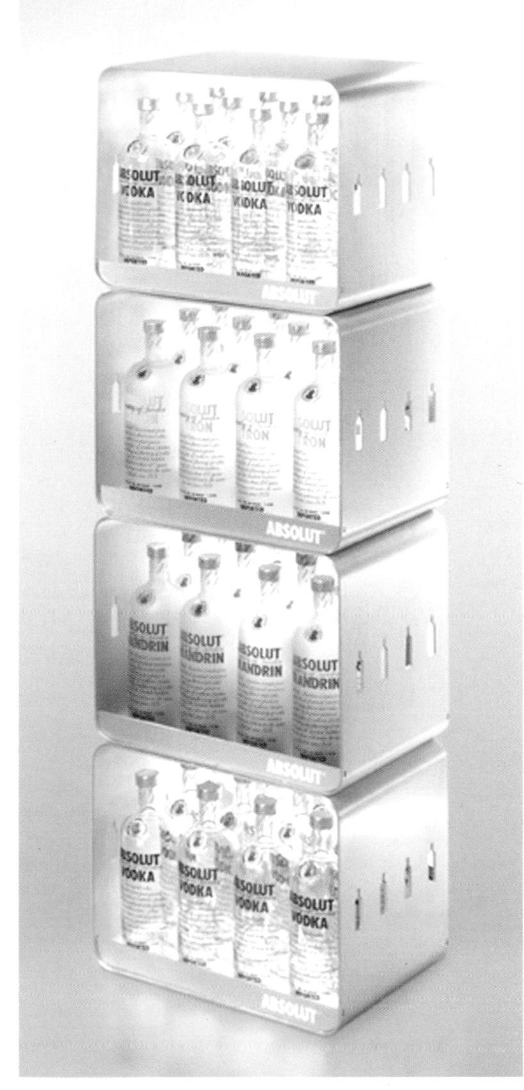

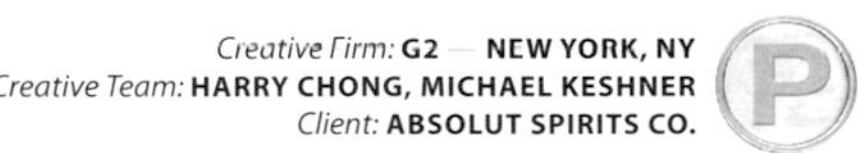

Creative Firm: **G2 — NEW YORK, NY**
Creative Team: **HARRY CHONG, MICHAEL KESHNER**
Client: **ABSOLUT SPIRITS CO.**

Creative Firm: **HBO OFF-AIR CREATIVE SERVICES — NEW YORK, NY**
Creative Team: **JOSE MENDEZ, IVY CALAHORRANO, LARRY BURNETT, VENUS DENNISON**
Client: **HBO MEDIA RELATIONS**

Creative Firm: **GAMMON RAGONESI ASSOCIATES — NEW YORK, NY**
Creative Team: **MARY RAGONESI, JUNG SUE LEE**
Client: **NESTLE**

Creative Firm: **ALCONE MARKETING — IRVINE, CA**
Creative Team: **LUIS CAMANO, SHIVONNE MILLER**
Client: **SAFEWAY**

Creative Firm: **G2 — NEW YORK, NY**
Creative Team: **HARRY CHONG, MICHAEL KESHNER**
Client: **ABSOLUT SPIRITS CO.**

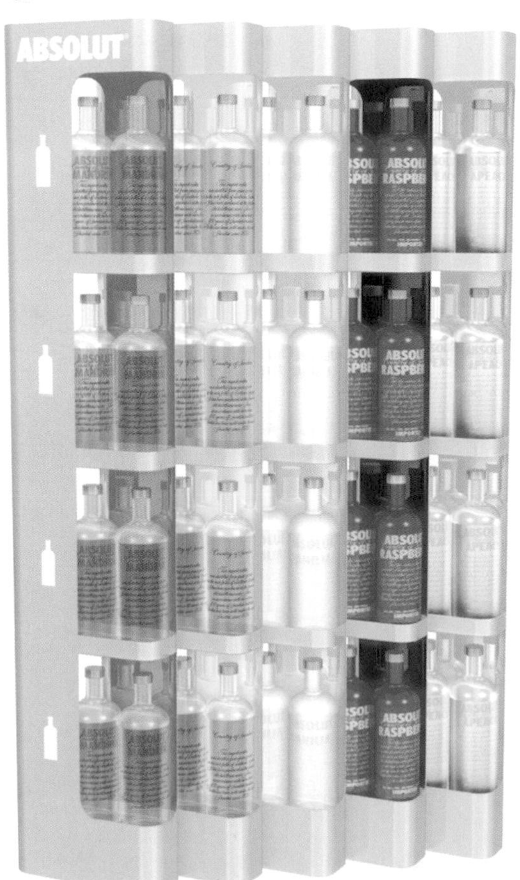

Creative Firm: **TOM FOWLER, INC. — NORWALK, CT**
Creative Team: **MARY ELLEN BUTKUS, BRIEN O'REILLY**
Client: **HONEYWELL CONSUMER PRODUCTS**

Creative Firm: **AGENCY X ADS — SAN FRANCISCO, CA**
Creative Team: **LOTUS CHILD, JENNIFER ELIAS**
Client: **SMARTSCO**

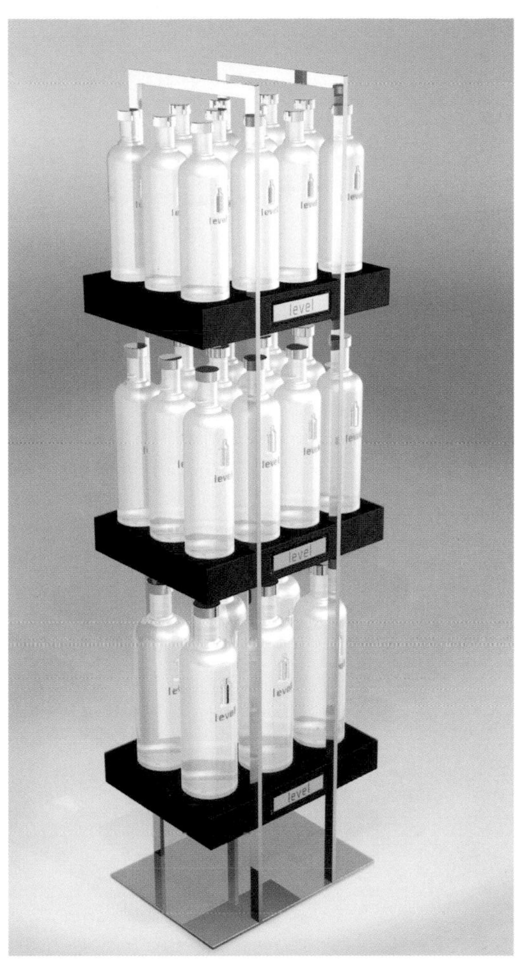

Creative Firm: **G2 — NEW YORK, NY**
Creative Team: **HARRY CHONG, MICHAEL KESHNER**
Client: **LEVEL**

Creative Firm: **LAUNCH CREATIVE MARKETING — CHICAGO, IL**
Creative Team: **MICHELLE MORALES**
Client: **KELLOGGS**

Creative Firm: **GAMMON RAGONESI ASSOCIATES — NEW YORK, NY**
Creative Team: **MARY RAGONESI, SANDRA PEREZ**
Client: **NESTLE**

Creative Firm: **GAMMON RAGONESI ASSOCIATES — NEW YORK, NY**
Creative Team: **MARY RAGONESI, DANIEL AU**
Client: **NESTLE**

Creative Firm: **GAMMON RAGONESI ASSOCIATES — NEW YORK, NY**
Creative Team: **MARY RAGONESI, JUNG SUE LEE**
Client: **NESTLE**

Creative Firm: **LAUNCH CREATIVE MARKETING — CHICAGO, IL**
Creative Team: **MICHELLE MORALES**
Client: **KELLOGGS**

Creative Firm: **GAMMON RAGONESI ASSOCIATES — NEW YORK, NY**
Creative Team: **MARY RAGONESI, KELLY CRISWELL**
Client: **NESTLE**

Creative Firm: **GAMMON RAGONESI ASSOCIATES — NEW YORK, NY**
Creative Team: **MARY RAGONESI, MICHAEL CAMPASANO**
Client: **NESTLE**

Creative Firm: **GAMMON RAGONESI ASSOCIATES — NEW YORK, NY**
Creative Team: **MARY RAGONESI, KELLY CRISWELL**
Client: **NESTLE**

Creative Firm: **JONI RAE AND ASSOCIATES — ENCINO, CA**
Creative Team: **JONI RAE RUSSELL, BEVERLY TRENGOVE**
Client: **THERMAFUSE**

Creative Firm: **LAUNCH CREATIVE MARKETING — CHICAGO, IL**
Creative Team: **MICHELLE MORALES**
Client: **KELLOGGS**

Creative Firm: **LAUNCH CREATIVE MARKETING — CHICAGO, IL**
Creative Team: **MICHELLE MORALES**
Client: **KELLOGGS**

Creative Firm: **NICOSIA CREATIVE EXPRESSO, LTD. — NEW YORK, NY**
Creative Team: **PATRICIA DOCAMPO, AILEEN RIORDAN**
Client: **PROCTER & GAMBLE**

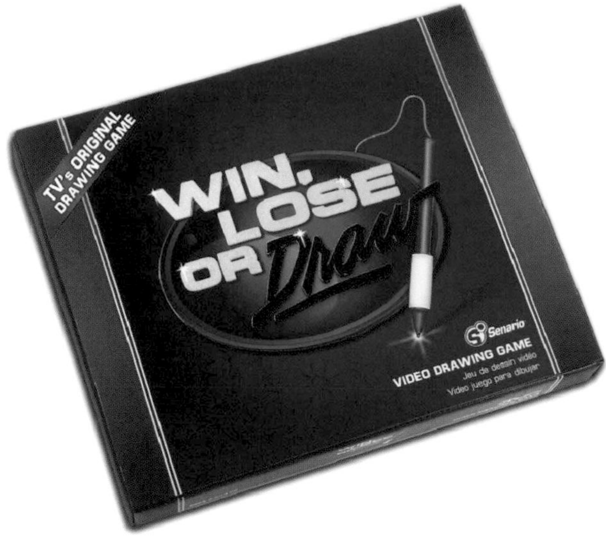

Creative Firm: **DESIGN RESOURCE CENTER — NAPERVILLE, IL**
Creative Team: **JOHN NORMAN, MELANIEGIBB**
Client: **SENARIO, LLC**

Creative Firm: **DESIGN RESOURCE CENTER — NAPERVILLE, IL**
Creative Team: **JOHN NORMAN, MELANIE GIBB**
Client: **SENARIO, LLC**

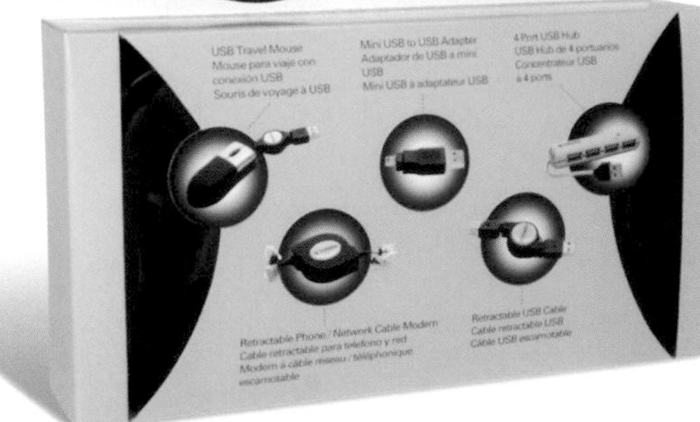

Creative Firm: **ADDISON WHITNEY — CHARLOTTE, NC**
Creative Team: **TREY WALSH, KIMBERLEE DAVIS, KRISTIN HAGER**
Client: **VERBATIM**

Creative Firm: **ACOSTA DESIGN INC — NEW YORK, NY**
Creative Team: **MAURICIO ACOSTA**
Client: **BIG ELECTRONIC GAMES LTD.**

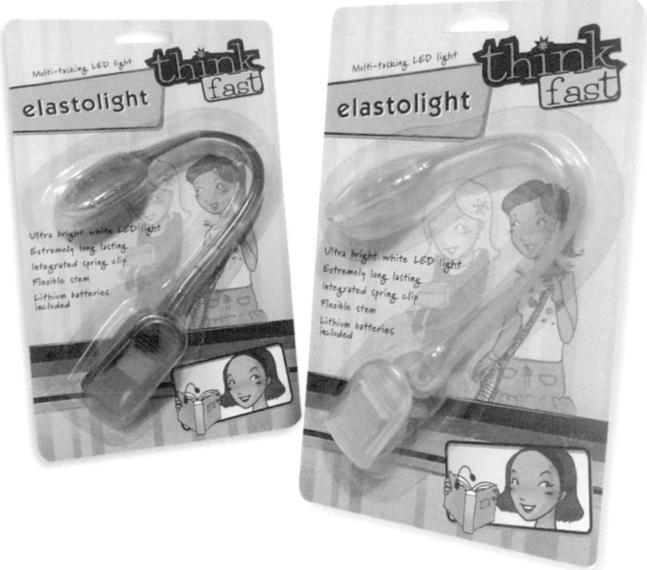

Creative Firm: **SILVER CREATIVE GROUP — SOUTH NORWALK, CT**
Creative Team: **PAUL ZULLO, TRACY WAXENBERG, LAURA TALLARDY**
Client: **ZELCO INDUSTRIES**

Creative Firm: **DESIGN RESOURCE CENTER — NAPERVILLE, IL**
Creative Team: **JOHN NORMAN, MELANIE GIBB**
Client: **SENARIO, LLC**

Creative Firm: **DESIGN RESOURCE CENTER — NAPERVILLE, IL**
Creative Team: **JOHN NORMAN, MELANIE GIBB**
Client: **SENARIO, LLC**

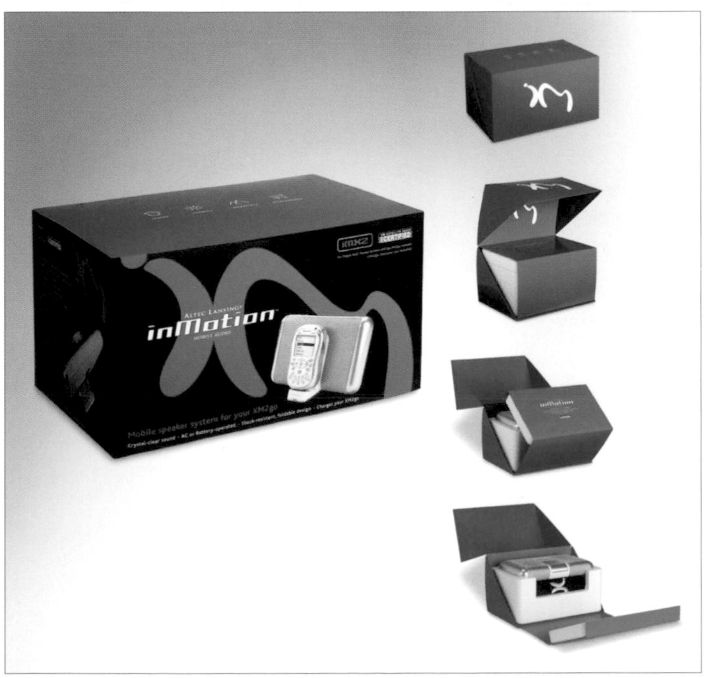

Creative Firm: **MNA CREATIVE — DANBURY, CT**
Creative Team: **HELEN MURPHY, KEN MACEY**
Client: **ALTEC LANSING**

Creative Firm: **ZUNDA GROUP LLC — SOUTH NORWALK, CT**
Creative Team: **CHARLES ZUNDA, GARY ESPOSITO, MICHAEL LELEUX, AMY DRESNER-YULES**
Client: **THE DANNON COMPANY, INC.**

Creative Firm: **VOICEBOX CREATIVE — SAN FRANCISCO, CA**
Creative Team: **JACQUES ROSSOUW, MELISSA MAUREZE**
Client: **FOSTER'S WINE ESTATES**

Creative Firm: **HORNALL ANDERSON DESIGN WORKS — SEATTLE, WA**
Creative Team: **JACK ANDERSON, LARRY ANDERSON, HOLLY CRAVEN, JAY HILBURN, CHRIS FREED**
Client: **COLD STANDARD**

Creative Firm: **STERLING CROSS CREATIVE — SONOMA, CA**
Creative Team: **PEGGY CROSS, REBECCA ESCALERA**
Client: **DIAGEO CHATEAU & ESTATE WINES**

Creative Firm: **CBX — NEW YORK, NY**
Client: **DEL MONTE FOODS**

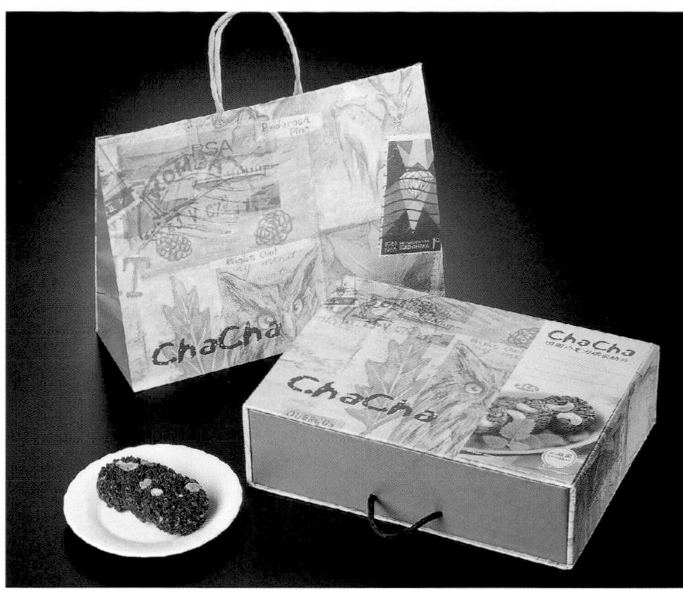

Creative Firm: **SCOTT VISION COMMUNICATION — TAIPEI, TAIWAN**

Creative Firm: **WALLACE CHURCH, INC. — NEW YORK, NY**
Creative Team: **STAN CHURCH, LAWRENCE HAGGERTY**
Client: **PEPPERIDGE FARM**

Creative Firm: **OPTIMA GROUP — HIGHLAND PARK, IL**
Creative Team: **CAROL GRABOWSKI-DAVIS**
Client: **LAKE CHAMPLAIN CHOCOLATES**

Creative Firm: **WILLIAM FOX MUNROE — SHELLINGTON , PA**
Creative Team: **AMY PARKER, MIKE AMOLE**
Client: **THE HERSHEY COMPANY**

Creative Firm: **CASSATA & ASSOCIATES — SCHAUMBURG, IL**
Creative Team: **JAMES MISKEVICS, JIM WOLFE**
Client: **THE WM. WRIGLEY COMPANY**

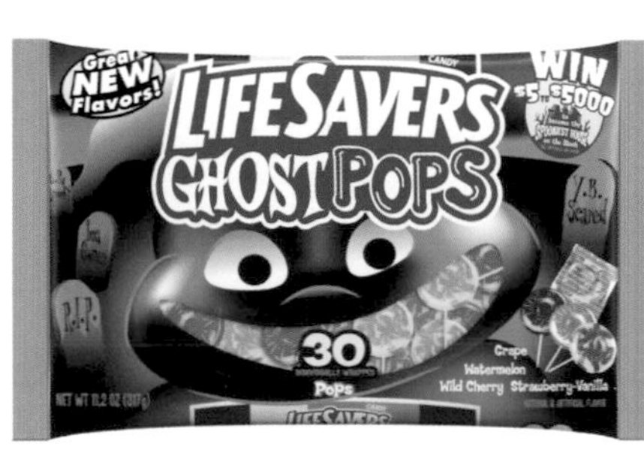

Creative Firm: **HORNALL ANDERSON DESIGN WORKS — SEATTLE, WA**
Creative Team: **JACK ANDERSON, KATHY SAITO, SONJA MAX, HENRY YIU, YURI SHVET**
Client: **AMES INTERNATIONAL**

Creative Firm: **BRAND ENGINE — SAUSALITO, CA**
Creative Team: **ANDREW OTTO, MEGHAN ZODROW, KONRAD TSE**
Client: **PLUM ORGANICS**

Creative Firm: **LIBBY PERSZYK KATHMAN — CINCINNATI, OH**
Creative Team: **BEN SAUER, DAVE BARRETTE, BRENDA MAHAN**
Client: **HERSHEY FOODS CORPORATION**

Creative Firm: **FAINE-OLLER PRODUCTIONS — SEATTLE, WA**
Creative Team: **CATHERINE OLLER, BRUCE HALE, CHRISTOPHER CONRAD, PATTY WITTMAN**
Client: **COLESON FOODS, INC.**

Creative Firm: **VOICEBOX CREATIVE — SAN FRANCISCO, CA**
Creative Team: **SEAN ZIEGLER, VOICEBOX TEAM**
Client: **FOSTER'S WINE ESTATES**

Creative Firm: **GAMMON RAGONESI ASSOCIATES — NEW YORK, NY**
Creative Team: **MARY RAGONESI, JILL SHELLHORN**
Client: **NESTLE**

Creative Firm: **LIBBY PERSZYK KATHMAN — CINCINNATI, OH**
Creative Team: **BEN SAUER, DAVE BARRETTE, DEREK RILLO, KELLY SMITH**
Client: **HERSHEY COMPANY**

Creative Firm: **WILLIAM FOX MUNROE — SHLLINGTON , PA**
Creative Team: **SCOTT HOUTZ, STEPHANIE BENNETT**
Client: **MURRY'S, INC**

Creative Firm: **OPTIMA GROUP — HIGHLAND PARK, IL**
Creative Team: **SARA BELSKIS, JIM PIETRUSZYNSKI, ADAM FERGUSON**
Client: **MILLER BREWING CO.**

Creative Firm: **ZUNDA GROUP LLC — SOUTH NORWALK, CT**
Creative Team: **CHARLES ZUNDA, DANIEL PRICE, GARY ESPOSITO, MICHAEL LELEUX, AMY DRESNER-YULES**
Client: **THE DANNON COMPANY, INC.**

Creative Firm: **FLOWDESIGN INC. — NORTHVILLE, MI**
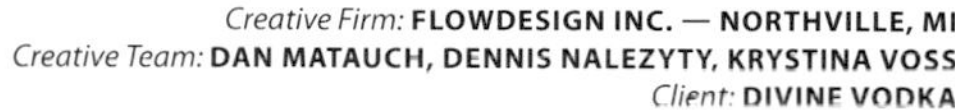
Creative Team: **DAN MATAUCH, DENNIS NALEZYTY, KRYSTINA VOSS**
Client: **DIVINE VODKA**

Creative Firm: **WALLACE CHURCH, INC. — NEW YORK, NY**
Creative Team: **STAN CHURCH, HEATHER ALLEN**
Client: **HJ HEINZ COMPANY**

Creative Firm: **SCOTT VISION COMMUNICATION — TAIPEI, TAIWAN**

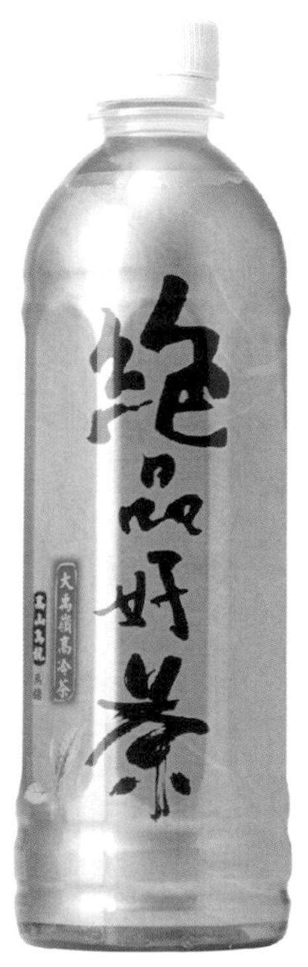

Creative Firm: **ASPREY CREATIVE — FITZROY, VICTORIA, AUSTRALIA**
Creative Team: **GEORGE MARGARITIS, PETER ASPREY**
Client: **PIZZA E BIRRA**

Creative Firm: **CBX — NEW YORK, NY**
Client: **GENERAL MILLS**

Creative Firm: **VOICEBOX CREATIVE — SAN FRANCISCO, CA**
Creative Team: **JACQUES ROSSOUW**
Client: **MARIN FRENCH CHEESE COMPANY**

Creative Firm: **FLOWDESIGN INC.— NORTHVILLE, MI**
Creative Team: **DAN MATAUCH**
Client: **ARCELLA PREMIUM BRANDS**

Creative Firm: **TANGRAM STRATEGIC DESIGN — NOVARA, ITALY**
Creative Team: **ENRICO SEMPI, ANTONELLA TREVISAN, ANDREA SEMPI, KENJI SUMURA**
Client: **CHIQUITA ITALIA**

Creative Firm: **FAINE-OLLER PRODUCTIONS — SEATTLE, WA**
Creative Team: **CATHERINE OLLER, STEPHANIE LANGLEY, BRUCE HALE**
Client: **H&N FOODS INTERNATIONAL**

Creative Firm: **HORNALL ANDERSON DESIGN WORKS — SEATTLE, WA**
Creative Team: **JACK ANDERSON, LARRY ANDERSON, JAY HILBURN, BRUCE STIGLER, ELMER DELA CRUZ, DAYMON BRUCK, HAYDEN SCHOEN**
Client: **WIDMER BROTHERS BREWERY**

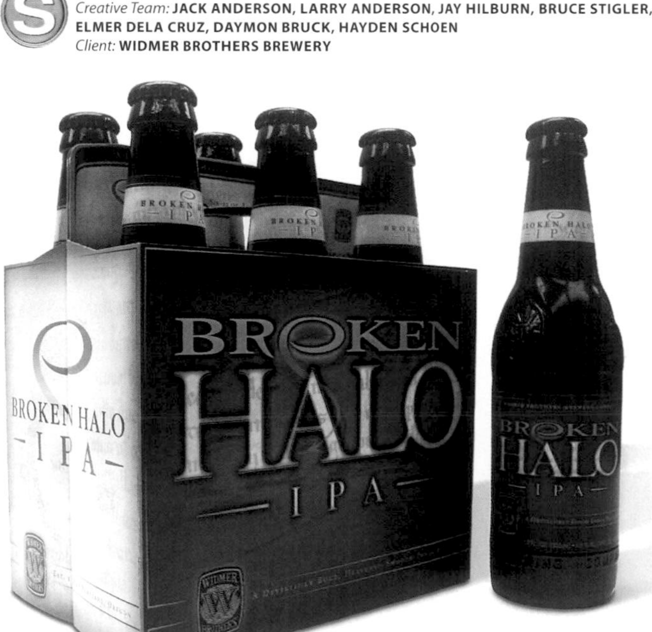

Creative Firm: **MAGNETO BRAND ADVERTISING — PORTLAND, OR**
Creative Team: **R. CRAIG OPFER, JEFF PAUL, JAY FAWCETT, MIKE TERRY**
Client: **ARGYLE WINERY**

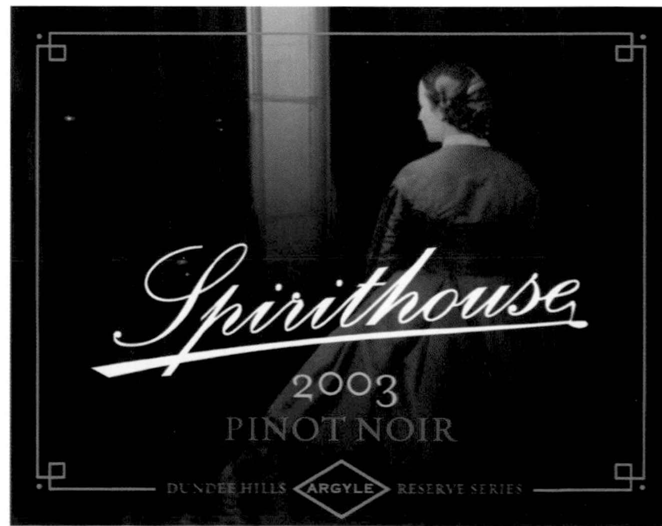

Creative Firm: **FLOWDESIGN INC. — NORTHVILLE, MI**
Creative Team: **DAN MATAUCH**
Client: **VARELA HERMANOS, S.A.**

Creative Firm: **VOICEBOX CREATIVE — SAN FRANCISCO, CA**
Creative Team: **JACQUES ROSSOUW, MELISSA MAUREZE**
Client: **FOSTER'S WINE ESTATES**

Creative Firm: **BRAND ENGINE — SAUSALITO, CA**
Creative Team: **ERIC READ, MEGHAN ZODROW, ROBERT BURNS, AILEEN KENDLE-SMITH**
Client: **PACKAGE DESIGN MAGAZINE: DESIGN CHALLENGE 2005**

Creative Firm: **SCOTT VISION COMMUNICATION — TAIPEI, TAIWAN**

Creative Firm: **WILLIAM FOX MUNROE — SHELLINGTON , PA**
Creative Team: **AMY PARKER, MIKE AMOLE**
Client: **THE HERSHEY COMPANY**

Creative Firm: **FUTURA DDB — LJUBLJANA, SLOVENIA**
Creative Team: **ZARE KERIN, MARKO VICIC, MARKO PISKUR**
Client: **DANA**

Creative Firm: **HORNALL ANDERSON DESIGN WORKS — SEATTLE, WA**
Creative Team: **LISA CERVENY, SONJA MAX, BELINDA BOWLING, ENSI MOFASSER, KATHY SAITO, BETH GRIMM, JULIE JACOBSON**
Client: **TAHITIAN NONI**

Creative Firm: **GAMMON RAGONESI ASSOCIATES — NEW YORK, NY**
Creative Team: **MARY RAGONESI, MICHAEL CAMPASANO**
Client: **NESTLE**

Creative Firm: **LEWIS MOBERLY — LONDON, UNITED KINGDOM**
Creative Team: **MARY LEWIS, JOANNE SMITH, PAUL CILIA LA CORTE**
Client: **ADRIATIC DISTILLERS**

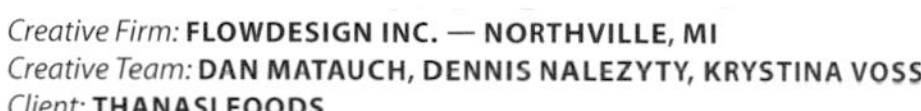
Creative Firm: **FLOWDESIGN INC. — NORTHVILLE, MI**
Creative Team: **DAN MATAUCH, DENNIS NALEZYTY, KRYSTINA VOSS**
Client: **THANASI FOODS**

Creative Firm: **TD2, S.C. — MEXICO CITY, D.F., MEXICO**
Creative Team: **R. RODRIGO CORDOVA, JOSE LUIS (PAT) PATIÑO, LAURA CORDOBA**
Client: **NATURITZ**

Creative Firm: **MARK OLIVER, INC. — SOLVANG, CA**
Creative Team: **MARK OLIVER, PATTY DEVLIN-DRISKEL**
Client: **OCEAN BEAUTY SEAFOODS**

Creative Firm: **ISLAND OASIS — WALPOLE, MA**
Creative Team: **PETE BUHLER**
Client: **ISLAND OASIS**

Creative Firm: **STERLING CROSS CREATIVE — SONOMA, CA**
Creative Team: **PEGGY CROSS, JULIE BUTTS**
Client: **DIAGEO CHATEAU & ESTATE WINES**

Creative Firm: **KELLER CRESCENT — EVANSVILLE, IN**
Creative Team: **GERRY ULRICH, LYNNE MLADY, RANDALL ROHN**
Client: **HEAVEN HILL**

Creative Firm: **ZUNDA GROUP LLC — SOUTH NORWALK, CT**
Creative Team: **CHARLES ZUNDA, DANIEL PRICE, GARY ESPOSITO, DONALD WINTMAN, JEAN LEGROS**
Client: **GREAT BRANDS OF EUROPE, INC.**

Creative Firm: **DESIGN NORTH, INC. — RACINE, WI**
Creative Team: **GWEN GRANZOW, FRANK ULLENBERG, KAYTEE MOSHER**
Client: **BIRDS EYE FOOD**

Creative Firm: **BAER DESIGN GROUP — EVANSTON, IL**
Creative Team: **DAVE SEIDLER, TODD BAER**
Client: **SOMMERS ORGANIC**

Creative Firm: **VOICEBOX CREATIVE — SAN FRANCISCO, CA**
Creative Team: **SEAN ZIEGLER, KRISTIE WISE, MIKE GRAY**
Client: **KV VINEYARDS / FOSTER'S WINE ESTATES**

Creative Firm: **FLOWDESIGN INC. — NORTHVILLE, MI**
Creative Team: **DAN MATAUCH, DENNIS NALEZYTY**
Client: **PIEDMONT DISTILLERS, INC.**

Creative Firm: **BAER DESIGN GROUP — EVANSTON, IL**
Creative Team: **DAVE SEIDLER, TODD BAER, MELISSA LANE**
Client: **LAZY DAYS TEA CO.**

Creative Firm: **LIBBY PERSZYK KATHMAN — CINCINNATI, OH**
Creative Team: **MATT BAUGHAN, KATE THOMAN**
Client: **PROCTER & GAMBLE**

Creative Firm: **DESIGN RESOURCE CENTER — NAPERVILLE, IL**
Creative Team: **JOHN NORMAN, MELANIE GIBB**
Client: **CHARMS MARKETING, COMPANY**

Creative Firm: **HORNALL ANDERSON DESIGN WORKS — SEATTLE, WA**
Creative Team: **JACK ANDERSON, LARRY ANDERSON, JAY HILBURN, HENRY YIU, BRUCE STIGLER, ELMER DELA CRUZ, BRUCE BRANSON-MEYER**
Client: **WIDMER BROTHERS BREWERY**

Creative Firm: **PRAXIS DISEÑADORES S.C. — MEXICO CITY, D.F., MEXICO**
Creative Team: **NADYA VILLEGAS, JUAN CARLOS ROJAS**
Client: **QUALTIA ALIMENTOS**

Creative Firm: **TD2, S.C. — MEXICO CITY, D.F., MEXICO**
Creative Team: **R. RODRIGO CORDOVA, MARIANA MORA, ADALBERTO ARENAS**
Client: **NESTLE BABY FOOD**

Creative Firm: **FLOWDESIGN INC. — NORTHVILLE, MI**
Creative Team: **DAN MATAUCH**
Client: **21ST CENTURY SPIRITS**

Creative Firm: **HORNALL ANDERSON DESIGN WORKS — SEATTLE, WA**
Creative Team: **LISA CERVENY, MARY HERMES, HILLARY RADBILL, TIFFANY PLACE, ELMER DELA CRUZ, BECKON WYLD, JOHN ANDERLE**
Client: **MILLENNIUM**

Creative Firm: **MARK OLIVER, INC. — SOLVANG, CA**
Creative Team: **MARK OLIVER, PATTY DEVLIN-DRISKEL**
Client: **OCEAN BEAUTY SEAFOODS**

Creative Firm: **LIBBY PERSZYK KATHMAN — CINCINNATI, OH**
Creative Team: **VICTOR JANTZEN, GARY CIERADKOWSK**
Client: **BIG RED COLA**

Creative Firm: **VOICEBOX CREATIVE — SAN FRANCISCO, CA**
Creative Team: **JACQUES ROSSOUW, KRISTIE WISE**
Client: **RODNEY STRONG VINEYARDS**

Creative Firm: **LIBBY PERSZYK KATHMAN — CINCINNATI, OH**
Creative Team: **ANDREW TESNAR, GARY CIERADKOWSKI**
Client: **PROCTER & GAMBLE**

Creative Firm: **PURE DESIGN CO. LLC — LEVERETT, MA**
Creative Team: **DAN MISHKIND, JOHN ROULAC**
Client: **NUTIVA**

Creative Firm: **SCOTT VISION COMMUNICATION — TAIPEI, TAIWAN**

Creative Firm: **GAMMON RAGONESI ASSOCIATES — NEW YORK, NY**
Creative Team: **MARY RAGONESI, JILL SHELLHORN**
Client: **NESTLE**

Creative Firm: **CBX — NEW YORK, NY**

Creative Firm: **FLOWDESIGN INC. — NORTHVILLE, MI**
Creative Team: **DAN MATAUCH**
Client: **HOBARAMA CORP.**

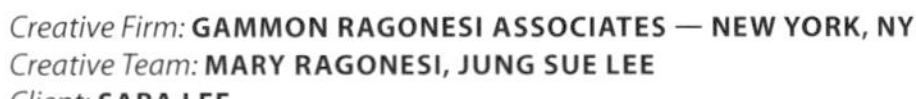
Creative Firm: **CBX — NEW YORK, NY**
Client: **SENECA FOODS**

Creative Firm: **FLOWDESIGN INC. — NORTHVILLE, MI**
Creative Team: **DAN MATAUCH, DENNIS NALEZYTY**
Client: **HAWAII SEA SPIRITS, LLC**

Creative Firm: **GAMMON RAGONESI ASSOCIATES — NEW YORK, NY**
Creative Team: **MARY RAGONESI, JUNG SUE LEE**
Client: **SARA LEE**

Creative Firm: **SHIMOKOCHI-REEVES — LOS ANGELES, CA**
Creative Team: **MAMORU SHIMOKOCHI, ANNE REEVES**
Client: **U.S. MILLS, INC.**

Creative Firm: **SCOTT VISION COMMUNICATION — TAIPEI, TAIWAN**

Creative Firm: **STERLING CROSS CREATIVE — SONOMA, CA**
Creative Team: **PEGGY CROSS, JULIE BUTTS**
Client: **DIAGEO CHATEAU & ESTATE WINES**

Creative Firm: **SCOTT VISION COMMUNICATION — TAIPEI, TAIWAN**

Creative Firm: **FUTURA DDB — LJUBLANA, SLOVENIA**
Creative Team: **ZARE KERIN, MARKO VICIC, MARKO PISKUR**
Client: **DANA**

Creative Firm: **ASPREY CREATIVE — FITZROY, VICTORIA, AUSTRALIA**
Creative Team: **GEORGE MARGARITIS, PETER ASPREY**
Client: **NATIONAL FOODS**

Creative Firm: **CBX — NEW YORK, NY**
Client: **GENERAL MILLS**

Creative Firm: **WILLIAM FOX MUNROE — SHELLINGTON, PA**
Creative Team: **AMY PARKER, MIKE AMOLE, JINGER BL ANTZ, RICK RHOADES**
Client: **THE HERSHEY COMPANY**

Creative Firm: **BERRY DESIGN INC — ALPHARETTA, GA**
Creative Team: **BOB BERRY, CHIP WALLER**
Client: **BISTRO FOODS INC**

Creative Firm: **MARK OLIVER, INC. — SOLVANG, CA**
Creative Team: **MARK OLIVER, PATTY DRISKEL, DOUGLAS SCHNEIDER, JOHN BURNS**
Client: **TRIBE MEDITERRANEAN**

Creative Firm: **VOICEBOX CREATIVE — SAN FRANCISCO, CA**
Creative Team: **JACQUES ROSSOUW, KRISTIE WISE**
Client: **SBRAGIA FAMILY VINEYARDS**

Creative Firm: **MARK OLIVER, INC. — SOLVANG, CA**
Creative Team: **MARK OLIVER, PATTY DRISKEL, LESLIE WU**
Client: **ALMA ROSA WINERY**

Creative Firm: **ASPREY CREATIVE — FITZROY, VICTORIA, AUSTRALIA**
Creative Team: **GEORGE MARGARITIS, PETER ASPREY**
Client: **MASTERFOODS SNACKFOOD**

Creative Firm: **HORNALL ANDERSON DESIGN WORKS — SEATTLE, WA**
Creative Team: **JACK ANDERSON, JAMES TEE, TIFFANY PLACE, LAUREN DIRUSSO, KRIS DELANEY, JOHN ANDERLE**
Client: **BOSTON MARKET**

Creative Firm: **WILLIAM FOX MUNROE — SHELLINGTON , PA**
Creative Team: **AMY PARKER, MIKE AM OLE**
Client: **THE HERSHEY COMPANY**

Creative Firm: **JONI RAE AND ASSOCIATES — ENCINO, CA**
Creative Team: **JONI RAE RUSSELL, BEVERLY TRENGOVE**
Client: **THERMAFUSE**

Creative Firm: **LIBBY PERSZYK KATHMAN — CINCINNATI, OH**
Creative Team: **NATHAN HENDRICKS, MICHELLE RAFIE, CATHY BAKER, ERIK PIETILA, AMY SCHWARTZ, MATT MOSES**
Client: **PROCTER & GAMBLE**

Creative Firm: **HORNALL ANDERSON DESIGN WORKS — SEATTLE, WA**
Creative Team: **LISA CERVENY, SONJA MAX, BELINDA BOWLING, ENSI MOFASSER, KATHY SAITO, BETH GRIMM, JULIE JACOBSON**
Client: **TAHITIAN NONI**

Creative Firm: **LANDOR ASSOCIATES — CINCINNATI, OH**
Creative Team: **TESSA WESTERMEYER, VALERIE AURILIO, TRACEY LANZ, EMILY MASON, KELLY LARBES, ANNE GIBBLE**
Client: **PROCTER & GAMBLE**

Creative Firm: **WALLACE CHURCH, INC. — NEW YORK, NY**
Creative Team: **STAN CHURCH, JOHN BRUNO**
Client: **THE GILLETTE COMPANY**

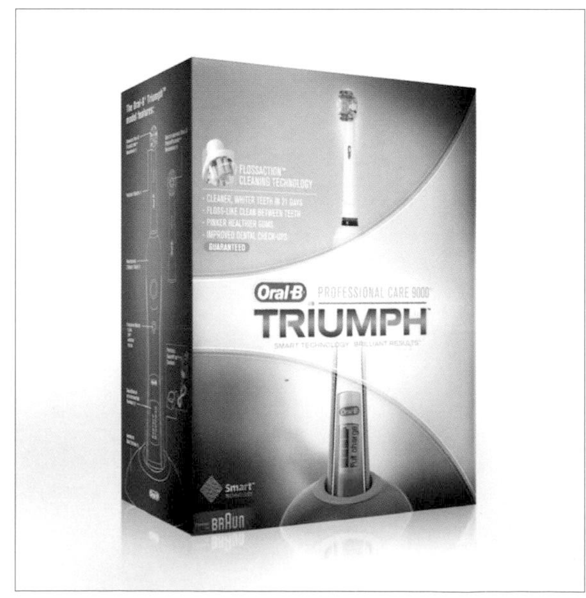

Creative Firm: **LIBBY PERSZYK KATHMAN — CINCINNATI, OH**
Creative Team: **JOHN METZ, JODI SENA, HOLLY SHOEMAKER, EMMA BRACEY, STEPHANIE CRAIR, ROBIN HORST**
Client: **PROCTER & GAMBLE**

Creative Firm: **WALLACE CHURCH, INC. — NEW YORK, NY**
Creative Team: **STAN CHURCH, JOHN BRUNO**
Client: **THE GILLETTE COMPANY**

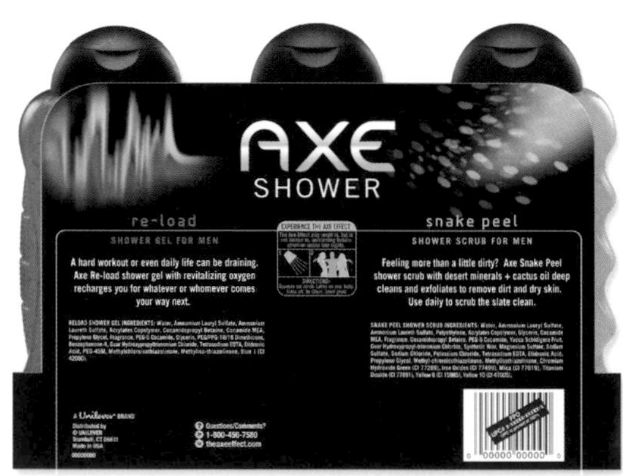

Creative Firm: **TOM FOWLER, INC. — NORWALK, CT**
Creative Team: **ELIZABETH P. BALL**
Client: **UNILEVER**

Creative Firm: **LIBBY PERSZYK KATHMAN — CINCINNATI, OH**
Creative Team: **BETH MALONE**
Client: **PROCTER & GAMBLE**

Creative Firm: **ZUNDA GROUP LLC — SOUTH NORWALK, CT**
Creative Team: **CHARLES ZUNDA, SIRI KORSGREN**
Client: **PRESTIGE BRANDS, INC.**

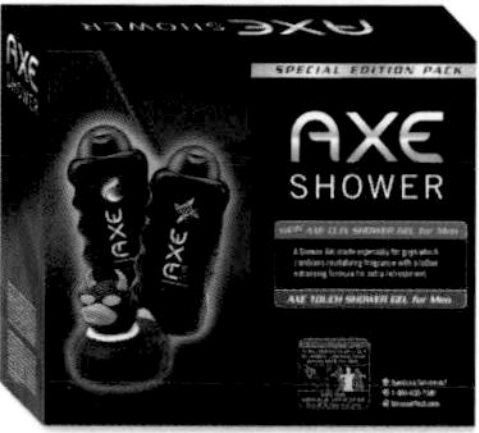

Creative Firm: **TOM FOWLER, INC. — NORWALK, CT**
Creative Team: **ELIZABETH P. BALL**
Client: **UNILEVER**

Creative Firm: **WALLACE CHURCH, INC. — NEW YORK, NY**
Creative Team: **STAN CHURCH, JOHN BRUNO**
Client: **THE GILLETTE COMPANY**

Creative Firm: **HORNALL ANDERSON DESIGN WORKS — SEATTLE, WA**
Creative Team: **LISA CERVENY, SONJA MAX, BELINDA BOWLING, ENSI MOFASSER, KATHY SAITO, BETH GRIMM, JULIE JACOBSON**
Client: **TAHITIAN NONI**

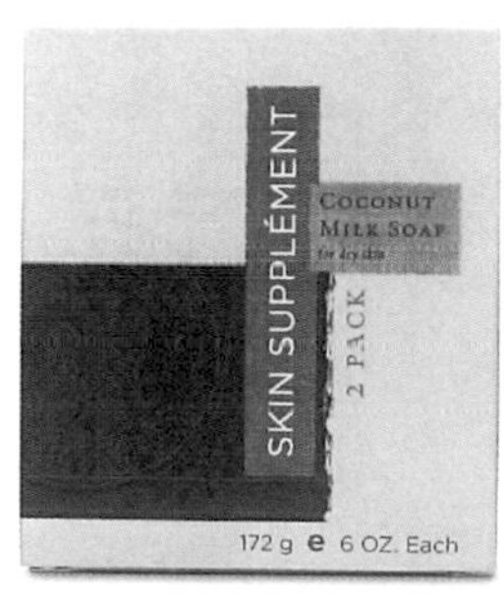

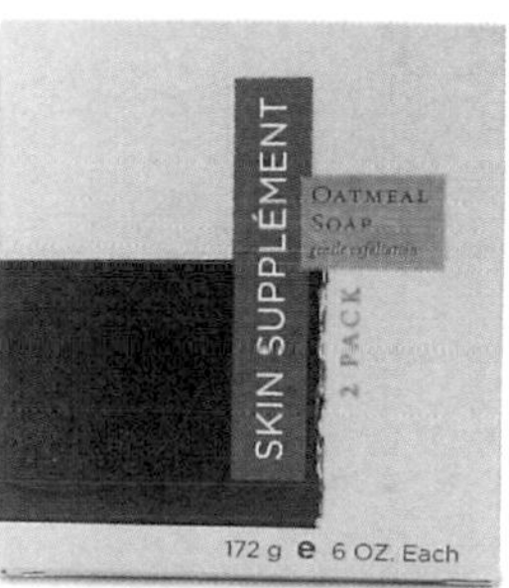

Creative Firm: **LIBBY PERSZYK KATHMAN — CINCINNATI, OH**
Creative Team: **LIZ GRUBOW, SUSAN ZINADER**
Client: **PROCTER & GAMBLE**

Creative Firm: **ZUNDA GROUP LLC — SOUTH NORWALK, CT**
Creative Team: **CHARLES ZUNDA**
Client: **SUPREME BRANDS, INC.**

Creative Firm: **LIBBY PERSZYK KATHMAN — CINCINNATI, OH**
Creative Team: **BETH MALONE**
Client: **PROCTER & GAMBLE**

Creative Firm: **PURE DESIGN CO. LLC — LEVERETT, MA**
Creative Team: **DAN MISHKIND, ROBYN TISDALE SCOTT**
Client: **PURELY SHEA**

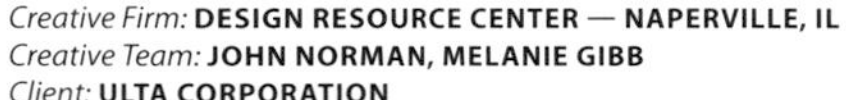

Creative Firm: **DESIGN RESOURCE CENTER — NAPERVILLE, IL**
Creative Team: **JOHN NORMAN, MELANIE GIBB**
Client: **ULTA CORPORATION**

Creative Firm: **LIBBY PERSZYK KATHMAN — CINCINNATI, OH**
Creative Team: **NANCY ANDREW, ALLY MCEWAN, JOHN MIKULA, DANE HEITHAUS**
Client: **NOVARTIS CONSUMER HEALTH, INC.**

Creative Firm: **PRAXIS DISEÑADORES S.C. — MEXICO CITY, D.F., MEXICO**
Creative Team: **FLORENCIA GUTIERREZ**
Client: **PROCTER AND GAMBLE BRAZIL LTDA.**

Creative Firm: **ALTERNATIVES — NEW YORK, NY**
Creative Team: **CARRI CORBETT, LYNN MARFEY**
Client: **SUDZ BY KISS MY FACE**

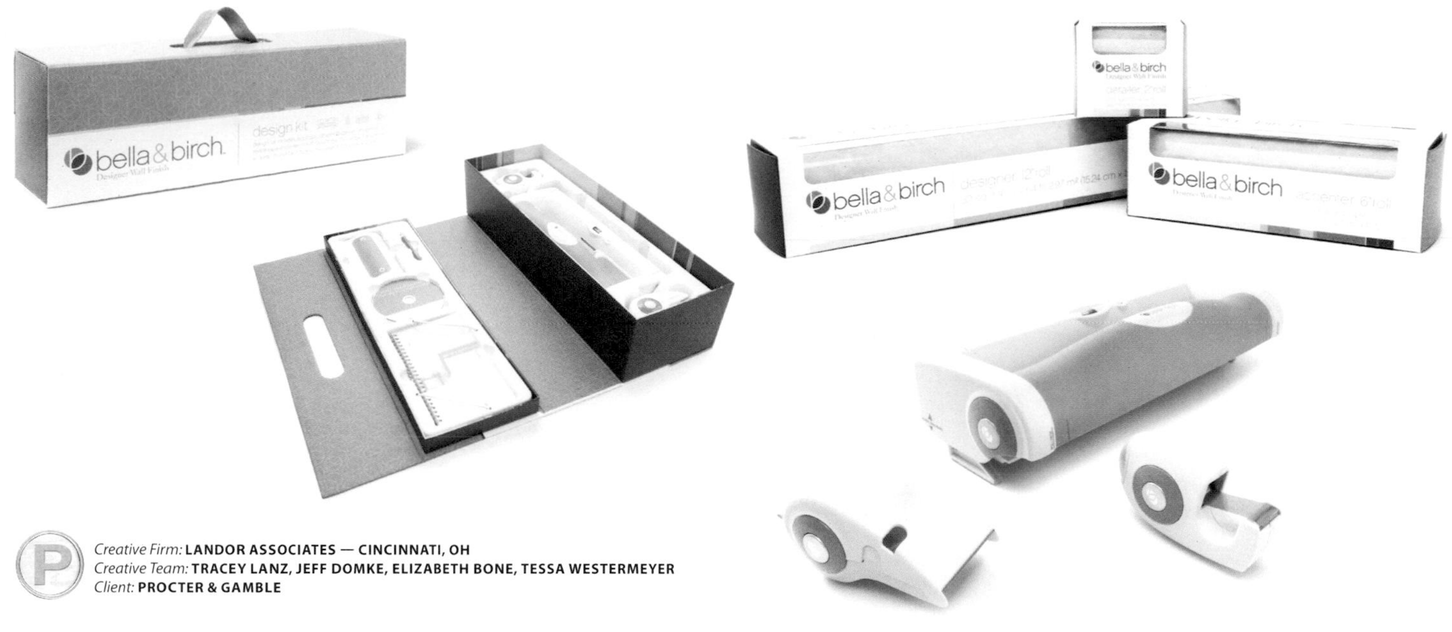

Creative Firm: **LANDOR ASSOCIATES — CINCINNATI, OH**
Creative Team: **TRACEY LANZ, JEFF DOMKE, ELIZABETH BONE, TESSA WESTERMEYER**
Client: **PROCTER & GAMBLE**

Creative Firm: **FUTURA DDB — LJUBLANA, SLOVENIA**
Creative Team: **ZARE KERIN, MARKO OMAHEN, RICCARDO CALIN**
Client: **BELINKA**

Creative Firm: **WILLIAM FOX MUNROE — SHELLINGTON , PA**
Creative Team: **BRIAN HARPER, MATT KENNEDY**
Client: **LOWES**

Creative Firm: **GAMMON RAGONESI ASSOCIATES — NEW YORK, NY**
Creative Team: **MARY RAGONESI, JILL SHELLHORN, JUNG SUE LEE**
Client: **MOEN**

Creative Firm: **KOLANO DESIGN — PITTSBURGH, PA**
Creative Team: **BILL KOLANO, TIM CARRERA**
Client: **SCOTT CALLAHAN — CALLAHAN & CHASE LLC**

Creative Firm: **CBX — NEW YORK, NY**
Client: **THE SCOTTS COMPANY**

Creative Firm: **CBX — NEW YORK, NY**
Client: **MASTER LOCK COMPANY**

Creative Firm: **FLOWDESIGN INC. — NORTHVILLE, MI**
Creative Team: **DAN MATAUCH, DENNIS NALEZYTY, KRYSTINA VOSS**
Client: **PUNATI CHEMICAL CORP.**

Creative Firm: **DESIGN RESOURCE CENTER — NAPERVILLE, IL**
Creative Team: **JOHN NORMAN, MELANIE GIBB**
Client: **DEFLECTO CORPORATION**

Creative Firm: **SUNSPOTS CREATIVE — FRANKLIN LAKES, NJ**
Creative Team: **RICK BONELLI, DAVE VIOREANU, DEENA HARTLEY**
Client: **SUPPLIES GUYS**

Creative Firm: **ISLAND OASIS — WALPOLE, MA**
Creative Team: **IAIN SHIPPERD**
Client: **ISLAND OASIS**

LABELS & TAGS

Creative Firm: **MORNINGSTAR DESIGN, INC. — FREDERICK, MD**
Creative Team: **MISTI MORNINGSTAR, MELISSA NEAL, EMILY POTTHAST**

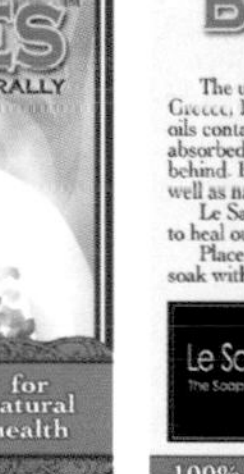

Creative Firm: **MORNINGSTAR DESIGN, INC. — FREDERICK, MD**
Creative Team: **MISTI MORNINGSTAR, MELISSA NEAL**

REGULATED MATERIALS

Creative Firm: **JACK NADEL INTERNATIONAL — LOS ANGELES, CA**
Creative Team: **SHELLEY SLUBOWSKI, AMYLIN PHARMACEUTICALS ART DIRECTION**
Client: **AMYLIN PHARMACEUTICALS / ELI LILLY**

Creative Firm: **TM&N DESIGN AND BRAND CONSULTANTS LTD. — HONG KONG**
Creative Team: **LEILA NACHTIGALL, JILLIAN LEE, SAMSON SUNG, VENUS CHAN, LIEM CHEUNG**
Client: **PURAPHARM INTERNATIONAL (HONG KONG) LIMITED**

Creative Firm: **ASPREY CREATIVE — FITZROY, VICTORIA, AUSTRALIA**
Creative Team: **RITA PALMIERI TRSAN, PETER ASPREY**
Client: **CARLSON HEALTH**

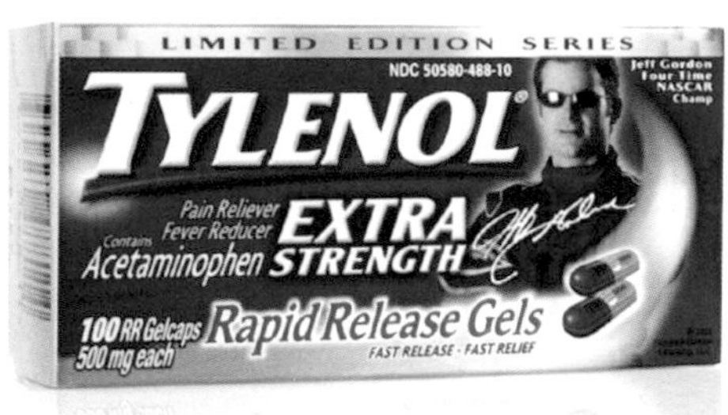

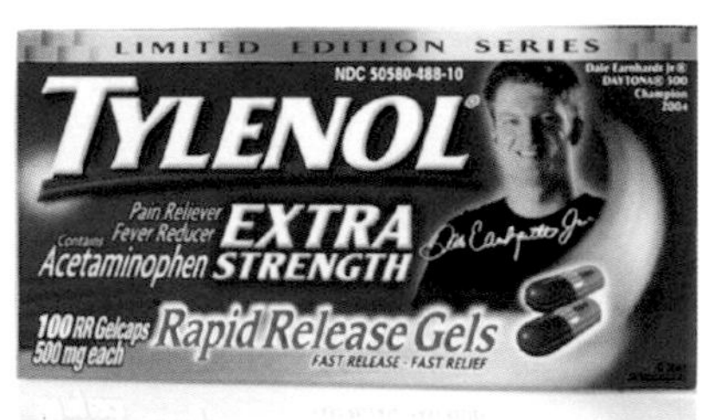

Creative Firm: **CBX — NEW YORK, NY**
Client: **MCNEIL CONSUMER & SPECIALTY PHARMACEUTICALS**

Creative Firm: **TRIPLE 888 STUDIOS — PARRAMATTA, NSW, AUSTRALIA**
Creative Team: **TRIPLE 888 CREATIVE TEAM**
Client: **SIRTEX MEDICAL**

Creative Firm: **ASPREY CREATIVE — FITZROY, VICTORIA, AUSTRALIA**
Creative Team: **RITA PALMIERI TRSAN, PETER ASPREY**
Client: **CARLSON HEALTH**

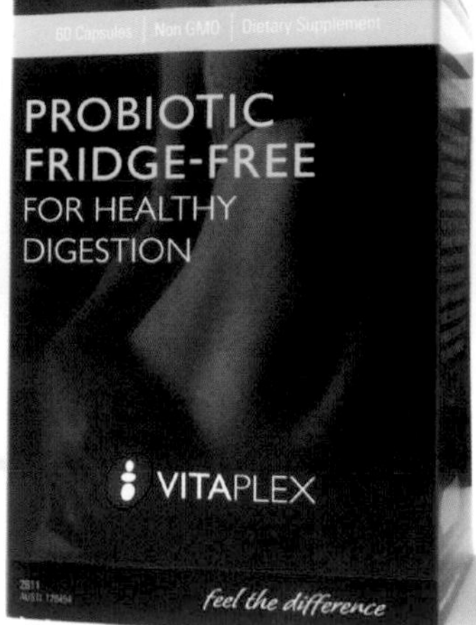

Creative Firm: **PATRICK HENRY CREATIVE PROMOTIONS, INC. — STAFFORD, TX**
Creative Team: **PHCP PRESTIGE ART TEAM, SMITH PHOTOGRAPHY**
Client: **INTERSTATE HOTELS AND RESORTS**

Creative Firm: **KARAKTER — LONDON, UNITED KINGDOM**
Creative Team: **CLIVE ROHALD, MEI WING CHAN, KAM DEVSI, SHAHAR SILBERSHATZ, PIERRE VINSOT**
Client: **CSA CZECH AIRLINES**

Creative Firm: **JOHN KNEAPLER DESIGN — NEW YORK, NY**
Creative Team: **JOHN KNEAPLER, COLLEEN SHEA, BOB SHEA**
Client: **HACKENSACK UNIVERSITY MEDICAL CENTER**

Creative Firm: **PATRICK HENRY CREATIVE PROMOTIONS, INC. — STAFFORD, TX**
Creative Team: **KENNETH WEAVER, CLEVELAND MENU PRINTING**
Client: **COLUMBIA SUSSEX CORPORATION**

Creative Firm: **PATRICK HENRY CREATIVE PROMOTIONS, INC. — STAFFORD, TX**
Creative Team: **DAVID ROCABADO, MICHAEL HASKINS PHOTOGRAPHY**
Client: **BENNIGAN'S GRILL AND TAVERN**

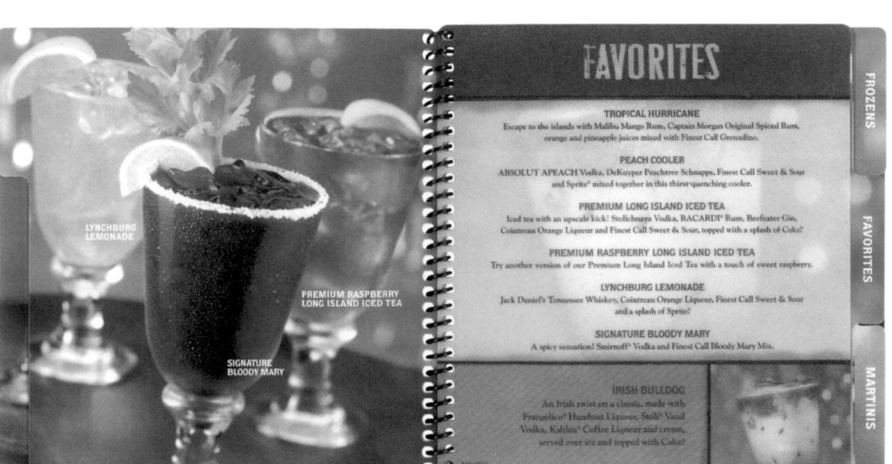

Creative Firm: **30SIXTY ADVERTISING+DESIGN, INC. — LOS ANGELES, CA**
Creative Team: **HENRY VIZCARRA, DAVID FUSCELLARO, LEE BARETT, JOHN LOTER**
Client: **KING'S SEAFOOD COMPANY**

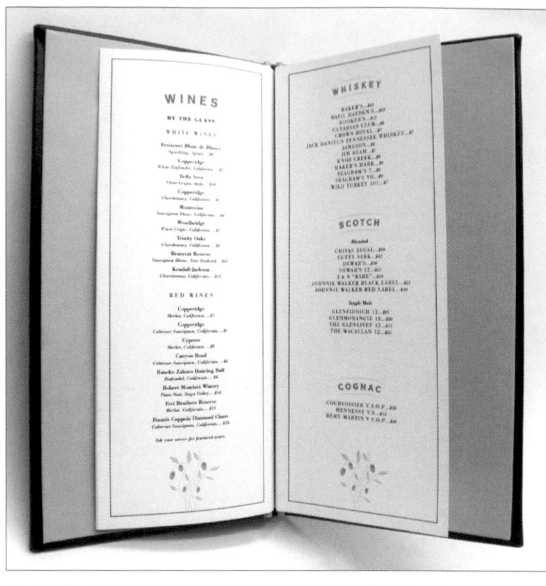

Creative Firm: **PATRICK HENRY CREATIVE PROMOTIONS, INC. — STAFFORD, TX**
Creative Team: **PHCP PRESTIGE ART TEAM**
Client: **HILTON HOTELS CORPORATION**

Creative Firm: **ISLAND OASIS — WALPOLE, MA**
Creative Team: **IAIN SHIPPERD**
Client: **ISLAND OASIS**

Creative Firm: **BERRY DESIGN INC — ALPHARETTA, GA**
Creative Team: **BOB BERRY, JULIE ACQUESTA**
Client: **UP THE CREEK**

Creative Firm: **ISLAND OASIS — WALPOLE, MA**
Creative Team: **IAIN SHIPPERD**
Client: **ISLAND OASIS**

Creative Firm: **PATRICK HENRY CREATIVE PROMOTIONS, INC. — STAFFORD, TX**
Creative Team: **PHCP PRESTIGE ART TEAM**
Client: **PHILLIPS SEAFOOD RESTAURANTS**

Creative Firm: **IGNITED MINDS, LLC — MARINA DEL REY, CA**
Creative Team: **OOGIE LEE, PERRY SIEWERT, KEU CHA, SCHAWK, INC.**
Client: **ACTIVISION**

Creative Firm: **HORNALL ANDERSON DESIGN WORKS — SEATTLE, WA**
Creative Team: **LISA CERVENY, MARY HERMES, JULIA LAPINE, JANA NISHI, BELINDA BOWLING, LAUREN DIRUSSO, ELMER DELA CRUZ**
Client: **O.C. TANNER**

Creative Firm: **HORNALL ANDERSON DESIGN WORKS — SEATTLE, WA**
Creative Team: **JACK ANDERSON, DAVID BATES, SONJA MAX, HOLLY CRAVEN**
Client: **NORDSTROM**

Creative Firm: **ACOSTA DESIGN INC — NEW YORK, NY**
Creative Team: **MAURICIO ACOSTA**
Client: **NCG**

Creative Firm: **WALLACE CHURCH, INC. — NEW YORK, NY**
Creative Team: **STAN CHURCH, JODI LUBRICH, RICH RICKABY**
Client: **WALLACE CHURCH, INC.**

Creative Firm: **ALL MEDIA PROJECTS LIMITED — PORT OF SPAIN, TRINIDAD AND TOBAGO**
Creative Team: **CATHLEEN JONES, KIRIE ISHMAEL, MARISA CAMEJO, JULIEN GREENIDGE, JOSIANE KHAN**
Client: **BP TRINIDAD AND TOBAGO (BPTT)**

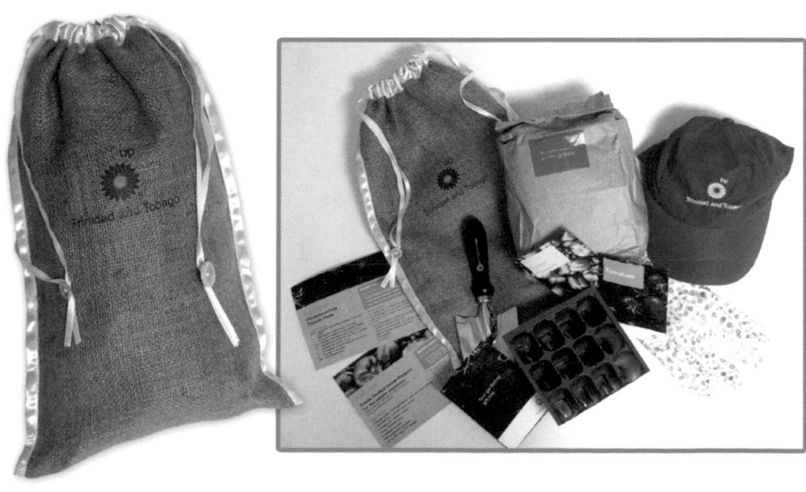

Creative Firm: **VH1 — NEW YORK, NY**
Client: **VH1**

Creative Firm: **MIND & MEDIA — ALEXANDRIA, VA**
Creative Team: **CHRIS AMMON, TROY THOMPSON, SARA ISACSON**
Client: **ARMY NATIONAL GAURD**

Creative Firm: **JACK NADEL INTERNATIONAL — LOS ANGELES, CA**
Creative Team: **SHELLEY SLUBOWSKI, AMYLIN PHARMECEUTICALS ART DIRECTION**
Client: **AMYLIN PHARMACEUTICALS / ELI LILLY**

Creative Firm: **JONI RAE AND ASSOCIATES — ENCINO, CA**
Creative Team: **JONI RAE RUSSELL, BEVERLY TRENGOVE**
Client: **THERMAFUSE**

Creative Firm: **TRIPLE 888 STUDIOS — PARRAMATTA, NSW, AUSTRALIA**
Creative Team: **TRIPLE 888 CREATIVE TEAM**
Client: **MAXWELL J. BUSHBY**

Creative Firm: **AOL | 360 CREATIVE — NEW YORK, NY**
Creative Team: **ANTHONY FARIA, MARIO ARIAS, RICHARD TAYLOR, AUDREY BREINDEL, ERIKA ALONSO**
Client: **AOL MEDIA NETWORKS**

Creative Firm: **JGA — SOUTHFIELD, MI**
Creative Team: **DAVID NELSON, TAMI JO URBAN, KATHI MCWILLIAMS**
Client: **KIRKLAND'S**

Creative Firm: **ZUNDA GROUP LLC — SOUTH NORWALK, CT**
Creative Team: **CHARLES ZUNDA, TODD NICKEL, MARK ISENHART**
Client: **HILL'S PET NUTRITION, INC.**

Creative Firm: **HORNALL ANDERSON DESIGN WORKS — SEATTLE, WA**
Creative Team: **LISA CERVENY, MARY HERMES, HOLLY CRAVEN, BELINDA BOWLING, MARY CHIN HUTCHINSON, TIFFANY PLACE**
Client: **BENJAMIN MOORE**

Creative Firm: **TOM FOWLER, INC. — NORWALK, CT**
Creative Team: **MARY ELLEN BUTKUS, ELIZABETH P. BALL, MARIE FORJAN**
Client: **ACME UNITED CORPORATION**

Creative Firm: **HEDGEHOG DESIGN LIMITED — NORTH POINT, HONG KONG**
Creative Team: **GARY MAN, KIT CHUNG, ANDY NEE**
Client: **HAPPY KID TOY GROUP LTD.**

Creative Firm: **JGA — SOUTHFIELD, MI**
Creative Team: **KEN NISCH, KATHI MCWILLIAMS**
Client: **LAURA SECORD**

Creative Firm: **AGENCY X ADS — SAN FRANCISCO, CA**
Creative Team: **LOTUS CHILD, JENNIFER ELIAS**
Client: **SMARTSCO**

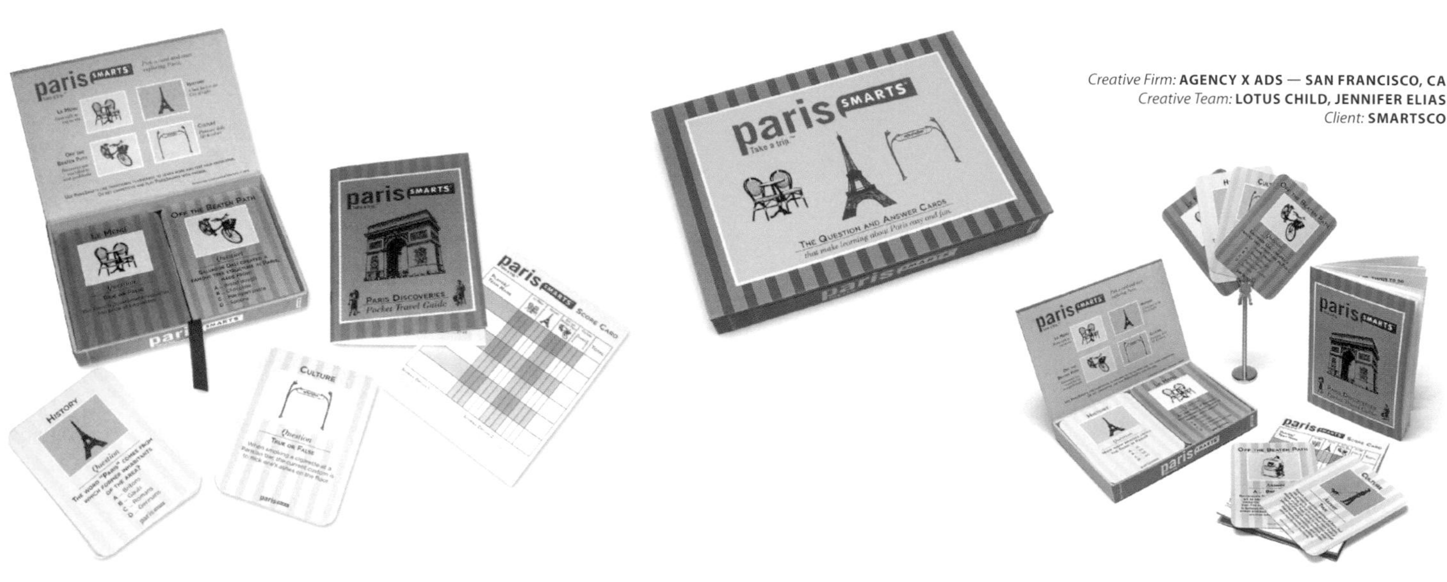

Creative Firm: **SCOTT VISION COMMUNICATION — TAIPEI, TAIWAN**

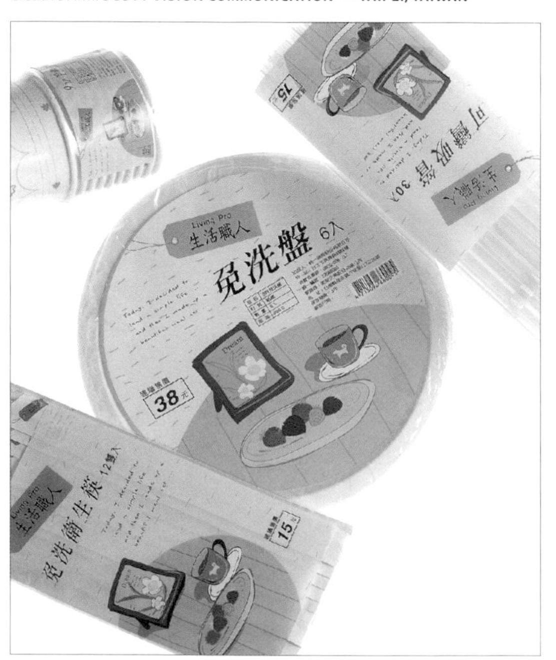

Creative Firm: **HEDGEHOG DESIGN LIMITED — NORTH POINT, HONG KONG**
Creative Team: **GARY MAN, KENNY KOON, ANDY NEE**
Client: **HAPPY KID TOY GROUP LTD.**

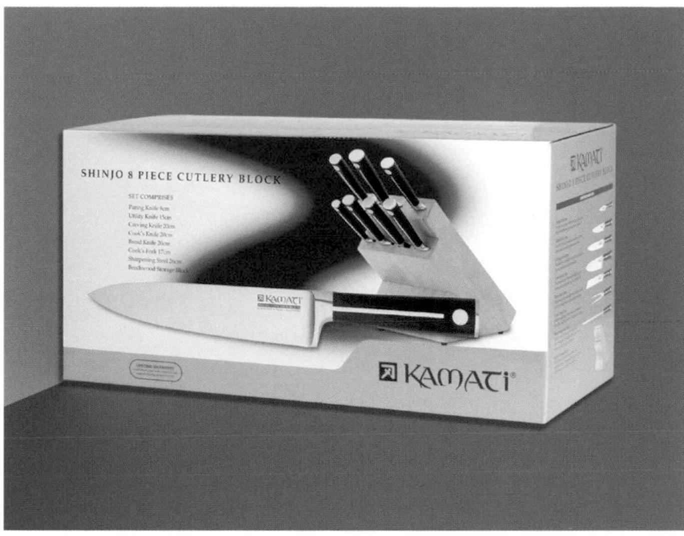

Creative Firm: **TRIPLE 888 STUDIOS — PARRAMATTA, NSW, AUSTRALIA**
Creative Team: **TRIPLE 888 CREATIVE TEAM**
Client: **SHELDON & HAMMOND**

Creative Firm: **WILLIAM FOX MUNROE — SHELLINGTON, PA**
Creative Team: **AMY PARKER, MIKE AMOLE**
Client: **WOODSCAPE ARTKITS, INC**

Creative Firm: **AGENCY X ADS — SAN FRANCISCO, CA**
Creative Team: **LOTUS CHILD, DENISE ST. LOUIS**
Client: **ALICE RADIO**

Creative Firm: **WILLIAM FOX MUNROE — SHELLINGTON, PA**
Creative Team: **MARY MALLIS, MATT KENNEDY, STEPHANIE BENNETT, JOSH SAMOLEWICZ**
Client: **EDUCATE, INC.**

Creative Firm: **CROSLEY RADIO — LOUISVILLE, KY**
Creative Team: **MARK GROVES**
Client: **CROSLEY RADIO**

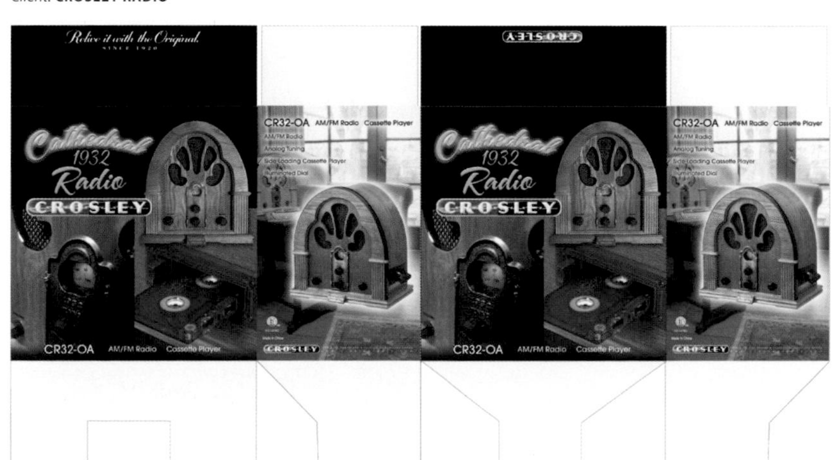

Creative Firm: **CROSLEY RADIO — LOUISVILLE, KY**
Creative Team: **MARK GROVES**
Client: **CROSLEY RADIO**

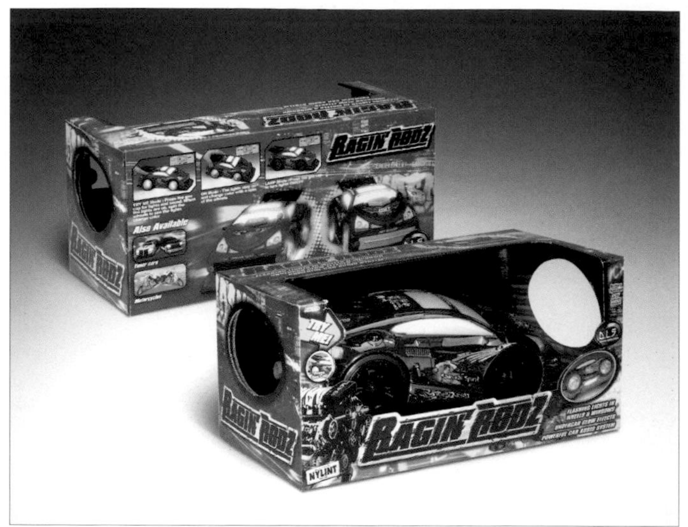

Creative Firm: **HEDGEHOG DESIGN LIMITED — NORTH POINT, HONG KONG**
Creative Team: **GARY MAN, KIT CHUNG, SCOTT NG**
Client: **FUNRISE TOYS LIMITED**

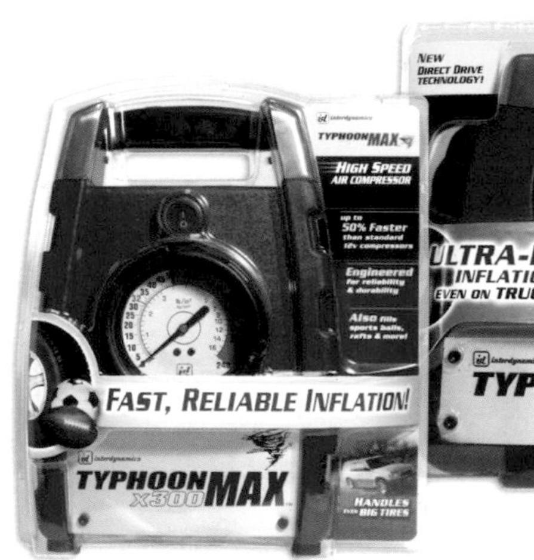

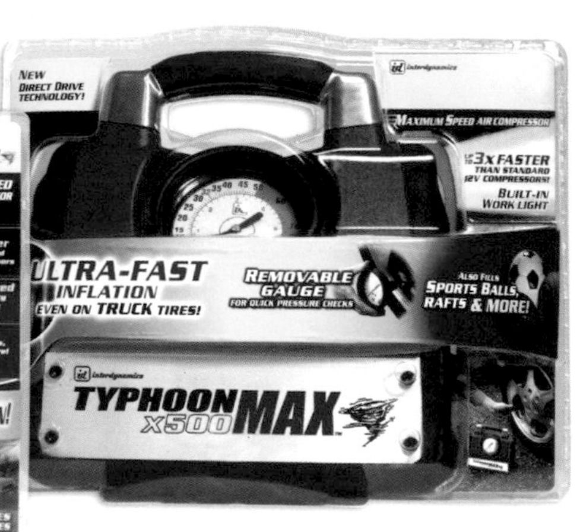

Creative Firm: **TOM FOWLER, INC. — NORWALK, CT**
Creative Team: **MARY ELLEN BUTKUS, THOMAS G. FOWLER**
Client: **INTERDYNAMICS**

Creative Firm: **INTERROBANG DESIGN COLLABORATIVE, INC. — RICHMOND, VT**
Creative Team: **MARK D. SYLVESTER**
Client: **TDK ELECTRONICS CORPORATION**

Creative Firm: **HEDGEHOG DESIGN LIMITED — NORTH POINT, HONG KONG**
Creative Team: **GARY MAN, KIT CHUNG, ANDY NEE**
Client: **HAPPY KID TOY GROUP LTD.**

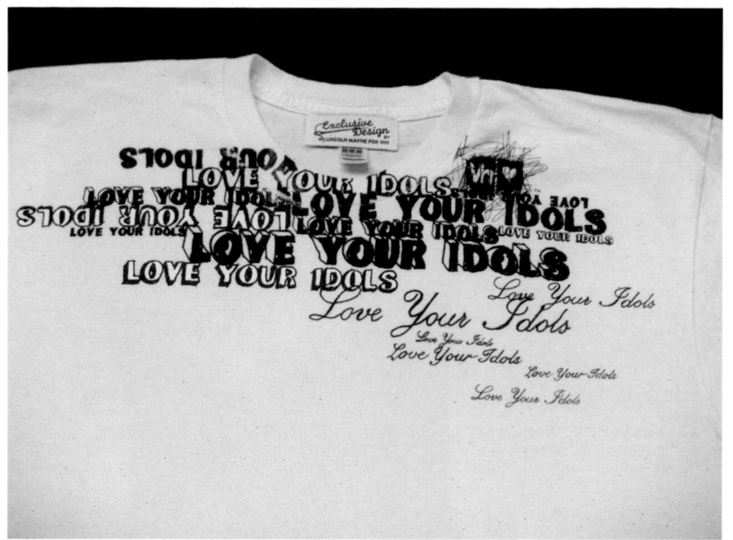

Creative Firm: **VH1 — NEW YORK, NY**
Client: **VH1**

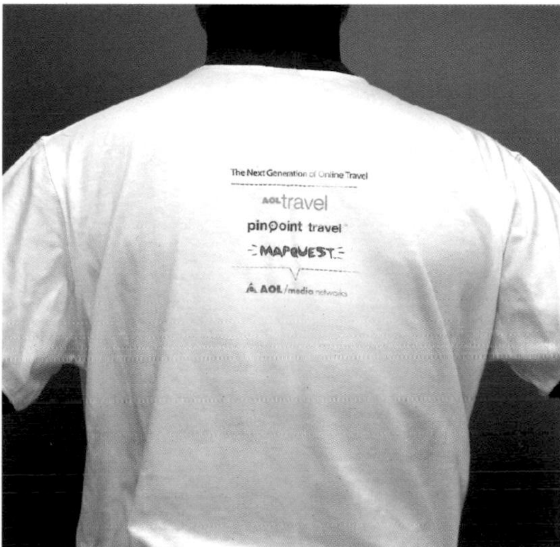

Creative Firm: **AOL | 360 CREATIVE — NEW YORK, NY**
Creative Team: **ANTHONY FARIA, KIMBERLY GEISER, TOM POLLEY, ERIKA ALONSO**
Client: **AOL MEDIA NETWORKS**

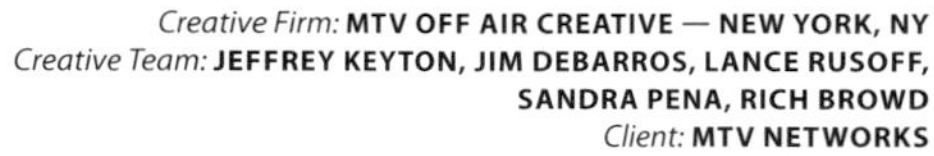

Creative Firm: **MTV OFF AIR CREATIVE — NEW YORK, NY**
Creative Team: **JEFFREY KEYTON, JIM DEBARROS, LANCE RUSOFF, SANDRA PENA, RICH BROWD**
Client: **MTV NETWORKS**

Creative Firm: **ISLAND OASIS — WALPOLE, MA**
Creative Team: **PETE BUHLER**
Client: **ISLAND OASIS**

Creative Firm: **JACK NADEL INTERNATIONAL — LOS ANGELES, CA**
Creative Team: **SCOTT BROWN**
Client: **D.A.R.E. AMERICA MERCHANDISE**

Creative Firm: **OCTAVO DESIGNS — FREDERICK, MD**
Creative Team: **SUE HOUGH**
Client: **THE TEMPLE, A PAUL MITCHELL PARTNER SCHOOL**

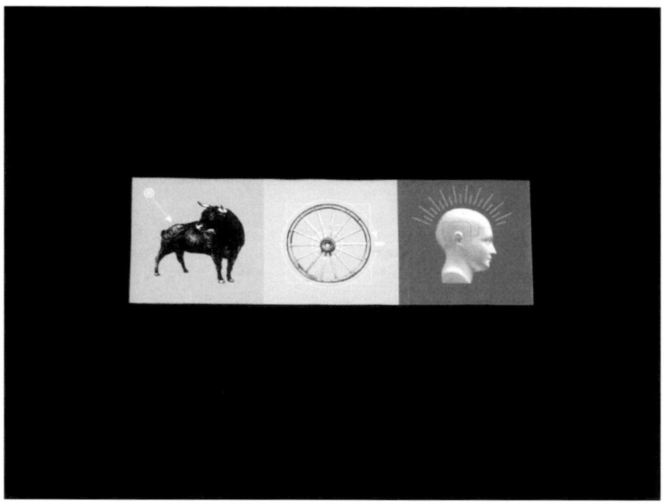

Creative Firm: **G2 — NEW YORK, NY**
Creative Team: **JASON BORZOUYEH**
Client: **G2**

Creative Firm: **MTV OFF AIR CREATIVE — NEW YORK, NY**
Creative Team: **JEFFREY KEYTON, JIM DEBARROS, RICHARD BROWD, SANDRA PENA**
Client: **MTV NETWORKS**

Creative Firm: **BBK STUDIO — GRAND RAPIDS, MI**
Creative Team: **MICHELE CHARTIER, KEVIN BUDELMANN**
Client: **SPOUT**

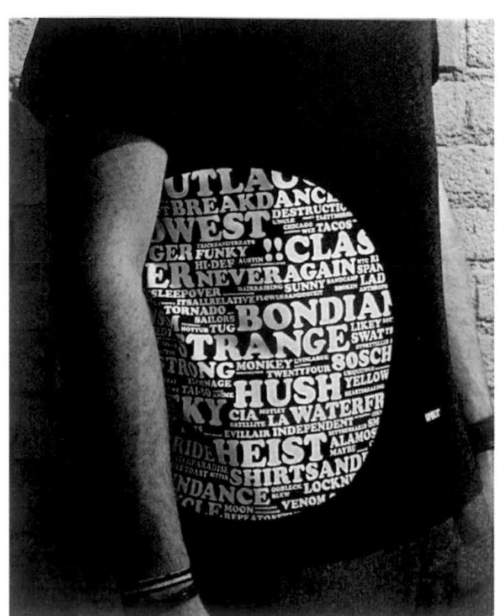

Creative Firm: **30SIXTY ADVERTISING+DESIGN, INC. — LOS ANGELES, CA**
Creative Team: **HENRY VIZCARRA, PÄR LARSSON, MOT POTIVES, BRUCE VENTANILLA, TUYET VONG**
Client: **UNIVERSAL STUDIOS HOME ENTERTAINMENT**

Creative Firm: **NEURON SYNDICATE INC. — SANTA MONICA, CA**
Creative Team: **RYAN CRAMER, SEAN ALATORRE, JASON BURNHAM, PHIL MCKENNA**
Client: **WARNER BROS. HOME ENTERTAINMENT**

Creative Firm: **NEURON SYNDICATE INC. — SANTA MONICA, CA**
Creative Team: **SEAN ALATORRE, RYAN CRAMER, JASON BURNAM**
Client: **20TH CENTURY FOX**

Creative Firm: **AMATO IMAGE DESIGN — TEMPE, AZ**
Creative Team: **TONY AMATO, MICHAEL WOODALL,**
Client: **THE BIG BOTTOM BAND**

Creative Firm: **NEURON SYNDICATE INC. — SANTA MONICA, CA**
Creative Team: **SEAN ALATORRE, RYAN CRAMER, JASON BURNAM, JUSTINA WANG**
Client: **20TH CENTURY FOX**

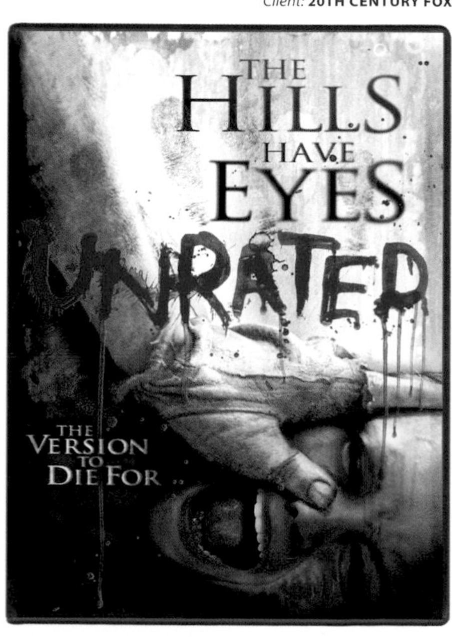

Creative Firm: **STUDIOERIN — JUPITER, FL**
Creative Team: **ERIN STARKS, FIELDS OF FOREL, ENRIQUE PALACIOS, ZAC COLLINS, STEVIE SAGER**
Client: **FIELDS OF FOREL**

Creative Firm: **NEURON SYNDICATE INC. — SANTA MONICA, CA**
Creative Team: **RYAN CRAMER, SEAN ALATORRE, JASON BURNAM, TIM CALIA**
Client: **20TH CENTURY FOX**

Creative Firm: **STUDIO FIVE — NEW YORK, NY**
Creative Team: **TATIANA AROCHA**
Client: **EXPANSION TEAM**

Creative Firm: **THE DESIGN STUDIO AT KEAN UNIVERSITY — UNION, NJ**
Creative Team: **STEVEN BROWER, BARBARA RÚSTICK**
Client: **THE AFFLIATE ARTISTS OF KEAN UNIVERSITY**

Creative Firm: **AMATO IMAGE DESIGN — TEMPE, AZ**
Creative Team: **TONY AMATO**
Client: **PHILLIP STRANGE**

Creative Firm: **AGENCY X ADS — SAN FRANCISCO, CA**
Creative Team: **LOTUS CHILD, DENISE ST. LOUIS**
Client: **ALICE RADIO**

Creative Firm: **COMPANY STANDARD — BROOKLYN, NY**
Creative Team: **MELISSA GORMAN, TATIANA AROCHA**
Client: **DEFINITIVE JUX**

Creative Firm: **BIGWIG DESIGN — SAN FRANCISCO, CA**
Creative Team: **RICHARD LEEDS, FRANCOIS BURLAND, PAUL MAHDER**
Client: **TOO FAR**

Creative Firm: **NEURON SYNDICATE INC. — SANTA MONICA, CA**
Creative Team: **SEAN ALATORRE, RYAN CRAMER, JASON BURNAM**
Client: **WARNER BROS.**

Creative Firm: **AMATO IMAGE DESIGN — TEMPE, AZ**
Creative Team: **TONY AMATO, MICHAEL WOODALL**
Client: **WARREN JONES**

Creative Firm: **BURROWS — BRENTWOOD, ESSEX, UNITED KINGDOM**
Creative Team: **ROYDON HEARNE, DARRYL SMITH, AARON HULSIZER, LUCY WELDON**
Client: **VOLVO CARS UK**

Creative Firm: **RIORDON DESIGN — OAKVILLE, ON, CANADA**
Creative Team: **SHIRLEY RIORDON**
Client: **PAUL BALOCHE / INTEGRITY MUSIC**

Creative Firm: **EPOS, INC. — SANTA MONICA, CA**
Creative Team: **KIMIYO NISHIO, GABRIELLE RAUMBERGER**
Client: **OLIVIA NEWTON-JOHN PRODUCTIONS**

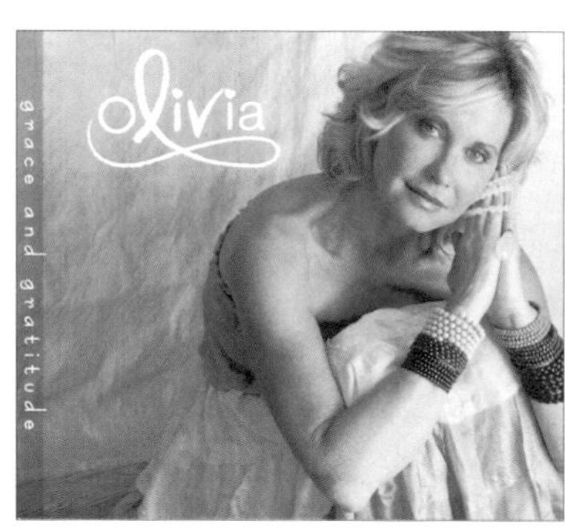

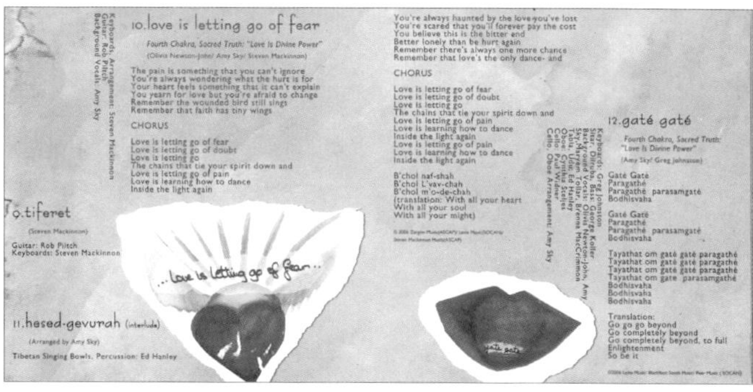

Creative Firm: **NEURON SYNDICATE INC. — SANTA MONICA, CA**
Creative Team: **SEAN ALATORRE, RYAN CRAMER**
Client: **BASEMENT RECORDS / MASTERGRIP LLC.**

Creative Firm: **AMATO IMAGE DESIGN — TEMPE, AZ**
Creative Team: **TONY AMATO, MICHAEL WOODALL**
Client: **JERRY DONATO**

Creative Firm: **TODD CHILDERS GRAPHIC DESIGN — BOWLING GREEN, OH**
Creative Team: **TODD CHILDERS, BRADLEY WILBER**
Client: **NINA ASSIMAKOPOULOS**

NORTHEAST DECIDUOUS FOREST

NATURE OF AMERICA

Creative Firm: **UNITED STATES POSTAL SERVICE — ARLINGTON, VA**
Creative Team: **ETHEL KESSLER, JOHN DAWSON**
Client: **UNITED STATES POSTAL SERVICE**

Creative Firm: **UNITED STATES POSTAL SERVICE — ARLINGTON, VA**
Creative Team: **ETHEL KESSLER, TIM O'BRIEN, GREG BERGER**
Client: **UNITED STATES POSTAL SERVICE**

Creative Firm: **RICK SEALOCK — KITCHENER, ON, CANADA**
Creative Team: **MICHAEL AUBRECHT, RICK SEALOCK**
Client: **SELLING POWER INC. MAGAZINE**

Creative Firm: **PLAYBOY ENTERPRISES INTERNATIONAL, INC. — CHICAGO, IL**
Creative Team: **TOM STAEBLER, DAVE MCKEAN**
Client: **PLAYBOY MAGAZINE**

Creative Firm: **UNITED STATES POSTAL SERVICE — ARLINGTON, VA**
Creative Team: **CARL HERRMAN, ART FITZPATRICK**
Client: **UNITED STATES POSTAL SERVICE**

Creative Firm: **PLAYBOY ENTERPRISES INTERNATIONAL, INC. — CHICAGO, IL**
Creative Team: **YUKO SHIMIZU, ROB WILSON, TOM STAEBLER**
Client: **PLAYBOY MAGAZINE**

Creative Firm: **DESIGN NUT — KENSINGTON, MD**
Creative Team: **BRENT ALMOND**
Client: **FAMILY TIES PROJECT**

Creative Firm: **UNITED STATES POSTAL SERVICE — ARLINGTON, VA**
Creative Team: **DERRY NOYES, JOHN MATTOS**
Client: **UNITED STATES POSTAL SERVICE**

Creative Firm: **WENDELL MINOR DESIGN — WASHINGTON, CT**
Creative Team: **WENDELL MINOR, FLORENCE MINOR, AL CETTA**
Client: **HARPERCOLLINS**

Creative Firm: **UNITED STATES POSTAL SERVICE — ARLINGTON, VA**
Creative Team: **PHIL JORDAN, WILLIAM S. PHILLIPS**
Client: **UNITED STATES POSTAL SERVICE**

Creative Firm: **PLAYBOY ENTERPRISES INTERNATIONAL, INC. — CHICAGO, IL**
Creative Team: **ISTVAN BANYAI, SCOTT ANDERSON, TOM STAEBLER**
Client: **PLAYBOY MAGAZINE**

Creative Firm: **SABINGRAFIK, INC. — CARLSBAD, CA**
Creative Team: **TRACY SABIN, BRIDGET SABIN**
Client: **SEAFARER BAKING COMPANY**

Creative Firm: **PLAYBOY ENTERPRISES INTERNATIONAL, INC. — CHICAGO, IL**
Creative Team: **CRAIG MULLINS, ROB WILSON, TOM STAEBLER**
Client: **PLAYBOY MAGAZINE**

Creative Firm: **MENDES PUBLICIDADE — BELÉM, PARÁ, BRAZIL**
Creative Team: **OSWALDO MENDES, MARCELO AMORIM**
Client: **TIM NORTE**

Creative Firm: **VH1 — NEW YORK, NY**
Client: **VH1**

Creative Firm: **PLAYBOY ENTERPRISES INTERNATIONAL, INC. — CHICAGO, IL**
Creative Team: **MIRKO ILIC, ROB WILSON, TOM STAEBLER**
Client: **PLAYBOY MAGAZINE**

Creative Firm: **AMERICAN RED CROSS BLOOD SERVICES, WEST DIVISION — POMONA, CA**
Creative Team: **BRIAN MEDINA**

Creative Firm: **UNITED STATES POSTAL SERVICE — ARLINGTON, VA**
Creative Team: **HOWARD PAINE, MICHAEL DEAS**
Client: **UNITED STATES POSTAL SERVICE**

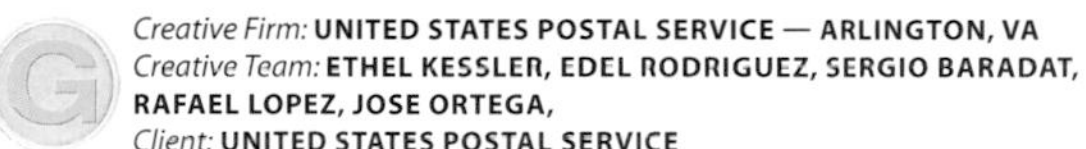
Creative Firm: **UNITED STATES POSTAL SERVICE — ARLINGTON, VA**
Creative Team: **ETHEL KESSLER, EDEL RODRIGUEZ, SERGIO BARADAT, RAFAEL LOPEZ, JOSE ORTEGA,**
Client: **UNITED STATES POSTAL SERVICE**

Creative Firm: **PLAYBOY ENTERPRISES INTERNATIONAL, INC. — CHICAGO, IL**
Creative Team: **TOMER HANUKA, TOM STAEBLER**
Client: **PLAYBOY MAGAZINE**

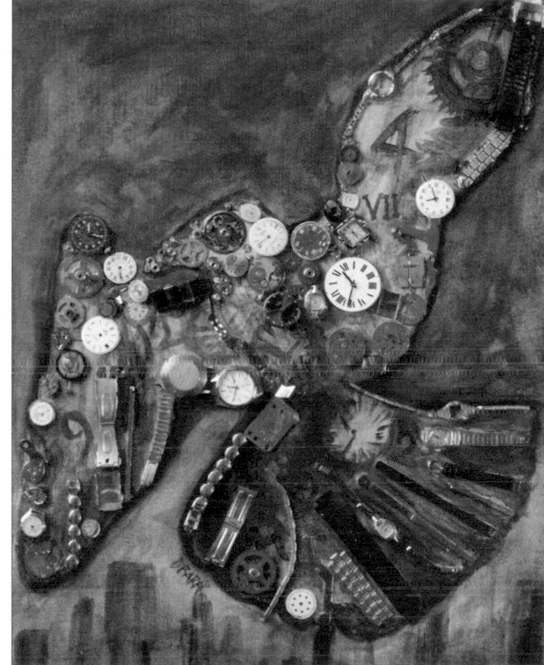

Creative Firm: **MPHASIS ON FRONTIER — DENVER, CO**
Creative Team: **DANA BARAK**
Client: **WILD BLUE YONDER MAGAZINE**

Creative Firm: **UNITED STATES POSTAL SERVICE — ARLINGTON, VA**
Creative Team: **RICHARD SHEAFF, ALBERT SLARK**
Client: **UNITED STATES POSTAL SERVICE**

Creative Firm: **PLAYBOY ENTERPRISES INTERNATIONAL, INC. — CHICAGO, IL**
Creative Team: **CATHIE BLECK, ROB WILSON, TOM STAEBLER**
Client: **PLAYBOY MAGAZINE**

Creative Firm: **UNITED STATES POSTAL SERVICE — ARLINGTON, VA**
Creative Team: **CARL HERRMAN, WILL WILSON**
Client: **UNITED STATES POSTAL SERVICE**

Creative Firm: **PLAYBOY ENTERPRISES INTERNATIONAL, INC. — CHICAGO, IL**
Creative Team: **NICHOLAS WILTON, TOM STAEBLER**
Client: **PLAYBOY MAGAZINE**

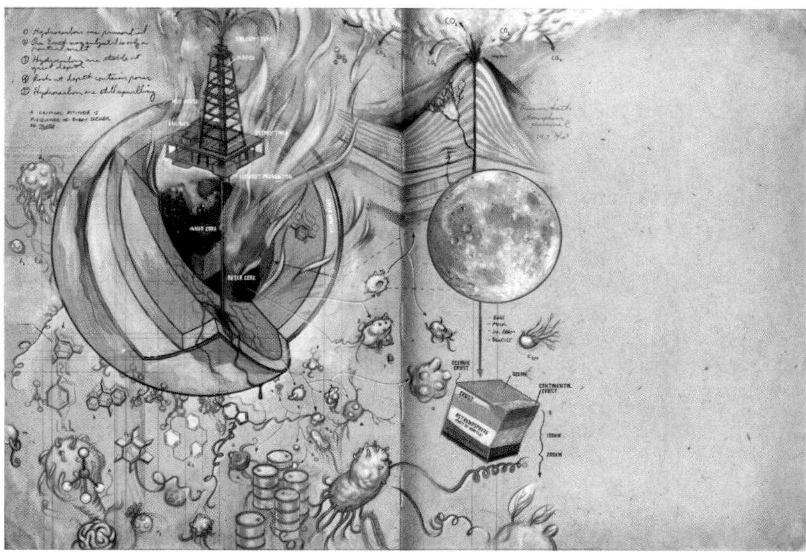

Creative Firm: **PLAYBOY ENTERPRISES INTERNATIONAL, INC. — CHICAGO, IL**
Creative Team: **JAMES JEAN, SCOTT ANDERSON, TOM STAEBLER**
Client: **PLAYBOY MAGAZINE**

Creative Firm: **WENDELL MINOR DESIGN — WASHINGTON, CT**
Creative Team: **WENDELL MINOR, CECILIA YUNG, GUNTA ALEXANDER**
Client: **PUTNAM**

Creative Firm: **PLAYBOY ENTERPRISES INTERNATIONAL, INC. — CHICAGO, IL**
Creative Team: **ROB WILSON, SCOTT ANDERSON, TOM STAEBLER**
Client: **PLAYBOY MAGAZINE**

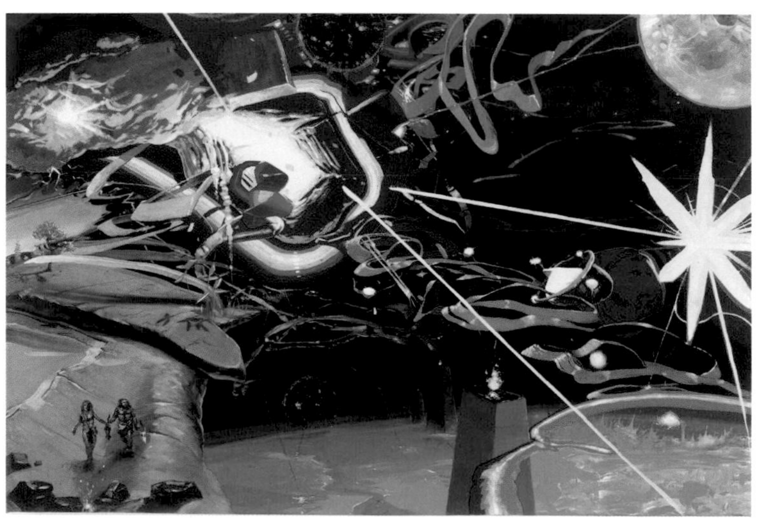

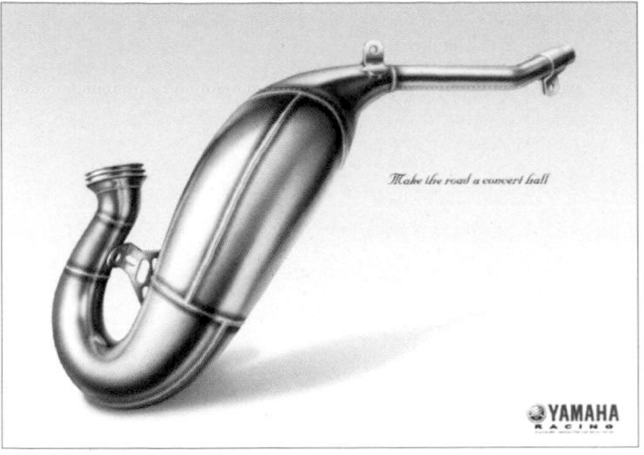

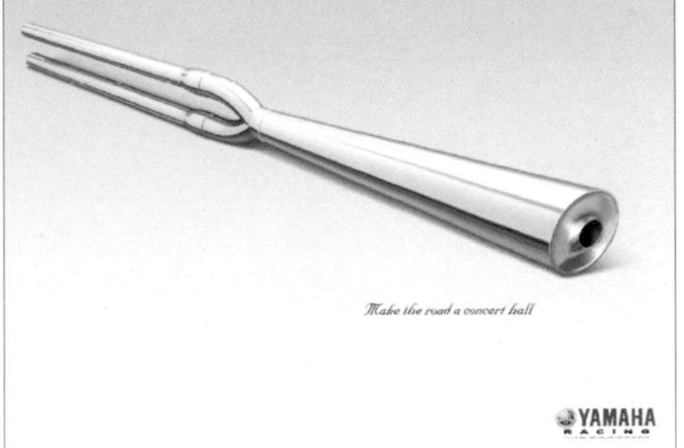

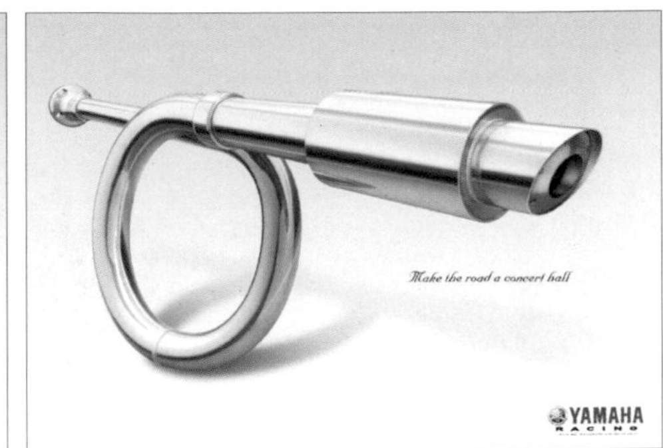

Creative Firm: **YOUNG & RUBICAM GMBH & CO. KG — FRANKFURT AM MAIN, HESSEN, GERMANY**
Creative Team: **CHRISTIAN DAUL, GUIDO MASSON, LOTHAR GRIM, KLAUS GERBER, CLAUDIA SCHOENHALS**
Client: **LUX AG**

Creative Firm: **RONI HICKS & ASSOCIATES — CARLSBAD, CA**
Creative Team: **TRACY SABIN, STEPHEN SHARP**
Client: **4S RANCH**

Creative Firm: **PERNSTEINER CREATIVE GROUP, INC. — ST LOUIS PARK, MN**
Creative Team: **TODD PERNSTEINER, ERIK LERVOLD**
Client: **SAINT MARY'S PRESS**

Creative Firm: **RICK SEALOCK — KITCHENER, ON, CANADA**
Creative Team: **MARK ALLEN, RICK SEALOCK**
Client: **TEMERLIN ADVERTISING INSTITUTE, SMU**

Creative Firm: **QUALCOMM — SAN DIEGO, CA**
Creative Team: **CHRIS LEE, MICHAEL SCHWAB**

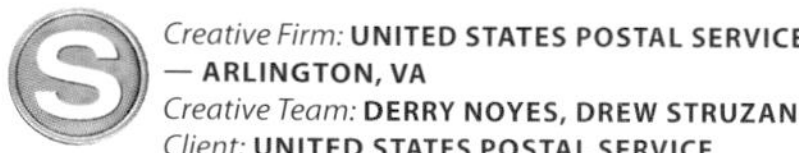

Creative Firm: **UNITED STATES POSTAL SERVICE — ARLINGTON, VA**
Creative Team: **DERRY NOYES, DREW STRUZAN**
Client: **UNITED STATES POSTAL SERVICE**

Creative Firm: **PLAYBOY ENTERPRISES INTERNATIONAL, INC. — CHICAGO, IL**
Creative Team: **ROBERTO PARADA, TOM STAEBLER**
Client: **PLAYBOY MAGAZINE**

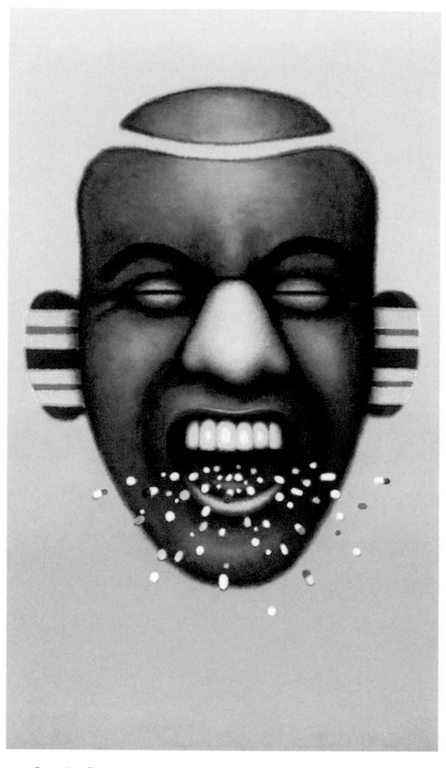

Creative Firm: **PLAYBOY ENTERPRISES INTERNATIONAL, INC. — CHICAGO, IL**
Creative Team: **ED PASCHKE, TOM STAEBLER**
Client: **PLAYBOY MAGAZINE**

Creative Firm: **WENDELL MINOR DESIGN — WASHINGTON, CT**
Creative Team: **WENDELL MINOR, JEAN CRAIGHEAD GEORGE, MARTHA RAGO, NEIL SWAAB**
Client: **HARPERCOLLINS**

Creative Firm: **PLAYBOY ENTERPRISES INTERNATIONAL, INC. — CHICAGO, IL**
Creative Team: **ROBERTO PARADA, TOM STAEBLER**
Client: **PLAYBOY MAGAZINE**

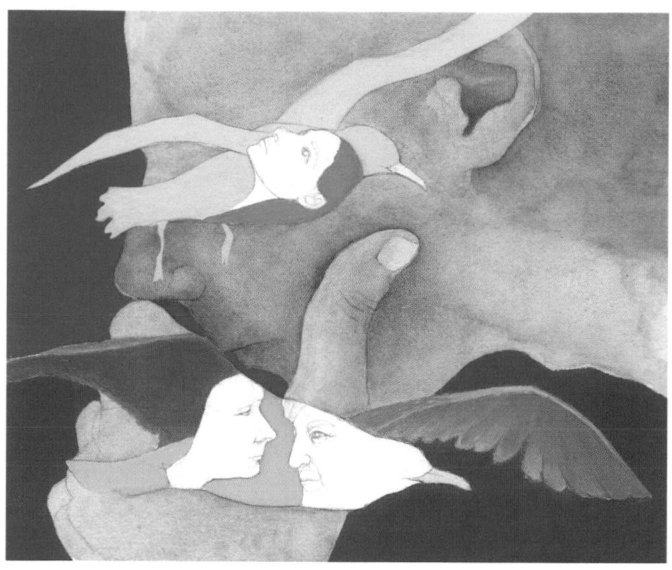

Creative Firm: **PLAYBOY ENTERPRISES INTERNATIONAL, INC. — CHICAGO, IL**
Creative Team: **TIFENN PYTHON, TOM STAEBLER**
Client: **PLAYBOY MAGAZINE**

Creative Firm: **ASPREY CREATIVE — FITZROY, VICTORIA, AUSTRALIA**
Creative Team: **GEORGE MARGARITIS, PETER ASPREY**
Client: **MASTERFOODS SNACKFOOD**

Creative Firm: **PLAYBOY ENTERPRISES INTERNATIONAL, INC. — CHICAGO, IL**
Creative Team: **JORDIN ISIP, TOM STAEBLER**
Client: **PLAYBOY MAGAZINE**

Creative Firm: **CHALMERS STUDIO — TRUMANSBURG, NY**
Creative Team: **CHERYL CHALMERS**
Client: **CHERYL CHALMERS**

Creative Firm: **PLAYBOY ENTERPRISES INTERNATIONAL, INC. — CHICAGO, IL**
Creative Team: **KENT WILLIAMS, TOM STAEBLER**
Client: **PLAYBOY MAGAZINE**

Creative Firm: **WALT DENSON — SAUSALITO, CA**
Creative Team: **WALT DENSON, STEVE PETERS**
Client: **WALT DENSON**

Creative Firm: **MANHATTAN GROUP LLC — NEW YORK, NY**
Creative Team: **RICK BARD**
Client: **MANHATTAN BRIDE**

Creative Firm: **DREW GARDNER PHOTOGRAPHY — NAPERVILLE, IL**
Creative Team: **DREW GARDNER**
Client: **DREW GARDNER**

Creative Firm: **STUDIO JMV LLC — MIAMI, FL**
Creative Team: **JOSE VIDAURRE, JASON VENTURA**

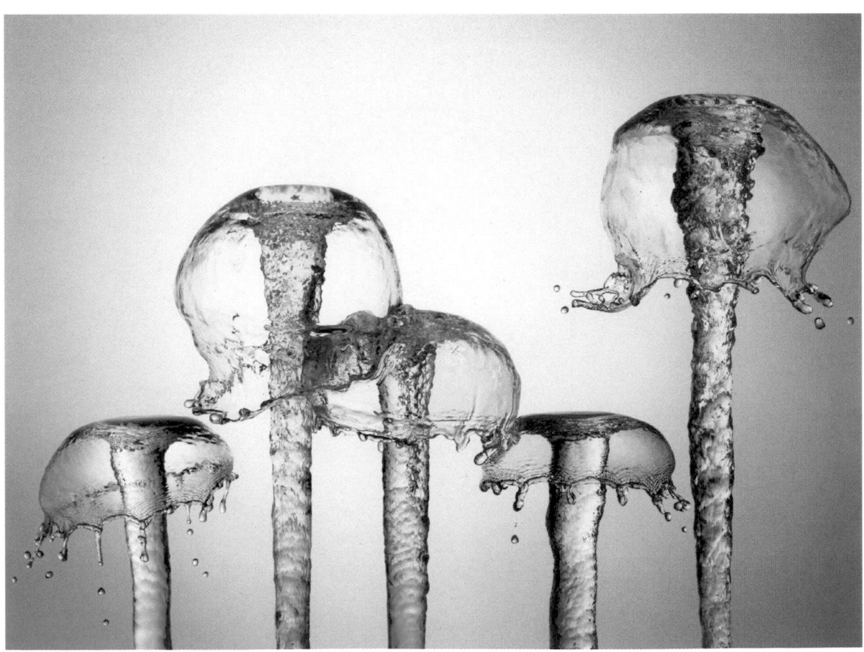

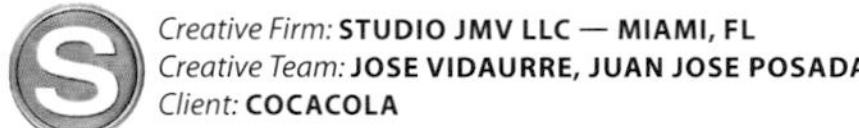

Creative Firm: **STUDIO JMV LLC — MIAMI, FL**
Creative Team: **JOSE VIDAURRE, JUAN JOSE POSADA**
Client: **COCACOLA**

Creative Firm: **EMERSON, WAJDOWICZ STUDIOS — NEW YORK, NY**
Creative Team: **JUREK WAJDOWICZ, LISA LAROCHELLE, YOKO YOSHIDA, MANNY MENDEZ, 17 MAGNUM PHOTOGRAPHERS**
Client: **MAGNUM PHOTOS AND SMART PAPERS**

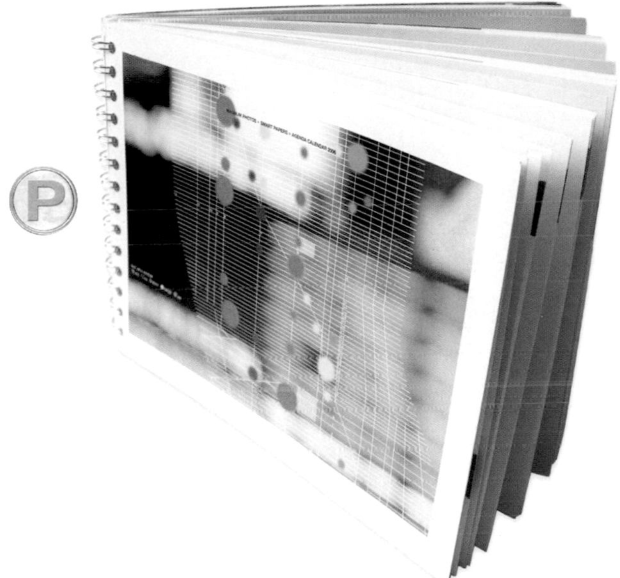

Creative Firm: **MANHATTAN GROUP LLC — NEW YORK, NY**
Creative Team: **RICK BARD**
Client: **MANHATTAN BRIDE**

Creative Firm: **MELAMED RILEY — NAPERVILLE, IL**
Creative Team: **DANA MOSES, STEVE PETERS**
Client: **SYNGENTA/MELAMED RILEY**

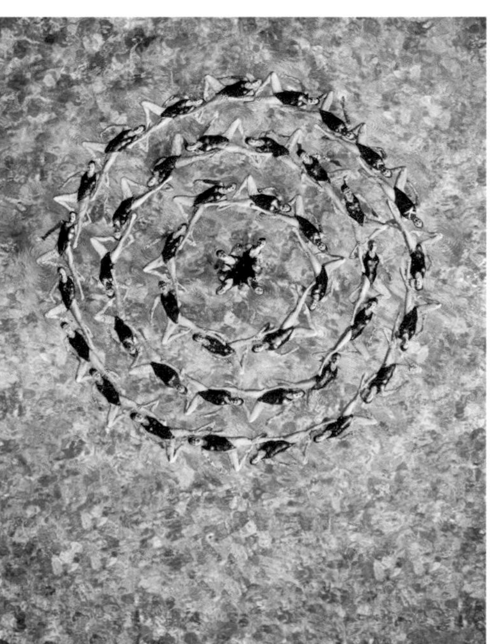

Creative Firm: **MANHATTAN GROUP LLC — NEW YORK, NY**
Creative Team: **RICK BARD**
Client: **MANHATTAN BRIDE**

Creative Firm: **WALT DENSON — SAUSALITO, CA**
Creative Team: **WALT DENSON**
Client: **WALT DENSON**

Creative Firm: **MANHATTAN GROUP LLC — NEW YORK, NY**
Creative Team: **RICK BARD**
Client: **MANHATTAN BRIDE**

Creative Firm: **DAVID J. BOOKBINDER — GLOUCESTER, MA**
Creative Team: **DAVID J. BOOKBINDER**
Client: **CRESCENT HILL BOOKS**

Creative Firm: **MANHATTAN GROUP LLC — NEW YORK, NY**
Creative Team: **RICK BARD**
Client: **MANHATTAN BRIDE**

Creative Firm: **RANDI WOLF DESIGN — GLASSBORO, NJ**
Creative Team: **RANDI WOLF**
Client: **MAIN STREET GLASSBORO**

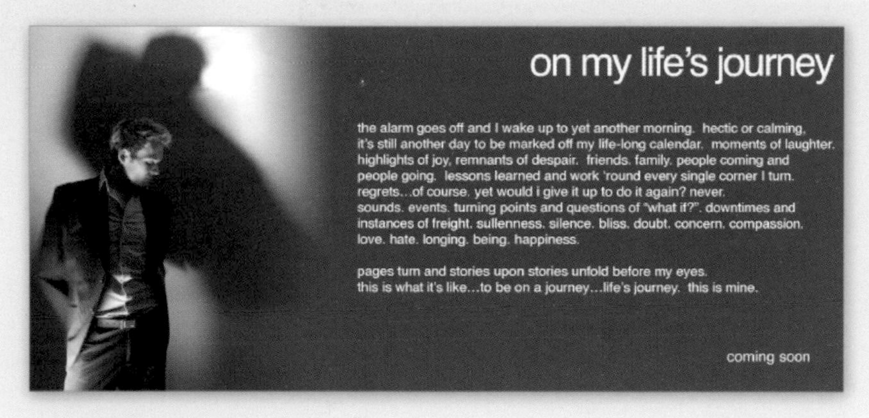

Creative Firm: **KELLY CARROLL — LOUISVILLE, KY**
Creative Team: **KELLY CARROLL, JOSHUA LAKES**
Client: **JOSHUA LAKES**

Creative Firm: **FAINE-OLLER PRODUCTIONS — SEATTLE, WA**
Creative Team: **CATHERINE OLLER, CHRISTOPHER CONRAD**
Client: **COLESON FOODS, INC.**

Creative Firm: **TV LAND — NEW YORK, NY**
Creative Team: **KIM ROSENBLUM, DOMINIQUE VITALI, KEVIN HARTMAN, CHELSEA MOST, TONY D'ORIO**
Client: **TV LAND**

Creative Firm: **EMERSON, WAJDOWICZ STUDIOS — NEW YORK, NY**
Creative Team: **JUREK WAJDOWICZ, LISA LAROCHELLE, MANNY MENDEZ, STEVEN MANNING, PETER BIRO, SCOTT ANGER AND OTHERS**
Client: **INTERNATIONAL RESCUE COMMITTEE**

Creative Firm: **AMERICAN RED CROSS BLOOD SERVICES, WEST DIVISION — POMONA, CA**
Creative Team: **SAUNDRA KEENAN DAVISON**

Creative Firm: **DEVON ENERGY - IN HOUSE — OKLAHOMA CITY, OK**
Creative Team: **SCOTT RAFFE, TIM LANGENBERG**
Client: **DEVON ENERGY CORPORATION**

Creative Firm: **MTV OFF AIR CREATIVE — NEW YORK, NY**
Creative Team: **JEFFREY KEYTON, JIM DEBARROS, CHRISTOPHER TRUCH, KAREN WEISS, NICK SONDERUP, MATHIAS CLAMER**
Client: **MTV NETWORKS**

Creative Firm: **MANHATTAN GROUP LLC — NEW YORK, NY**
Creative Team: **RICK BARD**
Client: **MANHATTAN BRIDE**

Creative Firm: **MANHATTAN GROUP LLC — NEW YORK, NY**
Creative Team: **RICK BARD**
Client: **MANHATTAN BRIDE**

Creative Firm: **MANHATTAN GROUP LLC — NEW YORK, NY**
Creative Team: **RICK BARD**
Client: **MANHATTAN BRIDE**

Creative Firm: **PETTINATO PHOTOGRAPHY — NAPERVILLE, IL**
Creative Team: **TONY PETTINATO**
Client: **TONY PETTINATO**

Creative Firm: **STUDIO JMV LLC — MIAMI, FL**
Creative Team: **JOSE VIDAURRE, JUAN JOSE POSADA**
Client: **DASANI/COCACOLA**

Creative Firm: **EMERSON, WAJDOWICZ STUDIOS — NEW YORK, NY**
Creative Team: **JUREK WAJDOWICZ, LISA LAROCHELLE, MANNY MENDEZ, JONAS BENDIKSEN**
Client: **THE ROCKEFELLER FOUNDATION**

Creative Firm: **EMERSON, WAJDOWICZ STUDIOS — NEW YORK, NY**
Creative Team: **L. LAROCHELLE, J. WAJDOWICZ, Y. YOSHIDA, M. MENDEZ, P. PETTERSSON, R. HAVIV, B. STEVENS, P. BONET, S. BOELSCH AND OTHERS**
Client: **MÉDECINS SANS FRONTIÈRES / DOCTORS WITHOUT BORDERS**

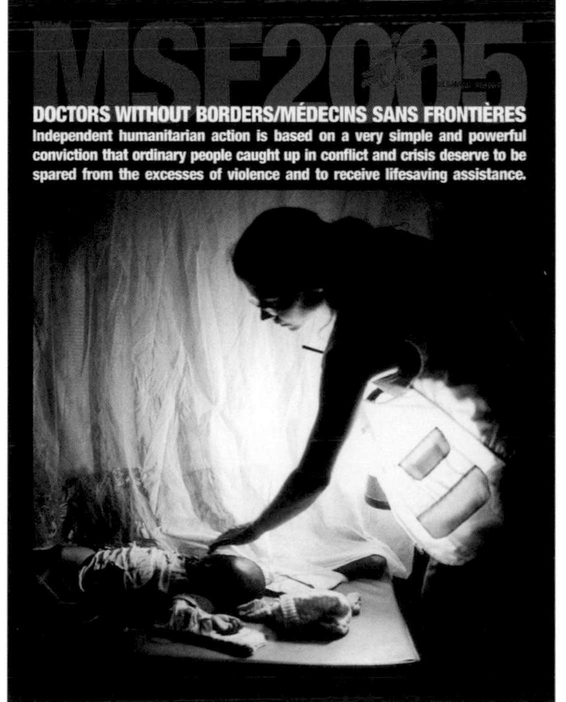

Creative Firm: **MANHATTAN GROUP LLC — NEW YORK, NY**
Creative Team: **RICK BARD**
Client: **MANHATTAN BRIDE**

Creative Firm: **PETERSON MILLA HOOKS — MINNEAPOLIS, MN**
Creative Team: **DAVE PETERSON, GAYLE MALCOLM, LISA MITCHELL**
Client: **TARGET**

Creative Firm: **MCCANN ERICKSON, NEW YORK — NEW YORK, NY**
Creative Team: **STEVE OHLER, GEORGE DEWEY, CHRIS QUILLEN, DAN DONOVAN, JOYCE KING THOMAS, BARBARA RESUA**
Client: **VERIZON WIRELESS**

Creative Firm: **DIESTE HARMEL & PARTNERS — DALLAS, TX**
Creative Team: **ALDO QUEVEDO, JESSE DIAZ, GABRIEL GUTIERREZ, ROSE GOMEZ, BORIS NURKO**
Client: **ED BOSQUES CLINIC**

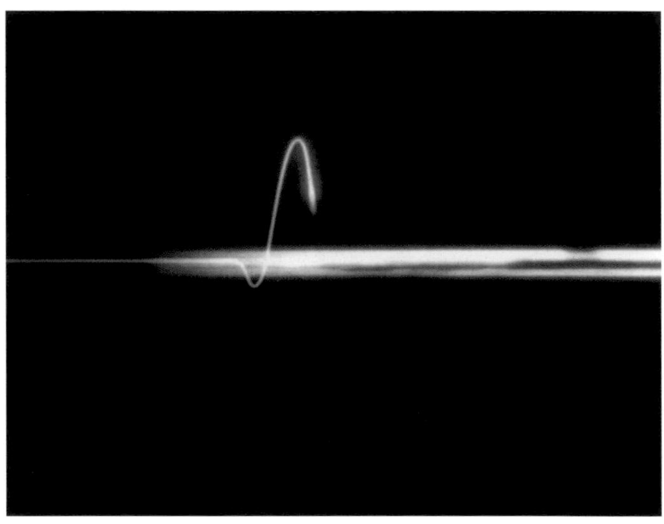

Creative Firm: **KELLER CRESCENT — EVANSVILLE, IN**
Creative Team: **RANDALL ROHN, LEE BRYANT, RANDY ROHN, JOHN CHADDOCK**
Client: **RIVERVIEW HOSPITAL**

Creative Firm: **BONNEVILLE COMMUNICATIONS — SALT LAKE CITY, UT**
Creative Team: **ERIC MORGAN**
Client: **DESERET FIRST CREDIT UNION**

Creative Firm: **HELFGOTT PRODUCTIONS — LOS ANGELES, CA**
Creative Team: **MATTHEW HELFGOTT, COLIN GLAUM, JESSE EISENHARDT, JORDAN MARKS, HOLLY LEIGH**
Client: **POKER.NET**

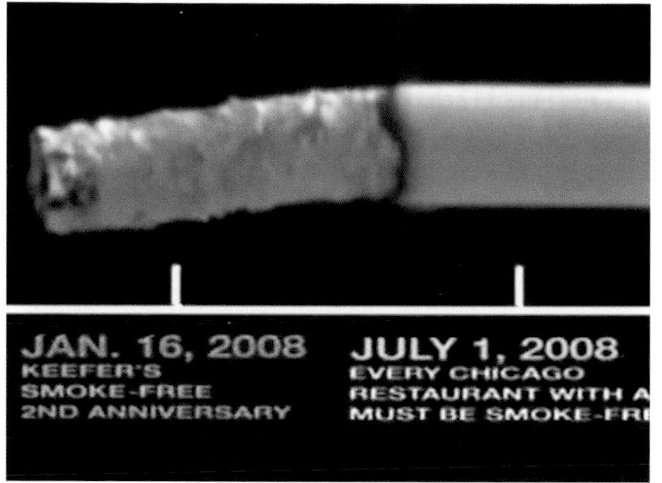

Creative Firm: **THE UNGAR GROUP — CHICAGO, IL**
Creative Team: **TOM UNGAR, ALLA DONINA, ASHLEY NATH, JONATHAN UNGAR, DAVE O'DONNELL**
Client: **KEEFER'S STEAK AND SEAFOOD**

Creative Firm: **BRUKETA&ZINIC — ZAGREB, CROATIA (HRVATSKA)**
Creative Team: **MOE MINKARA, TONKA LUJANAC, MIRAN TOMICIC, KOMAKINO, HOBO**
Client: **DUGRAF**

Creative Firm: **HITCHCOCK FLEMING & ASSOCIATES INC. — AKRON, OH**
Creative Team: **NICK BETRO, SCOTT KRISTOFF, GREG PFIFFNER, MARK COLLINS**
Client: **GEAUGA LAKE**

Creative Firm: **JWT DÜSSELDORF — DUESSELDORF, NRW, GERMANY**
Creative Team: **EDDY GREENWOOD, JOHN ABEL, MICHAEL FUETER, ELKE BOLL, CONSTANTINE WRAGE**
Client: **MAZDA MOTOR EUROPE**

Creative Firm: **MCCANN ERICKSON KOREA — SEOUL, KOREA (SOUTH)**
Creative Team: **JH CHO, SANGJIN KIM, MOONSUN CHOI, MINJUNG SONG, SANG YOUN KIM**
Client: **COCA-COLA KOREA**

Creative Firm: **MCCANN ERICKSON, NEW YORK — NEW YORK, NY**
Creative Team: **ERIC GOLDSTEIN, CHRIS CEREDA, JOYCE KING THOMAS, JULIE ANDARIESE, FRANK TODARO, ADAM BECKMAN**
Client: **MASTERCARD**

Creative Firm: **HITCHCOCK FLEMING & ASSOCIATES INC. — AKRON, OH**
Creative Team: **NICK BETRO, MAGGIE HARRIS, TODD MOSER**
Client: **GOODYEAR TIRE & RUBBER COMPANY**

Creative Firm: **NICKELODEON — NEW YORK, NY**
Creative Team: **FRANK CZUCHAN, HELENE MILLER- ALENSTEIN, KATIE FITZPARTICK, ANNA YOON**
Client: **NICK CREATIVE RESOURCES**

Creative Firm: **NICK AT NITE — NEW YORK, NY**
Creative Team: **KENNA KAY, PALOMA RAMIREZ, KURT HARTMAN, GEORGE BATES, LAURA BELGRAY, PENNY MAILANDER**
Client: **NICK AT NITE**

Creative Firm: **MCCANN ERICKSON, NEW YORK — NEW YORK, NY**
Creative Team: **GAIL BARLOW, SASHA SHOR, BILL OBERLANDER, JOYCE KING THOMAS, BONNIE BEDEL, JIM JENKINS**
Client: **AD COUNCIL**

Creative Firm: **NBC UNIVERSAL GLOBAL NETWORKS ITALIA — ROME, ITALY**
Client: **STUDIO UNIVERSAL**

Creative Firm: **PHP COMMUNICATIONS — BIRMINGHAM, AL**
Creative Team: **BRYAN CHACE, JASON RUHA, RUTH GREER**
Client: **BRADFORD HEALTH SERVICES**

Creative Firm: **DIESTE HARMEL & PARTNERS — DALLAS, TX**
Creative Team: **ALDO QUEVEDO, JAIME ANDRADE, GABRIEL PUERTO, ALEX TOEDTLI, JOSE SUASTE, JOHN COSTELLO**
Client: **BUDWEISER**

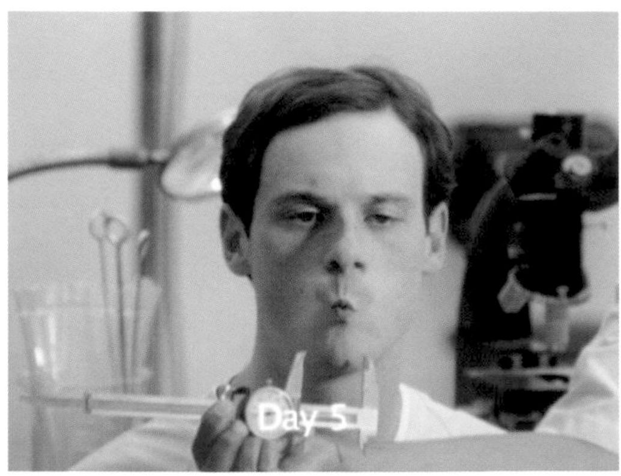

Creative Firm: **MCCANN ERICKSON, NEW YORK — NEW YORK, NY**
Creative Team: **JOYCE KING THOMAS, BILL OBERLANDER, JEFF TAYLOR, DAVID LEVY, TONI LIPARI, RICK LEMOINE**
Client: **SHARPIE MINI**

Creative Firm: **MCCANN ERICKSON KOREA — SEOUL, KOREA (SOUTH)**
Creative Team: **JH CHO, SANGJIN KIM, MOONSUN CHOI, MINJUNG SONG, SANG YOUN KIM**
Client: **COCA-COLA KOREA**

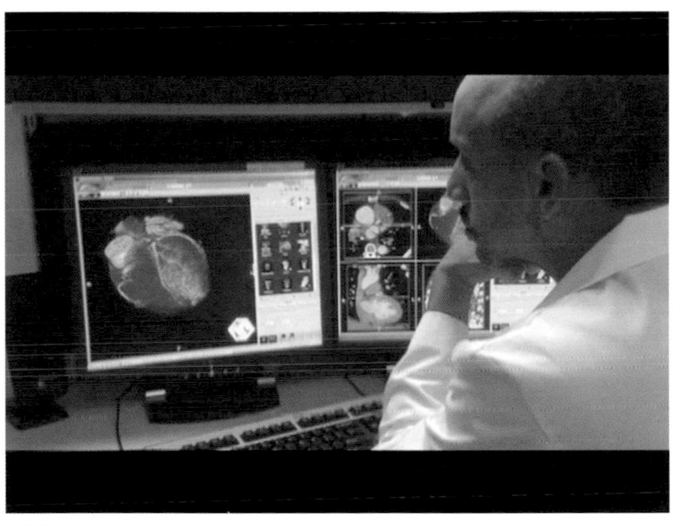

Creative Firm: **PENNY/OHLMANN/NEIMAN — DAYTON, OH**
Creative Team: **PAUL LINDAMOOD**
Client: **KETTERING MEDICAL CENTER**

Creative Firm: **DIESTE HARMEL & PARTNERS — DALLAS, TX**
Creative Team: **ALDO QUEVEDO, CARLOS TOURNE, PATRICIA MARTINEZ, RAYMUNDO VALDEZ, DIEGO DUPRAT**
Client: **CLOROX, PINESOL**

Creative Firm: **PETERSON MILLA HOOKS — MINNEAPOLIS, MN**
Creative Team: **DAVE PETERSON, JENNY SHEARS, GAYLE MALCOLM, ALDO HERTZ**
Client: **TARGET**

Creative Firm: **KELLER CRESCENT — EVANSVILLE, IN**
Creative Team: **RANDALL ROHN, NANCY KIRKPATRICK, NAIYANA HARDY, CARSON CATLIN, JOHN MENELLA**
Client: **MORGAN HOSPITAL**

Creative Firm: **MCCANN ERICKSON, NEW YORK — NEW YORK, NY**
Creative Team: **JOYCE KING THOMAS, PETER JONES, CHRIS CEREDA, GREG LOTUS, CHRISTIAN BERGER, ADAM PETOFSKY**
Client: **MASTERCARD**

Creative Firm: **DIESTE HARMEL & PARTNERS — DALLAS, TX**
Creative Team: **ALDO QUEVEDO, MACK SIMPSON, ROBERTO SAUCEDO, JUAN DANIEL NAVAS, IGNACIO ROMERO, JASSON TISSER, JOHN COSTELLO**
Client: **GATORADE**

Creative Firm: **BONNEVILLE COMMUNICATIONS — SALT LAKE CITY , UT**
Creative Team: **ERIC MORGAN**
Client: **DESERET FIRST CREDIT UNION**

Creative Firm: **SPIKE TV — NEW YORK, NY**
Creative Team: **SUE KIM, TERRY MINOGUE, CLIFF SCHWARTZ, JUSTIN GALLAHER, ALAN ROLL, NEILS SCHUURMANS**
Client: **SPIKE**

Creative Firm: **PETERSON MILLA HOOKS — MINNEAPOLIS, MN**

Creative Team: **DAVE PETERSON , DANIEL CHU, GAYLE MALCOLM, ALDO HERTZ**
Client: **TARGET**

Creative Firm: **MCCANN ERICKSON, NEW YORK — NEW YORK, NY**
Creative Team: **JOYCE KING THOMAS, BILL OBERLANDER, JEFF TAYLOR, DAVID LEVY, TONI LIPARI, RICK LEMOINE**
Client: **SHARPIE MINI**

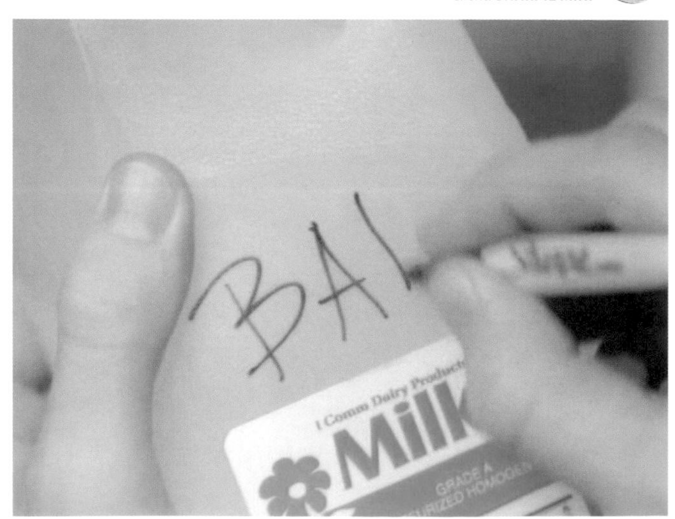

Creative Firm: **BONNEVILLE COMMUNICATIONS — SALT LAKE CITY , UT**
Creative Team: **ERIC MORGAN**
Client: **DESERET FIRST CREDIT UNION**

Creative Firm: **JWT DUESSELDORF — DUESSELDORF, NRW, GERMANY**
Creative Team: **EDDY GREENWOOD, JOHN ABEL, CHRISTIAN LYNGBYE, IGOR KARPALOV, ELKE BOLL, CONSTANTINE WRAGE**
Client: **MAZDA MOTOR EUROPE**

Creative Firm: **DIESTE HARMEL & PARTNERS — DALLAS, TX**
Creative Team: **ALDO QUEVEDO, JAIME ANDRADE, GABRIEL PUERTO, ALEX TOEDTLI, JOSE SUASTE, JOHN COSTELLO**
Client: **BUDWEISER**

Creative Firm: **MCCANN ERICKSON, NEW YORK — NEW YORK, NY**
Creative Team: **CINDY CASARES, KRISTAL KINDER, JOYCE KING THOMAS, JIM MCKENNAN, KATHY LOVE, MIKE BORIS**
Client: **WENDY'S**

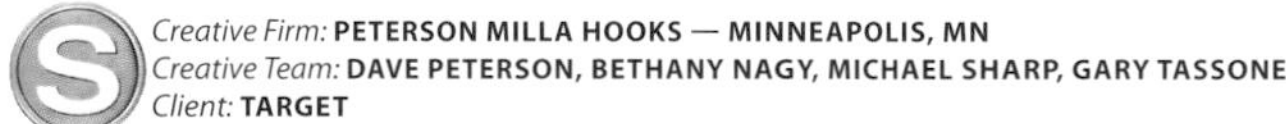

Creative Firm: **PETERSON MILLA HOOKS — MINNEAPOLIS, MN**
Creative Team: **DAVE PETERSON, BETHANY NAGY, MICHAEL SHARP, GARY TASSONE**
Client: **TARGET**

Creative Firm: **MCCANN ERICKSON, NEW YORK — NEW YORK, NY**
Creative Team: **JOYCE KING THOMAS, BILL OBERLANDER, LARRY PLATT, TOM SULLIVAN, JUDI NIERMAN, MARK ROMANEK**
Client: **NIKON**

Creative Firm: **FRY HAMMOND BARR — ORLANDO, FL**
Creative Team: **TIM FISHER, SEAN BRUNSON, SANDRA LAWTON, SHANNON HALLARE, NTH DEGREE**
Client: **ORLANDO SCIENCE CENTER**

Creative Firm: **MCCANN ERICKSON, NEW YORK/JOYCE KING THOMAS ECD/CCO — NEW YORK, NY**
Creative Team: **AUDREY HUFFENREUTER, LESLIE SIMS, PETER JONES, TIM DILLINGHAM, LISA BRANDRIFF, KATHY KUHN**
Client: **MASTERCARD**

Creative Firm: **TV LAND — NEW YORK, NY**
Creative Team: **KIM ROSENBLUM, DOMINIQUE VITALI, KEVIN HARTMAN, CHELSEA MOST**
Client: **TV LAND**

Creative Firm: **CMT — NEW YORK, NY**
Creative Team: **JAMES HITCHCOCK, MICHAEL ENGLEMAN, JEFF NICHOLS, AMIE NGUYEN, SCOTT MCDONALD, SCOTT GERLOCK**
Client: **CMT**

Creative Firm: **FRY HAMMOND BARR — ORLANDO, FL**
Creative Team: **TIM FISHER, TOM KANE, JOHN LOGAN, SEAN BRUNSON, MELISSA COONEY, RADIUM**
Client: **BRIGHT HOUSE NETWORKS**

Creative Firm: **MCCANN ERICKSON KOREA — SEOUL, KOREA (SOUTH)**
Creative Team: **JUNG-HYUN SHON, BH AHN, CU KIM, NAM-GIL KIM**
Client: **DAEDONG CONSTRUCTION**

Creative Firm: **CMT — NEW YORK, NY**
Creative Team: **JAMES HITCHCOCK, MICHAEL ENGLEMAN, JEFF NICHOLS, VALERIE CARRILLO, BRAND NEW SCHOOL (NY)**
Client: **CMT**

Creative Firm: **2 TICKS & THE DOG PRODUCTIONS, INC. — WARREN, OH**
Creative Team: **JIM FOGARTY, MATT SMITH**
Client: **BOB HAGAN**

Creative Firm: **BONNEVILLE COMMUNICATIONS — SALT LAKE CITY, UT**
Creative Team: **ERIC MORGAN**
Client: **DESERET FIRST CREDIT UNION**

Creative Firm: **MCCANN ERICKSON, NEW YORK / JOYCE KING THOMAS CCO — NEW YORK, NY**
Creative Team: **MARCO CIGNINI, JESSE POTACK, STEVE OHLER, SAM CERNICHIARI, PEIRRE LIPTON, TRAVIS BRITTON**
Client: **STAPLES**

Creative Firm: **CMT — NEW YORK, NY**
Creative Team: **JAMES HITCHCOCK, MICHAEL ENGLEMAN, JEFF NICHOLS, VALERIE CARRILLO**
Client: **CMT**

Creative Firm: **ACART COMMUNICATIONS — OTTAWA, ON, CANADA**
Creative Team: **TOM MEGGINSON, VERNON LAI, CRAIG CEBRYK, KELLY MACNAULL, CHANTAL VALLERAND**
Client: **OTTAWA SENATORS HOCKEY CLUB**

Creative Firm: **MTV ON AIR PROMOS — NEW YORK, NY**
Creative Team: **MATT JABLIN, JOE STEVENS, SHEREE SHU, PAT DONNELLY, REGINA CROWLEY, CRANDALL MILLER**
Client: **MTV**

Creative Firm: **BONNEVILLE COMMUNICATIONS — SALT LAKE CITY , UT**
Creative Team: **ERIC MORGAN**
Client: **HUNTSMAN CANCER INSTITUTE**

Creative Firm: **IM-AJ COMMUNICATIONS & DESIGN, INC. — WEST KINGSTON, RI**
Creative Team: **JAMI OUELLETTE, KRIS ALLARD**
Client: **CROSSROADS RHODE ISLAND**

Creative Firm: **IM-AJ COMMUNICATIONS & DESIGN, INC. — WEST KINGSTON, RI**
Creative Team: **JAMI OUELLETTE, KRIS ALLARD**
Client: **RHODE ISLAND HOUSING**

Creative Firm: **KELLER CRESCENT — EVANSVILLE, IN**
Creative Team: **RANDALL ROHN, LEE BRYANT, RANDY ROHN, JOHN CHADDOCK, CARSON CATLIN**
Client: **RIVERVIEW HOSPITAL**

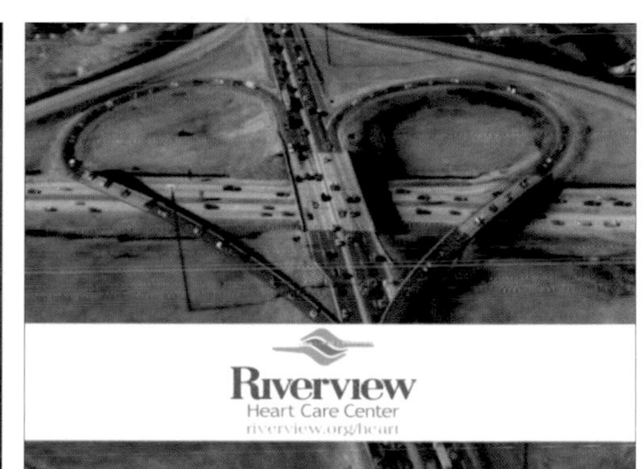

Creative Firm: **A3 DESIGN — CHARLOTTE, NC**
Creative Team: **ALAN ALTMAN, AMANDA ALTMAN**
Client: **MATTAMY HOMES**

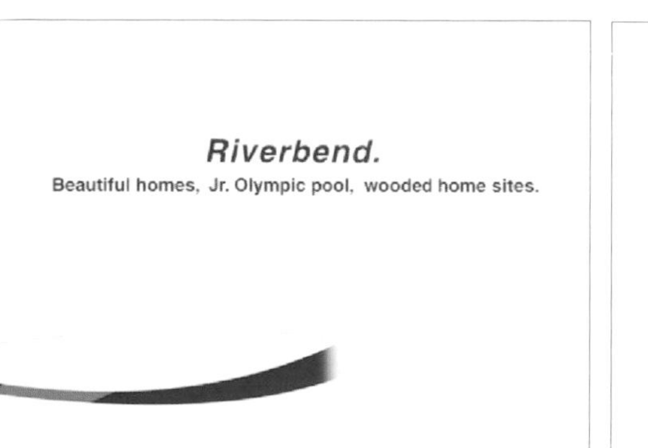

Creative Firm: **PHP COMMUNICATIONS — BIRMINGHAM, AL**
Creative Team: **BRYAN CHACE, JASON RUHA, RUTH GREER**
Client: **BRADFORD HEALTH SERVICES**

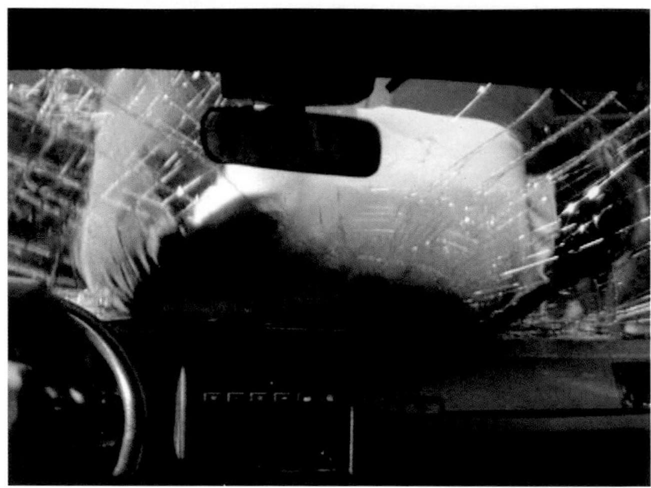

Creative Firm: **NBC UNIVERSAL GLOBAL NETWORKS ITALIA — ROME, ITALY**
Client: **STUDIO UNIVERSAL**

Creative Firm: **NICKELODEON — NEW YORK, NY**
Creative Team: **FRANK CZUCHAN, MARIANNE VOLCHEK, SAMANTHA BERGER, AARON MCDANNELL**

Creative Firm: **NICKTOONS — NEW YORK, NY**
Creative Team: **TERRY MCCORMICK, SUE KIM, YORK CAPISTRANO**
Client: **NICKTOONS NETWORK**

Creative Firm: **NBC UNIVERSAL GLOBAL NETWORKS ITALIA — ROME, ITALY**
Client: **STUDIO UNIVERSAL**

Creative Firm: **NICKELODEON — NEW YORK, NY**
Creative Team: **FRANK CZUCHAN, STACY KAPNER, AARON MCDANNELL, SAMANTHA BERGER, JASON ZEMLICKA**
Client: **NICK CREATIVE RESOURCES**

P

Creative Firm: **MTV ON AIR PROMOS — NEW YORK, NY**
Creative Team: **AARON STOLLER, MATTHEW GIULVEZAN, BART SMITH, BRYAN NEWMAN, CRANDALL MILLER, PAUL GOLDMAN**
Client: **MTV**

G

Creative Firm: **MTV ON AIR PROMOS — NEW YORK, NY**
Creative Team: **ANTONIO MCDONALD, KADINE ANCKLE, GRAYSON ROSS, DAVID FERRARA, ANDREA PURCIGLIOTTI, LUKE CHOI**
Client: **MTV2**

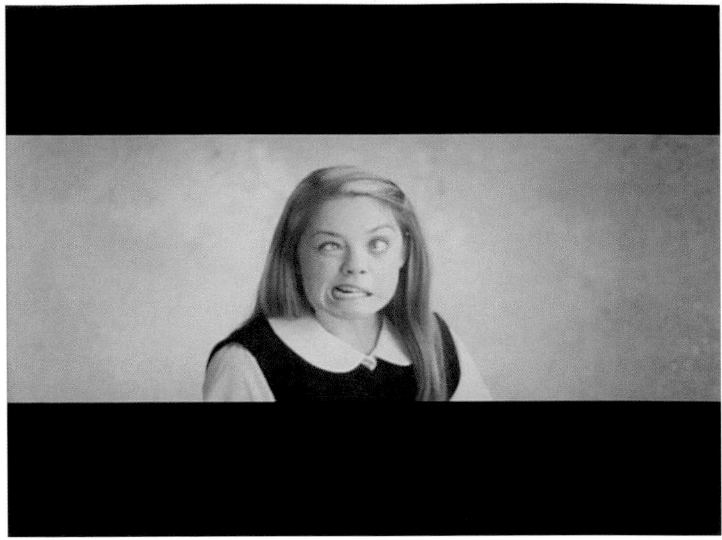

Creative Firm: **MTV ON AIR PROMOS — NEW YORK, NY**
Creative Team: **DAVID HOROWITZ, BETSY BLAKEMORE, MARTIN AHLGREN, NATHAN BYRNE, PAUL GOLDMAN**
Client: **MTV**

Creative Firm: **MTV ON AIR PROMOS — NEW YORK, NY**
Creative Team: **MATT JABLIN, SEYI PETER-THOMAS, SHEREE SHU, PAT DONNELLY, MARK SNELGROVE, REBECCA GWYNNE**
Client: **MTVU**

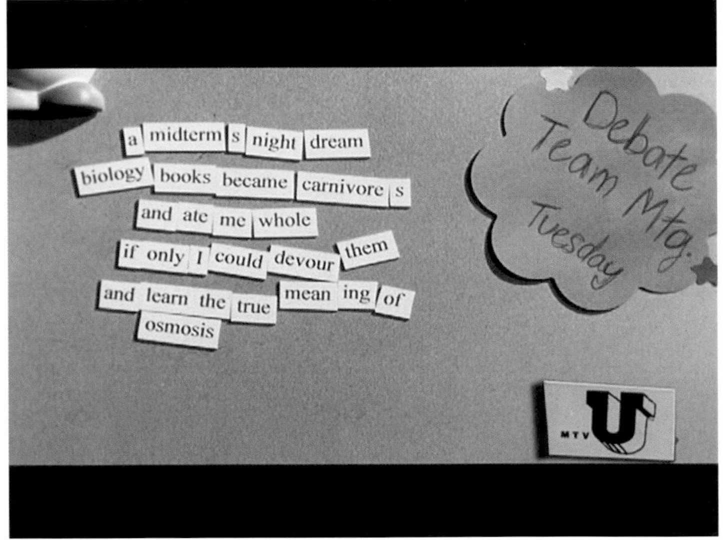

Creative Firm: **NICKTOONS — NEW YORK, NY**
Creative Team: **TERRY MCCORMICK, SUE KIM, KEN WEBB**
Client: **NICKTOONS NETWORK**

Creative Firm: **PENNY/OHLMANN/NEIMAN — DAYTON, OH**
Creative Team: **PAUL LINDAMOOD**
Client: **KETTERING MEDICAL CENTER**

Creative Firm: **RODGERS TOWNSEND — ST. LOUIS, MO**
Creative Team: **TOM HUDDER, MIKE DILLON, BOB WENDT, STEFAN WUERNITZER, DIGITAL KITCHEN**
Client: **AT&T**

Creative Firm: **RODGERS TOWNSEND — ST. LOUIS, MO**
Creative Team: **TOM HUDDER, MIKE DILLON, BOB WENDT, DIGITAL KITCHEN**
Client: **AT&T**

Creative Firm: **HERE! NETWORKS — NEW YORK, NY**
Creative Team: **ERIC FELDMAN**

Creative Firm: **TAXI CANADA INC. — TORONTO, ON, CANADA**
Creative Team: **ZAK MROUEH, ANNE MARIE MARTIGNAGO, REGINALD PIKE , CHRISTINA HUMPHRIES, TERRY TOMPKINS, RENEE MACCARTHY**
Client: **COVENANT HOUSE**

Creative Firm: **& WOJDYLA ADVERTISING — CHICAGO, IL**
Creative Team: **DAVID WOJDYLA, DONNA MARIE ARTUSO, BARRY SEIDMAN**
Client: **FOUNDATION FOR BIOMEDICAL RESEARCH**

Creative Firm: **BONNEVILLE COMMUNICATIONS — SALT LAKE CITY , UT**
Creative Team: **STEPHEN WUNDERLI**
Client: **DESERET INDUSTRIES**

Creative Firm: **BONNEVILLE COMMUNICATIONS — SALT LAKE CITY , UT**
Creative Team: **STEPHEN WUNDERLI**
Client: **DESERET INDUSTRIES**

Creative Firm: **BONNEVILLE COMMUNICATIONS — SALT LAKE CITY , UT**
Creative Team: **STEPHEN WUNDERLI**
Client: **DESERET INDUSTRIES**

Creative Firm: **& WOJDYLA ADVERTISING — CHICAGO, IL**
Creative Team: **MICHAEL JOHN, FRANKIE TRULL, DAVID WOJDYLA, BAXTER BLACK**
Client: **FOUNDATION FOR BIOMEDICAL RESEARCH**

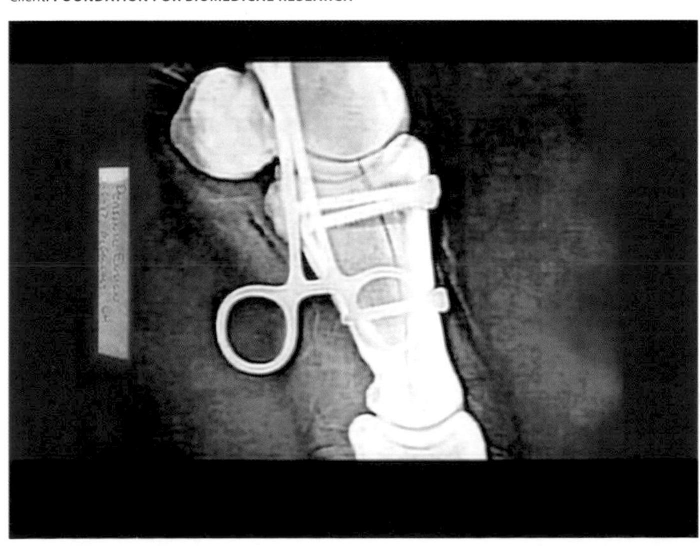

Creative Firm: **NICKELODEON — NEW YORK, NY**
Creative Team: **FRANK CZUCHAN, HOLLY GREGORY, SAMANTHA BERGER, ANNA YOON**
Client: **NICK CREATIVE RESOURCES**

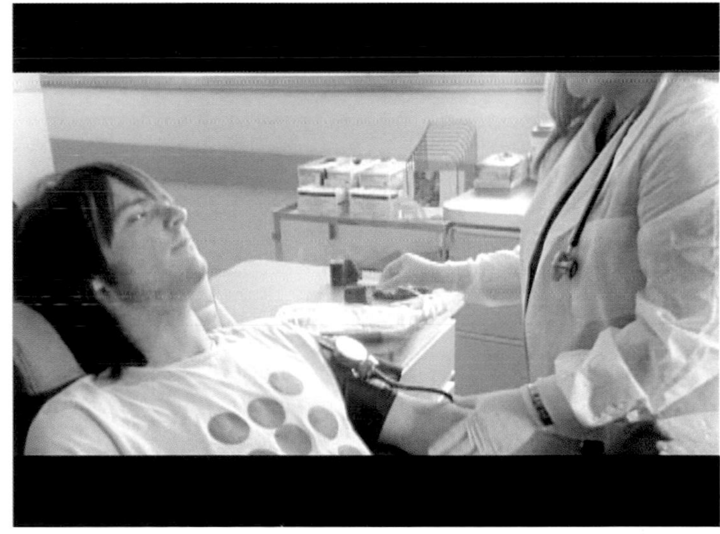

Creative Firm: **CAKE — POMONA, CA**
Creative Team: **KEVIN RAICH**
Client: **AMERICAN RED CROSS BLOOD SERVICES, WEST DIVISION**

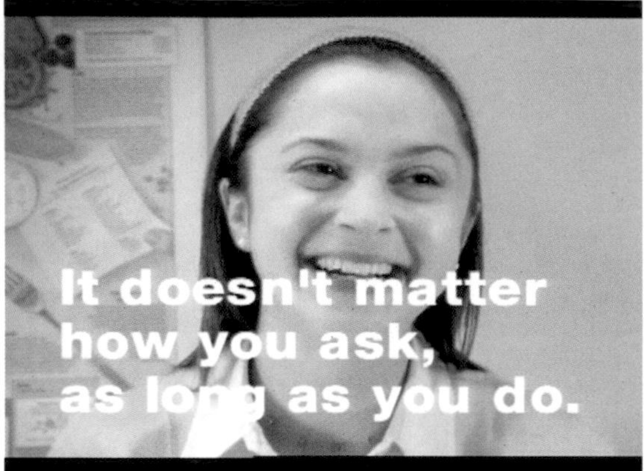

Creative Firm: **MTV ON AIR PROMOS — NEW YORK, NY**
Creative Team: **ALAN HARRIS, GINA HARRELL, MARYSE ALBERTI, RICHARD LASALLE, BRAD TURNER, DAN O'SULLIVAN**
Client: **MTV**

Creative Firm: **MCCANN ERICKSON, NEW YORK — NEW YORK, NY**
Creative Team: **STEVE OHLER, GEORGE DEWEY, REGAN WARNER, JOYCE KING THOMAS, DAVID SHANE, CORI H. RANZER**
Client: **UNITED NATIONS**

Creative Firm: **TV LAND — NEW YORK, NY**
Creative Team: **K. ROSENBLUM, D. NEWMAN, S. PETERSON, K. FIELDS, C. MOST, T. MONYEE, J. GOODE, B. SIA**
Client: **TV LAND**

Creative Firm: **SPIKE TV — NEW YORK, NY**
Creative Team: **LOEPOLTO GOUT, TERRY MINOGUE, OBI ONYEJEKWE, BOB SALAZAR, KEIF MATERA, NIELS SCHUURMANS**
Client: **SPIKE**

Creative Firm: **CMT — NEW YORK, NY**
Creative Team: **JAMES HITCHCOCK, MICHAEL ENGLEMAN, AMIE NGUYEN, ADOLESCENT**
Client: **CMT**

Creative Firm: **NBC UNIVERSAL GLOBAL NETWORKS ITALIA — ROME, ITALY**
Client: **STUDIO UNIVERSAL**

Creative Firm: **MTV ON AIR DESIGN — NEW YORK, NY**
Creative Team: **JEFFREY KEYTON, ROMY MANN, RODGER BELKNAP, RAFFAELA SACCONE, PSYOP**
Client: **MTV ON AIR DESIGN**

Creative Firm: **TV LAND — NEW YORK, NY**
Creative Team: **KIM ROSENBLUM, KENNA KAY, MARC NAHAS, MELISSA NEELEY, JOHN KARIAN, CATHERINE MULCAHY**
Client: **TV LAND**

Creative Firm: **KARACTERS DESIGN GROUP/DDB CANADA — VANCOUVER, BC, CANADA**
Creative Team: **MARIA KENNEDY, DANIEL JENETT, MONICA MARTINEZ, CATHARINE CHESTERMAN, CLINTON HUSSEY, HELEN WYNNE**
Client: **CANADIAN TOURISM COMMISSION**

Creative Firm: **SPIKE TV — NEW YORK, NY**
Creative Team: **BUCK , REG PUNLA, ALAN ROLL, JEN BROGLE, BOB SALAZAR**
Client: **SPIKE**

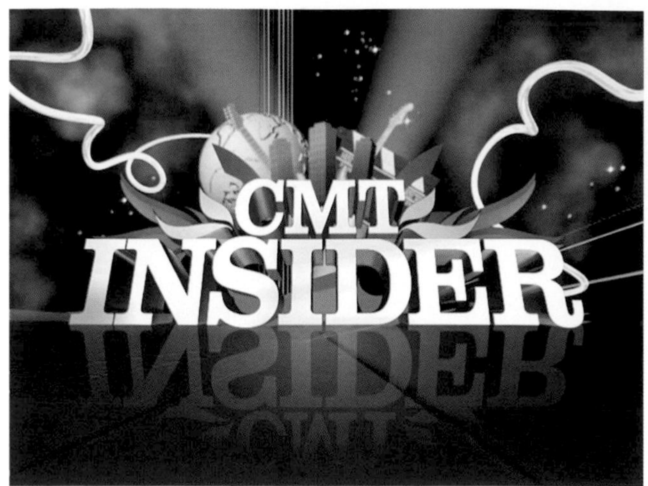

Creative Firm: **CMT — NEW YORK, NY**
Creative Team: **JAMES HITCHCOCK, MICHAEL ENGLEMAN, AMIE NGUYEN, DAVID BENNETT, FULLTANK**
Client: **CMT**

Creative Firm: **CMT — NEW YORK, NY**
Creative Team: **JAMES HITCHCOCK, MICHAEL ENGLEMAN, AMIE NGUYEN, DAVID WRIGHT, TRANSISTOR (LA) ,**
Client: **CMT**

Creative Firm: **NBC UNIVERSAL GLOBAL NETWORKS ITALIA — ROME, ITALY**
Client: **STUDIO UNIVERSAL**

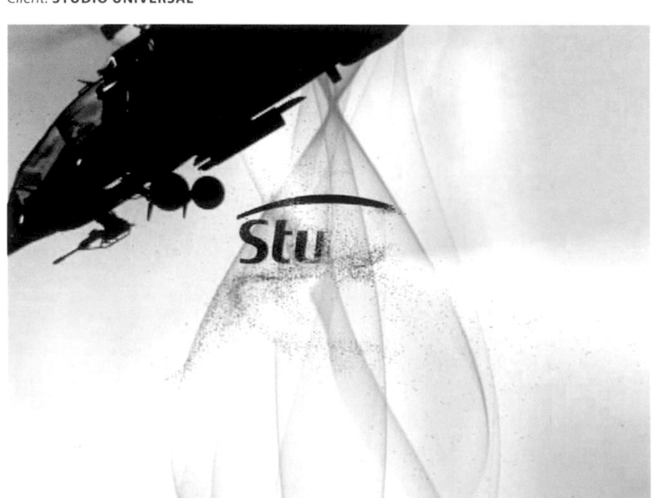

Creative Firm: **NICKELODEON — NEW YORK, NY**
Creative Team: **THERESA FITZGERALD, TAMAR SAMIR, ADOLESCENT, KATIE BRACK, MCPAUL SMITH, CHRISTINA AUGUSTINOS**
Client: **NICKELODEON ON-AIR**

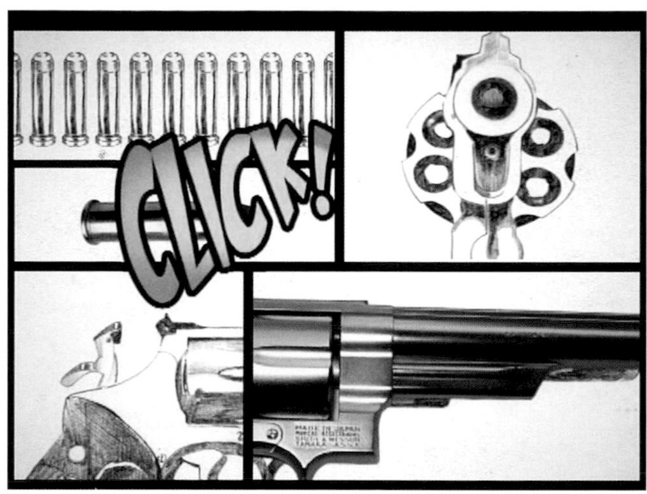

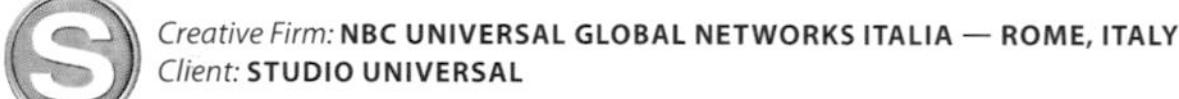
Creative Firm: **NBC UNIVERSAL GLOBAL NETWORKS ITALIA — ROME, ITALY**
Client: **STUDIO UNIVERSAL**

Creative Firm: **NBC UNIVERSAL GLOBAL NETWORKS ITALIA — ROME, ITALY**
Client: **STUDIO UNIVERSAL**

Creative Firm: **SPIKE TV — NEW YORK, NY**
Creative Team: **OBI ONYEJEKWE, TERRY MINOGUE, SCOTT FISHMAN, NIELS SCHUURMANS, JUSTIN GALLAHER, ALAN ROLL**
Client: **SPIKE**

Creative Firm: **NBC UNIVERSAL GLOBAL NETWORKS ITALIA — ROME, ITALY**
Client: **STUDIO UNIVERSAL**

Creative Firm: **NBC UNIVERSAL GLOBAL NETWORKS ITALIA — ROME, ITALY**
Client: **STUDIO UNIVERSAL**

Creative Firm: **CMT — NEW YORK, NY**
Creative Team: **JAMES HITCHCOCK, MICHAEL ENGLEMAN, AMIE NGUYEN, EYEBALL NYC**
Client: **CMT**

Creative Firm: **CMT — NEW YORK, NY**
Creative Team: **JAMES HITCHCOCK, MICHAEL ENGLEMAN, JEFF NICHOLS, EYEBALL NYC**
Client: **CMT**

Creative Firm: **NBC UNIVERSAL GLOBAL NETWORKS ITALIA — ROME, ITALY**
Client: **STUDIO UNIVERSAL**

Creative Firm: **NICKELODEON — NEW YORK, NY**
Creative Team: **THERESA FITZGERALD, TAMAR SAMIR, ADOLESCENT, RICH BARRY, MIKE SARNOSKI, VIRCILLO JOHN**
Client: **NICKELODEON ON-AIR**

Creative Firm: **CMT — NEW YORK, NY**
Creative Team: **JAMES HITCHCOCK, MICHAEL ENGLEMAN, CARLA DAENINCKX, BRAND NEW SCHOOL (NY)**
Client: **CMT**

Creative Firm: **NBC UNIVERSAL GLOBAL NETWORKS ITALIA — ROME, ITALY**
Client: **STUDIO UNIVERSAL**

Creative Firm: **NICKELODEON — NEW YORK, NY**
Creative Team: **THERESA FITZGERALD, TAMAR SAMIR, ANTHONY ZAZZI, TASO MASTORAKIS, JONATHAN JUDGE, ROSS ALVORD**
Client: **NICKELODEON ON-AIR**

Creative Firm: **MTV ON AIR DESIGN — NEW YORK, NY**
Creative Team: **JEFFREY KEYTON, ROMY MANN, RODGER BELKNAP, DAVID MCELWAINE, RAFFAELA SACCONE**
Client: **MTV ON AIR DESIGN**

Creative Firm: **LOGO — NEW YORK, NY**
Creative Team: **NANCY BENNETT, TOM BAYER, GARRETT WAGNER, GREG HAHN, DAVID BARRON**
Client: **LOGO PROGRAMMING**

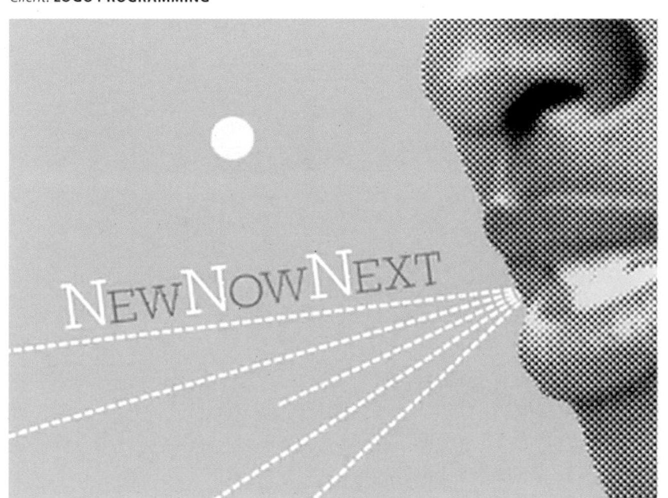

Creative Firm: **CMT — NEW YORK, NY**
Creative Team: **JAMES HITCHCOCK, MICHAEL ENGLEMAN, CARLA DAENINCKX, SCOTT GERLOCK, RYAN ROWLAND, FREESTYLE COLLECTIVE**
Client: **CMT**

Creative Firm: **TAXI CANADA INC. — TORONTO, ON, CANADA**
Creative Team: **ZAK MROUEH, DAVE DOUGLASS, PETE BRETON, JENNIFER METE, BRIAN LEE HUGHES, AARON DARK**
Client: **WORLD OF COMEDY**

CORPORATE FILM

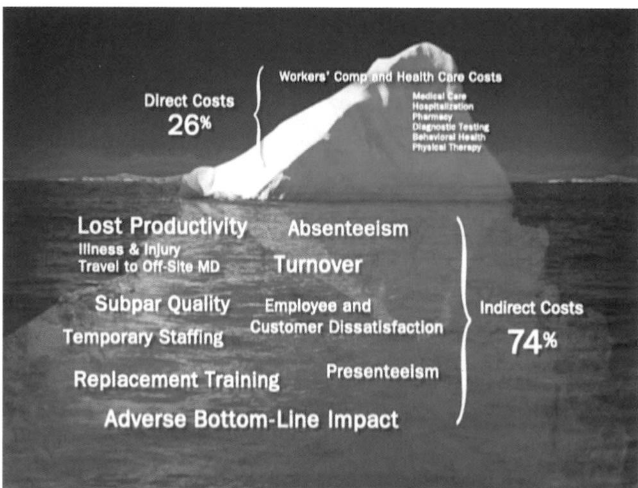

Creative Firm: **KAREN SKUNTA & COMPANY — CLEVELAND, OH**
Creative Team: **KAREN SKUNTA, RON GOLDFARB, JOHN LAGUARDIA, KEVIN PERLIC, JAMIE FINKELHOR, JENNIFER MAXWELL**
Client: **WHOLE HEALTH MANAGEMENT INC.**

PUBLIC SERVICE

Creative Firm: **EFFECTIVENESS THROUGH COMMUNICATION — EL CAJON, CA**
Creative Team: **ALLISON FIERLIT**
Client: **ELEMENTARY INSTITUTE OF SCIENCE**

Creative Firm: **NBC UNIVERSAL GLOBAL NETWORKS ITALIA — ROME, ITALY**
Client: **13TH FLOOR**

Creative Firm: **NBC UNIVERSAL GLOBAL NETWORKS ITALIA — ROME, ITALY**
Client: **SCI FI CHANNEL**

Creative Firm: **MTV NETWORKS CREATIVE SERVICES — NEW YORK, NY**

Creative Firm: **MTV NETWORKS CREATIVE SERVICES — NEW YORK, NY**

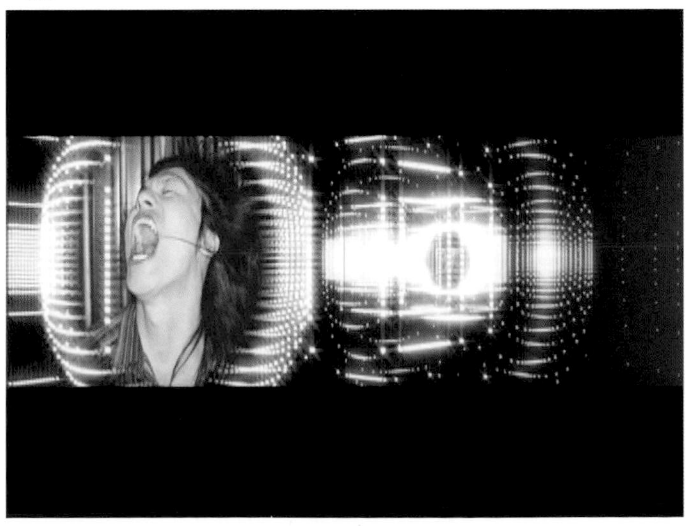

Creative Firm: **G2 — NEW YORK, NY**
Creative Team: **KC TAGLIANO**
Client: **G2**

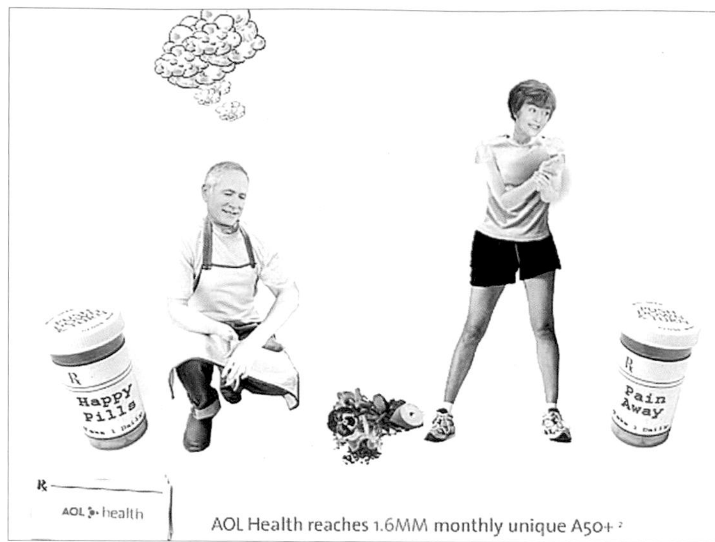

Creative Firm: **AOL | 360 CREATIVE — NEW YORK, NY**
Creative Team: **ANTHONY FARIA, RICHARD TAYLOR, ERIC LANE, HELEN LEE, ERIKA ALONSO**
Client: **AOL MEDIA NETWORKS**

Creative Firm: **AOL | 360 CREATIVE — NEW YORK, NY**
Creative Team: **DAVID DEBENEDETTO, MARIO ARIAS, JEFF BAYSON, ERIKA ALONSO**
Client: **AOL MEDIA NETWORKS**

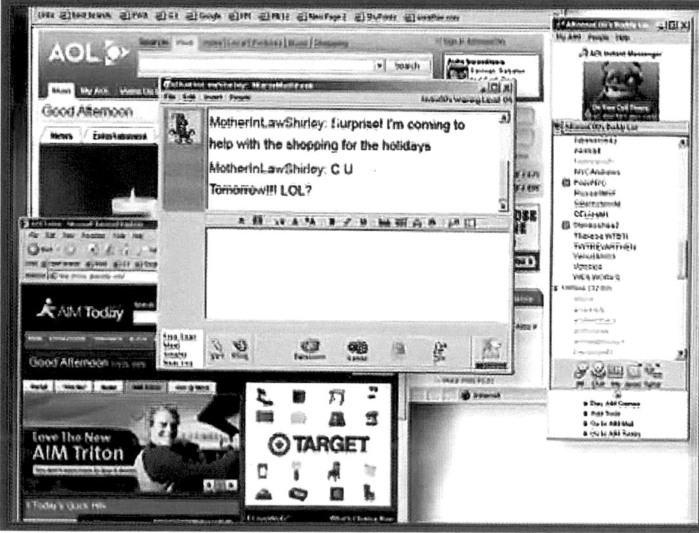

Creative Firm: **AOL | 360 CREATIVE — NEW YORK, NY**
Creative Team: **DAVID DEBENEDETTO, CHICO CONDE, JACK TIRANASAR, ERIC LANE, TOM POLLEY, ERIKA ALONSO**
Client: **AOL MEDIA NETWORKS**

Creative Firm: **AOL | 360 CREATIVE — NEW YORK, NY**
Creative Team: **DAVID DEBENEDETTO, ERIKA ALONSO**
Client: **AOL MEDIA NETWORKS**

Creative Firm: **AOL | 360 CREATIVE — NEW YORK, NY**
Creative Team: **ANTHONY FARIA, CHICO CONDE, CHANTAL BOTANA, ERIKA ALONSO**
Client: **AOL MEDIA NETWORKS**

Creative Firm: **EFFECTIVENESS THROUGH COMMUNICATION — EL CAJON, CA**
Creative Team: **ALLISON FIERLIT**
Client: **JACOBS CENTER FOR NEIGHBORHOOD INNOVATION**

Creative Firm: **AOL | 360 CREATIVE — NEW YORK, NY**
Creative Team: **DAVID DEBENEDETTO, CHICO CONDE, JACK TIRANASAR, ERIC LANE, ERIKA ALONSO**
Client: **AOL MEDIA NETWORKS**

Creative Firm: **AOL | 360 CREATIVE — NEW YORK, NY**
Creative Team: **DAVID DEBENEDETTO, RICHARD TAYLOR, CHICO CONDE, HEATHER IVINS, JEFF BAYSON, ERIKA ALONSO**
Client: **AOL MEDIA NETWORKS**

TRAINING FILM

Creative Firm: **MIND & MEDIA — ALEXANDRIA, VA**
Creative Team: **ROBERT DEEGE, BERRY BLANTON, JULIE NOONE, JASON HUNTER**
Client: **ARMY NATIONAL GAURD**

AUDIO-VISUAL

Creative Firm: **SNAP CREATIVE — ST. CHARLES, MO**
Creative Team: **ANGELA NEAL, HILARY CLEMENTS**
Client: **EPC**

RADIO, *SINGLE*

Entry Title: **JIMMY4 - YOUTH CENTS**
Creative Firm: **BONNEVILLE COMMUNICATIONS — SALT LAKE CITY , UT**
Creative Team: **ERIC MORGAN**
Client: **DESERET FIRST CREDIT UNION**

Entry Title: **JIMMY7 - 50TH ANNIVERSARY**
Creative Firm: **BONNEVILLE COMMUNICATIONS — SALT LAKE CITY , UT**
Creative Team: **ERIC MORGAN**
Client: **DESERET FIRST CREDIT UNION**

Entry Title: **JIMMY1 - 15YR MORTGAGE**
Creative Firm: **BONNEVILLE COMMUNICATIONS — SALT LAKE CITY , UT**
Creative Team: **ERIC MORGAN**
Client: **DESERET FIRST CREDIT UNION**

Entry Title: **JIMMY3 - HOME LOANS**
Creative Firm: **BONNEVILLE COMMUNICATIONS — SALT LAKE CITY , UT**
Creative Team: **ERIC MORGAN**
Client: **DESERET FIRST CREDIT UNION**

Entry Title: **TO HAVE & TO HOLD**
Creative Firm: **ADVANTAGE LTD — HAMILTON, BERMUDA**
Creative Team: **SAMI LILL**
Client: **WOMEN'S RESOURCE CENTRE**

Entry Title: **CALIFORNIA CLASSICS (:30)**
Creative Firm: **HOFFMAN/LEWIS — SAN FRANCISCO, CA**
Creative Team: **SHARON KRINSKY, PATTI BOTT**
Client: **BEV MO**

Entry Title: **DRIVE SAFETY-THINK!**
Creative Firm: **ALL MEDIA PROJECTS LIMITED — PORT OF SPAIN, TRINIDAD AND TOBAGO**
Creative Team: **ANTHONY MOORE, JOSIANE KHAN, RICHARD AHONG**
Client: **BP TRINIDAD AND TOBAGO (BPTT)**

Entry Title: **FIVE CENT SALE: HOOKED SALE ON (:60)**
Creative Firm: **HOFFMAN/LEWIS — SAN FRANCISCO, CA**
Creative Team: **SHARON KRINSKY, PATTI BOTT**
Client: **BEV MO**

Entry Title: **BUTTERFLIES, PANTHERS & BIRDS, OH MY!**
Creative Firm: **2 WOMEN & A COMPUTER — GAINESVILLE, FL**
Creative Team: **LINDA CONWAY CORRELL, LARRY LYALL, STEPHEN BAKER, MIRROR IMAGE**
Client: **DAY QUILTERS OF ALACHUA COUNTY**

Entry Title: **HAUNT RADIO (:30)**
Creative Firm: **HITCHCOCK FLEMING & ASSOCIATES INC.— AKRON, OH**
Creative Team: **NICK BETRO, GREG PFIFFNER, MIKE MICKLEY**
Client: **GEAUGA LAKE**

Entry Title: **OCTOBERFEST RADIO (:30)**
Creative Firm: **HITCHCOCK FLEMING & ASSOCIATES INC. — AKRON, OH**
Creative Team: **NICK BETRO, GREG PFIFFNER, MIKE MICKLEY**
Client: **GEAUGA LAKE**

Entry Title: **FIVE CENT SALE: HOOKED SALE ON (:30)**
Creative Firm: **HOFFMAN/LEWIS — SAN FRANCISCO, CA**
Creative Team: **SHARON KRINSKY, PATTI BOTT**
Client: **BEV MO**

Entry Title: **JIMMY8 - FOOTBALL**
Creative Firm: **BONNEVILLE COMMUNICATIONS — SALT LAKE CITY , UT**
Creative Team: **ERIC MORGAN**
Client: **DESERET FIRST CREDIT UNION**

Entry Title: **TWO-FERS**
Creative Firm: **KELLER CRESCENT — EVANSVILLE, IN**
Creative Team: **RANDALL ROHN, JOHN CHADDOCK, RANDY ROHN, JOHN MENELLA**
Client: **MCDONALDS**

Entry Title: **INNER VOICE**
Creative Firm: **KELLER CRESCENT — EVANSVILLE, IN**
Creative Team: **RANDALL ROHN, JOHN CHADDOCK, RANDY ROHN**
Client: **LOCAL MCDONALDS**

Entry Title: **WHOOPIE DOOPIE DOO**
Creative Firm: **KELLER CRESCENT — EVANSVILLE, IN**
Creative Team: **RANDALL ROHN, JOHN CHADDOCK, RANDY ROHN**
Client: **SPRINT/UBIQUITEL**

Entry Title: **SAME AS IT EVER WAS RADIO**
Creative Firm: **CREATIVE ALLIANCE — LOUISVILLE, KY**
Creative Team: **ERIC HAHN**
Client: **EON US**

RADIO, *CAMPAIGN*

Entry Title: **DESERET FIRST CREDIT UNION CAMPAIGN 05**
Creative Firm: **BONNEVILLE COMMUNICATIONS — SALT LAKE CITY , UT**
Creative Team: **ERIC MORGAN**
Client: **DESERET FIRST CREDIT UNION**

Entry Title: **DESERET FIRST CREDIT UNION CAMPAIGN 06**
Creative Firm: **BONNEVILLE COMMUNICATIONS — SALT LAKE CITY , UT**
Creative Team: **ERIC MORGAN**
Client: **DESERET FIRST CREDIT UNION**

Entry Title: **VOLVO - "YOU WON'T WANT YOUR FRIENDS TO KNOW"**
Creative Firm: **BURROWS — BRENTWOOD, ESSEX, UNITED KINGDOM**
Creative Team: **ROYDON HEARNE, AARON HULSIZER, LUCY WELDON**
Client: **VOLVO CARS UK**

Entry Title: **STOP HIV/AIDS DISCRIMINATION**
Creative Firm: **ALL MEDIA PROJECTS LIMITED — PORT OF SPAIN, TRINIDAD AND TOBAGO**
Creative Team: **ANTHONY MOORE, CARL HARDING, RICHARD AHONG**
Client: **SFA COMMUNICATIONS**

Entry Title: **QUIZ SHOW/NICKNAMES/SMALL BUSINESS/BIG THINKING**
Creative Firm: **MCCANN ERICKSON, NEW YORK — NEW YORK, NY**
Creative Team: **MIKE JOINER, YANA GOODSTEIN, JOYCE KING THOMAS, STEVE OHLER, KIRK CAMPION, JUDI NIERMAN**
Client: **BUDGET**

Creative Firm: **ALOFT GROUP, INC. — NEWBURYPORT, MA**
Creative Team: **MATT BOWEN, DON CRANE, BRENT MARTINO, ROBBIE MACDONALD, STEVEN BALESTA**
Client: **ALOFT GROUP, INC.**

ONLINE CATALOGS

Creative Firm: **SINGULARITY DESIGN, INC. — PHILADELPHIA, PA**
Creative Team: **CHRIS COUNTER, JOSHUA COHEN, JEFF GREENHOUSE**
Client: **CARLISLE WIDE PLANK FLOORS**

BANNER ADS, *SINGLE*

Creative Firm: **AOL | 360 CREATIVE — NEW YORK, NY**
Creative Team: **DAVID DEBENEDETTO, CHICO CONDE, CHANTAL BOTANA, BRUCE KIMERER, ERIKA ALONSO,**
Client: **AOL MEDIA NETWORKS**

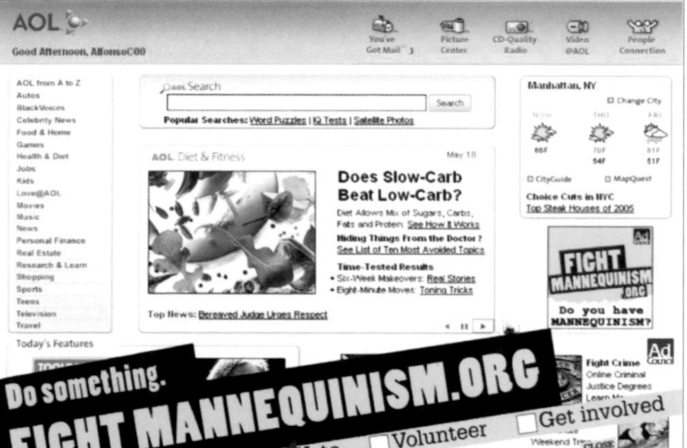

Creative Firm: **CRITICAL MASS INC. — CALGARY, AB, CANADA**
Creative Team: **ANDREW ZOLLER, ROB SAWCHUCK, SANJAI DAVE, DUANE WHEATCROFT, CHANTELLE ZANDBEEK,**
Client: **LAS VEGAS CONVENTION AND VISITORS AUTHORITY**

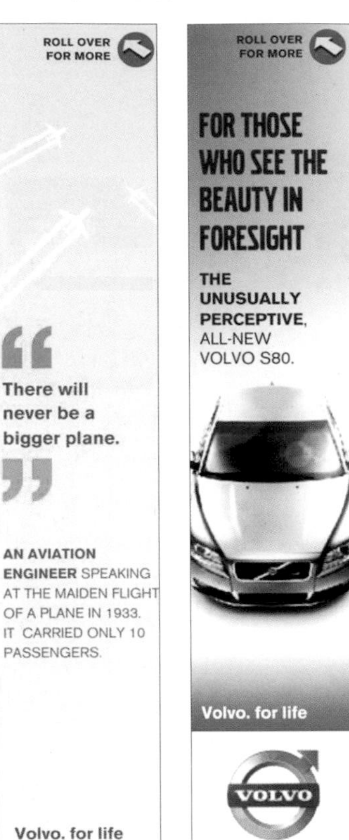

Creative Firm: **BURROWS — BRENTWOOD, ESSEX, UNITED KINGDOM**
Creative Team: **ROYDON HEARNE, MARK ELLIS, DARRYL SMITH, AARON HULSIZER, LUCY WELDON**
Client: **VOLVO CARS UK**

Creative Firm: **BURROWS — BRENTWOOD, ESSEX, UNITED KINGDOM**
Creative Team: **ROYDON HEARNE, ANDREW NICHOLSON, MICHAEL NAMAN, AARON HULSIZER, LUCY WELDON**
Client: **VOLVO CARS UK**

Creative Firm: **BURROWS — BRENTWOOD, ESSEX, UNITED KINGDOM**
Creative Team: **ROYDON HEARNE, DARRYL SMITH, AARON HULSIZER, DARREN POORE, LUCY WELDON**
Client: **VOLVO CARS UK**

Creative Firm: **BURROWS — BRENTWOOD, ESSEX, UNITED KINGDOM**
Creative Team: **ROYDON HEARNE, ANDREW NICHOLSON, DARRYL SMITH, AARON HULSIZER, LUCY WELDON**
Client: **VOLVO CARS UK**

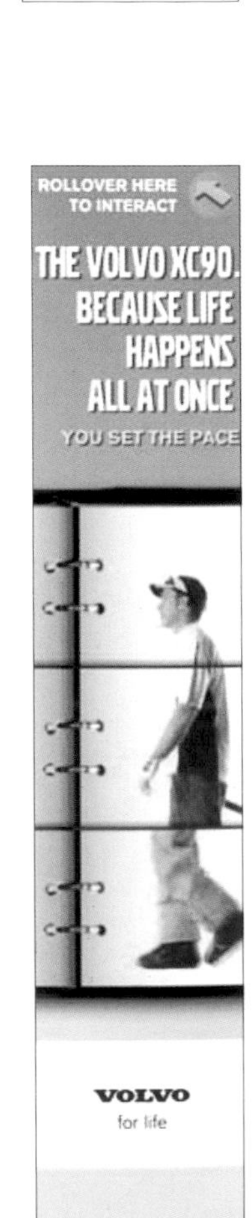

Creative Firm: **BURROWS — BRENTWOOD, ESSEX, UNITED KINGDOM**
Creative Team: **ROYDON HEARNE, DARRYL SMITH, AARON HULSIZER, LUCY WELDON**
Client: **VOLVO CARS UK**

Creative Firm: **GIDEON MULTIMEDIA — SPLIT, CROATIA (HRVATSKA)**
Creative Team: **ALEN ALEBIC, VEDRAN ELEZ, SINISA ERCEGOVAC, SANJA MIROSEVIC, VLADIMIR STERLE, MARIO BARICEVIC**
Client: **O'REILLY & JONES DISTRIBUTON**

Creative Firm: **GIDEON MULTIMEDIA — SPLIT, CROATIA (HRVATSKA)**
Creative Team: **ALEN ALEBIC, VEDRAN ELEZ, SINISA ERCEGOVAC, SANJA MIROSEVIC, VLADIMIR STERLE, MARIO BARICEVIC**
Client: **TOURIST BOARD OF BRELA**

Creative Firm: **GIDEON MULTIMEDIA — SPLIT, CROATIA (HRVATSKA)**
Creative Team: **ALEN ALEBIC, VEDRAN ELEZ, SINISA ERCEGOVAC, SANJA MIROSEVIC, VLADIMIR STERLE, MARIO BARICEVIC**
Client: **TOURIST BOARD OF SPLIT**

Creative Firm: **INFORMATION EXPERTS — RESTON, VA**
Creative Team: **RONA KILMER, MARK HENRY**
Client: **WORLD BANK**

Creative Firm: **ZUNDA GROUP LLC — SOUTH NORWALK, CT**
Creative Team: **CHARLES ZUNDA, DANIEL PRICE, JOHN GEOGHEGAN**
Client: **ZUNDA GROUP LLC**

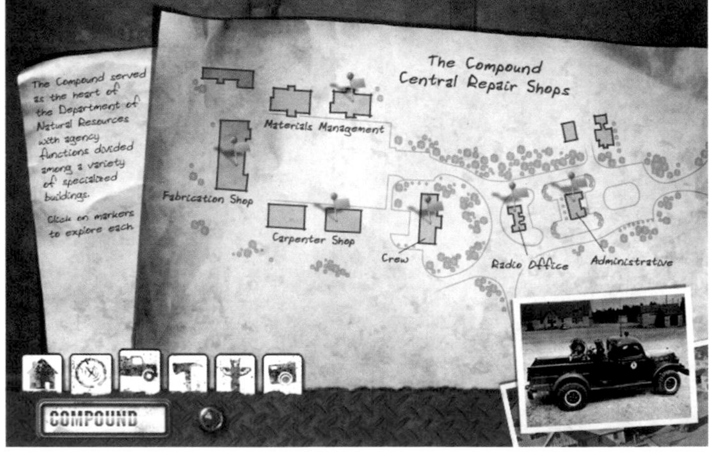

Creative Firm: **RUSTY GEORGE DESIGN — TACOMA, WA**
Creative Team: **BURT CRISMORE, RUSTY GEORGE DESIGN**
Client: **DEPARTMENT OF NATURAL RESOURCES**

Creative Firm: **KUTOKA INTERACTIVE — MONTREAL, QC, CANADA**
Creative Team: **RICHARD VINCENT, TANYA CLAESSENS, NADINE ROBERT, CHRISTINE MIMEAULT, ALEXANDER LESSARD**

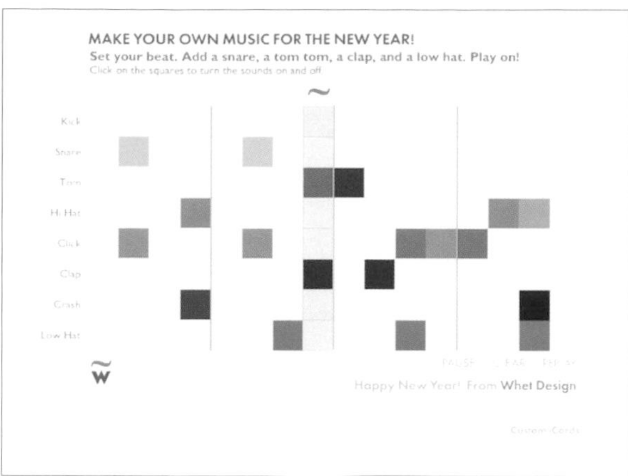

Creative Firm: **WHET DESIGN, INC. — NEW YORK, NY**
Creative Team: **CHERYL OPPENHEIM, YOHEI TAKESHITA, STEVE GU**
Client: **WHET DESIGN, INC.**

Creative Firm: **WHET DESIGN, INC. — NEW YORK, NY**
Creative Team: **CHERYL OPPENHEIM, JOHN WATERS, YOHEI TAKESHITA**
Client: **WHET DESIGN, INC.**

Creative Firm: **DESIGN 446 — MANASQUAN, NJ**
Creative Team: **BRIAN STERN**
Client: **DESIGN 446**

Creative Firm: **AOL | 360 CREATIVE — NEW YORK, NY**
Creative Team: **ANTHONY FARIA, CHICO CONDE, BARRY GARBARINO, ERIKA ALONSO**
Client: **AOL MEDIA NETWORKS**

E-MAILS, *CAMPAIGN*

Creative Firm: **JPL PRODUCTIONS — HARRISBURG, PA**
Creative Team: **CHELSIE MARKEL, KATY BASTAS, JAMY KUNJAPPU, SERENA FEDOR**
Client: **THE HERSHEY COMPANY**

Creative Firm: **CRITICAL MASS — CALGARY, AB, CANADA**
Creative Team: **RICHARD ALBORNOZ, COLIN LEACH**
Client: **ALBERTSONS**

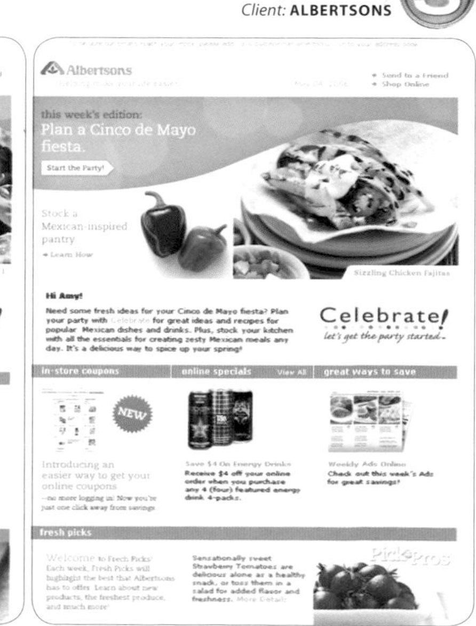

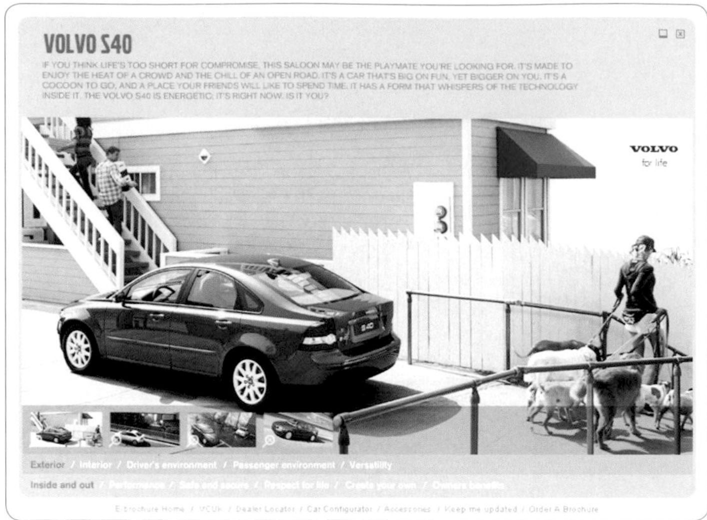

Creative Firm: **BURROWS — BRENTWOOD, ESSEX, UNITED KINGDOM**
Creative Team: **ROYDON HEARNE, ED SMITH, JON JUKES, AARON HULSIZER, LUCY WELDON**
Client: **VOLVO CARS UK**

Creative Firm: **STELLAR DEBRIS — HADANO-SHI, KANAGAWA-KEN, JAPAN**
Creative Team: **CHRISTOPHER JONES**
Client: **BYTWARE, INC.**

GAMES

Creative Firm: **LEVERAGE MARKETING GROUP — NEWTOWN, CT**
Creative Team: **DAVID GOODWICK, MIKE NOVIA, BECKY KOROL, MATT JAY, TOM MARKS, HARRIET POLANSKY**
Client: **NOVACHEM**

Creative Firm: **INFORMATION EXPERTS — RESTON, VA**
Creative Team: **ELICIA ROBERTS, ADRIENNE YOUNG**
Client: **BELLSOUTH**

Creative Firm: **COMEDY CENTRAL — NEW YORK, NY**
Creative Team: **KAREN LA CHIANA, BEN WINIARCZK, JESSE WILLMON, JULIE ANN PIETRANGELO, BETH LEWAND, PAUL BEDDOE-STEPHENS**
Client: **COMEDY CENTRAL**

Creative Firm: **ACART COMMUNICATIONS — OTTAWA, ON, CANADA**
Creative Team: **SOPHIE JALBERT, SARAH DESCHAMPS, VERNON LAI, TOM MEGGINSON, CASEY TOURANGEAU, JASON HAMILTON**
Client: **CANADIAN AUTOMOBILE ASSOCIATION**
WWW.CANADASROADS.COM

Creative Firm: **WHET DESIGN, INC. — NEW YORK, NY**
Creative Team: **CHERYL OPPENHEIM, YOHEI TAKESHITA, STEVE GU**
Client: **NATIONAL MUSEUM OF WOMEN IN THE ARTS**
WWW.COSTOMISPOT.COM/NMWA/DH

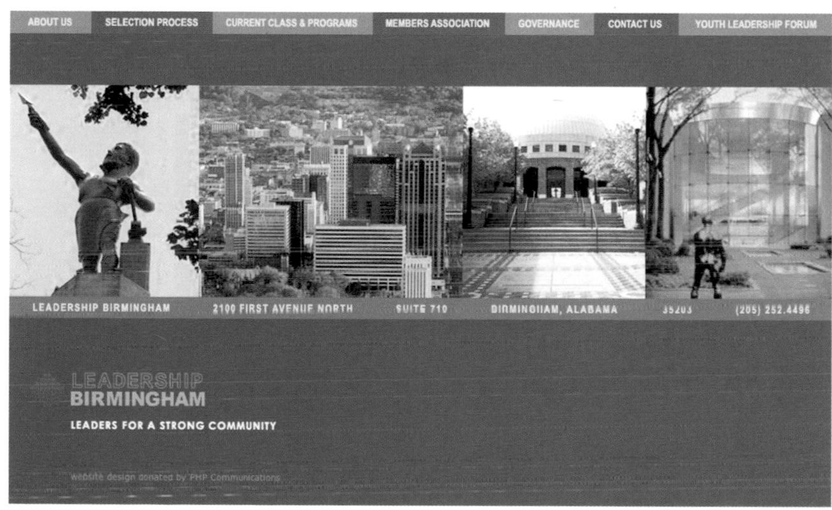

Creative Firm: **PHP COMMUNICATIONS — BIRMINGHAM, AL**
Creative Team: **BRYAN CHACE, LYNN SMITH, DREW SMITH**
Client: **LEADERSHIP BIRMINGHAM**
WWW.LEADERSHIPBIRMINGHAM.ORG

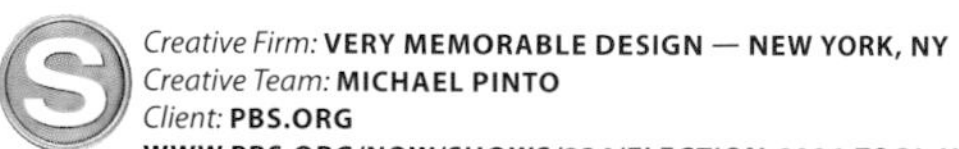

Creative Firm: **VERY MEMORABLE DESIGN — NEW YORK, NY**
Creative Team: **MICHAEL PINTO**
Client: **PBS.ORG**
WWW.PBS.ORG/NOW/SHOWS/234/ELECTION-2006-TOOL.HTML

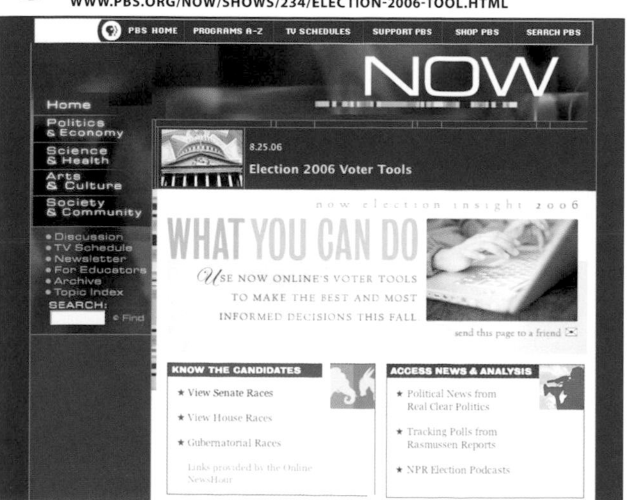

Creative Firm: **PHP COMMUNICATIONS — BIRMINGHAM, AL**
Creative Team: **BRYAN CHACE, KELLY POIRIER, DREW SMITH**
Client: **YOUTH LEADERSHIP FORUM**
WWW.YLFBHAM.COM

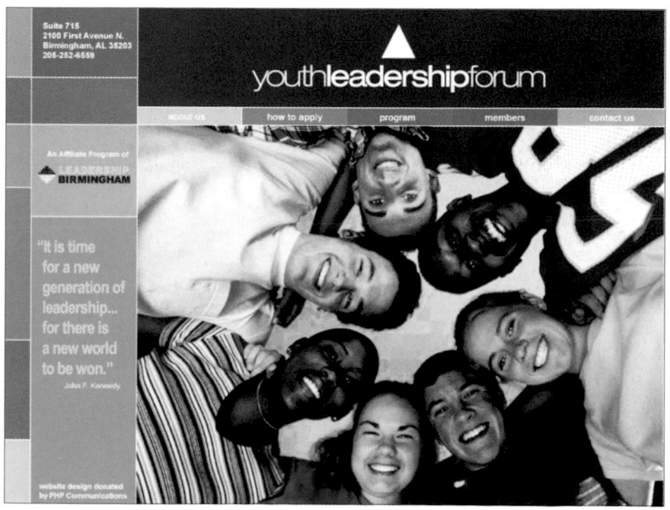

Creative Firm: **Q — WIESBADEN, GERMANY**
Creative Team: **THILO VON DEBSCHITZ, MARKUS REWELAND, GERHARD HEILAND, LAURENZ NIELBOCK, ALEXANDER WEINL**
Client: **BOEHRINGER INGELHEIM**
WWW.TINGUELY.SEEMEGROW.DE

Creative Firm: **LF BANKS + ASSOCIATES — PHILADELPHIA, PA**
Creative Team: **LORI BANKS, TRAVIS SCHNUPP**
Client: **FELDMAN SHEPHERD WOHLGELERNTER TANNER & WEINSTOCK**
WWW.SPINABIFIDALAW.COM

Creative Firm: **RODGERS TOWNSEND — ST. LOUIS, MO**
Creative Team: **TOM HUDDER, SCOTT LAWSON, MIKE HALBROOK, SHAUN YOUNG**
Client: **NETWORK FOR GOOD**
RODGERSTOWNSEND.COM/INTERACTIVE/NETWORK FORGOOD

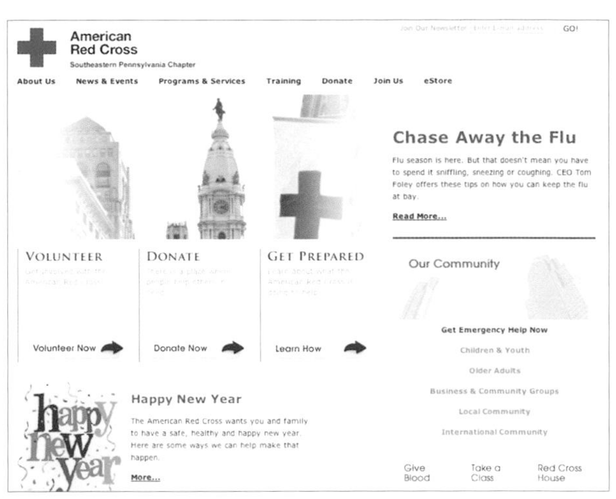

Creative Firm: **SINGULARITY DESIGN, INC. — PHILADELPHIA, PA**
Creative Team: **OWEN LINTON, JOSHUA COHEN**
Client: **AMERICAN RED CROSS - SEPA CHAPTER**
WWW.REDCROSS-PHILLY.ORG

Creative Firm: **Q — WIESBADEN, GERMANY**
Creative Team: **MARCEL KUMMERER, THILO VON DEBSCHITZ, MATTHIAS SCHAAB**
Client: **GALERIE Q**
WWW. ARTCOUNTDOWN.COM

Creative Firm: **MARK DEITCH & ASSOCIATES, INC. — BURBANK, CA**
Creative Team: **DVORJAC RIEMERSMA**
Client: **TEMPLE ALIYAH**
WWW.TEMPLEALIYAH.ORG

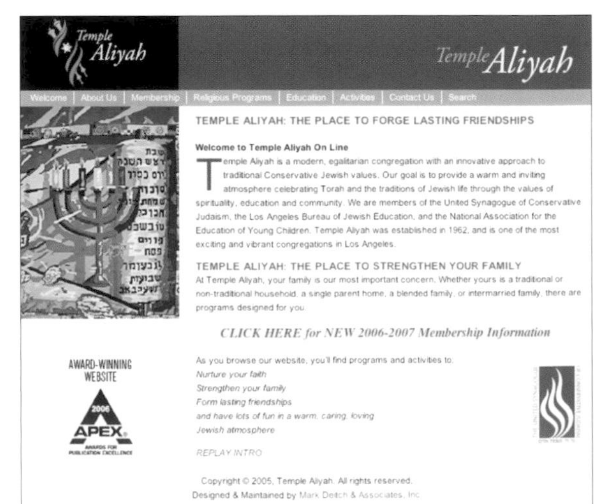

Creative Firm: **30SIXTY ADVERTISING+DESIGN, INC. — LOS ANGELES, CA**
Creative Team: **HENRY VIZCARRA, DUY NGUYEN, KASEY CHATILA, RICHARD HILARY**
Client: **PARAMOUNT HOME ENTERTAINMENT**
WWW.FERRISBUELLERONDVD.COM

Creative Firm: **JPL PRODUCTIONS — HARRISBURG, PA**
Creative Team: **CHRIS BUCHHOLZ, JIM ROBBINS, MATTHEW BYERS, JAMY KUNJAPPU, SERENA FEDOR**
Client: **THE HERSHEY COMPANY**
WWW.HERSHEYS.COM/SYRUPCAP

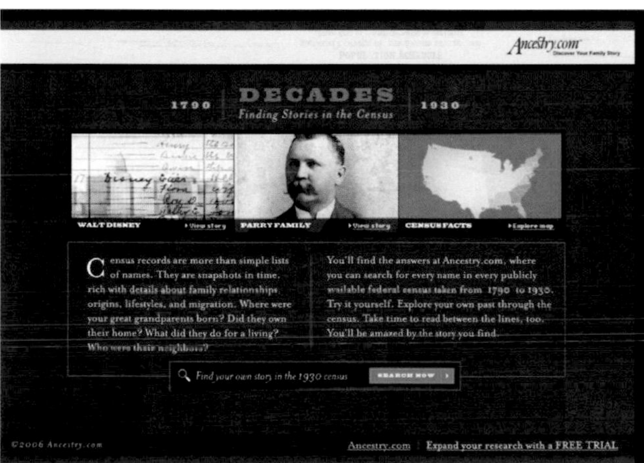

Creative Firm: **HORNALL ANDERSON DESIGN WORKS — SEATTLE, WA**
Creative Team: **JAMIE MONBERG, HANS KREBS, JOE KING, JASON HICKNER, ADRIEN LO, ERICA GOLDSMITH**
Client: **MY FAMILY**
CENSUS.ANCESTRY.COM/MICROSITE/CENSUS COMPLETE.ASPX

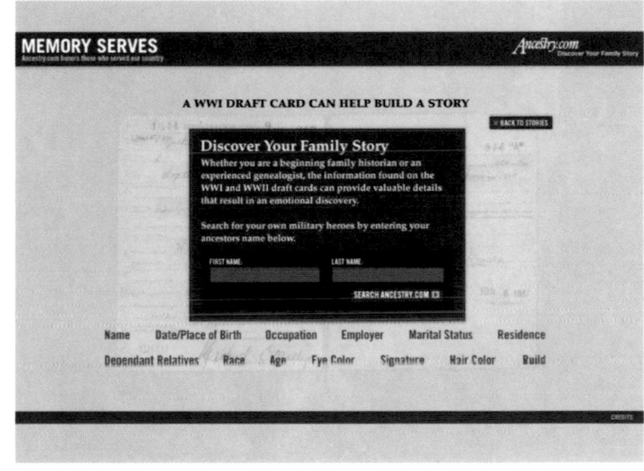

Creative Firm: **HORNALL ANDERSON DESIGN WORKS — SEATTLE, WA**
Creative Team: **NATHAN YOUNG, JOHN CLOSE, JAMIE MONBERG, ADRIEN LO, ROEL NAVA, MICHELE GODFREY**
Client: **MY FAMILY**
WWW.MEMORYSERVES.COM

Creative Firm: **VERY MEMORABLE DESIGN — NEW YORK, NY**
Creative Team: **MICHAEL PINTO, GWENEVERE SINGLEY**
Client: **SESAME WORKSHOP**
WWW.SESAMEWORKSHOP.ORG/PINKYDINKYDOO/

Creative Firm: **ZERO GRAVITY DESIGN GROUP — SMITHTOWN, NY**
Creative Team: **ZERO GRAVITY DESIGN GROUP**
Client: **WOLFFER ESTATE VINEYARD & STABLES**
WWW.WOLFFER.COM

Creative Firm: **PRIMARY DESIGN, INC. — HAVERHILL, MA**
Creative Team: **JEN DICKERT, VITA MARINOVA**
Client: **DIRK AND LUCY HERMAN**
WWW.DIRKANDLUCY.COM

Creative Firm: **ZERO GRAVITY DESIGN GROUP — SMITHTOWN, NY**
Client: **TONY D'MATTIA**
WWW.FIZBAND.COM

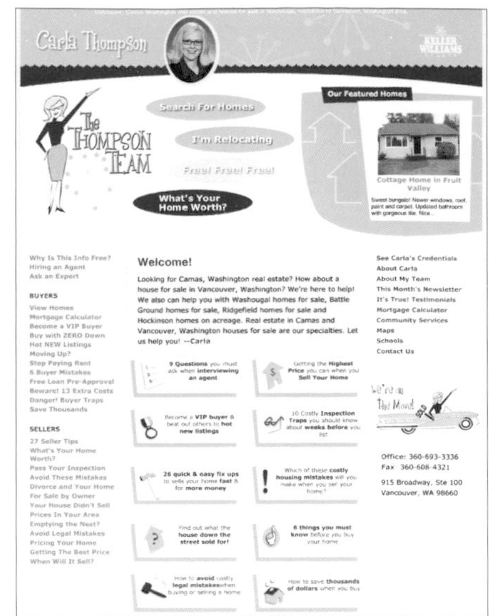

Creative Firm: **DOUG WILLIAMS & ASSOCIATES — VANCOUVER, WA**
Creative Team: **CASEY KRIMMEL**
Client: **CARLA THOMPSON**
WWW.CARLATHOMPSON.COM

Creative Firm: **CMT — NEW YORK, NY**
Creative Team: **MARTIN CLAYTON, DONNA PRIESMEYER, LORI REEVES, BEN FRANK, CALVIN GILBERT, JASON HILL**
Client: **CMT / CMT.COM**
WWW.CMT.COM/SHOWS/EVENTS/CMT_MUSIC_AWARDS/2006/INDEX.JHTML

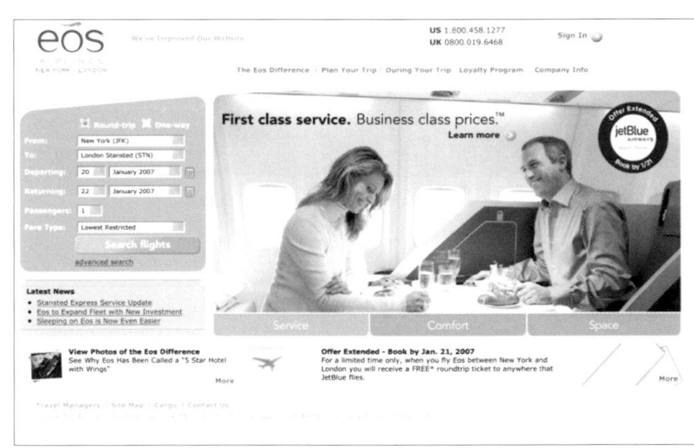

Creative Firm: **HORNALL ANDERSON DESIGN WORKS — SEATTLE, WA**
Creative Team: **MARK POPICH, HANS KREBS, JAMIE MONBERG, MOBIAM**
Client: **EOS AIRLINES**
WWW.EOSAIRLINES.COM

Creative Firm: **400LB.COMMUNICATIONS — PITTSBURGH, PA**
Creative Team: **NATHAN KRESS, CLINTON GODLESKY**
Client: **SHADY SIDE ACADEMY, PITTSBURGH, PA**
WWW.SHADYSIDEHOCKEY.COM

Creative Firm: **CMT — NEW YORK, NY**
Creative Team: **MARTIN CLAYTON, DONNA PRIESMEYER, LORI REEVES, MARSHALL WOKSA, CALVIN GILBERT, JASON HILL**
Client: **CMT/CMT.COM**
WWW.CMT.COM/MUSIC/EVENTS/ACM/2006

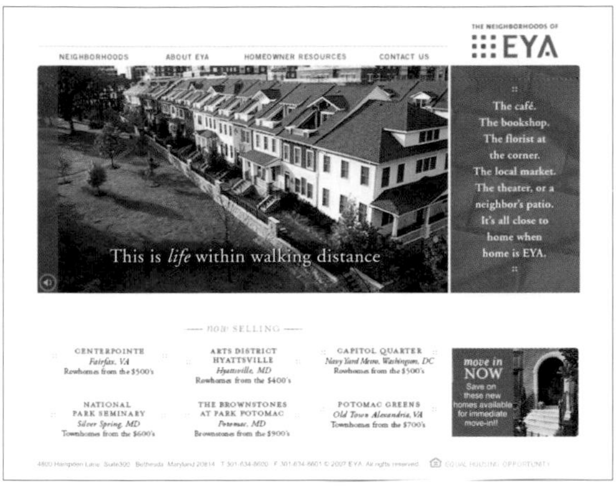

Creative Firm: **GRAFIK MARKETING COMMUNICATIONS — ALEXANDRIA, VA**
Creative Team: **ARTHUR HSU, JOHNNY VITOROVICH, KATHERINE SLACK, HAL SWETNAM, FABIO SILVA**
Client: **EYA**
WWW.EYA.COM

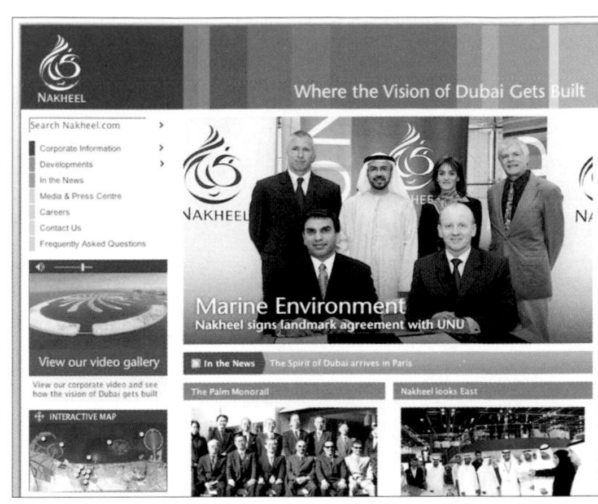

Creative Firm: **FUTUREBRAND — NEW YORK, NY**
Creative Team: **STEVE AARON, CARLSON YU, MIKE SHEEHAN, TOM LI, SEP SEYEDI, LYUTHA AL-HABSY**
Client: **NAKHEEL**
WWW.NAKHEEL.AE/

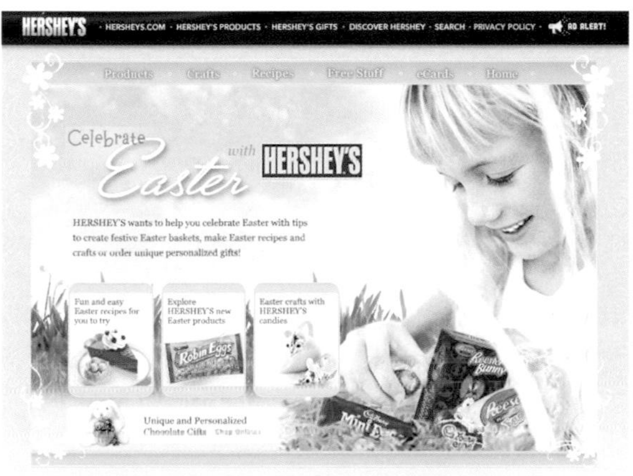

Creative Firm: **JPL PRODUCTIONS — HARRISBURG, PA**
Creative Team: **CHELSIE MARKEL, KATY BASTAS, JAMY KUNJAPPU, SERENA FEDOR**
Client: **THE HERSHEY COMPANY**
WWW.HERSHEYS.COM/EASTER

Creative Firm: **CJ DESIGN — SANTA CRUZ, CA**
Creative Team: **CHRIS MARK, JT MUDGE**
Client: **AZORES.COM**
WWW.AZORES.COM/

Creative Firm: **KIKU OBATA & COMPANY — ST. LOUIS, MO**
Creative Team: **TROY GUZMAN, TERESA NORTON-YOUNG, STEADY RAIN**
Client: **JAZZ CRUISES, LLC**
WWW.THESMOOTHJAZZCRUISE.COM

Creative Firm: **DESIGN 446 — MANASQUAN, NJ**
Creative Team: **BRIAN STERN**
Client: **RE/MAX**
WWW.SKYVIEWLIVING.COM

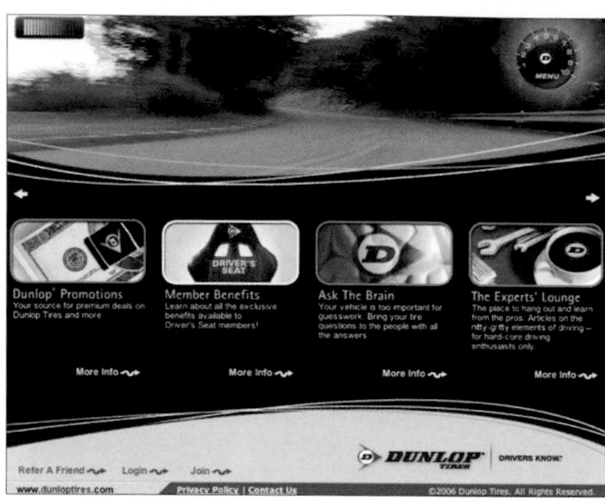

Creative Firm: **HITCHCOCK FLEMING & ASSOCIATES INC. — AKRON, OH**
Creative Team: **NICK BETRO, LARRY YODER, JAMES KIEL, MIKE MICKLEY, GREG PFIFFNER**
Client: **GOODYEAR TIRE & RUBBER COMPANY**
WWW.DUNLOPTIRES.COM/DRIVERSSEAT

Creative Firm: **LAUNCH CREATIVE MARKETING — CHICAGO, IL**
Creative Team: **JIM GELDER**
Client: **JARDEN**
WWW.DIAMONDBRANDS.COM

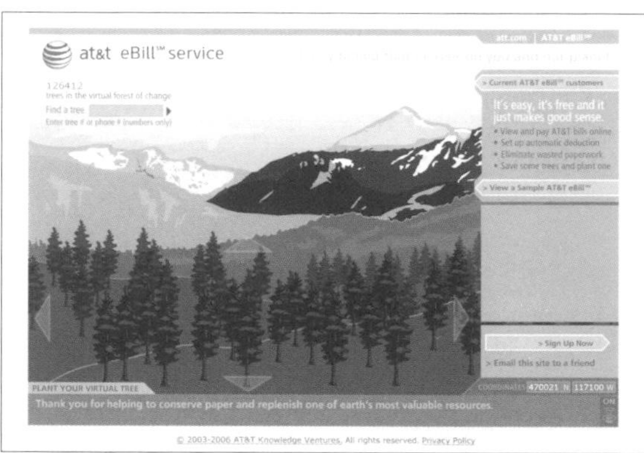

Creative Firm: **RODGERS TOWNSEND — ST. LOUIS, MO**
Creative Team: **ERIK MATHRE, RON COPELAND, RYAN MCMICHAEL, MIKE HALBROOK, MARK BATEMAN**
Client: **SBC COMMUNICATIONS, INC**
WWW.YOURATT.COM/DESTINATION/TREE/INDEX.CFM

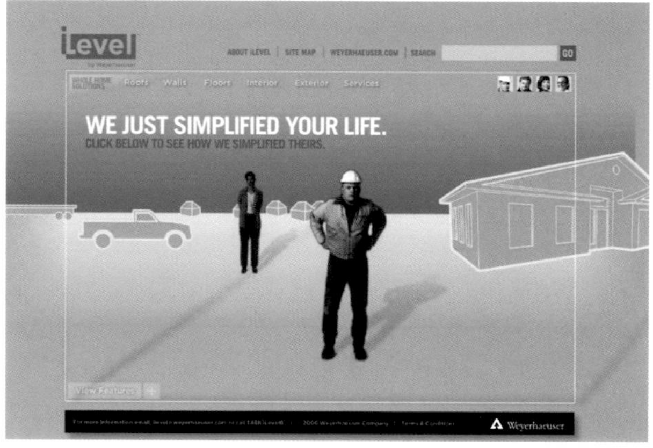

Creative Firm: **HORNALL ANDERSON DESIGN WORKS — SEATTLE, WA**
Creative Team: **J. MONBERG, C. COLLINSWORTH, A. LO, N. YOUNG, J. HICKNER, J. KING, D. ROBINSON, J. HILBURN, D. KENOYER, E. GOLDSMITH, J. TEE**
Client: **WEYERHAEUSER CORP.**
WWW.ILEVEL.COM

Creative Firm: **HITCHCOCK FLEMING & ASSOCIATES INC. — AKRON, OH**
Creative Team: **NICK BETRO, RENE MCCANN, JAMES KIEL, STEVE LAMB, ERIC HARTLINE**
Client: **GOODYEAR TIRE & RUBBER COMPANY**
WWW.GOODYEARFORTERA.COM./TRIPLETRED

Creative Firm: **TODD CHILDERS GRAPHIC DESIGN — BOWLING GREEN, OH**
Creative Team: **TODD CHILDERS, BONNIE MITCHELL, SUE WEISSHAAR**
Client: **BOWLING GREEN STATE UNIVERSITY SCHOOL OF ART**
WWW.BGSU.EDU/DEPARTMENTS/ART

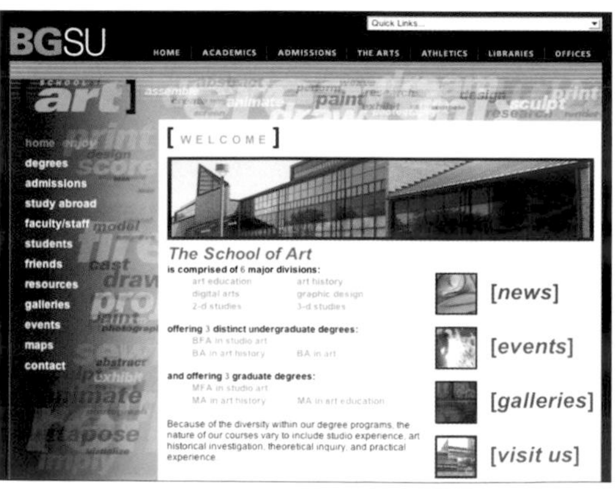

Creative Firm: **KIKU OBATA & COMPANY — ST. LOUIS, MO**
Creative Team: **TROY GUZMAN, TERESA NORTON-YOUNG, STEADY RAIN**
Client: **JAZZ CRUISES, LLC**
WWW.JAZZCRUISESLLC.COM

Creative Firm: **KIKU OBATA & COMPANY — ST. LOUIS, MO**
Creative Team: **TROY GUZMAN, TERESA NORTON-YOUNG, STEADY RAIN**
Client: **JAZZ CRUISES, LLC**
WWW.THEJAZZCRUISE.COM

Creative Firm: **MCCANN ERICKSON, NEW YORK — NEW YORK, NY**
Creative Team: **CRAIG MARKUS, SHALOM AUSLANDER, JOYCE KING THOMAS, CORI H. BOUDIN , BRENDAN GIBBONS, PETE FRITZ**
Client: **VERIZON WIRELESS**
HTTPS://VERIZONSUBMISSION.WGEXCHANGE.COM

Creative Firm: **STUDIOERIN — JUPITER, FL**
Client: **RAYMOND ACEVEDO/AFTERWORLD RECORDS**
WWW.AFTERWORLDRECORDS.NET

Creative Firm: **TAXI — MONTRÉAL, QUÉBEC, CANADA**
Creative Team: **DOMINIQUE TRUDEAU, JESSICA MANCHESTER, ÉMILIE TRUDEAU-RABINOWICZ, MECANO, LA FABRIQUE D'IMAGES, APOLLO**
Client: **DERMETK PHARMACEUTIQUE (ROBERT LAVOIE-PRESIDENT)**
WWW.SEEMORESIDEEFFECTS.CA

Creative Firm: **BOSTON WEB DESIGN — BOSTON, MA**
Client: **NEW ENGLAND COFFEE**
WWW.NEWENGLANDCOFFEE.COM

Creative Firm: **SPIDERTEL, INC. — OVERLAND PARK, KS**
Creative Team: **JOE LIEBERMAN**
Client: **DRI DUCK TRADERS**
WWW.DRIDUCKTRADERS.COM

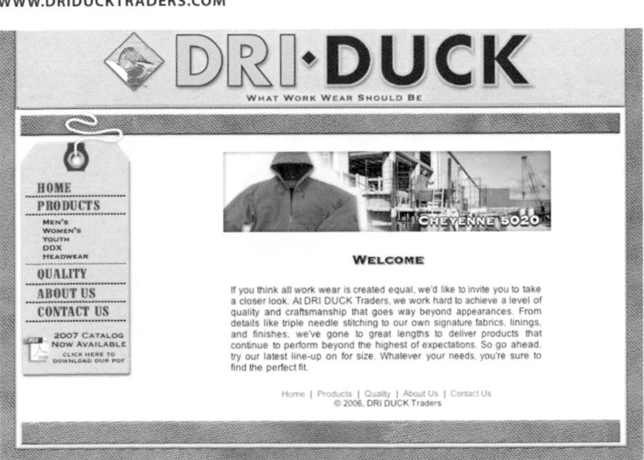

Creative Firm: **CMT — NEW YORK, NY**
Creative Team: **MARTIN CLAYTON, DONNA PRIESMEYER, LORI REEVES, MARSHALL WOKSA, CALVIN GILBERT, JASON HILL**
Client: **CMT / CMT.COM**
WWW.CMT.COM/MUSIC/EVENTS/CMA_MUSIC_FESTIVAL/2006

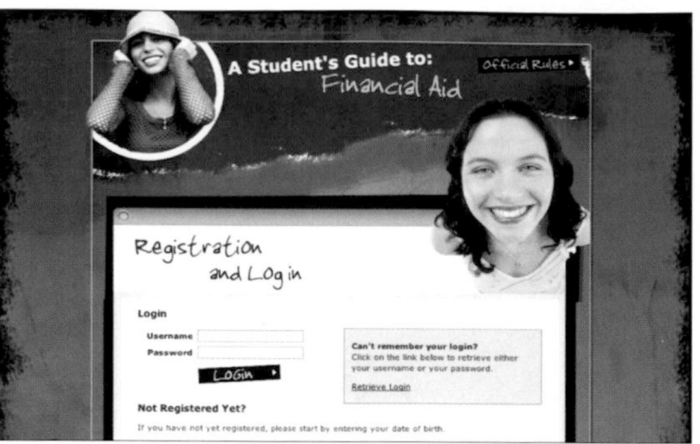

Creative Firm: **JPL PRODUCTIONS — HARRISBURG, PA**
Creative Team: **SHANE HOFFA, KATY BASTAS, JIM ROBBINS, JIM MITCHELL, CAROL HUNT**
Client: **CAMPUS DOOR**
WWW.INTERNETSTUDENTLOANS.COM/GAME

Creative Firm: **MALONEY & FOX — NEW YORK, NY**
Creative Team: **BRIAN MALONEY, MARGIE FOX, DUVAL HOPKINS, GILES HANSON, DAVID ORCHARD**
Client: **DRAMBUIE**
WWW.SIGNATURESPIRIT.COM

Creative Firm: **JPL PRODUCTIONS — HARRISBURG, PA**
Creative Team: **BRANDON CRAIG, CHELSIE MARKEL, JIM ROBBINS, JAMY KUNJAPPU, SERENA FEDOR**
Client: **JERR-DAN CORPORATION**
JERRDAN.COM/INDEX.ASP

Creative Firm: **CJ DESIGN — SANTA CRUZ, CA**
Creative Team: **CHRIS MARK, JOHN BENEDETTI, QUAN DO**
Client: **AIKANE**
AIKANE.ILUMINADA.COM/

Creative Firm: **SINGULARITY DESIGN, INC. — PHILADELPHIA, PA**
Creative Team: **OWEN LINTON, JOSHUA COHEN**
Client: **CBSW CORPORATION**
WWW.SUBWAYCEDARBROOK.COM

Creative Firm: **30SIXTY ADVERTISING+DESIGN, INC. — LOS ANGELES, CA**
Creative Team: **HENRY VIZCARRA, DAVID FUSCELLARO, KASEY CHATILA, MARISA GHIGLIERI**
Client: **PARAMOUNT HOME ENTERTAINMENT**
WWW.TOMMYBOYONDVD.COM

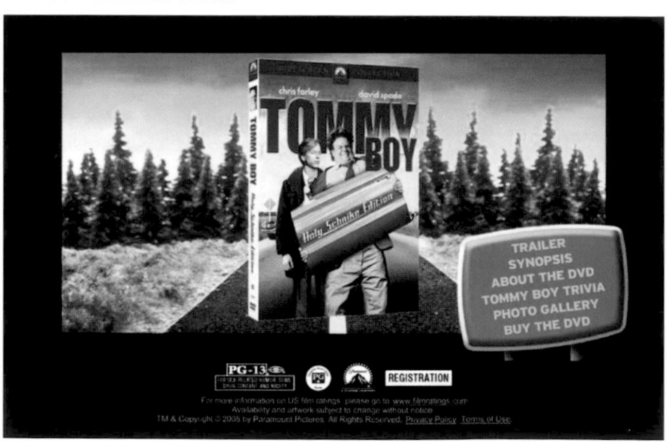

Creative Firm: **HITCHCOCK FLEMING & ASSOCIATES INC. — AKRON, OH**
Creative Team: **NICK BETRO, STEVE LAMB, ERIC HARTLINE**
Client: **GOODYEAR TIRE & RUBBER COMPANY**
WWW.DUNLOPTIRES.COM

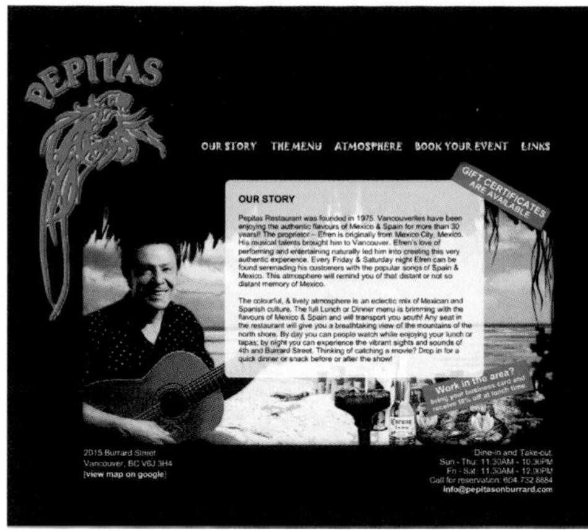

Creative Firm: **KIMBO DESIGN — VANCOUVER, BC, CANADA**
Creative Team: **KIM PICKETT, BUDIANTO NASRUN**
Client: **PEPITAS - MEXICAN SPANISH RESTAURANT**
WWW.PEPITASONBURRARD.COM

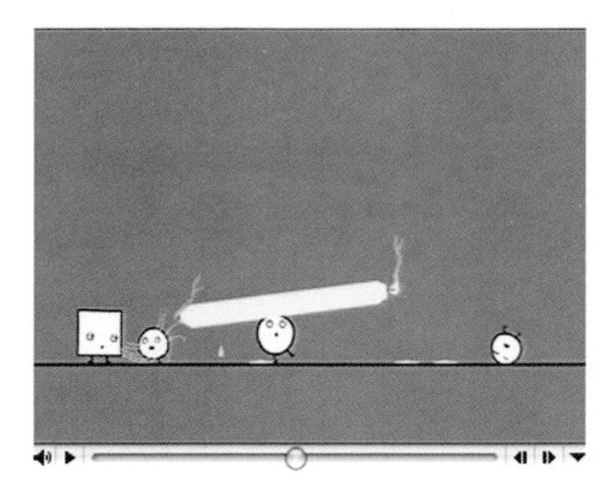

Creative Firm: **MCCANN ERICKSON, NEW YORK — NEW YORK, NY**
Creative Team: **SHARON EHRLICH, DANNY RODRIGUEZ, JOYCE KING THOMAS, KATHY LOVE, AARON STEWART, MIKE BORIS**
Client: **WENDY'S**
HTTPS://WENDYSSUBMISSION1.WGEXCHANGE.COM

Creative Firm: **SINGULARITY DESIGN, INC. — PHILADELPHIA, PA**
Creative Team: **JOSHUA COHEN, CHRIS COUNTER, JEFF GREENHOUSE**
Client: **CARLISLE WIDE PLANK FLOORS**
WWW.WIDEPLANKFLOORING.COM/

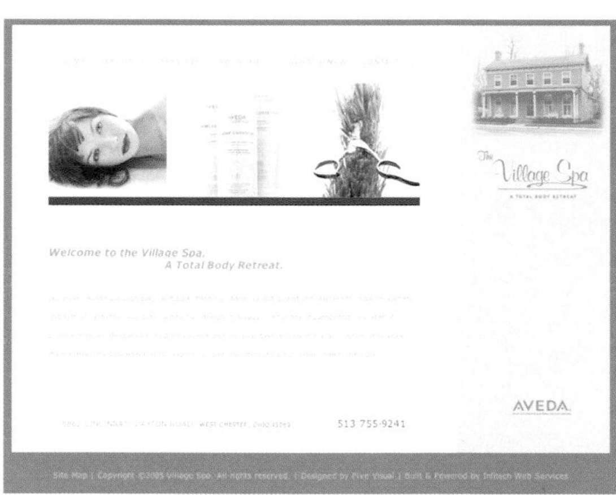

Creative Firm: **FIVE VISUAL COMMUNICATION & DESIGN — WEST CHESTER, OH**
Creative Team: **RONDI TSCHOPP**
Client: **THE VILLAGE SPA SALON**
WWW.THEVILLAGESPASALON.COM

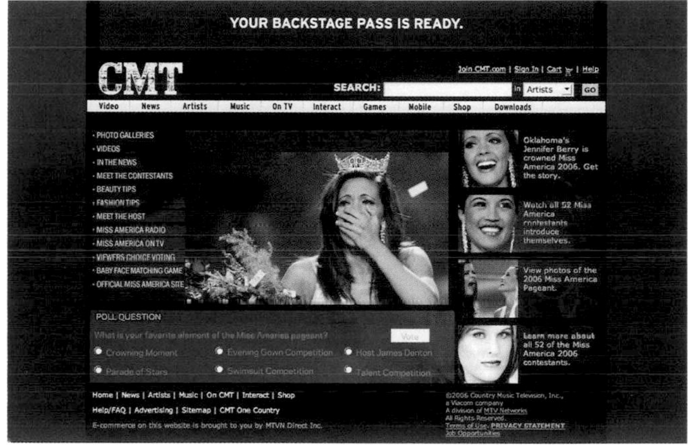

Creative Firm: **CMT — NEW YORK, NY**
Client: **MARTIN CLAYTON, DONNA PRIESMEYER, KIM SORENSEN, MARSHALL WOKSA, STEPHANIE PENDERGRASS, CALVIN GILBERT**
Client: **CMT / MISS AMERICA ORGANIZATION**
WWW.CMT.COM/SHOWS/EVENTS/MISS_AMERICA/2006/

Creative Firm: **JPL PRODUCTIONS — HARRISBURG, PA**
Creative Team: **CHELSIE MARKEL, PEGGY BRUCK, MICHAEL WETZEL, DAVE ROBERTSON, DAN THOMPSON**
Client: **HARSCO CORPORATION**
WWW.HARSCO.COM

Creative Firm: **LISKA + ASSOCIATES — CHICAGO, IL**
Creative Team: **STEVE LISKA, MEGHAN MCCLAIN**
Client: **SCHATZ DEVELOPMENT**
WWW.600NORTHFAIRBANKS.COM

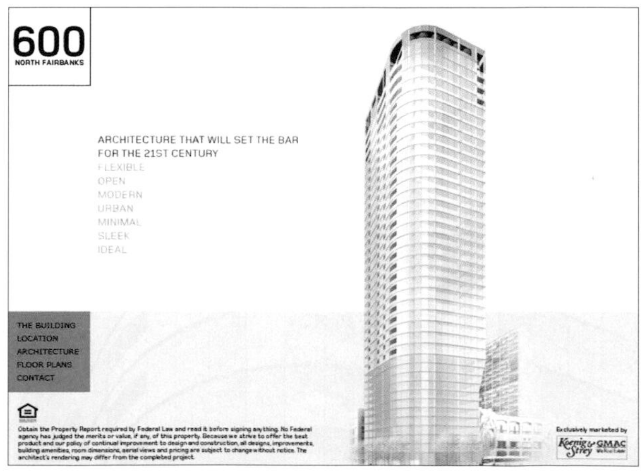

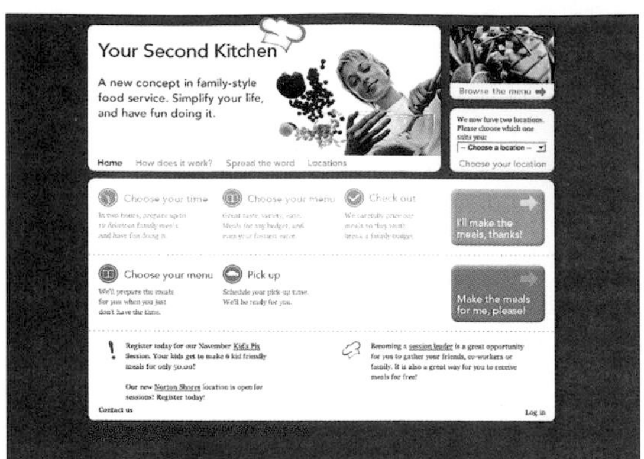

Creative Firm: **BBK STUDIO — GRAND RAPIDS, MI**
Creative Team: **KEVIN BUDELMANN, ALISON POPP, MARIE-CLAIRE CAMP**
Client: **YOUR SECOND KITCHEN**
WWW.YOURSECONDKITCHEN.COM

Creative Firm: **FLUILINK SRL — ROME, LAZIO, ITALY**
Creative Team: **GIULIO GIORGETTI, SARA QUINTORIO, ALFREDO CELAIA, FABIO PALLOTTA**
WWW.STUDIOUNIVERSAL.IT/REPLAY

Creative Firm: **KIKU OBATA & COMPANY — ST. LOUIS, MO**
Creative Team: **TROY GUZMAN, TERESA NORTON-YOUNG, STEADY RAIN**
Client: **JAZZ CRUISES, LLC**
WWW.DAVEKOZCRUISE.COM

Creative Firm: **JPL PRODUCTIONS — HARRISBURG, PA**
Creative Team: **KATY BASTAS, CHELSIE MARKEL, ALISON FETTERMAN**
Client: **THE HERSHEY COMPANY**
WWW.HERSHEYS.COM/PLEDGE

Creative Firm: **CMT — NEW YORK, NY**
Creative Team: **MARTIN CLAYTON, DONNA PRIESMEYER, LORI REEVES SR. PRODUCER, MARSHALL WOKSA, CALVIN GILBERT, JASON HILL**
Client: **CMT / CMT.COM**
WWW.CMT.COM/MUSIC/EVENTS/CMA/2005

Creative Firm: **HITCHCOCK FLEMING & ASSOCIATES INC. — AKRON, OH**
Creative Team: **NICK BETRO, JAMES KIEL, STEVE LAMB, ERIC HARTLINE, MARCK COLLINS**
Client: **GOODYEAR TIRE & RUBBER COMPANY**
WWW.GOODYEAREAGLE.COM

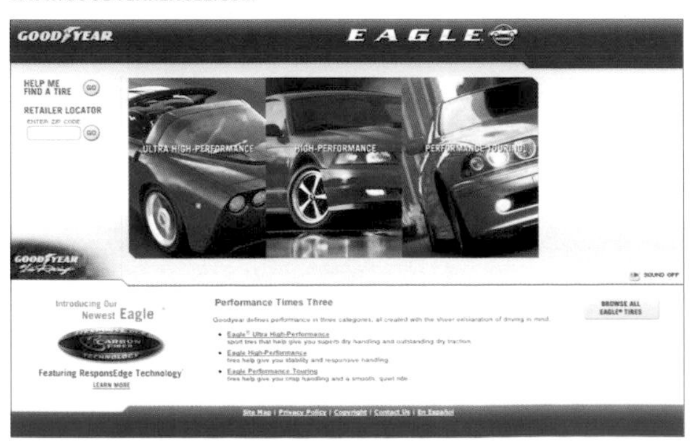

Creative Firm: **ZERO GRAVITY DESIGN GROUP**
Client: **WOLFFER ESTATE VINEYARD & STABLES**
WWW.WOLFFERESTATESTALES.COM

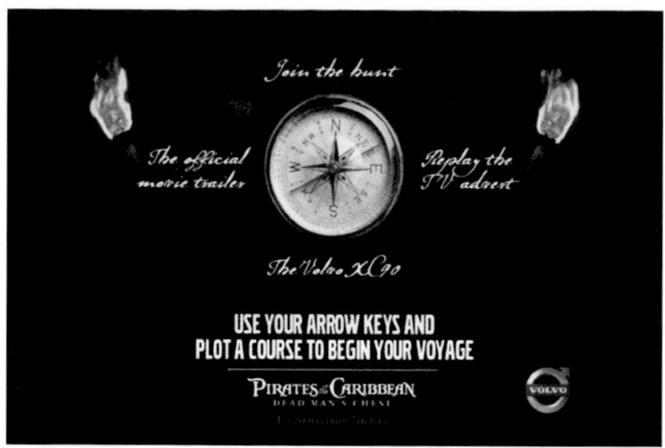

Creative Firm: **BURROWS — BRENTWOOD, ESSEX, UNITED KINGDOM**
Creative Team: **ROYDON HEARNE, DARRYL SMITH, AARON HULSIZER, LUCY WELDON**
Client: **VOLVO CARS UK**

Creative Firm: **BURROWS — BRENTWOOD, ESSEX, UNITED KINGDOM**
Creative Team: **ROYDON HEARNE, ED SMITH, JON JUKES, AARON HULSIZER, LUCY WELDON**
Client: **VOLVO CARS UK**
WWW.VOLVOCARCAMPAIGNS.CO.UK/GOLFCLUB/

Creative Firm: **JPL PRODUCTIONS — HARRISBURG, PA**
Creative Team: **CHRIS BUCHHOLZ, CHELSIE MARKEL, MATTHEW BYERS, JAMY KUNJAPPU, JIM ROBBINS, SERENA FEDOR**
Client: **THE HERSHEY COMPANY**
WWW.HERSHEYS.COM/TIMANDFAITH/HOME.ASPX

Creative Firm: **GODBE COMMUNICATIONS — HALF MOON BAY, CA**
Client: **FERRET COMPANY**
WWW.FERRETCOMPANY.COM

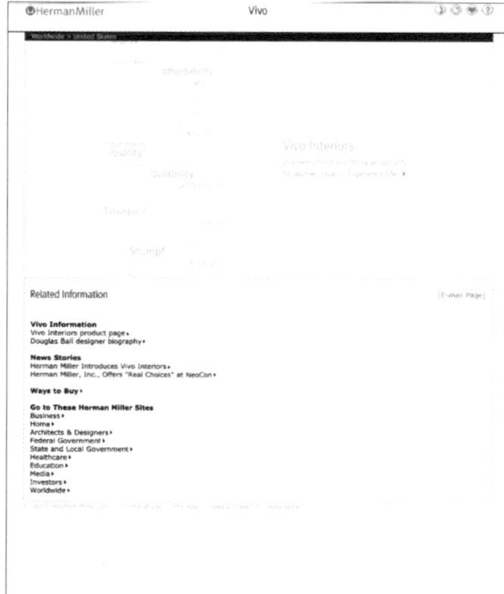

Creative Firm: **BBK STUDIO — GRAND RAPIDS, MI**
Creative Team: **GEOFF MARK, RYAN LEE**
Client: **HERMAN MILLER**
WWW.HERMANMILLER.COM/VIVOEXPERIENCE

Creative Firm: **KELLER CRESCENT — EVANSVILLE, IN**
Creative Team: **CARSON CATLIN, LYNNE MLADY, RANDALL ROHN**
Client: **HEAVEN HILL**
WWW.KELLERCRESCENT.COM/PAMA

Creative Firm: **MCCANN ERICKSON, NEW YORK — NEW YORK, NY**
Creative Team: **CRAIG MARKUS, SHALOM AUSLANDER, JOYCE KING THOMAS, JONATHAN SHIPMAN, SIMON BLAKE**
Client: **LEVI'S**
HTTPS://LEVISSUBMISSION.WGEXCHANGE.COM

Creative Firm: **ISLAND OASIS — WALPOLE, MA**
Creative Team: **PETE BUHLER**
Client: **ISLAND OASIS**
WWW.ISLANDOASIS.COM

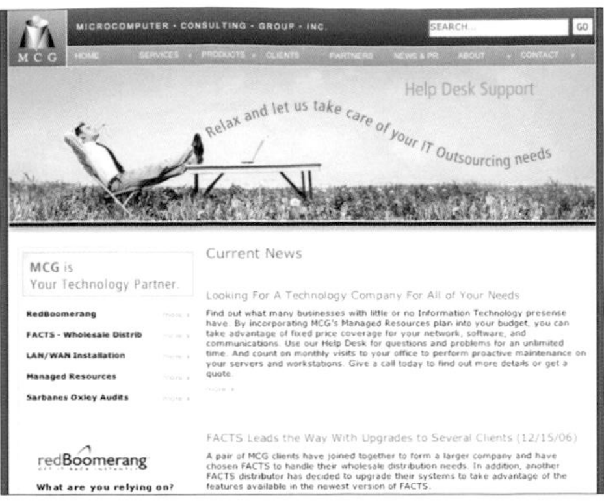

Creative Firm: **ZERO GRAVITY DESIGN GROUP — SMITHTOWN, NY**
Creative Team: **ZERO GRAVITY DESIGN GROUP**
Client: **MICROCOMPUTER CONSULTING GROUP**
WWW.MCGNET.COM

Creative Firm: **HUGHES HUNTER, INC. — THOUSAND OAKS, CA**
Creative Team: **JIM HUGHES, BRUCE POLKES, LIZ FIELDS,TIM SCHMIDT, STEPHANIE SCHMIDT**
Client: **TOYOTA MOTOR SALES USA**

Creative Firm: **HITCHCOCK FLEMING & ASSOCIATES INC. — AKRON, OH**
Creative Team: **NICK BETRO, RENE MCCANN, KIM BRUNS**
Client: **VERITAS**
WWW.VERITASIDEAS.COM

Creative Firm: **ZERO GRAVITY DESIGN GROUP — SMITHTOWN, NY**
Creative Team: **ZERO GRAVITY DESIGN GROUP**
Client: **DIGITAL WATERWORX**
WWW.WATERWORX.COM

Creative Firm: **HORNALL ANDERSON DESIGN WORKS — SEATTLE, WA**
Creative Team: **HILLARY RADBILL, DAYMON BRUCK, DON KENOYER, ALAN DRAPER, ROEL NAVA**
Client: **BLRB ARCHITECTS**
WWW.BLRB.COM

Creative Firm: **BBK STUDIO — GRAND RAPIDS, MI**
Creative Team: **GEOFF MARK, KEVIN BUDELMANN, MARIE-CLAIRE CAMP, JOHN WINKELMAN, CHUCK SHOTWELL**
Client: **CUMBERLAND FURNITURE**
WWW.CUMBERLANDFURNITURE.COM

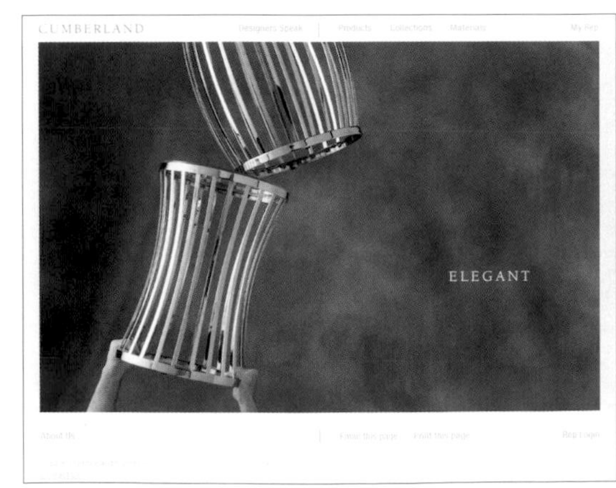

Creative Firm: **KELLER CRESCENT — EVANSVILLE, IN**
Creative Team: **CARSON CATLIN, RANDY ROHN, RANDALL ROHN**
Client: **KELLER CRESCENT**
WWW.KELLERCRESCENT.COM/

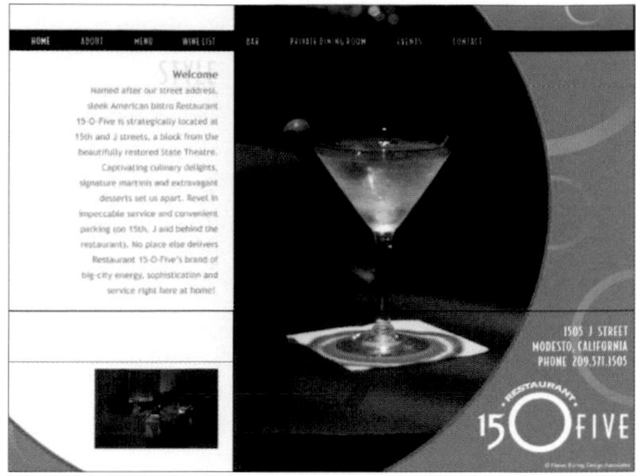

Creative Firm: **NEVER BORING DESIGN ASSOCIATES — MODESTO, CA**
Creative Team: **DAVID BORING, SHAWNA BAYERS**
Client: **RESTAURANT 15-0-FIVE**
WWW.RESTAURANT1505.COM

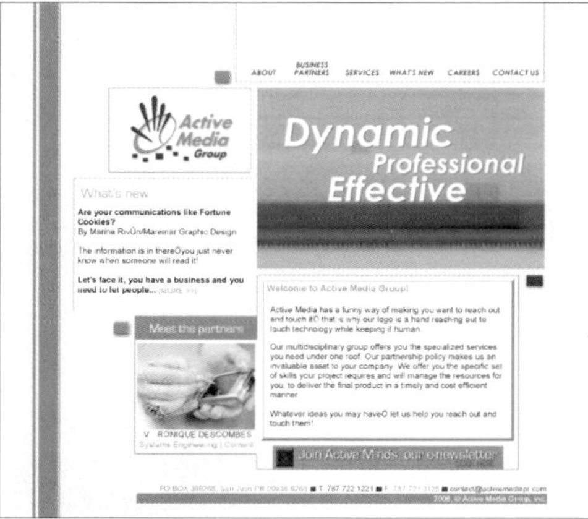

Creative Firm: **ACTIVE MEDIA GROUP — BAYAMON, PR**
Creative Team: **VERONIQUE DESCOMBES, GONZALO ARANIBAR, MARINA RIVON**
Client: **ACTIVE MEDIA GROUP**
WWW.ACTIVEMEDIAPR.COM

Creative Firm: **FITTING GROUP — PITTSBURGH, PA**
Creative Team: **ANDREW ELLIS, JEFF FITTING, TRAVIS NORRIS, AMY CHIAVERINI, BECKY THURNER**
Client: **BLACK KNIGHT SECURITY**
WWW.BLACKKNIGHTSECURITY.COM

Creative Firm: **SNAP CREATIVE — ST. CHARLES, MO**
Creative Team: **ANGELA NEAL, SARAH E.G. WATERS**
Client: **ENVIRONMENTAL MANAGEMENT ALTERNATIVES**
WWW.EMA-ENV.COM

Creative Firm: **HUGHES HUNTER, INC. — THOUSAND OAKS, CA**
Creative Team: **JIM HUGHES, BRUCE POLKES, LIZ FIELDS, CALLIE MILLER, TIM SCHMIDT, STEPHANIE SCHMIDT**
Client: **LEXUS**
WWW.LEXUS.COM/CPODEMYSTIFY/

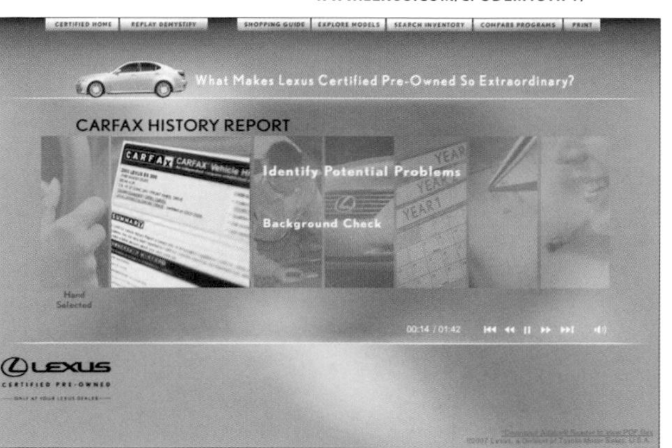

Creative Firm: **OCTAVO DESIGNS — FREDERICK, MD**
Creative Team: **SUE HOUGH, MARK BURRIER**
Client: **PLATINUM PR**
WWW.PLATINUMPUBLICRELATIONS.COM

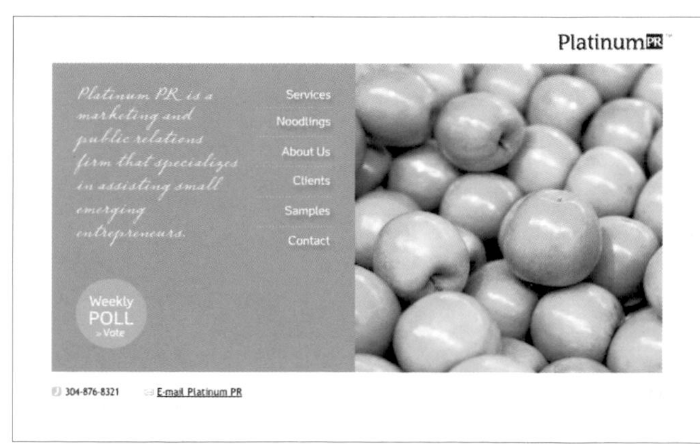

Creative Firm: **NICKTOONS — NEW YORK, NY**
Creative Team: **CHRISTINA VANN, ALLISON TUOHY, TAMI HEATON**
Client: **NICKTOONS NETWORK**
WWW.NICKTOONSNETWORK.COM

Creative Firm: **LEVINE & ASSOCIATES — WASHINGTON, DC**
Creative Team: **GREG SITZMANN, MONICA SNELLINGS**
Client: **LEVINE & ASSOCIATES**
WWW.LEVINEDC.COM

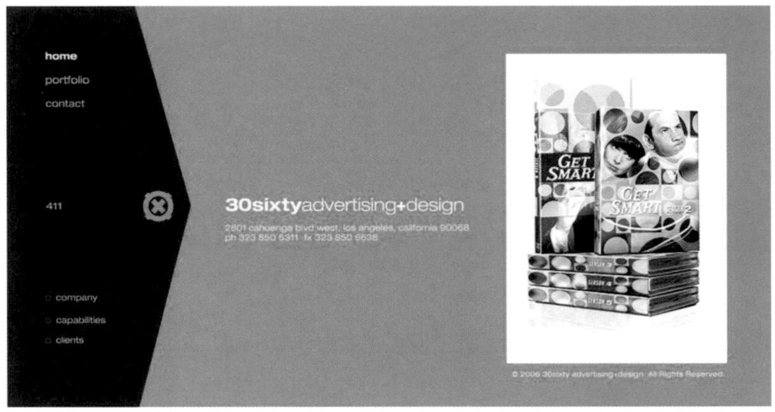

Creative Firm: **30SIXTY ADVERTISING+DESIGN, INC. — LOS ANGELES, CA**
Creative Team: **HENRY VIZCARRA, PÄR LARSSON, KASEY CHATILA, SCOTT HENSEL**
Client: **30SIXTY ADVERTISING+DESIGN, INC.**
WWW.30SIXTYDESIGN.COM

Creative Firm: **CONNIE HWANG DESIGN — GAINESVILLE, FL**
Creative Team: **CONNIE HWANG, KAI RADER, CELESTE ROBERGE**
Client: **CELESTE ROBERGE**
WWW.CELESTEROBERGE.COM

Creative Firm: **BRANDOCTOR — ZAGREB, CROATIA (HRVATSKA)**
Creative Team: **MOE MINKARA, SINISA SUDAR, ANJA BAUER MINKARA, MAJA BENCIC, HELENA ROSANDIC, DARIJE JURAJ**
Client: **BRANDOCTOR**
WWW.BRANDOCTOR.COM

Creative Firm: **DESIGN 446 — MANASQUAN, NJ**
Creative Team: **BRIAN STERN**
Client: **DESIGN 446**
WWW.DESIGN446.COM

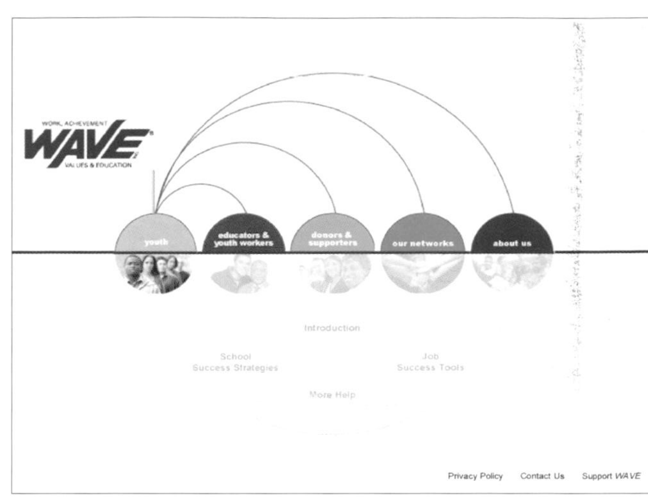

Creative Firm: **CRABTREE & COMPANY — FALLS CHURCH, VA**
Creative Team: **SUSAN ANGRISANI, ROD VERA**
Client: **WAVE**
WWW.WAVE.ORG

Creative Firm: **LF BANKS + ASSOCIATES — PHILADELPHIA, PA**
Creative Team: **LORI BANKS, CARRIE PAUL**
Client: **LF BANKS + ASSOCIATES**
WWW.LFBANKS.COM

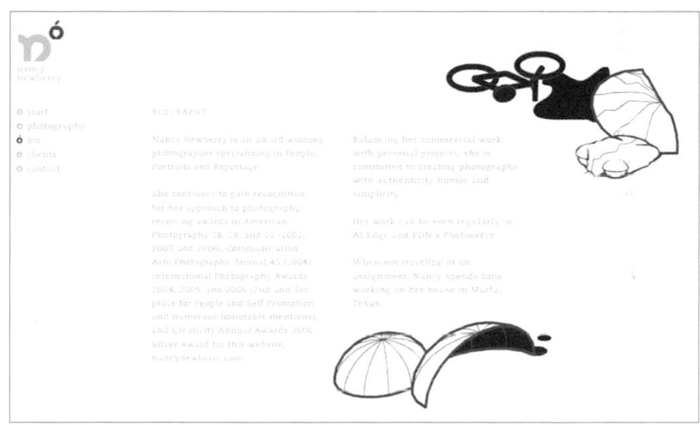

Creative Firm: **NANCY NEWBERRY PHOTOGRAPHY AND DAS PLANKTON — DALLAS, TX**
Creative Team: **NANCY NEWBERRY, ANNIKA HAMAN**
Client: **NANCY NEWBERRY PHOTOGRAPHY**
WWW.NANCYNEWBERRY.COM

Creative Firm: **HUGHES HUNTER, INC. — THOUSAND OAKS, CA**
Creative Team: **JIM HUGHES, BRUCE POLKES, LIZ FIELDS, TIM SCHMIDT, STEPHANIE SCHMIDT**
Client: **ACURA**

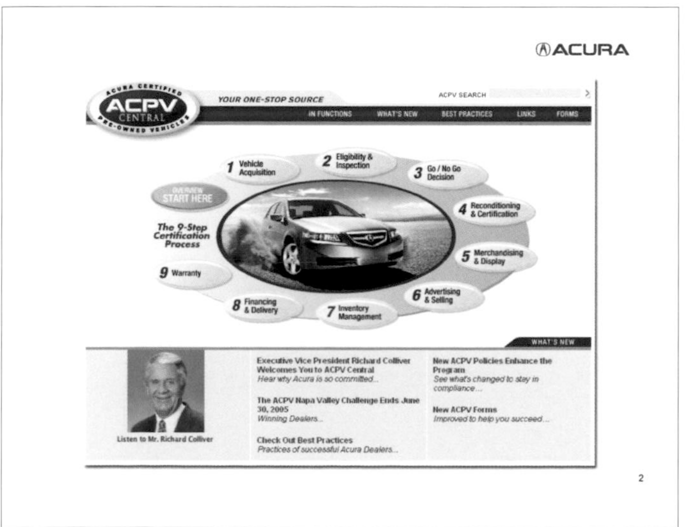

Creative Firm: **COMEDY CENTRAL — NEW YORK, NY**
Creative Team: **KAREN LA CHIANA, JULIE ANN PIETRANGELO, JARRETT BRILLIANT, JESSE WILLMON, BETH LEWAND, PAUL BEDDOE-STEPHENS**
Client: **COMEDY CENTRAL**
WWW.COMEDYCENTRAL.COM/SHOWS/ROAST_ANDERSON/INDEX.JHTML

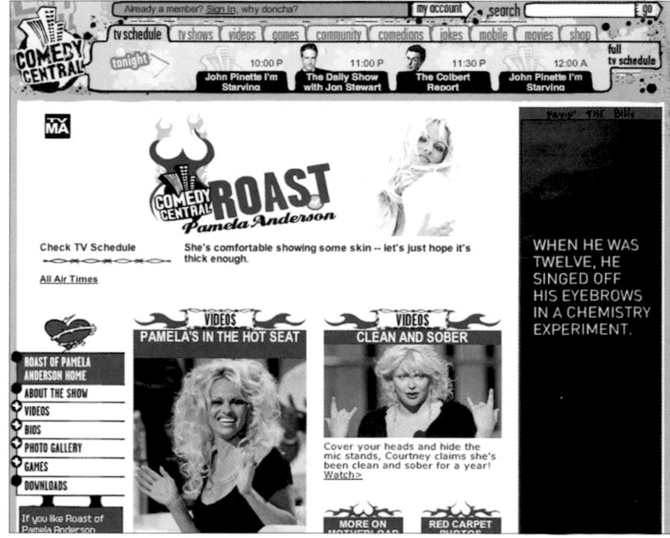

Creative Firm: **OCTAVO DESIGNS — FREDERICK, MD**
Creative Team: **SUE HOUGH, MARK BURRIER**
Client: **OCTAVO DESIGNS**
WWW.8VODESIGNS.COM

Creative Firm: **FIVESTONE — BUFORD, GA**
Creative Team: **JASON LOCY, PATRICIO JUAREZ**
Client: **EWALD-SIGAMONEY PRODUCTIONS**
WWW.EWALDSIGAMONEY.COM

Creative Firm: **KIMBO DESIGN / FRESH STRATEGY — VANCOUVER, BC, CANADA**
Creative Team: **KIM PICKETT, BUDIANTO NASRUN, MARINA PERCY, SARAH KIEHNE, JENNIFER MAH**
Client: **MINDSET MEDIA**
WWW.UGANDARISING.COM

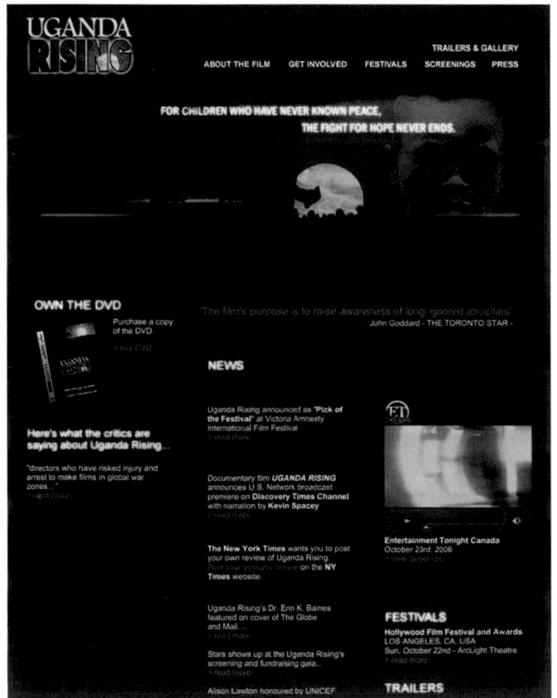

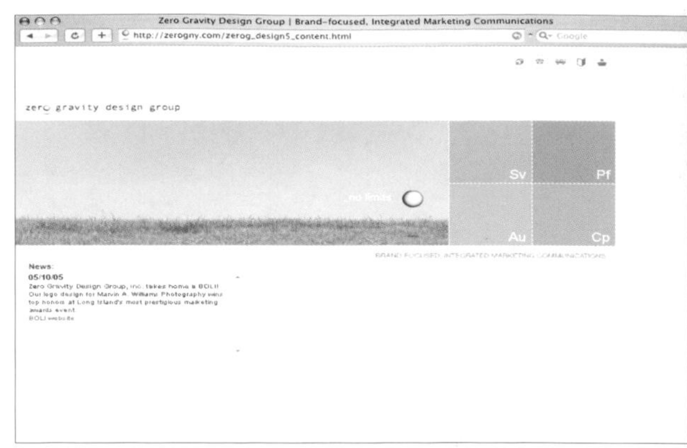

Creative Firm: **ZERO GRAVITY DESIGN GROUP — SMITHTOWN, NY**
Client: **ZERO GRAVITY DESIGN GROUP**
WWW.ZEROGNY.COM

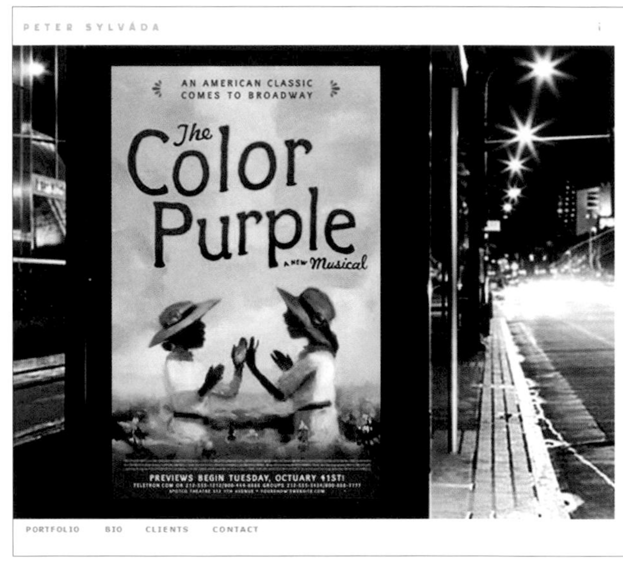

Creative Firm: **RED CANOE — DEER LODGE, TN**
Creative Team: **DEB KOCH, CAROLINE KAVANAGH, PETER SYLVADA**
Client: **PETER SYLVADA**
WWW.PETERSYLVADA.COM

Creative Firm: **GRAFIK MARKETING COMMUNICATIONS — ALEXANDRIA, VA**
Creative Team: **JAMES SMITH, DAVID COLLINS, GREGG GLAVIANO, FABIO SILVA, JUDY KIRPICH**
WWW.GRAFIK.COM

Creative Firm: **ZUNDA GROUP LLC — SOUTH NORWALK, CT**
Creative Team: **CHARLES ZUNDA, ROBERT R. THOMAS, JOHN GEOGHEGAN**
Client: **ZUNDA GROUP LLC**
WWW.ZUNDAGROUP.COM/

Creative Firm: **LEVERAGE MARKETING GROUP — NEWTOWN, CT**
Creative Team: **DAVID GOODWICK, MIKE NOVIA, TOM MARKS, BECKY KOROL**
Client: **LEVERAGE MARKETING GROUP**
WWW.LEVERAGE-MARKETING.COM

Creative Firm: **CONNIE HWANG DESIGN — GAINESVILLE, FL**
Creative Team: **CONNIE HWANG, NEAL HORSTMEYER, ARNOLD MESCHES**
Client: **ARNOLD MESCHES**
WWW.ARNOLDMESCHES.COM

Creative Firm: **ROBINLANDA.COM — NEW YORK, NY**
Creative Team: **MICHAEL SICKINGER, NEIL ADELANTE, ROBIN LANDA**
Client: **ROBIN LANDA**
WWW.ROBINLANDA.COM

Creative Firm: **THE LUDLOW GROUP — VIRGINIA BEACH, VA**
Creative Team: **NICK GLENN, MARCK WEISS, PAUL BELOTE, LEONARD ZANGS, JOSH HARRELL**
Client: **THE LUDLOW GROUP**
WWW.THELUDLOWGROUP.COM

Creative Firm: **ZERO GRAVITY DESIGN GROUP — SMITHTOWN, NY**
Creative Team: **ZERO GRAVITY DESIGN GROUP**
Client: **MARVIN A. WILLIAMS PHOTOGRAPHY**
WWW.MARVINAWILLIAMS.COM

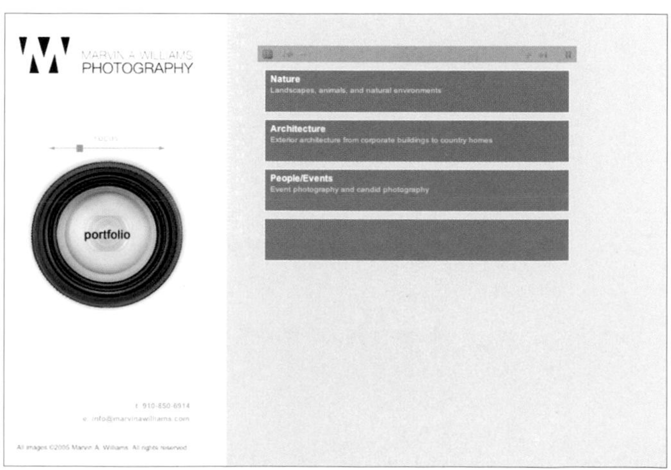

Creative Firm: **OCTAVO DESIGNS — FREDERICK, MD**
Creative Team: **SUE HOUGH, MARK BURRIER, BETTINA STRAUSS**
Client: **BEST FOTO LLC**
WWW.BEST—FOTO.COM

Creative Firm: **FITTING GROUP — PITTSBURGH, PA**
Creative Team: **TRAVIS NORRIS, ANDREW ELLIS, C. SCOTT GILBERT**
WWW.FITTINGGROUP.COM/AD-O-MATIC

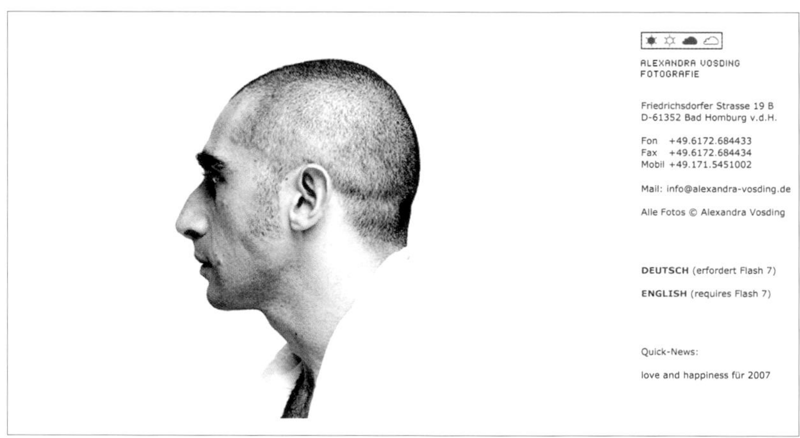

Creative Firm: **Q — WIESBADEN, GERMANY**
Creative Team: **MARCEL KUMMERER, LAURENZ NIELBOCK**
Client: **ALEXANDRA VOSDING**
WWW.ALEXANDRA-VOSDING.DE

Creative Firm: **RED CANOE — DEER LODGE, TN**
Creative Team: **DEB KOCH, CAROLINE KAVANAGH, DAVID VOGELEER, JAMIE BERGER, STEVE ROMANENGHI**
Client: **POTTERING AROUND**
WWW.POTTERINGAROUND.COM

Creative Firm: **ZYGO COMMUNICATIONS — WYNCOTE, PA**
Creative Team: **SCOTT LASEROW, ROE LASEROW**
Client: **SCOTT & ROE LASEROW**
WWW.REMROX.COM

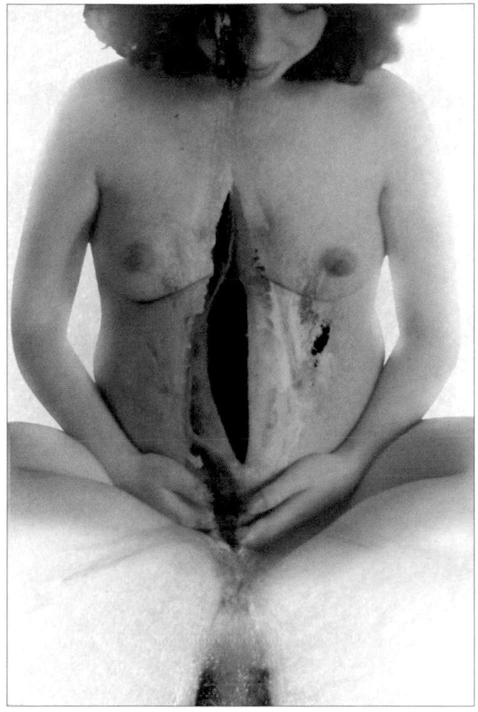

Category Name: **ART & ILLUSTRATION**
Student Name: **YULIA KOLONIA**
School Name: **STEPHEN F AUSTIN STATE UNIVERSITY**

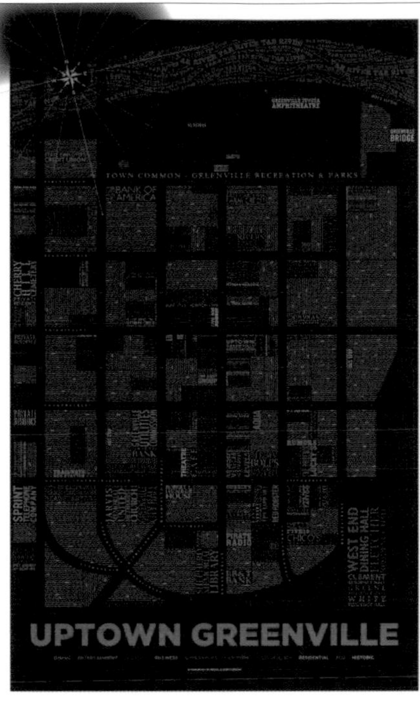

Category Name: **POSTERS**
Student Name: **COURTNEY ANN BARR**
School Name: **EAST CAROLINA UNIVERSITY OF ART AND DESIGN**
Other Creatives: **GUNNAR SWANSON**

Category Name: **POSTERS**
Student Name: **DON HARING, JR.**
School Name: **DREXEL UNIVERSITY GRAPHIC DESIGN PROGRAM**

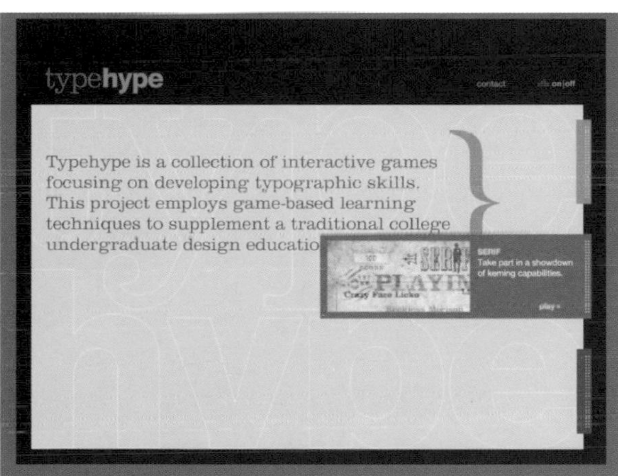

Category Name: **WEBSITE DESIGN**
Student Name: **JEANNE KOMP**
WWW.TYPEHYPE.NET

Category Name: **DIMENSIONAL PROMO**
Student Name: **SHANNON EARY**
School Name: **ART INSTITUTE OF CALIFORNIA-SAN DIEGO**
Client: **DISNEY DVD**

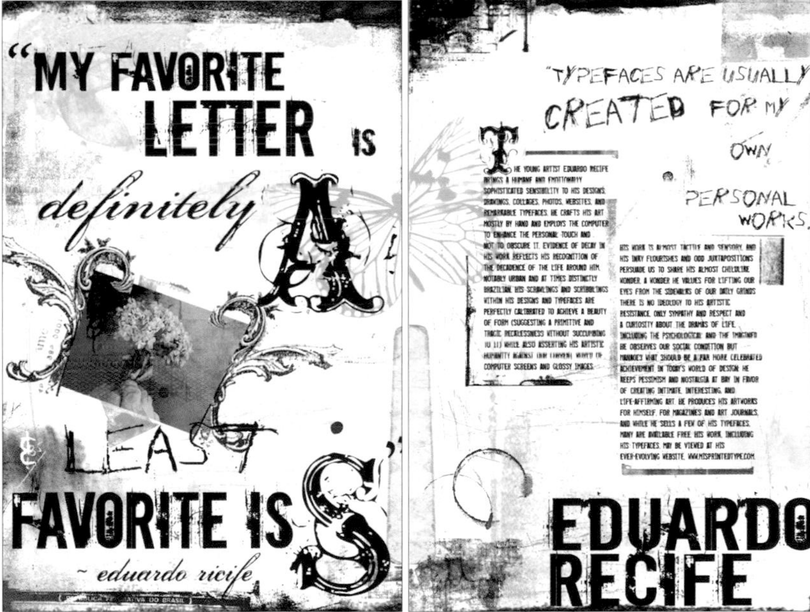

Category Name: **POSTERS, CAMPAIGN**
Student Name: **CHRISTINE MEAHAN**
School Name: **ENDICOTT COLLEGE**

Category Name: **LOGOS & TRADEMARKS**
Student Name: **JEANNE KOMP**

Category Name: **LETTERHEADS**
Student Name: **LESLIE HANSON**
School Name: **SUSQUEHANNA UNIVERSITY**

Category Name: **LOGOS & TRADEMARKS**
Student Name: **TREVOR HARKEMA**
School Name: **IOWA STATE UNIVERSITY**
Client: **CLUB KB DJ SERVICES**

Category Name: **POSTERS**
Student Name: **MARCELLA ZUCZEK, MARK WILLIE**
School Name: **DREXEL UNIVERSITY GRAPHIC DESIGN PROGRAM**

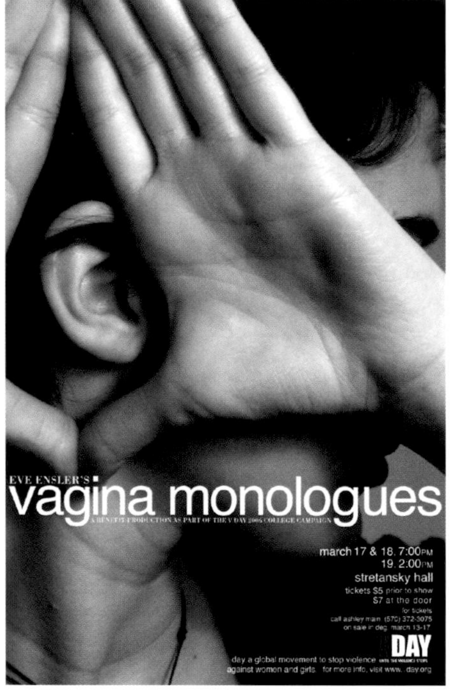

Category Name: **POSTERS**
Student Name: **LESLIE HANSON**
School Name: **SUSQUEHANNA UNIVERSITY**

Category Name: **SIGNS**
Student Name: **IN-SIL HAN**
School Name: **PRATT INSTITUTE**

Category Name: **POSTERS**
Student Name: **ZVONIMIR MINTAS**
School Name: **UNIVERSITY OF ZAGREB**
Other Creatives: **ANDREA SRECKOVIC**

Category Name: **POSTERS**
Student Name: **DANIEL JACOB**
School Name: **MIAMI AD SCHOOL/ESPM**
Client: **WILATI**
Other Creatives: **DANIEL SCHEINER**

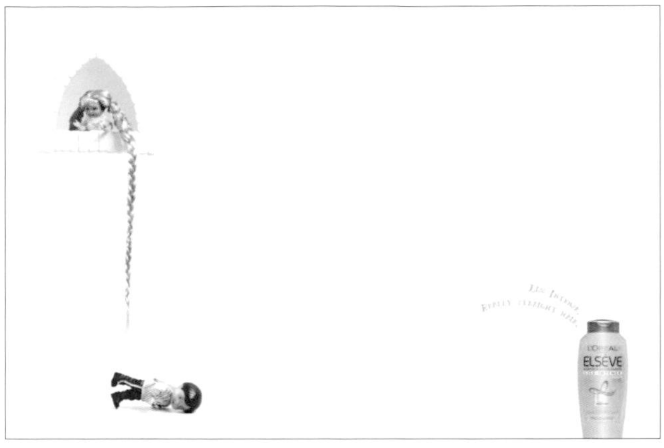

Category Name: **POSTERS**
Student Name: **DANIEL JACOB**
School Name: **MIAMI AD SCHOOL/ESPM**
Client: **L 'OREAL**
Other Creatives: **ALEXANDRE AMARAL, DANIEL SASSO**

Category Name: **POSTERS, CAMPAIGN**
Student Name: **YOO-KYUNG HAN**
School Name: **OTIS COLLEGE OF ART AND DESIGN**
Client: **WORLD HEAL TH ORGANIZATION**

Category Name: **POSTERS**
Student Name: **GINA LAMANNA,MARK WILLIE**
School Name: **DREXEL UNIVERSITY GRAPHIC DESIGN PROGRAM**

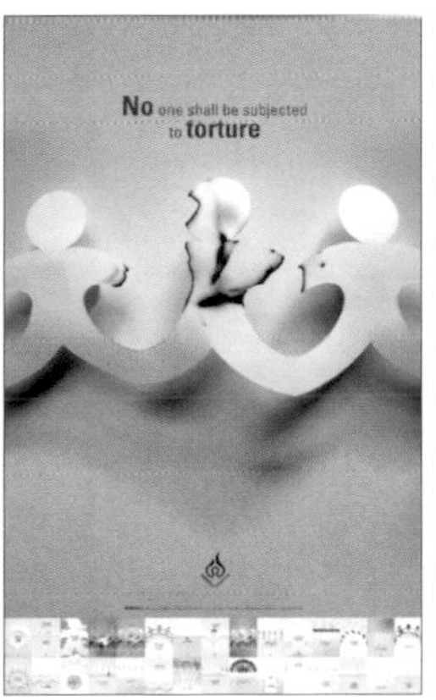

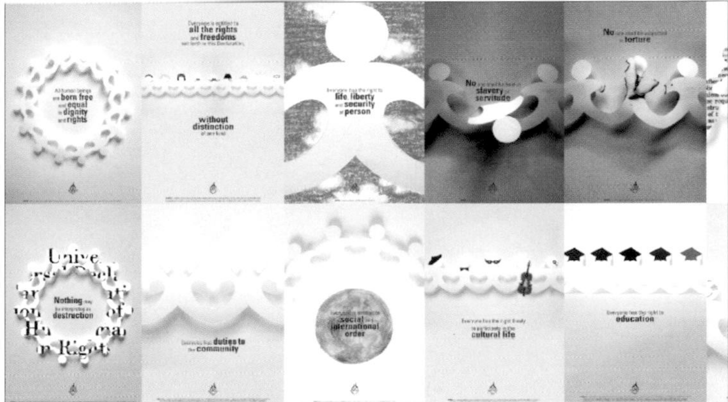

Category Name: **POSTERS, CAMPAIGN**
Student Name: **IN-SIL HAN**
School Name: **PRATT INSTITUTE**

Category Name: **LOGOS & TRADEMARKS**
Student Name: **IN-SIL HAN**
School Name: **PRATT INSTITUTE**

Category Name: **POSTERS**
Student Name: **IN-SIL HAN**
School Name: **PRATT INSTITUTE**

Category Name: **BOOK DESIGN, INTERIOR**
Student Name: **KELLY LARBES**
School Name: **OHIO UNIVERSITY**

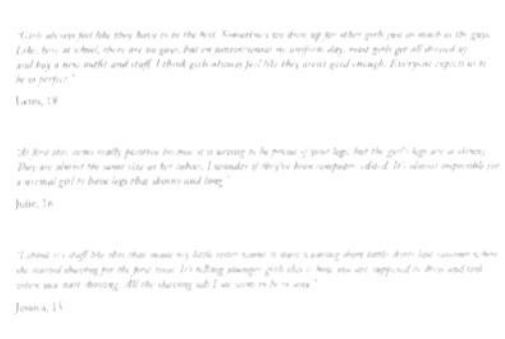

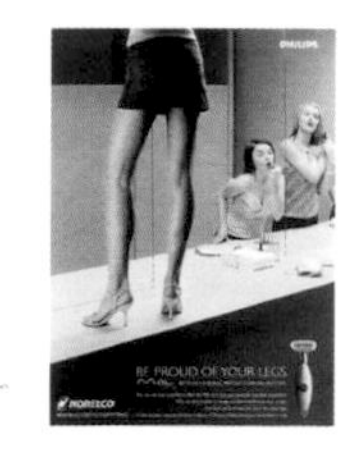

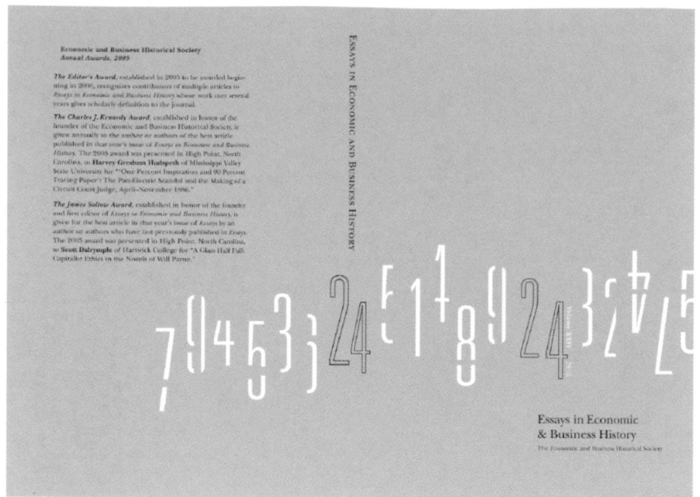

Category Name: **BOOK DESIGN, JACKETS**
Student Name: **SHELBY SPEARS**
School Name: **AUBURN UNIVERSITY**
Client: **DAVID O. WHITTEN**
Other Creatives: **KELLY BRYANT, DAVID WHITTEN**

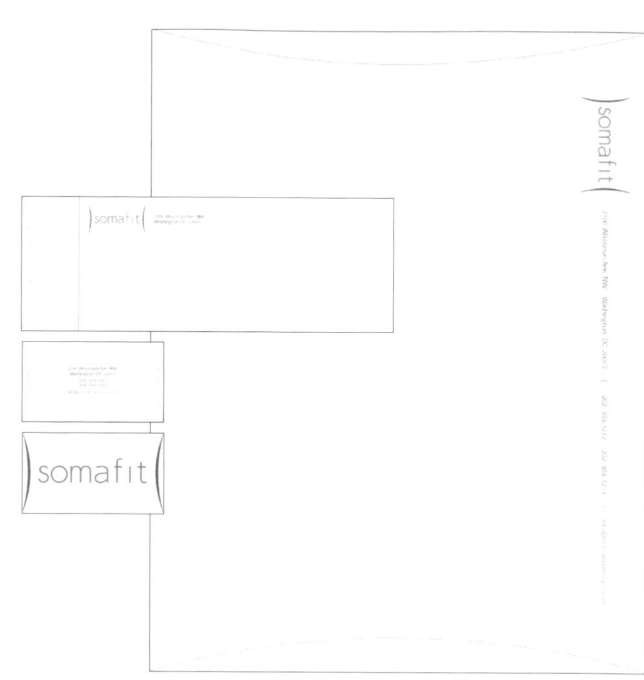

Category Name: **LETTERHEADS**
Student Name: **LESLIE HANSON**
School Name: **SUSQUEHANNA UNIVERSITY**

Category Name: **POSTERS, CAMPAIGN**
Student Name: **DANIEL JACOB**
School Name: **MIAMI AD SCHOOL/ESPM**
Client: **GATORADE**
Other Creatives: **ALEXANDRE AMARAL, PEDRO BORTOLINI**

Category Name: **RADIO**
Entry Title: **NATURAL**
Student Name: **DANIEL JACOB**
School Name: **MIAMI AD SCHOOL/ESPM**
Client: **TWEEZERMAN TWEEZERS**
Other Creatives: **DANE ROBERTS, MIKE LAZARUS, AMY JARRARD**

Category Name: **BROCHURES, CONSUMER PRODUCTS**
Student Name: **DIANA LOMONACO**
School Name: **ROGER WILLIAMS UNIVERSITY**

Category Name: **MAGAZINE AD, CONSUMER, SINGLE**
Student Name: **DANE ROBERTS**
School Name: **MIAMI AD SCHOOL**
Client: **COTTON GROWERS OF AMERICA**
Other Creatives: **JASON TEBBE, JENNIFER JOHNSON**

Category Name: **PROMOTIONAL PACKAGING**
Student Name: **GAVIN COOPER**

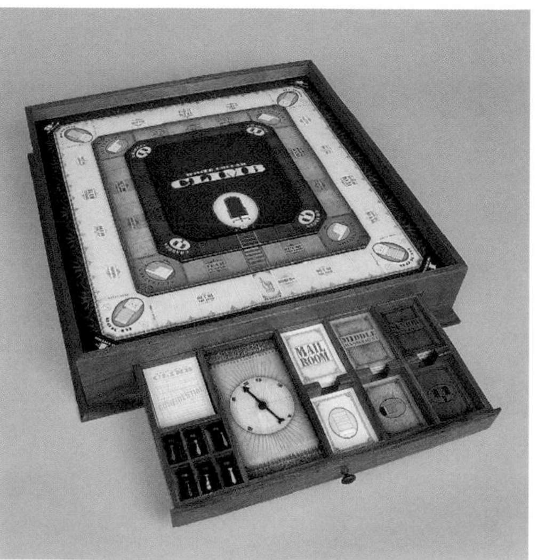